'This is a wonderful, exciting book. In this time of austerity, it is easy to despair, but this book offers lots of examples of how to get involved in working with others to create a better world. It moves beyond theory to describe different forms of collective action and inspires hope about social change. Another world, a better world is possible but action without reflection can threaten progress. This book explores the underlying theories, values and different forms of social action in a lucid and stimulating format.'

Michael Murray, Emeritus Professor of Social & Health Psychology,
Keele University, UK

'The second edition of this ground-breaking volume maintains the excellent approach of the first volume; it is honest, self-reflective and comprehensive in describing and elaborating this vastly important approach to understanding behaviour, institutions, societies and processes of change. It has been updated with modern cases and developments on the global stage and goes into detail of how change can be achieved without simply trying to shout louder than others.

As young people become increasingly aware of their rights and of the crucial importance of altering the direction of travel if their futures are to be more secure than they currently appear, so increasing numbers of university courses (and not just Psychology degrees) will need to offer modules that provide the sort of thoughtful and lucid analyses outlined in this volume. This will make an excellent source book for such modules.'

Roger Ingham, Professor of Health and Community Psychology,
University of Southampton, UK

Critical Community Psychology

This accessible textbook draws upon progressions in academic, political and global arenas, to provide a comprehensive overview of practical issues in psychological work across a diverse range of community settings.

Interest in community psychology, and its potential as a distinctive approach, is growing and evolving in parallel with societal and policy changes. Thoroughly revised and updated, this new edition covers crucial issues including decolonial approaches, migration, social justice and the environmental crisis. It has a new chapter on archive research, working with data, policy analysis and development, to reflect the continuously developing global nature of community psychology. Key features include:

- sections and chapters organised around thinking, acting and reflecting;
- case examples and reflections of community psychology in action;
- discussion points and ideas for exercises that can be undertaken by the reader, in order to extend critical understanding.

Aiming to provide readers not only with the theories, values and principles of community psychology, but also with the practical guidance that will underpin their community psychological work, this is the ideal resource for any student of community, social and clinical psychology, social work or community practice, and for people working in community based professions and applied settings.

Carolyn Kagan is a Professor Emerita Community Social Psychology at Manchester Metropolitan University. Having retired from the university she now works as a scholar activist on local participation and community development projects and on climate/economic/social justice policies at the regional level, through the collective, Steady State Manchester. @CarolynKagan

Mark Burton is a scholar activist, working on a variety of environmental, economic and political issues. Among other activities he is part of the Steady State Manchester collective which explores and promotes a post-growth approach to economy and society in the city-regional context. For many years he worked as a psychologist and manager in health and social care services. @MarkHBurton

Paul Duckett is an academic community psychologist at Central Queensland University, Australia. He works in the fields of disability and mental health and has worked alongside disabled people including people with mental health difficulties and people with learning difficulties since 1988. He has a YouTube channel where he posts videos on topics and issues relevant to critical community psychology – just search for Paul Duckett.

Rebecca Lawthom is Professor of Community Psychology in the Faculty of Health, Psychology and Social Care at Manchester Metropolitan University. She co-directs the Research and Knowledge Exchange Centre entitled Health, Psychology and Communities. Her research embraces creative, participatory methods. @rebeccalawthom

Asiya Siddiquee is Senior Lecturer in the Department of Psychology at Manchester Metropolitan University. Her research has centred around well-being in various contexts – digital technologies, refugee women and arts for health. Working with mixed methods research, her future aspirations are to explore issues regarding equality, social justice and cultural diversity.

Critical Community Psychology

Critical Action and Social Change

Carolyn Kagan, Mark Burton, Paul Duckett,
Rebecca Lawthom and Asiya Siddiquee

Routledge
Taylor & Francis Group
LONDON AND NEW YORK

Second edition published 2020
by Routledge
2 Park Square, Milton Park, Abingdon, Oxon OX14 4RN

and by Routledge
52 Vanderbilt Avenue, New York, NY 10017

Routledge is an imprint of the Taylor & Francis Group, an informa business

First edition published by John Wiley & Sons 2011

British Library Cataloguing-in-Publication Data
A catalogue record for this book is available from the British Library

Library of Congress Cataloging-in-Publication Data
A catalog record has been requested for this book

ISBN: 978-1-138-36405-9 (hbk)
ISBN: 978-1-138-36412-7 (pbk)
ISBN: 978-0-429-43150-0 (ebk)

Typeset in Sabon
by Wearset Ltd, Boldon, Tyne and Wear

For our community partners and our students past and present

Contents

Contents

Contents

Figures

Tables

Part 1
Think!

Contents

This section is concerned with the theoretical context of critical community psychology. Key ideas and concepts are introduced which underpin the chapters on critical community psychology action and reflection. We explore the nature of critical community psychology; the core elements of critical community psychology; the contested nature of community; and the nature of social ties and participation. By the end of this section you will have had a lot to think about, and will have some ideas about what we mean by *critical* community psychology.

Chapter 1

Introduction

Summary

In this chapter we explain the origins of the book, both in our relationships to each other and in the place where we all worked and lived, Manchester, UK. We talk about the importance – or not – of Manchester as the place in which we developed our critical community psychology approach, characterised by learning through action (action learning) and action through learning (action research). We consider issues to do with language and representation throughout the book and what we mean by critical. Finally, we give an orientation to the three parts of the book and to the importance of Think! Act! Reflect! as the organising theme for the book, and the critical disruptions that are used throughout.

Critical community psychology in Manchester, UK

When we wrote the first book we all worked and lived together in or near Manchester, UK. Things have changed. Rebecca still works and lives near Manchester. Paul lives and works in Australia; Asiya lives and works in China; and Carolyn and Mark still live in Manchester but are retired from paid employment and working as activist scholars or scholar activists. With the advances in internet facilities we have still been able to co-operate over revising the text. This means that this is now a book about critical community psychology, written by a mixed group of academics and scholar activists or activist scholars. When we wrote the first edition of the book, four of us – Carolyn, Rebecca, Paul and Asiya – all worked together at Manchester Metropolitan University, on curriculum design of award bearing undergraduate and postgraduate courses as well as short courses; teaching; supervising; researching; writing, and doing the myriad other things that working in the university entailed. Mark held a visiting professorship at the university, collaborating on research projects, writing and some teaching, whilst managing a complex multi-professional service for people with learning difficulties in the city. We had the largest critical mass of community psychologists in the UK, probably in Europe, in our department, along with critical psychologists and people working in innovative areas of psychology. We were (and are) also friends. We are able, still, to draw on the experiences of our undergraduate, postgraduate and doctoral community psychology students, our various research teams and the many community groups and organisations and people we work with and with whom we have struggled, and continue to struggle, in solidarity for greater social justice and to create a better world.

In the past seven years the challenge of impending climate catastrophe has become clearer, so we work, not only for social justice but for climate justice too. Other things have changed during this period as well, some local, some national and some international, including:

1 There has been a move to right wing, nationalist, populist and some fascist regimes around the world, including the election of Trump in the USA.
2 The full aftermath of the Global Financial Crisis has played out, leading to ramped up austerity and letting the bankers off the hook – this is marked in the UK but evident in other places too.
3 The Hoffman Report – relating to USA based American Psychology Association (APA) ethics guidelines, national security interrogations and torture, but with reverberations around the world – was published and we mobilised around an anti-torture position within the British Psychological Association (BPS).
4 The BPS Division of Clinical Psychology wrote a report that asked for psychology to move away from the biological model of mental illness.
5 Fake news, alternative facts, have become rife, and there has been a push back from positivist science to reclaim the narrative on fact and fiction.
6 There has been increased momentum in the neoliberalism of higher education – the introduction of teaching quality and knowledge exchange quality frameworks, to sit alongside the research quality framework in the UK, and higher education funding cuts in UK and Australia.
7 There is rising inequality everywhere, particularly income inequality in many places, leading to destabilisation and the normalising of extreme right wing discourses.
8 Indigenous communities from around the world have found their livelihoods more threatened than ever as big corporate business tears up the spaces in which they live, and those of us living in the rich parts of the world continue to consume to excess, thriving on the products of this destruction.
9 There is instability in many regions, leading to war, conflict, displacement and famine.
10 Nuclear brinkmanship is taking place between various combinations of Russia, China, North Korea and the USA.
11 Islamophobia has become a fully matured form of state-sponsored violence in the UK and elsewhere.
12 A referendum was held in the UK with a narrow margin between those who voted for the UK to leave the European Union (Brexit) and those who didn't, with considerable turmoil, division and chaos in both Parliament and the country following.
13 Seventy-two people lost their lives as a fire engulfed Grenfell Tower in London – almost certainly corporate greed will emerge as a contributory factor as the inquiry into the disaster proceeds.
14 Psychology was at the heart of a science crisis – the scandal about faking data in replication studies had reverberations across the scientific world with seepage into the public consciousness and contributing to greater mistrust of institutions and expertise.

All of these changes have had a direct impact on us all, but most particularly on those already marginalised in different ways. Despite this, though, people have expressed voice, resilience, courage, solidarity, continued to bring joy to each other and to their children and, most importantly, promoted hope. We struggle, though, along with many, with the realisation that the list of threats nearly overwhelms the sites of resistance and us! We hope that our critical community psychology approach remains relevant, and supports people working for progressive change.

The book is the result of many years working, teaching and thinking together – even at a distance – and realising that we have developed a form of praxis (the inseparable union of theory and practice) that remains firmly grounded in our time and place together, but enriched with the life changes we have undergone. One of the many questions we have asked ourselves, in relation to our praxis, is *"to what extent is it important that we were bound together through time and place and that the place is Manchester?"* When we discussed this, we thought about other developments of which we have been a part and asked ourselves the same question. When we worked together, it was at Manchester Metropolitan University (MMU), which prior to 1992 was Manchester Polytechnic. The kind of institution we worked in is firmly embedded in the history and policies affecting university–community relations (Kagan & Diamond, 2019). We were lucky to have had, at times, an enabling context, in terms of opportunities for innovative practice in academia, but also in public services. We were lucky to have been friends and to have shared the same value base. At Manchester Polytechnic we developed the first Psychology of Women course in the country (Kagan & Lewis, 1990). Whilst place was important in bringing like-minded people together to work, discuss and create, we do not link this development to Manchester in particular, but rather to women's networks and the women's movement more widely. Whilst this is not a feminist community psychology book, we continue to work with, and be inspired by, feminist thought and the bravery of much feminist struggle. Feminist theory and principles underpin our work. Manchester has distinguished itself this year by erecting (through public subscription) a statue of Emmeline Pankhurst, who led the more militant suffragette movement in the UK at the turn of the twentieth century – the second statue of a woman in the city (the first being of the imperialist queen Victoria).

Our department produced the first book on qualitative research methods in psychology (Banister, Burman, Parker, Taylor & Tindall, 1997) but again, although being in the same place at the same time was important for the group of authors, we do not link this development specifically to Manchester, but rather to the critical turn in social psychology following the so-called 'crisis of social psychology' in the 1970s and 1980s. For a period of more than 20 years our department was known for its critical work. During this period, we developed the first Masters programme in community psychology in the UK. The situation, now, is not so enabling. There is no longer a named Masters programme in community psychology at MMU. Departmental developments have reflected routes to professional psychology status (community psychology has no formal route to professional recognition in the UK), maximising student recruitment. Undergraduate programmes retain community psychology for all students, which is good, but pressure is on to demonstrate how this part of their course contributes to their 'employability', as university priorities are drawn ever more close to government priorities. Research, teaching and even third stream activity is subject to national metrics, and time is mapped on to them. It is difficult to find space to develop community relationships, and yet, as we have shown, some remarkable work still emanates from academia (Benneworth, 2013; Kagan & Diamond, 2019). Indeed, Levin and Greenwood (2018) argue that action research promises the only meaningful frame of action for university–community work. From outside in, it is relatively easy for community groups to collaborate with academics from the elite, research intensive universities, who have additional funds and seemingly more time, but, ironically, it is less easy to collaborate with those traditionally working well with communities (Brown & Carasso, 2013).

Even though our horizons have broadened in terms of time and space, and we are influenced by colleagues and friends from around the world, we link the development and evolution of our work in critical community psychology firmly to Manchester: a modern city with a past littered with collective struggles. Bauman (2007a) draws attention to the importance of place, an importance that underpins our experiences:

> It is around <u>places</u> that human experience tends to be formed and gleaned, that life-sharing is attempted to be managed, that life meanings are conceived, absorbed and negotiated. And it is

<u>in</u> places that human urges and desires are gestated and incubated, that they live in the hope of fulfilment, run the risk of frustration – and are indeed, more often than not, frustrated and strangled.

(Bauman, 2007a, p. 81)

Why Manchester?

Manchester is in the North West of England. As a site for manufacturing and heavy engineering works, Manchester was at the heart of the industrial revolution and local people became catalysts for free trade in the nineteenth century. It is the place where Engels lived and wrote *The Condition of the Working Class in England* in 1844 and where Elizabeth Gaskell wrote *Mary Barton*, *Cranford* and *North and South* between 1848 and 1854. It is the home of the modern Co-operative Movement (which emerged in Rochdale just north of Manchester in 1844). In 1868 the first Trades Union Congress was held in Manchester's Mechanics' Institute. During the latter half of the nineteenth and first part of the twentieth centuries, the campaign for women's franchise was led by Emmeline Pankhurst and her daughters, who were born and lived in Manchester. Manufacturing industry was supported by the world's first passenger train line, between Manchester and Liverpool; in 1761 the first artificially cut waterway, the Bridgewater Canal, had been built to carry coal into the city. During the

Figure 1.1 New Manchester: Spinningfields.

eighteenth and nineteenth centuries, the history of Manchester was linked to the history of collective struggles for political representation, underpinned by a growing recognition of the powers held by working people. 2019 is the 200 year anniversary of the Peterloo Massacre – when cavalry charged into a crowd of approximately 70,000 working people who were demanding political representation (Phythian, 2018). In the city centre stands a statue of Abraham Lincoln with an inscription thanking the Manchester cotton workers for supporting the anti-slavery movement of the unionists in America, even though this meant that the cotton grown in the Southern states could not reach the Lancashire cotton mills, creating extreme hardship amongst the cotton workers. In addition to its political and industrial heritages, Manchester has more recently been a centre for creativity and cultural activity, leading the country in music, poetry and art. It has a radical past and its local government continues to innovate on both the national and the European stage. It is now common to talk of it as a city region (Ravetz, 2000), an emphasis that will become ever more important as the twin challenges of 'peak oil' and climate change (Holmgren, 2008; New Economics Foundation [NEF], 2008a) bring profound changes to the economy and to human settlements, forcing us all to look to our local region as the main source to support prosperity and well-being. Figures 1.1 and 1.2 show the old and new faces of Manchester, which, whilst not sitting side by side, co-exist within a mile of each other.

Despite its radical and challenging past, Manchester experiences some of the same tensions as other large cities worldwide. We (the authors) share, with other urban elites, as we have seen, the capacity

Figure 1.2 Old Manchester: Moss Side.

to move from the city as and when we like, due to our privileged economic, cultural, social and political positions. In many ways we have become separated from the city in which we live and work, and through cyberspace and travel the global has become local. This book, in part, attempts to re-centre us – and our students and those of you reading the book who may also be at risk of becoming part of the urban elite – into the city where those most marginalised by our social systems live and experience the world.

Many of those with whom we work are not connected to cyberspace but are physically rooted firmly in the city. Their struggles take place inside the city where they battle on a daily basis for a better place to live. Many of the problems they face are not of their making but need to be understood in a much wider context. As Bauman (2007a) says:

> To cut a long story short: cities have become dumping grounds for globally conceived and gestated problems. The residents of cities and their elected representatives tend to be confronted with a task which by no stretch of imagination can they fulfil: the task of finding local solutions to globally conceived troubles and quandaries.

(Bauman, 2007a, p. 83)

As the divide between the rich and the poor increases at an ever more rapid pace (Figure 1.3), the flight of the elite, both physically and psychologically, from their urban dwellings becomes ever more

Figure 1.3 Barriers around or against the community?

stark in comparison with the anchored grounding, both physical and emotional, of the urban poor. Whilst the elite have their lifestyles and aspirations moulded into (and moulded by) the mass media the poor live their lives in its shadow.

So, our text is caught between the local and the global. We cannot ignore the global issues that are shaping our discipline, at least calling it increasingly to account (such as global warming, global economic inequality and pillage, global migration and so on). We cannot ignore the global issues that shape our lives and those with whom we work, via the spread of global capitalism and the clutch of neoliberal social and economic policies. However, equally, we cannot escape the rootedness of the struggles of the urban poor around us. Whilst the work we are engaged in is mostly local, it speaks to issues of wider, global concerns.

Learning through action and action through learning

The approach we take to practising and learning about critical community psychology is an action learning one, wherein we, and our students, learn by doing. We believe that critical community psychology is not a discipline that can be learnt and then applied, but instead we need to continually reflect upon and learn from our experiences. The very subject matter requires us to move beyond pedagogic, didactic approaches to learning to andragogic, critical approaches (Freire, 1972a, 1972b; Knowles, 1980), which value and build on the experience learners bring. In the UK the undergraduate curriculum is circumscribed by the British Psychological Society and the Higher Education Authority (essentially the same group of people drawing the boundaries around what is covered by the undergraduate curricula (Kagan, 2008)). At present, the formal definitions of a psychology curriculum do not include community psychology. Radford (2008) acknowledges that other disciplines also offer understanding of human behaviour, and within the UK academic framework, many of the underpinning values and insights of community psychology would fit more easily within the curricula areas of social work and social administration. This does not deter us, but in making the case for growing community psychology, Kagan (2008) asks:

> Where is psychology's visibility in the social exclusion analyses and debates; world poverty; war, conflict resolution and recuperation; the soul destroying effects of the imposition of neo-liberal economic and social policies world wide; violence towards women and children; population movements and displacement: and so on? What can and does psychology contribute to the rhetoric of choice and involvement in public policy, especially amongst those most affected, the poor and the marginalised? What can and does psychology contribute to the vision held by regeneration professionals and policy makers of the so called mixed social economy – where middle class families will live happily alongside drug users and 'neighbours from hell' who have previously been confined to the peripheral ghettos of council estates? If the answer is that these issues are not within the boundary of psychology, the riposte must be: why not when they have a fundamental impact on so many people's experience, wellbeing and quality of life?
>
> (Kagan, 2008, p. 29)

She goes on to discuss the implications of introducing a psychology that deals with some of these matters into the mainstream curriculum and suggests that to do so will be:

> …to challenge and make explicit, through our curricula and learning processes, not only the moral dimensions underlying psychology but also the political ones. At the heart of the human causes and consequences of contemporary social problems are issues of power and powerlessness; of dominance and oppression; of wealth and poverty; of exploitation and resistance. Not

only do we – and our students – need to understand our 'positionality', ... we also need to become reflective and reflexive as practitioners and learners, and to be aware of our overlapping roles as citizens, experts and workers...

It is this that leads us to the approach we have to learning and doing critical community psychology action and critical reflection (Kagan, Lawthom, Siddiquee, Duckett & Knowles, 2007) and that is reflected throughout this book. It is worth noting that at the time of writing there is still no professional route to training and employment as a community psychologist in the UK, although a community psychology section has been formed within the British Psychological Society with good links to the wider European Community Psychology Association. Burton and Kagan (2003) offer some explanations for why, historically, there was a gap in Britain, linked to the social policy context; the ideological and theoretical character of psychology; the availability of appropriately oriented people to become community psychologists; and the presence of other community practitioners. Many other community practitioners, such as community development workers, youth workers and so on, have been cut as part of the austerity measures imposed for over ten years, which means the space has opened up for those with community psychological training, whether this is as a part of other professional roles or free standing. At policy levels, the concept of well-being has grown in public discourse, and even community well-being is now being discussed. The *What Works for Wellbeing Centre* programme on community well-being, seeks to address the following questions:

How do the places we live, and our participation in local decision-making, influence personal and community wellbeing? What does community wellbeing actually mean? What can be done to improve wellbeing by voluntary organisations, businesses, local and central government?
(https://whatworkswellbeing.org/our-work/community/, retrieved February 7, 2019)

Action learning

At the core of action learning (Revans, 1980) is <u>doing something</u>; getting involved with and working on a real issue or concern outside of the academy – a theme that we pursue through research via action research (see below). Other features include: collaboration; facilitation of learning; reflection; discussion with and learning through peers; exploration of values, assumptions and feelings underpinning the learning experience; and critical and collaborative thinking, informed by theory (McGill & Brockbank, 2004; O'Neil & Marsick, 2007). These features of action learning were implemented in our community psychology courses, insofar as students:

- negotiated and worked in collaboration with a community partner;
- worked on a change agenda and issue identified by the partner;
- formed action learning groups with other students for continual discussion about their work;
- followed an action research cycle – reflection at the heart, and evaluation and sustainability built in from the outset;
- approached tutors and other students as resources for learning.

We, as tutors, provided theoretical frameworks for thinking and facilitating the extension of students' learning. We use the same processes of learning ourselves and hope that the examples we give throughout the book give a flavour of what this is like in practice. Whilst you, as reader, can explore the issues we present on your own, your learning will be more powerful if you work with others on the subjects we cover and, if possible, apply your learning to a practical task you are facing in partnership with other community partners.

Action research

In the 'doing' part of action learning, we encourage an action research process. Whilst there are many variations of action research, at its heart is some intentional action which is reflected upon in the light of evidence of change and modified in the light of experience. It is a process rather than a method and in its simplest form it combines understanding, or development of theory, with action and change through a participative process, whilst remaining grounded in experience (Kagan, Burton & Siddiquee, 2017). Action research is not necessarily a progressive process, and more technical approaches can lead to control and constraint rather than empowerment and liberation. The key stages of an action research process are *thinking* – defining and understanding the problem or issue, planning and decision making; *acting* or doing – implementing strategies for change; and *reflecting* – evaluating progress and impact and reflecting on the skills and processes of change. It is easy to see that the thinking, doing and reflecting stages resonate with action learning. The stages are distinct but also overlap, so many of the concerns of one stage are repeated in others. A good example of this is the place that participation plays – participation is relevant to all stages of action research but raises different dilemmas and ways of thinking about it at planning, doing or evaluating stages. We have organised the book according to the stages of thinking, acting and reflecting. Whilst we have separated the stages out for the purposes of the book, the overlapping and common elements of each stage need to be borne in mind. Although we have placed action research centrally in our practice and in this book, we do not intend to write a book on methods of research. There are many volumes already devoted to this and we favour using whatever methods are most suitable for the task in hand, and, if there are none, creatively inventing them! Of course we need to think carefully about the epistemological and ontological assumptions underpinning different kinds of information. This means we need to consider carefully the assumptions underpinning the nature of knowledge revealed through different methods, and the assumptions about the nature of the world and people in it. However, we do not want to get involved, here, with the esoteric arguments that have made many a psychologist's career and are captured in the many textbooks on methods. If we are assiduous about thinking and planning, skilled in execution and careful in reflection, we suggest that any method can serve the purpose of community psychology (Burton & Kagan, 1998): it is the purpose and the use to which methods are put that is important. By way of illustrating the utility of action research as an orientation for critical community psychology we can examine what Reason and Bradbury (2001, p. 2) suggest the purposes of action research to be:

> to produce practical knowledge that is useful to people in the everyday conduct of their lives;
> to contribute through this knowledge to increased well-being – economic, political, psychological, spiritual – of individuals and communities and to a more equitable and sustainable relationship with the wider ecology of the planet;

and

> to combine practical outcomes with new understanding "since action without theory is blind, just as theory without action is meaningless".

In addition to the cyclical pattern of the different stages within action research, its underlying features, in common with critical community psychology, include:

- being a deeply collaborative process of inquiry, operating at one and the same time at individual, interpersonal, group, organisational, community (and indeed societal) levels;
- focusing on practical (and political) issues;
- including reflection on one's own practices and the involvement of others in the research;
- involving collaboration between researcher and participants;
- being a dynamic process of spiralling back and forth among reflection, data collection and action;
- enabling the development of a plan of action to respond to a practical issue and/or create change;
- incorporating careful, planned sharing of findings with all relevant stakeholders.

It is not always necessary to be explicit about action research stages as there is an argument that can be made that all research involves action (Parker, 2005) and all action can be researched. Whilst this may be true, action research reminds us of the political dimension to our work and the need for participation and reflection. We are acutely aware that we have practised in the global North most of our lives, whilst drawing on work from other parts of the world. Nevertheless, we are sensitive to the fact that the imposition of Western ideas and worldviews has led to what has been called 'epistemic injustice' (Fricker, 2007) and attempt to take a decolonising stance in our work (see Kessi (2017) for decolonising possibilities).

Language, discourse and representation

There are many texts too that focus exclusively on language, discourse and social representations. We cannot do justice to these fields here. Rather, we need to explore briefly how language usage, discourses and representations of our work and of community can impact upon thinking around critical community psychology, public engagement and policy development. In the United Kingdom, in the 1980s, Margaret Thatcher (the then prime minister) claimed that there was no such thing as society, only individuals and families.

> I think we've been through a period where too many people have been given to understand that if they have a problem, it's the government's job to cope with it. 'I have a problem, I'll get a grant.' 'I'm homeless, the government must house me.' They're casting their problem on society. And, you know, there is no such thing as society. There are individual men and women, and there are families. And no government can do anything except through people, and people must look to themselves first. It's our duty to look after ourselves and then, also to look after our neighbour. People have got the entitlements too much in mind, without the obligations. There's no such thing as entitlement, unless someone has first met an obligation.
>
> (Prime Minister Margaret Thatcher, talking to *Women's Own* magazine, October 31, 1987)

In exploring this claim, we can see that language is not a transparent medium which conveys and communicates, rather language is hugely important. The (in)famous speech above locates gendered individuals (individual men and women) and families, indicating that there are the people who need to 'look to themselves first'. This is presented in opposition to 'casting problems on society' as 'there is no such thing as society'. Now this bald and bold statement appears to suggest a 'society' is a 'thing' which does not exist 'you know'. There is little nuance in the claim and by making society a thing, the speaker rejects its existence.

During the 1980s, too, there was a so-called 'turn to language' in the social sciences. This movement originated alongside increasing recognition that the transmission model of communication (Wertsch, 1990) provided an over simplistic model of language. The transmission model of communication assumes that meaning is carried through words being shared and encoded, implying a rather static view of the meanings carried by language. However, language is more flexible that this and its uses and meanings are continually changing.

Act!

Write down what you think critical community psychology is and how it differs from other psychologies and/or other community practices. As you go through the book, periodically review your ideas about critical community psychology. Try and document how your understanding of 'critical community psychology' changes throughout the text as you encounter different chapters.

If language is not a static system, how is it used? – language is an important mechanism for doing things, greeting, praising, denying, doubting and claiming (see Potter, 2001). It colours everything we do and say. We can see this process very clearly impacting upon common community descriptors, such as a 'rough estate', a 'sink estate', a 'gypsy community', a 'cohesive community', or an 'organised community'. All of these terms are laden with meaning and do not function as transparent shared understandings. Different people may interpret the terms differently. Crucially, these terms imply judgement: judgements that differ according to the speaker of the term and the context in which the terms are used, reflecting social power in many possible ways. Consider for example how the same term might convey different meanings in different circumstances.

Think!

Consider the following newspaper headlines and statements made by prominent people or organisations. Think about their position of power, the social power of their words and the potential impact.

a   Swedish politician forced to resign after saying Muslims are 'not fully human' (*The Independent*, November 27, 2017)
b   "It's really cold outside, they are calling it a major freeze, weeks ahead of normal. Man, we could use a big fat dose of global warming!" (Tweet by Donald J. Trump, President of the USA, 9.30 p.m., October 19, 2015)
c   Oscar nominated actor Benedict Cumberbatch apologises after calling black actors 'coloured' (*Guardian*, January 26, 2015)
d   "If you tell me that the burka is oppressive, then I am with you … I would go further and say that is it absolutely ridiculous that people should choose to go around looking like letter boxes." (Boris Johnson, prominent Conservative MP (ex-Mayor of London and ex-Secretary of State for Foreign and Commonwealth Affairs), *Telegraph*, August 5, 2018)
e   Texas school removes 'sexist' quote … "The more you act like a lady, the more he'll act like a gentleman" (*USA Today* Network, August 18, 2018)
f   Church of England plan for welcoming trans people under fire. One member of the archbishops' council, the Rev Ian Paul, suggested church leaders were "allowing themselves to be hijacked by these very small special interest groups" (*Guardian*, January 29, 2019)

In our work – and in the writing of this book – we know that we must take care about how we talk about people, situations, analytic concepts and incidents. Some of the terms we have used seem unproblematic, but need some explanation. Below we illustrate some of the choices we have made in the use of language in the book.

We: any combination or all of the five authors. When used to denote our approach to critical community psychology, or to illustrate community psychological practice, 'we' may often give the impression of unity when in practice there are differences, and discussions and arguments take place all the time.

Community partners: the people with whom we work outside the academy or formal services on projects and struggles to improve life in their communities and with whom we strive to increase social justice.

Poverty, oppression, marginalisation: descriptors that come from a political analysis about the objective positions that people occupy and not necessarily people's own estimations of themselves or their situations. This analysis takes as given that societies are conflictual and that there are differentials in power and experience.

Reflect!

Over the time we have been working in critical community psychology, there have been changes in the meanings of words and phrases, and changes in the words used to describe the same phenomena. How have you reacted to these changes (or indeed, if you did not know about them, what sense can you make of the changes)?

- mental handicap, the intellectually disabled, people with learning disabilities, people with learning difficulties, people with the label of a learning difficulty;
- the handicapped, the disabled, people who are disabled, differently abled, disabled people;
- homosexual, gay, queer;
- coloured, black, African heritage, mixed race, dual heritage;
- females, girls, women;
- poverty, deprivation, disadvantage, social exclusion;
- tramps, vagrants, homeless, precariously housed;
- migrants, immigrants, refugees, asylum seekers, trafficked people;
- mad, insane, mentally ill, people with mental health difficulties or mental health issues, psychiatric survivors;
- riots, civil disturbances, civil grievances;
- bigotry, prejudice, racism.

Consider how where we are positioned in the world also informs the terms and meanings.

Throughout the book we try to define or explain where we think there might be confusion over the use of specific terms. One term, though, warrants greater attention here, namely 'critical'.

What do we mean by 'critical'?

We use this word 'critical' throughout this book. The term 'critical' is being used as an additional description for versions of a number of disciplines (including community psychology). It has multiple origins, but perhaps the most significant one is from its use in 'critical theory'. This itself refers to several things – in some contexts it was used as code for Marxism, or rather for historical materialist analysis. It became best known in referring to the Frankfurt School of Marxist intellectuals concerned with questions of culture and its relation to society – e.g. Adorno, Horkheimer, Marcuse, Fromm, Habermas. Here what is meant by the term 'critical' is an approach that tries to understand a social reality through introduction of another, more penetrating frame of reference, one that has to do with a general theory of human society (or at least late capitalist society) understood in terms of contradictions between different social interests and economic processes of exploitation, capital accumulation and so on. So these critical theorists apply a powerful set of practical-theoretical tools to social phenomena to try to get a more thorough understanding that can help foment progressive social change.

But this way of using 'critical' need not be restricted to a Marxist approach. It could also apply to any approach that seeks to redefine, rework, or give direction to a discipline through this appeal to 'another more penetrating framework', but this would need to be characterised by an attempt to look beyond appearances, beyond accepted explanations and rationalisations. It would almost certainly imply an analysis of the underlying social interests and the use of the idea of a wider frame of reference than the discipline in question. Examples would be feminist theory or the use of the social model of disability to question dominant professional frameworks and their understanding of women or disabled people in relation to male and patriarchal or 'ableist' values, respectively.

Another common use of 'critical', however, seems to come from the lay notion of the 'critic'. At its worst (and most post-modern) that almost seems to mean 'say what you like', and 'pose as the most critical voice of all'. There is no method, just individual opinion. This can be destructive rather than constructive. It could be seen as part of the 'society of the spectacle', of consumerism, of capitalism itself (Debord, 1983).

Here we've set up two ideal types, with a clear bias as to the one that we are more comfortable with, and why. But nevertheless, the idea of being a critic is also contained within the first version of what 'critical' means, simply because the work of those who follow an orthodox, non-critical path is being criticised, if not explicitly then implicitly. However, we see no value in *ad hominem* critiques that attack the writer, or other bearer (for example through policy and practice) of an a-critical approach.

Reflect!

If you want to check whether you are being critical in the best sense, ask yourself:

"Is your analysis one that requires stepping outside the dominating frame of reference of this society and its dominant social science (including psychology)?"

"Where is your argument taking us and in whose interests are you making it?"

"What's the action – and what's your action?"
and
"Are you doing this in a spirit of enquiry, respect and solidarity?"

Although we have discussed language here, and there is no doubt that language is important in maintaining social relationships and contributes to the construction of social worlds, we do not want to press the point and suggest that it is more important than it is. Whilst our use of language may serve to reproduce the social system, we can also use it as a tool for transformation. Language is a cultural resource we can use, alongside others, to connect with other people, to exchange world views, to clarify intentions and meaning. It can be just as much a tool for liberation as for oppression (Williams, 1980).

Orientation to the book: structure of the book and changes for the second edition

We have not made a great number of changes to the book in the second edition, which will be a relief to some but a disappointment to others. We have responded to feedback we have received over the years and to the ideas of the anonymous reviewers of the second edition proposal. We have a new publisher: Routledge is committed to expanding its community psychology list, whereas our former publisher had no interest in a second edition, clearly thinking community psychology was not a growing field. We believe Routledge has a more accurate view of the future! Throughout the book we have continued to use an action research and action learning process to organise material and to illustrate one approach to critical community psychology, namely the one we developed in Manchester, UK.

The book is still organised in three, interrelated sections with an emphasis on theory, or Thinking (Part 1), strategies for action, or Acting (Part 2) and skills and resources brought to bear on a critical praxis, or Reflecting (Part 3).

Chapters 2, 3, 4 and 5 make up Part 1 – Think! Here, we are trying to stimulate thought about the nature of community psychology and what it is that constitutes critical community psychology. We go on to consider the contested nature of community, looking at different dimensions of community but also community asocial ties and sense of belonging. We consider, too, whether or not community and communities are benign and always a power for good or not. Towards the end of Part 1 – Think! we examine the nature of participation, a concept and a practice that appears throughout the book. We move on, in Part 2 – Act!, in Chapters 6, 7, 8, 9 and 10, to discuss what it is that we **do** in community psychology. We do not attempt to cover every possible thing that can be done, but rather we focus on those frameworks and practices that we have found useful. Following an action research cycle, we start Part 2 – Act! with ways of defining whatever issue we are concerned with. We then go on to look at decision making – how to plan an action. This is then followed by chapters on furthering critical consciousness and the creation of new social settings; development of alliances and accompaniment and advocacy. Following this, we have included a new chapter on the use of archives and big data and policy analysis, development and implementation. The final section, Part 3 – Reflect!, continues with the action research cycle to introduce different frameworks for evaluation (Chapter 11), including decolonising methods that have a relevance beyond evaluation itself. In Chapter 12 we re-visit the nature of power and social change – key ideas for critical community psychology. Once all the practical and theoretical ideas have been discussed, we move on to look at the roles and skills needed to put critical community psychology into practice, refusing to accept the idea of competencies, with their suggestion of measurement and assessment, but accepting that critical community psychology competence can be promoted.

Think!, Act! and Reflect! are the cornerstones of our approach and, as you have already seen above, within each chapter you, the reader will be invited to think, act or reflect and we hope these invitations help extend your learning and critical overview of the activity that is critical community psychology. Many of these invitations to think, act or reflect have stayed as they were in the original edition although there are also some new ones. We have anchored our discussion in our experiences of working in critical, community psychological ways, and the text is illustrated with examples from some of the work that we and our students have been involved with. This means that there will be lots of references to our own work in the text. We have thought carefully about which examples to retain in this edition: some of them go back many years, but we think the lessons to be drawn from the total corpus of our work are relevant to today's practice. We have tried to ensure that the work we present is still available. We do, of course value other people's work, but are making no claims to provide a comprehensive overview of critical community psychology. Indeed, many other examples of community psychology practice can be found in the journals and textbooks and we do not set about reproducing or reviewing them here. We have provided new references in many sections, but unapologetically we have kept many the same. Again, this inevitably means that some work we cite might seem dated: however, we do not take the view that social science is an incremental science, with today's publications overriding yesterday's. Rather, we see it as an expanding mosaic: work published in 1970 sits alongside work published in 2017, to provide a rich and complex understanding of the world around us. Again, we have tried to ensure that all the work we cite is still available.

We are rarely entirely satisfied with the work we do – not because we do it badly but because in all critical community psychological work there are tensions to be overcome and dilemmas to be faced. We have tried to include some of these as we illustrate the approach with our examples. As a further aid to this, we have included, at the end of each Part some 'critical disruptions'. We are aware that by doing this we leave ourselves open to the charge that we are not committed to a critical community psychological perspective. However, on the contrary we believe that a continual process of questioning and offering alternative ways of thinking, via reflection on theory and action, leads to a stronger critical community psychological praxis. We would encourage you to add your own. At the very end of the book, we have included a further critical disruption (Chapter 14) which raises some questions about the whole approach taken in this book: of critical community psychology itself.

Chapter 2

What is critical community psychology?

Summary

In this chapter we explore the foundations of a critical community psychology. We present an overview of the nature and origins of community psychology and go on to examine different definitions and their emergence in different places. We suggest some of the key themes and global trends in critical community psychology. Lastly we explore the role of social movements in relation to critical community psychology and the core values that characterise the practice.

The nature and origins of community psychology

What is psychology? Where does our answer to this come from? Had psychology been developed in a different type of society would it look different?

Modern psychology developed over a period starting in the second half of the nineteenth century, establishing a more or less stable form as early as the 1930s. Of course there have been developments since then, but we would argue that the main assumptions of the discipline and its overall style of approach have changed little since then. What we mean is that over that period, the dominant approaches, whether behaviourist, cognitivist, social or biological in flavour, have tended to assume that the discipline is about understanding the way the individual person functions. It has been assumed that the answer to this lies in general characteristics of the human being that can be identified through psychological research that uncovers such processes. Even when looking at people in interaction (as in social psychology) the emphasis is still on the way the individual functions.

Think!

Before going on, quickly define your understanding of the schools of thought identified above: cognitivist, behaviourist, social and biological. Consider the extent to which they position individuals at the centre and how they consider the social.

This idea of individual-centred psychology is not inevitable. It is no surprise that psychology as a discipline emerged following the establishment of a social system (capitalism). Here, individual people were freed from the traditional bonds of obligation, membership, responsibility, duty, location, and increasingly from adherence to the traditional systems of ideas that defined who they were and where they would normally remain. In this new 'world turned upside down' people were seen as separate disconnected 'atoms', free to enter into contracts with one another (but normally with the owner of the means of production), in arrangements that could be as transient as they were binding. This was a massive shift in thinking about individuals which impacted upon work, social life and of course the social sciences. Psychology, along with the other social sciences mirrored this new way of understanding the human condition. The new social system had created the conditions for the emergence of these new ways of understanding people and society (replacing a former approach where religion, philosophy, ethics, science and economy were much less distinct). But the new disciplines worked under the overall domination of the way of thinking (ideology) that corresponded to the new system of social relations. This is what Marxists have called 'bourgeois individualism' – a way of thinking that emerges from the interests of the owners (the bourgeoisie) of the resources (the means of production) in the new system and which sees this new idea of the free human atom as the unit of analysis, the fundamental reality. It was on this way of looking at the relationship between person and society that psychology was built.

Think!

As a mental experiment, consider what a discipline of psychology might have looked like if, instead of emerging in the universities of Europe, and then reaching its mature form in the business-driven context of the United States' universities, it had:

i   emerged within the autonomous city states of the Italian renaissance (where Galilean science emerged caught between the new demands of the mercantile system and the traditions of the Roman Catholic Church)?
ii developed in Muslim Córdoba (where, as part of the Arab world, the traditions of Semitic and Greek philosophy and science had survived, developed and led to advances in medicine, science and philosophy in a relatively tolerant intellectual and cultural space)?
iii been a part of the emerging labour and co-operative movement of the new industrial cities (where the key tasks were to understand how to build a strong movement with its own values, proposals and ways of being with one another, in resistance to the theft of wealth by the capitalists)?

In each case it seems unlikely that the model of the atomic individual would have held centre stage, and in some cases it seems unlikely that it would have occurred at all. But then, since it was the context of late nineteenth century/early twentieth century capitalism that was the cradle of psychology, those counterfactual examples remain just that – as the 'psychology that got away'.

This is a book about a form of psychology that did not 'get away', but that has the somewhat contradictory properties of being both a derivative from mainstream psychology and an alternative approach. Community psychology is the applied psychology of working with communities, both whole communities and sections of communities, and with people in the context of their community. Starting not (just) from the individual, but also from collectives of people, it can also be seen as an alternative approach to psychology, part of a family of approaches themselves alternative to mainstream psychology – especially its applied forms. We must be careful here, since this text neither provides an alternative programme for psychology, nor a theoretical basis for it. What we want to do in this introduction is say something about how our approach to applied psychology, *really social psychology* (Burton & Kagan, 2009) draws on and develops the work of others, in community psychology and allied fields (inside and outside what we regard as the false boundary of the discipline), and how through its concepts and its practice, it systematically rejects a way of thinking and doing psychology known as *individualism (focusing on processes and behaviours within individuals)*, instead understanding the psychological as both emerging from and dependent on social relations, not just interpersonal ones but collective and social-systemic relations too.

Psychology in general has often put social and economic factors beyond its disciplinary boundary, preferring instead to look to intra-psychic explanations (Danziger, 1994; Smail, 1993). This minority that tried to adopt and develop a social approach has included G.H. Mead, W. Reich, L.S. Vygotsky, A.R. Luria, E. Pichon-Rivière, L. Sève, M. Jahoda, I. Martín-Baró, A. and N. Caparrós, and P. Leonard, of whom only Mead and Leonard came from an English speaking country. The alliance of knowledge with language is interesting and indicates a relationship between power, language and norms. It is a theme we will return to around issues of globalism and colonialism.

These minority socially oriented approaches have always been outside the mainstream individualistic approach. In keeping with these writers, we see human beings as becoming who and what they are through the process of interacting in a socially organised and socially defined world. This is not to deny the bodily reality of humans as a kind of great ape with brains, eyes, ears, hands and so on, but to suggest that the nature of our species is such that we are pre-prepared to enter into a social milieu, *and* that in doing so we become what is distinctively human, and our psychology (including our most private and personal or inner experiences) is rooted in, dependent on and structured by this. But these social relations are not just a matter of interactions between people, or even between groups. This is where psychologists have had most difficulty understanding the nature of the social, and in trying to articulate a social approach that is distinct from individualism. We have to understand how the social system is structured and how it works, how social phenomena that exist at a level of analysis beyond the interpersonal nevertheless enter into the construction and functioning of human actors, their ideas, desires, prejudices, feelings, preferences, habits, customs and culture. The really social approach then opposes reductionism, where social phenomena are nothing more than the combined actions of individual people.

Reflect!

Consider yourself as a human actor over the course of a day. What kinds of activities comprise a 'normal' day in your life? Now try to figure out what shapes those activities that you engaged in. Can you explain them in terms of individual characteristics and processes such as desires or personality traits, or are some of the behaviours rooted in the relations among and between social groups such as families, friendship groups, identity groups (defined by religion, ethnicity, gender, sexuality, place for example), classes, nations and so on?

Community psychology has emerged in a variety of places at different times, and under varying influences, but each time it can be seen as a manifestation of unease with mainstream psychology. To give a flavour of community psychology's various points of emergence, some examples follow. We should note that here we are restricting ourselves to those developments that have used the term 'community psychology' but as we have noted elsewhere (Burton, Boyle, Harris & Kagan, 2007) there is also a lot of work that does not use this term but which could be described as community psychology since its concepts, aims, methods and value-orientation would put it firmly within the range of community psychology as usually understood.

Definitions

Pretorius-Heuchert and Ahmed (2001, p. 19) make the important point that:

> There is no consensus among the different paradigms in the discipline about a single definition for the field. The different approaches to Community Psychology, for example mental health, social action, ecological, and organizational, and the different perspectives within these approaches ... demonstrate the heterogeneous nature of Community Psychology.

We know community psychologists who resist any attempt to define the discipline, seeing such definition as the unwarranted exercise of power. However, while acknowledging that definitions are not fixed or final, and that they should be taken as only provisional, we see them as necessary in capturing the essential characteristics of what can be included when talking about critical community psychology, for example when writing a book about it. That the meaning of terms shifts, and connects with other meanings and social interests, must be taken as read (Williams, 1976).

Think!

Every year, the major dictionaries revise their word lists to reflect the way the meanings of words shift along with their uses in the population of speakers and writers. On the other hand, "When I use a word," Humpty Dumpty [In Lewis Carroll's *Through the Looking Glass*] said in a rather scornful tone, "it means just what I choose it to mean, nothing less, and nothing more." To what extent do you think that each approach could be used in defining a field such as 'community psychology'. What might be the advantages and disadvantages of each?

Table 2.1 presents a range of recent definitions. These are informative since they embody not only the orientation of community psychology but also its methods, principles and values, although we recognise there will be other definitions of community psychology elsewhere, and that the field is constantly shifting.

Levine and Perkins from the USA define community psychology largely in terms of the prevention of psychopathology and community intervention for mental health problems (Levine & Perkins, 1997). But Levine himself in the introduction to a book by Thomas and Veno that set out to define community psychology for the distinctive Australia and Aotearoa/New Zealand context (Thomas & Veno, 1992, p. 9) notes that even at Swampscott (1965) there was already a broader conception – "...a vision of community psychologists contributing much more broadly to community well-being...". He notes that since then much of what was proposed has become common sense and therefore community psychology has a "...new struggle to rediscover the uniqueness of our field". (The 1965 Swampscott conference is considered the birthplace of community psychology in the

Table 2.1 Definitions of community psychology used in different parts of the world

Country/region	Definition of community psychology (CP)
Latin America	A dynamic and complex notion of community as CP's object and active subject of research and action is at the basis of understanding of the field in Latin America. … CP has as one of its bases the *active conception* of the people integrating the communities; … CP is made with them, not just for them, or carried out in a community environment … awareness of the need to work on de-ideologizing and strengthening, or empowering, community groups, movements and stakeholders in order to foster social change [is] one of the main tasks for CP in Latin America. … Transformations are then decided with the community as well as influenced by the political character of the processes leading to them. (Montero & Varas-Díaz, 2007, p. 62)
Norway	CP is rooted in an ecological theoretical framework … [it is] an intrinsically critical discipline focusing on the prevention of human suffering, therefore, having to critically analyze and take into consideration how historical, cultural, social, economic and political contexts contribute to oppression and suffering. CP has, therefore, an ethical obligation to fight against macro arrangements that foster human indignity and injustice … ideological awareness, critical analyses, and concepts such as solidarity, equality and concern for communality should therefore constitute central issues of CP. (Carlquist, Nafstad & Blakar, 2007, pp. 284, 294)
Turkey	CP is a field that takes ecology and community seriously. In all this, what is particularly desirable and useful in the local context is the focus on empowerment, liberation, social justice, and dignity, the explicit acceptance of the role of scientist as a social agent and social action as a part of science. (Değirmencioğlu, 2007: 357)
Italy	Connections between individual and collective processes [are seen as] the core features of the discipline … much attention [has been given] to exploring the historical link between the process of valorisation of individual freedoms and collective struggle; to promoting socio-political empowerment and social capital; and to examining the multiple meanings of community and sense of community. (Francescato, Arcidiacono, Albanesi & Mannarini, 2007, p. 263)
Aotearoa/ New Zealand	CP is a context sensitive, applied social science that attempts to promote social justice and enhance the life circumstances of groups of people, especially those who are oppressed stigmatised or marginalised. Although its origins lie in psychology, CP favours interdisciplinary approaches. It has permeable boundaries, owing as much to sociology, community development, education and the policy sciences as it does to the 'parent' discipline. (Robertson & Masters-Awatere, 2007, pp. 140–141)

Country/region	Definition of community psychology (CP)
Britain	Community psychology offers a framework for working with those marginalised by the social system that leads to self-aware social change with an emphasis on value based, participatory work and the forging of alliances. It is a way of working that is pragmatic and reflexive, whilst not wedded to any particular orthodoxy of method. ... It is *community* psychology because it emphasises a level of analysis and intervention other than the individual and their immediate interpersonal context. It is community *psychology* because it is nevertheless concerned with how people feel, think, experience and act as they work together, resisting oppression and struggling to create a better world. (Burton, Boyle, Harris & Kagan, 2007, p. 219)
Canada and Ghana	Community psychology concerns the relationships of the individual to communities and society. Through collaborative research and action, community psychologists seek to understand and to enhance quality of life for individual, communities and society. (Dalton, Elias & Wandersman, 2001, p. 5)
USA	CP [is] a field that engages in research and action to promote individual, relational and societal well-being while working to reduce suffering and oppression. CP values (a) diversity, (b) ecological analyses, (c) a critical perspective; (d) methodological pluralism, (e) interdisciplinary collaboration, and (f) social change. (Angelique & Culley, 2007, pp. 37–38)
Australia	Community psychologists ... have advanced training in understanding the needs of people in their communities. They focus less on 'problems' and more on the strengths and competencies of community members. The aim of community psychologists is to work in partnership with people to achieve the goals and aspirations of their community or social groups. (Gridley & Breen, 2008, p. 121, excerpt from APS College of Community Psychologists' brochure)
India	Communities are social systems that serve to meet human needs. Therefore, community psychology can be defined as understanding the needs of a people and the resources available to meet those needs. Understanding a community helps CP to focus on formulating interventions that provide opportunities for optimum growth of its people ... (Bhatia & Sethi, 2007, p. 180)

Anglo-American tradition – psychologists came together to discuss mental health issues and other concerns around social change.)

Thomas and Veno (1992, p. 28) emphasise:

- an ecological approach to the understanding and prevention of social problems;
- knowledge about how social systems operate;
- enhancing the competence of individuals, groups and organisations in community interventions;
- prevention rather than treatment – within an overall orientation to social change.

Dalton, Elias and Wandersman (2001, p. 5), also from the USA, succinctly define it in terms of the relationships between people and collectivities while emphasising a collaborative orientation:

> Community Psychology concerns the relationships of the individual to communities and society. Through collaborative research and action, community psychologists seek to understand and to enhance quality of life for individuals, communities, and society.

Montero, from Venezuela, who has written extensively on community psychology from a Latin American perspective rooted in social and political psychology, sociology and the philosophy of liberation, defined community psychology as:

> The branch of psychology whose object is the study of psychological factors that allow the development, promotion and maintenance of the power and control that individuals can exercise over their individual and social environment in order to solve the problems that bother them and to obtain changes in those environments and in the social order.
>
> (Montero, 1982, cited in Montero 2004a, p 70)

Later, after 25 years' practice in the field, she points out the need to emphasise psychological praxis (action linked to theory linked to action) and social and cultural factors (Montero, 2004a, p. 71). However, she also cautions against a 'river-definition' that tries to include everything. Nelson (from Canada) and Prilleltensky (who was in Australia at the time of writing), in a text that embraces a radical agenda of liberation, similarly note that community psychology is evolving and diverse and that a concise definition cannot really capture its complexity (Nelson & Prilleltensky, 2005).

Reflect!

Which of the definitions summarised above appeal to you most? Why do you prefer some rather than others? Do your preferences for some perspectives on community psychology rather than others indicate you would find some ways of working hard? Why might this be?

But while acknowledging that community psychology is today a diverse discipline, here we want to approach it in a particular way that owes a lot to our experience in Manchester, while still drawing concepts, methods and inspiration from a breadth of experience from elsewhere in the world.

So, with all this in mind we have defined critical community psychology as

> ... (offering) a framework for working with those marginalised by the social system that leads to self-aware social change with an emphasis on value based, participatory work and the forging of alliances. It is a way of working that is pragmatic and reflexive, whilst not wedded to any particular orthodoxy of method. As such, community psychology is one alternative to the dominant individualistic psychology typically taught and practised in the high income countries. It is <u>community</u> psychology because it emphasises a level of analysis and intervention other than the individual and their immediate interpersonal context. It is community <u>psychology</u> because it is nevertheless concerned with how people feel, think, experience and act as they work together, resisting oppression and struggling to create a better world.
>
> (Burton et al., 2007, p. 219)

Think!

The emergence of community psychology in different parts of the world

In North America (and here we mean the USA and also Canada, but not Mexico, which we include under Latin America) the key event in the establishment of community psychology as a discipline was a conference in 1965 at Swampscott near Boston. The Swampscott conference was called to consider the education of psychologists for new roles in community based mental health services, but the conference took on a wider brief, calling for a change in role from working solely with individuals to one that also focused on prevention, service development and social action. This led to the establishment of a defined field and soon a separate division within the American (sic) Psychological Association, which later (1989) became the quasi-autonomous Society for Community Research and Action (Angelique & Culley, 2007). The context of the Swampscott initiative was that of an increasing national interest in social change. The civil rights movement was gathering momentum; opposition to the Vietnam war and nuclear arms was beginning, while the beginnings of a counter-culture were also being heard. Society and social science knowledge tend to be linked as problems tend to generate knowledge. Perhaps more important was the explosion of community work projects in the USA in the context of the Kennedy–Johnson administration's 'war on poverty' and its initiatives on mental health, leading to the establishment of community mental health centres with some emphasis on prevention: this was a fertile ground for an expanding profession of psychology imbued with liberal values, although the subsequent swing to the right and budget cuts strengthened the emphasis on non-psychologists as providers of social support (Dalton et al., 2001, p. 47). In this context 'liberal' is interpreted in social rather than economic terms: an orientation to and tolerance of personal freedom and diversity. Its mirror image is economic liberalism which can be characterised as an orientation to and advocacy of freedom for capital, free markets and the autonomy of the worker as commodity. The two strands of liberalism are at times in tension with each other. Liberalism can be traced to the context of the establishment of modern capitalism with its need for individual freedom to invest and enter into contracts.

The community psychologist would be a 'participant-conceptualiser' with the dual role of change agent and researcher, developing the new discipline that would try to understand the relationships between social systems and the behaviour of individual people. North American community psychology has been characterised by an emphasis on liberal values, prevention and the ecological metaphor. In our view the activist orientation has been subordinate to the orientation to research, much of it descriptive (the *American Journal of Community Psychology* is full of multivariate correlational studies). Community psychologists in other regions have often defined their approaches in contrast to North American traditions in community psychology, while nevertheless taking key ideas from there. North American community psychology has provided significant contributions to conceptualisation in the community psychology field, with key ideas such as 'the ecological metaphor', the psychological sense of community', 'the construction of social settings', and some excellent examples of praxis. Yet at times its vision of community psychology has been narrow – some of our work, for example has been rejected without review by one of the main North American community psychology journals on the grounds that the work was not considered by the editors to be community psychology. To define is to exert power.

Community psychology, as a self-identified sub-discipline, emerged later in Australia and New Zealand than in North America. There psychology in general is often largely indistinguishable from North American psychology, and indeed in Australia at least the US influence kick-started the (community psychology) field in the 1970s. Nevertheless, Australian and New Zealand community psychologists tended to increasingly structure their discipline around the ideas of social responsibility, social justice and cultural and ethnic issues, including combating the oppression of the respective indigenous populations (e.g. Gridley & Breen, 2008; Robertson & Masters-Awatere, 2007). In both contexts, there has been a strong base in professional practice although the published literature is again dominated by university-based practitioners.

Think!

Why might Australia and New Zealand have this particular form of community psychology? Consider the relationship between indigenous people and migrants to the respective countries.

Meanwhile, in Latin America, community psychology developed not from applied psychology but from academic social and political psychology. As in Europe and North America, the late 1960s and early 1970s saw a so-called 'crisis in social psychology' (Armistead, 1974; Montero, 2000a, 2000b) with fundamental critiques on the basis of its irrelevance to real social problems, its habit of generalising from laboratory studies of university students to other social groups and its conceptual barrenness especially in relation to the understanding of person–society relations. In Latin America this led to the development of a more politically aware practice oriented to the 'popular majorities', the poor, the marginalised and the excluded that make up the majorities in many of these countries. The example of the Cuban revolution in 1959, the work of popular educators informed by the methodology and theory of Paulo Freire (Freire, 1972a, 1972b; Kane, 2001; Mayo, 1999; McLaren, 2000; McLaren & Leonard, 1993) and of community researchers developing Participative Action Research (Fals Borda, 1988; Fals Borda & Rahman, 1991), together with ideas from liberation theology (Gutiérrez, 1973) and the economics of dependency (see Flores, 2009), were important defining influences, as were the experiences of state and imperialist repression from Puerto Rico to Chile, from Mexico to Argentina (Burton & Kagan, 2005; Montero, 1982, 1996; Montero & Varas-Díaz, 2007; Freitas, 2000). Latin American community psychology has had a relationship of mutual influence with the approach and field of liberation psychology, sharing a number of lead practitioners and common roots in specifically Latin American styles and innovations in theory and practice (Montero, Sonn & Burton, 2016).

In South Africa, community psychology similarly addressed itself to inherent societal problems, with its history of apartheid, reconciliation and continued inequality and oppression. There, as in Latin America, the Marxist influence has been significant, in part because of its role in the leadership of the liberation struggle (Bhana, Petersen & Rochat, 2008; Lazarus, Bulbulia, Taliep, & Naidoo, 2015; Seedat, Duncan, & Lazarus, 2001; Hook, Kiguwa & Mkhize, 2004).

The development of community psychology in Europe has also been diverse, varying in extent and character between countries. The influence of German philosophers and social theorists – e.g. the Frankfurt School – has been an important contrast with the English speaking world. However, in each case there has been a focus on a distinctive national and/or European style of community psychology, not assimilated to the dominant North American paradigm (see the chapters in Part 4 of Reich, Riemer, Prilleltensky, & Montero, 2007, pp. 217–443). In the UK, the development of community psychology has been slow, with distinct waves of development, some pre-dating the North American genesis (Mackay, 2008), but since the 1990s an enthusiastic network of community psychologists has emerged with origins in social and environmental, educational, clinical and health psychology (Burton et al., 2007). This book (originally appearing in 2011) is the third text on community psychology published in Britain: the other two were by Bender (1976) and Orford (1992, now in its second edition, 2008).

Act!

Plot a timeline for the emergence of community psychology. A timeline (with dates and places in the world) should pick out types of approaches, possible drivers for the development of community psychology and key terms. Is this historical context a global one?

Think!

Notwithstanding the differences in community psychology between and within the world's regions, there are some important commonalities in all the variants. These can be summarised as follows, and as a safeguard to the temptation to seek a generalised unity where maybe one does not exist, each common feature we identify also comes with a caveat that points to the limits of those commonalities.

- A focus on the community as the focus for the discipline and in theoretical terms an interest in the wider context in which people live their lives – although the way that context is understood can vary from the merely the psychological context of interpersonal behaviour to the entire socio-economic system as it penetrates psychological space.
- A stance critical of dominant mainstream psychology, even though in some instances that critical-ity may be timid (at least methodologically) when compared with the more politically radical ver-sions that flourish elsewhere.
- An interest in power, ethics, doing what is right – although there are multiple perspectives on how to understand these questions and how to discharge one's social responsibility. This is almost always associated with a focus on the situation of those living in conditions of deprivation, poverty, oppression, discrimination.
- An emphasis on giving psychology away and making its disciplinary boundary less hard, rather than on its ever increasing professionalisation – although sooner or later groupings of community psychologists themselves tend to get organised as sub-professional groupings, albeit often with res-ervations about the ethics and politics of doing so.
- An interest in the prevention of social ills rather than in offering remedial treatment – although there is a continuum from a community psychology that allies itself with 'prevention science' and one that emphasises liberation from oppression.

This international emergence of community psychology can be looked at in terms of two levels of explanation – (a) why psychologists sought an alternative, and (b) what the conditions were that allowed or facilitated that alternative to establish itself. Elsewhere, based on our research into the emergence of the British variants (Burton & Kagan, 2003), we have proposed a model of emergence for community psychology in any context. This is summarised in Figure 2.1.

Community psychology needs a space in which to exist within society and the existence of that niche depends on a favourable social policy climate, or other supportive societal conditions. However, psychologists can only occupy such niches if they have an appropriate (theoretical, ideological and practical) orientation. Whether or not they have that in turn depends on both the wider societal context and on the experiences they have had, both in their education as psychologists and in subse-quent practices. Finally, their ability to successfully occupy those niches for practice depends on the relative absence of competition from other workers. This is a simplified picture but it does appear to hold for all the cases of the development of community psychology that we have considered.

All this talk of the establishment of community psychology might suggest that it is well established as a discipline, at least in some parts of the world. The reality is rather different. In every location it is still a marginalised field. In one sense there is not such a thing as community psychology – not every-thing that would meet our definition calls itself community psychology (for example, Hook et al., 2004) and not everything that does adopt the name would meet our definition. There is no 'discipline' here, and we mean this in the sense of discipline as order and control, but maybe also in the other sense, that of a field of endeavour. Yet, despite and because of this state of diversity and space for debate, community psychology – and critical community psychology – certainly does exist if enough of us believe in it and do it.

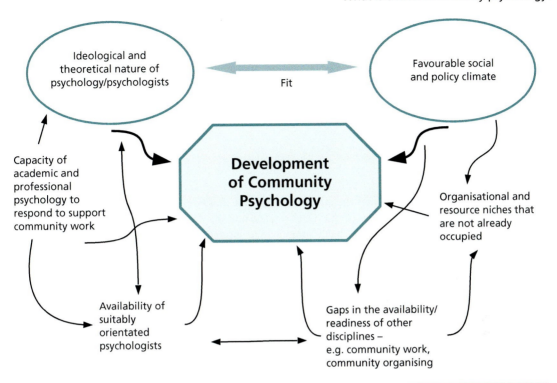

Figure 2.1 Conditions for the emergence of community psychologies.

Source: Burton & Kagan, 2003, p. 17.

Key themes in critical community psychology

In mapping the terrain, we position ourselves within it and the approach we take is critical community psychology. To explore further our understanding of critical community psychology we will now outline some of the key themes in this approach to community psychology. These themes reflect our approach to and imposition of order on a field that is far from unified.

From prevention to liberation

From its early days, community psychology has emphasised prevention as a corrective to individual treatment. This emphasis is based on several ideas. First, it is better to prevent problems than to have to treat them later – better for the victim better for the community. Second, community psychologists have pointed out the inefficiency and indeed the impossibility of treating everyone. With levels of mental health disorders, for example, at epidemic levels, and with finite psychological resources, there just will never be enough psychologists to offer psychological treatments to everyone that might benefit. Third, community psychology has pointed to the relative ineffectiveness of professional intervention when compared to lay intervention (although the evidence is mixed on this point). Finally, by treating the victims but not the environmental or systemic causes of their suffering, there is the prospect of relapse when people go back and again face those same 'envirogenic' forces that caused their problems in the first place.

These arguments are sound, but it is possible to go further through a critique of 'prevention' just as community psychology has criticised treatment – as having a limited horizon on the causes of human distress and suffering.

29

> ## *Think!*
>
> Prevention is universally thought to be a good thing. What might be the critiques which can be applied to prevention? For example, if there is a hole in the road, a barrier erected round it might stop people falling in but might mean that attention and energy is diverted from repairing the hole in the road. Can you think of examples like this that relate to people's lives and the work that community psychologists might do?

An emphasis on prevention alone can mean that there are now prevention experts, in place of treatment experts, who do all the work. This may be more efficient, but it does not generally engage the potential victims in taking control of the circumstances that make them ill. Allied to this, prevention can mean a social engineering approach that does not include the action of people themselves. It often ends up reverting to an individualistic behaviour change model in which interventions (typically as training) now become preventative rather than ameliorative but do little to deal with the root causes.

Prevention can also be used as a resource saving strategy to justify the cut in public spending and in public service provision. As the costs of healthcare increase and the financial crisis in public expenditure deepens it is interesting to correlate the rediscovery of an interest in prevention, once a subversive concept suppressed for example by the Thatcher regime in the early 1980s. An emphasis on prevention on its own, and especially if it takes a positivist or technical approach to knowledge, can be a way of sidestepping the underlying socio-economic disease, the ever expanding accumulation of capital at whatever cost to human welfare. Thus, we see successful industries based on the production and marketing of tobacco, sugar, alcohol, toxic chemicals, arms, the private car and so on.

The missing concept here is that of *liberation*. A perspective that seeks to support the liberation of people from the forces that counter their interests and needs broadens the field of view beyond the prevention concept, while nevertheless including it as an essential element. We are here dealing with a redefinition of the boundaries of what critical community psychology can consider as its remit. (For further discussion of boundaries, and boundary critique, see Chapter 7).

> ## *Act!*
>
> A key word which re-occurs in different forms is liberation. Write down your understanding of the term and consider if this definition shifts as you read through the book.

A liberatory orientation brings in the affected, the victims, or survivors, as actors and not just passive recipients of prevention or treatment programmes. It makes explicit the need for a campaigning approach, not just a Fabian presentation of knowledge to decision makers. It is useful to note that The Fabian Society, established at the end of the nineteenth century took its name from the Roman general Quintus Fabius Maximus whose tactics of repeated guerrilla type assaults on the invading Carthaginians were ultimately successful. The Fabians sought a gradualist, reformist path to socialism, eschewing class struggle. Their approach has tended to be based on presenting ideas and proposals, often backed with social scientific research in order to convince those in positions of power, a style of engagement not dissimilar to the dominant one of the psychology profession, to the extent that it does concern itself with social issues.

A liberatory orientation also brings into view dimensions of human well-being and distress, challenging the dominant consensus over what is right. Certainly, community psychology has not been responsible for any of the great social gains of the last 50 years, with the possible exception of a significant contribution to the ending of impunity for torturers in some Latin American countries (Agger & Buus Jensen, 1996; Burton & Kagan, 2005; Hollander, 1997; Lira, 2000).

But we also argue that *liberation* can be misunderstood as a liberal-individualistic concept unless it is explicitly and rigorously linked theoretically and in practice to society-level categories such as conflict of interest/class, exploitation, propaganda and ideology and to collective action on a shared project whereby people are the agents of their own liberation.

Liberation and decolonisation

Allied with the emphasis on liberation is an emphasis on decolonising psychological theory and practice. What does this mean? As it happens, the term 'liberation' is also associated with the many liberation movements that arose in the global South in response to the colonisation of lands and peoples by the European empires, and latterly by the United States, Australia and Japan. The experience of colonisation had profound impacts on the societies of colonised lands but also back home in the imperialist countries too. The structures of life, social practices and ways of thinking were all profoundly defined by the economic facts of exploitation and the justifications that arose which both shaped European modes of thinking and being and privileged them over those of colonised peoples (Dussel, 2000; Escobar, 2007; Quijano, 2000). These relations are complex, multi-layered and multi-faceted (Grosfoguel, 2008). The colonial powers established forms of administration that distinguished different classes of person, redefining ethnicity and gender in more fixed and biological terms. Moreover, a set of administrative practices and systems were developed. The social sciences were particularly influenced by the legacy of colonisation. In addition, the forms of social administration that emerged in the North to manage 'inconvenient populations', for example in the orphanages, prisons and mental institutions, had commonalities with the patterns of administration of colonial populations (Bhambra & Holmwood, 2018). So when critical community psychologists talk of decolonising the discipline (Bell, 2016; Moane, 2011), they are referring to a set of linked forms of colonisation, all underpinned by the casting of 'the other', the inconvenient, the weak, the rebellious, the non-white, non-male, into subordinate categories. This decolonisation, then is simultaneously concerned with racism–imperialism, with patriarchy and sexism, with accumulation versus the natural world, with dominant versus subordinate knowledge and belief systems, and with the assimilation of coloniality into the heart of the social sciences, including psychology (Burton, 2013a). Critical community psychology takes the imperative of decolonisation seriously, seeking, beyond mere psychological practice, which is always going to be a marginal pastime, a renegotiating of relations between us all and the natural world on which we depend, with the ambition of ultimately eliminating the domination of established power and ownership interests.

Global trends and critical community psychology

It is a cliché to say that we live in a globalised world. All this means to us is that the processes of international economic integration and domination are accelerating. This follows the recovery of capitalist accumulation starting in the 1970s (with the implementation of what has become known as neoliberalism), leading to the collapse of the counterbalancing socialist bloc 15 years later. This is one of the periods of advance in a process we now call globalisation, based on domination and theft that started with the first empires, and accelerated in a stepwise fashion with the key catalysing events such as the invasion of the other continents by Europeans, starting with the Americas (Dussel, 1995, 2000), the exploitation of fossil fuels (Malm, 2016), and the development of combustion engines, telecommunications and computers (Wallerstein, 1996a, 1996b).

What it means is that the impact of the dominant economic system is increasingly brought into communities everywhere. We can see ways in which this occurs in the examples below.

1   The closure and run down, and at times development of new manufacturing, agricultural and extractive industries (i.e. those based on the removal of environmental resources such as logging,

mining, water diversion) in accordance with the dictates of profitability. This has a direct consequence for employment and the pattern of life in communities, including the renewed emergence of people surplus to the needs of the system whether as alienated youth or vulnerable elders.

2 The arrival of people from other countries, either displaced by the same processes of capital accumulation (and the associated conflicts and trauma) or newly able to move as a result of deregulation of some borders and the integration of nations into super economic units (like the European Union – EU) which continues to alter the cultural make-up of communities, changing communities and establishing new communities.

3 Involvement of our citizens in wars, in occupying armies mainly to protect national economic interests (for example, Iraq) although sometimes to manage the consequences of broader economic and political policy decisions (Sierra Leone, Yugoslavia), or through the manufacture and sale of weapons.

4 The vulnerability of us and our communities to violent political revenge for the political and economic policies of this country and its allies (popularly referred to as terrorism).

5 The impact of tourism and international travel, internet etc., meaning that many of us have friends and relations from other countries and cultures and that new, rapid relationships between strangers develop.

6 The impact of changes in production and distribution on our everyday lives, changing the way we eat, drink, socialise and live as families, right down to the feel and look of people and neighbourhoods, the pattern of our days, and the things people believe in.

7 The breaching of the safe planetary and ecological limits, imposed whether we like it or not, by the finite nature of the one planet that we live on. The most salient of these is the existential crisis of climate change, which menaces us all with annihilation: as Naomi Klein (2015) puts it, "This Changes Everything".

It is these realities that set a challenging context for community psychology (Sloan, 2005). At this moment the world is faced with a set of interlocked crises – the financial crash and recession, the food crisis, the energy crisis, the water crisis, climate change, and the accompanying legitimation crises that take differing forms in different global locations and in different social sectors. It has to be against this pressing reality that critical community psychology's relevance must be tested.

Example: Steady State Manchester

We have been active in arguing for a response to the economic crisis that simultaneously begins to address challenges of climate change and the other planetary boundaries along with the failure of the standard economic prescriptions to deliver equitable and decent living conditions and livelihoods in our post-industrial city region. This work is part of a wider set of actions, in alliance with environmental activists and others, for rapid and principled political change. As change agents we use a variety of skills and knowledge sets that owe a lot to our critical community psychology experiences, but we do not explicitly frame the project in those terms. In effect, the community psychology becomes part of a broader social practice (Burton, 2013b, 2015, 2016b; Burton, Irvine, & Emanuel, 2014; Kagan & Burton, 2014, 2018).

Psychology is itself a product of a particular set of social systems – first industrial capitalism, then welfare capitalism and now neoliberal capitalism, all of which existed within national and global chains of expropriation and exploitation. It bears the marks of its origins and its memberships of these social systems, in ways that are complicated. It is not just that it reflects the system: the successive and contradictory ideologies of these systems co-exist within psychology as ideology, method, knowledge and values. Yet critical community psychology purports to offer an alternative approach, characterised by an opposition to that most fundamental stain of capitalism, individualism, and the search for a more adequate approach, that is cognizant of the broader contexts in which people live their lives. But without a well grounded understanding of the overall, global, systemic, context, we suggest that these attempts are doomed to be at best ameliorative only and at worst a waste of everyone's time.

Think global, act local?

But if we are concerned with community, how can we at the same time be concerned with the global plane? That question supposes that communities exist in a local space. While that can be challenged to some degree (see Chapters 4 and 5) it is fair to say that 'community' is generally to be found at a relatively local scale of social organisation (and hence social analysis). Yet if our ethics are concerned with social justice, and our praxis is liberatory and transformational it is not possible to be concerned solely with the local context. One slogan sometimes used by community psychology (borrowed from the green movement) is '*Think global, act local!*' This is helpful insofar as it focuses on feasible practical action while retaining a wider consciousness, but as it stands it fails to articulate the linkages. The fear is that a multitude of actions at a local level will remain just that – uncoordinated local actions that fail to carry a transformative force to do anything to fundamentally alter the design of a system that keeps people poor, alienated, exploited, frightened, hurt and hurting. There has to be an explicit way of connecting these local actions together with a broader movement for principled change. We address this in a number of ways.

LOCALISM AS A PHILOSOPHY

A focus on the local can in itself be a response to globalisation, and indeed it is fatal to continue sourcing the things we need to live from around the world or to fly thousands of miles for our leisure, while local farms lie fallow, factories are derelict and communities formerly based on workplaces have no longer a reason for existing. If it is not sustainable, then alternative ways of living need to be constructed where, for example, most food eaten in a region is produced there; where mutual aid and co-operation join with the endogenous development of a replacement economy, a reborn popular culture and new forms of community welfare. This 'localism', if strategic (North, 2010), is the very stuff of a worthwhile critical community psychology and as such is part of the response to the global crises (see Burton, 2009a; Desai & Riddlestone, 2002; Kropotkin, 1912; Sale, 1985; Junqué & Baird, 2018).

Sharing experiences, strategies and programmes

It has been the experience of community psychologists that making links with others doing the same or similar things strengthens the activity across these different sites. For this reason it is important that community psychologists make and keep contacts, networks, communication channels, with other community psychologists nationally and internationally. However, as leaders in principled social change, it is crucial that we all recognise the damage done to the planetary climate system by the emissions from flying to international locations. For that reason some of us no longer go to intercontinental gatherings (having already used far, far more than our fair share of the remaining global carbon budget) and travel to European destinations by train. Digital technology does now provide viable alternatives to travel, for example for making conference presentations.

BEING PART OF A WIDER MOVEMENT

However, it is really important that critical community psychology does not just look to other community psychologists for giving and receiving this support. Critical, liberatory community psychology sees itself as part of much wider development of social alternatives and the struggle for them. It is difficult to assess the prospects for such engagement – this will depend on both internal and external contexts, and if we know anything it is that prediction is difficult. But the key question here is, "how best can community psychologists contribute to wider struggles and campaigns?" Campaigning groups will rarely say: "let's invite a community psychologist to work with us and advise us" (although there are exceptions (Kagan, Lawthom, Knowles & Burton, 2000; Sánchez, Cronick, & Wiesenfeld, 1988)). Indeed there is understandable suspicion as to what psychological expertise could contribute. So, it is often necessary to approach struggles and campaigns in other roles that we also play, for example those of citizen and worker, not making a big thing of the psychological role. In other cases, the campaign emerges while the community psychologist is already engaged in a community based project and here the task may be to re-negotiate the role. The caution to observe in all of this is that while we have a certain expertise, if we are truthful it may be that it is not all that great, or at least the seduction of applying it across contexts can lead to error.

It is also wise to be aware that the space (in liberal societies) for committed action to change the present reality is conditional – the implicit contract issued by the state or other power interests being "yes you can organise and lobby, but only so long as you don't try to fundamentally change the system" (Petras & Veltmeyer, 2001). This is why ultimately this kind of activity must be part of a broader political strategy and coalition.

However, there are some things that seem to potentially constrain the current effectiveness of community psychologists seeking to engage politically:

1 Psychologists are mostly dependent on the state and its agencies for their income and position power, and can be constrained in taking on a more open political role. Indeed, in some circumstances it will be dangerous for one's employment.
2 Psychology is not traditionally political in orientation – its very construction has been that of the science of the general individual, abstracted from anything but the most proximal social context (Danziger, 1990; Sève, 1975). So political analysis and activity does not come easily to psychologists, nor in many cases does the formation of alliances with others (as discussed above). Critical community psychology is in many ways the counterfactual case, but we should not underestimate the extent to which it carries the traits of its parent.
3 Particularly in the universities, but also via the attack on public services, there is an increasingly vocal movement against thinking and practice that challenges the status quo and promotes the interests of oppressed and exploited groups. Criticism from the so-called 'Alt. Right', for instance argues university teachers and researchers who advocate for social change and who offer critiques of capitalism and patriarchy are left wing ideologues or 'cultural Marxists'.

Nevertheless, if critical community psychology is to keep the pretension of transformational community change, it does have to engage with global issues and their local impacts and dimensions and do this consciously and with a good understanding of how the global system works (Collective of Authors, 2007). Our conclusion is that in place of the slogan *'Think global, act local!'*, we need to think in terms of: *'Global is local and local is global: challenge oppression and build social and ecological justice at all levels!'*

The role of social movements

Working with communities means engaging with the bodies that operate in that terrain, in some cases embodying the communities. In some instances this means the third sector (in the UK this refers to charities, voluntary organisations, social enterprises and community groups whose mission is to contribute to the social good: they are distinguished from public sector organisations, which are national or local state run, and private sector organisations, which are answerable to shareholders and exist to make profits) and non-governmental organisations (NGOs). However these formal organisations are often colonised by the state – that is to say they have become arms of the state, delivering the state's policies and services: many NGOs have changed in nature from being campaigning or advocacy organisations to being compromised by their dependence on public authorities, for example through contracts to provide public services on behalf of government agencies.

An alternative orientation to the organisational basis of community life emphasises the role of social movements, which might include some NGOs as well as other organisations and associations. It is these movements that are typically concerned with transformational change rather than implementation of ameliorative policy initiatives or service provision. Examples from history and the present time include the labour movement, women's and gay movements, the disabled people's movement, the civil rights and anti-war movements, anti-racism movements and the green movement.

Reflect!

What do you know about those movements identified above? How did they contribute to social change? Why is it you know more about some of them than others? Would you consider yourself a member of any social movement? Why or why not?

Community psychologists in search of transformational, liberatory change need to look to the linkages of change projects with social movements, and ensure that there is an embedding or at least a connection with them. This provides a safeguard against projects that do little more than confirm the hegemonic paradigm. One example from the UK is the work of British psychologists in collaboration with the parents of intellectually disabled people in pioneering new community based supports in the 1970s and 1980s (Burton et al., 2007). The work of Elizabeth Lira and colleagues at ILAS in Chile is another example of how psychological work has linked up with a broader movement to seek and obtain justice for the oppressed – in this case the victims of torture under the Pinochet regime, challenging the culture and institutional embedding of impunity (Agger & Buus Jensen, 1996; Lira, 2000; Lira & Castillo, 1991; Lira & Weinstein, 2000).

Social movements are communities in motion. While the dominant forces create motion and change, so do the social movements that arise to create better conditions.

Social justice and a just society

Most community psychology has emphasised the pursuit of social justice. We take this further by stating that critical community psychology is part of a wider movement for a just society. It is fundamentally an ethical project. These aims of social justice and a just society are the standard against which the adequacy of critical community psychology should be evaluated. We therefore emphasise what we call the 'so *what?*' question. For every community psychology project, process or output (especially academic outputs like books and articles and conference papers) we ask the questions:

So what has changed for those that participated in the project, those from the community in question? Did their life materially improve? Or at least did their prospects improve? Are they better able to influence what happens to themselves, to their families, neighbours? Is the community stronger, more sure of itself, more able to understand its situation and act on it?

Despite a recent tendency to disparage approaches that identify universal social realities, we believe that community psychology needs to be firmly grounded in an understanding of poverty, oppression, disadvantage, exclusion and exploitation. As of the period 2014–2016, the average life expectancy at birth for men in Manchester is 75.5 years, and for women is 79.5 years of age, some 10 years less than those in the country's wealthiest borough, London's Kensington and Chelsea (83.7 for males, 86.4 for females). Life expectancy is 8.1 years lower for men and 7.0 years lower for women in the most deprived areas of the city of Manchester than in the least deprived areas. While life expectancy in Kensington and Chelsea is, on average, much higher than in Manchester, there is more inequality: life expectancy is 13.8 years lower for men and 7.5 years lower for women in the most deprived areas of Kensington and Chelsea than in the least deprived areas (Public Health England, 2018). These differences are closely associated with income. Over 2017, the percentage of households in the city that were without employment was 20.7, compared to a Great Britain rate of 14.5 per cent (Office for National Statistics, 2018). Figures from the Australian Bureau of Statistics (2018) showed that life expectancy estimates for Aboriginal and Torres Strait Islander Australians remain lower than for the non-Indigenous population (by 8.6 years for men and 7.8 years for women). We could go on, but this is enough to illustrate what Göran Therborn has called the "killing fields of inequality" (Therborn, 2009; see also Wilkinson & Pickett, 2009, and www.equalitytrust.org.uk/). Beyond this recognition of the existence of humanity-deforming inequalities it is necessary to know something of the 'motor' that produces them.

This is an economic system based on exploitation and its ideological justification (Collective of Authors, 2007). It is this state of injustice that is the premise for action of critical community psychology and a contrast from other areas of psychology where, for example, the themes of social exclusion and marginalisation are rarely considered.

Think!

The Manchester example above starts with local knowledge (statistics and inequality) but links to global concerns (of the economy). Consider your local context – how does the picture here link to the global context. If you do not know, how might you find out?

Core values underpinning a critical community psychology

All community psychology is characterised by the explicit recognition of the guiding role of values. This contrasts with the dominant approach in psychology which models itself on a positivist concept of science wherein there is a strict distinction between facts and values (Kolakowski, 1972), whilst failing to recognise that facts about people, and the society they live in, are themselves value laden. Values organise social behaviour – without them it is difficult to conceive of any order in social relations (Kelvin, 1971).

For critical community psychology, clarity about values is fundamental. Knowing one's values – where one stands – does not guarantee ethical coherence, but without this self understanding it is very difficult to negotiate the dilemmas of community practice.

Reflect!

Consider your personal set of values. Can you articulate them? Do they translate into how you live your life – for example buying free trade goods? To what extent do your values extend to different parts of your life – do different values underpin your relationships, your work, the decisions you make about holidays and so on? Does your community psychology practice differ from other areas of your life? Why is this?

Example: Community leadership: the challenge of racist attitudes

We and a group of students were invited into a marginalised community by a group that was trying to set up a community organisation. The community was characterised by chronic unemployment, a large number of single parent families, what looked like neglect by public services and a popular discourse of being embattled. The community was also almost entirely white. Members of the community group from time to time expressed racist views. We were uncomfortable with this. One member of the team wanted to withdraw since she found it very offensive (she has black family members). She believed that a zero tolerance approach is the only way to deal with this kind of racist behaviour. The others regarded this kind of expression as inevitable given the deprivation, low educational attainment and marginality of this neighbourhood.

Reflect!

The community leadership example above exemplifies the interplay between values, social analysis and action. What would your resolution to the dilemma be? What theoretical ideas would you bring to bear on the dilemma?

The 'zero tolerance' psychologist, in the above example, has very strong anti-racist values based on personal commitment and experience. Her analysis is that verbal statements of this kind structure overt racist behaviour. Her prescription for action is therefore that collusion would lead to a worsening situation not retrievable through other community benefits from engagement of the team. The other team members believe that a more inclusive and anti-racist society will come about from the inclusion and valuing of everyone and they see the racist attitudes of the community members as arising from their social situation, and manipulation. Their prescription for action is to put the racism question to one side and focus on strengthening this community through its new neighbourhood association.

Our approach would be to take the best from both these approaches. We would almost certainly raise the issue, but do this gently at first in order to not antagonise the community members and to keep the door open. This could lead to a resolution whereby the community members see that this behaviour is frowned on and are encouraged to explore other viewpoints – without exerting a morally superior posture, which would be belittling. Nevertheless we would be persistent in this stance, finding ways to promote anti-discriminatory thinking from a number of angles (for example, some community members are disabled, some are drug users, some are old, some young, women are the main activists, and it turns out that some also have family connections with other ethnicities and are also offended by the racist talk). The social analysis which links the twin values of anti-racism and acceptance of deprived people as people is one that tries to work with people to understand the forces that instil racism and that keep it alive, together with the ways that people can be helped out of this cul de sac thinking, something that is increasingly being exploited by extreme right wing authoritarian political movements.

Critical community psychology, then, is a moral project – not just a matter of psychological research in the community context for example. The challenge for mainstream community psychology ideas factories (such as journals – and indeed this book) is to reflect this in their publishing practice.

For critical community psychology we can identify some overall value stances. These do not substitute for the community psychologist making a careful consideration of their own value base – a list such as this cannot substitute for the assumption of a value stance from the basis of life experience (which includes what we above described as social analysis – how we understand why things are as they are and what can be done about this).

Social justice

We have already discussed the emphasis on social justice as constitutive of the field of critical community psychology. Here we look at its implications as a value.

If we are serious about justice as a value, we are serious about people's rights to self-determination; to a fair allocation of resources; to live in peace, with freedom from constraints; and to be treated fairly and equitably.

In pursuit of justice, we would be concerned with personal control or agency as well as with social influence, political power and legal rights. We might, for example, expose the ways in which authorities, established to be of service to people, wield their power and authority to effectively silence them; we might highlight inequities in how human services operate; we might work with people to secure access to the necessary supports, or work with services on a change agenda so that they work in a more inclusive and non-discriminatory way. In addition we would seek to adopt a decolonising stance, whereby we seek to expose the domination of particular schools of thought and practices, in particular the hidden forces of colonial power – both past and present. Further, we would endeavour to ensure that marginalised and indigenous voices get heard and that local struggles, practices and resistances are understood, not through a colonial lens, but in terms of people's own understandings, attempting to achieve epistemic justice as opposed to the silencing of those experiences.

Stewardship

Stewardship means being careful about the use of resources, natural resources, economic resources, as well as people's time and effort. While the concept is understood in the fields of ecological design and permaculture (the design, installation and maintenance of indefinitely sustainable human communities set in balanced ecologies, both urban and rural e.g. Holmgren, 2007), it is not usually mentioned explicitly in connection with community psychology. Nevertheless, for us it is a crucial element. Stewardship has been an important aspect of many indigenous traditions, not surprisingly given that in these non-industrial societies, people live closer to and in more immediate interdependence with, the natural world. In complex, industrial societies (which includes the post-industrial landscapes of parts of rich countries) human interdependence with the natural world is less obvious, but is nevertheless fundamental, as the field of ecological economics has made clear (D'Alisa, Demaria & Kallis, 2014; Daly & Farley, 2011; Davey, 2015; Odum & Odum, 2001). Moreover, in a number of locations, those indigenous traditions have provided key elements in the development of alternative proposals and visions for the future of complex modern human societies (Ahmed Iqbal Ullah Race Relations Resource Centre, 2013; Kothari, Demaria & Acosta, 2014; Tanguay, 2012).

If we are serious about stewardship as a value, we are serious about our duties to look after our world and the people in it; to enable people to make a contribution and gain a sense of social belonging; not to waste things, people's lives, or time; and to think long term, make things last longer than us and do things as right as we can.

In pursuit of stewardship, to make the best use of resources, we would work as efficiently as possible, maximising both human and material resources and work in ways that will lead to long lasting sustainable change and not just short term fixes. We would involve other people as fully as possible in innovation, sharing our expertise but not privileging it. Our emphasis would be on helping people change the context of their lives, through an emphasis on their creativity, strengths and potential. We would engage in a continual cycle of doing, learning and reflection.

Community

Inevitably, critical community psychology is about *community*, but what might 'community' mean as a *value* rather than as an object of study or a focus for action? To consider community in these terms indicates the role of critical community psychology in the collaborative construction of better lives, better societies.

If we are serious about community as a value, we take seriously the different hopes and desires that people have, including the hope for companionship, love, acceptance and tolerance; the hope to be included, and for diversity to be welcomed and celebrated; the hope that our histories will be understood, and the hope that our individual and collective flaws will not hide our potential, and that we will all be accepted for who we are.

In pursuit of community, the focus of our work would be to strengthen people's sense of social belonging, respect and commitment to each other, irrespective of their history and social position. We would be in a position to explore, expose and possibly bridge the rifts within communities, and to understand ways in which strong communities can be excluding and intolerant of diversity. We would stress conflict resolution via mediation and negotiation, and would be concerned to be reflective and to evaluate our work constructively and critically.

See Figure 2.2 for a summary of the key points about these three core values.

This chapter has explained how critical community psychology as an (in)discipline and an orientation is situated, ideologically, geographically and historically and has suggested some of its key foundations. The next chapter goes on to look in more detail at some of the key concepts characterising critical community psychology.

Social Justice

Stewardship   Community

Social Justice as a value leads to the articulation of the following rights:
- to have more equal and equitable distribution of resources
- to live in peace and in freedom from constraints
- to equality and fair treatment
- to self-determination

Each of these rights can be pursued in our praxis, underpinned by the value of justice.

Stewardship as a value leads to the articulation of the following duties and responsibilities:
- to look after our world and the people in it
- to enable people to make a contribution and gain a sense of belonging
- not to waste things, people's lives or time
- to think long term make things last longer than us and to do things as right as we can

Each of these duties can be reflected in our praxis, underpinned by the value of stewardship.

Community as a value leads to the articulation of the following hopes and desires:
- for companionship, love, acceptance and tolerance
- for our histories to be understood
- to be included and for diversity to be welcomed and celebrated
- that our individual and collective flaws will not hide our potential and that we will be accepted for who we are

Each of these hopes can guide our praxis, underpinned by the value of community.

Figure 2.2 The three core values of critical community psychology.

Chapter 3

Core elements of a critical community psychology

Summary

The previous chapter has set out the basis for critical community psychology, historically, contextually and ethically. In this chapter we continue setting the scene, first exploring key elements that inform the praxis of critical community psychology, drawing on the ecological metaphor; systems perspectives; multiple levels of analysis; the person-in-context thinking; working together; and prefigurative action. We then summarise these two chapters in terms of what we understand to be the key principles underlying a critical community psychology, namely diversity; innovation; liberation; commitment; critical reflection; and humility.

Elements of critical community psychology

Here we are concerned to identify those bases of critical community psychology praxis that help distinguish it from other fields of applied psychology. Critical community psychology does have elements in common with other fields of applied psychology, both conventional and critical – there is no need to construct an entirely new edifice. These common elements with mainstream psychology include a variety of mainstream social psychological concepts such as social roles and rules, norms and the dynamics of influence and persuasion as well as a variety of methodological assumptions such as the distinction between observation and interpretation or basic psychological principles of learning and development and an understanding of the role of emotion in everyday life. Shared elements with critical variants of psychology include an emphasis on power, on the value laden nature of facts, as well as assumptions about the capacity of everyone to grow and develop given the right conditions. We will touch on all these in this book but not explore those aspects that are adequately treated elsewhere. Moreover, the elements we will pick out in this chapter are not necessarily unique to critical community psychology, although we do generally have a distinctive angle on them. See Figure 3.1 for a depiction of these relationships.

Think!

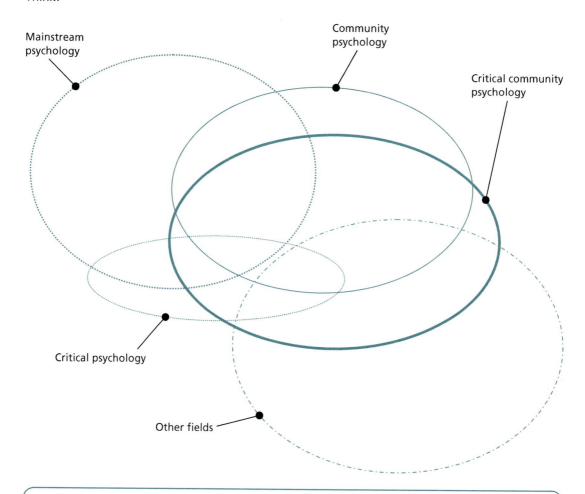

Figure 3.1 Relationships of critical community psychology with related fields.

Many of the concepts and frameworks we will consider do not come originally from the discipline of psychology. However, that is not unusual in psychology in general where a variety of metaphors and concepts has been borrowed from philosophy, the natural sciences, engineering, the social sciences and the arts at various times in its evolution.

The ecological metaphor

Community psychology is concerned with people in their community contexts. It is therefore not surprising that ideas should have been borrowed from the field of ecology – the study of organisms and their environment in interaction.

In the USA, Kelly, in 1968 (reproduced in Kelly, 2006) wrote an influential early paper about the use of the ecological metaphor in community psychology. There have been frequent mentions of the metaphor but surprisingly little articulation of it and use of it as an organising concept. Exceptions can be found in the work of Trickett (e.g. Trickett, Barone, & Watts, 2000) and Revenson (Revenson et al., 2002). Trickett refers to Adaptation, Cycling of resources, Interdependence and Succession as guiding principles (we describe these below). These are sound principles and ones we would also endorse. However, we make the claim for an ecological approach on a broader basis and also cite some additional principles. Ecological thinking can promote a non-individualistic understanding of systems (see section below on the systems metaphor) in that it considers all the elements of a community as interdependent and interacting in complex ways. The whole ecosystem is more than the sum of its parts and it is this kind of thinking that is needed if the complex systems called communities are to be understood. Ecological principles can also be used as a productive source of ideas for the design of interventions and of settings. This can be done through taking principles from the biological study of ecosystems directly to the critical community psychology context (as in our use of the edge effect (Burton & Kagan, 2000), but note that we are not suggesting that a biological model of human social functioning is particularly helpful) or through the intermediary field of human ecology which studies groups, communities and systems of human beings and their resource usage and interchange in the context of the natural environment.

To Trickett's quartet of (1) Adaptation, (2) Cycling of resources, (3) Interdependence, and (4) Succession, we add (5) Unintended consequences, (6) Non-linearity, (7) Ecological fields and edges, (8) Nesting of ecosystems, (9) Ecological design and (10) Ecological priority. We will briefly outline each of these ten principles here.

Adaptation

Organisms in an ecosystem adapt to their surroundings. Similarly, people also adapt to their context. This has both positive and negative aspects. Positively, people can adapt to a new set of circumstances, showing resilience, imagination and organisation. Negatively, people can get used to an unacceptable situation – indeed internalise aspects of it, for example in communities with high levels of civil strife coming to regard violence as normal (Estrada, Ibarra & Sarmiento, 2007).

Cycling of resources

Most ecosystems are relatively closed in terms of the fundamental resources that sustain them. These resources flow in a cyclical manner, being used again; for example, with leaf fall the fibre and mineral content of the leaf goes back into the soil through the action of micro-organisms, fungi, insects and earthworms. It is later used by plants, so continuing the cycle. Human communities often have similar characteristics, for example at cultural level where stories are transmitted and reworked as ways of giving meaning and direction to collective activity. This concept is explicit in the idea, prevalent in Latin American community and liberation psychology of 'the recovery of historical memory', where the collective history of a people is brought into focus as inspiration and a source of practical ideas for addressing the social realities confronting the community (Burton, 2013c; Martín-Baró, 1996; Montero, Sonn & Burton, 2016). The principle is also relevant to the design of effective social settings, reducing dependence on external inputs that may be costly for the community or render it dependent.

Interdependence

In an ecosystem all the organisms are interdependent, forming chains and webs whereby outputs from one life process (including waste products) are the inputs for others (animals breathe out carbon dioxide and green plants use it in photosynthesis to make sugars). Other forms of interdependency exist where one species performs a service for the other while using some asset or product from it (e.g. bees and pollination).

In communities there also are high levels of interdependence. Understanding how this is structured and how it functions is key to understanding the systemic nature of a community.

Think!

Succession

Two kinds of succession can be identified in ecosystems. Organisms have their life cycles and are replaced by others – for example when a forest tree falls, dormant seeds germinate in the area that is now sunlit and more prone to wetting by rain. At the level of the habitat there is often a process of succession, for example from herbs via scrub through low woodland to climax forest.

Succession is similarly an important principle in understanding how community groups, community leaders and whole communities change over time. Different generations of community leaders, for example, may have very different styles and stances as a result of the changing context and maturity of the community. In some cases the transition is from reformist, conservative, to radical and in others the change goes in the other direction. Similarly, the characteristics of a community change over time; for example, a new housing development may begin with many young families but 30 years later these have grown up and there is a high proportion of retired people. An immigrant community starts its life in inner city neighbourhoods and with the passing of generations it becomes established, using the language of the new country, modifying cultural practices, dispersing or translocating to wealthier suburbs. The evolution of this book into its second edition is an example of succession, where an artefact is produced through an interdependent set of social processes: something similar happens in the variety of cultural artefacts, practices, traditions of any community.

Unintended consequences

Since the publication of Silent Spring (Carson, 1962) in the early 1960s, there has been an increasing understanding of the fragility of ecosystems and their propensity to experience unintended consequences of human intervention. So, large river dams, for example, lead to salination of irrigated land, can change the prevalence of parasites such as bilharzia and affect fisheries downstream (Darling, 1970).

Unintended consequences are also a result of interventions in human systems including communities and while they are difficult to anticipate it is vital to try to do so, to be in a position to identify them when they occur and to at least minimise the damage.

Example: Tenant management of housing

A poor community was supported to develop the skills to take over the management of a social housing complex in the North of Manchester. This led to an increased sense of community identity, confidence and skill in negotiating with public authorities, as well as skills and responsibilities. Before long they began to take decisions that reflected hostility towards other groups. For instance, they developed policies not to allow drug users to obtain tenancies: this was followed by the exclusion of families with children and those with mental health difficulties. They became even more inward looking and stronger in their own identity.

In environmental protection the concept of unintended consequences leads to the 'precautionary principle' (e.g. European Environment Agency, 2013).

Non-linearity

The effects of changes in ecosystems are typically not linear or simply cumulative. The rapidly increasing global concentrations of greenhouse gases do not just lead to radiative forcing – the increased retention of solar radiation – but also to increasing ocean acidity (and reduced ability to absorb carbon dioxide). At the same time, the increased temperatures lead to melting of permafrost, releasing the potent greenhouse gas methane, and the melting of ice sheets decreases the reflectivity of the earth. In all these cases the feedback effects are positive.

Similar effects take place in human communities. For example, it may seem little progress is being made on social issues, but then a number of mutually reinforcing developments take place in short succession producing a 'quantum leap' and real change. Such changes are experienced as unantici-pated breakthroughs or cultural change, for example in the social treatment of formerly excluded groups (e.g. the revolution in attitudes to disabled people, or gay people in the later twentieth century in particular minority world contexts); the almost universal adoption of anti-smoking norms in public places, extending even to many private homes; or the sudden collapse and fall of a regime (e.g. Apart-heid South Africa, the Soviet Union) that had seemed impregnable.

Fields and edges

A key concept in ecology is that of the ecosystem. This describes both a field and a system. As a field, we are considering a terrain that has a boundary and within which interactions happen. Field concepts have been used in psychology from time to time (Gestalt psychology and hence Lewin, and J.R. Kantor's interbehavioural psychology, show some manifestations of environmental psychology, for example) although it has not been a customary recourse for psychologists – for critical community psychology it is through the ecological metaphor that field thinking enters. When the ecosystem is considered as a system, we are considering those interactions within the field as having a structure and complexity that cannot simply be reduced to the sum of those interactions. There is more on the system concept later in this chapter.

The field we call the ecosystem does not generally have a 'hard' boundary that totally encloses it. There are transactions between adjacent ecosystems. The edge or 'ecotone' is where two ecosystems meet. This area tends to have characteristics of both ecosystems with a resulting richness of species and energy transactions. The edge concept is used extensively in permaculture (Holmgren, 2007; Mol-linson, 1988) as a design principle to maximise yield. It can also be applied to social systems. We have used the concept in this way to maximise available resources for social change (Burton & Kagan, 2000; Kagan, 2007; Kagan et al., 2000). Edge is also arguably an ethical principle – looking to work with and to maximise edge between social groups facilitates contact, interaction, learning and respect between them. As a strategy for maximising the use of community resources it can increase people's prospects for making sustained changes.

Nesting

Nesting here does not refer to the behaviour of birds but to the way habitats and ecosystems can be defined on various scales. So, while a rotten tree is a habitat for a wide variety of organisms, the tree itself is part of a wood, and the wood is part of a wider ecosystem. In a similar way, communities can also be thought of in these terms. On a spatially defined scale, this will range from the household to the street, to the neighbourhood, to the city, province and so on. On a scale defined by identity and belonging, the following communities are nested within each other: from the family and friendship group, to the social network, to the community of (e.g. religious, political, ethnic, occupational) inter-est, to the regional group (e.g. Mancunians – a term to describe people from Manchester, UK, North-erners), to that of nationality and beyond (e.g. Welsh, British, Muslim, anti-capitalist, Latin American, Asian). In working with communities, we need to understand these multiple forms of nesting to avoid oversimplifying.

Ecological design

Since a key role for critical community psychology is in the construction of better ways of living (the creation of social settings) in various ways, *design* is a neglected but important part of practice. In this, ideas from ecologically based design can be helpful. These include:

- the use of endogenous resources (creating, sharing and using wealth locally and not depending on inward investment);
- the exploitation of the edge effect (discussed above);
- strengthening community resilience;
- creating elements that produce multiple yields (e.g. a community building might serve several practical functions as well as more psychological functions in terms of community identity and cohesion);
- attention to the community's carrying capacity, for living within the limits of an ecosystem depends on three factors:
  i the amount of resources available in the ecosystem;
  ii the size of the population or community; and
  iii the amount of resources each individual within the community is consuming.

Our borrowing from ecological concepts and the modelling of interventions on ecological design has two motivations. First, it offers us a rich set of metaphors and concepts to enrich critical community psychology practice. Second, the global ecological crisis in any case forces us to actively consider how to live within our ecological resources, the carrying capacity of our home ecosystem or bioregion. As Holmgren (2008, p. 1.1) reminds us:

> Archaeology records a series of civilisations that rose and fell as they depleted their bioregional resource base.

Ecological priority

The ecological model also sets a priority for us in our studies, professional work, personal lives and activism. That priority is guided both by facts and values. It is that protection and restoration of the ecosystem that has a fundamental importance. Without it, human life, human society, human endeavour, become untenable. We are currently living through an ecological crisis, an emergency. This can be expressed in a variety of ways. The 'ecological footprint' measures how fast 'we' (humanity in the aggregate) use resources and generate waste in comparison to the rate at which they are regenerated by natural processes.

> Each city, state or nation's Ecological Footprint can be compared to its biocapacity. If a population's Ecological Footprint exceeds the region's biocapacity, that region runs an ecological deficit. Its demand for the goods and services that its land and seas can provide – fruits and vegetables, meat, fish, wood, cotton for clothing, and carbon dioxide absorption – exceeds what the region's ecosystems can renew. A region in ecological deficit meets demand by importing, liquidating its own ecological assets (such as overfishing), and/or emitting carbon dioxide into the atmosphere. If a region's biocapacity exceeds its Ecological Footprint, it has an ecological reserve.
>
> (Global Footprint Network, n.d.)

The Global Footprint Network calculates that globally, 1.7 earths are being used to provision humanity and deal with its wastes, and that "more than 80 percent of the world's population lives in countries that are running ecological deficits, using more resources than what their ecosystems can renew". This ratio can also be expressed as an 'overshoot day', and the calculation can be made at global, nation-state, city and personal levels. The ecological footprint, then, is a powerful heuristic tool for highlighting the nature of the ecological crisis and the priority of the ecological for humanity.

In a programme of work at the Stockholm Resilience Centre, Johan Rockström and colleagues have developed the concept of planetary boundaries (Rockström et al., 2009a, 2009b). These define the safe operating space for humanity with respect to the planet's biophysical subsystems or processes. Many of these react in a non-linear, often abrupt manner, with particular sensitivity near to threshold levels of certain key variables. Crossing these thresholds could shift important subsystems, such as a monsoon system, or the North Atlantic Drift/Gulf Stream current that warms Western Europe, into a new state, with threatening and potentially even catastrophic consequences for people. The Stockholm team identified nine of these planetary subsystems and proposed boundaries and thresholds for each. On reviewing the situation in 2015, they concluded that two of the boundaries, genetic diversity (i.e. biodiversity) and biochemical flows (nitrogen and phosphorous cycles), were beyond the zone of uncertainty, i.e. at high risk (Steffen et al., 2015). Two others, climate change and land system change, were in the range of uncertainty, i.e. at increasing risk. The latest data on global climate change (including greenhouse gas concentrations, average temperatures, sea ice loss and ice-cap and glacier melt, permafrost loss and methane release) suggest that climate change is now past the zone of uncertainty and presents a very high risk (Intergovernmental Panel on Climate Change, 2018). Furthermore, Rockström and colleagues did not have data for all the boundaries. 'Novel entities', for example, concerns chemicals introduced into the ecosystem by human activity with unknown consequences. Increasing concern on plastics, and especially incorporation of synthetic plastics molecules into all life forms, indicates the likelihood that these 'known unknowns' also present a serious risk to the ecosystems and hence to humanity.

These ecological system crises are unprecedented. While former civilisations have succumbed to destruction of their ecological substrate, it now seems a strong possibility that human civilisation as a whole (if we should really call it that) could meet the same fate. This is what we mean when we identify this tenth principle of 'ecological priority'. Ecological priority is, because it underpins human survival, a deeply ethical question. Crossing ecological boundaries will threaten the lives of not only future generations but also people living today, and those in precarious environments (coastal cities, low lying islands, high altitude settlements, hurricane zones) disproportionately so.

Reflect!

Explore the ecological footprint for your country and you personally at www. footprintcalculator.org/. One of the authors is using the equivalent of 1.1 earths. It's still too much but can you do better?

Act!

See what you can find out about the meaning of the concepts of (a) anthropocene and (b) capitalocene. Both suggest ecological systems collapse – what do you think are the inequalities in both causation and receipt of this ecological systems collapse?

Think!

Community psychologists share ideas, research and practice at an international level. This includes going to international conferences, at a continental and intercontinental level. However, a jet flight emits a vast amount of carbon dioxide, which is particularly potent at high altitudes, contributing to global warming. One intercontinental flight will wipe out all of a person's emission savings through cycling, not eating meat, turning down the heating or use of natural ventilation in preference to air conditioning.

Supposing these international exchanges have some value, what alternatives can you envisage that avoid the harmful ecological impacts?

> ## Reflect!
>
> Have you encountered any of these concepts before in your psychological education? Which ones? If you haven't, why do you think that might be?

The systems perspective

> A system is a set of things – people, cells, molecules, or whatever – interconnected in such a way that they produce their own pattern of behavior over time. The system may be buffeted, constricted, triggered, or driven by outside forces. But the system's response to these forces is characteristic of itself, and that response is seldom simple in the real world.
>
> (Meadows, 2009, p. 2)

Community psychology is always concerned with social 'systems', whether at the level of the group, the neighbourhood, the organisation, a dispersed community or on a wider territorial basis. Typically, these systems intersect, so for example, the neighbourhood is shaped by and subject to influences and forces from the economy, government, associations and so on. It is therefore essential that critical community psychology has an understanding of systems, not just as the sum of their separate elements (for example the people in the neighbourhood) but of the way these parts work together as an interconnected whole. We therefore contrast the needed 'systems thinking' with 'atomistic thinking' that fails to take account of the nature of the systemic properties of community systems, and therefore often fails because it is unprepared for the complexities that arise. For example, an atomistic intervention will try to alter one aspect of concern in a community, in isolation and without being prepared for the reactions of other parts of the system.

Systems thinking can be difficult to articulate as there are many different accounts, but the following key ideas are shared by all schools of systems thinkers. (For a more comprehensive list, though very much from the systems dynamics variant of systems theory, see Meadows (2009, pp. 188–191)).

1   Complex systems involve interconnected parts.
2   The organisation of complex systems can be understood in terms of a series of levels, where elements of one level can be dependent on the superior and inferior levels.
3   The properties of systems are emergent, that is they cannot be predicted from the properties of individual elements in themselves.
4   Systems are characterised by feedback, recursion, boundaries, nested subsystems and responsiveness to the environment in which the system is located.

Moreover, the kinds of systems that we are concerned with in critical community psychology have some further typical properties.

5   They are open – that is they are subject to outside influences and they themselves affect other systems.
6   They are 'soft' rather than hard, which means that they cannot be understood in terms of mechanical-like processes of input–output and prediction: they involve people and people have ideas, beliefs and attitudes and these enter into the system as properties.

These open and soft aspects come together when we call community social systems 'loosely bounded'. Their boundaries are flexible, permeable and changeable. We therefore require a particular kind of systems thinking to appreciate and work with the kinds of systems that we meet in critical community psychology, and this has been variously described as soft and critical systems thinking (Midgley &

Ochoa-Arias, 2004). We will meet some examples from these systems disciplines later in the book as helpful tools for critical community psychology. It is also worth noting that the previous section on the ecological metaphor has already introduced several principles of systems thinking.

While on the systems metaphor, we should also make the point that all psychology is properly a systems discipline, since it is concerned with human beings who are themselves open systems, consisting of sets of subsystems, influenced by, or constructed by, super-ordinate social systems (family, peer group, community, economy, state).

Multiple levels of analysis

The above discussions of the systemic nature of people and their communities indicates the need for multiple levels of analysis in critical community psychology. To take an example, a project on friendship patterns of disabled young women (Burton & Kagan, 1995) could look at the different levels of analysis as shown in Table 3.1.

Table 3.1 Different levels of analysis and issues in relation to friendships

Level	Issues
Individual	How do the participants themselves look at and understand the question of friendship? What are their expectations, attitudes, beliefs, values and competences? What do they want to change?
Dyad	In specific interactions, what goes on? How could this be different?
Group	What is the pattern of friendships among the group? How do these change over time?
Neighbourhood	What is the neighbourhood like? How easy, and safe, is it to get out and about? Are there settings that offer opportunities to meet and get to know people, and to do things with them as friends?
Service system	Does the service system have friendship on its agenda? Does it encourage or discourage citizen involvement?

Think!

See if you can extend the levels that might influence the friendship patterns of a young disabled woman (see Table 3.1) by identifying the following:

Level of analysis	Issues
Family	
Economy	
State	

The primary focus of a critical community psychology intervention might be any one of these, but an intervention that did not take account of the others would not be critical community psychology.

The person-in-context

Strangely enough, for all the thousands of books and articles by psychologists there is surprisingly little discussion of what a person is, perhaps because the person (in the general sense) seems like a given, an unproblematic category or concept, which is therefore not subjected to further theorisation. Maybe this is more properly a philosophical question, and indeed philosophy has treated the question in various ways. Fundamental here is the relation between the person as individual and their social context – the relationship between person and society or in mainstream psychology that between person and situation. As indicated in the last chapter, critical community psychology does start from the idea that the psychological is best understood as both emerging from and dependent on social relations, not just interpersonal ones but collective and social-systemic relations too. Here we will outline some of the dimensions of this understanding.

An ontology of individual and society

Following Bhaskar (1998) we are not simply replacing the individualism we criticised in the last chapter with its opposite – collectivism. While a pure form of individualism tries to explain social phenomena solely in terms of facts about individuals, a pure collectivism would explain individuals solely in terms of the social system. Instead, we adopt what Bhaskar (1979, p. 120) terms the transformational model:

> [People] do not create society. For it always pre-exists them. Rather it is an ensemble of structures, practices and conventions that individuals reproduce or transform, but which would not exist unless they did so. Society does not exist independently of conscious human activity (the error of reification). But it is not the product of the latter (the error of voluntarism).

So people construct their world but not under the circumstances of their choosing, and they themselves are constructed through their own social context (see Figure 3.2).

These linked processes happen over time and can be analytically separated into the socialisation of people, and the activities by which they then reproduce and also transform their world. A community psychology that does not understand the fundamental nature of these three processes, socialisation, reproduction and transformation cannot be truly critical since it will not be able to understand the following:

● the way in which people become the way they are – imperfect, bearers of tradition, yet potentially capable of amazing feats of resilience and creativity;

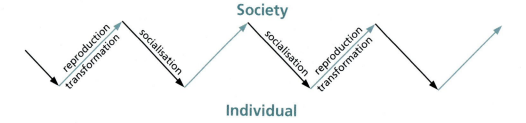

Figure 3.2 Representation of the reproduction and transformation of the person and society in a continuous process.

- the way in which social systems act, through their members to preserve the status quo, to reproduce themselves while nevertheless adapting to changed circumstances;
- the imperfect nature of social reproduction, which depends on human subjects who think, decide, act and reflect, can use the tools the system gives them (like people saying new things in a language they have learned) to make (transformational) changes in their circumstances whether in their personal lives, their community context or more widely through societal change (Burton, 2014b).

The person–situation formula

Just as we avoid a simplistic individualism and a simplistic collectivism in favour of the transformational account, so we also avoid attributing people's actions merely to characteristics either of themselves or of the settings in which they find themselves. This may seem an obvious point, that action, thought, behaviour, decision, emotion are all the joint product of the person themselves and of the setting which the person inhabits. But understanding this is fundamental, especially when the critical community psychologist is confronted with the inevitable frustrations encountered in trying to help people make real change in their community. Why do people act irrationally, selfishly, cruelly? Armed with some understanding of the person × situation formula it is possible, indeed imperative, to always analyse. The problem is never the person and never just the situation but a complex mixture of the two, conditioned through the wider processes of socialisation and reproduction.

For the purposes of analysis we can distinguish between two broad levels of the social context, that of the person–situation and that of community–society. While helpful for purposes of analysis and exposition, this split does break down in practice since even the immediate context of the person is deeply affected by societal level factors which saturate not just the social settings we encounter as social beings but also the very being of all people. We will therefore conclude with a brief treatment of these person–society relationships too. Figure 3.3 maps out this 'analytic terrain' for critical community psychology.

Person–situation level elements of analysis

Mainstream social psychology can provide us with helpful concepts for understanding the person-in-context. Let us present some examples of such concepts, not as a complete list but to indicate how mainstream social psychology can be drawn from as part of the toolkit for a critical community psychology.

ROLE-RULE CONTEXTS

Some social scientists (e.g. Goffman, Harré and Secord) have made much of the idea that social life can be likened to a play where actors have roles that are relatively predictable, indeed scripted in terms of social rules and norms. Putting the idea of social role and social rule together enables us to identify role-rule contexts, relatively predictable ways in which as social actors we decode the implicit rules of a situation and adopt behaviours that fit our expected roles. Some of these role-rule contexts are episodic or short term, for example taking part in a job interview, being at a party, listening to a speech. Others are more enduring, for example being a parent. For the community psychologist, having an idea of what the rules of a situation or of a community are can help interpret the actions of those therein. It can prevent unrealistic expectations – for example for people to break out of the straitjacket of expectations – while also giving clues as to where the role-rule-norm complex is less strong, whether temporarily weakened or maybe unclear and in flux. If we are working to help the weaker members of communities to take more control of their life situation, understanding these factors can make a difference between setting them up to fail or giving helpful catalytic support to transcend the nexus of expectations and internalised, quasi-automatic patterns of thought, emotion and action.

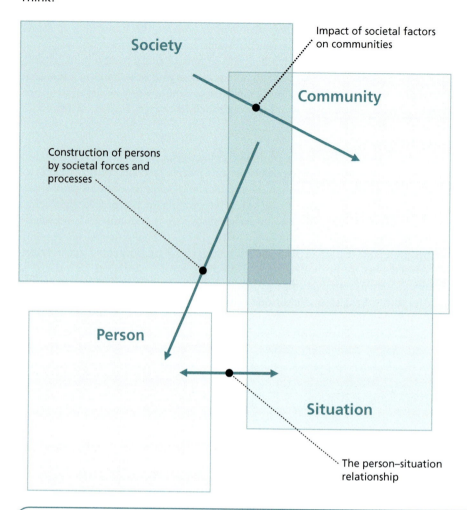

Figure 3.3 Analytic terrain for critical community psychology.

Example: South Asian families: mismatch between behavioural style and role-rule context

We (MB) were invited to contribute to a workshop event organised by parent carers of disabled children and young adults of South Asian (mainly Pakistani) heritage. He (MB) assumed his usual style of interaction with family members which is to work collaboratively, following their lead as to what is most important for them. Only later did he find that this had been interpreted as being diffident in the workshop because in their cultural context 'health professionals' are high status people who are expected to take on a more directive and high profile role. There was a mismatch between the role-rule context and the behavioural style adopted so that in effect some social rules were inadvertently broken.

GROUP DYNAMICS

The social group is a key element of most social settings. Groups, like role-rule contexts, have many forms, from the transient situation of a bus queue (which might only just qualify for the label 'group') through loose groupings of friends and colleagues to more organised groupings such as a street gang or tenants' group. In all cases there are phenomena that arise from the fact of being a group and which do not appear to be reducible to the individuals in the group. The study of 'group dynamics' has been for many years part of the tradition of mainstream social psychology, although the approach to study has often been rather artificial. Nevertheless, having some grounding in the typical group processes and patterns can be very helpful. For example:

- Understanding something of how groups tend to evolve (the stages of forming, norming, storming…) can help to distinguish between transient conflict that is an essential part of group formation and more threatening discord that may damage or destroy the group in question.
- Understanding something of how groups act under pressure, for example in defining in-group and out-group identities, can help the community psychologist to understand that it is not always possible to insist on universal tolerance, for example in a situation where a community group is coming under attack from other community members or official bodies.
- Understanding something of group decision making – phenomena such as 'group-think' and the polarisation of judgements (Janis, 1982; Moscovici & Zavalloni, 1969) – is a resource for the community psychologist to support a community group to think through carefully the decisions that it is making and to avoid the common traps.

These three examples are all examples of mainstream psychological concepts that can be shared with community colleagues, not as some kind of arcane mind-reading or 'psycho-analysis' but as practical tools for strengthening those in the thick of principled struggles.

> ## Think!
>
> Why has a great deal of social psychology been considered irrelevant to real-life situations? To what extent has the 'crisis in social psychology' that arose in Anglo-American psychology in the 1970s been resolved? Why do you think this is?

LEADERSHIP

Social groups tend to have those that lead and those that follow, and so do communities and groups within them. Working with communities requires an understanding of leadership, its typical dimensions – how it can be strengthened or undermined. A large social psychological literature on leadership is relevant here. For example, the relationship between concern with task and concern for people (Blake & Mouton, 1961) helps us understand the balance between effectiveness and popularity, how the two can mutually reinforce one another, but also how the pursuit of one at the expense of the other can lead to failures of leadership. Ideas from the study of leadership, for example, have been applied by Venezuelan community social psychologists to the leadership dilemmas of community leaders (Farias & Perdomo, 2004), who have also developed interventions to support such leaders (Hernández, 2004, and see also other articles in this issue of the journal). Leadership is, however, a fundamentally relational concept, rather than being a quality of an individual, and it is a mistake to think that community leaders can be identified or that 'once a leader, always a leader'. The dynamic process of community leadership can be nurtured, though, and it is quite possible for different people to assume leadership at different times and in different ways.

Reflect!

Describe some situations in which you have shown leadership. When this happened, who followed? What enabled you to assume the role of leader at this time? Now see if you can describe some situations where you were happy to be led. What was different about these situations?

Community–society level elements of analysis

At this level of analysis, social psychology has little to offer the community psychologist, critical or otherwise. The task is to understand something of the forces that shape, destroy and reconstitute communities together with the ways dominant ideology both describes and disguises these processes. Not having an understanding of these factors can lead to two kinds of error. The first, one that can apply to community psychologists who do not take account of wider societal forces, can lead to a voluntaristic optimism, where change seems possible, particularly where people on the ground are enthusiastic, committed and act with integrity. Short and medium range change can be achieved in such contexts but the community psychologists can be unprepared for the forces that come along and alter the rules of the game. Having seen traditional working class communities in our city, Manchester, destroyed through the de-industrialisation of the Thatcher years and by successive urban regeneration schemes, we are very aware of the scale of these forces that shake and remake the very terrain on which communities exist. Further afield we can point to the systematic destruction of communities in places as far apart as Palestine and Colombia. For survivors of the psychiatric systems and those harmed by psychotropic medication, the rapid growth of the pharmaceutical industry into a billion dollar monolithic structure has very much changed the rules of the game for those working for social justice in the mental health field. The resistance put up by the pharmaceutical industry against any impute of corporate irresponsibility or against the broader critique of the biomedical model of mental health is now swift and brutal and the impotence of government regulators stark. Many of the previous systems of protection and representation for those receiving mental health systems have effectively been lost or rendered ineffective.

The other error though is to fall into the trap of a highly 'structural' understanding that supposes that nothing can be done either to resist wide scale societal economic and political forces or to construct better social arrangements. Such an understanding would run counter to the transformational ontology described above.

So what are the conceptual building bricks for building an understanding of the society–community relationship? We can begin to answer this by suggesting some propositions about the relationship between communities (however constituted, conceived and bounded – see Chapter 4) and the economic and political systems – the broader societies in which they exist:

1   Communities are created, shaped and ultimately reconstituted and destroyed as a consequence of broader economic relations.
2   Communities, while to greater or lesser extent enjoying a relative autonomy from the wider societal scale, are nevertheless affected by economic, political and policy initiatives, particularly those from government.
3   Communities intersect with the processes and structures of political representation and mobilisation.
4   Communities have within them conflicts of interest, which at times become manifest as behavioural conflicts, that represent in microcosm some of the structural conflicts in the host society.
5   Communities may themselves have interests that are consistent or contradictory with the dominant interests in the host society.
6   As historical products, communities include layers of influence, power, interest, conflict, commonality that reflect the wider society and also the historical process of community formation and development. These elements can be in conflict.

Reflect!

Think about your community (or one you know well). In what ways has it changed over the years? What do you think caused those changes? What effects has that had on the people – who lives in the community, where they live, what they do in work, social reproduction and leisure, and what they think, feel and believe? How do you see this continuing to change?

Act!

With some friends or colleagues, collect some magazine pictures that you think reflect your idea of community. How much overlap was there in the images you chose? Why were there differences between you? How do these images link to the wider society of which they are a part? How is power revealed through these images (for example who is included and who is not)?

Society and the individual

Finally, we need to also understand something of the process linking society and the individual. We have already established the overall ontological assumptions here, but, specifically, through what kinds of social institutions and processes do socialisation, reproduction and transformation occur? We find Leonard's (1984) framework useful here. He identifies three social spheres in which individuals are formed, State, Family and Economy. These three spheres saturate the social worlds of people, every encounter, and the obtaining of any resource depends on one or more of them. Take economy for instance: from the earliest years, aspirations and expectations as to who we will be are dependent on the options that the economy affords. Even for those who are not in work, who are still in preparation for work roles, who can't access them or who have now finished working, the economy is constitutive of who they are. In just the same way, the family and the state have similarly saturating influences on who we are, how we think, what we feel, what options we have open to us. This understanding of the *societal* construction of the individual (Burton & Kagan, 2008) provides a necessary corrective to the largely intra-psychic and individualistic paradigm that dominates conventional psychologies.

However, these relations of the 'big three' – state, economy and family – are also typically mediated through other social domains – community, workplace, school, club, group, church and so on – some of which themselves enjoy a relative autonomy from the fundamental trio.

Reflect!

How are you, just now, at this point in your life, affected by the state, the economy or your family? What else influences who you are and where you are going in life?

To consider how these spheres and domains work to construct persons, we would also need to identify some mediating social processes and phenomena. For us, key building blocks in an analysis would be relations of exchange, including those of exploitation, other types of interaction, ideology and communication. These then operate differentially depending on the distinctions among people and their social position (power, resources, identity, social linkages and belonging) on the dimensions of class, race, religion, sex and gender, age, ability and disability and so on.

Finally, we need to understand something of how these societal forces and phenomena are 'interpolated' (Leonard, 1984; Therborn, 1980) or subjectively configured (González Rey, 2015, 2017), that is, the way they enter, now as psychological entities, into customary ways of thinking, acting, feeling, being. Elsewhere we have proposed a model of ideology–action–structure complexes (IASCs) as a way of understanding the interrelated nature of society-wide ideologies, customary practices and policies and social structures. These IASCs operate at all three levels (individual, community, society) and can help us understand typical patterns in their interrelations (Burton, 2013a; Kagan & Burton, 2014, 2018).

Reflect!

Do these ways of thinking about the construction of persons in society alter the way you think about those around you? In what ways?

The above, albeit schematic, overview of the relationships between person, community and society is rarely attempted, either in other fields of pure or applied psychology or generally in community psychology, or in related fields which if they consider the societal sphere may tend to neglect the psychological. One of the few attempts to do this was that of Ignacio Martín-Baró in the two text-books of: *Acción e Ideología: Psicología social desde Centroamérica* [Social Psychology from a Central American Perspective: Action and Ideology] (Martín-Baró, 1983); and *Sistema, Grupo y Poder* [System, Group and Power] (Martín-Baró, 1989). Unfortunately, neither has been translated into English. Rather as we have outlined above, but over the course of two substantial books, he integrated insights from mainstream social psychology with a more political–economic analysis, correcting the short-sightedness of Anglo-American social psychology with an analysis that took account of wider structural inequalities and the processes that underpin them. In so doing he tried to establish a social psychology that was adequate for the real project of social reconstruction and community empowerment in which he and colleagues were engaged in war torn El Salvador. His work is one inspiration for our own approach (Burton, 2004a; Burton & Kagan, 2005).

Think!

What psychology texts have you read that were written in the global South (the 'third world', 'developing countries', 'periphery')? What do you consider to be the factors that prevent work from those parts of the world becoming part of the mainstream literature of psychology?

FACING THE NATURE OF OPPRESSION AND LIBERATION: IMMERSION IN THE LIVED EXPERIENCES OF PEOPLE OPPRESSED BY THE SOCIAL SYSTEM

In the previous chapter we identified the key theme of social justice. Here we present the same issue but in negative terms as point of departure for critical community psychology. Oppression, exclusion, exploitation, marginality are experiences affecting millions of people throughout the world. Being poor, unemployed, discriminated or disabled in an ableist society are serious risk factors. Being excluded from economic, social and political life can have adverse effects on individuals and communities alike. Critical community psychology makes a direct confrontation with this reality, for much of the time hidden from view by the obscene bonanza of consumption and squander of resources, and by the propaganda of the dominant system of social relations. This reality is hard to face. It involves recognising the pain of the majority. It requires strength and commitment, and a refusal to accept the excuses, the lies, the myths that make normal and acceptable that daily reality of theft, pillage, neglect, cruelty and violence.

The existence of oppression and its pervasive and persistent nature give reason for the existence of critical community psychology as part of a wider family of liberatory praxis. It makes liberation the central aim, at all levels of the system, defining the relevance, the effectiveness and the truth of psychological concepts and tools.

While not religious (most of the present authors are atheists) we follow liberation psychology in adopting from liberation theology the 'preferential option for the poor' which we redefine as follows,

> There is a need to test psychology against the experiences of those whose lives are distorted by the accumulation process and its correlates – the excluded, the marginalised and the oppressed. But it is also important to recognise that those groups are diverse and fragmented. Disabled people in an urban suburb, migrant workers in a country town, 'surplus' people in a poor neighbourhood, victims of domestic violence, Indonesian textile workers producing cheap clothing for a high street chain in the middle to high income countries, Iraqis and Palestinians bombed by weapons from the core capitalist countries, or traditional farmers (for example in Mexico and India) impoverished and displaced by cheap grain imports from the US: all these are part of the oppressed majority that are the proper focus of engagement for a globally literate, liberatory psychology, practised from the core capitalist countries.
>
> (adapted from Burton & Kagan, 2009, p. 58)

Because critical community psychology starts from the position and the experience of the oppressed it takes as inherently problematic, as chronically contested, the role of the <u>expert</u> – in this case that of the community psychologist. The professional expert does not live the same reality as the oppressed person, although they may themselves experience some forms of oppression. Nevertheless, we do not fall into the trap of rejecting expertise. Instead we adopt the notion taught us by Latin American colleagues which distinguishes between popular and scientific knowledge. In this formulation, popular knowledge is that which comes from the lived reality of the people, the community members or, in terms of this discussion, the oppressed. Scientific knowledge, on the other hand is the specialised concepts, the technical knowledge, the metaphors and models and tools that the psychologist brings, not as a superior expert who knows best, but as the junior part of the dialectical relationship with the community. In keeping with that idea we constantly move back and forth from the 'scientific', the specialist, to the ordinary, from ideas taken from the academy to the reality (and ideas) in the field, putting them together, blending them, contrasting them always seeking a productive relationship, even where that is tense and uncomfortable.

There are various ways of managing the inherent tension in roles and social situation between expert and community member. One idealisation of this is Fals Borda's model of 'inserción', where the professional lives as part of the community, sharing the day to day problems and issues, but nevertheless maintaining a distinctive role of expert facilitator or 'animator' (Fals Borda, 1988; Fals Borda & Rahman, 1991). Freire's model of popular educator is similar (Freire, 1972b; Kane, 2001; Mayo, 1999; McLaren & Leonard, 1993). We may not be in a position to adopt these models, and indeed they may not be entirely appropriate in different contexts, yet they do throw into relief some kinds of community psychology practice that has little real presence in the community and remains alienated from the lives of the oppressed.

A dialectical relationship between people and systems: conscientisation

In keeping with the above ideas we also want to emphasise what may be called the dialectical relationship between people and systems. This notion of a dialectical relationship can be difficult to pin down since as a philosophical idea it stands outside the dominant approach in psychology which, for example, distinguishes between 'independent and dependent variables'. The dialectical approach instead emphasises the dialogue between opposites – which here includes system and individual. In keeping with the transformational account outlined above, the dialectical account stresses the co-constitution of the two terms. As Seidman (1986, p. 8) suggests, this is what defines the distinctive niche of community psychology:

> ...reciprocal relationships and interdependencies between individuals and social systems that represent a unique and emergent synthesis of community and psychology.

Freire (1972a, p. 73) put it like this:

> It is as transforming and creative beings that men [sic – *he later acknowledged that his language in the early 1970s was not sufficiently inclusive in terms of gender*], in their permanent relations with reality, produce not only material goods – tangible objects – but also social institutions, ideas and concepts. Through their continuing praxis, men simultaneously create history and become historical-social beings.

Freire introduced the concept and method of 'conscientisation' as the key to enabling people to become conscious of the processes by which they and their social contexts are constructed together, and what needs to happen to remove not solely external oppression but also the psychological habits of the oppressed that help perpetuate injustice – socialisation and reproduction that once conscientisation takes place can be shifted towards a process of transformation.

As Martín-Baró (1996) describes it, conscientisation involves a person or people being transformed through changing their reality, through an active process of dialogue. In this there is a gradual decoding of the world, as mechanisms of oppression and dehumanisation are grasped. Thereby new possibilities for action open up as the people's new knowledge of the surrounding reality leads to new self understanding about the roots of what people are and what they can become. This process is what we aspire to in critical community psychology and at times we do indeed witness it, even contribute to it in reality.

Act!

Imagine you are talking to a group of six-year-olds. How would you convey to them the idea of a dialectical relationship between people and systems? How could you link this complex idea to a relatively uncomplicated outlook on the world? How would you explain the same idea to your grandmother?

Working together

By now there should be no doubt that critical community psychology sets itself ambitious goals for system change. Indeed, such goals may seem ridiculously out of proportion for professional psychologists. The key here is that psychologists can indeed achieve little, either on their own, or merely within their job role. Just as we emphasised building up networks of support in the last chapter, here we emphasise that critical community psychology is done together, in partnership with other colleagues and with community members.

Interdisciplinarity

We have already noted some of the relationships between critical community psychology and other disciplines and acknowledged that many of the concepts and tools in our own practice come from outside the conventional disciplinary boundary of psychology. But successful programmes of work require the input of other specialists. We, for instance, have recently worked with urban planners and regeneration professionals, public health specialists, social services managers and professionals, visual and performance artists, educationalists, health workers and systems practitioners. Colleagues elsewhere work with economists, architects, ecologists, engineers and anthropologists. These relationships, interchanges, borrowings and divisions of labour strengthen and enrich critical community psychology, which has to be secure and confident enough of its own disciplinary identity to maintain its own distinctive contribution as part of a collective collaborative effort.

Agency, power and collective action

We have seen that critical community psychology adopts the 'preferential option for the oppressed'. It sides with the weak, the disadvantaged, the excluded and the marginalised, and those who struggle to improve the quality of life of those in their communities. In so doing it allies itself with those who have relatively limited power. But in doing that it is always alert to how the power of the oppressed and disadvantaged can be maximised. Elsewhere (Burton & Kagan, 1996) we have reviewed the nature of empowerment and identified a number of propositions both about the nature of power and as guides to increasing the relative power of those who are relatively powerless. These are reproduced in Table 3.2. They emphasise increasing social power through collective action and the formation of alliances and coalitions. We recommend the approach to this in the work of Antonio Gramsci (Devine, Pearmain & Purdy, 2009; Gramsci, 1971), which although written more than 70 years ago, attains a level of sophistication that is hard to match. Other work that is relevant is the work on social movements from the North American resource mobilisation school, European writers on the new social movements and commentators on social movements in the global South (Burton, 2000; Foweraker, 1995; Petras & Veltmeyer, 2005; Touraine, 1988; Zald & McCarthy, 1988; Vergara-Camus, 2014). We will return to the question of power in later chapters because power underlies everything and is revealed as soon as we try to change anything.

Table 3.2 Propositions on power and empowerment

1. Power is a relative attribute: some have more than others.
2. However, power is primarily systemic in nature, tied to material relations between groups of people with irreconcilable interests.
3. Power is all around us, in our everyday practices and speech, and in our understanding of the world. As such its exercise is greatly hidden.
4. Power decays: it has to be continually regenerated through social interaction.
5. Power is not in our gift, although we can alter social relations on a small scale to catalyse the winning of more power.
6. Power can be acquired by joining with others: the more diverse the social movement, the more powerful, but the more prone to fragmentation. This involves sharing power.
7. Power to change things rests on a vision of what things could be like, and a criticism of the world as it is.
8. While power exists on a societal level, it (or its absence) also exists in the consciousness of individuals, and this self perception of power can, within limits, become a self-fulfilling prophecy.

Think!

Participation

Finally, as implied in the above, this work in the interests of disadvantaged and oppressed people and communities cannot be 'done to' or 'for' them – it has to be part of a joint venture. This raises the question of participation, a key element (although not an unproblematic one: see Kagan, 2006a) for critical community psychology and one that runs through the following chapters (see in particular Chapter 4).

Prefigurative action

We have been clear that critical community psychology is about more than ameliorative change, aspiring to transformational change for people and communities that are disadvantaged or oppressed. We have couched this in relation to social justice. Nevertheless, much of the work of critical community psychologists is, in reality, small scale and often time-limited. It is much easier to aspire to transformational practice than to engage in it. There are a number of reasons for this:

- Social life (relationships, ideology, practices, communities, and so on) is shaped by forces (e.g. socio-economic factors, social policy, hegemonic ideologies) that are located outside the boundaries of both the community contexts and the projects within them that community psychologists and others are typically involved with. Those forces act as constraints on locally based social change yet they are relatively invisible and inaccessible to interventions at a local level.
- While aspiring to transformational change the work of community psychologists is often disconnected from social movements whose project is such systemic (or anti-systemic) change.
- Methodologies, developed largely from a social psychological knowledge base, that are used in local action projects do not contain either analytic or action frameworks for the societal level.
- In the case of community psychology, despite its emphasis on units of analysis that are greater than the individual and the immediate interpersonal context, there has been relatively little in the way of a theorisation of the societal level, either in terms of the societal construction of the individual and the group, or in terms of action frameworks for systemic, macro or societal level change.
- Increasingly, the work of human service workers and academics, including psychologists, is audited so they are expected to provide evidence of the impact of their work. Psychologists employed in human service settings are typically audited in terms of individual level and pathology oriented indicators, such as number of clients seen. Academics are increasingly being asked to evidence the social impact of their work. Impact on broad social systems is both difficult to achieve and difficult to evidence, while psychologists' work and its effects cannot be easily separated out from the work of others who are simultaneously working for change in the social system.

How can the connection be made between the local, project-based working typical of community psychology and a broader agenda or programme of principled social change? We have addressed this question elsewhere (Kagan & Burton, 2000) through the Gramscian concept, that of 'prefigurative' action. Gramsci pointed to the importance in struggle of exploring, defining and anticipating the new social forms to which the struggle itself aspires. So, as we work in ways that develop innovations, anticipating a Just Society we will not be immediately creating this society: instead we experiment (in partnership and solidarity) with change and learning from the process in a systematic way. In any radical intervention and change there will be two opposing processes.

The prefigurative, creative, explorative, radical processes and achievements will be pitted against 'recuperative', retrogressive, traditionalist, unimaginative, conservative tendencies. The sources for the reactionary tendencies are likely to be multiple – in the external environment, and its impact on the setting itself, but also in the ideological and psychological baggage that the participants inevitably bring with them. There is never a clean break with the past (Kagan & Burton, 2000, pp. 75–76).

Prefigurative praxis, then, explores the possibilities of prefiguring a just society, while at the same time identifying the limits of reform and hence the need for transformation. We assume that through this action learning about social change, resources for more fundamental social change will be developed. This understanding and learning itself forms part of a higher order change project that goes beyond merely interpreting the world.

Prefigurative praxis is not a methodology in itself (we discuss some specific methodologies that are relevant to it in the Act! section of the book), but rather an organising orientation that guides our roles as collaborators and co-learners within complex social environments. A prefigurative orientation includes learning about constraints, society, social power, the change process and capacities for change. It includes learning how to innovate, and what it takes to develop strategic interventions. It includes learning by people in professional and non-professional roles, and by participants and those peripheral to the intervention. It includes learning that is both manifest and latent.

Whilst our prefigurative stance has its origins in Gramsci's writings (Gramsci, 1968), a similar stance was taken by the pragmatists (see also Zúñiga, 1975). The very foundation of the democratic procedure is dependence upon experimental production of social change: and experimentation directed by working principles that are tested and developed in the very process of being tried out in action (Dewey, 1946, p. 157).

There are a number of ways in which the learning from prefigurative work is used or stored. Sometimes the new learning about social relations is released into the wider society in a variety of ways, including through the lived experiences of those that participated, were challenged, grew or benefited in some way. Sometimes the new learning is stabilised in new social institutions, and sometimes not. Sometimes the new learning will be stored amongst people and accessed later in ways that cannot be predicted (Ray, 1993). Even apparently failed social projects can contribute to the wider programme and movements for principled change.

Core principles underlying a critical community psychology

To finish this introductory exploration of the Think! section of the book we will briefly summarise some principles that guide the practice of critical community psychologists. Needless to say, these principles are not always easy to live up to but they do provide direction and guidance, especially when there are dilemmas to face.

Diversity

Critical community psychology takes seriously the need to respect and work with diverse people, groups and communities. It recognises the importance of such variety of need, interest, aspiration, culture, ability and identity. It aims to oppose those who would either try to homogenise the rich diversity of our communities (e.g. neo-fascist groups like the English Defence League, the Australian One Nation party, the Italian Lega or the German Alternative für Deutschland, but also those in the mainstream who impose what some of them have called a 'hostile environment' fleeing war or terror, or who create a 'hostile environment' for those fleeing war and terror, or seeking better options as the consequence of the impacts of historical and modern imperialism and the global ecological and climate crisis on their livelihoods in their countries of origin). Similarly, critical community psychology will oppose those who now exclude, oppress or otherwise imperil the human rights of any group (obviously fascist organisations, but also mainstream media such as the popular UK daily newspapers, like the *Sun*, *Mail* and *Express* (and similar outlets in other countries) and mainstream politicians who play to that agenda – for example through the policies that pauperise asylum seekers).

Think!

Innovation

Critical community psychology seeks to invent, to develop and to support those who also try to innovate. We know that while many traditions are valuable resources, our society and its communities are far from perfect and there is a great need to improve settings and the social practices within them. Critical community psychology therefore takes an active interest in social innovations, while being aware of the lure of the new, the glib and the superficial as proffered fixes for social ills. It seeks to support and promote good innovations in communities as well as to innovate in its own practice.

Liberation

As discussed in the previous chapter, critical community psychology aims to be a liberatory praxis, working to free people and communities from oppression, discrimination and pain. It aims to work with people on their own projects of liberation – always within the overall parameters of ethical practice. To do this requires a decolonial stance – understanding the ways in which colonial power continues to be exerted over and above local frames of reference and understandings.

Commitment

Critical community psychology cannot be just a job. As one of our students once put it, it is '*a practice for liberation with responsibilities*'. It requires commitment and integrity. In this it makes a contrast with positivist psychology which stresses the separation of fact and value, practitioner and 'subject', AND with academic critical psychology which typically denounces without constructing a better alternative to that which is denounced (Burton, 2013b). Critical community psychology aspires to ground itself in the life of people in community, getting its bearings from there. It does not do in–out projects, but should always try to maintain some degree of relationship and follow-up even when (especially when) funding for a project finishes.

Critical reflection

Critical community psychology learns from its practice, its successes and failures, and from those with whom it allies. It refuses complacency, being restless in its search for learning from multiple sources. It guides its reflection with a critical analysis that tries always to see the bigger picture, the dynamic of social forces that create, transform and ultimately destroy communities.

Humility

Finally, critical community psychology tries to be humble. It knows (from the ecological principle of unintended consequences) that it will get things wrong and it is therefore alert to that risk, working to prevent damage, to detect it and to put it right. It can only do that by interpreting professionalism as service, expertise as relative and reality as flawed.

Table 3.3 summarises the key characteristics of critical community psychology as we understand it, then, in comparison with other related approaches. This builds on a table offered by Montero (2004b) in which she contrasted the fields of community social psychology, critical psychology (both in their Latin American versions) and liberation social psychology. To her categorisation we have added mainstream community psychology and our version of critical community psychology (or as we have described it elsewhere, really social psychology). This then puts side by side a family of approaches among which there are similarities and differences.

Think!

In what order of priority would you place the above principles and why?

Conclusions

In this chapter we have presented a landscape of concepts with which to understand critical community psychology. The map is geographically diverse (spanning vastly different contexts), deep (focusing on different layers and units of analysis) and wide (embracing interdisciplinarity). This fertile landscape (echoing the ecological metaphor) presents possibility and complexity. You may need to re-visit elements covered here when they are used in context later in the text. To maximise your learning, it might be worth maintaining your own glossary of terms. In the next chapter we untangle the concept of community (a term used and abused) to understand its usage.

Table 3.3 Comparison between mainstream community psychology, community social psychology, critical psychology, liberation social psychology and critical community psychology

Category of analysis	Mainstream community psychology	Community social psychology (Montero)	Critical psychology (Montero)	Liberation social psychology (Montero)	Our version of critical community psychology (or really social psychology)
Characteristic concepts	Critique of laboratory and clinic-based science	Critique of positivism	Critique of positivism	Critique of positivism	Critique of positivism
		Social criticism	Social criticism	Social criticism	Social criticism
	Community service	Use of Freirean concepts	Revision of psychological concepts	Use of Freirean concepts	Use of Freirean concepts
		Notion of social participation	Oppressed social categories as active social subjects	Oppressed majorities as social actors and subjects of this psychology	Revision of psychological concepts
		Incorporation of new social actors into praxis			Oppressed and deprived social groups and communities as actors and co-producers of praxis
	Absence of the category of ideology	Presence of the category of ideology	Presence of the category of ideology	Presence of the category of ideology	Presence of the category of ideology
	Liberal reformism	Political character of community action		Political character of social phenomena	Community action linked to politico-economic realities
	Prevention	Change in the role of psychologists			
	Addressing social problems				
	Multivariate understanding of social psychological phenomena	Holism, dynamism and complexity	Holism, dynamism and complexity	Holism, dynamism and complexity	Holism, dynamism and complexity

Fundamental principles	Prevention Addressing social problems Psychological sense of community Resilience Empowerment Building on strengths and strengthening people and communities	Redefinition of the dominant notions of power and power relations in the social sciences Introduction of the notion of strengthening Power and control in the community Dialogical relations between external agents (researcher interveners) and internal agents (community members)	Critique the exercise of power in science and social relations Critique of concepts and procedures disconnected from the needs of the subjects of the study	Critique of the exercise of power in Latin American societies Asymmetrical conception of power Valuing of popular knowledge Listening to the voice of the people	Critique of power relations in society with a focus on strengthening the power and resources of oppressed and deprived groups and communities Asymmetrical conception of power Contextualisation in structures and relations of economic and social power in the community Conception of power linked to dialogic coalition of oppressed and deprived groups and communities and community actors

continued

Table 3.3 Continued

Category of analysis	Mainstream community psychology	Community social psychology (Montero)	Critical psychology (Montero)	Liberation social psychology (Montero)	Our version of critical community psychology (or really social psychology)
	Involvement of non-professionals Relationships between individual and community Giving psychology away Training community members and leaders	Incorporation of popular knowledge Praxis: union of theory and practice based on reflection Sharing the knowledge produced with: • community where working • scientific community Commitment of both agents to social transformation	Psychological praxis for individual and social transformation	Freeing psychology from its preoccupation with its status in favour of concerning itself with those in need Democratisation	Incorporation of popular knowledge; psychological praxis for individual and social transformation; and rejection of psychology from its preoccupation with its status in favour of concerning itself with those in need – the three elements in dialectical relationship with each other Sharing the knowledge produced with: • community where working • scientific community Prefigurative action for social transformation
Principal external influences	Interdisciplinary Community organising (Alinsky) Community mental health	Transdisciplinarity Popular education (Freire) Marx and Engels	Marx, Engels and Marxian writers	Transdisciplinarity Popular education (Freire) Marx and Engels	Transdisciplinarity Popular education (Freire) Marx and Engels and Marxian writers including, Gramsci, Bhaskar, Leonard, Dussel, Williams

	Community mental health	Phenomenology	Phenomenology	Liberation theology (Gutiérrez, Ellacuria, Boff, Cardenal and others)	Feminism Disability studies
Methods	Social anthropology	Berger and Luckman	Critical social science	Social theory and psychology	Critical social science
	Mainstream sociology	Critical Sociology (Fals Borda)	Frankfurt School	Critique of methods and generation of other new ones	Ecology and permaculture
	Ecology	Dependency theory	Critique and rejection of traditional quantitative methods	Preference for participative and qualitative methods in psychosocial research	Systems thinking
	Organisational studies	Critique and rejection of traditional methods	Preference for qualitative methods as well as novel traditional methods	Methodological pluralism	Organisational studies
	Methodological plurality	Redefinition and generation of methods			Action research as an organising framework: participative, systemic, prefigurative
	Questionnaires and surveys	Methodological plurality			Methodological pluralism and community members as co-researchers
	Action research (Lewin)	Development of new participative methods			
	Qualitative methods	Participative action research			
	Multivariate statistics (e.g. multiple regression)				

continued

Table 3.3 Continued

Category of analysis	Mainstream community psychology	Community social psychology (Montero)	Critical psychology (Montero)	Liberation social psychology (Montero)	Our version of critical community psychology (or really social psychology)
Orientation and aims	Prevention Addressing social problems Creation of social settings	Social transformation Building a psychology responsive to the needs of society Development of social consciousness Strengthening and development of citizens Equality with respect to diversity Freedom Autonomy of communities with limited resources	Transformation of social sciences Developing legitimacy Recognising diversity and strengthening of oppressed social groups Social transformation	Centring psychology in the problems of the oppressed majorities in Latin America Conscientisation Liberation	Centring psychology in the problems of oppressed and deprived groups and communities Conscientisation Liberation Prefigurative development of social settings for social transformation

Source: from table in Montero (2004b), our translation. The final column is our addition. With the permission of the journal *Psykhe*.

Chapter 4

The contested nature of community

Summary

In this chapter we explore the contested nature of community – essential for an understanding of critical community psychology. We examine different ways of describing community and its key dimensions of sentiment (including psychological sense of community and the symbolic construction of community), space and social structure. We make the case for an understanding of the multi-dimensional nature of communities and consider what we mean by 'social exclusion'.

'Community' can be the warmly persuasive word to describe an existing set of relationships, or the warmly persuasive word to describe an alternative set of relationships. What is most important, perhaps, is that unlike all other terms for social organisation (state, nation, society etc.), it seems never to be used unfavourably, and never to be given any positive opposing or distinguishing term.

(Williams, 1976, p. 76)

There is no one definition of community. Indeed, in the social sciences, it is one of the most highly contested terms. Hillery (1955) concluded that of the 94 different definitions of community he reviewed the only thing that was in common to them all was that community involved people. That situation does not seem to have altered significantly in the intervening six decades. Because it is such a central concept in community psychology it is worth spending some time examining the different ways in which it is understood, however a complex task this might be.

It is actually quite difficult to find explicit definitions of community in many of the widely used (in the global North) reference texts for community psychology. It appears that many texts avoid too close a scrutiny of what community means as often neither an explicit definition nor a historical analysis of the concept is offered. For example, Orford's (1992) authoritative and influential text on community psychology does not provide a conceptual or historical definition of community, in spite of attempting to demonstrate that the discipline of psychology has not just thoughtlessly attached the word 'community' to itself. Sometimes the definition of community that is offered is only made explicit towards the end of a text. For example, In Rappaport and Seidman's *Handbook of Community Psychology* (2000) a definition of community is not cited until page 941 of 982 pages. When one does find an attempt to define community in a community psychology textbook, it is often scant (e.g. little more than three pages of Dalton, Elias and Wandersman's 441-page text on community psychology is spent on defining 'community'). Taking a broader perspective across the public profile of the discipline of community psychology (its textbooks, journals, research projects and conferencing activities), definitions of community are hard to find and when we do find them they tend to offer a somewhat limited definition – one that primarily focuses upon its psychological dimension – 'the psychological sense of community' (which we describe later in this chapter).

We have found that the definitions of 'community' offered by community psychology often fail to capture the multifarious, slippery and complex nature of the concept and are often positioned in ways that suggest the concept might not be of central theoretical concern. This contrasts, for example, with the way community is defined by those working in the fields of politics, social anthropology and sociology (e.g. Cohen, 1985). This is not to say those who publish in the field of community psychology lack a full understanding of the concept. It does, however, at the very least highlight some interesting editorial decisions in terms of the value that is placed on publicly discussing the concept that is the discipline's namesake. It also creates the risk that community psychology largely operates with, at worst, an erroneous and, at best, an obfuscated idea of what community is. In this chapter, we seek to make some of the complexities of the concept of community more transparent.

What is community?

The concept of community is obviously central to community psychology but also to the social sciences in general. It is prominent in policy circles too, invoking the communitarian romantic notions of integration and harmony, building capacity and integrating this notion of community. In psychology, community is the backdrop against which we study individual behaviour and where social identities and a sense of self are negotiated and realised. In politics it is the boundary that is placed around people (such as a national identity) that informs social policies and programmes (such as immigration policies). In anthropology it is a unit of study – a social grouping that permits us to explore and understand culture. Community is important to study in the social sciences because it:

- provides meaning and identity and contributes to a sense of self;
- has material effects on people's lives;
- is made up of a wide variety of social processes;
- generates social behaviour and social relationships;
- feeds into and is fed by social policy and social programmes.

Community is usually contrasted to the more formal ways of organising social life, especially those of state and market. Its meaning overlaps with the increasingly popular (but often vacuous) term civil society. Community can be used to indicate more or less organised and intentional social units (the 'Findhorn Community', the 'European Community'), or a less organised diffuse network ('Care in the Community', the 'Jewish Community'). In its more amorphous senses it overlaps with some senses of the term 'culture' and concepts such as 'lifeworld' (from phenomenology) or the idea of the 'core economy' as introduced to indicate something similar, the social resources inherent in social capital rather than in the formal community or the state (see NEF, 2008b). Community is also utilised when referring to movements – the Transition Network is a movement of communities coming together to re-imagine and rebuild our world (www.transitionnetwork.org).

Community is not an abstract concept. It is a lived experience, something which gives meaning to ourselves and gives us an understanding of others. The way community is constructed, and where we are located within it, can have very real, material effects on our lives. Communities can enhance and empower our lives, but they can also lead us into becoming stigmatised and marginalised. In this chapter, we consider both of these sides of community.

One thing is certain: community is complex (see the example below). It is often initially used as a means to describe a group of people who have something in common that makes them different, in a significant way, from other groups of people. Indeed, community is rooted to the word 'common' (through the Latin word 'communis'). 'Community' thus describes the many different things that are common and not common between people and this is where we encounter the first level of complexity. The commonality between people could be based on some form of an objective assessment (such as living in the same neighbourhood as other people) or subjective assessment (such as feeling a sense of being the same as other people). The second complexity is the distinction between the concept acting as a description of groups (telling people what they *are* doing) and the concept acting as a prescription for groups (telling people what they *ought* to be doing). These assessments can be made through a group of people defining themselves as a community themselves or through a group of people being defined as a community by others. We begin by first focusing on how people assess whether a group is or is not a community by examining the different dimensions used in defining what is in common between people that could bind them together into a 'community'. We consider how various writers have provided different ways to classify these dimensions through developing different 'theories of community'. In Chapter 5 we discuss how the concept of community is used to prescribe rather than describe how groups of people form and behave.

Example: Inner city disturbances – understanding the complexity of community

In 1981 there were civil disturbances in a number of English cities, leading to injury and extensive damage to local businesses and community facilities. Disturbances occurred most notably in London, Bristol, Manchester, Liverpool and Leeds. In Manchester a Committee of Enquiry was established and we (CK) were invited to be a member of it, along with a community worker, barrister, senior police officer and youth worker (Hytner, D'Cocodia, Kagan, Spencer & Yates, 1981). As we took evidence from witnesses and read documentary material, we were able to make sense of the historically located divisions within the communities affected by the disturbances. We drew on our different knowledge and experience – all of us insiders to Manchester in one way or another – and combined these with lots of very different perspectives from those caught up in or affected in some way by the disturbances. The communities were divided by race, employment and wealth and suffused with longstanding antagonisms between different sectors, particularly between local people and the authorities. We made a number of recommendations which led to the creation of a community liaison worker to act as a bridge between local people and the police to repair the trust that had been lost between them. Continued community psychological involvement in this process stood us in good stead when the opportunity arose some 25 years later to work on projects seeking to address conflicts and schisms amongst different kinds of communities, this time labelled as problems with community cohesion (Kagan & Duggan, 2009; Worley, 2005).

Reflect!

How would you answer the question: what community do you come from?
What communities do you think other people would say you belong to?

Theory descriptions of community

One of the mostly widely cited theories of community is that of Tönnies (1887/2002). Tönnies made the distinction between two forms of community living which he called *Gemeinschaft* and *Gesellshaft*. Gemeinschaft is community formed through shared fellowship where connections between members are intimate and based on close personal knowledge about one another and where members live co-operatively with one another. Here, community resembles a large family and is often structured by blood ties and patriarchal status. Gesellschaft, in contrast, is community formed by association. Here, the connections between members are impersonal and unattached. Life in such a community is fragmented and devoid of co-operation and social cohesion. Tönnies associated Gemeinschaft with a pre-industrial world and Gesellschaft with a post-industrialised world. The distinction between these two forms of community has been drawn out by others as a continuum between rural and urban ways of living (e.g. Nisbet, 1967). Typically, the rural community is defined as provincial and idyllic and the urban community as cosmopolitan and impersonal.

A different dimension to community was captured in Willmott's work on the distinction between 'communities of attachment' and 'communities of interest' (Willmott, 1989). Here, rather than focus on a physical, geographical area to which people belong (such as to a rural or an urban area), community is defined more in terms of the social relations that exist between people. Willmott defined communities of attachment as neighbourhoods which function along lines of loyalty, belonging and identity. He contrasted this with 'communities of interest' where people are not bound so much by social attachment, but by sharing common interests. Examples of 'communities of attachment' are those that make up the Association of Camphill Communities. For Camphill communities, the concept of 'communities of attachment' is used to emphasise the mutual interdependence of disabled and non-disabled people and offer alternatives to the professional care model that led to disabled people becoming dependent upon professionals for social support (Grover, 1995). An example of 'communities of interest' could be, say, book clubs where people who might ordinarily not have an attachment to one another are brought together with a common interest in literature. Much of the research into 'communities of interest' initially focused on workplace settings (e.g. Klein & D'Aunno, 1986; Lambert & Hopkins, 1995), and more recently the online sphere (e.g. Hu, Zhao & Huang, 2015; Chouchani & Abed, 2018) with some critical commentary (Locke, Lawthom & Lyons, 2018).

Think!

From the literature, newspapers, online searches or through discussion, identify the meaning of community in the following:

community assets; community care; community policing; community hubs; Department of Housing, Communities and Local Government; community health; community interest company; Business in the Community; community schools; community participation; community shares; community energy; community-led housing; Community Development Trust, LGBT community, online communities.

How meaningful is the concept of community?

The variety of theories of community offered reflects the many different ways that community is defined. Thus, a community might have a geographical dimension where it is defined by the physical space in which people live. This could be a building (e.g. a tenants' association), a neighbourhood (e.g. a neighbourhood watch area), a city or settlement (e.g. a village community), a region, a nation or even a supranational state (e.g. 'the European Community'). Community might also be constructed around social identity, such as a person's age, disability, gender, ethnicity, professional status, sexual identity, social class and so on. Recently there have been a number of movements which cohered around a sense of shared identities or a recognition of minority identities. The #METOO movement enabled women globally to out sexual predators and recognise harassment globally. It has been utilised in protests, award ceremonies and in the twittersphere to raise consciousness and shed light on practices. Community might be a combination of geography and social identity (such as national identity) and can be constructed through the sharing of material goods that bonds people together. Examples of such materially based bonds might be shareholders in a commercial corporation and members of Credit Unions or Trading Schemes (though the extent to which such bonds leads to the creation of 'community' is subject to debate – see Silverman, 2001; Williams et al., 2001). People might be viewed as a community if they share common interests, lifestyles and so on (e.g. cat lovers). Community might also be something that operates at a purely symbolic level such that it exists when people share a common belief that it does exist or desire that it should exist.

Reflect!

What does community mean to you? Think about where you live – is this a community? Why? Is there a distinction between sense of community and sense of place – if so, what is it?

Dimensions of community: sentiment, social structure and space

One way to organise the various ways of defining community that we find particularly useful is that suggested by Campbell (2000) who offers three dimensions to community: sentiment, space and social structure. Figure 4.1 illustrates how these dimensions overlap. Indeed, each of these dimensions might be inseparable from the others, but for the sake of clarity in exposition, we describe each of these dimensions separately.

Sentiment

'Sentiment' refers to the way community operates in a psychological, cultural and symbolic sense. It captures the way community exists in the minds of those who belong to it and those who desire to be in it as well as in the minds of those who exist outside of it. A sense of community can be felt but also communicated through becoming attached to particular symbols (such as the picture of an idyllic rural village or notion of community as an extended family through which Tönnies' description of Gemeinschaft has come to symbolise community) or community becoming a symbol to communicate a sense of safety and protection (such as through neighbourhood 'community watch' schemes that seek to protect householders, who live in a common physical space, from robbery or violence).

Thus, this dimension captures the way community operates as an idea (as a symbol) but also the way it is directly experienced by its members and non-members (as an experience and a feeling). Here a community comes into existence through people having a common sense of being 'a community' or a shared acceptance of what objects can symbolise community. In this way, community comes to be understood by the emotional and psychological connections that exist between people and the groups they form and the means by which people communicate the idea of community – it exists through shared meaning.

Think!

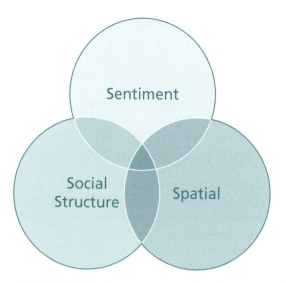

> **Figure 4.1** Dimensions of community.
> Source: taken from Campbell, 2000.

These emotional, psychological and communicational connections can develop through the experience of living close together with others (we describe the spatial dimension to community later) as well as through people sharing common beliefs and interests. As mentioned earlier, Willmott based his theory on this dimension – communities of interest. Here, interest is broadly interpreted to also include shared social identities based on the ascription of age, disability, ethnicity, gender, sexuality, spirituality and so on.

It is the sentimental dimension to community that has attracted the attention of a number of community psychologists and has developed into a whole field of empirical and theoretical work on the 'psychological sense of community'.

Psychological sense of community

The Psychological Sense of Community (PSoC) (Sarason, 1974, 1988) is a long standing and central concept in community psychology (Fisher, Sonn & Bishop, 2002; McMillan & Chavis, 1986). You will find many contemporary references to the 'psychological sense of community', as researchers try to explore the limitations and applications of the term. PSoC is said to capture the strong attachments between people and their communities, be those attachments geographical (such as neighbourhoods) or functional (such as workplaces or self help groups). Early on in the history of community psychology as a distinct discipline in the US, Sarason (1974, p. 157) described PSoC as:

> the perception of similarity to others, an acknowledged interdependence with others, a willingness to maintain this interdependence by giving to or doing for others what one expects from them, and the feeling that one is part of a larger dependable and stable structure.

McMillan & Chavis similarly stated that it is

> a feeling that members have of belonging, a feeling that members matter to one another and to the group, and a shared faith that members' needs will be met through their commitment to be together
> (McMillan & Chavis, 1986, p. 9)

The four characteristics of PSoC originally posed were:

- a sense of belonging;
- a sense of mattering to one another;
- a shared faith that all members needs are met;
- a commitment to be together.

Taken together, these characteristics are known as the 'solidarity of the social group'. Without this, it is believed that people feel alienated and isolated – they do not feel they belong.

There have been lots of attempts to measure PSoC and there are debates as to whether this is an entity that can be measured or an experience which has to be captured in other ways. What is consistent is the belief that PSoC is something, however it might exist, that needs to be strengthened and that doing so will enhance the natural helping and problem solving capacity of social groups. In other words, promoting PSoC helps us look for assets and strengths amongst the people inside a community rather than relying on the expertise of professionals who live outside a community. It is also believed that once communities have coped with one problem they are more likely to be resilient and to be able to cope with others. Similarly, once people have pulled together for one purpose they are believed to be more likely to pull together for other purposes. So, where there is a history of collective action (for example, a campaign to save a local public amenity, stop a road being built, save a woodland and so on) the density of voluntary activity and other forms of collective behaviour in a community will be greater. This is reflected in Willmott's (1989) argument that communities of interest are strengthened when they experience external threats, and is an argument that is commonly developed from community psychology's deployment of the PSoC concept.

The cultural and symbolic sense of community

When community is talked about there is often the assumption that those who belong to a community have shared underlying values, moral codes, norms of behaviour and social activities. This is the meaning of community for anthropologists – people become a community if there are signs and symbols that bind them together: a shared understanding (Cohen, 1986). Sometimes this kind of community might coincide with a particular place (such as a village) or a particular social structure (such as a group of employees at a workplace). For example, street signs that declare you are now entering such and such a place can be signs of shared identity (either assigned or experienced) amongst the residents of that place).The street sign symbolises (communicates meaning to others) that the group of people you are encountering may be a community. If, when people talk, they locate themselves as from one place rather than another, this can be indicative of their shared identity with others from that place. For example, the statement "I am from Sao Paulo" can be taken to mean more than a statement about where a person lives. It can be taken to be a statement about the person's social and cultural heritage. It can also position that person as an insider (I come from Sao Paulo, that is where I belong) or an outsider (I come from Sao Paulo, I do not belong here, in Fortaleza). It can also be used by others to position that person as an insider or an outsider.

The complex ways in which people conceive their community identity can be illustrated with reference to Maori people. In Aotearoa/New Zealand Maori people traditionally introduce themselves not as an individual, but as a member of a community through describing their connections to relations, to ancestors as well as to the physical spaces their ancestors occupied. The connection to land is particularly strongly expressed in Maori culture. Thus, a formal Maori introduction might first identify the mountain or the river in the place of the person's ancestors (indeed, such physical features can be described in the same way as they would their human ancestors), and then describe their tribe and their family. This cultural practice has helped to maintain Maori people's collective memory of their land and their connections to their land in the context of being displaced by white settlers since the eighteenth century. Introducing yourself through your tribal associations is also important given the historical internecine violence between tribes that requires reconciliation in the present or might require preventative actions to ensure past antagonisms do not re-erupt once more.

The insider–outsider aspect of community identity is important in some cases, with roots to such distinctions often being embedded historically. Incomers (those outsiders who move into the boundaries of a new community) may be spurned, or they may be welcomed (Crow, Allan & Summers, 2001). Both might result from strong pre-existing ties within the host community. When moving to a new village, a new town or a new country, it can take a long time – even decades – to feel accepted as an insider. In the case of moving to a new country, this is complicated by immigration policies that might give you a political status that reinforces your identity as an outsider. This insider–outsider dimension of community experience is closely linked to the idea of a private and public community face. Those signs and symbols that represent the community to the outside world contribute to the *public* face of a community. That public face is often one that emphasises the commonalities between its members. The messages of coherence and homogeneity that are often conveyed are frequently different from those understandings that insiders themselves hold of community life, with its factions, different interests and social relations. For example, the women's movement is often seen from the outside as a social movement of women who are involved in a common struggle to gender quality (public face). From the inside, the movement can be experienced as a group of people who are divided by ideological belief (there are many distinct forms of feminism some forms of which are antagonistic to others) and by their other social identities (such as age, class, disability, ethnicity, sexuality and so on). The private face is that experienced by insiders and the public face is the outer representation of a community (Mewett, 1986). We describe this more fully later when we discuss the social marginalisation that can result from the construction of 'community'.

Act!

Walk around your neighbourhood. Try to work out what the public face of the neighbourhood is. What signs indicate you are in this particular neighbourhood, town or city, country? Is there anything that will tell outsiders what this place is like? How does it feel to be an insider to this place? Does this differ from the public face? Why do you think this is?

The sentiment dimension to community is increasingly promoted as an area of interest for social scientists and social policy makers. Cohen (1985) argued that if one wishes to understand what community is, one has to study the symbolic construction of the boundaries people use to distinguish their group from others and that the reality of the boundaries that separate people into distinct communities resides in the minds of the people who are bound by them, not in their structural features. The sentiment dimension of community has been associated with the growth of interest in 'community activism' since the 1970s in which groups forge strongly politicised identities (as in the identity politics of the women's movement, the black movement, the lesbian, gay bisexual and transgendered movement and, most recently, the disability movement). It has also become more popular following the increased rates of globalisation, urbanisation and migration that have dislocated community from its historical bond to geographical space (Meyrowitz, 1986) as more and more people have begun to physically relocate to new urban settings and to new countries. More recently, the growing spread of virtual communities and new forms of social networking spawned by the development of new forms of broadcast (the mass media) and narrowcast (the internet) by increasingly powerful media and technology corporations may have helped spotlight the sentiment dimension of community over and above its other dimensions.

Put simply, people were moving so far, moving so often and communicating across such large distances in an instant that locating a community in one physical space became impossible. This has been described as the increasing liquidity of people's lives (Bauman, 2005; Jurgenson, 2009). This not only refers to patterns of migration and communication, but also to social transformation such that as well as people moving into and out of communities, communities were also shape shifting at a rapid pace around people. For example, coal mining communities transformed dramatically in the UK following the national programme of coal-pit closures under the Thatcher government during the 1980s and 1990s. Once thriving, vibrant communities frequently became transformed rapidly into holding camps for the unemployed, and sites of economic and social deprivation and ill-health. The national programme of coal-pit closures along with an accompanying move away from an industrial base for the UK's economic activity caused a swift and dramatic social transformation of communities across the UK (Bennett, Beynon & Hudson, 2000). These were massive shifts in the symbolic meaning of community to inhabitants of those villages, but driven largely by material changes in the economic fabric of community life.

The symbolic shifting of community caused by such material changes notwithstanding, the trend to consider community as it is constructed inside people's heads (through sentiment) might take attention away from that other dimension of community which has historical significance and still informs contemporary understandings of what community means – space. Indeed, as much as there has been a shift in focus in understanding community towards its sentiment component, the dimension of space continues to have a strong hold on how the concept is popularly understood.

At the time of revision, media attention in Europe has focused on community membership of the European Union. The new term 'Brexit' refers to the process by which Britain, following a referendum, is leaving the European Union. Strong feelings and contested notions of membership have been played out leading to difficult discussions which are about sentiment, membership and control of space and borders.

Space

Space is the second of Campbell's three dimensions of 'community'. The constant state of flux that people are in, captured in the notion of 'liquid life' is, however, largely about the lives of those who live in resource rich industrialised societies and who have access to technology and transport. It also has resonance to the lives of (at least in the biographies of if not the present lived experience of) people caught in the various diasporas (dispersions of populations) created by political and economic instability. Examples of such diasporas include the Jewish people who fled Eastern Europe during successive waves of anti-Semitism during the nineteenth and twentieth centuries; the dislocation and relocation of Muslims and Hindus as India and Pakistan were (re)created in the mid nineteenth century; the conditions of modern slavery that result in undocumented, vulnerable and exploited workers from many different countries moving across Europe and North America (Craig, Gaus, Wilkinson, Skøivánková & McQuade, 2007); Latin Americans seeking refuge from political oppression and economic deprivation and so on. Though such movements of people appear to have freed 'community' from its physical dimension, the spatial dimension exists through both the national identity that people may carry with them – and that may obstruct their future movement across national borders (due to immigration policies) and negatively impact upon their social circumstances (through the racist effects of the cultural norms and social practices of their host community) – and the sense of place that migrants may carry with them (a sense of their homeland as a physical space from which they have become separated). For some, however, the spatial dimension to community dominates and this might be particularly so for those who have become locked down to the physical space in which they dwell due to economic and political factors.

Example: Forced labour amongst Chinese migrant workers

In a project exploring forced labour and work for migrant Chinese workers (Lawthom et al., 2015), we worked with a respected Chinese social enterprise. Within the project team, we were a mix of nationalities and the project enabled embedding a Chinese Mandarin and Cantonese speaking researcher to work alongside the organisation. Despite this attention to language and culture, the Chinese researcher was from Hong Kong: all but one of the participants were from mainland China. Despite having a shared language, the Chinese participants did not always want to share stories with the Hong Kong born researcher (although it was not clear if participants were reluctant to tell their stories to anyone!). History and judgements of space made a difference when sharing personal stories.

As much as the removal of barriers such as the Berlin Wall may have increased freedom to travel in one part of the world, the erection of barriers such as the construction by the Israeli political administration of a wall around the Occupied Territories of Palestine, or Trump's anti-immigration fences and wall on the US–Mexico border, and around the North African Spanish colonies of Melilla and Ceuta, have restricted the freedom to travel in another part of the world. For people who live in territories occupied by hostile forces, controlled by hostile political administrations and contained by hostile socio-economic conditions (poverty and social marginalisation), people's ability to take part in liquid life may be considerably curtailed and many who are caught in the global population flows can find themselves suddenly frozen and locked back down to space (for example, in detention centres in the UK; migrant camps in Greece and Italy; and detention centres both on mainland Australia and in Manus Province, Papua New Guinea where refugees began to be imprisoned upon entry into Australia under the Liberal government of John Howard).

The spatial dimension of community is also important because it is central to public policy, to much of modern sociological theory and to many people's understanding of the term. Often that space is geographical – the physical space that groups of people occupy and proximity to the space occupied by others. Indeed, geographical space and community are often conflated in terms of the terms being used interchangeably. So, for example, the 'community shop' and the 'community hall' refer to amenities that serve a particular geographical location (rather than a particular interest group). Community hubs or anchors are those local facilities that are designed for use by people living nearby. Often, when people refer to their community, they are referring to the geographical space in which they live (their neighbourhood, or village or city). The space is thus often a social and physical space: a socio-spatial entity that refers to a collection of people, in face to face contact, often living in close proximity to one another.

This socio-spatial dimension of community is one the meaning of which is most often employed in policy incursions into social development. Community development workers would not try to work with a whole town; nor would they work only with a small group. They might, however, work with a number of groups to help them see that if they worked together there would be maximum gain for local people. The notion of 'local people' is deployed to identify those groups who are the key stakeholders in the physical and economic regeneration of an area. Thus, physical parameters are set around the concept of community to identify both the geographical area that needs an intervention and the people who live there, who will be affected. In many projects which focus on the alleviation of poverty, it is this meaning of community that is at the heart of the work and that is work grounded in a particular geographical space such as a particular part of a city that is targeted for 'renewal' or 'regeneration'. Here, there is a deliberate policy to symbolically shift a community in a positive way through transforming the material resources available to it (such as improved housing, amenities and transport links) but one that is dependent upon community being defined in a particular territorial space (such as an inner city area). However, critics of regeneration policies see it as more a deliberate policy to permit the purchase of public housing by private commercial companies (where the policy is used to lever open opportunities for commercial property developers to profiteer from 'problem' communities). Also, social policy and public administration can lead to the dividing up of territory into community blocks such as through the practice of zoning and the establishment of jurisdictional boundaries such that resource allocation can be targeted, audited and effectively managed (the management of health, social and educational services and the control of property development and business growth).

Sometimes the geographical space that community signifies is as 'space outside'. Community care, for example, refers to care that is not within institutions – it is a place other than an institution like a hospital or a residential home. However, it does not normally mean care on the streets: it means care in family homes, domestic size units or even in mini-institutions housing 100 people. For elders, for example, it is community care that is meant to enable people to live for as long as possible in their own homes, despite increasing frailty. Community care for people with a diagnosis of a severe mental illness is non-hospital based care: although this could be supporting people in hostels or in their own homes. There may be residential staff or there may not be. The important thing is that community is defined as 'not institution' – other than that it is used vaguely – in a policy process that has been described as more like 'walking backwards out of the workhouse' than in terms of positive inclusion in community life. Here, community as a concept begins to operate less as a way of describing what is common among people who are located in a particular physical setting, and starts to resemble more a way of defining the characteristics of a particular social policy or social programme. We discuss this more towards the end of this chapter where we examine how community is used in social policy.

As well as geographical space, communities can be defined in terms of time (or temporal space) such as at a time in history. In this respect, the 'global community' whilst joining everyone together, separates them from the people of a previous era – it describes the global population at a particular point in time (such as people located in the new era of globalisation or the new era of the global threat of climate change). Global community also has a rhetorical and ideological function (we discuss this later) where community becomes a vehicle for socio-political change (such as through the environmental movement). Here, time as well as space is key to how 'community' is being employed – we are a community because we live together in the same physical and temporal space – the 'here and now'.

Reflect!

Identify a local facility that is known as a community facility – for example, community school, community centre, community hospital, community policewoman, community outreach service and so on. What is the sense of the descriptor 'community' in relation to this facility? Is it defined as outside something else or as different from a similar facility that is not called a 'community' thing? Does it refer to a locality? What are the connections between people who might use this facility – in other words what is the common bond that people share in using the facility?

Social structure

Social structure is Campbell's (2000) third dimension of community and it refers to the way groups are organised. In describing a social structure, such things as the size and membership of the group are cited as well as the nature of the social ties that exist between group members that are determined by the organisational structure of the group (such as power relations). Communities defined by social structure might include the social ties between people that are created through formal membership rules (such as in a formally constituted club or society or by a contractual arrangement between an employer and employees) or through rules, rituals and norms that may be less explicit and acquired through an extended period of social learning (that is, through familiarisation with cultural practice and tradition). Where social structures primarily promote equality and collegiality (such as in a non-hierarchical organisation) the social ties that form might be those of affection (such as in friendship groups) or functional independence (such as in a workers' co-operative). Where social structures primarily promote discipline and authority (such as in a hierarchical organisation) social ties of coercion might dominate (for example, in the military). It might be difficult to fully understand the nature of the bonds that exist between people; indeed, those bonds can be extraordinarily complex, as are the effects of social structures upon them. However, it is possible to discern the ways that bonds of affection, functional interdependence and coercion can come to inform the assumptions researchers and policy makers carry when they think about the concept of community. In Chapter 5 we explore these social ties in more detail. Here, we briefly outline how the social structural dimension permits us to see community in a different way.

The social structural dimension provides an insight into how community can be constructed out of social identities (such as those based on age, ethnicity, gender, impairment, nationality, professional status, sexuality, social class and so on) in a way that imposes particular social conditions on who can be a member, how members should behave and who can speak for whom and make decisions for whom. For example, some parts of the disability movement would stipulate that you must be disabled before you can act with or speak for their community (in reaction to the oppressive ways non-disabled people speak for disabled people), that you must avoid oppressive organisational structures (in reaction to the hierarchical organisation of social institutions that provided health and social care in a way that denied choice or autonomy to disabled people), and that you behave in a way that helps to challenge the medical model (that locates the cause of problems with the impaired individual) and that helps to promote the social model (that locates the cause of problems with a disabling social environment). Thus, social movements based on identity politics (such as the disability movement but also the black movement, the lesbian, gay, bisexual and transgendered movement, the women's movement and so on) can often impose 'club rules' on its 'members'. This is also true for the labour movement and for conservative social movements such as the Freemasons or the Orangemen, not usually thought of in terms of identity politics. These communities can assert that to belong is to adopt a particular social identity, a particular way of thinking and acting or a particular social history. But this extends well beyond social movements and can apply to all forms of group activity. As with all social structures, such implicit and explicit rules are debated and, at times, resisted by both insiders and outsiders and it is often such points of debate and resistance that signify the splitting of a community into separate factions that then go on to operate as separate communities. For example, as mentioned, there is continual debate in the disability movement over membership rules: do you need to be disabled to be part of the disability movement (Duckett, 1998)?

What is particularly interesting for community psychologists is that this dimensional aspect to community raises the spectre of how social policy can play a key role in how communities are formed. This may happen through social policy that seeks to treat one group of people differently to another based on the distinct social identity they are given (such as in the distribution of 'disability benefits' from social welfare institutions which helps construct the notion of a community of disabled people) or can happen by people taking over a pre-existing social identity constructed by social policy (such as the social status of 'refugee') to achieve collective action and social change (such as the social movements described earlier). We consider this in Chapter 5 where we describe in more detail how these social structures are important for understanding how the concept of community can be used to create the political conditions that permit both social exclusion and social inclusion – key focal areas for critical community psychology.

> ## Think!
>
> Are there any other ways of thinking about community that are not covered by the above? How does community differ from social networks which could be said to be close knit? Do online communities function in the same way as physical communities?

Multi-dimensional communities

As we stated earlier, the dimensions (sentimental, spatial and social structural) by which we can define communities are multiple and overlapping and transformable. Indeed, the way people talk about their communities often contains elements of all three dimensions. For example, a teenage mother who joins a support group for young mothers might experience all three dimensions to community through her membership of such a group. She attends the group because of shared social experiences (being a parent) where those social experiences are determined by her life stage (being a teenager) and by social identity (being a woman) and thus she may experience the group as a community across three overlapping dimensions: sentiment (shared interest), space (shared life space) and social structure (shared social role).

Not only can the different dimensions of community overlap, so too can one dimension have a causal connection to another. Thus a community that is defined by the spatial proximity between its members might give rise to a community defined by sentiment where the spatial proximity between people gives rise to a community being created through its members feeling close to (emotionally) as well as feeling close by (spatially) others. Also, changes to one dimension of a community can create changes to the other dimensions. A loss of sense of community with others can arise from physical relocation (such as the fracturing of work relationships when some workers are moved to work on another site); changes to the social structure (through the promotion of some workers or rendering of other workers redundant, altering relationships between colleagues); and through changes to the symbolic meaning of community (such as when an employer changes from being a workers co-operative to a shareholder corporation). Such transformation in the social structure of communities (that creates changes in the social ties between people), or changes in the spatial governance of communities (where people are drawn physically or temporarily together or apart through processes of immigration or intergenerational movement) and in the sentimental dimension of community (through changing how people think and feel about community) can occur through processes of social and political change (which we describe later).

Though the symbolic and sentimental nature of community is an important dimension, without consideration of the social structural dimension, we might only obtain a muted recognition of the causes for and points of potential resistance against the political marginalisation of certain groups in society such as women, children, disabled people, elders, gay people, migrants and so on. Further, an analysis of community that fails to capture the importance of social structure may make it harder for us to understand how resistance builds in the system and gives rise to social movements such as the disability movement, the women's movement, gay pride and so on. It is also crucial to understand how such movements form through bonds of mutual aid and affection, but also are a product of relations of coercion and exploitation.

Many countries like the UK carry a heavy inheritance of deep social inequalities, and those inequalities continue (though transformed) under the present political and economic context. The voting patterns in the recent UK referendum, about whether or not to leave the European Union, in part reflected these inheritances. Populist governments, aided by the ways social media construct community identity, in, for example the USA, Turkey, Hungary and Brazil, are, as we write, exploiting notions of community, identity and historical inequalities to promote their right wing agendas. This is manifest most clearly in Trump's call to 'build the wall' between the USA and Mexico. If we fail to acknowledge the negative side of community we might fail to understand the anger that swells among the ranks of such social movements against power elites but we might also fail to capture how social movements might themselves grow in a way to build walls of marginalisation themselves and we might overlook the fractious nature of many such movements. For example, there have been fractures in feminism (Gray-Rosendale & Harootunian, 2003), in disability studies (Deal, 2003; Priestley, 2006), in gay and lesbian politics (Humphrey, 2000) and in trans politics (Keenan 2017), as well as fractures between these movements (Lloyd, 2001). Barriers function to serve the interests of those who have power and are often constructed by the powerful to marginalise the powerless. Equally, the powerless might erect their own barriers to protect their own interests, and within those groups powerlessness might not be distributed evenly. Thus, progressive social movements might be marred by the divisive nature of boundary making and the construction of borders to entry that caused the very problems they fight against. To understand such divisions, we need to understand the nature of social power.

Power and community

Power is important to consider in relation to understanding the concept of community because community, particularly along its symbolic dimension, is open to manipulation by groups who have monopolies of economic, political and cultural power. As Foucault's work shows, such groups have the power to impose their version of reality upon others through the social institutions they control (such as those that regulate economics, politics, family/kinship, education, employment, health and religion) and through the use of the military and the mass media to instil certain ideas in a population. Such groups have the power to make certain meanings stick (Thompson, 1990) and to disrupt other meanings as a way to promote and protect their interests.

Constructions of community can be transmitted through the ways a society's culturally dominant social institutions decide how people's material needs and desires are met, and how goods are produced and distributed (economics), how disagreements between people are resolved and which punishments and threats of punishment should be used (jurisprudence), which social behaviours to proscribe (legislature), which public social goals and values should be promoted (politics), how procreation, marriage and child-rearing is supported (family or kinship), how personal meaning develops and impacts upon the meaning of life and death (religion) and how support to sustain or attain positive social functioning and a high quality of life is provided (social welfare). Where each of these involves the attribution of roles and social relationships, community can be employed as a 'catch-all' concept.

Critical community psychology, perhaps more so than community psychology, offers the potential to disrupt the ideological use of the concept community when it is used in the interests of those sectors of society who accumulate economic and political capital at the expense of others. A focus on communities as ghettos (see Chapter 5) may help us to question the propriety of the social borders that are placed around certain groups and may urge us towards either finding ways of removing those borders or finding ways to bridge across them. We discuss the importance of attending to boundaries and, unlike McMillan and Chavis, describe ways in which we can work on the edge of those boundaries and across boundaries in Chapters 7 and 9. By focusing on community as ghetto we can highlight an important problematic aspect of community – the latent pernicious process of social division upon which it operates.

Communities can be positioned relative to one another with a history of unequal access to resources of both material and symbolic power, and each can become involved in a struggle for representation so as to gain access to or to retain access to power. Bridging social capital (see Chapter 5) occurs across these struggles and such inequalities can temper the ability to successfully get different communities working together. Often the struggle that community psychologists engage in is to gain influence over those communities that have attained concentrations of social power that act to disadvantage others and to get such communities to consider goals that extend beyond their own immediate self-interests. In the present cultural context in the (once) industrialised West, this is also a battle against a dominant ideology that has put the interests of power elites at the core of society (a neoliberal, free market system that places the self serving interests of the powerful as the standard by which all other values and morals are judged such that the value of an individual is measured by their present or future contribution to the fiscal economy). Critical community psychology can be as much about working with politically marginalised groups against powerful interest groups who harm them as it can be about working with non-dominant discourses (such as anti-capitalism).

Social exclusion

Social exclusion can result when individuals, groups and whole communities find they are restricted from taking a full and active part in society. Burchardt, Le Grand and Piachaud (1999) define this as happening when people find that they cannot participate in the 'normal' activities of the society in which they are resident, when such people would like to participate but they are prevented from doing so due to factors that are beyond their control and the non-participation is involuntary. So, people who purposefully exclude themselves from society – such as those who live in gated communities (we describe this more fully in Chapter 5) or those whose actions lead them to be excluded (such as people who commit crime and are then incarcerated in a penal institution) are not considered to be 'socially excluded'. Of course, this definition opens up areas of debate in relation to the role of agency (a person has control over their social circumstances) and determinism (a person's social circumstances have control over them) as well as debates as to what one considers to be 'normal activities' and how normal varies depending on cultural norms. Leonard (1984, p. 181) more satisfactorily characterises the involuntarily excluded as remaining outside 'the major arena of capitalist productive and reproductive activity' (which of course would include those in prison). Burchardt, Le Grand and Piachaud go on to set out four dimensions of social exclusion:

- consumption – income that enables the purchase of goods and services to sustain a good quality of life;
- production – opportunities for employment;
- political engagement – opportunities to vote in local and national elections and to take part in local and national political processes;
- social engagement – a social network that can offer social support when needed.

So, indicators of social exclusion could include poverty (consumption), unemployment (production), political under representation (political engagement) and loneliness (social engagement). These dimensions might be differently emphasised depending on the socio-economic context. In societies dominated by capitalist consumer economic systems (such as the UK) there is a greater emphasis on the dimensions of consumption and production (focusing on the contribution people make to the national economy through their employment status and spending power) than on political and social engagement (focusing on improving the social fabric through promoting community engagement and political activism). Though the latter is viewed by a capitalist state as important, it can be overshadowed by the concern to service the needs of the economy.

Indeed, the consumption and production dimensions to social exclusion dominate governmental and non-governmental organisations' approach to social exclusion (income poverty and lack of employment). This is linked to social justice – ensuring opportunities are open to all. The problem with under-emphasising the importance of social and political engagement and emphasising the importance of agency (those who are excluded against their will) is that the notion of social exclusion does not capture the reasons why it is a problem for society. Not only is social exclusion viewed as problematic because it is unjust to deny people opportunities, it is socially corrosive because of the effect it has on social solidarity (Wilkinson & Pickett, 2009). Definitions that concentrate on poverty rather than wealth, for example, omit from consideration the problems caused to society by those who withdraw from society because they have the financial resources to do so (those who choose not to use services provided by the state and in turn refuse to contribute to the state through tax avoidance and so on). Some commentators are beginning to talk of decisions made by the wealthy, rather than the poor, and the ways in which government policy demonising particular groups exacerbates the situation, obscuring the sources of inequality. For example, Austin (2018) summarises a recent report into social exclusion in the USA. He says:

> As Connie M. Razza [the report's author] states, "Social exclusion is a set of decisions and actions" by the "economically and politically powerful" to "[deploy] white supremacist and racist ideas to further concentrate their wealth and power. They have deputized others – including people who are not white – to enforce the social exclusion of black people through simple and seemingly individual acts, as well as through sweeping rules." While the Trump administration has fanned the flames of xenophobia, Islamophobia, and racism, convincing many white, Christian Americans that they need to fear immigrants, Muslims, and African Americans, the richest 1 percent of Americans continue to amass wealth at a rapid pace. ...
>
> A recent analysis of anti-Muslim hate found a dramatic rise in anti-Muslim violence and hate speech since the election of Donald Trump. The study finds that 20 per cent of people involved in documented instances of hate violence "referenced Trump, a Trump policy, or a Trump slogan."
>
> Here we see a clear example of social exclusion at work. As Razza states, the processes of social exclusion "[draw] the lines of who belongs – in the broad national community and in very particular places – and *how* they belong there. It deliberately deploys racist ideas to justify and naturalize ... economic disadvantage, democratic disqualification, and even further social deprivation – in order to distract the public from who is responsible for inequality."

A limited notion of social exclusion can offer a limited mandate for social change to address the problems it causes society. In keeping with the foregoing analysis, Kagan and Burton (2010, pp. 313–327) present an analysis of social marginalisation (another way to describe social exclusion) in terms of its dimensions and its sources, enveloped in an 'ideological cloud' that makes it difficult to apprehend the social processes that create the reality of marginalisation.

Conclusions about community

The task of defining community is not an easy one. Neither theoretical nor empirical work in the social sciences has actually settled on an agreed definition of what community is: nor can it, since the nature of community is itself fluid and determined along multiple dimensions. Community psychology, however, has been largely disengaged from theoretical debates on what community is and has tended to concentrate instead on documenting what it means to people living in a community (its sentimental or symbolic dimension) through seeking to understand people's 'psychological sense of community'. However, this is just one dimension to community. Other dimensions include space, time and social structure. All these dimensions intersect and one can transform into another. Considering them separately allows us to question whether one dimension might be more ascendant than another in the academic literature and social policy development, as well as in practices. It appears that the sentimental dimension of community has captured most attention recently and this might be due to increased patterns of migration (people move in and out of different physical spaces, often) and advances in communication technology that allows communities to form over widely dispersed locations. Both trends might have weakened the importance of a spatial dimension to community. However, the spatial dimension to community is still important to those who are not able to move freely and those who have no access to communication technology. Moreover, the spatial and social structural dimension of community might make it easier to connect the concept of community to public policy and social structures. It is important to consider power when defining community, as the nature of community is open to manipulation by those groups in society that hold monopolies of economic, political and cultural social power.

While this chapter has asked what community is, it has not fully explored the question of what the concept of community does and how it is used. These are questions that have resonance with the philosophy pioneered by Wittgenstein (1953), which focuses on the use of language in relation to forms of life. However, it is also a dimension to community that comes from the influence of critical theory and critical texts. It is to these questions that we turn in Chapter 5.

Chapter 5

Community as social ties

Summary

In the previous chapter we examined theories of community and explored its various dimensions, including sentiment (the way community exists symbolically), space (the way community is defined by a physical or temporal space) and social structure (the way community is defined by social features of a group – such as its membership rules). In this chapter, we explore in more detail the social structural dimension to community by examining the nature of the social ties between people that define the concept of community and then consider how the concept is employed to prescribe rather than describe the behaviours of its members.

Social ties

Social ties are the social connections that bond people. These might be both malign and benign. The nature of the social ties that we are bound by (the relationships we have with our family, friends, peers, community and so on) has a dramatic impact upon our psychological and our physical health (Kawachi & Berkman, 2001; Wilkinson & Pickett, 2009). Underpinning theories of social ties is importance of others' perception of us for our sense of self.

> Other people's perception of us is evaluative and judgmental: they like or dislike, they accept or reject, they trust or don't trust, they look up to or down on us. So essential is this intimate monitoring of others' reactions to us for our security, safety, socialization, and learning that instead of experiencing it as their reactions to us, we often experience it as if it were our experience of ourselves. When we do something that is shameful in others' eyes, we can hate ourselves for it, and when we do something that others admire, value, and appreciate, we can get a glowing sense of self-realization.
>
> (Wilkinson, 2005, p. 91)

Think!

More generally, the studies of social networks point to the importance social ties play in our sense of well-being.

> ...being embedded in a network of supportive relationships is associated in general with health and psychological well-being.
>
> (Dalton et al., 2001, p. 234)

The social ties between people are greatly influenced by social systems and, as such, the social structural dimension to community both teases out the nature of those ties and suggests ways in which those ties are formed. Below, we examine three types of social tie: those based on affection (such as in social groups), functional interdependence (such as shared needs) and coercion (such as in work places where an employee might be punished for failing to attend work). The nature of social ties might be seen as extraordinarily complex. However, it is easier to discern the ways that bonds of affection, functional interdependence and coercion inform the assumptions of researchers and policy makers and how these theories that relate to community carry assumptions about the social ties that constitute community. After a brief introduction to these three types of social ties, we consider how each might become expressed in social policy – as prescriptions of how people should live.

Reflect!

Do you like to spend time alone – how might the amount of time you spend alone be related to life stage? Babies, school age children, young adults, adults, older adults participate differently in family life and institutional life.

Social ties of affection

Studies of affection refer to the ways people are bonded together through a concern for one another's welfare, built out of a liking for each other. Here we find friendship groups but also philanthropic groups. Often, when bonds are believed to be largely based on affection, we find studies that search for the existence of informal, sustained voluntary associations between people and social policies that see community as built on voluntarism (such as active citizenship, volunteering schemes, the role of the charitable sector and so on). Here people are bonded together because they want to help others. So, to trace the degree to which a group forms a community when carrying these assumptions, we would measure the degree to which the group engages in voluntarism and philanthropy. These social ties are most likely to be affected by homophily – the love of sameness. Thus, such ties can become concentrated in groups that share characteristics based on gender, ethnicity, class, disability status and so on. People form ties of liking because they feel they are alike. The social identity upon which likeness is based can be manipulated – such as the manipulation of national identity to increase or decrease social ties of affection within and between groups. In the UK, the 'Leave' campaign behind 'Brexit' in the UK was quite successful at manipulating social ties of affection at a supranational level – creating antagonism between UK citizens and citizens in the European Union. In the USA, the Trump administration's pledge to 'Build the Wall' on its border with Mexico invoked and inflamed existing racial tensions in the populace. In Australia, social ties of affection between indigenous and non-indigenous people have been effectively disrupted to such an extent that Australia has, for 200 years, avoided establishing a treaty with indigenous people to negotiate sovereignty and has sustained a perverse cultural ritual of celebrating the invasion of Aboriginal and Torres Strait Islanders' land each year on 'Australia Day'.

Social platforms like Facebook and Twitter have been criticised for manipulating people's social ties of affection by asking users to like or dislike other users' content and then building communities on the basis of this that sharpen differences between group members and non-members; enable victim-isation and social exclusion through 'unfriending' a member; create content feed algorithms that reduce the contact between group members and non-group members; and create toxic spaces where groups can engage in confrontation and antagonism with non-group members. All of this is done not to forge communities but to monetise social ties through selling to advertisers information on the social ties that the platform has created. These social platforms remind us how creating communities through ties of affection can create sharp boundaries between those that are alike and those that are not and how for those outside, the severance from a group's ties of affection can lead to indifference at best and hatred at worst (e.g. online 'trolling'). Political discourses around immigration in the USA, UK and Australia, as well as elsewhere, can also be seen as direct manipulations of social ties of affection, essentially severing those ties by exaggerating differences between immigrants and non-immigrants. In Australia, these discourses have sustained the practice of the indefinite detention of asylum seekers in off-shore processing centres.

Social ties of interdependence

Where the belief is that social ties are based on interdependence among members, research often searches for patterns of exchange between group members such as through LETS (Local Exchange Trading Scheme) and self help organisations. It is here that we see theories of social capital. Thus, when networks between people are strong and there are strong norms of reciprocity (people helping each other out) it is said there is strong social capital amongst people. This is generally thought to be a good thing and to lead to positive well-being and good health, with lots of people being involved with others in different ways and on a range of activities (Gilchrist, 2004). In the UK an example of community forming through the social ties of interdependence was the tragedy of the Grenfell Tower in London in 2017. Grenfell Tower was a 23-storey residential tower block where a fire in the early hours of the morning of July 14, 2017 spread rapidly through the whole tower block, killing 72 people. The fire was initially blamed on the use of dangerous cladding and insulation on the building, poorly maintained fire safety equipment in the building and an inadequate fire evacuation plan for the building. During the tragedy people living in the tower block and in the surrounding community assisted in the rescue of tower block residents and in the aftermath, the surviving residents and people in the surrounding community worked together to support each other materially and to hold to account those who were responsible for the tragedy politically.

These ties can develop between people not because they like one another, but because they feel they need one another.

It is easy to see that such strong links between people could easily turn inwards and the distinction between those inside and those outside the community becomes important. Indeed, strong inward looking communities might positively exclude new people, leading to conflict, or make excessive claims on 'insiders'; restrict access to opportunities and individual freedoms; and promote a 'downward levelling of norms' (Evans, 1997). The most obvious manifestation of this can be seen in the 'gated community'. Gated communities have become more prevalent across Australia, Europe, the United States of America and major cities in China (see Figure 1.3 in Chapter 1 for a gated community in Manchester). Hutton (2002) reported that at the turn of the century 3 million people in the USA were living in gated communities. Branic and Kubrin (2018) stipulate that more recent estimations of the number of people living in gated communities is difficult to obtain; but there is little doubt that the figure has considerably increased from earlier estimations. Some of these have high levels of interdependence between residents and independence from the state such that residents organise their own community tax to pay for rubbish collection and policing and do not pay state taxes for such services. Thus, residents of these gated communities become highly dependent upon one another in terms of relying on each other to provide the funding to keep their neighbourhood clean and secure. They also become bound together by their own membership rules which can include specific bylaws. The latter can, for example, specify a minimum age for children who are permitted to enter the community, and security provisions.

Social ties of coercion

When the assumption is that social ties will be coercive, the focus of research is often on the imposition of structures on a group that seek to maintain social order or of social ties that operate as a form of resistance against patterns of exclusion and domination. Typically, the focus is on a community as a place of confinement from which people cannot escape rather than a place where people are bonded by affection or co-dependence: the processes that bind people together are negative. Pahl (1970) outlines a form of community to which people have strong allegiances, due to shared social and economic disadvantage. These communities are often close knit but are difficult to leave due to the circumstances people find themselves in. Pahl notes that such communities can be stifling for some but comforting to others, anticipating the UK Government's framing of neighbourhoods as communities experiencing different levels of social deprivation, as described through the Indices of Deprivation (UK Government, 2015). Whilst these descriptions offer objective assessments of some dimensions of community life, they do not necessarily correspond to perceived deprivation by those living in particular neighbourhoods. In Australia, government assessments of indigenous social deprivation identified the neglect and abuse of indigenous children in indigenous communities. That assessment justified the imposition of 'the intervention' in 73 indigenous communities in Australia's Northern Territory that made, inter alia, changes to welfare provision, law enforcement and land tenure. This was enacted through enforced alcohol and pornography bans, compulsory health checks and increased social and economic surveillance, and gave the government the right to seize indigenous land. In 2010, a United Nations investigation concluded that many of those measures constituted racial discrimination and violations of human rights against indigenous people.

In reality, the different kinds of social ties co-exist and might evolve into each other. For example, a community bound together by ties of coercion might transform into ties of affection and mutual interdependence if the cause for the negative effects of their being bound together as a community becomes focused on those outside. This can be realised in scapegoating of other marginalised groups in one form and in another more progressive form can be the development of political awareness of the social structures that causes the problems people are experiencing, as in processes of 'conscientisation' (see Chapter 3). So, the ties between people can be multi-layered but also transitional.

Theory prescriptions for community

It is said that philosophers, politicians and the 'public' provide prescriptions of community while social scientists provide descriptions and definitions of community which are prescriptions in disguise. Thus, theories of community and theoretical frameworks used to study communities are often normative and ideological – they say something about how the theorists or researchers think community should be.

Since the early 1900s, social scientists have increasingly moved from making theoretical venturings about what communities might be to empirical observation of what communities are. Some of these studies have sought to understand the complexity of community by having researchers immerse themselves in a community for substantial periods of time. There have been a number of such intensive studies (for example Lynd & Lynd, 1929; Jahoda, Lazarsfeld & Zeisel, 2002; Whyte, 1943; Harrison 2008). Such studies point to the complexity of community and how different dimensions of community become meaningful for people at different times and in different contexts. What is perhaps clearer to define is how the different dimensions of community affect the empirical and theoretical work of social scientists and social policy makers, that is how social scientists perceive community rather than necessarily how people experience community. This gives us an insight into the preconceptions of those who study community, including community psychologists, as well as the socio-economic context in which those preconceptions develop.

For example, Tönnies' theory of community (see Chapter 4) was located in conservative thought at the time of the industrial revolution in the West. This was a time of dramatic social upheavals during which the regulation of society by nature (employed at the time when the economy was organised around the farming community and the traditions of the craftsperson) was shifting to a regulation of society by bureaucratic social administration and the mechanisation of working practices (production lines and factories). Conservative thought was hostile to the growing process of urbanisation and the fear that the destruction of rural communities and their replacement by urban communities could loosen social control and lead to a threat to the social order by the masses. Thus, the theory that Tönnies gave voice to was grounded in a normative prescription that was against forms of social regulation that were at that time new.

Thus, the distinction between Gemeinschaft and Gesellschaft draws our attention to the role that social structures play in defining our sense of community. People's sense of shared identity, loyalty, allegiance and so on changes as their patterns of work and mobility change. In making those distinctions, Tönnies was berating the loss of one type of sense of community (Gemeinschaft) that was happening under the rapid process of economic and social change through industrialisation.

Up until the 1970s, much of what was written about communities based in Europe and North America continued to focus, in one way or another, on the transformation that has happened to urban and to rural life through the social and economic changes that occurred during the industrial revolution. Prior to this, danger was perceived to largely exist outside of the city walls. The city protected you from harsh conditions of rural life (where you were at risk of being raided by bandits, attacked by wild animals and battered by storms). Since the 1900s, the perception of danger has shifted to inside the city walls (Bauman, 2007a). The spatial dimension of community was central to such work. As we describe in Chapter 4, since the 1970s we have seen an increasing focus on the importance of the symbolic nature of community following the latest major economic and social transformation (the shift in the West from a capitalist producer society to a capitalist consumer society).

Both the focus on the spatial dimension of community and that on the symbolic nature of community could be viewed as based upon changes in social structure (in terms of global socio-economic transformations). These social structures have had a dramatic impact upon the social ties between people in communities and it is here that we can perhaps see at its most pronounced how theorists can prescribe rather than describe what those social relations might be. Thus, we contrast two approaches to theorising and researching community based first on social ties of affection and co-operation and second on social ties of coercion.

Ties of affection and co-operation: community as social capital

Social support has usually been understood and measured as a process occurring between two individuals. This has kept much of the research on social support at the individual level (Felton & Shinn, 1992). The various types of support are described in Table 5.1. Clearly, social support also occurs in groups (Maton, 1989), especially in microsystems (focusing on friendships). Those groups provide support to their members even when the individual members change. The sense of belonging within such organisations or microsystems may be as important as social support from individuals (Felton & Shinn, 1992). Recognition of this has led to increasing interest in the concept of social capital.

In 1995, Putnam reflected upon the decline of organised bowling leagues in the USA and how these were being replaced with people going to bowling alleys to bowl with friends and family instead. This

Think!

<table>
<tr><td colspan="2">**Table 5.1** Types of social support</td></tr>
</table>

Type of support	Example
Material	Child care, money lending, running errands, help with transport, DIY jobs
Social integration	Companionship
Emotional	Informal counselling, 'a shoulder to cry on'
Esteem	Making someone feel good about themselves by complementing them and displaying other forms of respect towards them

became a metaphor to describe what many commentators saw as US citizens' withdrawal from actively engaging in civil life (in sports clubs, voluntary organisations, neighbourhood associations and so on). Putnam's work is part of a body of social commentary that has focused on the consequences of modern individualism that characterises the dominant cultural mode of living in the US the UK, Australia and elsewhere (see Chapters 2 and 3) and the loss of social support at community and societal levels.

Reflect!

If you were asked to tell someone who had come to live in your country from abroad about how to take part in community groups, interest groups or local politics, what would you tell them? How did you learn about this?

Putnam's work created a considerable level of interest from academics and social policy makers who have used the concept to promote various policies (such as active citizenship in the UK).

> By 'social capital' I mean features of social life – networks, norms, and trust – that enable participants to act together more effectively to pursue shared objectives ... To the extent that the norms, networks, and trust link substantial sectors of the community and span underlying social cleavages – to the extent that the social capital is of a bridging sort – then the enhanced cooperation is likely to serve broader interests and to be widely welcomed.
>
> (Putnam, 1995, pp. 664–665)

For Putnam, increasing levels of trust between people arises from the strengthening of norms of cooperation such as the belief in the importance of reciprocity (the belief that if you do good acts for others, others will do good acts for you) and the growth of networks of civic engagement. Putnam identified two forms of social capital. Bonding capital is that which occurs between people who are 'like' one another (that is, it happens within the one community rather between two different communities). Bridging capital occurs between people and groups where co-membership of one particular community plays no necessary part (that is, it happens between different communities). For Putnam, bridging social capital was the key to promoting civil life (increased civil engagement in a democratic political system).

Putnam's thesis is that increases in social capital and increased levels of trust among people will all lead to higher levels of civic engagement (see Figure 5.1) and that this will result in a society characterised by high levels of democratic polity (a political system that seeks to promote high levels of citizen representation and participation in executive decision making processes).

The epidemiologist Richard Wilkinson incorporates the notion of social capital to explain his findings that societies that are less egalitarian are less healthy.

> ...egalitarian societies ... have ... social cohesion. They have a strong community life. Instead of social life stopping outside the front door, public space remains a social space ... People are more likely to be involved in social and voluntary activities outside the home...
>
> Social capital ... lubricates the working of the whole society and economy. There are fewer signs of anti-social aggressiveness, and society appears more caring. In short, the social fabric is in better condition.
>
> (Wilkinson, 1996, p. 4)

Wilkinson's work would add to the conceptual model proposed by Putnam, as illustrated by Figure 5.2.

So, researchers such as Wilkinson point to the corrosive effects on social cohesion of income inequalities. However, the popular focus upon social capital has tended to neglect this aspect, and discussion about social capital by social policy makers and social scientists alike often fails to acknowledge how social capital might be largely dependent upon levels of social equality and that declines and rises in social capital are likely to be inversely related to the declines and rises in social inequalities (Wilkinson,

Figure 5.1 Income equality and social capital.

Figure 5.2 Income equality, social capital and democracy.

2005). Another element that is largely absent from Putnam's work, highlighted by drawing upon Wilkinson's work, is the importance of 'respect' and a consideration that respect might precede trust. Thus, before you can establish trust between people, there needs to be mutual respect and that the feeling that you or your group is disrespected by others is reason for a deterioration of social cohesion (Szreter, 2002; Wilkinson, Kawachi & Kennedy, 1998). That feeling of respect might be read by the ways your community is valued in comparison with another group or in comparison with how your group appeared valued in the past to how it is now. This might be measured by the degree to which your community is represented in the political system (is your voice heard in Parliament or are your people recognised in your country's constitution?), in cultural institutions (are your stories told through the popular arts and the mass media?) and the degree to which your community has access to economic and material resources (are you paid a decent wage, do you have access to good education, health, housing and social services?).

The criticism here is that the theory of social capital is somewhat blinkered to the broader socio-economic and political context and insufficiently engages with the problem posed by political and ideological systems that create social inequalities. For example, Putnam's thesis that increases in social capital result in increased civil engagement and a more democratic political system somewhat ignores the structural and ideological systems in which such processes occur. Moreover, civic engagement can be widespread in non-democratic political systems and such engagement is not bound to result in an increase in democratic political processes (Boggs, 2001). Also, highly democratic systems can lead to social inequalities and discrimination (such as the Swiss deciding in 2009 through a democratic referendum to ban the building of minarets, various European countries since 2004 banning the burqa, and in the UK a referendum on membership of the European Union leading to a result that has produced political turmoil and strong political divisions across the UK – known as Brexit). Indeed, increases in social capital and civil engagement can result in a deterioration of democratic polity if that engagement is through street gangs, religious cults and reactionary political movements. The fact that norms of reciprocity might develop between members of a community, and a community becomes increasingly interconnected by social networks and becomes trusting, does not necessarily mean that the activity of that community will be beneficial to others. Indeed, that community might become quite self serving and unhelpful to those who are not members – it might exploit and damage the interests of non-community members. Putnam later recognised the negative purposes to which social capital might be employed (see Portes & Landolt, 1996). However, the 'dark side' of social capital is an area that is largely overlooked in the literature, while the positive aspects of social capital are commonly emphasised by social policy makers and academics alike.

Think!

Draw up a table of positive and negative aspects of social capital. On balance, do you think social capital should be encouraged? Why is this?

This lack of understanding of the importance of socio-political and economic context – namely the influence of power, economics, politics and ideology – is also highlighted in the way Putnam writes about the deterioration in social capital in the USA since the 1960s. Putnam believed that the major reason for the decline was the effect of generational succession whereby the pre-war generation (those born between 1910 and 1940) were succeeded by later generations who have been less engaged in civil life, placed less value on duty and held less faith in the ability and appropriateness of government to intervene in the life of the individual. However, Putnam fails to consider why this has happened and to consider the socio-political events and processes that might have contributed to this change in values and loss of faith in political institutions and a growing culture of competitive individualism.

The notion of social capital has also been criticised in a number of other ways. For example, it is somewhat gender blind. Much of the initial research into social capital focused on support systems used largely by men during the 1970s (such as sports clubs) and women's systems of support were largely ignored and/or considered irrelevant to the political world and to citizenship (James cited in Lowndes, 2000).

Also, most social support research has been middle class focused and biased against non-dominant groups (Mickelson & Kubzansky, 2003). The privatised and individualised lifestyle of middle class USA may seem less familiar to those who are not middle class and not living in the USA (Szreter, 2002) where the 'we' is used by and to signify a liberal/cosmopolitan elite. The 'Me Too' movement is an interesting case in point. The movement began in 2006 and was focused on black women's experience of sexual abuse, particularly in socio-economically deprived communities. In 2017 the movement effectively became re-appropriated by middle class American women – notably by Hollywood actors. The reframing of 'Me Too' has led critics to berate dilution of the movement as its focus has shifted away from issues of race and class. Class also impacts upon the way social capital is distributed, valued and used. Writers like Bourdieu (1986) have pointed out how the poor generally have more access to social capital because they have little access to any other form of capital. Also, by accessing social capital the poor might in fact find that it might lock them into poverty (such as on housing estates where social capital is provided by street gangs and so on, which might disconnect them from other social networks that might offer them a way out of their poverty). This is the problem of bonding social capital (which links us together with those in our designated community) in comparison with bridging social capital (which links us to people outside of our specified community). Both the rich and the poor tend to have more bonding social capital than bridging social capital which results in people becoming locked into poverty or wealth and power being locked up with small pockets of elite groups. Indeed, bridging capital may be difficult to create where deeply embedded and somewhat change resistant social inequalities and historical antagonisms create distrust and disrespect between groups.

We now consider what might happen if the social ties are strong between people but that these are largely characterised as ties of coercion rather than affection and co-operation.

Reflect!

Consider your local community – can you discern bridging and bonding ties? How do they come about? Which is stronger, bonding or bridging capital? Why is this?

Ties of coercion: community as ghetto

A contrasting vision of a community tied together by bonds of affection and co-operation is that of people being connected by ties of coercion and exploitation and such a picture of a community is provided by descriptions of communities as ghettos.

> Ghettos and prisons are two varieties of the strategy of 'tying the undesirables to the ground', of confinement and immobilization. In a world in which mobility and the facility to be on the move have become principal factors of social stratification, this is (both physically and symbolically) a weapon of ultimate exclusion and degradation.
>
> (Bauman, 2001, p. 120)

A ghetto is a community into which people are placed involuntarily and from which people are prevented from leaving. Ghettos contrast with gated communities (described earlier) where residents cut themselves off from the outside voluntarily and residents are free to leave, but non-residents are not free to enter. Gated communities are constructed to keep those inside secure and free from threat and their residents are usually resource rich, while ghettos are constructed to keep those outside secure and free from threat and the residents are usually resource poor.

Among the most prominent historical examples of ghettos are the Jewish ghettos (for example, Budapest, Kovno, Łódź, Vilna and Warsaw), in Nazi occupied Europe during the 1930s and 1940s. These ghettos were internment areas built on the previously existing ghettos where Jewish people had been required to live in Eastern Europe.

Conditions in these Jewish ghettos under Nazi control were wretched. Large numbers of people were crammed into small areas where food was scarce and amenities were minimal. For example, the Warsaw ghetto was just over four hundred hectares in area and housed 400,000 Jewish people. Ironically the most prominent contemporary examples of a ghetto are parts of the Occupied Territories of Palestine – the Israeli political administration subjecting the Palestinians to the treatment Jewish people were subjected to by the Nazis.

Among modern day ghettos are the 'black ghettos', particularly prevalent in the USA, and immigrant ghettos that are becoming widespread across Europe. In Australia, ghettos were created for indigenous people when they were moved onto small parcels of land (reserves, missions and stations). This was the Australian government's political response to the dispossessions of indigenous people from their native lands.

Ghettos are often those communities that are experiencing multiple levels of economic deprivation. It is not the absence of resource per se that makes such communities ghettos, but the effect such material deprivation has on their residents' ability to leave. The situation faced by some people living on council (or public housing) estates in the UK reflects this. These estates have long been characterised as places of heightened crime and delinquency and those that live there are commonly caricatured as criminals and delinquents (they are often called 'sink estates'). Such representations have continually been reinforced through mass media portrayals (in documentaries, dramas, literature, music and cinema). These communities gain negative reputations which are then transferred onto those who live there. It is difficult to find a city or a town in the UK that does not have an area within it stigmatised in this way.

Example: Community leadership

We worked, and a group of students, worked with some residents who lived on the edge of a prosperous market town in the North West of England. There were few facilities in this area: no schools, doctors' surgeries, community meeting places, or libraries. There was a small parade of shops with most units empty and one rough public house. The estate was called Broadheath (a pseudonym). All the houses and flats were simply called Broadheath no. 1 or 203, or 1,130. There were no names to the roads. Residents were of the firm belief that as soon as they gave their address as Broadheath, when applying for jobs and so on, they got no further, due to the negative reputation attached to Broadheath. They could not give their address without naming Broadheath, whereas everywhere else in the town could just give their house number and road and did not need to name the district.

Blanden, Gregg & Machin (2005) reported on the decreasing levels of intergenerational social mobility in the UK, showing that a child born in the 1970s was less likely to move out of the poverty of its parents than a child born in the 1950s. The report further concluded that social mobility in the UK and USA were both lower than in Germany, which had the middle rate of social mobility in the countries surveyed by the report, and were substantially lower than in Canada and the Nordic countries, which had the highest level of social mobility. To be poor in the UK is to inherit the poverty of parents and to bequeath poverty to children. Sprigings and Allen (2005, p. 389) argue that one of the paradoxical effects of the UK Government's policies on community building

> restricts the residential mobility of poorer households and exacerbates (rather than combats) their social exclusion because a key indicator of social inclusion is their ability to take advantage of the social, cultural and economic opportunities that so often exist elsewhere.

As we briefly described in Chapter 4, people can also find that while they themselves do not move, their communities (both social settings and social identities) move (or shape-shift) around them, transformed by socio-economic and political forces into something unrecognised and unwanted. You might find that you are not placed into a ghetto, but that the place in which you live or the social identity you are given becomes transformed in such a way that you become ghettoised. For example, many communities that developed around the coal mining and manufacturing industries were economically and socially devastated following the policy of disinvestment in manufacturing in the UK. Another example is how the social identity of Muslims has shifted since the terrorist attacks on the USA in 2001 such that racism and Islamophobia can make daily life difficult for many Muslim people in the West. Here a ghetto does not need to be a physical space – it can be a symbolic space, a representation or stereotype (see section on ghetto walls below).

The restrictions on the freedom to leave can make ghettos resemble a form of prison or mental institution. Indeed, the process of 'ghettoisation' runs in parallel with a penal system with an ongoing mutual exchange occurring between residents in each as part of a systemic criminalisation and pathologisation of the poor (Duckett & Schinkel, 2008). Bauman (2001) argues that the ghetto serves as the dumping ground for those for whom society has no economic or political use.

The ghetto walls

Ghettos can exist without the need for physical barriers to keep people inside. Barriers can be attitudinal or social. For example, there may be no physical barrier that stops black residents from crossing the street and walking into a nearby white neighbourhood. But if they do, they may be watched and then reported by white residents, and then trailed, stopped and searched by the police.

Social attitudes can ghettoise. Whilst physical barriers to social inclusion for disabled people, for example, have greatly reduced in the UK, their exclusion is maintained through attitudinal barriers. Similarly, a diagnosis of 'mental illness' can transform social identity to the extent that employment is restricted and people are perceived as a potential threat to others. They become ghettoised by a medical label. People can find themselves locked into a social identity (based on ethnicity, disability, gender, sexuality, social class and so on).

Reflect!

Which social identities do you have which:

- You have chosen?
- Have been chosen for you?
- You can change?
- You cannot change?

In this way, a community might be a bad place to be because of the people who you are placed there with (whether that is a place or a social identity). To be placed in a ghetto often means you are being placed in with those whom society has either labelled as 'bad' or 'mad'. This is the way that problem places are seen as inhabited by problem people (Johnston & Mooney, 2007). So, people find themselves placed in these physical settings or social identities against their will and once there are unable to leave.

> The truth is that council housing is a living tomb. You dare not give up the house because you might never get another, but staying is to be trapped in a ghetto of both place and mind.
>
> (Hutton, 2007, www.guardian.co.uk/commentisfree/2007/feb/18/comment.homeaffairs)

The 'favelas', 'barrios', 'bustees', 'townships' and 'slums' which characterise majority world cities (Neuwirth, 2006) all illustrate similar processes of ghettoisation.

Think!

Can you think of people who lack the social mobility to move out of their stigmatised identity? What might be the reasons for this? What consequences does this have for their lives?

In a ghetto, social relations will often be characterised more by antagonism than by affection and co-operation. Ghetto residents can turn in on themselves and distance themselves from others to whom they attribute blame for the stigma their place (or identity) attracts. Newly arrived immigrants, disabled people, people diagnosed with a mental illness, unemployed people and so on may all be targeted for discrimination in disadvantaged communities. Bauman (2001) captures this process:

> To regain a measure of dignity and reaffirm the legitimacy of their own status in the eyes of society, residents ... overstress their moral worth as individuals (or as family members) and join in the dominant discourse of denunciation of those who undeservingly 'profit' from social programmes, faux pauvres and 'welfare cheats'. It is as if they could gain value only by devaluing their neighbourhood and their neighbours. They also engage in a variety of strategies of social distinction and withdrawal which converge to undermine neighbourhood cohesion.
>
> (Bauman, 2001, p. 121)

Here, the social relations between people are not characterised by affection or co-operation but by antagonism. Indeed, the whole analysis rests on the assumption that the social ties between people in such settings are hostile, not harmonious. These different ways of thinking about social ties can also be found in how social boundaries around communities are seen.

Social boundaries: benign or benevolent?

The construction of social and cultural borders can be a reminder of the benign side to community – social safety – or of its less than benign side – social division. The identification of the very things that people have in common with each other (whatever that might be) also has the effect of marking out those with whom people have less in common. Thus, the construction of community around 'sameness' (shared interests, shared space, shared identity and so on) denotes a place where you are around people who are similar to you and apart from people who are dissimilar to you (the Other). Often the homogeneity of both those inside and those outside of a community becomes amplified, as does the perceived deviance of the outsiders and righteousness of the insiders. In this way, community can involve the construction of barriers (not only physical, but also social and cultural) that are closely monitored to maintain the protection of those on the inside and the persecution of those outside. Uncritically constructing community as a place of safety and security can lead to a justification for this process of 'Othering' and boundary making.

> ... the unrelenting processes of social differentiation which reflect and amplify social hierarchy are fundamentally important in any analysis of social integration and community. It is these processes which create social exclusion, which stigmatise the most deprived and establish social distances throughout society.
>
> (Wilkinson, 1996, p. 171)

If we assume that the social ties between people in communities are based on affection and co-operation we might see those boundaries as more benevolent than benign. Community psychologists often do just that – focusing on the positive effects of community and the barriers that are created around them. For example, McMillan and Chavis point to the positives of constructing boundaries as a means to offset the harmful effects such social divisions might create:

> Social psychology research has demonstrated that people have boundaries protecting their personal space. People need these barriers to protect against threat ... While much sympathetic interest in and research on the deviant have been generated, group members' legitimate needs for boundaries to protect their intimate social connections have often been overlooked ... the harm which comes from the pain of rejection and isolation created by boundaries will continue until we clarify the positive benefits that boundaries provide to communities.
>
> (McMillan & Chavis, 1986, p. 4)

Here, the Other becomes the deviant whom 'we' (the cosmopolitan elite) need to be protected against with boundaries. However, McMillan and Chavis interpret social barriers as providing emotional safety.

These differences in perspective and lived reality (whether we view or experience communities as sites of social capital and places which can enable and empower, or as ghettos which marginalise and stigmatise) are inextricably linked to social power at a structural level. One of the criticisms of Putnam's theory of social capital is that communities are largely seen as doing it for themselves and the role of the state in creating the conditions for this to happen or not to happen is largely overlooked (Szreter, 2002).

Community and social policy

Not only is it possible to trace the ideological and theoretical underpinnings of the various ways community is defined, it is also important to consider how the concept of community has been employed to achieve particular political ends. Indeed, 'community' has largely been defined over the last two hundred years for political and administrative purposes and once placed in its historical context we find that it is a concept that "... *has been contested, fought over and appropriated for different uses and interests to justify different politics, policies and practices*" (Mayo, 1994, p. 48). This perspective states that the concept of community conveys not a description of but a prescription for social organisation. Below we list a number of examples of how community has been prescribed in this way.

- Under colonial direct rule in East Africa in the late nineteenth and early twentieth centuries, the concept of 'community' was used to classify and regulate South Asian immigrant skilled manual workers. The construct 'tribe' was used to administer the African workforce but this was inappropriate for the South Asian workers so a new concept had to be created and used to classify and regulate the Asian population (Bauman, 1996).

- In the UK during the mid twentieth century the concept of community was used in urban planning as a tool for social engineering. Community was invoked to smooth social resistance against a social programme that sought 're-development' of working class areas and mass movement of working class neighbourhoods to new housing estates following 'slum clearances'. These urban planning initiatives deployed the symbolic association of community with safety, security and extended family to promote their social planning agenda and placate working class concerns that their lives were being re-ordered at the behest of and for the benefit of the political classes.
- In Europe during the 1950s 'community' was used in the Paris Treaty of 1951 and the Rome Treaty of 1957 to proffer an organisational structure that would supersede the concept of the 'nation state' – the European Community. The use of the concept of community functioned to focus attention on mutual aid and protection and deflect attention from the attempts to create a superpower to compete economically, politically and militarily in global order.
- In the UK, the disappearance of 'community' from the political lexicon during the neo-conservative emphasis on individualism was epitomised by Thatcher's 'no such thing as society' speech (see Chapter 1). When the Labour Party came to power in the UK in 1997, the concept of community became re-introduced into social policy discussion and was used, specifically in programmes of 'urban regeneration/renewal', to signify 'bottom up' programmes of social and economic reform and the political process of decentralisation and devolution. More generally, it was used to promote the development of 'third-way politics' – a transfer of responsibility away from the social institution and from the individual and onto the collective of individuals – the community. Thus, 'community' became the site of a political project that sought to leave society unbound from both the tyranny of being governed by the dictates of social institutions and the self-interest of the individual and thus 'community' would mediate between the individual and the social institution and become the site where the individual would become re-shackled by moral responsibility to the political economy of the nation state.

Thus, it is important to understand the socio-economic and cultural context in which attempts are made to anchor the meaning of the concept of community and the ideological purposes for which it is invoked. Such an understanding points to the historical and political malleability of the concept (for example, in the policies of 'community care', 'urban regeneration' and 'New Deal for communities' in the UK, and 'community renewal' in Australia, Canada and the USA). Common to all of these modern initiatives that invoke community is the notion of 'participation', a key process in critical community psychology.

Nature of participation

As with the concept of 'community', participation is a complex and problematic concept (Cooke & Kothari, 2001; Cornwall, 2008). Cooke (2001) distinguished between participation as a means and as an end. Participation as means, he argues, builds a sense of commitment and enhances effectiveness of service delivery. This kind of participation would be as part of externally defined, top down agendas. Participation as an end, on the other hand, is said to increase empowerment, or control over development activities from which people had hitherto been excluded. This kind of participation is driven bottom up and will often originate with marginalised people themselves. Beetham, Blick, Margetts and Weir (2008) suggest that participation can be characterised along four different dimensions: individual versus collective action or initiative; unstructured versus structured through existing organisations and channels; time-bound or one-off versus ongoing through time; and reactive versus proactive.

Although they argue that widening and deepening participation leads to greater social justice, they point out that any form of participation in the UK is as unequal as the distribution of power and resources throughout society. Participation does not necessarily have a levelling effect.

Reflect!

Think about your own participation in any activities or groups which aim to contribute to social change. What do you do and with whom?

In much of community psychology action there are elements of both types of participation. Kagan (2006a, 2006b) suggests that it is bottom up participation and collective action or those participation practices that include bottom up processes that are likely to have the greatest impact on both well-being and potential for changing the material circumstances of life. This type of participation does several things (Campbell & Jovchelovitch, 2000; Campbell & Murray, 2004).

First, the group's critical awareness and development of critical thinking is enhanced. Second, members of the group re-negotiate their collective social identity and varied, associated perspectives and views of the world. They do this by people developing shared understanding, information and ways of talking about themselves and others. Lastly, people's confidence and ability to take control of their lives is reinforced. People are *empowered* to make changes to their lives. With this type of participation it is necessary to have access to power, and resources, and this is the role of the external agents, community psychologists or other professionals.

Montero (2004a) discusses participation from the perspective of those who are participating. She conceptualises participation as a process closely connected to the concept of 'commitment'. Rather than a linear ladder with its metaphor of higher and lower forms of participation, Montero conceptualises a dynamic system of concentric circles with the nucleus of maximum participation and commitment at the centre. The circles radiate through different levels of participation-commitment to the outer layer of positive friendly curiosity with no commitment (see Figure 5.3).

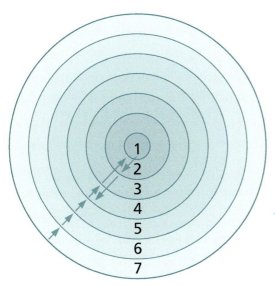

1. Nucleus of maximum participation and commitment
2. Frequent participation and high commitment
3. Specific participation, medium commitment
4. Sporadic participation, low commitment
5. New and tentative participation, low commitment (e.g. financial support material)
6. Tangential participation, unclear (e.g. approval, agreement)
7. Positive, friendly curiosity. No commitment.

➚ People moving in and out with greater or lesser levels of commitment

Figure 5.3 Levels of participation and commitment in the community.
Source: Montero, 2004a. Reproduced with permission of the author.

Think!

Level of participation	Activity
1. Information	Tell people what is planned
2. Consultation	Offer a number of options and listen to the feedback
3. Deciding together	Encourage others to provide some additional ideas and options, and join in deciding what is the best way forward
4. Acting together	Not only do different interests decide together what is best, they also form a partnership to carry it out
5. Supporting independent community initiatives	Others are helped to do what they want (perhaps within a framework of grants advice and support provided by the resource holder)

Source: adapted from Wilcox, 1994, p. 4. Licensed under CC BY-ND-NC 1.0.

Note: Levels 3–5 involve substantial participation.

Thus, for Montero, participation is a dynamic system wherein individuals or groups can move in and out. Part of the task of trying to gain participation is to enable movement from the outer to the inner levels, and a further task is to support those at the inner levels so that they are able to retain their levels of commitment.

Wilcox (1994) builds on Arnstein's (1969) 'ladder of participation' to suggest a more static five levels, or stances towards participation, which offer increasing degrees of control to those involved. Table 5.2 summarises the five levels. It is the levels of 'deciding' and 'acting together' and 'supporting community initiatives' that are most likely to lead to transformative change.

Act!

Using a variety of methods (e.g. the web, newspapers, television or word-of-mouth) identify a number of social action or social justice groups. Using Table 5.2 decide what their key features are and what level of participation they involve.

We have combined these approaches and think of participatory work along two dimensions of participation (proactive and passive) and commitment (high to low) (Kagan, 2006a).

We can then map different activities and degrees of involvement along these dimensions, as in Figure 5.4. We can position the types of participation required by policy (similar to Wilcox's levels) as well as participation roles in practice (similar to Montero's positions) in the participation space.

Community activists, who identify their own needs and set their own agendas, would typically find that their own strategies for achieving change are in the proactive participation, high commitment quadrant. Community members and representatives who work in partnership with agencies on policy agendas can also be situated in this quadrant, whereas those self-appointed community representatives who get co-opted into activities with agendas set by professionals could be situated in the proactive participation, low commitment quadrant. Professionals who are committed to working on community issues but who work weekdays only and go home at night can also be placed in this quadrant. This mapping of participation and commitment can be useful for exploring movement over time, and for

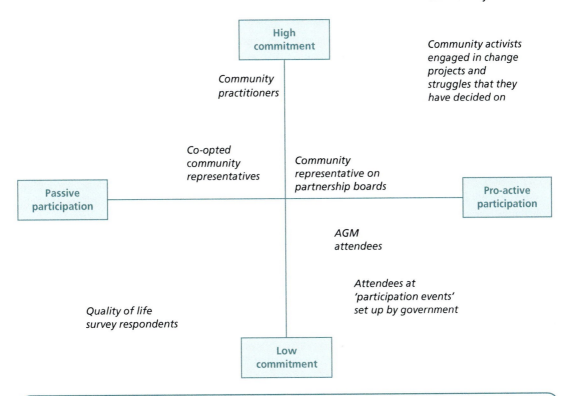

Figure 5.4 Mapping participation in terms of pro-activity and commitment.

identifying those most at need of support for their activities, lest they risk stress, disaffection or burnout – those in the top right, high commitment, proactive participation quadrant.

One of the difficulties inherent in the term 'participation' is that the term is contested and used in different ways by different people. Brodie, Cowling and Nissen (2009) distinguish between public, social and individual participation. Public participation is *"the engagement of individuals with the various structures and institutions of democracy"*. Sometimes this is referred to as political or civic participation or participatory governance. Examples of public participation include voting; becoming an elected politician or joining a political party; becoming involved in the governance of a school, hospital or other public institution. Social participation refers to collective activities that people might get involved in, such as residents' groups, clubs and societies, solidarity groups, local protest campaigns and so on. Individual participation refers to the choices and actions that individuals make and which are reflections of their values and concerns. They include, for example, buying fair trade goods, volunteering time to a local good cause, donating money to charities, writing letters in response to a campaign and so on. Clearly the modes of participation overlap. Community psychology might be concerned with them all, though perhaps is more focused on social and public participation.

Ife (1995) identifies a number of conditions under which people are most likely to participate and these can help to assess the likelihood of genuine participation being achieved.

1 People will participate if they feel the issue or activity is important. Clearly, this is more likely if people themselves have been involved in identifying the issue and had a say in any action to be taken, from the outset. It will be more difficult to encourage participation in relation to an issue that others have defined as important, and more difficult still if people have been given an

opportunity to express their views – often through consultation processes, rather than genuine participative processes – only to be overruled by 'experts'.

2 People must feel that their action will make a difference. If there seems to be little opportunity of success it will be difficult to encourage people to participate. This is linked to the ways in which people have been involved in deciding on action to be taken, but also to the degree to which they can see that they or people close to them will benefit. In this case, there may be a role to be played in helping translate a general community benefit into tangible benefits for individuals or groups.

3 Different forms of participation must be acknowledged. Formal participation, in committees and formally constituted groups, is only one kind of participation. It is important that people's different skills, talents, interests, available time and energy are taken into account and more informal forms of participation recognised. This might include posting leaflets, stuffing envelopes, providing refreshments for events or meetings, art work, childminding, helping with transport, sympathetic listening, contributing to discussions, keeping notes of events and so on.

4 People must be enabled to participate and be supported in their participation. This means that help with care (of children, elders etc.), transport, availability of translation and interpretation as necessary, the timing and location of events, the involvement of gatekeepers and community leaders, or advocates as necessary will all need to be taken into account to enable participation.

5 Structures and processes must not be alienating. Participation that relies on writing, confidence in speaking in a group, involvement in formal meetings, the articulation of complex experiences and ideas, and so on may be alienating to those not used to such activities. On the other hand, participation that is linked to an activity or the development of more naturally occurring relationships might be more enabling. It is possible to make participation fun and stimulating so that the activities themselves can be positive experiences.

Example: Gardening as a tool for participation

A community group was concerned with the appearance of the local environment. There was little interest from local people in doing anything about it. A small group of activists began clearing and planting up some of the flower beds around the residences. Gradually more residents got involved as they saw the results of the work and how the environment around people's homes improved. Children with reputations for troublesome behaviour locally also showed interest and were given tasks to do. Other residents began to offer refreshments to the 'gardeners', including the children with whom they had recently been in some conflict. When the group entered and won awards in a local competition, still more people got involved and the project extended beyond gardening to other physical improvements of the locality. After two years the most active people had not participated at the start and the original activists were able to withdraw.

As participation is a relational and dynamic process, it is particularly important that we engage in constant processes of reflection to ensure we are inclusive, enabling and supportive, and can recognise signs of exhaustion and fatigue, due to the emotional toll that participating in community action can take (Kagan 2006a, 2006b). Boundary critique (see Chapter 7) can help us reflect upon whether there are some people whose participation is essential, without whom the problem will be defined in a restrictive way and the action implemented will be inappropriate.

Working participatively does not mean that we ask people what they want and how in an uncritical way, and then go and make this happen. Instead, it is a process wherein expert (community psychological) knowledge is combined with lay knowledge through processes of collaborative working (Kagan, Duggan, Richards & Siddiquee, 2011). Through this process,

> ...two forms of knowledge merge: the 'ordinary' or common knowledge, transmitted through traditions and everyday life contributed by community members; and the scientific knowledge of the community psychologists, derived from their learning and experience.

Montero (1998) argues that this process of sharing different forms of expertise is guided by the principles of reality (how circumstances are perceived and experienced) and possibilities (assessment of what kinds of changes are needed and goals to be sought). Both are necessary.

> 'Reality' without 'possibilities' leads to helplessness and passivity. 'Possibilities' without 'reality' lead to confusion and loss of perspective, therefore inducing failure and helplessness.
>
> (Montero, 1998, p. 66)

Thus, participation is more a process of facilitating discussion, exploring differences and reaching agreement amongst people affected by an issue, where people hold different world views, attitudes and beliefs about the issue, themselves in relation to it, and possibilities for change.

However, there are dangers in focusing on participation in this way which are connected to our critique of community. The danger is if community psychologists carry with them the idea that community is largely a positive, safe place where people are bonded together by a sense of affection and functional interdependence, they may either be shocked or be unable to understand those communities (and there are many of them) that do not function in this way.

As critical community psychologists we need to take care we do not inadvertently use processes of participation to promote the illusion of choice and voice for those whose social reality is that they have neither, whilst remembering that participation can still serve as route to empowerment (Zambrano, 2007).

In this chapter we looked critically at the nature of social ties and how the different ways of thinking about connections between people are used to prescribe community in a variety of ways. We examined the ways in which communities are boundaried, in particular in relation to ghettoisation, and the links between community and social policy. Lastly we looked positively and critically at the notion of participation and its role in critical community psychology.

The importance of maintaining a critical perspective on both the concept of community and the concept of participation is part of the process of challenging oppression and marginalisation and we need to maintain this perspective as we move into Part 2 of the book, Act!

Part 1

Critical disruption of Think!

In this first critical disruption chapter we seek to problematise some of the material in Part 1 so as to illustrate how theory (thinking) can lead us into problems if our thoughts are not accompanied by action and reflection. That is not to say that the materials in Part 1 are based solely on theory (much of what we have written is grounded in action and reflection), but that action and reflection are not so much discussed here as in Parts 2 and 3.

In Part 1 we have discussed the importance of systems thinking for critical community psychology and how psychology should be considered a 'systems discipline' and have at its focus the social systems (family, peer group, community, economy, state and so on) that shape and are shaped by human behaviour. The question this begs is: 'to what extent have we acknowledged the social systems that have shaped the content of our book?' Such a question allows us to critically disrupt the explicit and implicit historical accounts we provide in Part 1 (both the construction of the history of community psychology and historical accounts of the theories and applications of 'community') and the critique of individualism embedded throughout Part 1. We hope to show how our thoughts might result in unintended action and how our arguments take on a different appearance once situated into their cultural and political context. We first consider how our thoughts on individualism might be disrupted by reflecting on where such thoughts come from. We then consider how our history of community psychology might be used (that is, put into action) in ways we do not intend.

Critically disrupting the challenge to individualism

Our critique of mainstream psychology is that it is individualistic at its heart because it purports to study individuals decontextualised from their historical, social, political, economic and cultural surroundings. In this, we share our perspective with other critical thinkers (who are cited throughout our book). Our challenge to individualism is not just about method or about theory, but is also an ideologically based challenge to the dominant cultural norms carried by the most economically and politically powerful social institutions (such as corporations and government bodies). However, such challenges against the ideology of individualism largely come from academics located in the university systems of the core capitalist countries, who are relatively well funded and have privileged access to publish their work in the dominant journals in the field.

This is a problem because one of the main concerns about the dominance of individualism in psychology (and more broadly in the social sciences) highlighted by such critical thinkers is that individualism promotes the belief that you can separate the observer from the observed (that is, the belief that psychologists can objectively rather than subjectively study individuals and that such observations can be held as 'facts' that exist independent of the social conditions under which the 'facts' were gathered). This results in the work of psychologists being stripped of its cultural and political heritage and obscures the way that the gender, class, race, disability status and so on of those who practise psychology impacts upon their work. But, in rejecting this doctrine of neutral observers, critical thinkers become subject to their own critique – we need to consider how their criticism of individualism is shaped by the individualistic culture in which they operate. Thus, we cannot hold up our own criticism of psychology without subjecting ourselves to our own critique. The critique we need to consider is whether our thoughts on individualism are themselves individualistic (given we are located in an individualistic culture) and to more broadly consider the impact of individualism on our own work.

It has been argued that a discussion of individualism can only be entertained under an individualistic framework – that the dichotomy between individualism and collectivism (which we allude to often in our book) is an individualistic construct (Sampson, 2000). A collectivist perspective would view both the individual and the collective as part of an indivisible whole and would thus view individualism and collectivism as not separate processes, but part of one process with neither the individual nor the collective having the possibility of dominating over or having conflict with the other. Thus, under a collectivist framework the notion of individualism as an alternative to collectivism is based on a false dichotomy – in essence, it cannot exist. We deal with this issue in Chapter 3 (see the treatment of Bhaskar's approach which argues for a transformational approach to the individual–society question), but it is for the reader to judge how successful this is.

The second problem is that the case against individualism is likely to have become somewhat exaggerated. We believe it to be true that the doctrine of individualism has been adopted wholesale by the dominant political and economic social institutions in the West. For example:

- Government: the marginalisation of socialism and promotion of active citizenship (whereby responsibilities for promoting well-being are shifted from the state and onto the individual); personal freedom is given precedence and public spaces and public services are increasingly privatised.
- Economic institutions: the adoption of a model of human behaviour that views consumers as autonomous actors who are motivated by self-interest.
- Mass media: the cult of the celebrity where individual life stories dominate and personality supplants politics.
- Science: the dominance of positivism which has promoted the view of the scientist as independent, objective observer detached from culture and politics and from the observed, mimicking the way self is conceptually separated from society.

Yet none of this means that individualism is the only cultural *value* in the West. As Billig (2008) points out, the modern era was never fully individualistic and this remains so. Outside of dominant political and economic systems and of the epistemological paradigms deployed by scientists, collectivism thrives – people are still willing to pay taxes that fund health services and education and to engage in mass participation (such as through mass boycotts, petitions and protests). The collective continually confounds the individualistic culture that capitalism was supposed to have spawned.

So, despite the relative dominance of individualism as normative model and theory of society, we are able to find ways to disengage from the imposed cultural norms. Indeed, our focus on the dominance of individualism might say more about how we, the authors of this book, are particularly dominated by powerful institutions. This might be because we work closely with (or at least in similar social circles to) people in positions of power who can influence us, we have money and reputations that can be lost if we upset those in power, and we read lots so we are at risk of soaking up the propaganda produced by the system.

> Propaganda very often works better for the educated than it does for the uneducated. This is true on many issues. There are a lot of reasons for this, one being that the educated receive more of the propaganda because they read more. Another thing is that they are the agents of propaganda. After all, … they're supposed to be the agents of the propaganda system so they believe it. It's very hard to say something unless you believe it. Other reasons are that, by and large, they are just part of the privileged elite so they share their interests and perceptions, whereas the general population is more marginalized. It, by and large, doesn't participate in the democratic system, which is overwhelmingly an elite game.
>
> (Chomsky, 1992, p. 119)

So, it might be the case that those who are working in those social institutions (such as ourselves as academics working in the scientific community) might find disengagement from an individualistic culture harder as recipients of the most intense individualistic propaganda – we matter more to the people in power as we write, we teach and are in positions of influence.

Critically disrupting our history of community psychology

The way we have laid out our account of individualism might function rhetorically, using hyperbole to strengthen our argument or at least to make our arguments clearer. So too our construction of a history of community psychology and a history of the contested nature of community needs to be reflected upon. Our histories, and those we have inherited from others, might say as much about what we would like the history to be rather than describe what the history is (if the latter is ever possible).

It has been said that history is written by the victor (an aphorism sometimes attributed to Churchill who did write such history). We might extend that to saying that history is written by the powerful – those who have the cultural, economic, political and social resources to ensure their version of history sticks. Historical accounts are always subject to disagreements; for example, feminists have renamed history as herstory when analysing the past with a gendered lens. This is because history is as much about the discarding of information as it is about archiving information – separating out the trivial events (such as what you ate for breakfast) from the important events (such as decisions made by Parliament). But decisions over what is and is not important are based on the presumptions and preferences of particular interest groups and on their particular tastes, values, politics, belief systems and so on. So, history can become a series of distortions bent towards the interest of particular social groups (and by the features of the archiving processes). At worst, historical events might be based on fabrications of or denial of events for the purpose of propaganda.

Think!

Many of the struggles of the powerless against the powerful, which we describe in this book, are not only for an adequate share of resources, but also to ensure recorded history does justice to their stories. Kundera summed this up in the following quote that has become a clarion call for the poor and dispossessed around the world:

The struggle of man against power is the struggle of man against forgetting.

(Kundera, 1978, p. 3)

The version of history that wins is likely to be the one that portrays those who have the greatest power in the most benign light. So, the history of the Second World War portrays the Germans and Japanese as war criminals (the Holocaust, the torture and summary execution of prisoners and so on), while the British, US and Soviet armies have their actions extolled as virtuous. Thus, the bombing of Dresden has not been recorded in history as a war crime, nor was dropping the atomic bomb on Hiroshima and then on Nagasaki three days later, nor the collateral damage – for example the Bengal famine. Churchill himself, rather than being cast as a racist, drunken war criminal has been cast as a hero (even though there is as much evidence to support the former as a more accurate characterisation). Churchill's involvement in war crimes is largely written out of the history books and only exists in radical texts that sit at the edge of mainstream consciousness.

This critical reading of history recalls Foucault's work that connects power and knowledge (see Chapter 11), that is, it is always possible to take apart an intellectual system and trace its component parts to the interests of certain social groups (Parker, 1999). The feminist community psychology approach emphasises the following characteristics:

A willingness to make explicit the implicit assumptions embedded in our most sacred and taken for granted concepts; an acceptance that all knowledge is socially produced and therefore can never be value free; interests, however implicit, are always being served; an awareness that there is an inescapable relationship between knowledge and power.

(Cosgrove & McHugh, 2000, p. 817)

So, what is important is not what is said, but *who* says *what* about *whom*. Applying this reflection we can consider how our history of community psychology might be enacted in a way that serves particular interest groups. In turning to the histories of community psychology that have been written, the one history that is most dominant is that of the Swampscott conference (see Chapter 2). This became the globally dominant account of where community psychology came from; it has become dominant as Swampscott is regularly cited as the birthplace for community psychology and manifestations of community psychology outside of the USA are largely described as developing after Swampscott (see Fryer, 2008). Whose interests does this serve? Well, to be cited as a founder of community psychology can accrue for you and those associated with you (your colleagues, your institution, your publisher, your students and so on) considerable social prestige within the field of community psychology. Indeed, in the USA there are regular events and projects that celebrate the achievements of the great, founding fathers (they were all men) of community psychology who were present at Swampscott (a history not a herstory). Given the dominance of the USA in the world, due to the power and reach of its publishing industry and the relatively resource rich status of its academic institutions, it might be difficult to unseat the way Swampscott has been written into the history of community psychology.

Finally, is there a problem in the histories we have constructed or reconstructed because we might have constructed our history of community in a way distorted by the encroachment of an individualistic perspective? For one, as academics we are locked into a convention of academic practice where ideas are believed to belong to individuals who need to be cited and referenced. Indeed, not to do so is viewed as at best either academic sloppiness or at worst plagiarism. That is why throughout this book you will see this practice observed (our text would not be published otherwise). For an interesting cultural and political critique of plagiarism see Martin (1994). This can lead to history being structured around individual biographies (individual academics or small groups of academics) and about singular events (an individualised history). As Eskin (1999 cited in Sampson, 2000) put it, we write our own autobiographies as though they are about a person who is in full command of his or her own person, thereby deleting the cast of hundreds (perhaps thousands) who make our own life stories what they are. This is notable in how we recognise scholarship with individual degrees predicated on the concept of the autonomous worker. Recent doctoral candidates of Maori origin in Aotearoa/New Zealand have articulated the need to author their work in a culturally appropriate way, invoking a historical family tree indicating where one comes from and multiple authors. Universities are struggling with this notion as individual ownership of intellectual property is a fundamental plank of scholarship.

Think!

Only five names appear in the authorship of our book. Can you think of any feasible way in which we could have given recognition to the wider network of those who have contributed to its genesis and production?

Here is a collection of some resources with a short description to assist in your reading of Part 1 (Chapters 1, 2, 3, 4 and 5).

Films

- Works by documentary maker Adam Curtis: http://watchdocumentaries.com/tag/adam-curtis/
- *Peterloo* (2018). Directed by Mike Leigh: a film about everyday people caught up in the 1819 Peterloo Massacre, Manchester. Good for some of the speeches on why political representation matters and for thinking about the similarities with contemporary pro-democracy protests. www. peterloofilm.co.uk/
- *Embrace of the Serpent* (2016). Directed by Ciro Guerra. This is a highly acclaimed film that tells the story of the invasion of a sacred site in the Amazon jungle from an indigenous perspective. Prepare to be mesmerised.
- *Raining Stones* (1993). Directed by Ken Loach. This is a film set on the outskirts of Manchester (in an area where we have worked with residents) during the 1990s. It tells the story of a family's experience of poverty. Dealing with life on the margins, it shows how unemployment and money impact upon the whole family.

Think!

Watch these two films together:

- *Crude* (2009). Directed by Joe Berlinger, this is a documentary on the class action suit against Chevron/Texaco by indigenous people in the Amazon region of Ecuador. The film is available at a number of sources on the internet – try searching for 'Crude', and 'film' or 'movie'.
- *Erin Brockovich* (2000). Directed by Steven Soderbergh, this film is based on the real-life story of a woman's legal battle against a California power company accused of polluting a city's water supply.
- *The Boy in the Striped Pyjamas* (2008). Directed by Mark Herman. This film focuses on issues around the treatment of Jewish people in Nazi Germany by telling the story of a friendship between a Jewish boy in a concentration camp and a German boy who is the son of the camp's commandant.
- *The Children of Gaza* (UK Channel 4 documentary) by documentary filmmaker Jezza Neumann. This documentary looks at the lives of children in Gaza who live under the occupation of the Israeli government.
- *The BlacKkKlansman* (2018). Directed by Spike Lee, this is both funny and a thought-provoking and provocative examination of racism in the USA. It is based on a true story of a black police officer in the 1970s who infiltrated the Ku Klux Klan. The film concludes with footage from the 2017 'Unite the Right' rally in Charlottesville which powerfully connects the racism of the past to the racism of the present.
- *Wall Street* (1987). Directed by Oliver Stone. A young and impatient stockbroker is willing to do anything to get to the top, including trading on illegal inside information taken through a ruthless and greedy corporate raider who takes the youth under his wing. The 'Greed is Good' speech in the movie came to symbolise the excesses of neoliberal economic politics.
- *The Big Short* (2015). Directed by Adam McKay. The story of the events behind the Global Financial Crisis. It tells the story of four financial outsiders who saw the corruption of the financial dealings of banks in the USA and how they saw it as an opportunity to make some money out of the impending global collapse. The story is both funny and shocking.
- *Jellyfish* (2018). Directed by James Gardener. With a life under duress as a teenager responsible for siblings and a mother with mental health difficulties, stand up comedy is the road to survival.

Theatre

- *Les Miserables*. If you can, go and see the musical theatre production of *Les Miserables* (or get hold of a DVD – or even read the book!). What does this tell us about power and powerlessness, the ways in which marginalisation and misery can be turned into commodities for commercial organisations to gain profits?

Books

- Davies, N. (1998). *Dark Heart: The Shocking Truth about Modern Britain*. London: Vintage. Nick Davies' *Dark Heart* is a wonderful book that shows how appalling life for the poor in the UK is.
- Fanon, F. (1967). *Black Skins, White Masks*. New York: Grove. Classic text on the damage of coloniality.
- Hanley, L. (2017). *Estates: An Intimate History*. London: Granta Books. This is an account of what it is like growing up and living on a social housing estate near Birmingham, UK. Read it and you can really feel what it must have been like. How might you design an area of social housing?
- Klein, N. (2015). *This Changes Everything*. London: Penguin Books/Simon Schuster. Klein argues that the climate catastrophe facing us cannot be dealt with by the neoliberal, high consumption patterns of living in the rich world. Essential reading about climate change.

There is a documentary directed by Avi Lewis of the issues raised in the book at https://this changeseverything.org/the-documentary/

- Mckenzie, L. (2015). *Getting By: Estates, Class and Culture in Austerity Britain*. Bristol: Policy Press. A good ethnographic account of how women and men live poverty differently in austerity Britain.
- Wainwright, H. (2009). *Reclaim the State: Experiments in Popular Democracy*. London: Seagull Books. This book gives example of popular participation that has contributed to transformational change in different ways in different parts of the world. Well worth a look!

Other relevant resources

- *Wars With and Without Bullets*: a *Special Issue* of *The Journal of Critical Psychology, Counselling and Psychotherapy* (March 2019). *The Journal of Critical Psychology, Counselling and Psycho-therapy* 19(1), 1–85. All the contributions are written from an anti-capitalist standpoint and contributions include those from community, disability and human rights activists.
- See what you can find out about the philanthropic work of Bill and Melinda Gates' use of profits from the Microsoft industry. What does this tell you about participation, people's voice and autonomy? The Bill and Melinda Gates Foundation is at www.gatesfoundation.org
- How do you think the approaches promoted by the World Bank contribute to transformational change (or not)? Look at the website of the World Bank Academy which houses online courses at https://olc.worldbank.org/wbg-academy. You might also like to look at some of their documents, such as the *World Bank Participation Sourcebook*, http://documents.worldbank.org/curated/en/289471468741587739/The-World-Bank-participation-sourcebook. As you look at these resources ask yourself *"what is the wider agenda here?"*
- If you want to check information about a think tank or similar organisation try Source Watch at www.sourcewatch.org/. Look at their critical reviews of the Bill and Melinda Gates Foundation and the World Bank Institute. What does this add? You might also find the Corporate Watch site interesting: https://corporatewatch.org/
- Look at the Climate Psychology Alliance (CPA). Central to the vision behind CPA is that they are seeking to place human science alongside natural science in the cause of ecologically informed living, through understanding and facing difficult truths. Members set out to understand the unconscious feelings and attitudes preventing human action on climate change. Try exploring the site and discuss the extent to which the approach taken by the Climate Psychology Alliance is, or is not, community psychological. What makes it so? www.climatepsychologyalliance.org
- See what you can find out about the Zapatista revolution by looking at some of the websites listed below. Ask yourself *"why is the Zapatista revolution of relevance to critical community psychology?"* See http://la.utexas.edu/users/hcleaver/Chiapas95/zapsincyberwebsites.html

Relevant networks/online groups

- http://communitypsychologyuk.ning.com/
- www.bps.org.uk/member-microsites/community-psychology-section
- www.compsy.org.uk/
- www.jiscmail.ac.uk/cgi-bin/webadmin?A0=COMMUNITYPSYCHUK
- http://libpsy.org
- www.ecpa-online.com
- http://list.waikato.ac.nz/mailman/listinfo/compsychwaikato
- www.scra27.org
- https://psysr.net/

Part 2
Act!

Contents

In Part 1, *Think!* we examined the conceptual basis of critical community psychology. In this section of the book, *Act!* we discuss critical community psychological praxis in relation to the different parts of an action research process. In particular, we present ways of understanding and defining a community psychological issue or problem, planning a piece of critical community psychological work, and then implementing six key strategies for change: furtherance of critical consciousness; creation of new social settings; development of alliances; accompaniment and advocacy; archive research; and policy analysis and development.

Chapter 6

Framing the issue

Summary

In this chapter we will discuss the concepts of social issues and social needs, and explore how needs assessments can form part of critical community psychological work. In doing this we will argue that our critical community psychologists' positions, in relation to, and in partnership with, those with whom we are working are central to understanding issues. We will discuss some of the tensions of getting to know and making contact with complex communities. We will offer ways of developing understanding of multi-faceted community issues and problem situations – as human systems, each with multiple stakeholder interests.

Reflect!

Do you think that action research should always start with the identification of an issue, concern or problem? If so, who should identify the issue? If not, how else might you get started with your action research project? What is the difference between framing and identifying an issue?

It should be clear from Part 1 that we adopt a social justice approach to critical community psychology, embracing decolonising perspectives and underpinned by specific values and principles. This helps us to work *with* people to prioritise issues on which to work and to clarify the nature of any particular concern or issue being addressed. We have called this 'framing the issue' rather than defining a problem. Defining a problem assumes that the situation under consideration is objectively knowable and in some way fixed, whereas framing the issue or situation acknowledges that purposeful choices can be made (Collins & Ison, 2009). Furthermore, the term 'problem' often implies some kind of deficiency, requiring a technical solution to be fixed – or an ameliorative intervention (Nelson &

Prilleltensky, 2005, p. 144). The problems we refer to here are the issue or matter under consideration, viewed from a particular standpoint, at a particular moment in time, and in terms of the principles and values underpinning critical community psychology, including sources of power and oppression. We are not talking of problems as entities for which there is a simple solution, but rather as more complex, situated dilemmas, for which there might not, in fact, be any straightforward solution. Broadly, a social issue is an undesirable and unwanted disturbing situation, which adversely affects particular groups, compounding their marginalisation and oppression, social and collective well-being, or human flourishing within planetary boundaries.

It is useful to consider the origins of the issues that surface. For example, from a university base, collaborative research will nearly always start with the identification of a research issue. Sometimes this will originate in the university (and may or may not be linked to research priorities), and external collaborations are then sought: sometimes the issue will originate from the community and research partners are then sought (Kagan & Diamond, 2019). From a service base, issues may be defined by service providers (and may or may not be linked to service priorities) and collaboration with service users sought; or by service users and collaborations with providers or other groups of service users sought. Inside-out drivers may include priorities set by institutions themselves or by funders, or by individual (groups of) researchers. If the issue is identified from outside in, drivers may be due to individual assertive citizens, as part of a group or not, groups or community organisations, or, again, by funding opportunities. The issues may have arisen as a result of some community engagement process, or be a reflection of a small niche interest.

When considering a problem situation, a key question to ask, then, is "from whose perspective is this what kind of an issue?" Fore-fronting this allows us to approach the task of problem definition in terms of at least four features:

1 Substantively or materially ("What is actually going on here in this patch of reality? Who suffers, who gets what they need, and why?"). To address this, we assess social issues and needs analysis.
2 Politically ("From whose perspective, in whose interests, and how is power and advantage structured?"). A core aspect of a political stance is that of positionality, which enables us to explore how perspective shapes the problem definition.
3 Normatively ("What is the consensus about the problem, and how can this be enlarged?" – versus "Can it be enlarged/Is there any basis for consensus? Which is the political question?"). Here, stakeholder analysis, and seeing communities as systems, allows a rich understanding of the problem at hand.
4 Methodologically and/or epistemologically ("Which techniques are helpful in exploring a problem and in coming to a defensible definition of it? What are their strengths and limitations? What kind of knowledge do they produce and how can it be validated?" – back to the normative, political and substantive perspectives).

To consider these issues, getting to know the community and the tools to accompany this are explored.

Social issues

The social justice approach adopted in critical community psychology work should fit the type of social issue identified. Ife (1995), drawing on the work of Taylor-Gooby and Dale (1981) identifies a four fold classification of 'accounts of social issues', each with a different perspective on the problem, sources of 'blame', and potential solutions. Table 6.1 summarises these individual, institutional reformist, structural and post-structural perspectives.

Table 6.1 Classification of accounts of social issues

Perspective accounting for social issue	Source of blame	Perception of problem	Potential solution or level of intervention for change
Individual perspective	Victim	Individual frailty, pathology, psychological, moral or character defect	Individual therapy, medical treatment, punishment and control, behaviour modification, moral exhortation
Institutional Reformist perspective	Rescuer (usually in the form of human services)	Institutions established to deal with the problem: courts, schools, human service organisations	Reorganise institutions, more resources, service development and expansion, professional training
Structural	The system	Structural disadvantage or oppression: class, race, gender, age, disability, income distribution, economic opportunity, power	Structural change, changing basis of oppression, social transformation liberation and social movements, revolution
Post-structural	Discourse	Modernity, language, formation and accumulation of knowledge, shared understandings, processes of naturalisation through discourse	Analysis and understanding of discourse, access to understandings, challenge the 'rules' and what is taken for granted

Source: adapted from Ife, 1995.

Whilst each of these accounts may be based on some valid insights, a transformative, critical community psychology would focus on the third perspective, offering a structural account and change solution. However, in our sophisticated and tight welfare system, it is often necessary to work with institutional reformist change as well, or sometimes as the means towards an aim of structural change. One of the challenges facing community psychology is how to turn what could remain a theoretical analysis of oppression into the identification of needs, problems and priorities that lead to practical action for change.

> ## Think!
>
> Do you understand the distinction between the perspectives summarised in Table 6.1? Imagine you are required to talk on a daytime TV show about the differences in approach. Using climate change as the social issue, explain how the four perspectives position climate change. Once you have done this, map the different strategies of intervention or change linked to each perspective. Which of these interventions is community psychological?

Need

Needs assessment forms the bedrock of much professional practice leading to the rationing of welfare resources. This notion of need implicitly assumes need is a fixed, objective quantity, requiring professional expertise to identify and measure it, both strengthening professional power and at the same time disabling those whose needs are being assessed, by excluding them from the process (Illich, Zola, McKnight, Caplan & Shaiken, 1977). Needs assessments are at the core of the critique of welfare professionals, which argues that professional practice is ultimately disabling, through the exclusion of those whose needs are being assessed (Illich et al., 1977) whilst at the same time increasing the power of the professionals.

The demand of the International Disability Rights Movement (Bell, 2014), taken up in relation to other impairments such as dementia and HIV, for example, is 'Nothing about us without us'. It has underpinned a move for a more collaborative process of needs identification, in this case closely linked to rights. From this standpoint, needs are arrived at more participatively and explicitly using a rights agenda.

> ## Think!
>
> In September 2015, 170 world leaders adopted the 2030 Agenda for Sustainable Development. This Agenda covers a broad set of 17 Sustainable Development Goals (SDGs) and 167 targets which are to serve as the overall framework to guide global and national development action for the next 15 years. To read about this see www.un.org/sustainabledevelopment/development-agenda. According to the UN,
>
> > The SDGs are the result of the most consultative and inclusive process in the history of the United Nations. Grounded in international human rights law, the agenda offers critical opportunities to further advance the realization of human rights for all people everywhere, without discrimination.
>
> 90 per cent of the SDGs are underpinned by the human rights enshrined in the Universal Declaration of Human Rights.
>
> Are you aware of the SDGs or the human rights underpinning them? What do you think of this framework? How do they reflect your everyday life or aspirations for the future? How well do you think your country does on this progress to meeting any of the SDGs? Or human rights?

Nevertheless, this rights approach can be undermined by overarching ideological ambitions and social policies, such as the austerity policies in the UK that have propelled many disabled people into hardship and poverty and distress (Committee on the Rights of Persons with Disabilities, 2017; Psychologists Against Austerity, 2015).

Bradshaw (2015/1972), outlined a much adopted typology of overlapping social need, which is summarised in Table 6.2.

This categorisation still elevates the role of the expert, either in identifying the need through measurement of some kind or in interpreting the expression of need. People themselves may or may not agree they have a need. Comparative needs that are assessed by people themselves might lead to feelings of relative deprivation (Walker & Smith, 2002), contributing to a sense of dissatisfaction that others are better off in some way.

With regard to the communication of need, people will be positioned differently: they will have different interests, knowledge and information on which to base their assessments, and the best approach is to work towards consensus. This can be achieved if a genuine dialogue is established between: (i) those with popular knowledge (the general population and those who will be affected by any proposed service or facility and who infer need on the basis of their experiences); and (ii) those with professional, expert or scientific knowledge (professionals with access to resources, such as social workers,

Table 6.2 Taxonomy of social need

Category of need	Description	Source of needs identification
Normative need	Need as identified according to a norm, defined by an accepted authority (expert) in accordance with an accepted standard (e.g. welfare benefit levels)	Expert, not necessarily with lay agreement
Comparative need	Needs inferred from comparison with others who are not in need. Comparative needs may emerge via comparison with regional or national norms, for example the comparison of different areas in terms of their relative deprivation and need for services	Expert, not necessarily with lay agreement
Felt need	Need expressed by the people concerned, from their own perspectives, generally accessed through surveys. Includes wants, wishes and desires	Lay but with expert interpretation
Expressed need	Need expressed by people who say they have this need. They may be seeking some kind of service in which case waiting lists might give an indication of unmet need	Lay but with expert interpretation

Source: after Bradshaw, 2015/1972.

community workers, clergy, local politicians; and planners or researchers who infer need on the basis of available data).

A two-pronged approach is required to reach a consensus about need. First, the general public can be helped to gain expertise and resources to make more informed judgements; and second, the professionals can be helped to become more sensitive to the experiences and lived realities of the people concerned.

Example: Space, place and older people's needs

We are part of a local action group working to ensure the community (people, services, amenities, geography, facilities) are such that people with dementia find it a good place to live. Some members of the group walked around the district with people living with dementia and their carers, listening to their experiences and ideas for change; others talked to the local traders about dementia. Following this, we ran several workshops in the locality, bringing together people living with dementia, their carer and service workers, as well as local citizens. With the use of maps and pictures to aid the discussion, we set out to imagine a better place for people living with dementia and their carers and explored how the different dimensions of the community might change. The outcomes of the workshops are being made into an exhibition to be placed in different venues in the area so as to widen the awareness of the needs of people living with dementia and their carers – and how the community might respond. The whole process is designed to enable the different stakeholders in both place and quality of life for people living with dementia and their carers to share perceptions and move towards a common understanding. Some similar processes were used in another, international project we are involved with, concerning older adults' sense of place (Fisher, Lawthom, Hartley, Koivunen & Yeowell, 2018).

Thus, the identification of need is a negotiated process and arrived at through genuine dialogue between the different definers of need. Burton and Kagan (1995, p. 6) summarise this process of shared learning as one in which all parties "start out from a position of mutual relative ignorance and over time become more knowledgeable". The negotiation and re-negotiation of need can take place over time and does not have to be seen as a once and for all assessment. Figure 6.1 summarises the process of negotiated awareness of need. Through negotiation, all parties begin to look differently at the issue, and their shared understanding of the matter in hand increases.

This negotiated understanding of need is at the core of participative approaches to needs assessments and to people's involvement in decision making about matters that affect them. Various methods of participative needs assessments have been used in the health, community and social development fields. Most draw on processes of participative rural appraisal (PRA) and participative learning and action (PLA). Participative needs assessments are subject to the same criticisms of co-optation and tokenism as other forms of participation (see for example, Cooke & Kothari, 2001). However, there are recent examples of some of the more innovative qualitative methods being used, particularly to engage more difficult to reach groups, such as older people (see, for example, Lawthom et al., 2018). The alternative of non-participative needs assessment is not, however, acceptable. We examined some ways of thinking about participation in Chapter 5.

There is a danger, in talking about the negotiated assessment of need, that need is understood in relativist terms, belying the existence of universal human needs. Doyal and Gough (1991) present a

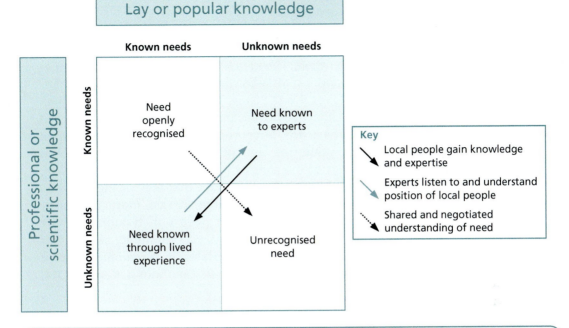

Figure 6.1 CAROMA window.

Source: adapted from Burton & Kagan, 1995 after Luft, 1969.

Note: Caroma – Just as the Johari window was named after Jo Luft and Harry Ingram (Luft, 1969), the Caroma window is named after Carolyn Kagan and Mark Burton (Burton & Kagan, 1995).

persuasive argument for recognising the universal needs of health and autonomy of agency, and a right to their optimal satisfaction. Needs fulfilment is understood in structural terms. Dussel (2013), placing the victims of the dominant social and economic system at the heart of his thinking, makes a similar point. The social and biological maintenance and reproduction of human life is fundamental, and this can only be satisfied if there are adequate arrangements for dialogue, for making things happen, and for dealing with the inevitable unintended consequences of action. It is impossible to talk of human need at this point in time without reference to the planetary boundaries in which we live. Indeed, Gough (2017) has developed his earlier theory of human need to show how human well-being and need fulfilment, capitalism and climate change are all interrelated. He also advocates a participative and deliberative approach to agreeing on needs and needs satisfiers, based on the collaboration between lay and expert actors. Büchs and Koch (2017) also draw on the theory of human need in their analysis of the impact of post economic growth on human well-being, where an alternative to economic growth is necessary in order to live within planetary boundaries (see also Natale, di Martino, Procentese and Arcidiacono (2016), who link some of these ideas to community psychology). These writers (from the perspectives of philosophy, social policy or community psychology) remind us that any negotiation of need should include discussion and exploration of structural disadvantage and social justice, as well as planetary boundaries and climate change, thus retaining a moral and political edge.

Needs assessments may be the start of a development of change process or may emerge from existing processes and herald a change in direction. Below we outline different ways of working with others to assess need.

Example 1: Community organising

Community organising is a bottom up process of needs assessment. Community organisers work in a small locality and approach people individually, or in families, to listen, and connect people with others. The idea is that once people get together to identify their shared concerns and interests (maybe needs, but not always), they will be motivated to take action to resolve the issue. The community organiser then works to help people build their collective power and their capacity for action and to become and stay motivated. There are, of course, different models of community organising, some relatively value-free and others underpinned by explicit values and complex understandings of the context in which issues arise. In the UK, community organising explicitly seeks solutions to issues that are for the common good of the whole community. In the name of being bottom up, most community organising starts with individuals and households. It need not, though, and the starting point could easily be a collective starting point, via community associations and interest groups. Community organising is best located in communities and is hard to initiate from university or service bases (Fisher, Lawthom & Kagan, 2014, 2016).

Example 2: Capacity building for evaluation

A multi-disciplinary team (including team members from management, operational research, industrial chemistry, health and safety at work, psychology, nursing, and community work) was commissioned to develop capacity for evaluation amongst community and voluntary sector groups (Boyd et al., 2001). We had expertise in different forms of evaluation in the community and voluntary sectors, but nevertheless were reluctant to go ahead and design a process without wide consultation and involvement of the sector in defining their capacity building needs. We wanted to negotiate the needs for capacity building in order to design different events to reach a wider range of third sector organisations. We also wanted to work in such a way that the participating organisations got something useful from the process which might otherwise have been an extractive one whereby we gained information from them. Altogether, we consulted with 50 voluntary organisations, community groups and statutory services about their views on evaluation and what they wanted from a series of capacity building events. Each workshop lasted about three hours and involved five to ten people. The consultation process was a participative one. Looking back over the experience of facilitating these workshops, and taking into account the evaluation feedback, we agreed that this proved to be a useful approach to managing the consultation process and identifying capacity building needs for evaluation.

This needs assessment took the form of structured, facilitated, participative workshops.

Example 3: Asset based needs assessment

Asset based approaches have been gathering momentum in recent years. These start with local assessment of needs, valuing the positive capacity, skills, knowledge and connections in a community. The kinds of assets that might be explored include:

- the practical skills, capacity and knowledge of local residents;
- the passions and interests of local people that give the energy to change;
- the networks and connections in a community;
- the effectiveness of local community and voluntary associations;
- the resources of public, private and third sector organisations that are available to support a community; and
- the physical and economic resources of a place that enhance well-being.

Clearly in disadvantaged areas these kinds of assets might be spread quite thinly and even before any needs assessment there may need to be a process of capacity building. Nevertheless, a needs assessment based on assets is quite different from one based on deficits or problems (Foot & Hopkins, 2010; O'Leary, Burkett & Braithwaite, 2011). Nel (2018) compared an asset based with a traditional problem based needs assessment and concluded that whilst both led to positive outcomes, there were greater community gains for the former and the initiatives that followed were more sustainable.

Example 4: Appreciative inquiry

Appreciative inquiry is another opportunity-centric (Boyd & Bright, 2007) process, initially applied to organisational development, introducing an appreciative approach in contrast to a deficit one. The process involves identifying, elevating and expanding community strengths through a structured process of four steps – discover, dream, design and destiny. The method goes beyond discussions, interviews, focus groups and inventories of assets, to include a whole systems 'summit', wherein participatory creative activities break down boundaries between different stakeholders with varying degrees of power and authority. Fynn (2013) illustrates in detail the process of an appreciative inquiry as part of an evaluation of an NGO in Soweto, South Africa. Whilst this is framed as an evaluation, it doubles as a needs assessment insofar as it exposes systemic, organisational blocks that need to be overcome for the group to continue (in true action research style). Appreciative inquiry can be particularly useful where there is conflict at the start of a piece of work, and Fynn points out some of the political and structural difficulties that can arise when there are low levels of trust and cohesion among stakeholders (in his case, funders and the NGO). We used the process with rather more success in initial stages of our research with community, when there were also difficulties to overcome in terms of trust and common identification of needs underpinning the research (Sixsmith & Kagan, 2005).

> ## Act!
>
> Locate a report on a social issue (using a local newspaper or the web) – this may be from a local or national government body. Can you see (a) if needs are explicitly referred to? And (b) how these were assessed? What are the implications of using different needs assessment processes?

Positionality and the definition of issues or problems

We can see from the four examples listed above that the position of the community psychologist (and 'expert') varies and any needs assessment must take account of their positionality. Positionality is concerned with how any particular person is situated in relation to an issue, and it is sometimes referred to as their standpoint. Our positionality is important in all aspects of reflexive work and needs to be under scrutiny on a continuous basis. It not only defines what we know in relation to others, but also our ideological position and insider–outsider status. Whilst the insider–outsider dichotomy has given way to a more complex understanding of positionality in terms of multiple positions held at the same time (for example, Merriam et al., 2001; Suffla, Seedat & Bawa, 2015; Sultana, 2007), it remains a powerful way to understand different routes to identifying issues on which to work. From the needs assessment examples above, we can see different routes depending on our positionality.

As insiders to an issue, we may have a good idea about what is needed, but may or may not be able to act, due to constraints of time, priorities of employers and so on. As outsiders to issues, we may become involved as a result of commissioning or by invitation. Once work is commissioned we will often have to negotiate access to relevant communities or groups, and the important thing is to take time to develop meaningful, trusting relationships, irrespective of how these are initiated. When we are invited in, we will often have to clarify and even re-negotiate the work to be undertaken, which might, in the end, differ considerably from the original request. We will continue this discussion of initial involvement later in the chapter.

Figure 6.2 maps different kinds of work according to the insider vs. outsider position of the critical community psychologist and the formal or informal status of the work.

Over time, and as the work evolves, different facets of our positionality may change and assume different degrees of importance.

Whose need?

Implicit in the above discussion of needs assessment and problem identification is the importance of clarifying whose issue it is that we are identifying.

> ## Think!
>
> Choose any three methods of assessing community needs from the Community Toolbox at https://ctb.ku.edu/en/table-of-contents/assessment/assessing-community-needs-and-resources. review these methods and consider (a) whether they assess collective need; (b) whether they are participative, or could be participative; and (c) what skills you have to use any of these methods.

In practice, needs and issue identification might be at individual, interpersonal, group, organisational or community levels. It is the last three that we, as critical community psychologists, are most

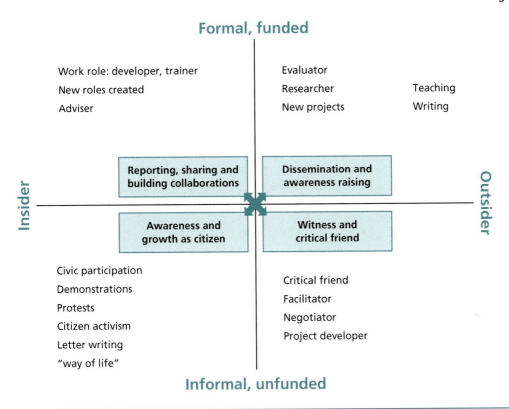

Figure 6.2 Key dimensions of positionality for community psychologists in terms of roles in relation to issues and the processes involved.

concerned with, although we recognise that groups, organisations and communities are all made up of individual people interacting in different ways, so individual and group levels of analysis cannot be ignored. Having said this, groups, organisations and communities are not mutually independent from each other, and in one way or another we are usually working with groups of people who at the same time belong to families, organisations and communities.

Reflect!

Consider what kinds of groups, communities and organisations you belong to. Consider whether and how these different groups or organisations meet your differing needs.

Getting to know the community

Getting to know the community depends in large part on what kind of community we mean and, as we have seen, the extent to which we already have contact and our insider–outsider status or positionality. Even so, there are some frameworks that can be used and adapted to whatever kind of community is under consideration, and whatever our relationships with it might be. Hawtin, Hughes and Percy-Smith (1994) draw a distinction between needs assessments, community consultations, social audits and community profiling. The choice of which to use should, they suggest, be guided by answers to the questions: What is the purpose of the exercise? Who is initiating the project? To what extent is the community involved? What is the scope of the exercise?

Nearly all approaches to understanding the community involve the use of objective and subjective assessments of community involvement.

Door knocking and social media (ask and listen)

One of the most basic ways of getting to know a community is to ask local people about it. Those who live or work in an area know what is good about it and what is lacking. Table 6.4 (see later in chapter) includes a number of ways of asking people who live or work in an area about what it is like. Stalls in public places, questionnaires, focus groups, charts, games, community walks, the use of photo-voice and video diaries, online surveys are all ways of asking people. Going along to community groups, local consultations and so on all provide information about the area – not just what people think of it but what resources there are, that can be built on, as well as what appetite for change there is. The foundation of community organising (see above) is knocking on people's doors and talking to them about what is good and not so good about the area in which they live. In the internet age, valuable information about a community can be obtained from blogs, vlogs, podcasts, community forums, online news and social networking sites. It must be remembered, though, that social media are used by a subset of any community and whilst they may create a lot of 'noise', this does not always reflect the wider nature of the community. It would be folly, though, not to take account of social media traffic in any assessment of a community and its issues. Door knocking and social media give subjective views of the community, and it is important to get as broad a cross section of views as possible and to ask the questions "whose voice is not being heard?" and "how might it be made easier to be heard?"

Reflect!

Have you ever been asked about your local area? Why or why not? What dimensions do you think are important to describe it? What importance do you place on physical, social or emotional aspects of the area? How important are open and green spaces to you? Do you think your friends and families would describe the area in the same way? Why might they differ?

Community audit

Audits of communities typically involve some kind of measurement, that can be repeated over time to assess change on key dimensions. At first glance these do not appear to be congruent with critical community psychological practices. However, the social auditing process has shifted audit practice to include, for example, measurement of progress towards equal opportunities and environmental sustainability, and not just the financial bottom line (MacGillivary, Weston & Unsworth, 1998; Pearce, Raynard & Zadek, 1996). Community audits may or may not involve community members, but can be powerful ways of listening to community voices when they do (Hodgson & Turner, 2003; Murtagh, 1999).

Taylor and Burns (2000, pp. 2–5) have drawn on the social audit approach to examine local community participation. They argue that such an approach draws on many perspectives, not just one; reflects local circumstances – for example, political context, and organisational capacity; encourages enquiry and learning; can be peer driven rather than top down; and can be qualitative rather than just

Table 6.3 Audit of community participation: tools for measurement	
Audit stage and method	*Content and purpose*
1. Baseline Mapping	exercises to establish the context within which participation is being introduced.
2. Relevant Checklists	• activities or approaches that contribute to effective community involvement; • questions that need to be asked if community involvement is to be effective.
3. Measurement Scales	to help stakeholders think through the quality and extent of the participation activities that they are putting in place.

Source: Taylor & Burns, 2000.

quantitative. In their manual, explaining the audit process, Taylor and Burns suggest three main types of audit tool, as summarised in Table 6.3. Whilst these address community participation, they can be adapted to assess any dimension of community life.

Many community audits use survey methods on a regular basis to establish baseline records of activity and to assess change, particularly against targets set, and in relation to regular interventions. For example, in England, local authorities have an obligation to improve the quality of life of people living in their areas. Regular ward level surveys enable changes to be monitored and progress assessed (wards are areas with boundaries that are identified for administrative and electoral purposes).

Example: Leisure advocacy

When we sought to develop a project promoting the inclusion of adults with learning difficulties in local leisure activities, we began by undertaking a survey of the nature and extent of involvement in local leisure activities by adults living in the same district (a community audit). We wanted to know what local people did in their leisure time, how often and with whom. We were then able to design a project that reflected other people's patterns of leisure, and not have over-optimistic or pessimistic expectations for the disabled people involved (Kagan, 1986).

Whilst community audits might provide valuable information, and can involve local people in more than the collection of quantifiable data, a more comprehensive approach to understanding a community is offered by community profiling.

Community profiling

Community profiling can be undertaken as an exercise in gaining knowledge and understanding about an area. However, it is most usefully employed as a process through which community members can set an action plan for change.

Hawtin et al. (1994, p. 5) define a community profile as follows.

> A comprehensive description of the needs of a population that is defined, or defines itself, as a community, and the resources that exist within that community, carried out with the active involvement of the community itself, for the purpose of developing an action plan or other means of improving the quality of life in the community.

A community profile can both draw on existing information and collect new information, but it is important to be clear about what dimension of community life might be relevant to a specific profile. Hawtin et al. (1994, p. 70) suggest four types of information that might be needed: contextual and background information; detailed description of the community and its resources; details of the needs of the community; existing policies and alternative strategies for the community. Table 6.4 offers a summary of relevant dimensions, all or some of which might contribute to a profile.

Act!

Undertake a community profile of the area in which you live, or one in which you have lived. Walk around and look at the different kinds of spaces, resources, buildings, transport links. Using local reports explore how the community is framed and seen in terms of public statistics (in areas such as education, poverty etc.). How does this outside view compare with an insider's position? What have you learnt from this exercise?

It is important to include specific groups from the community who might use and/or understand space and places differently, such as older people, disabled people, carers, new mothers, teenagers – even dog walkers – and to continue to ask the question "whose voice is not being heard?"

Cheong (2006), drawing on the work of Habermas (1984) argues for the importance of understanding the communication action context. In any neighbourhood or locality there are pre-existing conditions which affect people's communication within and between individuals, households and groups. The communication action context may be relatively open (encouraging people to interact and participate in community building) or closed (discouraging such encounters and civic engagement opportunities). Any neighbourhood is likely to have elements of both openness and closedness (see discussion of space and place, and the penetrability of situations, in Chapter 8). Contextual conditions constrain or enable interactive discourse, trust and civic norms (ingredients of social capital – see Chapter 5).

In getting to understand a community, Cheong suggests gaining information about physical, psychological, socio-cultural, economic and technological aspects of the community (see Table 6.5).

Any neighbourhood can be described in these terms. Indeed, any meaningful community (such as workplaces) can be described in these terms.

Think!

Read Cheong's (2006) article and see if you can describe how this interpretation would differ from the community profile undertaken above? What advantages might there be in adopting this framework for understanding a community?

In Chapters 4 and 5, we examined different ways of thinking about community, some of the problems in attempting to define community, the differences that can exist between insider and outsider constructions of community and both the benign and malign sides of community. It is important to bear these tensions

Table 6.4 Examples of relevant dimensions of community life for a community profile

Dimension	Existing sources of information	New sources of information	Purpose of collecting this information
Characteristics of the community or population	Public statistics e.g. Census information Indices of Deprivation Labour market statistics	Observation Community walk	Understand diversity within or boundaries around the groups of interest
Local views and priorities	Local authority surveys – e.g. quality of life, Best Value Local newspapers	Resident led survey Focus groups Street interviews Community consultation events Community walk Diaries Video diaries Participant observation Resident led films or documentaries	Different perspectives on priorities for change
Housing	Census information Local authority housing department Crime statistics	Observation Community walk Estate agent business figures	Turnover and mobility within a locality Understanding of social networks and of divisions of wealth
Education	Inspection reports Local authority reports National information about attainment levels, exclusion rates, local access to higher education rates	Young people's fora Young people's parliaments Community walks around schools Creative writing workshops	Understanding of class divisions and future aspirations
Environment	Local environmental health department Local newspapers Wildlife and biodiversity surveys	Citizen land use surveys Focus groups	Challenges facing sustainability issues

continued

Table 6.4 Continued			

Dimension	Existing sources of information	New sources of information	Purpose of collecting this information
Facilities and services	Local service directories Best Value surveys Waiting lists	Observation – attendance at meetings Community walk Focus groups and interviews Video diaries	Opportunities and supports for different groups of people Quality of infrastructure and sources of community pride
Crime and safety	National and local crime surveys and statistics Local community safety surveys Content analysis of local newspapers	Observation Street interviews Focus groups Resident led video diaries	Health and well-being of local people
Physical environment	Maps Weather reports and patterns	Observation of physical infrastructure, graffiti, public notices Community walk – land use and sites of neglect and dereliction, shops and local facilities	Ease of access for different groups such as elderly, disabled people
Transport and communications	Passenger transport authority reports Local newspapers Maps of public transport routes Traffic surveys Local newspapers, radio, television and websites	Observation – pedestrian and cycle routes, patterns of road and other usage (e.g. areas for play, young peoples' gatherings, rubbish dumping etc.) Interviews Focus groups Meetings with local transport users' organisations	Patterns of movement and use of local facilities Close or dispersed networks
Health	Population mortality figures Public health information	Reports from lobby groups	Life expectancy Health aspects of quality of life and well-being

Table 6.5 Dimensions of the communication action context

Dimension	Information required
Physical	how area is constructed via street designs, places that bring people to meet and talk – parks, libraries, etc.
Psychological	extent to which people feel free to engage with each other (fear of safety issues, neighbourliness etc.)
Socio-cultural	degree of class, ethnic, cultural similarity; individualism or collectivism; discrimination etc.
Economic	time and resources available to engage in everyday interaction. Includes work opportunities, work-family support policies and services such as childcare, health care etc.
Technological	older and newer technologies such as internet facilities and transport, car ownership etc.

Source: after Cheong, 2006.

in mind when planning and making sense of community audits and profiles. Both community audits and community profiles can be undertaken participatively, with negotiation over methods of collecting information and involving local people in different ways to collect and make sense of the information, thereby effectively engaging in community development through auditing or profiling (Packham, 1998).

The final challenge to any form of community profiling is how best to record the information gathered. This is linked to the purpose of undertaking the work in the first place. If it is to gain understanding, it may be sufficient to summarise the main issues identified and the methods of gaining information as general context to the subsequent work carried out. It may be used for discussion about the priorities of any subsequent work and be linked to other techniques such as rich picturing and stakeholder analysis, which we discuss in more detail below.

Community profiling can become, itself, an intervention, as illustrated by the work of Francescato, Gellini, Mannarini and Taurino (2004) and Arcidiacono, Tuozzi and Procentese (2016), who have used community profiling as a means to community development. Their comprehensive framework consists of both qualitative and quantitative information gathered about seven key community characteristics – territorial, demographic, economic, service oriented, institutional, anthropological and psychological. By collecting information collaboratively and sharing analyses, people's awareness and understanding of their communities change. Hawtin et al. (1994, p. 35), too, claim that community profiling can be a means of empowering the community. It not only brings people together, and enables them to develop new skills, but also leads them to a greater understanding of the nature of their oppression and to be active in trying to create change.

Use of official information and statistics

Official sources (government and government agencies, including national, regional and municipal level government) can be valuable sources of information about the community for use in conjunction with the other methods described here. The use of official statistics, its possibilities and problems, is discussed more fully in Chapter 10. As with all sources of information, it is important to understand who is providing the information and the purpose for which the information is being presented, and hence the potential biases and gaps in it.

Observation

There is a lot to be said for noticing things around us and asking questions of what we take for granted. We often do not see until we look carefully. Initially it can be useful to have an open agenda as it is not always clear what is worth observing. After some time, though, observations can become more structured.

> ### Example: Community resources
>
> One of our mature students who had lived in a particular area all her life asserted that there were few local community projects in her area. We knew this was not the case and asked her to go and walk around her neighbourhood, looking carefully at what was familiar to her and asking herself what went on in each building and if she really knew what the different projects listed in the library and community centre did. She returned a week later, somewhat sheepishly, and said there was a whole layer of life in her area about which she had previously known nothing. Her eyes were now 'open' and she had a richer understanding of what was going on in her area, by whom and with whom.

This example blurs the distinction that is often made between direct and participant observation: the observer is part participant and part independent observer. This of course has implications for the ways in which we are positioned and the roles we adopt.

Reflect!

Building on the above example, consider how you might help yourself to see your local area differently, as if through different eyes. What different places would you go to, at what times? How would you dress and travel? How would you make it easy to get into conversations with people that you might otherwise not have? How would you do that without being over-intrusive or putting yourself at risk (for example if you chanced on illegal activities)?

Community walks

The community resources example above was also a community walk. The student walked around her community noticing what was there. Community walks can include local people with different kinds of local knowledge who are then able to tell the community psychologists about the area and what is important to them. If community walks are undertaken with people from different groups, we gain different perspectives on the nature of the locality. For example, a group of older residents may have a rather different perception of an area than do young people.

Community walks can be actual, that is literally walking around the community. They can also be virtual, for example discussion around a map of the area. This in turn can be an actual map or a cognitive map, where those we are working with draw their perceived community for us.

Example 1: Well-being in schools

In a study we undertook about children's well-being in school we asked groups of children to take us round the school to places that were important to them in different ways (Duckett, Sixsmith & Kagan, 2008). As we went round, they talked about the places, what went on and how this made them feel. Although we were able to walk around the school ourselves and observe, the guided walks added subjective and affective information to our understanding of each school community. This is an actual walk where the community is the school and the literal movement around the school undertaken with children allowed richer information.

Example 2: Slums of Kolkata

We undertook some work in the slums of Kolkata that aimed to improve the supports given to families with disabled children (Kagan & Scott-Roberts, 2002; Sen & Goldbart, 2005). Part of the initial stages of the work involved walking around different kinds of slum areas which enabled us to get a sense of the challenges facing people. We were shown quite different aspects of the communities when we were shown round by health workers, by political activists or by children. The positions people hold in communities will affect what is seen and, from this, what is shown to others.

Example 3: Psychogeography and new ways of seeing

Bridger, Emmanouil and Lawthom (2017) describe a project which used ideas and methods from psychogeography to walk with people around a neighbourhood, collecting artefacts and then discussing these via a public exhibition. Walking around a neighbourhood does not need to be arduous – it can be playful.

Example 4: The nature of a community through the eyes of people living with dementia and their carers

To understand the nature of a local community for people with dementia and their carers, we walked and talked around the area. We listened to what people had to say about spaces and places, about their ease of use or scariness, about their friendliness and their hostility, about their safety and their risk. The information we gathered from these walks became part of an action programme to make the area dementia- and age-friendly, involving traders, health and social care services, civil society, families and the general public. We subsequently held some events where a range of different people discussed the area and placed comments on maps, indicating where changes were needed.

Act!

Community walks can become interventions in themselves – interventions as people gain insight into their own surroundings, which may then lead to social action. Community walks can become processes of conscientisation (see Chapter 8). During the process of getting to understand the community we may find out who the best people to link with in a community might be or who might be important to get to know as a step in being accepted by the community. Making a start and gaining entry to a community, whether by invitation or not, is a key step in any community psychological process.

Making contact and gaining entry in the community

Some of the methods of getting to know the community also help gaining entry if we are outsiders to the area. Indeed, it can be useful to think about different routes into communities, as illustrated in Table 6.6.

It would be rare in critical community psychology praxis for entry to communities to be direct. All of the other routes to entry ensure the project is grounded in the needs of the community and not in the academic desires of the professional or academic researcher.

Reflect!

What routes to enter a community would you be most comfortable with? Why? Which would you find most difficult? Why? What skills do you think you would need for the different routes to community entry?

Table 6.6 Routes into communities

Route	Starting position	Issues to consider
Organic	Insider: already a member of the community	What networks are you a part of? What levels of trust are there? What is your visibility in the community?
Invited	Outsider: invited in	Who has issued the invitation? What is their agenda? Who is excluded?
Mediated	Outsider: via key community leaders as brokers or gatekeepers	What levels of credibility do gatekeepers have and what is their agenda? What levels of trust do gatekeepers enjoy? Is there any opposition to these gatekeepers and their agendas? Are any people silenced by these gatekeepers?
Direct	Outsider: parachuting into community with a clear agenda	What justification is there for your involvement? Could you work with community partners more?

Table 6.7 Stages of entry into a community

Stage	Impact
Stopping	Informal or formal means may be used to prevent access to community. Trust based on the development of authentic relationships begins at this stage, enabling following stages to be completed. If this stage is foreclosed too quickly, subsequent relationships may be damaged and progress will not be possible. It is often at this stage that we realise that those who we thought could enable good entry to the community do not, in fact, have these powers.
Waiting	Being present but keeping a low profile. Continuing to get to know people and to explain who we are. Community members assess whether we are to be trusted or not and whether or not we are worth spending time with.
Transition	Access to some enabled but not usually the most important community members is given but not to all. Participation in meaningful community activities begins.
Acceptance	Trust is established and feelings and reflections are shared openly with the community psychologist.

Source: after Kowalsky et al., 1996.

Wherever we are positioned, as insiders or outsiders, we will have to gain entry to all or some aspects of the community – not just physically but most importantly through developing relationships with community members. We need to do this as sensitively as possible and our entry cannot be rushed, as illustrated by Crespo, Pallí and Lalueza (2002) with reference to working with a Spanish Roma community. The slowness of this process can be a source of frustration and irritation if we are bound by deadlines (as nearly always students or those working on research projects are). Nevertheless, it is important to recognise that all aspects of our work as critical community psychologists stem in one way or another from how we enter and are received by communities.

Kowalsky, Verhoef, Thurston and Rutherford (1996), with reference to Canadian First Nation communities, draw attention to four stages of entry into a community: stopping stage, waiting stage, transition stage and acceptance stage. Community entry is time consuming, takes tact, diplomacy and patience. Sometimes we will be at different stages with different groups in the same community and it is well worth trying to understand this (see Table 6.7).

Over time, we have come up with a list of rules, or guidelines, for entering and working with communities. Our list, derived from experience, discussion with community partners and others' work, including Kowalsky et al. (1996) includes:

- Never say you want to help a community.
- Be honest about your motives.
- Be yourself and participate in the community.
- Walk, talk and listen.
- Contribute to the community in economic terms where possible.
- Consider what facilitates interaction with community members.
- Respect confidences and guard against taking sides.

Act!

- Be aware of general etiquette and expectations.
- Follow the lines of authority and thus show respect for it.
- Recognise and respect the spiritual and cultural components to people's lives.
- Recognise that community members are in charge and be patient.
- Take care not to develop preferential relationships.
- Allow for time.
- Be ready to teach and share ideas.
- Be ready to learn.
- Be sensitive.
- Enjoy and allow humour.
- Monitor your feelings.
- Reassess relationships on an ongoing basis.
- Be prepared for the uncertainty of the process and for the unexpected.
- Be prepared to change tack if necessary.
- Recognise that community members are in charge and be patient.
- Be honest about your motives.
- Monitor your feelings.
- Reassess relationships on an ongoing basis.
- Have a clear and shared exit and/or continuity plan.

Reflect!

Some of these lessons seem to be in conflict with 'professional' codes of conduct which assume expertise lies with the professional. Do these rules constitute a code for community psychologists? How might you resolve any tensions between these and your professional code of practice?

Latin American community psychologists describe the process of '*inserción*' within communities (not quite insertion, but nearly so – Montero, 2006). In one form, inserción means becoming one of the community, living there and experiencing life alongside other community members. For most of us, though it means being authentic and gaining the trust of those we are, or are about to be, working with. It is difficult to do this on one-off projects, bound by funding and time.

Inserción can take different forms.

Example 1: Accessible environments

A student was exploring the physical and social accessibility and inclusion of disabled people in a particular locality. He was unfamiliar with the area. He spent a lot of time in the local pubs and shops, buying drinks or goods, and talking to local people, not about disability, but just talking. Over time he was recognised as a regular visitor. Only then could he begin to talk to people about disability and only then had he built sufficient trust for people to tell him what they really thought.

Example 2: Social capital and health

A colleague was working in a small community in a Northern town, exploring the links between social capital and health. She had employed a researcher who was new to the area and did not live there. He spent a lot of time in the area, getting to know people and helping in the building and decoration of a community centre in his spare time alongside doing his research.

Example 3: Co-research on forced labour in the Chinese Community

The very work of co-producing a research proposal with members of a key NGO in the Chinese community served to develop relationships and build trust. Further-more, the initial stages of what we hoped would be participative research involved some workshops for potential co-researchers, on different ways of thinking about research. This served to further build trust amongst the community (and also con-vinced most people that they did not want to be co-researchers, so we had to change our research design!) (Lawthom et al., 2013).

These examples illustrate the importance of gaining trust and demonstrating commitment to listening to what local people want and to their accounts of their experiences. This is often a new way of working for them as they are more used to having researchers and professionals imposing their demands and expertise on them. The relationships built through these processes can become long term and this has advantages for understanding and working with people over long periods of time, not restricted to a particular project and its funding. If inserción is not achieved, projects can be jeopard-ised. The example below is one where we did not really achieve inserción, and, although the research progressed well, in the end we were limited in the change we could facilitate.

Example: Well-being in schools

We (PD and CK) and a colleague undertook a project about children's well-being in schools. Our community links were from a school support service and we relied on them for all the practical arrangements for the work. Once it came to discussion of our findings with the authorities we still had to go through the support service. As we had not developed these links ourselves, we were unable to make this stage happen and the change aspects of the work faltered (Duckett et al., 2008).

Gaining entry to a community is the first stage in community engagement. It will often include offer-ing something to the community. The examples above show that initial entry might include:

- learning: offering skills or training, leading to new ways of acting or confidence in further engagement;
- information: providing background knowledge or information about an issue affecting communities;
- emotion: having fun and enjoyment together.

Act!

There are a number of methods of community entry, which could include participative methods. They all are aimed at opening doors, developing trusting relationships and enabling further participation. Some of the methods are the same as general methods of engagement, and some are best suited to the early stages of gaining entry. Methods might include:

- public meetings, ensuring constructive, considerate and respectful participation;
- talking to knowledgeable people, who could be community leaders but could also be elders, youth, children, shopkeepers and so on;
- networking, building lists of contacts and their contacts (that is, snowballing), but taking care not to get sucked into exclusive networks;
- spending time in informal community places, watching and talking to people, including, for example, bars, cafes, places of worship, streets, festivals, protests;
- making contact with community organisations and civil society groups, attending their meetings and talking to their members;
- joining and contributing to local social media groups;
- organising community fun days or assisting in community activities like school fairs and other community events.

Act!

Write a list of the pros and cons of these different methods of gaining entry to a community, thinking about your own neighbourhood. How would these pros and cons differ if the issue was (a) what would make this neighbourhood better, or (b) how to increase active travel (walking and cycling) in this neighbourhood? Why?

Problem situations as human systems

Whilst communities, in the sense of localities, can be defined by bricks and mortar, as in many urban neighbourhoods, it is of more use to us to understand them as complex human systems, or soft systems. It is people that use buildings to live, work or spend time in. It is people who form groups, take action or inaction over injustice, deliver services and so on. Community groups and organisations are made up of people in complex and multiple forms of interaction with each other – the essence of an ecological systems perspective, as discussed in Chapter 3.

We have drawn on both soft systems and nested systems thinking to help in our understanding of problems within their wider contexts. Clarifying the 'problem situation', from the different perspectives of those involved, is a key component of soft systems methodology (Foster-Fishman, Nowell & Yang, 2007).

The starting point of any systems analysis is to identify the elements of the system and their interrelationships, with a view to understanding how these change over time, as the system adapts to changes in the environment.

The different elements of a **particular** system and the relationships between them can be represented visually as a 'rich picture'. To draw a rich picture, first start with a focal group, person or role, issue or activity and then add to the picture other relevant groups, services, roles, facilities and so on. Different kinds of symbols can be used for different parts of the system. For example, services could be shown as triangles, people or roles as circles, groups or organisations as squares and so on. Relationships between different parts of the system can be represented by different kinds of lines (for example straight lines for positive and jagged lines for conflictual relationships, dotted lines for weak and double lines for strong links and so on).

Act!

Draw a picture of all the elements of a system with which you are familiar. For example, if you are a student, what does the education system look like? What are the elements and how are they connected? Include as many parts of the system and their relationship with each other as possible. Do not worry if it all looks a bit messy – 'messy pictures' are another way of describing rich pictures. The realities of human systems are that they are usually messy and complex and seldom simple or organised. Drawing the picture enables you to capture some of the complexity that would be difficult to do if you just described the situation. Consider sharing your picture with someone else who knows the system too: do they see it differently? Can they add things you hadn't thought of? Using rich pictures collaboratively is a good way to build a shared understanding of a particular set of issues.

Different rich pictures can be drawn by different people involved in the problem at hand, or a composite picture could be compiled, drawing on the different perspectives involved.

We have used rich pictures to aid our understanding of complex links and interactions within a given community or to show the strengths and weakness within a system, which in turn feeds into decision making as to what action could be taken.

Example: Slums of Kolkata

The rich picture shown in Figure 6.3 was drawn up to aid understanding about the context in which families with disabled children living in slums of Kolkata (formerly known as Calcutta) lived (Kagan & Scott-Roberts, 2002). We worked with other members of the interdisciplinary project team, to draw this picture. Together we identified some of the community resources and the connections between them. It became clear where there were good, existing links; where there were weak connections at the moment but, had the links been strengthened, disabled children and their families might have been better included; and where there were potential connections but we did not know the nature of these connections.

As we collectively compiled the picture, we could begin to see where connections could be strengthened and community resources harnessed. One such example stemmed from our observation that children were playing a lot in groups, often carrying younger children and babies with them: it did not seem as if disabled children were part of these groups as families kept them inside a lot, but there would be potential to encourage greater inclusion through play. An important thing to note, here, is that in each of the slum areas in which we worked, different health and social agencies worked differently, and whilst this is a composite rich picture across all projects, we drew separate pictures for the different slums. These rich pictures enabled the different parties to highlight those resources that were and that could potentially be used to support families and aid their inclusion in everyday life. As we noted (Kagan & Scott-Roberts, 2002, p. 9),

'Any particular part of a social system can be, at the same time, both oppressive and supportive. For example, families, health, education and welfare agencies, hospitals, neighbourhood agencies and institutions, all have the potential to provide support to enable disabled children to maintain identity, and secure material resources. However, they also have the potential for oppression. Thus, for example, whilst the families in this project have the potential to facilitate the inclusion of their disabled children into community life, they may also serve to restrict them through over-protectiveness, lack of expectation and hope and so on.'

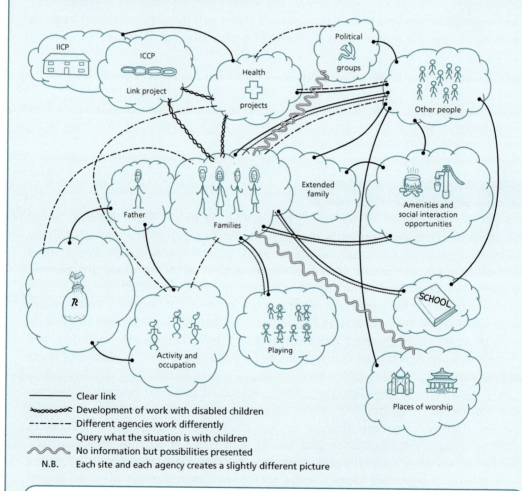

Clear link
Development of work with disabled children
Different agencies work differently
Query what the situation is with children
No information but possibilities presented
N.B. Each site and each agency creates a slightly different picture

Figure 6.3 Resources available for families with disabled children living in slums of Kolkata.

Source: Kagan & Scott-Roberts, 2002. Reproduced by permission of Manchester Metropolitan University.

Rich pictures can help disentangle complicated power relationships between parts of a system. The connections between different elements give an indication of where there are strengths and weaknesses in the system and where action might be best targeted. We will sometimes use rich picturing to represent best understanding of how things are at the moment, and contrast this with a rich picture of how things might be in the future. The change project then becomes one of how to move towards the envisaged future. It is through rich picturing that the problem situation can be encapsulated. Different people inside and outside the system might represent the problem situation differently, and we think it is important that as many people with different views about what is going on as possible together work on a rich picture. The very process of rich picturing aids understanding and insight into other positions. The decision about what to include in a rich picture will depend on the situation and the issue at stake. Indeed, systems can be described in different ways (Shiell & Riley, 2017). Hawe, Shiell and Riley (2009) suggest it is useful to consider linkages, relationships, feedback loops and interactions between elements of the system in relation to:

- activity settings (time–space boundaried patterns of behaviour focusing on roles, people, symbols, time, financial and physical resources);
- social networks (in the usual sense, not necessarily but possibly linked to social media) connecting both people and settings;
- time (past present and future – any intervention is a critical moment in the system's history).

The concept of ecological nested systems gives a different way of articulating the components of a problem situation. Bronfenbrenner (1979) developed the idea of an ecological systems perspective in relation to child development and it has been widely applied to other problem situations. The metaphor has been adopted within community psychology as a means of understanding the multiple influences of the environment, at different levels, on human experience and social change. Bronfenbrenner initially proposed four levels of the environment – or systems – affecting children directly and indirectly: the microsystem, mesosystem, exosystem and macrosystem. He suggested that the microsystem, or more proximal components of the overall system, had most impact, but that this was embedded in and powerfully shaped by conditions and events during the historical period of people's lives, but also in the circumstances leading to their social position, such as class. In recognition of this, in later work a fifth system, the chronosystem, was added.

> (The Chronosystem) encompasses change or consistency over time, not only in the characteristics of the person but also of the environment in which that person lives (e.g. changes over the life course in family structure, socioeconomic status, employment, place of residence, or the degree of hecticness and ability in everyday life).
>
> (Bronfenbrenner, 1994, p. 40)

People are not passive recipients of things that happen in their environments, but actively create these environments too – thus, there is a reciprocal relationship between people and their environments. Bronfenbrenner argued that the power of forces operating at any one system level depends on the nature of environmental structures existing at the same and higher levels and that culturally defined expectations and opportunities (found in the more distal parts of the system) had a defining impact on all levels. It is not always easy to see how the more distal level environments influence people: however, ideology, cultural norms and beliefs suffuse everything that we do, acting on human consciousness and becoming embodied in the reality of human relationships. Thus, for critical community psychology it is particularly important to retain an understanding of the influence of macro systems on every other system, as we are often contending with unspoken assumptions and beliefs about how the world is in supporting social change. Some people have argued (for example Seidman, 1988) that it is the meso-level interventions that stand to contribute to transformative change and that should be the focus of community psychological work. We tend to agree.

We will overview the different systems in relation to a particular issue we have encountered.

Example: Community leadership in a modern day ghetto

In this project, we worked with a newly formed group of activists who were trying to get more participation by people living locally in order to improve the area both physically and socially (Kagan et al., 2000).

Microsystem: the immediate and principal context of people's experiences. This level of system includes other people with whom the focal people have direct contact, in various groups or organisations. Elements of this system include the activist group; activists' families; existing residents' association; other residents in the area; local politicians; local youth and community development workers; schools; shops; church; people living in the local town; public sector workers such as refuse collectors, housing officials; community psychologists.

Mesosystem: the web of relationships between the different parts of the micro system and within which experience takes place. For example, the relationships between the schools and the youth workers; between existing residents' association and housing officials; between residents and shops; between police and residents, and so on.

Exosystem: environments which are external to the people at the centre of concern but in which other people within the microsystem take part. This includes links between different elements of the microsystems, only some of which people have direct contact with. For example, the local political groups to which elected members belong but that affect how they relate to residents; residents' families' workplaces which might contain practices and procedures that make it difficult to support aged or sick family members; the employing organisation of the community development worker or the refuse workers which determines how they work in this district; the housing agency in which the housing officials work and that influences the time they spend with residents; the local airport and its development plans which relate to longer term strategies for redeveloping the area. These more distant elements of the system still have an influence on what the activists do and can do, although they do not have direct contact with them.

Macrosystem: this system includes the wider policies which surround the activists' lives; broad ideological values; norms and cultural patterns. In our example, national changes in the organisation of housing, policies and practices related to community involvement, subcultural patterns of paid and non-paid work and regional development policies on economic development were all part of the wider environment exerting indirect influence on those attempting change.

Chronosystem: this system refers to the patterning of environmental events and transitions over time and includes socio-historical contexts. In our example, it was necessary to understand the history of the area, the conflicts as well as the previous experience of participation in local issues of both activists and other residents. We also had to take note of changes in the activists' lives throughout the project – such as moving into employment – and of key events that altered the course of the work, the key points of transition in the past that affected the course of history, as well as future projections as they related to all the other subsystems.

Think!

Look back at Chapter 3 and ask yourself whether such a nested systems approach can incorporate all the aspects of systems that were summarised there. If anything is missing, why is this?

Figure 6.4 illustrates the different layers of this nested system model.

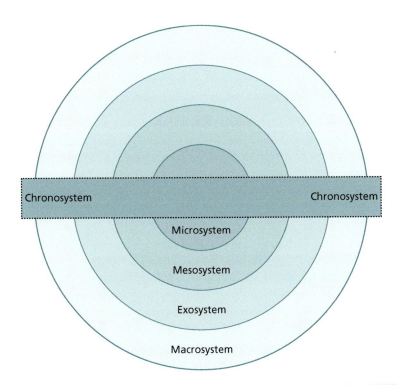

Figure 6.4 Nested systems: different levels of environment.

Example: The context of service responses to sexual assault

One of our students undertook a community psychological approach to explore the adequacy of the service response to people who had experienced serious sexual assault. He summarised the existing system in a nested systems diagram (Figure 6.5). This enabled him to see if the service response operated at all levels.

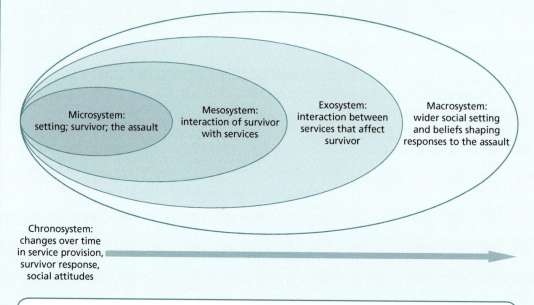

Figure 6.5 A nested systems picture of the response to serious sexual assault.
Source: with kind permission of Iain Mclean.

Example: Complexity of an evolving system of homelessness

One of our students undertook an immersive, participatory and ethnographic research into the changes that Manchester's homelessness sector was undergoing over a two-year period (2016–2018). During this time there was a concerted effort to embed co-production – the equal collaboration between policy makers and service users – in all aspects of service design, delivery and evaluation. Co-production is both elusive to conceptualise and difficult to implement. It relies on trust between volunteer citizen groups and the paid representatives to form deep working relationships and undertake the hard work of enhancing services. In order to re-imagine services, a series of action groups were formed around specific topics such as mental health, prevention and emergency shelter. These small groups brought together experts by experience with front line staff from across the sector to co-produce new ways of working that could be implemented across the sector.

This rich picture (Figure 6.6) shows the complexities that arise when a new sector-wide approach (like the Manchester Homelessness Partnership – MHP) is implemented alongside traditional inter-organisational relationships, and helped in the conceptualisation of the complex system.

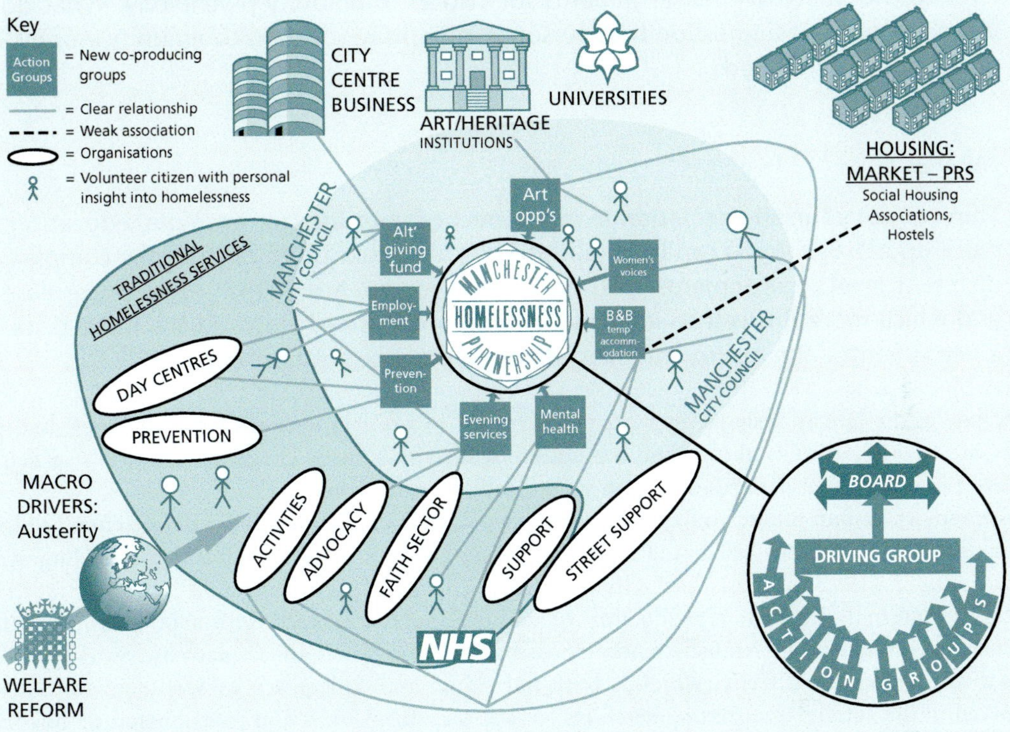

Figure 6.6 A rich picture of the evolving system around homelessness in Manchester.

Source: with kind permission of Nigel Allmark.

It is possible to combine both types of picture in the same project, giving different types of information and yielding different kinds of insights.

Foster-Fishmann, Nowell and Yang (2007) suggest that interrogating systems norms, resources, regulations and operations allows an exploration of how different parts interact with each other. The examples we have given are of projects within neighbourhoods. Just as important is working with organisations to strengthen them to pursue goals of social benefit. Francescato and Aber (2015) give an overview of how systems thinking can be applied to organisational empowerment. Drawing on work carried out initially in Italy, they show how different facets of an organisation can be understood and assessed, including the following dimensions:

- structural, strategic;
- functional;

- psychodynamic and cultural;
- psycho-environmental.

Act!

Write a review of the article by Francescato and Aber (2015) with particular reference to the utility of their arguments for critical community psychology. What do you think of their suggestion that personal, organisational and community empowerment are all required?

Reflect!

Think about yourself in relation to any aspect of your life (for example, education, work, sport). See if you can draw a nested system diagram to capture the complex, different level environments relating to your experience. Which levels were easy and which more difficult to identify? Why might this be? How did the more distal environments – the macro and exosystems – influence your experience?

Soft systems are human systems: they are characterised by the relationships between people and patterns of activities. Activity theory and the notion of activity systems (Engeström, 1999) can help us understand more about patterns of activities that lead to social change.

An activity system focuses on the achievement of social change through goal oriented, individual and collective actions, mediated by and creating changes in socio-cultural forces. Engeström and Miettinen (1999) suggest that activity systems consist of two continuously interacting processes: the internalisation or reproduction of culture and the externalisation or creation of new artefacts making cultural transformation possible. The elements of an activity system include: object (or goal of the activity, which is both individual and collective); subject (actor and actors involved in the activity); mediating artefacts (or socio-cultural signs and tools, including historical factors); rules (again, culturally determined); community (wider group of actors potentially engaged in the activity); and division of labour (ways in which collective action is achieved through the execution of different actions). Within an activity system, there is always tension between individual motivation, collective motivation and culturally mediated tools and conditions surrounding the action.

Thus, to understand an activity system it is necessary to take different perspectives into account, and to make sense of the cultural context in which the activity takes place. This is a potentially fruitful analysis for critical community psychology as it combines systems perspectives with actor perspectives, and also considers the role of the outside agent, or researcher, in the process of change.

> Activity system as a unit of analysis calls for complementarity of the system view and the subject's view. The analyst constructs the activity system as if looking at it from above. At the same time, the analyst must select a subject (or better yet multiple different members), of the local activity, through whose eyes and interpretations the activity is constructed. The dialectic between the systemic and subjective-partisan views brings the researcher into dialectical relationship with the local activity under investigation. The study of an activity system becomes a collective, multi-voiced construction of its past, present and future zones of proximal development.
>
> (Engeström & Miettinen, 1999, p. 10)

Example: Gardening as a tool for participation

We worked with a local group of residents living in what had been designated an area of multiple deprivation – indeed, at the time of the project the locality was considered the most deprived area of the country. The aim of the project was to improve the environment through gardening activity linked to a national horticultural competition, the In Bloom competition (www.rhs.org.uk/get-involved/britain-in-bloom). At the same time the project sought to generate greater participation by local people (Stewart & Kagan, 2008). The main features were to develop a new cultural practice (in this case participation via the gardening project) requiring alignment with three types of local factors:

- Social – largely relationships, … e.g. power, support. Support of the local environmental officer and the enthusiasm and encouragement of initially the organiser and subsequently neighbours.
- Cultural – ways things happen, what they mean … e.g. whether or not residents or the Council should tend the gardens; gardening as a legitimate household activity; In Bloom as a cultural process.
- Historical – current context, arrangements … e.g. resources, the availability of materials and the presence of the In Bloom competition.

Figure 6.7 illustrates the elements of the gardening activity system.

Figure 6.7 Gardening activity system.

Activity theory perspectives suggest that the relationship between human agents (residents) and objects of environment (in this case participation, but the gardens may also be seen as objects in the environment) is mediated by cultural means, tools and rules (gardening, the In Bloom competition). Not only this, but it is suggested that the human mind (experience) develops, and can only be understood, within the context of meaningful, goal oriented and socially determined interaction between human beings and their material environment. Thus, it is through the gardening that residents' understanding of the importance of 'community' and their role in building it develops. It is through the activity that those around the residents (professionals in particular) come to understand the capacity of local people to be involved, without the need for capacity building.

Soft (human) systems are dynamic systems and change over time. It is, therefore, worth drawing rich pictures at different stages of a project. Implicit in the thinking about the complex system in which an issue is embedded is the concept of stakeholder. Indeed, some of those roles and people identified in the above pictures can be said to be stakeholders in the issue. Part of understanding the problem is to understand the different stakeholders' positions and their potential for blocking or enabling an intervention.

Stakeholders and stakeholder analyses

Stakeholders are all those with an interest in the issue, people or activity contributing to the problem. A stakeholder analysis is vital in any initial attempt to understand a problem. Like the systems descriptions outlined above, stakeholder analyses can be revisited throughout an intervention. At initial stages though, a stakeholder analysis gives a relatively superficial understanding of who (or what groups or organisations) have what kind of power and influence in a particular situation. This in turn can help make decisions about best courses of action to take and in what order of priority.

There are a number of ways in which a stakeholder analysis can be undertaken. Checkland and Scholes (1990) use the mnemonic CATWOE to differentiate different groups of stakeholders. With reference to the Slums of Kolkata project described above, CATWOE stands for:

C The 'customers of the system', that is those on the receiving end of whatever it is that the system does. 'Customers' are those who stand to gain or lose from the system activities. They would include families with and without disabled children – those without always have the potential for one of their children to become disabled. They would also include other local residents.

A The 'actors', meaning those who would actually carry out the activities envisaged in the notional system being defined. This refers to the health workers and their home organisations that work directly with families. In this case the Indian Institute for Cerebral Palsy, and the funders of the project are actors.

T The 'transformation process'. What does the system do to the inputs to convert them into the outputs? This is the process through which health workers who are trained to work with families of disabled children and other social institutions (churches, mosques, temples; schools for example) receive guidance about including disabled children.

W The 'world view' puts the system into a wider context. In the case of poor families with disabled children in India this might refer to their potential for economic activity versus support by the state; it might tie in with disability and rights agendas. In this example, gender impacts upon the world view related to economic activity and cost to family. The consequences for systems failures can be made explicit here.

O The 'owner(s)'. These are those who have sufficient formal power over the system to stop it existing if they so wished (though they won't usually want to do this). This often will refer to those who fund a particular project. Owners for the India project may be some of the actors, they may be religious leaders or employers. They have the power to stop things changing or to enable them.

E   The 'environmental constraints'. Resources (financial, time, staffing etc.), regulations, activities by other organisations that overlap, relevant social policies might all be environmental constraints.

Other ways of identifying stakeholders are via lists specifying what it is that particular people or groups have to gain or lose, or the power and influence they wield. Figure 6.8 enables stakeholders to be rated according to impact (importance and influence) and status. A somewhat different way of mapping stakeholders in terms of the power and influence they hold is shown in Figure 6.9, in which the different stakeholders can be listed in the different quadrants.

Stakeholders	Stakeholder interests	Impact Importance High, Medium, Low	Impact Influence High, Medium, Low	Status High, Medium, Low	Current relationship
Etc.					

Figure 6.8 Basic stakeholder analysis framework.

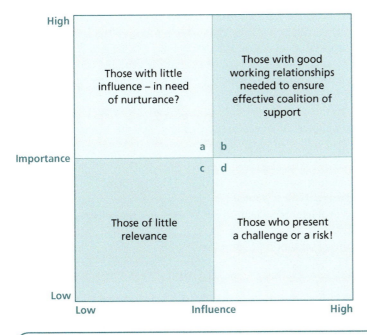

Figure 6.9 Importance and influence of stakeholders.

153

Act!

Think of something you want to change (If you cannot think of anything choose one of the following: increasing financial support for students; halting the spread of genetically modified seed in poor countries; increasing the amount of cycling in your local town). See if you can complete the different stakeholder analyses for the issue you have chosen. Which one worked best and why?

Stakeholder perspectives acknowledge that different people have different positions in relation to an issue: they have different world views. (Stakeholder analyses are returned to in Chapter 7).

Reflect!

Consider your position on your home government's position on asylum seekers and refugees. How is your thinking informed? How close are you to the issue? How might your stake in this impact upon your beliefs?

In this chapter we have tackled:

- mapping the issue (identifying what is real through needs analysis), emphasising assets rather than problems;
- exploring positionality and perspective;
- finding methods which work (getting to know a community; gaining entry; systems and stakeholder analyses).

The case examples discussed bring some of the theory alive but this is no substitute for 'inserción'. These techniques are given life once they are applied.

We have spent a lot of time exploring, here, the nature of the issue or problem to be addressed. In any intervention this is time well spent, as it frames not only the understanding of the issue, but also the nature of the intervention and even its evaluation. Archibald (2019) links the definition of the issue directly to evaluation (see Chapter 11), by suggesting that 'problem definition critique' can, itself, be a form of evaluation. He draws on six questions posed by Baachi (2012, p. 21) that problematise the very definition of the issue and should be asked at the start of an intervention and that will then guide evaluation. These are somewhat similar to the questions posed at the beginning of the chapter, and to boundary questions discussed in the next chapter. As new ways of defining the issue are identified (for example in Question 4 below), they are also subjected to the same interrogation. The questions are:

1 What's the 'problem' represented to be in a specific policy or policy proposal?
2 What presuppositions or assumptions underpin this representation of the 'problem'?
3 How has this representation of the 'problem' come about?
4 What is left unproblematic in this problem representation? Where are the silences? Can the 'problem' be thought about differently?
5 What effects are produced by this representation of the 'problem'?
6 How/where has this representation of the 'problem' been produced, disseminated and defended? How has it been (or could it be) questioned, disrupted and replaced?

Having identified the issue and gained some understanding of both the complexity of the problem and the system or community with which we are working, the next stage is action planning.

Chapter 7

Action planning

Summary

In this chapter we are concerned with ways of thinking about decision making and action planning. We will look at a number of different frameworks for thinking about who should – and could – be involved in decision making and at participatory decision making. We will consider some of the processes involved in making choices about action in complex decision-making circumstances.

Action planning is about making decisions for action, based on the information gleaned from the problem identification stage. Once the problem has been mapped and we have understood something about its context, action for change can be planned. There is not always a clear distinction to be made between identifying or framing the issue situation and planning the action and we will see that the two stages interlink in complex ways. Action planning involves having in mind the kind of change to be achieved as well as the ways of getting there, in other words, understanding the nature of change. It also involves making different kinds of decisions, which sounds easy but can be complex when there are different people with different interests involved. In this chapter we will explore decision making and the nature of change.

Decision making

Decision making builds on the identification of the problem to identify alternatives for action: there is rarely only one possibility for action. These alternatives are then assessed and choices made about what to do and in what order, leading to action. In community psychological praxis, there are different kinds of decisions to be made with community partners. In making choices from options it is possible to set the various alternatives against values, to try to ensure that decision making is ethical.

Decision making can cover a variety of areas. Table 7.1 shows some of those we have encountered.

Table 7.1 Areas of decision making and options in community praxis	
Area for decision making	*Options, alternatives and choices*
What is the purpose of the work?	Who decides?
	Who is involved in this decision?
	Who is excluded?
Is this to be a large or small piece of work?	Short and focused
	Longer term and more complex
	Different stages or phases to evolve over time
	Partial or comprehensive
What kind of work is it?	Research
	Facilitation
	Support
	Advocacy
	Education
When and where should it be done?	Geographical location or group base?
	Have environmental issues been taken into account?
	Timescale
	Physical locations in or outside community
	Is anywhere excluded?
Who should be involved?	Who and why of:
	Community members
	University staff and or students
	Professionals
	Is anyone excluded?
How should the work be done?	What methods will be used?
	Are methods culturally safe?
	What scope is there for evolution of methods?
	Are any methods excluded?
What is the timescale?	Fixed from start or negotiable as work proceeds?
Do we have the necessary resources?	Knowledge
	Skills
	Cultural knowledge
	Physical resources
	Funding

Table 7.1 Continued

Area for decision making	Options, alternatives and choices
How will the work be evaluated?	What plans for evaluation Internal or external Extent of stakeholder involvement Formative and/or summative Methods of capturing information Who is responsible for what? What should be done with evaluation? Is reflexivity built in?
What kind of reporting will be needed?	Written, visual, auditory Formal, informal Academic, professional Dissemination events or workshops
How will information be captured and by whom?	Who will collect information? Who will analyse information? Who will write or prepare presentation of information?
What other kinds of dissemination will be required?	Exhibition Website Posters Other products (training materials etc.)
Is funding available?	What is needed by whom to enable the work to proceed? Sources of funding – are they ethical? Funding bids written Dissemination and sustainability included in funding bids

Decisions have to be made, not only at the outset of a piece of work but also as the work proceeds and new dilemmas emerge. Some decisions will have already been made by those who have identified the need for change; others will have to be taken by the project workers; but many decisions need to be made jointly between project workers and project partners, including funders. Like all other forms of participation there are degrees of participation (as described in Chapter 6). We advocate a critical stance to all decisions made at whatever stage in a project and by whomsoever. A critical stance on decision making enables values to be embedded in our work and exposes alternative values that might be at play. By doing this we remain aware of the ethical dilemmas we face and the extent to which we are able to resolve them. It is possible that resolution does not always happen but working in this way highlights these issues of difference.

Reflect!

Consider a decision you have made recently. It could be an academic decision, a career issue or a personal life decision. Use the dimensions identified in Table 7.1 to consider how you made this decision and what the implications are. Now imagine your decision has to be done in collaboration with others and accepted by others. What dimensions of the above table did you use and why? Did any of the dimensions affect the outputs or impact of the decision? You can see that working participatively can take time and effort – no wonder people make individual decisions and act upon them.

Critical community psychological work will often involve us in working with people who have different types of understanding about the issues we are working on, and may have different life experiences, perspectives, values and attitudes. It takes time to explore points of mutual interest and concern in order to find ways of working together. The fashion, now, is to call participative decision making co-production – whether this is of need, framing of an issue, decision making, or action – and this is explored further in Chapter 8. It is not our place to impose our own world view on community partners, even when we think that we are right! However, given the values and principles of working as critical community psychologists, we should not be afraid to challenge others who are in a position to undermine, belittle or oppress, or otherwise distort the scope, direction and form of the project. It is best to expose, negotiate and work through these kinds of differences at the problem identification and planning stages of work where possible – however, sometimes differences in values only emerge as the work progresses. In this case, it can be useful to take time out from the main project in order to reconcile differences, find points of compromise and proceed to work together constructively.

Example: Living with multiple sclerosis

One of our doctoral students was investigating the ways in which health and social care services contributed to quality of life and promoted independence for people living with long term, chronic disabling conditions. He spent a long time negotiating with representatives of the public services and third sector or non-governmental organisations how to go about this and who to involve. During the course of these discussions it became clear that different parties had different agendas and were interested in being involved for different reasons. Managers wanted information they could use for service transformation, as required by a recent policy initiative. Front line professionals were anxious to be shown in a good light and wanted control over which service users were involved. Some health professionals wanted full partnership with the research in order to secure funding from a pharmaceuticals company. Negotiations took over a year and involved discussion about methods as well as what the most useful focus of the research might be. During this period, some tensions in the care system were revealed, relating in particular to how people who needed support got information and contact with services, and the rather haphazard way in which different services kept information about the prevalence of chronic disability in their area. This meant that the research took a different course and included a strong focus on service users' satisfaction with services. It also led to a focus on the experiences of living with one condition, multiple sclerosis, which had not been part of the original intention. During the course of the research, further adjustments had to be made to its direction, as more compromises between the different parties had to be made and the research focused less on quality of life than on social relationships.

Who makes what kinds of decisions?

In planning any kind of action we need to consider who makes what kinds of decisions about projects, interventions or any other piece of work, and to what extent decision makers re-enact colonial power relations. We can understand decision making in terms of two dimensions: individual–collective and emancipatory–directive, which results in four quadrants: individual/emancipatory, individual/directive, collective/emancipatory and collective/directive (See Figure 7.1). The individual–collective dimension refers to whether decisions are made individually or collectively (though we need to recognise that this binary distinction might be problematic – see our critical disruption of Part 1). The emancipatory–directive dimension includes decisions which are imposed or directed, through to those which can empower others. In progressive praxis, we strive for the decisions we make to be in the collective/emancipatory quadrant, but this is not always possible. By mapping the decisions we make in this two-dimensional space we can remain aware of the kinds of decisions we are making and thus monitor our praxis.

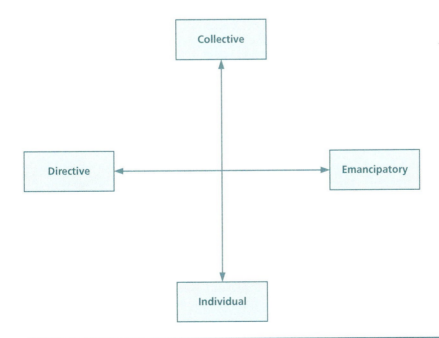

Figure 7.1 Mapping decision making.

Act!

The more our decision making is in the upper right quadrant, the more it reflects critical community psychology values. Participatory means of planning action, involving different stakeholders in devising different actions, would normally fall in the collective–emancipatory field.

Dialogue and discussion are important tools in planning. This can be face to face as in joint planning and decision making. Alternatively, it can be over time, with suggestions laid out, offered to others, responses coordinated and circulated for further comment, and so on.

At the planning stage, collaborative processes not only help decide options and ways forward, but also serve to find a common ground for working. It is at the planning stages that teambuilding across the different partners, including exploration of the range of different perspectives and values held, can be most useful. Although we examined different stakeholder interests in the issue identification stage, these can be revisited in slightly different ways in planning.

Think!

Visit or re-visit a published piece of work (a report or journal article). Consider whether the process of decision making is made explicit or not. If the process is explicit, can it be categorised according to the quadrants identified above? If it is not explicit, why do you think this is?

Stakeholder analysis and action planning

A stakeholder analysis (see Chapter 6 for further discussion of stakeholder analyses) can assist with planning of an intervention, and, indeed, can help identify who might best be involved at the action planning stage. Analysing stakeholders can highlight where there are potential allies for or powerful blocks to change, which in itself can shape an intervention. For example, it may be necessary to weaken power blocks as part of an intervention. Second, during the stakeholder analysis itself, an anticipated change can be included. In part, this involves the assessment of how ready different stakeholders are to get involved with a change project and how much power they have, but also includes an idea about how changes in their positions are anticipated and built into the change project. Readiness is the amount a stakeholder knows about the issue at stake or their view of it (positive or negative). Power is the influence a stakeholder has over the success of the change project. See Figure 7.2.

Example: Witness support

Kagan, Caton and Amin (2001) explored the feasibility of developing a scheme to support witnesses of crime who were scared to come forward and report what they had witnessed. The net result of this was not only that crime continued, but the official statistics of reported crime were low, making it look as if local policing was effective. Major stakeholders were the police, who had low readiness for change and high degrees of power at the start. Ideally, over time, their readiness would increase and their power diminish, enabling witnesses to be prepared to come forward. Local perpetrators of crime and disorder did not want change at the outset and had a lot of coercive power. Over time it was hoped they would see change was in their interests and that their coercive power would decrease. Local people affected by crime and disorder wanted change to happen but initially had little power. The intervention was designed, in part, to empower them. Other crime prevention projects that were around had only a moderate interest in change, that over time should increase, and medium levels of power, which again should increase over time. The stakeholder analysis helped the decision making process for how to go about the work, particularly in terms of using a process that contributed to residents' empowerment.

X = position from which they start. O = ideal position if they are to assist with making change happen

Stakeholder's stakeholder group	Readiness			Power		
	High	*Medium*	*Low*	*High*	*Medium*	*Low*
Police	–	O	X	X	O	–
Local perpetrators of crime and disorder	–	O	X	X	–	O
Local people affected by crime and disorder	XO	–	–	O	–	X
Other crime prevention projects	O	X	–	O	X	–

Figure 7.2 An example of stakeholder analysis in planning: a readiness–power matrix.

Sometimes it is useful to combine stakeholder analysis with power analysis, particularly to assess the extent to which different stakeholders have influence and offer the potential for support which can be helpful. Power analyses at the start of a process can help ensure against neo-colonial interventions – ones which, far from being liberatory, resuscitate and re-enact colonial dynamics and dominations. Figure 7.3 offers a framework for identifying these different levels of influence and support.

Placing these different stakeholders in the power matrix helps us see: (a) who it might be useful to recruit to the cause; (b) who needs further persuasion; or (c) sources of resistance to be understood, overcome or avoided. It can also help us identify potential supports who have not yet been hooked into the change process, and hidden opponents (who appear to be in support of an issue but who either have little actual influence or work to effectively sabotage a change process).

Watson and Foster-Fishman (2013) looked at collaborative decision making in order to best understand how it is that despite their best intentions, collaborative decision making bodies often fail to ensure that stakeholders from disadvantaged populations can authentically participate. They suggest that two processes, with power at their heart, are at play:

1 The exchange of resources: participatory decision making involves the activation and sharing of assets in a setting, assets such as relationships, time, knowledge, experience and skills – this exchange can be enabled or denied.
2 Internalised social boundaries: all participants bring with them beliefs that constrain and enable what they feel able to do or say, through historical and social divisions between different groups

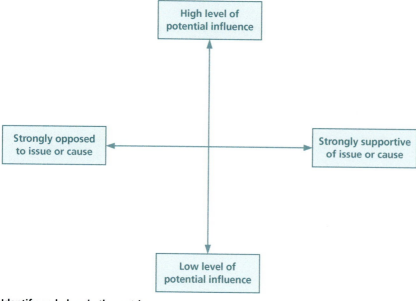

Identify and place in the matrix:
a.   allies
b.   beneficiaries
c.   blockers or opponents
d.   decision makers
e.   influencers

Figure 7.3 Power in terms of influence and support for an issue, cause or person.

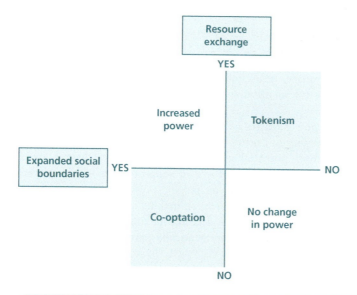

Figure 7.4 Power, resources exchange and the expansion of social boundaries.
Source: derived from Watson & Foster-Fishman, 2013.

(age, race, gender, class etc.), ranging from confidence in privileged entitlement to a lack of confidence and reserve.

The ways in which these two processes play out in collaborative or participatory decision making affect the degree to which participants are empowered or power is retained by existing power brokers. Figure 7.4 summarises how different degrees of resource exchange and expanded social boundaries define the nature of participation.

Authentic participation, then, requires the development of capacity to activate and value not only one's own assets but also those of other people, and a willingness to share; and the expansion of social boundaries through critical reflection and consciousness, and discussion of existing boundaries and a determination to expand those boundaries.

Power mapping is another way of trying to assess a situation or issue with a view to identifying not only possibilities for change but also resistance to change. Hagan and Smail (1997) suggest that at any moment in practice it is possible to map power with respect to particular people. The same could be suggested for groups or communities. Figure 7.5 offers a framework for mapping both proximal (close to) and distal (further away) power. Once the analysis is completed, it is a good idea to summarise the main positive and negative forces of influence.

When reflecting upon our own power in an advocacy situation, for example, especially to try to minimise this, it can be useful to think of the different forms of power that can be exercised over others, and which we want to exercise, bearing in mind our liberatory quest. There are a number of sources of social power, and these are discussed further in Chapter 12.

Boundary critique – towards value based decision making

Decision making as a process has implications – if we go one way, then 'x' may happen, if we choose another then 'y' becomes possible. In this way, every project is in some way arbitrary. What the project consists of (its scope, for example) is only one in a universe of possible versions. Likewise, in terms of the people involved in a project, it is reasonable to ask *"why these people and not those?"* These boundaries around any particular project are never fixed and decisions made about them both limit the possibilities of any particular piece of work and reflect the values underpinning the work. Changing the boundaries of an issue or a project may change the very nature of the project: it may also change our understanding of who may be considered a decision maker. Identifying boundaries involves mapping the issue or problem as a system (we explored this in Chapter 6) Foster-Fishman and Behrens (2007, p. 193) draw attention to the importance of exploring boundaries.

> … the process of defining a system's boundary [may be] the most critical step in a systems change endeavour … Boundaries clarify what is important and valued: they make explicit the focus of inquiry (including the problem definition) and the potential range of impact of a change initiative … more attention is needed to how community psychologists define the problem situation and the boundaries around the targeted system

Reflecting on how the boundaries are drawn around a targeted system is a key part of our community psychological practice, and is known as 'boundary critique'. Boundary critique is a process, borrowed from the field of critical systems thinking (see Midgley, 2000), that invites critical reflection on key decisions made about a project. Boundary critique involves:

> Maintaining a stance of critical awareness … considering the different possible boundaries that might be used in analyses, and taking account of their possible consequences for intervention.
> (Midgley, Munlo & Brown, 1998, p. 467)

Act!

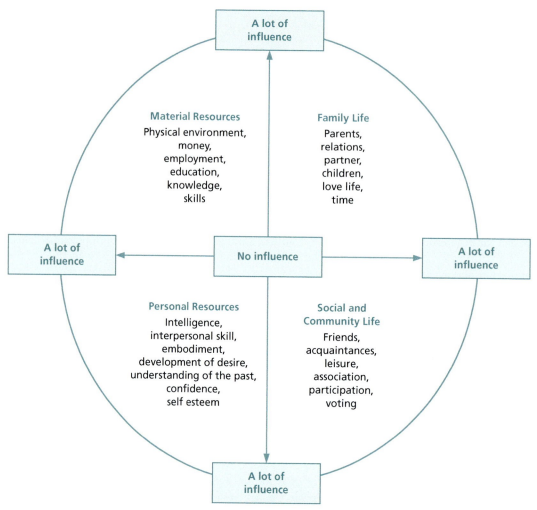

For each segment, estimate the influence of each aspect (rate 1 = little influence... 5 = considerable influence), and estimate whether this influence is positive or negative. Also consider:

Economics: explain how the capitalist system and global economics has direct and indirect influence over life chances and wellbeing.

Politics: explain how current local, national and international policies influence life chances and wellbeing and frame ideological forces.

Culture: explain how national, age, gender, religious culture influence life chances and wellbeing.

Information: explain how information, including the media frames experiences and influences life chances and wellbeing.

Figure 7.5 Distal and proximal power mapping.

Source: based on Hagan & Smail,1997; Burton & Kagan, 2008.

Table 7.2 Checklist of critical boundary questions

SOURCES OF MOTIVATION	(1)	*Who is (ought to be) the client or beneficiary?* That is, whose interests are (should be) served?
	(2)	*What is (ought to be) the purpose?* That is, what are (should be) the consequences?
	(3)	*What is (ought to be) the measure of improvement or measure of success?* That is, how can (should) we determine that the consequences, taken together, constitute an improvement?
SOURCES OF POWER	(4)	*Who is (ought to be) the decision-maker?* That is, who is (should be) in a position to change the measure of improvement?
	(5)	*What resources and other conditions of success are (ought to be) controlled by the decision-maker?* That is, what conditions of success can (should) those involved control?
	(6)	*What conditions of success are (ought to be) part of the decision environment?* That is, what conditions can (should) the decision maker *not* control (e.g. from the viewpoint of those not involved)?
SOURCES OF KNOWLEDGE	(7)	*Who is (ought to be) considered a professional or further expert?* That is, who is (should be) involved as competent provider of experience and expertise?
	(8)	*What kind expertise is (ought to be) consulted?* That is, what counts (should count) as relevant knowledge?
	(9)	*What or who is (ought to be) assumed to be the guarantor of success?* That is, where do (should) those involved seek some guarantee that improvement will be achieved – for example, consensus among experts, the involvement of stakeholders, the experience and intuition of those involved, political support?
SOURCES OF LEGITIMATION	(10)	*Who is (ought to be) witness to the interests of those affected but not involved?* That is, who is (should be) treated as a legitimate stakeholder, and who argues (should argue) the case of those stakeholders who cannot speak for themselves, including future generations and non-human nature?
	(11)	*What secures (ought to secure) the emancipation of those affected from the premises and promises of those involved?* That is, where does (should) legitimacy lie?
	(12)	*What world view is (ought to be) determining?* That is, what different visions of 'improvement' are (should be) considered, and how are they (should they be) reconciled?

Detailed explorations of boundary judgements and boundary critique can be found in the writing of Ulrich (see, for example, Ulrich & Reynolds, 2010), for whom boundary judgements and value judgements are intimately linked. Our decisions about how we boundary our work reflect our values.

Ulrich developed a set of 12 questions (Ulrich, 2005) which can be used heuristically to question what a system currently is and what it ought to be, thus bringing to the surface the value judgements that underpin boundary decisions. One of Ulrich's core ideas is that of 'legitimacy' – who is making what decision and who ought to be. Thus, decision making can be examined in terms of what *is* and what *ought* to be. Table 7.2 provides a checklist of questions in relation to purpose, power, knowledge and legitimation within a project. Each question is asked in two forms: the '*is*' mode – what is the present situation? And the '*ought*' mode – what ought to be the arrangements in this change project?

At its most simple, boundary critique asks *"who or what is involved in and who or what is left out of a project?"* This seemingly simple decision can reflect underlying values and the ethics of praxis, exposing ethical dilemmas, which in turn have to be resolved.

Example: Witness support

As discussed above, we were asked to examine the feasibility of a witness support scheme for residents in a neighbourhood who experienced high degrees of intimidation and were afraid to report crime and disorder (Kagan, Caton & Amin, 2001). Our initial brief was to discuss this with those stakeholder groups who had already been involved with local regeneration professionals and the police and who had identified the need for the project. Thus, boundary decisions had already been made about who should be involved. There seemed to be internal consensus that there would not be any need to trawl more widely for information.

Ethical Dilemma: These groups had all been involved in the initial survey and recommendation to develop a project. If the range of stakeholders involved was not broadened, then the project would risk being unable to add to their understanding of the problem, and hence of what the project needed to do. Excluded groups included many other people affected by the crime levels and experiences of acting as witnesses. These included residents not linked to associations (the vast majority in the area), young people and children, people from minority ethnic groups and employers and people working in the area, other projects and agencies operating in the locality (including faith organisations, youth organisations, sports organisations and so on). So, if we were to work with integrity we would have to re-negotiate these boundaries in order to include more people. We proposed a project design that differed from the initial one to be commissioned, and that would be more complex and take longer – and thus be more expensive. We considered whether we would go ahead if the boundaries could not be re-negotiated. This involved us reflecting upon what the consequences for local people would be if a different team were commissioned to follow the original project brief closely. We decided to keep an open mind and, on balance, thought that people would be better off if we undertook the work.

We managed to re-negotiate a broadening of the boundary of those to be involved, as well as a broadening of the methods to be used. We successfully extended the time period by a third but did not manage to procure more resources. So, we ended up with a more complex, slightly longer timescale project to be completed within the same resources.

During this process of negotiation, the marginalised status of some of the stakeholders was emerging. When it came to youth and children, those who had commissioned the study were unanimous in their being outside the remit of the study.

<u>Ethical Dilemma</u>: We faced the ethical decision as to whether we should go ahead without involving young people when they clearly should be involved. We decided that the involvement of youth project workers and our own knowledge of young people's issues might be sufficient at this stage to advocate for a youth perspective throughout the project. This was preferable to not undertaking the project.

The first major boundary dispute, then, was in terms of decision making over the remit and involvement in the project. We were able, through dialogue (and the passing of time) to agree new boundaries for the project (Kagan, Caton & Amin, 2001; Kagan, Caton, Amin & Choudry, 2004).

Midgley (1992), draws attention to the dilemmas posed when there is a conflict between groups of people who have different values (or ethical stances) relating to the same issue and then make different boundary judgements. He describes how a marginal area exists between a narrow and another wider boundary judgement (as in the views of those with different values). The marginal area contains elements excluded by the first boundary judgement but included in the wider, second analysis. He suggests that when two such ethical boundary judgements come into conflict, the situation is resolved by the valuing or devaluing of the marginal elements. Resolution of boundary disputes, therefore, either require compromise and new boundaries agreed (usually through dialogue) or require one boundary to dominate the other. In the course of resolving boundary disputes, the different value bases of the parties involved are exposed.

Reflect!

You can consider boundaries around who is inside and outside all kinds of decisions. Family decisions, for example, can be subject to the same kind of analysis around boundaries. Occasions such as family weddings, funerals etc. tend to elicit different views of who should come or not, and how they should contribute. Imagine the difficulty of boundaries when multiple stakeholders are involved. Think of a recent situation where a decision was made that involved boundary disputes. How were they resolved? If you were an inside party to the dispute, how did you feel about the way it was resolved? Why did you feel this way?

In community psychological work, boundary decisions may refer to the focus of investigation or to the intervention techniques.

> ## Example: Arts and mental health
>
> We were commissioned to undertake evaluations of a number of different partici-
> patory projects using arts for mental health and well-being (Lawthom, Sixsmith &
> Kagan, 2007; Sixsmith & Kagan, 2005). These projects had been running for some
> time when we were invited in by the overall manager. Our preference was to
> undertake participatory evaluations and work in collaboration with those benefit-
> ing from the projects. However, it soon became clear that project funders wanted
> 'hard evidence' of mental health gain; and that the artists running the projects
> were uncomfortable with the active involvement of project participants. Thus, our
> stance was of involvement and participation, using the strengths and experiences
> of project participants; funders wanted a positivist approach, using standardised
> questionnaires in order to demonstrate 'real change'; and artists challenged the
> idea of framing mental health as the important issue and were protective of their
> project participants. There was then a boundary dispute over epistemology,
> methods and involvement of project participants. The compromise reached was for
> a multi-method evaluation that contained substantial elements of participation
> and participant observation by the researchers. We were able to show evidence of
> mental health gain but not through the use of standardised methods, so did not
> fully meet the funders' agenda. The compromise was achieved through dialogue
> and through an appreciative inquiry process involving researchers and artists (Coop-
> errider & Whitney, 2005; Kagan & Kilroy, 2007). (Appreciative Inquiry is a collabora-
> tive process through which participants are able to explore their positive values and
> attitudes towards an issue and come to mutual understanding. It was particularly
> appropriate in this case as it combines an investigatory process with creative activi-
> ties, promoting shared innovative thinking.) The involvement of project partici-
> pants in these decisions was by proxy, as they were never present in the discussions,
> but were represented by project managers and to a certain extent by artists. Our
> reflections as a research team became important sources of data in themselves and
> formed the basis of our team discussions, enabling us to adopt the stance of reflex-
> ive participants, throughout. We participated in the art, rather than as project par-
> ticipants participating in the research.

Act!

Read the case example above. See if you can apply the critical boundary questions
from Table 7.2 to this situation. Remember to ask both sets of questions: what is
and what ought to be? What values does this reveal? Which were easier and which
more difficult questions to answer and why was this?

Whilst evaluation is often thought to occur at the end of a project (see Chapter 11) it can also form
part of the planning of work, and we try to build evaluation into the start of a project to help with the
planning of what is to be done. The boundary question of 'what to evaluate', near the start of the
project influences the way in which the nature of the project itself is defined (see Chapter 6).

> ### Example: User led mental health services
>
> One of our students was working with an innovative user led mental health service. She had negotiated with them a piece of work that would be useful to them, namely an evaluation, through participant observation and discussions with group members, of a hearing voices group that was facilitated by someone who had used mental health services. She thought about how her evaluation might contribute to overall change. By only focusing on the hearing voices group, she realised that any recommendations she made could only result in small scale improvements to the group – ameliorative change. By moving the boundary and seeing the group as a part of the overall innovative service, she could see how her evaluation might contribute to the overall challenge being made to the mental health system by a user led project – far more of a transformative change.

Whilst techniques for evaluation are covered later, here we present one system of evaluation that is particularly valuable at planning stages, and that involves different stakeholders in an organised way, namely fourth generation evaluation (Guba & Lincoln, 2001).

Fourth generation evaluation

Fourth generation evaluation examines the different meanings and interpretations of different stakeholders, each with different perspectives. It is a constructivist approach, based on meanings and discussions. Guba and Lincoln suggest:

> The basic methodological assumption of constructivism is hermeneutic-dialecticism, that is, a process by which constructions entertained by the several involved individuals and groups (stakeholders) are first uncovered and plumbed for meaning and then confronted, compared, and contrasted in encounter situations.
>
> (Guba & Lincoln, 2001, p. 1)

This then is a process that has a lot in common with boundary critique and the negotiation of understanding of the nature of problems, and of action to be taken, when different stakeholders are involved. At the heart of fourth generation evaluation are processes of discovery and assimilation. Discovery refers to the surfacing of existing meanings about the situation and topic to be evaluated. Assimilation refers to attempts to incorporate new understandings into existing constructions or generate new understandings. Both these processes are achieved by negotiating, defining, elucidating, mediating, illuminating, challenging and testing individual, group and collective constructions. This is achieved:

> …through a series of steps which … may well be iterative and reiterative in practice as constructions evolve and as particular claims, concerns, and issues are dealt with.
>
> (Guba & Lincoln, 2001, p. 5)

Example: Evaluation of training needs

One of our students was employed in a large voluntary residential organisation for people with brain injury. She was charged with developing a training strategy and training programme to help the organisation move from a paternalistic one to one which engaged with residents as active agents with empowerment as a core principle. The organisation was a long standing one and several groups of staff and residents had worked there for a long time. In addition, family members were by and large happy with how the organisation functioned. Instead of taking a managerialist approach to the development and training strategy, she used a Fourth Generation Evaluation process to arrive at an agreed set of goals and priorities for training. This involved interviews and surveys of different stakeholder groups, clarifying their appraisal of the current situation and what needed to change and how, introducing to each group any differences from other stakeholder perceptions. As the process continued, different stakeholder groups were brought together for face to face discussion and gained insight into the different perspectives held. After a process of about nine months, agreement was reached about the future direction of the organisation and the development needs of all involved. She thereby used an evaluation process to plan for action.

Reflect! & Think!

Imagine how different stakeholders may see the case example on evaluation of training needs above. How might a relative see the issue of empowerment, as distinct from a paid worker or a client who is brain injured? Who participates in order to decide? Read the article by Langer and Rodin (1976) who discuss the value of participation and autonomy for older people in an institutional setting. Do you think anything has changed in terms of stakeholder involvement in decision making around older people?

A different, but linked, iterative process for agreeing community priorities and gaining the views of marginalised groups was described by Jackson, Burgess et al. (2018). They used a feedback loop process to ensure that all the different views within a culturally diverse community could be heard in the identification of priorities, through a co-production process, but also in implementing action solutions and collecting feedback on the implementation. The process can be described in a number of steps:

1 Hold a community conversation about neighbourhood priorities and agree them.
2 Co-design a way to get community feedback on these priorities.
3 Collect the data from different groups within the community about the priorities.
4 Have another community conversation about the data to determine the appropriate actions based on the identified priorities.
5 Implement the chosen action(s)/solutions(s) and keep the group updated on the progress.
6 Co-design a second way to collect feedback on how the solution is going.
7 Collect this data.
8 Facilitate a community conversation about the successes and failures of the project as well as the feedback process.

Think!

Look at the steps proposed by Jackson, Burgess et al. (2018). Can you see which pairs or groups of three steps might need to be repeated more than once in the process of engagement and co-production of priorities, implementation solutions and evaluation? How will you know when there is no more need to repeat the steps?

Participatory appraisal of needs and development of action (PANDA)

Taket and White (2000), again working from a systems and constructivist stance, have linked the collaborative assessment of needs with priorities for action. They offer a framework known as participatory appraisal of needs and development of action (PANDA). Their work is based on multi-agency settings but is relevant to any complex, diverse, problem solving situation. At the heart of their framework is what they call pragmatic pluralism (broadly, doing what works). They adopt a pluralist approach to: community partners or clients, recognising diversity and differences; the creative use of methods; modes of representation employed, moving from attempts to capture the reality of the world to capturing impressions of the world from different perspectives; and facilitation processes, involving flexibility over time. Within this framework three processes are continually at play: deliberation, debate and decision making. It is by bringing different groups of people together in dialogue and discussion that shared understanding and assessment of priorities can take place. Thus, there are close similarities with fourth generation evaluation. Within this framework, Taket and White move beyond discussion and dialogue to include a variety of techniques enabling those involved to move forward collaboratively. Those we have found most useful will be summarised below and will be familiar to those of you working in organisational or community development.

Think!

Use internet sources to find out as much as you can about appreciative inquiry and fourth generation evaluation. What do the processes have in common and how do they differ? Are they based in realist or constructivist paradigms?

Strengths, weaknesses, opportunities and threats (SWOT)

This is a simple process wherein different stakeholders are brought together to assess the current situation and its context in terms of existing strengths but also weaknesses, and opportunities and threats. Strengths and weaknesses can be anything, including external influences, human, financial and physical resources, knowledge and skills and so on. Opportunities and threats might be changes in the external environment, availability of new staff, competing demands on time and so on. The grid shown in Figure 7.6 can be a useful way to summarise the information, especially if the analysis is done on a group basis.

The challenge for the group is then to discuss and plan how to build on the strengths, in the light of opportunities, taking account of threats and weaknesses. This might mean that original ideas are abandoned whilst weaknesses are repaired, for example. It is through the SWOT analysis that priorities for action emerge.

Act!

Strengths	**Weaknesses**
Opportunities	**Threats**

Figure 7.6 SWOT analysis.

Reflect!

Think about what it might take for you to work as a community psychologist. Use a SWOT analysis to organise your ideas. What are the strengths and weaknesses (these might include your skills and knowledge, personal attributes or be more broadly related to the employment situation)? What are the opportunities and threats to becoming a community psychologist? How does the SWOT analysis help you clarify your ideas?

A related process is force field analysis.

Force field analysis

Force field analysis derives from Lewin's work (Lewin, 1943, republished in Lewin, 1997). Lewin understood behaviour to be a function of both the person and the environment (see Chapter 3). In order to understand any behaviour it was necessary to look at the total situation, which Lewin understood as combinations of forces coming together as a field (employing the scientific metaphor of magnetism, popular at the time). A 'field' is defined as *"the totality of coexisting facts which are conceived of as mutually interdependent"* (Lewin 1951, p. 240).

Some of these forces would be driving forces and some restraining forces. By analysing the ways in which the driving and restraining forces work together, through a force field analysis, it is possible to identify what might make a difference in progress in one direction or another.

In a force field analysis, therefore, the driving forces and restraining forces are identified and the way they operate on one another assessed. The planning task then is to strengthen or increase driving forces and weaken or reduce restraining forces. The different forces can be grouped together or not. We have found force field analyses useful at different stages in a project, in planning, progress review and further recommendations for change stages.

Example: Witness support

Staying with the example discussed earlier in the chapter we can illustrate a partial SWOT analysis and a force field analysis as part of the project. We used these in order to identify priorities for change. Table 7.3 summarises this process.

Table 7.3 Partial SWOT analysis: opportunities and threats within the existing context for the prospects of a witness support scheme

Aspect of the context	Opportunities	Threats
Regeneration Policy and Practice: • Local involvement • Housing	• enthusiasm and commitment • strong ties in some areas • consultation over developments • work with private landlords	• some lack of awareness and involvement • participation fatigue • empty properties • attitudes of landlords
Lack of Confidence in the Police • Legal Procedures	• some positive changes seen • local officers valued • channels of communication open • awareness of need for positive results • awareness of local differences • experience of supporting witnesses in court	• negative attitudes throughout the force • lack of change in attitudes in mainstream policing • priorities not always shared with residents • limited vision of collaborative working • perceived double standards • lack of knowledge and understanding
Identity: • Locality	• commitment and enthusiasm for change • commitment to the locality • some awareness of local differences in confidence	• perception that others are better off • some areas particularly sparse in terms of facilities
• Insider-outsider	• strong local networks • recognition that each group of residents has its own problems that need to be worked through	• some people do not have strong ties • reputations spread and fuel negative attitudes
• Seriousness of incidents of crime, nuisance and disorder • Youth	• diversity of views about impact of incidents • crimes against the person drive people to report • it is recognised that young people want to participate in local improvements • energy and commitment of young people	• some people have ceased to notice incidents • the impact of apparently less serious incidents is unknown • youth seen as a problem not a solution • little intergenerational work • limited facilities

Source: reproduced by permission of Manchester Metropolitan University.

Act!

The major themes around which the opportunities and threats are organised emerged from initial information gathering. We argued that any development of a witness support scheme should take account of the opportunities and threats in the context. A second force field analysis was undertaken to clarify what enabled and what prevented people coming forward as witnesses (see Figure 7.7). The different forces are organised around categories that emerged from initial data gathering. A witness support scheme should strengthen the supports and reduce the barriers, in order to increase the likelihood that people would act as witnesses.

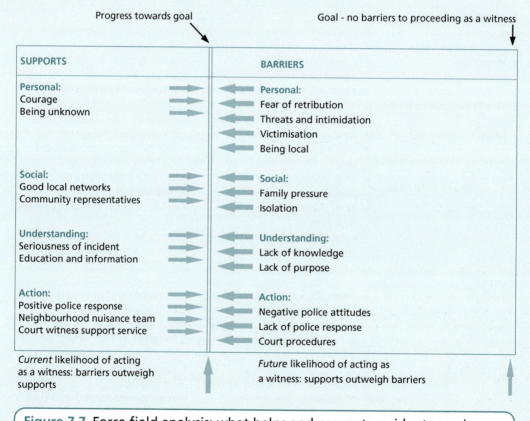

Progress towards goal

Goal - no barriers to proceeding as a witness

SUPPORTS

Personal:
Courage
Being unknown

Social:
Good local networks
Community representatives

Understanding:
Seriousness of incident
Education and information

Action:
Positive police response
Neighbourhood nuisance team
Court witness support service

BARRIERS

Personal:
Fear of retribution
Threats and intimidation
Victimisation
Being local

Social:
Family pressure
Isolation

Understanding:
Lack of knowledge
Lack of purpose

Action:
Negative police attitudes
Lack of police response
Court procedures

Current likelihood of acting as a witness: barriers outweigh supports

Future likelihood of acting as a witness: supports outweigh barriers

Figure 7.7 Force field analysis: what helps and prevents residents coming forward as witness to crime and disorder?

Act!

Look at the supports and barriers in Figure 7.7. List ideas for how the supports could be strengthened or increased, and the barriers weakened or reduced. How might you build these ideas into a project to support witnesses?

In this project, the feasibility study ended up with eight options that were put to the different stakeholder groups. Following this, a final recommendation was made which took features from several of the original options. This process of careful selection among potential options, usually using an explicit set of criteria, is known as 'option appraisal'.

Reflect!

If you are not familiar with force field or SWOT analysis try it for a decision you are making. Consider what are the strengths, weaknesses, opportunities and threats to the issue. When plotting the goal, what are the barriers to achievement of that goal and what are supports?

Option appraisal

Part of any decision making process involves making choices between alternatives and examining the consequences of decisions. In the witness support example above, we went through a process of option appraisal. Each option was summarised and through group discussion relevant criteria for appraising them in order to prioritise or choose between them were drawn up. Sometimes the criteria for choosing particular options are clear. Sometimes they involve further discussion and exploration between different stakeholders, making a diversion from the main task in hand. However, the stage cannot be rushed: if criteria for choosing between options are not agreed, then ownership of the decisions will be weak and proposed action may not follow the taking account of alternatives and/or understanding the consequences of particular decisions that are made.

Example: Witness support

In our Witness Support project discussed throughout this chapter, we thought we had agreement on the best way forward. From discussion with different stakeholders around different options, we had come up with a proposal that combined support for individual witnesses of crime but at the same time engaged in organisational and community development to facilitate greater community cohesion and involvement in strategic decision making in the locality. Thus, the proposal was for more far reaching change than just ways of supporting individual witnesses. However, when the final proposal was taken to the relevant committee (the members of which had all been involved in different ways with the feasibility study) the proposal was not ratified, and further data were sought. This perplexed us greatly but provided the opportunity to think about and understand more about the context of the work, particularly the vested political interests. Our action research project became a prefigurative action research project (Kagan & Burton, 2000). It was also a timely reminder that we, the community psychologists, could not and should not own the process of change and that our work, report and proposals were part of a process that the community had to own. Two years later a community conciliation project was developed, building on our recommendations.

An important lesson from the example above relates to the ownership of change. Change is not ours (the critical community psychologists') to own and celebrate as our achievement. If we take seriously the involvement of those affected by the change we must find ways of handing control to them – and of living with the consequences. If we have successfully built good rapport and trusting relationships, we have found that even when change does not happen at a particular time, we will often be invited back to work with those affected by the issue on further changes sometime later. We see critical community psychologists playing important catalysing roles in change and the more other people own any change, the better. However, this can produce tensions. Our employers, for example, may need to have examples of change we have created in order to justify our salaries. We need to understand the contexts in which we are working and share this with those we work with from the start, without detracting from the issues in hand. This sounds easy but is not always so.

Compromise

Many of the processes of problem identification and action planning involve the negotiation of understanding, meaning and priorities and lead to compromise. Sometimes the compromise will be a redefinition of the 'problem' – changing the boundary. Burton and Kagan (1995) point out that there are different kinds of compromises, some more desirable than others. Cop-outs and retrograde compromises do not enable progress to be made. Cop-outs either involve little attempt to achieve a satisfactory outcome, or address irrelevant issues; retrograde compromises also involve action that has little to do with the matter in hand. Of those compromises that help make progress for action, a distinction can be made between selective, comparative or progressive compromises. It is progressive compromises that move us furthest in the desired direction: they may not be ideal but they are a good first step and sometimes a better alternative than any other options. Comparative compromises lead to action that is better than expected; and selective compromises are those where a part of an objective is pursued at any particular point in time. Progressive compromises are the ones to aim for, but we often find ourselves in the situation of going along with a selective compromise. Our values and principles can act as aids in thinking about compromise, but they can only be reached through constructive dialogue with the parties concerned.

Dialogue in and of itself can lead to change. It is not always possible, however, or even desirable to encourage face to face dialogue between different parties from the start. If different groups of people have very different degrees of power in relation to an issue it will often be preferable to facilitate the understanding each has of the other. It might only feel 'safe' to meet face to face after considerable work has been done helping the different parties to articulate their positions and have these represented to the others. Guba and Lincoln (2001) (as discussed above) refer to hermeneutic dialoguing. Through a process of gathering views from one group, representing them to another and gathering their views and so on, mutual understanding is gained. This process leads not only to understanding but to a shift towards greater shared values. It is not always necessary to broker a face to face encounter of some kind, but we think it is highly desirable: only then do the different parties have the opportunity to hear and believe in their common ground. This joint meeting is often an emotional experience as the different participants gain insight and reflect, not only on what they hear, but on their own preconceptions of the others.

> ### Example: Living with multiple sclerosis
>
> In the research that explored the experiences of people living with multiple sclerosis (MS) and their satisfaction with services and supporting their well-being, referred to earlier, service users and the different professionals involved were interviewed separately and the different perspectives on what it was to live with MS were gathered. A large stakeholder conference, including all interested parties was held and it became quite clear that although they stated separately that they valued the views of people with MS and their carers, some of the medical professionals present really wanted to assert their expert views if they disagreed with what people were saying. Without the meeting, this would not have been apparent. After this meeting some of the people who had MS and their carers were upset about what they perceived to be a lack of progress in being 'heard' by professionals, and the researcher did some more work to enable the positions of each group to be heard and understood by the others.

When such meetings are planned, careful preparation and support of those with least power is needed. The way such meetings are organised can also affect their outcomes. When there are strong power differentials between different parties, it is useful to use a levelling process of some kind.

> ### Example: Urban regeneration, health and well-being
>
> We worked with residents of a district undergoing substantial urban renewal over several years (Woolrych, Sixsmith & Kagan, 2007). The focus of the work was on how urban renewal impacted upon residents' health and well-being. A number of different studies had been carried out, using a variety of methods, including interviews, focus groups, and video diaries, and some different reports had been produced. After a recent cycle of the research a meeting of different stakeholders was convened to share perspectives and to decide if there was to be another round of research. A World Café process was used in which residents and professional could meet on equal terms and listen to each other. Some of the feedback from residents who had been involved in lots of different ways with the projects, was that this was the first time they felt they had really been heard (Woolrych & Sixsmith, 2008).

Decision making cannot be separated from views about the direction of change. Kagan and Burton (2000) suggest that community psychological praxis is always moving towards greater social justice – an unattainable end point but an essential ideal for providing a sense of direction. We have found visioning to be a useful process in working with groups to clarify the direction of change and hopes for the future.

Visioning

Visioning processes can be introduced at team, project or even community level. They are often included as part of a wider ranging process of consultation and decision making. It can sometimes be difficult to turn a collective vision of a more desirable future into strategy and action, but we have found that it is

Table 7.4 Steps in PATH planning process

Steps of the PATH process (adapted from Pearpoint, O'Brien, & Forest, 1993)	Practical questions linked to each step (adapted from different projects in practice)
1. Dreaming: Using probing questions, the facilitator tries to elicit a picture of the future.	Imagine a future, 5 (or 10) years ahead. If this project goes well what will the world/people's lives/this neighbourhood etc. be like?
2. Sensing the Goal: The facilitator encourages people to look backward, pretend success has already been achieved, and describes what changes would have happened as a result.	In order to have made this happen, what will have changed after 3 (or 5) years, and then after 1 (or 3) years?
3. Grounding in the Now: An honest description of the present is sought with agreement from those involved.	If that is where we are aiming to get, let's try and describe what things are like now.
4. Identifying People to Enrol: A list is drawn up of those who are committed to the change and the contributions they can make.	In order to move from where we are now to where we are trying to get to in 1,3,5 years, whose help do we need – who can we enlist and what will they contribute?
5. Recognising Ways to Build Strength: A summary is made of the strengths needed for the dream to be realised.	What strengths do we have to help us move from where we are now to where we are trying to get to? These might include personal qualities (skills, commitment, knowledge, contacts etc.).
6. Charting Action for the Next Few Months: An action plan is drawn up specifying who will do what and when, covering the next three months. A check is made that this will lead to progress towards the dream.	So how do we build on our strengths and harness the commitments of others to make the changes happen? Who will do what and by when? Are we sure this will help us make the changes we have identified in the first year?
7. Planning the Next Month's Work: Working backwards a more detailed action plan is prepared for the first month.	Given our action plan, who is going to do what in the next month – what difficulties might there be and how can these be overcome?
8. Committing to the First Step: A commitment is made about who will do what to start, ensuring there is support to enable this to happen.	What is the very first thing to be done, and how can we ensure it is likely to be successful?

usually possible if consensus can be reached about the future goals. If it cannot, more work is needed to develop a common perspective on a piece of work or to identify the points of compromise. Typically, a visioning process invites participants to close their eyes and imagine a future beyond the life of the project. Creating a picture of both the goals and the steps towards achieving them is an accessible way to ensure that participants from different walks of life reach consensus about what has been agreed.

One process we have found useful because it combines action planning with visioning is the PATH process (the acronym comes from 'planning alternative tomorrows with hope'). Initially designed as a tool for person centred planning with people with learning difficulties (Pearpoint, O'Brien & Forest, 1993), we have used it in a number of situations to gain agreement and a common sense of purpose. The PATH process encourages groups to collectively dream about an ideal future, then identify what is realistic within a particular time frame and identify key initial stages to make this happen. It works best (as do all visioning processes) if the ideas and imaginings can be captured visually – either through graphic facilitation (see for example Hanks & Belliston, 2006) or the creative use of post-it notes or similar. Colourful, imaginative recording of the discussion that can be copied for all participants is a good way to consolidate the work carried out through the process. We have even used these pictures as project planning tools. The steps of the PATH process are illustrated in Table 7.4.

Mixing methods

In practice, different methods for decision making can be combined, as advocated by Taket and White (2000) for their PANDA process (see above). We have combined visioning with SWOT, force field analysis, a modified CATWOE – BATWOVE, with beneficiaries replacing customers, and a category of victims included in the stakeholder analysis (see Chapter 6) within a PATH framework.

> ### Example: Capacity building for evaluation
>
> The culmination of a project with community and voluntary organisations on capacity building for evaluation (Boyd et al., 2001, 2007) was a series of workshops where community and voluntary groups worked together to identify how to continue to build evaluation capability in the sector. We used a number of different facilitation techniques to identify not only the current situation but also what needed to change and how. These were drawn together through graphic facilitation as summarised in Figure 7.8. We started by filling in the clouds on the right, identifying what the future might hold and then imagining what might be in place in three years' time. With this in mind we then looked at the obstacles and opportunities in the current situation via a force field analysis, and the strengths of the project in terms of a SWOT analysis. Following this, as the first steps to action, we considered the stakeholders via the BATWOVE mnemonic, and this in turn led to the articulation of an action plan to be implemented. By the end of each workshop all participants had clarified what they could do next and by the end of the series of workshops the team were in a position to make a number of recommendations for further change. We undertook some follow-up work a year later and were able to confirm that many of the actions had been taken, including the development of the North West Evaluation Network which continues to support evaluation capability in the sector and which has become the North West hub of the UK Evaluation Society.

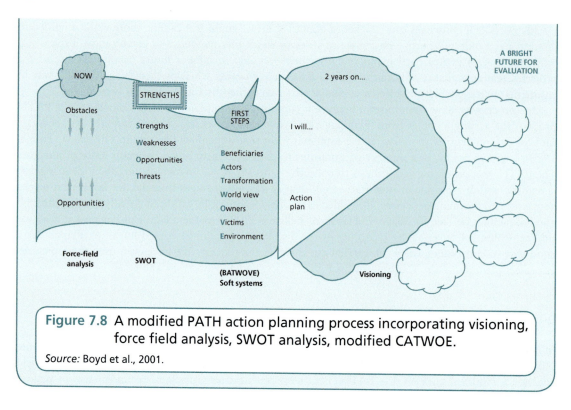

Figure 7.8 A modified PATH action planning process incorporating visioning, force field analysis, SWOT analysis, modified CATWOE.

Source: Boyd et al., 2001.

Synnot and Fitzgerald (2007) provide an excellent digest of different tools for change including many of these discussed above.

Complex decision making: polarity management

Decision making is rarely a choice between two simple alternatives. Taket and White (2000) make the important point that consensus might not always be possible; they prefer to talk of a 'system of consent', which will often lead to different people taking different courses of action in relation to future action. Another way to think about this is to see alternatives as options not to be considered separately, but to be addressed together. What at first glance seem to be contradictory options are interlinked and can sometimes both be addressed at the same time. 'Polarity management' (Johnson, 1992) is a process for recognising that seemingly opposing positions can be held at the same time and the task then is not of choosing between them, but of holding the complexity. Figure 7.9 captures the complexity of a decision making process in a community development team.

Example: Communication, change and community development

We were asked to facilitate some decision making within a community develop-ment team. The starting point was that at a time of rapid and complex change there was a problem with existing communications that led to perceived stress for staff. Team discussion highlighted: the concerns with existing communications; fea-tures of more open communications; down-sides of open communications and the strengths of existing communications. These seemingly contradictory issues were summarised in a 'polarity map'. The team moved forward recognising that closed and open systems of communication could co-exist and presented an ongoing

(A = initial situation leading to problem; B = initial solution. But C = problems arising from initial solution and thus look to D = positive aspects of initial situation, but this has problems (A) … and so on.)

+	+
Communication structure – good	Being listened to and pressures reviewed
Business planning and budget management	Knowing what goes on
Team meetings	*Explicit valuing of staff*
Censor speculation and rumours	Face to face communication
Huge amount of information received – choose what	Positive framing of issues
to pass on. Management makes decision about who	Honest about alternatives
needs to know what	Trust
Sometimes have to find out more information	Answers are clear
Scan horizon for information	It's OK to say 'we don't know'
Talk to people – 1:1 if necessary	All have access to e-mail
Some have knowledge of understanding and	Continual improvement of skills and learning
working with change	*Discussion of and support for change for all*

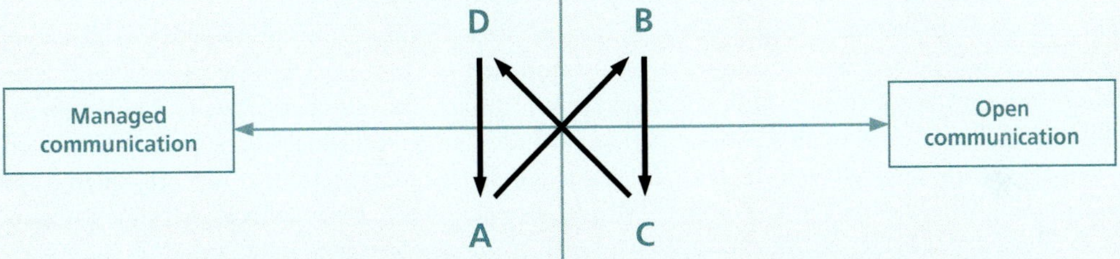

D   **B**

Managed communication ⟷ Open communication

A   **C**

–	–
Rumours abound: cuts? Loss of jobs?	People may be worried with partial information
Fear and fantasy if facts are not known	Blame culture could be damaging
Stress	Possible overload
Absence and sickness	Some people don't need to know some things
Increased mental ill health	Speculation can be divisive
Lack of communication	People may be exposed to budget vulnerability
Lack of trust	
Answers are unclear	
Information not available	
Some managers don't tell people what's going on	
Frustrating not to know	
Big picture not known	

Figure 7.9 Polarity map – moving from a managed to an open communica-tion system.

dilemma to be managed or worked with, rather than a problem to be solved. Figure 7.9 summarises the discussion in a 'polarity map'.

Quadrant A represents the initial problem about which a decision was to be made. It was described as a 'managed system of communication' as opposed to a more desirable 'open communication system'. The open communication system (Quadrant B) was seen as the system that was more desirable. However, as the discussion proceeded, the disadvantages of an open system (Quadrant C) were highlighted and in order to deal with these disadvantages, a more closed system (Quadrant D) was required. But as we had seen from the outset, this managed system had disadvantages (Quadrant A). This discussion could have resulted in the team members feeling despondent and caught in a cycle of negativity from which they could not escape. However, instead through the discussion, which then went onto sketch out the complexities of the communication context in which they were working, they saw that the advantages and disadvantages would remain of both communication systems and it was the balance between them that was the task ahead, not the choice of moving from one to the other. It was recognised that there were multiple channels of communication and vested interests in withholding and directing communications that would not always be apparent to people in different parts of the overall system.

The relationships between stakeholders, either people or groups, are not always friendly: they can sometimes be hostile and irreconcilable. All too frequently we find ourselves working in situations of collaboration and co-operation within a context of conflict and competitiveness. The business networking field has a term for this – *co-opetition* (Brandenburger & Nalebuff, 1996). Whilst competitiveness in community settings is not the same as in business settings, we are often working collaboratively with partners who compete with us, or each other, for resources, making co-operation difficult (Blickstead, Lester & Shapcott, 2008). Once all those concerned understand the limits to their co-operation in the context of competition, it is easier to proceed to work positively together.

Example: Citizen advocacy

We were working closely with a citizen advocacy project who had been asked to develop a region wide brief for citizen advocacy. It made sense for them to work on this in collaboration with other relevant projects in the region. However, each of the separate projects was a competitor for financial support from the body that had requested the work. There was reluctance on all sides to work openly together (a) in case another project stole ideas from them; or (b) preparing a regional brief undermined their individual case for further financial support. It was several months before a joint project idea was developed and even then not all the relevant parent projects were a part of the consortium.

During the planning stages, additional priorities and issues can emerge that have not been thought about previously, and planning can be part of further 'problem identification'. It is sometimes through planning that different stakeholders come together for the first time, and it is useful to have some means of jointly exploring options. We can see, therefore, that planning can itself become an intervention and lead to change as people begin to share perspectives and identify priorities.

Reflect!

It should be clear that collaboration and participation are key ideas for working in community psychology. The case examples demonstrate some of the difficulty in working in this way. Think of times when you had to work collaboratively – for paid work, academic projects or in voluntary settings. How did you make decisions about what to do, who with and how to do it? Were there any problems during the collaboration? How did you approach the task – competitively, choosing a single course of action? What can you learn about yourself from these situations?

There are a number of different, large systems planning processes in widespread use now, not just in the social development field, but also in what has been called deliberative decision making about issues such as public science and technology policy, health service priorities and so on (see INVOLVE, www. invo.org.uk). Sometimes it appears that these processes are little more than a cynical attempt to preempt opposition to decisions that have already been made by politicians or policy makers. Indeed, Cooke and Kothari (2001) titled a critical collection of reflections on participation in social development projects, the 'tyranny of participation'.

Example: Participation in town and district development

We were involved with a number of town and district centre redevelopment programmes. Our role was to develop a framework for centre managers to assess their progress in involving local people in participating in decision making over the changes. The project researcher attended one public meeting on a Friday night where some 60 people, citizens of the town, had turned up. The Chair opened the meeting by saying there were 24 things they had not come to discuss and proceeded to list them. On several occasions if a member of the public spoke, he foreclosed on their issues by saying, "no, we're not here to discuss that". By the end of the meeting there were a lot of disaffected people. When asked how he thought the meeting went by the researcher, the Chair said "Just great. The point of these meetings is that you start by knowing what you want to do and you manage the meeting so they agree with you."

At other times, though, there seems a genuine concern to introduce change that is grounded in the grass roots, and for participation to be authentic. In England, each local administration or council is required to have a community engagement strategy. Salford City Council, on the edge of Manchester, has a fully developed community engagement strategy which is comprehensive and thoughtful, not pushing any particular form of engagement, but reflecting upon the pros and cons of different types of engagement. The strategy distinguishes four different types of engagement, used for different purposes, namely devolved responsibility, information giving, community consultation and community involvement (see also Chapter 5). The different activities that address each type of engagement are:

- Devolved responsibility: development trusts, participatory budgeting.
- Information giving: broadcast media; events; e-consultation; printed media.
- Community consultation: appreciative inquiry; broadcast media; citizen's jury; citizens'/user/community panels; events; e-consultation; focus groups; future search; interviews; mystery shopper; open space; overview and scrutiny; participatory appraisal; Planning for Real; public meetings; questionnaires; World Café.
- Community involvement: arts based involvement; citizen's jury; citizens'/user/community panels; development trusts; events – meals, fun days; focus groups; Planning for Real.

In the UK – outside of community psychology – there are some interesting examples of large systems participatory work (Taket & White, 2000; Burns 2007; NEF, 1998). From systems perspectives, Jackson (2003) and Taket and White (2000) give good summaries and guidance about implementation of large group methods and it is certainly worth following these up if your work includes this scale of activity. Even if it does not, the techniques can be adapted successfully.

Think!

Look up any one of the techniques for large systems work identified above. How might you use these or encourage others to use these in your work? What dilemmas might you face in trying to implement a large group process and how do cultural traditions influence them?

In this chapter we have considered planning for action, in particular processes of participative decision making for change. The next three chapters will consider action itself.

Chapter 8

Action 1: Furtherance of critical consciousness and creation of new forms of social settings

Summary

The issue framing and action planning stages, discussed in the previous two chapters, are both action oriented – they involve doing things with people, and may even constitute interventions in their own right. In this chapter we will outline the 'action' stage of action research and will consider both ameliorative and transformative change. We will introduce two strategies for change (the furtherance of critical consciousness and the creation of alternative social settings). We will follow this by considering four more strategies for change in the next two chapters.

Action for change

Action in critical community psychology is inextricably linked to change: change in the direction of a more just society that betters the life opportunities and experiences with and of those oppressed and marginalised. Given that marginalisation is a product of structural forces, unequal distribution of resources and inequitable exertion of social power, this kind of change cannot be achieved without social transformation. Thus, the ultimate goal of critical community psychology action, often in the form of intervention, is social transformation.

Reflect!

Consider an aspect of **your** community or locality that requires change to promote social justice for a particular marginalised group. What actions could be taken to try to achieve this change? What could you do to make this happen? How easy would you find this? How would these changes influence wider social processes (or not)?

Act!

Nelson and Prilleltensky (2005, p. 144) distinguish between ameliorative and transformative interventions:

> Ameliorative interventions are those that aim to promote well-being. Transformative interventions, while also concerned with the promotion of well-being, focus on changing power relationships and striving to eliminate oppression. ... First order change, amelioration, creates change within a system, while second order change, transformation, strives to change the system and its assumptions. ... Ameliorative interventions tend to frame issues as problems and as technical matters that can be resolved through rational-empirical problem solving ... Transformative interventions, on the other hand, frame issues in terms of oppression and inequities in power and emphasise strengths of people rather than their deficiencies. Whilst research and problem-solving are used to address the issue, the overall focus is on liberation from oppression ...

Nelson and Prilleltensky suggest that, to date, most community psychology action is ameliorative. Whilst ameliorative action is not a bad thing – after all it can make a situation better – they argue for a greater emphasis on transformative action in order to promote social justice. Transformative action tackles the root causes of social problems and as such is consistent with critical community psychology's emphasis on prevention and lasting, sustainable change.

Think!

Using your previous examples of actions to achieve change for a particular marginalised group, try to decide whether these are ameliorative or transformative. How might ameliorative changes become transformative ones?

Change needs to involve those people affected by an issue and will also often involve those with vested interests in ensuring that nothing does change. This is not to promote an abdication of responsibility or of specialist knowledge on the part of critical community psychologists. Instead our concern is with the way in which the expertise of critical community psychology is deployed. Our position is elegantly summarised by Freitas (1994) who distinguishes four 'community practices' in terms of their theory of determination of the phenomena studied (horizontal axis), and the degree of specificity in the disciplinary contribution – by psychologists (vertical axis) (see Figure 8.1).

Practice 3 corresponds to critical community psychology. It is a position that combines the specificity of psychological practice, and the belief in socio-historical determination of social phenomena

Figure 8.1 Four community practices.

Source: from Freitas (1994), our translation, reproduced with permission of Universidad de Guadalajara Editores.

(see Durkheim (1894/1982, p. 129) who said *"Whenever a social phenomenon is explained directly in terms of a psychological phenomenon, you can be certain that the explanation is false"*). It involves setting out to demystify or de-ideologise difficulties faced by people that they take for granted and explain psychologically. It employs both the use of psychological techniques already existing in psychology and the creation of new ones in a joint process of participation with the population concerned.

If change is to be more than local then networks and links must be developed, not only as a means of increasing resources for change but as a means of extending the reach and impact of change. Change must be multi-level and combine the resources of those affected by the change and external agents with particular knowledge and expertise. This means the *co-creation of consciousness and change* which is achieved through a process of reflection–action–reflection–action–reflection on the part of both internal and external participants.

Strategies of critical community psychological action

Our stance, then, is that action research (participative where possible) constitutes social action, and that this action can be best understood in terms of different strategies, each focusing on a specific aspect of change. Within each of these strategies a mind-set of 'giving psychology away' is embedded, which means sharing knowledge, making practices and concepts accessible, being receptive to the knowledge of others, and working in partnership with marginalised people and other change agents wherever possible. Whilst psychological expertise is not denied, it is seen as only one kind of expertise to be combined with that of other disciplines or professions and a range of life experiences – all equally valuable. Action takes place through a collaborative and joint process of mutual learning and development; and learning takes place through action. This means that it is not possible to learn (about) community psychology or social change without trying to enact it. Thus, in the context of formal learning, community based learning (CBL) and service learning are the best vehicles for introducing community psychology.

Reflect!

Service learning and community based learning are frequently included in critical community psychological training. If you have taken part in either service or community based learning, what did you learn that you could not have learned in other ways? If you have not taken part in these forms of learning, think of any topic you have learned about recently and consider what else you might have learned if the learning setting was service or community based learning.

The action strategies are interrelated and, in practice an intervention may include elements of more than one. The strategies are summarised in Table 8.1.

Furtherance of critical consciousness (conscientisation)

As Moane (2009, p. 140) notes, "a key process in liberation is the development of consciousness, which includes a social analysis of the systemic nature of oppression and a capacity for action". The term 'conscientisation', emerged from the work of Freire (for example 1972a, 1972b; Freire & Faundez, 1989) and embraces a continual process wherein awareness and action are inseparable:

Table 8.1 Strategies of critical community psychology action

Strategy	Focus of change
Furtherance of critical consciousness	people's knowledge, understanding, beliefs, critical reflection on their worlds and experiences and political awareness
Creation of new forms of social relations (or new social settings)	new ways of bringing people together that disrupt the 'natural' way of doing things and creatively devise new activities and opportunities that give insights into possibilities for wider change
Development of alliances and counter systems	expanding and maximising the resources for change and for spreading change beyond the local issue and context, and for building a counter system that can be a part of wider emancipatory social movements
Accompaniment and advocacy	solidarity and representations of and exposure of oppression through direct observation and experience, and via both direct and indirect advocacy
Working with archives and big data	challenging hegemonic views and sources of power that are embedded in the social fabric
Policy intervention	development, implementation and analysis of policies which expose processes of oppression at more macro levels and seek to promote positive alternatives

action follows from awareness and creates further action and so on. This process of gaining awareness is achieved through an educational process that differs from the more familiar, one-way, expert driven learning of traditional education. Freire argues that it is dialogue between people that leads to conscientisation for all those involved.

Conscientisation was explained by Martín-Baró (1996), as a process in which the human being is transformed through changing his or her reality, by means of an active process of dialogue in which there is a gradual decoding of the world, as people grasp the mechanisms of oppression and dehumanisation. This opens up new possibilities for action. The new knowledge of the surrounding reality leads to new self understanding about the roots of what people are at present and what they can become in the future (Burton & Kagan, 2005).

It is by different people sharing their perceptions of the world that dialogue can begin. Francescato (2000), too, argued for interventions that encourage pluralistic interpretations, and that unite different kinds of knowledge: different types of knowledge, that is, that emanate from different people, different workers and different social discourses.

Conscientisation, then, is a cyclical process grounded firmly in people's lived experiences and starting at people's own levels of consciousness and ability to take action. As critical awareness develops over time, through dialogue and reflection, people's agency increases and their potential and ability to take action for social justice is enhanced. Change is bottom up, not imposed, and emanates from the people themselves. As Moane (2009) points out, such change challenges the role of the psychologist working with people to understand the ways in which they are caught in the cycle of oppression, the structural forces that give rise to it, and how they might move to action for liberation.

Luque-Ribelles, García-Ramírez and Portillo (2009) note that oppression has both political and psychological dimensions, which co-exist and are reciprocally determined. The first dimension includes the mechanisms whereby people are prevented from accessing social privilege. This could be through direct violence, the erection of legal, economic or material barriers, socio-cultural restrictions, ethnocentrism and support for a victim blaming culture where social marginalisation is considered the responsibility of the marginalised. The psychological consequences of sustained social subjugation are the internalisation of inferiority and lack of worth and the conviction that it is the natural order of things to be denied resources and rights. Under these conditions, several processes occur:

> At the personal-psychological level, people are likely to develop a fatalistic attitude towards life and experience feelings of anxiety, depression and anger. At the relational level, people may become less responsive to the needs of others and favor conflict resolution through violence. Finally, at the community level, it is common to find litter, vandalized property, abandoned buildings, overcrowding, noise, organized crime and the presence of gangs.
>
> (Luque-Ribelles et al., 2009, p. 279)

Thus, conscientisation is a process of mobilising awareness about social reality, enabling people or groups of people to move from an uncritical acceptance of their lives to being able to envision ways in which their lives could be transformed into better living conditions. It enables them to understand different forms of oppression and to question what they have hitherto taken for granted about their own personal and social inferiority. This process is known as a dialogic process, and assumes that *"radical change can only come from consciousness developed as a result of exchange rather than imposition"* (Leonard, 1975, p. 59). Through dialogic practice, the learner assumes the role of knowing subject in dialogue with the educator, so reality is demythologised: those who had been 'submerged' in oppressive social relations begin to understand these relations and the ideology that hides them, so recasting their social role with critical awareness. It is through this process that learning takes place, and it is with greater conscientisation that action for change is possible. As an intervention for change, group conscientisation is the most effective.

The development of a critical consciousness, by which the demystification of political structures and economic relations takes place, enables a group and the individuals within it to assert their own humanity and to confront dehumanisation systems (Leonard, 1975, p. 60).

Problematisation

As we have argued, above, critical awareness arises through dialogue and exchange between people. Not all social exchanges bring about conscientisation. Freire (1972a, 1972b) suggested that the key to liberatory education was dialogue between the educator and those being educated, not through the transference of knowledge from the educator to those being educated, but through dialogue – in particular through a form of dialogue that encouraged critical reflection, a process called 'problematisation'.

Problematisation sensitises, denaturalises, and establishes the cognitive and affective bases necessary to motivate changes thus inducing concrete transforming actions. In community social psychology to problematise is to generate situations in which the people involved are forced to review their actions and opinions about daily life events considered not only as ordinary circumstances, but also as inevitable because of their attributed essential way of being. This happens is such a way that their critical discussion leads them to being aware of the oppression, exclusion, underevaluation, or uncritical reproduction of information received which has negative effects for their daily lives. And, in so doing they also examine the relation between that knowledge and other temporally and spatially contextualised possibilities for living and knowing, and their possible transformation. (Montero, 2009, p. 80).

There is no one method of problematisation, although there are some principles to be followed by problematising agents (in our case, critical community psychologists) who seek to expose socialised beliefs and broaden understanding. This is a two way process, not one of the external agent instructing others about social reality, but one of engaging in a process of mutual discovery. Montero (2009) summarises the principles of problematisation as follows:

1 Listening. It is through listening that the socialisation and naturalisation processes underpinning people's views and opinions can be exposed, and challenged, thereby creating the conditions for problematisation and furthering critical awareness.
2 Dialogue. Listening is not enough. A dialogic relationship that is fully inclusive, supported by an ethical stance of respect for difference, is needed.
3 Inclusion. Conversation should be pitched in ways that can be understood, not using jargon or forms of speech that confirm people's inferiority. Care should be taken to clarify understanding of technical terms and to use examples to illustrate abstract and new ideas. Dialogue can take symbolic forms, and creative methods – beyond verbal methods – of enabling people to express ideas will sometimes be useful.
4 Communication. The dialogic exchange should be two way and opportunities made for disagreements, discussion, questions and so on. All those involved must be open to new ideas and ordinary features of conversations should be encouraged, such as curiosity, humour, creativity and emotion. Thus, it is essential that the external agent participates, not as expert, but as an equal, willing to share and be open about her own life experiences, thoughts and beliefs.
5 Humility and respect. As this is an exchange, no one is superior to any other and mutual respect for difference should underpin the relationships.
6 Critique. Critical analysis is fundamental to the process of problematisation and it is through this that participants can be encouraged to question their own beliefs and opinions. It is important that the critiques are not destructive or close down enthusiasm for debate, for it should arise from questioning and debate.
7 Concrete situations. Dialogue should refer to specific, concrete situations. Problematisation is grounded in real-life experiences of different situations and the sense people make of them.
8 Reflexive. Problematisation has a reflexive character, as its main function is to generate critical examination of actions or situations.

In community groups (or similar spaces) where a review of work often prompts the question "what have we learnt today?", Montero advocates that this is turned on its head. The learning is transformed into teaching – "what have you taught someone today?" This can prompt a consideration of how knowledge has been transferred and that everyone has knowledge to bring. Sometimes a shared conscientisation arises from joint action and working together.

> ## Example: Constructions of disability
>
> We have been involved for a number of years in a project, working in Malaysia and the UK around constructions of disability, which aims to uncover thinking and practices around disability using local knowledge. Involving field work in each country and working with local experts we are starting to uncover very different understandings of disability. In a rural setting in Borneo, researchers stayed with a local family and were told that "no-one was disabled here". A visit to a school and coming across a disabled entrepreneur who had set up a business in the community suggested that disability was not seen as a problem in the same ways – it was invisible in certain contexts. Working with a UK parent activist organisation, we see that disability labels can be and are used for advocacy purposes around services (Goodley & Lawthom, 2011). The meaning of using very diagnostic and clinical labels has been discussed with the Malaysian team.

In this example, critical consciousness is shifting across the team.

Montero and Montenegro (2006, p. 259) note:

> So critique, or what is considered 'critical', aims to make uncomfortable that which is considered adequate and natural. Its function is not to generate patterns of action or social categorization. It does not canonize modes of acting nor does it produce norms. In this sense it does not generate that calming sensation of security for us that comes from believing that we have, finally, produced *The Knowledge*. Such a thing can lead us to naturalize modes of doing, with which our critique would have been a new form of essentializing a specific form of knowing.

In shifting away from essential forms of knowledge we can start to share and shift consciousness.

Reflect!

Do you think you have the necessary skills listed as being needed for facilitating conscientisation? In what ways could you further develop these skills?

As we have seen, dialogue is a key component of conscientisation and some learning processes depend on this entirely. Close to Manchester, David McNulty (2005) pioneered neighbourhood learning groups which followed Freirean principles and processes. People in neighbourhoods were brought together to share their life experiences, discuss and learn about themselves in the context of the wider system – government, social policy, public services and so on. As McNulty describes in a newspaper interview (Guardian, 2004):

> This is about starting a dialogue to enable people to tell and retell their stories as the basis for empowering themselves, both through a better understanding of their lives and world and through enhanced skills and capability.

Any process that relies heavily on dialogue and discussion has the potential to build conscientisation. Thus, popular education, community philosophy (Tiffany, 2009), community or adult education, and, in the UK, youth work can all serve conscientisation functions (Crowther, Martin & Shaw, 1999).

These processes all lead to personal and group development: in and of itself conscientisation does not lead to wider change unless, through the process, people gain a sense of collective understanding of sources of oppression, and the knowledge and confidence to go on and take further action.

The neighbourhood learning project outlined above enabled people to go on to take new roles, challenge those in authority and engaging in advocacy for themselves and others living locally. It is through the knowledge, and confidence gained through the learning process that action is possible. In our own work we have seen that one of the most important bridges between conscientisation and action is hope (Kagan & Lewis, 1995).

Example: Collective action by parents of disabled children

The Federation of Local Supported Living Groups is an umbrella organisation formed in the 1990s to support local family members living in the North West of England to plan and design new, innovative and appropriate supports for their learning disabled sons and daughters living at home. It arose from groups of parents getting together, sharing life experiences, engaging in facilitated dialogue through various workshops and getting to understand more about how the system worked to keep them in a state of despair about the future (Riley, 1998). The collective awareness about sources of disempowerment and the potential for change led to raising levels of hope, which then underpinned collective action for change. The federation experimented with models of supported living for people with learning difficulties (creating new social settings) which have now become mainstream.

Hope is fundamental to conscientisation and to change. Indeed, Freire too explored the role of hope and considered that a central task for the progressive educator was to *"unveil opportunities for hope, no matter what the obstacles may be"* (Freire, 1994, p. 9) in recognition of its importance for empowerment.

Experiential learning

Sometimes, it is difficult for people to put their experiences into words and dialogue is not enough. There are other techniques of active, experiential learning that are useful to consider, that build on different kinds of experiences and use a variety of different media for exploration in addition to words. Experiential learning has its roots in different traditions, including those of action research (after Lewin – see Johnson & Johnson, 1996), humanistic development (after Rogers, 1969), organisational change (after Kolb, 1984; Argyris & Schön, 1996) and adult learning (re: the theories of androgogy see Knowles, 1980) and situated learning (Lave & Wenger, 1990). Experiential learning is learning from experience: this could be the experience derived from participation in everyday life; learning from an immediate and relevant setting through which specific problems are directly encountered (such as on a professional placement as part of a course); or learning from structured learning experiences designed to create new experiences and to lead to changes in knowledge and beliefs, behaviour, attitudes and feelings, informed by theoretical frameworks. Weil and McGill (1989, p. 3) describe four 'villages' of experiential learning:

1. *Village One* is concerned particularly with assessing and accrediting learning from life and work experience as the basis for creating new routes into higher education, employment and training opportunities, and professional bodies.

2. *Village Two* focuses on experiential learning as the basis for bringing about change in the structures, purposes and curricula of post-secondary education.
3. *Village Three* emphasises experiential learning as the basis for group consciousness raising, community action and social change.
4. *Village Four* is concerned with personal growth and development and experiential learning approaches that increase self awareness and group effectiveness.

When we use experiential learning in critical community psychology we may want to visit all the villages, but it is the last two that connect most closely with conscientisation.

Reflect!

Think back to your own experiences of education and of learning. How much was built on your own experiences? Which parts challenged the way you thought about the world? What knock on effects did this kind of education have on the rest of your life? If you have experienced any form of education where you were a passive recipient of information drummed into you by an 'expert', how did this make you feel? What knock on effects did this kind of learning have on the rest of your life?

There are a number of common features of different models of experiential learning. These include:

- a degree of self initiation by learners;
- learners having theories of action which can be changed;
- learners being motivated to learn;
- learning being most effective when undertaken in groups and social interaction being a key process;
- novices being able to learn from those with greater experience;
- learners learning best when the topics have immediate relevance;
- mistakes contributing to learning;
- deep involvement of participants;
- making it possible for tacit knowledge and socialisation to be challenged and made conscious;
- deeply held cultural beliefs being able to be uncovered and challenged;
- learners moving through a process of action, reflection, conceptualisation and further application of learning; and
- learning being a combination of experience and conceptualisation of that experience.

Structured experiential learning (Village 3) requires facilitators to design learning experiences for a group of people, recognising that learning can take place through any of the senses – vision, hearing, movement or kinaesthetics, and touch – and that learners will vary in their preferred mode of learning. Thus, well designed sessions include a variety of methods of learning – which also helps to keep people's attention and their motivation strong. Whilst most experiential learning frameworks discuss stages of learning, these are not stages that have to be adhered to rigidly, and there can be freedom of movement between them. However, effective learning includes:

1   Experience – asking the question "what is?" This involves activity, doing something that leads to discovery. With a group the experiences could be the same for all or different. There are a number of different methods that can be used to structure experiences and these are summarised in Table 8.2. What they all have in common is enabling experience to be had, from which discussion and dialogue can be generated.

2 Sharing – asking the question "what happened and did we all experience it in the same way?" This stage allows responses to the experience to be made. Group members can share their reactions and observations within the group. This can feel risky for some group members and it is important that a safe and trusting learning environment has been created.

3 Processing – asking the question "what does it mean?" During this stage patterns from the experiences can be analysed and commonalities and differences explored. Facilitators enable questions to be asked that extend learners' thinking and insight into themselves and their social worlds. Links can also be made to theoretical ideas and learners helped to conceptualise their experiences.

4 Generalising – asking the question "so what?" This enables links to the wider world to be made and the reality or limitations of the structured experience to be discussed. In addition, the implications of the learning for personal experience can be explored.

5 Applying – asking the question "what now?" If learning is to contribute to social change, it is important it does not stay in the learning session. The group can identify plans for the future, what is to be done with the knowledge or insight they have gained. The possibility of specific action or further learning can be considered.

Figure 8.2 illustrates the circular nature of experiential learning.

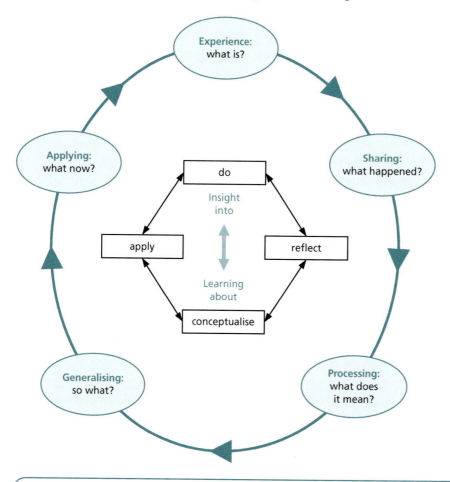

Figure 8.2 The circle of experiential learning.

The methods that can be used for experiential learning are as varied as your imagination. They can include word based activities such as panel discussions or debates, and these work particularly powerfully if participants are invited to adopt a position other than their own natural position in discussion. Other techniques cluster around spending time in different places; role plays, games and simulations; problem solving; physical activity; creative activity; and large group events such as World Café processes. There is not space here to go into these in detail, but resources are given at the end of this Part 2 of our book for you to follow some of these up. Table 8.2 summarises the different activities we have used successfully in different contexts.

There are skills involved in designing and facilitating learning experiences, in the techniques you can use to promote dialogue and discussion. Nevertheless, it is always important to plan carefully and to have a theory of why the particular experience you are creating should lead to learning. It is also important to leave plenty of time for discussion – you cannot expect learning to just happen without giving people the opportunity to process their experiences. Key to all these methods are processes of dialogue, interaction and reflection (Moon, 2004). In community settings it is often possible – and usually desirable – to harness the wide range of expertise through experience that will be present in any group, and to build on pre-existing knowledge of people from a variety of situations. The experience and the discussion are not, however, enough and help is sometimes needed for participants to see how their learning can lead to action.

Act!

Design a one-day development workshop about a particular community issue (such as stigma, social exclusion, race relations, crime). What are the objectives of the workshop? Decide who the participants will be and how many might attend. What information and activities will you put into the workshop? What opportunities for building on past experience and for collective activity will there be? What beliefs might be challenged? How will you challenge them? How will you make sure the day ends on a positive note for participants?

'Capacitation'

Taking action also requires capability and closely linked to conscientisation and problematisation is the process of 'capacitation' (translated imperfectly from the Portuguese and often wrongly interpreted in the English language literature as training – see Burton, 2009b). 'Capacitation' was promoted by Clodomir Santos de Morais (who for a while shared a prison cell with Paulo Freire), a social activist involved with workers' organisations and peasant land reclamation movements (Carmen & Sobrado, 2000). The ability to earn a living through effective operation in the economic sphere was, for Morais, an essential aspect of empowerment. Carmen (2000, p. 48) describes the roots of the concept of capacitation:

> ...the theoretical roots for 'capacitation' can be traced to the Russian School of Social Psychology in the 1930s, i.e. Leont'ev, Luria, Vygotsky's concept of active subjects whose knowledge of the pre-existing material reality is founded on their interactions with it.

'Capacitation' is more than training. It is the learning that comes from engagement in productive activity, or enterprise. This very activity 'teaches' participants to become organisationally and entrepreneurially literate, and to be able to make use of opportunities that arise for community (not just self-interested) change. Resources are pooled for collective use (not individual ownership), and

Table 8.2 Examples of experiential learning techniques

Technique	Example
Spending time in different places: e.g. going on trips, visits to other places, or projects, shadowing or mentoring relationships.	Residents who were thinking of forming into a new residents' association visited other associations in similar areas to experience, discuss and consider how this linked to their own situations.
Discussion: panel discussions and debates.	We held a panel discussion about the role of regeneration professionals and the empowerment of residents. Each panel member (including a resident) gave a short talk reflecting a unique position and there then followed a lot of audience involvement (again involving residents). Variations of this have included making available Twitter comments posted on a large screen, in real time, from both within the room and outside the event. Panel members were then able to address the comments (in real time) as they emerged.
Creative activities: painting, sewing, arts and crafts activities.	We held a large community participation event wherein groups were invited to make collages of pictures from old magazines to capture their hopes for the future of the area. These were then discussed and reflected upon in terms of what was missing and what needed to be done next.
Role play, games and simulations. These can include spontaneous role plays or scripted ones; active games, computer games, board or card games, large commercial or locally invented simulations experimenting with different future scenarios or re-enacting past scenarios. There are many handbooks that guide facilitators in how to design and run sessions (for example, Aldrich, 2005; Brandes & Norris, 1998).	When the Human Rights Act was introduced into national legislation it was important the citizen advocates and their partners with learning difficulties understood its main features. We worked with an advocacy organisation to invent a game that involved a bit of role playing and a lot of fun so that different possibilities of the Act could be explored. On other occasions we have adapted well known board games in order to explore, for example, person centred planning in the context of people with learning difficulties; urban regeneration and community cohesion; poverty; and life opportunities.

continued

Technique	Example
Drama and performance. This can vary from static or 'living' sculpts, where participants use their bodies to form shapes or images of the matter under consideration, to improvised or scripted sketches. There are lots of examples of performance being used as tool for conscientisation, particularly in the work of Augusto Boal (1995).	On working with a group of students on poverty in the UK we created a class 'sculpt'. All those students who wanted to took part and formed a collective image, bit by bit, of different social institutions and their connections with each other. It became clear to students where hegemonic power lay and those who represented unemployed people, migrants, people living in poverty were invisible to the main nexus of power.
Media activities leading to specific products e.g. film making, radio programme production, magazine production, creative writing anthology; song writing.	Film making was the main vehicle used on one part of a complex project about the experience of migration. Recent migrants to the UK got together, learnt film making techniques and made a quasi-documentary about their lives in the UK. The processes of discussion and decision making as well as the end film contributed to greater political awareness and action.

Source: reproduced by permission of Manchester Metropolitan University.

through shared learning, understanding grows and the tendencies towards individualism and self sufficiency are minimised. People do not become the possessors of skills, they become active learners in change. Kagan (2002) points out that whereas conventional training works to try to ensure errors are not made, in 'capacitation' it is through struggling to make something work and making mistakes that learning takes place. There are three central strands to this enterprise learning: (i) learning from the collective activity of developing an enterprise, (ii) large group learning about organisational theory, and local business contexts (regulations, formal requirements and so on) and (iii) involvement in and understanding of inter-group and intra-group communication. The large group learning format encourages linking with other groups of people who have similar experiences.

Unlike some other enterprise development processes, 'capacitation' is not imposed by outside experts, but learnt by insiders. Local, 'lay' people can become facilitators of the learning process: the process is not one of individualised self help, but rather collective growth. The 'organization workshop' is one such vehicle for facilitating 'capacitation' (Carmen & Sobrado, 2000; Labra, 2001). Capacitation involves local participation and shared commitment to change. It implies an investment in human capital, not just in knowledge and skills but also in the social relations and social supports necessary for the realisation of the benefit from training and education. The important point to make here is that 'capacitation' is not a property of an individual (as skill might be), but is a property of the individual within a social context – elsewhere we have referred to this as social capability (Burton & Kagan, 1995). The nearest term in popular usage in community development work is capacity building: even this, though, will often refer to an individual's ability to do something. Capacitation is a form of situated learning (Lave & Wenger, 1990).

> ## Example: Organisation workshop
>
> The first example in the UK of introducing a 'capacitation' approach to community and enterprise development was in Marsh Farm, a social housing estate near Luton (Imagine, 2016). In 2007, a group of community activists prepared the ground and initiated an 'organisational workshop' – or OW – facilitated by an experienced Latin American OW facilitator, Ivan Labra from Terra Integra. After a great deal of difficulty and Government interference (possibly due to the way the media responded to the initiative as a radical, subversive initiative (Topping, 2008)), funding was obtained and permission given to run the full workshop in 2014/15. Forty-five people participated (250 people had expressed interest in 2008 but this momentum could not be maintained over such a long time), and after two years 77 per cent of them were either in work or in the process of establishing a new enterprise. As we write another group, Heart of Hastings Community Land Trust, in another part of the country, is also planning an organisational workshop, having learnt from Marsh Farm the power of collective enterprise development (one of the trustees was responsible for one of the early grants to Marsh Farm, and one of the community leaders from Marsh Farm is involved in the Hastings project). (https://d3n8a8pro7vhmx.cloudfront.net/hohclt/pages/1269/attachments/original/1542979203/OW_Flyer.pdf?1542979203).

Think!

See if you can find definitions of some of the key terms we have used here so that you can clarify the differences between them. Define:

conscientisation; problematisation; empowerment; learning; training; personal development; capacitation; capacity building.

Deideologisation

The collective and challenging processes of problematisation, conscientisation and capacitation share not only an emphasis on active involvement and building on the material realities of people's existence but also the function of 'deideologising' (Montero, 1994). Deideologisation is the process through which firmly held, ideologically constructed beliefs are challenged, questioned and understood. Many of these beliefs are deeply ingrained and have come to be thought of as natural – 'how the world is'. Montero, again, puts it thus:

> Deideologisation consists of rejecting the hegemony of certain ideas justifying and naturalising forms of social oppression, by showing how certain interpretations and senses, socially constructed and taught, operate in people's daily life.
>
> (Montero, 2009, pp. 78–79)

Reflect!

Think back to your own experiences of education and of learning. How much was built on your own experiences? Which parts challenged the way you thought about the world? What knock on effects did this kind of education have on the rest of your life? If you have experienced any form of education where you were a passive recipient of information drummed into you by an 'expert', how did this make you feel?

Through all of these processes people begin to change their beliefs and understand some of the forces that have constructed them in the first place. This is, perhaps a familiar process in feminist consciousness raising, but also applies to other walks of life. Those beliefs that have hitherto immobilised – perhaps imprisoned – people in their social circumstance begin to be challenged and they are liberated for action. Whilst this action could be individual action for change, the very collective nature of the action methods discussed above make collective action more likely.

A change in beliefs and understanding underpins critical community psychological approaches to collective trauma due, for example to displacement, war, genocide, slavery or colonialism. The recovery of historical and cultural memory goes beyond deideologisation to enable the recuperation of collective identity and, in some cases, resistance to social oblivion and fight against impunity (Vidales, 2014). There is a danger of considering trauma as individual pathology, rendering people as autonomous victims to be assisted through individual therapy. Instead, methods such as those outlined above, broadly analectic (see Montero, Sonn & Burton, 2016, for more examples of analectic methods) position people as agentic, connected, and highlight the importance of both affirmation and collective processes of recovering historical and cultural memories – enabling groups to collectively reject hegemonic representations of them and their pasts. It is important to recognise that what we hegemonically consider to be traumatising may not always be so, and collective processes of memory restoration help to challenge this.

Example: Anti-hegemonic view of trauma

Meari (2015) draws on her work collecting accounts from Palestinian political captives who had experienced interrogation and torture. She challenges the idea of psychiatric and human rights conceptions of trauma, instead introducing the discourse of sumud. Sumud is

> a Palestinian anticolonial construct promoted by Palestinians living under the colonial order, which constantly subjects Palestinians to arrest, interrogation and torture. The discourse of sumud is the praxis of struggle wherein the subject can be a victim and resisting hero [p. 76]. ... Sumud embodies a radical alterity to the conceptions, sensibilities, attachments and practices of humanitarian psychiatry. Sumud is the refusal to confess or reveal secrets to interrogators despite the cruelty of the physical and psychological torture employed by the interrogators. In an enactment of sumud, the Palestinian voluntarily endures the suffering of the continual torture to protect the secrets regarding the self, the comrades, and the revolutionary organization [p. 77].

This particular discourse could be seen to underplay the impact of trauma. Meari anticipates this and says

> I suggest that a dismissal of the critique I offer here as irresponsible arises from an assumption that psychological–human rights-oriented work is the only imaginable and legitimate way of enacting political and human emancipation. The hegemonic liberal gaze of psychological–human rights work inordinately dwells on the 'oppressed' and their redemption from oppression [p. 78].

The alternative is to dwell on the collective and on resistance.

Reflect!

How did you feel when you read the above example? If you felt uncomfortable, why do you think this is? If it felt familiar to you, why do you think that was? Can you think of any examples from your own life where other people look at you as an individual but you feel more a part of a wider group or community? What is that group or community and where did these feelings of identity come from?

Think!

It is one thing to work with conscientisation and deideologisation with those who have little social or economic power. What do you think the advantages of working on these processes with the powerful might be? List the pros and cons of doing this. How would this change the nature of critical community psychology?

Systematisation of experiences

The systematisation of experiences emerged in Latin America, initially as a part of the development of social work, then linked closely to Freirean critical pedagogy and community learning, and liberation theology, but now extended to other places and other interventions (Falkembach & Torres, 2015; Streck & Jara, 2015). It is used in part for learning from an intervention but also as a tool for furthering critical consciousness, leading to new actions. The idea is that the recording, recuperation and sharing of people's different interpretations of common experiences leads to new insights (rather like the idea of "the whole is greater than the sum of the parts") and new ways of understanding and theorising about the world – all based on concrete actions and experiences. At an organisational level, systematisation of experiences is the "process of reflection about the organisation's own accumulated historical experience, and, more specifically, the collective construction of knowledge through a critical analysis of how to achieve the proposed change" (Mantilla, 2010, p. 368). More than this, systematisation supports the production of a kind of knowledge that transforms realities, as through the process it contributes to the construction of social subjects, empowering and maximising the potential capabilities and capacities of those involved in the intervention.

Furthermore, it gives impetus to new knowledge, which, when shared, supports groups and organisations working for greater social justice.

We describe the process of systematising experiences more fully in Chapter 11 where we discuss evaluation and in Chapter 13 where we go into more detail about reflexivity. Systematisation of experiences can take place at any point in an action project: it can be an isolated activity after an intervention has taken place or integrated throughout. However it is to be done, systematisation requires a commitment from all involved to register, log or record experiences as they happen. These data then provide the basis for collective exploration and explanation. A historical strand is an important aspect of systematisation and if data are not recorded in real time, Mantilla (2010) argues that there is a risk that valuable information that can explain the experience might be lost. There is no one way of recording experiences, and Table 8.3 outlines some well tried methods.

Act!

Think of an area of your life – it could be studying, as aspect of working, sports, community volunteering – anything in fact. Try keeping a diary for a week focusing on this activity. How easy was it to do this? Do you think you could keep this up over a year – why or why not? What was it you included about other people in your diary and why? Has this given you any ideas about how best to record experiences in a community psychological intervention?

Usually some discussion is needed in order to agree the best forms of recording experiences and at this point, it might be useful to also introduce some discussions about ethical issues. Given that later on in the process, people will be sharing their experiences, including personal observations and recollections, recordings should be made in ways that are respectful of others.

Reflect!

What are the ethical issues in recording experiences that you will then share with others? Do the values of community psychology help you decide how and what to include? What other guidelines might help?

It is not easy to record experiences. Not everyone involved in an intervention will be used to writing and it might be necessary to include other ways of enabling people to log their experiences. Keeping video or audio diaries, drawings, or even finding ways of interviewing people throughout the intervention might help it to be inclusive. Luger and Massing (2015) remind us that it is not usually possible for everyone connected to an intervention to be involved in the systematisation. They identify three groups of participants: project managers or implementers; direct and indirect beneficiaries; other stakeholders (such as funders and other organisations linked to the intervention).

At the root of the process is the sharing of different perspectives on the same experience, so it is important that each of these groups is represented in the systematisation process, which highlights the importance of clarifying who in any project or organisation will be involved. It is generally agreed that the process of systematisation will need to be facilitated and that this is best done by those who have shared the experiences. However, Luger and Massing (2015) suggest that outside facilitators may be needed when a systematisation is undertaken for the first time.

We have overviewed the nature of a systematisation of experiences and included here some ideas about both the importance of, and methods of recording experiences throughout an intervention. More details will be given in Chapter 11 about what then to do with these experiences. Sometimes the

Table 8.3 Methods of registering experiences

Field diary	Many researchers will be familiar with the process of keeping a field diary. If this is to be used in a systematisation, it is essential that good records of actual activities – what, when, how they took place – are included, in addition to personal reflections. Other people involved in an intervention may be less familiar with keeping a diary and may need some guidance. The structured recordings of experiences below may help with this.
Daily record of individual activity	Name:_____Date:_____

What I did today	Time taken	Purpose	Who else took part	Outcomes	Observations and impressions

Team weekly record (can be agreed at a short weekly meeting at which people share their diverse perceptions)

Name of project/locality/programme

Activities developed	Date	Objectives	Who is responsible	Who participated	Outcomes

Activity record (to be completed for a particular activity either by an individual or jointly as part of team work)

Name(s):
Project/locality/programme: ...
Date:
Overview:
1. Title or type of activity:
2. Where it took place:
3. Who and how many people participated:
4. Duration:
5. Description of the activity (1 page maximum):

If the activity had been planned in advance:
1. Planned objectives:
2. Outcomes obtained:
   a. In relation to the planned objectives
   b. Unanticipated outcomes

If the activity was not planned in advance:
1. How and why was it decided to do this activity?
2. Outcomes obtained:

Impressions and observations about the activity:
Documents available about this activity (for example, designs, methods, photos, recordings, publicity, materials used etc):

Other means of recording experiences

It should be clear that in addition to notes being kept, as above, linking specific activity to the people involved and the dates on which they occurred, other records of activities, that can include visual (photos, videos, drawings etc), spoken (writings, recordings etc) and formal (minutes of meetings, workshop materials, publicity for events and so on) can and should be kept.

Source: adapted from Jara, n.d.

simple matter of recording of experiences leads to new insights, but it is the collective sharing and critical analysis of experiences that result in conscientisation, and the communicating of new knowledge and understanding that contributes to social transformation.

Example: Systematisation of experiences of an arts intervention

Daher and Haz (2011) report a systematisation of experiences conducted with women who participated in a ten-session arts project. The aim of the intervention was to deepen the personal and emotional knowledge held by the women, recognising this as an important area of their lives, and it was part of a wider intervention to increase inclusion via education and social development. The intervention and investigation of experiences took place simultaneously, with ongoing group discussions and recordings of sessions, as well as post-intervention interviews. Daher and Haz describe the sessions, which each ended with extensive group work which entailed…

> …contemplation and description of participants' artistic work and discussion about their feelings and the connection with aspects of their lives. This moment was crucial for the intervention because participants could externalize their inner world (expressed through artistic creation) and received feedback from their partners and facilitators (reflection and contention mainly). It is important to note that the intervention ended with an exhibition of the artistic work carried out by participants. … This exhibition was prepared by participants during the activity … and involved the revision of the work done during the intervention through a collective reflexion.

Critical analysis of the data followed a grounded theory method and revealed the core aspect of women's experiences as being the fact that they were women living in urban poverty. This in turn influenced all other aspects of experience. New collective understanding was gained of how the women's context influenced their levels of confidence and inclusion but also of how they were strengthened through the arts process.

Whilst this systematisation was not a fully collective and participative one, relying more than usual on the researchers' grounding of their analysis, it does give some idea of how experiences can be explored and shared.

We have seen that furthering critical consciousness is complex. To be an effective practitioner, we need to be able to employ flexible ways of learning and be able to facilitate others' learning, building on their lived experiences. At different times we need to engage in: active listening, expression and storytelling; use of metaphors and symbolic communication; creative and expressive work; group formation, development and facilitation practices; different registers of communication, encouragement and facilitative conflict management; resource procurement; and reflection. It is helpful to have a general approach that is open, with a willingness to share, to have persistence and a sense of humour, whilst also being able to challenge and support others in questioning what they take for granted.

Creation of new forms of social relations (new social settings)

One feature of an ecological perspective is to see behaviour and experience as inseparable from their context – their physical, social, organisational and wider historical context. Much community psychological work, particularly that with an Anglocentric bias, neglects the historical dimension of context and of how settings are understood (see Chapter 6 for the role that time plays in an ecological systems analysis). An understanding of social situations and settings is necessary to make sense of what others and we experience and to apply it as a strategy for change. Social settings go beyond the physical to the relational aspects of situations (the social ties between people – see Chapter 5) and the meaning they hold. This means we are not only talking about creating new physical situations but also finding new ways of people relating to each other (Sarason, 1972). Social situations, and the meanings of social situations, influence people's behaviour and experience and at the same time people create and modify social situations. We advocate considering the multi-dimensional nature of social situations, as well as the concept of behaviour settings and the meaning held by social actors of the situations of which they are a part.

Multi-dimensional nature of social situations

Argyle, Furnham and Graham (1981) draw attention to the physical features, boundaries, props, modifiers and spaces within social situations, all of which impinge upon behaviour and experience. The physical features of a setting might restrict or enable access; the internal layout of a room may inhibit or encourage interaction and so on. Boundaries are the physical enclosures of a situation and it is partly by noting and making sense of the boundary markers that we understand the purpose of the setting. Neighbourhood signs, for instance, might encourage a sense of community identity and belonging, but they also define who it is that does not belong, who are outsiders. Walls around a property or a housing estate also signify insider–outsider status (see our discussion of gated communities in Chapter 5). Props too can serve the same function. Racist or homophobic graffiti in a neighbourhood sends messages about social attitudes held within the setting. Litter left to lie on the streets and near people's houses tells us the neighbourhood (and the people who live and work in it) is uncared for and may not be a priority for the authorities. Props are temporary features of a situation, contained within a boundary, that define the purpose of a space. They also signify personal and social identities: for example, the notices and decorations of a community centre tell us something about who is welcome there. A community centre that has a notice board with lots of notices about local churches but none about local temples or mosques might suggest some people are more welcome than others. The artefacts that migrants bring and keep in their homes enable them to preserve connections across fragmented identities (Pahl, 2004).

Reflect!

Look around any room in your home – what do the things that are there say about you? Would a stranger coming into this room get a different impression from someone who knows you well? Why might this be? What kinds of things might the stranger infer about you from your room?

Modifiers are those physical features that affect the quality of a situation – noise, heat, smell, light, for example. Different participants will experience modifiers differently – some might find some smells aversive, others enervating. It is the perception and the meaning attributed to modifiers that are important.

Spaces refer to the distances between people and the meanings that are attached to them. Acceptable distances between people vary with the nature of the situation as much as with the space. For example, the same sized space might be considered crowded by five people if it were a bedroom but relatively empty if it were a meeting room. The acceptability of social distance is also culturally determined – someone from a Western culture typically feels less comfortable with touching and close physical proximity when conversing than might someone from an Arab culture.

Some aspects of the physical environment contribute to what is known as the portable environment (Burton & Kagan, 1982). Our clothes, hairstyle, type of car or bicycle, all tell onlookers something about us.

Act!

Stand in a busy place such as a shopping centre or student refectory. Watch people and decide who has what role in that place (for example as shopkeeper or shopper; student or lecturer etc.). How do you know? What aspects of their portable environment tell you something about them?

Think!

In the UK police officers wear an identifying number on their uniforms. It has been noted that in some police operations – particularly those in which protests or demonstrations are being policed – these are (illegally) removed. Why do they have them in the first place and what does it mean if they are removed? What psychological explanation might there be for police brutality when they are not wearing identification numbers?

Our portable environments convey information about our identity – about who we are and sometimes about our interests, although these signs can be misread.

The physical features of social situations can be relatively easily detected. The meanings of these situations, however, are derived from the cultural contexts in which they are embedded and from the purposes for which they are used. Sometimes the transition from one meaning to another is marked by a change in the physical features. For example, a family café might mark its transition to an adults-only bar by turning the lights down and lighting candles on the tables. A church that is now used as a Hindu temple might erect signs and notices and change the facade.

Harvey (2005b) argues that spaces are socially produced: whereas absolute space refers to bounded territories with a strong degree of permanency, relational space–time refers to the ways in which spatial meanings come through the memories and attachments we forge through relationships, but also to the sense of socially sanctioned entitlement we feel we have to occupy particular spaces.

Reflect!

Consider any area of public space – a street, park, shop, bus, for example. Have you ever been discomfited by either the presence or the behaviour of other people in this space? Why did you feel uncomfortable? What did you do about it (for example, walk on embarrassed, leave the situation)? What does this tell you about the social rules underlying this space?

Behaviour settings

Barker (1968) introduced the ecological concept of behaviour settings, in which behaviour patterns could be observed, that then defined the meaning of the setting beyond the characteristics of participants in that setting. The individuals participating in a setting are thought to be interchangeable – the behaviour is similar whoever is there. For example, the exchange that takes place in a shop between customer and seller is pretty much the same whoever the actual people are. Furthermore, the very performance of particular behaviours in the setting enables the setting to continue, and participants in a setting are expected to conform to expectations of their behaviour (or achieve behaviour–environment congruence). Thus, settings both determine and are determined by behaviour. This idea is closely linked to what Harré (1993) describes as role-rule contexts of situations: explicit or implicit cultural and subcultural expectations about how people occupying formal or informal roles (should) behave in particular situations. We manage our social situations by understanding the role-rule contexts and if we get them wrong, some kind of disruption in the interaction will occur. The more formal the setting, the clearer the role-rule contexts and the less important the characteristics of the people involved.

All social settings invite participation to greater or lesser degrees, with varying roles available for people to take within the setting. If a situation is penetrable by a wide cross section of people and serves a number of different functions, it is known as a rich setting. Settings that are difficult to penetrate are more likely to exclude people than those whose penetrability is loose. Credit unions, for example, are community finance projects in which people can save on a regular basis and apply for low interest loans. All decisions are made by members of the credit union and individual circumstances can be taken into account. The membership of a credit union is defined by what is known as the common bond between people. The common bond might be as workers in a workplace or as residents in a locality. Once the common bond is agreed, the credit union membership is open to all (fully penetrable). However, it is not open to people who do not share that common bond. A credit union is not a particularly rich setting as there are a limited number of roles and functions. Increasing the penetrability, and the richness of a setting might be a strategy for community action.

Example: Inclusion in community associations

One of our students worked with a residents' association in an inner city district which was home to a very mixed population including sex workers and drug users. He noticed that membership of the residents' group was broad but that sex workers and drug users were seen as problems for the area. The group was not open to them. He worked tirelessly to try to include some sex workers and drug users in the work of the residents' group but met with a lot of resistance from existing members of the group. This setting was difficult to penetrate. Another student, however, worked with a victim support project (supporting victims of crime) in a multicultural part of the city. She noticed very few people from ethnic minority communities making use of the project and raised this as a concern with the management committee. With their support she developed a culturally sensitive extension service and successfully enabled many more people from the local community to penetrate the setting. It could also be said she had created a new social setting.

These different aspects of social situations and settings can be taken into account when creating new social settings for change. Sarason (1974, p. 269) defines social settings broadly:

By a new social setting I mean any instance in which two or more people come together in new and sustained relationships to attain stated objectives.

Traditionally, the impetus of new social settings has come from professionals who seek to do things differently. However, participation need not only be in the setting itself – it can and should involve a wide range of people (especially those who might benefit from the creation of an alternative, new social setting). We call this the co-production of new social settings, borrowing from work on co-production of both services and knowledge (Durose & Richardson, 2015; Filipe et al., 2017; Pearce, 2010).

Reflect!

Do you think you have ever been a part of a new social setting? How would this differ from simply getting to know new people?

New or alternative social settings

The creation of a new social setting, then, involves bringing people together in ways that are new, sometimes outside the existing social order. New service developments or projects could be considered new social settings. They can also be transformations within existing services, the creation of non-service forms of association such as residents' groups or self help groups, the use of existing settings for different purposes, the transplantation of ways of relating from one physical setting to another; or they can be a completely new entity.

The inclusivity of the victim support example given above is an example of a transformation of an existing service or project. Third sector organisations (the term used in the UK to include community groups, voluntary organisations or NGOs and charities) will usually have started out as a new social setting – people getting together to create a new activity, often in relation to social marginalisation. For example, all the local supported living groups that are affiliated with the Federation of Local Supported Living Groups, discussed above, are new social settings, designing and implementing new ways of supporting disabled people to live independently.

The replication of a successful project but in a different physical location is another example of the creation of a new setting, such as the replication of a successful community intervention in another place.

The use of a familiar setting for a new purpose, thus creating a new setting in which people came together in new ways, was described by Chatterjee and Camic (2015). They reported an innovation wherein a well known national art gallery became the place in which mental health workers and art therapists worked with carers of people with long term serious mental health difficulties. Walker, Hart and Hanna (2017) suggest that a considerable amount of invaluable mental distress work is undertaken in spaces in our communities that are not understood as mental health venues or treatments. Ordinary spaces and activities, from fishing to cycling, to meeting in community centres are enriched by the function they serve in supporting people living with mental distress and preventing its escalation. As they say:

> Informal spaces, community groups and actions of people who weren't mental health professionals repeatedly revealed themselves to be fundamentally important to people's recovery.
>
> (Walker, Hart & Hanna, 2017, p. 44)

Many of these ordinary places will be what Oldenburg (1989, 2001) calls 'third places'. They are not home (first place) or work (second place), but public space where people can mix and interact. Oldenburg (1997) summarises the features of 'third places':

- are local-valued and within walking distance of those they serve;
- unify neighbourhoods – are open to all;
- provide a point of entry for those new to a neighbourhood – are welcoming;
- act as sorting areas where like-minded people can be introduced or find each other and people can encounter a range of different other people;
- can bring older and younger people and different social classes together;
- help care for the neighbourhood and act as gathering spaces;
- foster political debate;
- are sites of support and mutual aid;
- are entertaining through the activities of those using the spaces;
- give the gift of friendship, making it possible for superficial as well as deep encounters.

Third places are places for people to spend time with each other, interact, exchange ideas, build relationships and have a good time, and are essential parts of any neighbourhood infrastructure. Despite their role in underpinning the vitality of a community and in combating loneliness, in many parts of the advanced economies, 'third places' are disappearing. Libraries, leisure centres, recreation fields, district shopping streets, cinemas are all disappearing as people retreat into their homes and shop via the internet or as privately owned shopping malls place restrictions on who can or cannot enter. Increasingly, people's social lives are contracting into silos where we only meet those who live and think like us and chance encounters become increasingly rare.

Reflect!

What 'third places' do you use? Has there been a reduction in the number of 'third places' near where you live? Why is this? How might you support the increase in 'third places' in your neighbourhood?

Support for, and facilitation of, new 'third places' can be a community psychology intervention.

Example: Third places and positive mental well-being

Feeney (2019) describes a project – Tea in the Pot – which provides a safe place for women to meet in which they can enjoy the company of other women, while developing new skills if they wish. They found that attending Tea in the Pot enabled positive interaction, which in turn engendered a sense of belonging, helped alleviate feelings of loneliness and isolation and helped connect members to the wider community. Not only did individual members benefit from Tea in the Pot, it in and of itself became a non-stigmatising part of the urban infrastructure and contributed to the vitality of the neighbourhood.

Sometimes the creation of new social settings, or 'third places' puts a strain on work roles and staff are prohibited from undertaking this form of action in work time. This happens when the values of the workplace do not resonate with those of critical community psychology or chime with the idea of creating and maintaining new social settings. When they do, new social settings are often created through alliances and partnerships.

> ### Example: Active parenting project
>
> Building Bridges was a community psychology project in Liverpool. The local migrant Somali and Yemeni communities identified a problem that was putting strain on families, namely the ways in which fathers and sons related to each other. Building Bridges facilitated some meal based, narrative workshops (alternative settings) wherein older and younger men from the communities could relate to each other differently, via the medium of storytelling. By preparing and telling stories, and then discussing the implications of the stories for their lives in Liverpool, the older and younger men listened differently, and discussed differently. The narrative workshops enabled the same people to connect in new ways through the narrative process. This led to increased understanding and willingness to listen and learn more about each other's experiences. The narrative workshops were followed by other activities (the making of a film for the young Yemeni men; the production of a magazine by the young Somali men; and group discussions, meetings with different service agencies and role play activities for the two groups of older men). Each of these follow-on activities could also be described as a new social setting. (Hassan, Fatimilehin & Kagan, 2019).

Another kind of tension encountered in the creation of new settings can occur when the people involved are trying to work in different and new ways – trying to create new ways of relating to each other. Another way of thinking about this is that alternative role-rule contexts are established. The force of familiarity may make it difficult for new roles to be played.

New social settings, whilst challenging the mainstream as they begin, may become mainstream over time – they are no longer new (as in the example of The Federation of Independent Supported Living Groups, above). When this happens it can be useful to look for new opportunities to create new social settings! Many new social settings evolve, not only into the mainstream, but into further alternative social settings.

> ### Example: Intergenerational activity in schools
>
> A local intergenerational project sought to link retired persons with schools linked together in a neighbourhood. After a number of years of running successfully and learning from evaluation, the Chair of the local group resigned and formed a national umbrella organisation to support and enable the development of similar projects elsewhere. Whereas the original project was established as a small local charity, the national organisation is established as a social enterprise in the form of a community interest company (Raynes, Kagan, Varela-Raynes & Bolt, 2013).

This example illustrates the importance of understanding and working with different organisational forms. Whilst many new settings will emerge organically in an unstructured and non-incorporated form, others will need to develop some kind of organisational entity in the longer term. Social enterprises and community interest companies are popular in the UK at the time of writing, but co-operative forms of working together have a longer and probably more enduring history. There will often be choices about what kind of organisational form a new setting should take. Different organisational forms may be needed if there are clear tasks that need to be accomplished quickly from those where the tasks are less clear and there is a stronger emphasis on participation, engagement and relationships. Often, during the creation of a new social setting, advice may need to be taken on what kind of organisational form will best serve the project.

New social settings are closely linked to cultural practices. Over the last decade there has been an explosion of the creation of new settings based on internet technology or social networking. Not only have self help and interest groups proliferated, providing new opportunities for gaining a sense of community, net-based settings form an alternative basis for social support and social action (Goodings & Tucker, 2019). Whilst at first glance, these settings appear to be rich settings, and function, sometimes as 'third places' they are impenetrable to those without internet connection or the skills and experience to access them. Furthermore, Blanchard (2006) points out that what she calls 'virtual behaviour settings' interact closely with physical situations.

Example: Social capital and the internet

One of us (AS) worked with migrant women who were learning internet skills through the radically new, community based settings of 'electronic village halls', part of the emerging social and community informatics movement. The benefits to the women in terms of identity and providing the base for action, particularly in terms of advocating for greater inclusion in service provision, were substantial (Siddiquee & Kagan, 2006).

Act!

Imagine you are promoting the concept of new social settings to the mayor of your town. Design a poster or leaflet to capture the main points of new social settings and their links to social change.

Think!

What kind of spaces or places do social media and other virtual reality spaces occupy? Are contemporary ways of thinking about spaces and places adequate to explain the complexity of virtual reality? What else might be needed?

Sometimes the new social settings fail – in these circumstances it is important to learn what we can about the prevailing social forces and blocks to change – see Kagan and Burton's (2000) model of pre-figurative action research. The reasons why new settings might fail include:

- competition from traditional or mainstream settings;
- inadequate preparation with partners and allies about the core values underpinning the change process – conflict needs to be dealt with, not avoided;
- failure to include key power holders as allies to the project;
- inadequate local support base – more community engagement and support is needed;
- a pressure to complete the project before it is ready – sometimes for political, sometimes financial reasons;
- lack of resources – human, material (often property) and financial;
- weak penetrability of the setting leading to some people feeling excluded;
- attempts to establish traditional practices (albeit in a different place) rather than embrace new activities or ways of working;
- the alternative setting is premature and there are insufficient enabling conditions;
- difficulty conveying and communicating alternative ways of doing things.

Think!

What can the field of organisational development contribute to our understanding of the creation of new social settings? See if you can find some literature on organisational development that reflects the values of critical community psychology. Why might this be hard to find?

The radical nature of alternative social settings

Alternative social settings will often pioneer alternative social relations (and conversely new ways of relating will often create alternative social settings), while still located within a dominant social context which puts pressure (passive and active, implicit and explicit) on the alternative setting. Table 8.4 illustrates this with reference to some different types of social innovations, some small scale, some large scale (Burton, 2000).

Table 8.4 New social settings: new social relations in the context of dominant social forces

New social setting	New social relations attempted	Forces within dominant social context
1. LETS (Local Exchange Trading Schemes)	Alternative labour exchange relationships.	• Orthodox exchange/exploitation relations. • Non-local markets.
2. Supported living for impaired persons	Support as a right to enable inclusion in communities.	• Societal exclusion and devaluation of impaired persons.
3. Co-operative movement	Social ownership of means of distribution and production.	• Market where big capital dominates and drives down costs.
4. UK National Health Service	Health care taken out of the commodity market.	• Capitalist economic system prone to fiscal crises. • Entrenched professional interest groups. • Increased hegemony of market model.
5. Social revolutions in post colonial countries	Social ownership. Empowerment of peasants and workers (politically, and through redistribution).	• Global system of postcolonial exploitation. • Local elites with stake in exploitative relations. • Imperialist policing/superpower conflicts.

Source: Burton, 1999.

We can call these alternative social settings that challenge, 'prefigurative' (see Chapter 3 for a discussion of prefigurative action).

In any new social setting, there will two opposing processes. The prefigurative, creative, explorative, radical processes and achievements will be pitted against 'recuperative', retrogressive, traditionalist, unimaginative, conservative tendencies. The sources for the reactionary tendencies are likely to be multiple – in the external environment, and its impact on the setting itself, but also in the ideological and psychological baggage that the participants inevitably bring with them. There is never a clean break with the past.

Given the constant tension between prefigurative and reactionary tendencies in new social settings, it is not surprising that such settings are often threatened, in terms of either their existence or their ethos. It is tempting to want to defend such innovatory social settings, and often this is a precondition for the maintenance of change. Sometimes, however, it may be not be a particularly high priority to defend a new setting. Two such cases can be identified.

1   Sometimes the setting really was prefigurative, and although it is now under threat, its insights and innovations are carried on into more mainstream social relations. Short term grant aided projects sometimes have such widespread success, although they themselves are not sustained.
2   Sometimes energy would be better expended elsewhere because the prefigurative battle has already been lost in the particular setting.

In the latter case, however, the setting has not necessarily failed. New social settings engender new learning about social relations, which is not just retained in that setting, but released into the wider society (Ray, 1993) in a variety of ways including through the lived experience of those who participated, were challenged, who grew, or benefited. Sometimes that social learning is successfully stabilised in new social institutions (services, customs, laws, rights, democratic processes), and sometimes not. Yet that learning is always stored among people, and can and will be accessed later, at times and in ways that cannot be predicted. So even apparently failed social settings can, despite the degeneration of democracy, contribute to a more informed and reflexive society.

Reflect!

If you were going to initiate the creation of new social setting, what might your strengths and weaknesses be? Where might you seek assistance to help you succeed?

In creating new social settings we need to be able to work with organisations. Much of the face to face work will involve negotiation and mediation; resource maximisation; organisational development thinking and practice; and understanding of different organisational forms. We will be most effective if we are flexible, open to new learning but also able to communicate, clearly, the possibilities for change.

In this chapter we have considered action, exploring in particular detail the furtherance of critical consciousness and the creation of new forms of social settings. The next chapter will consider other aspects related to action.

Chapter 9

Action 2: Development of alliances, accompaniment and advocacy

Summary

In the previous chapter, we have seen that in furthering critical consciousness and in the creation of new social settings, linking people together with similar interests, working in groups and making links across organisations in order to secure resources for change are important. In this chapter we consider in more detail change processes founded on the development of alliances and coalitions, drawing on the ecological metaphor to consider working at the 'edge', and the nature of social movements. We then go on to consider the characteristics of accompaniment and advocacy and their place as part of social change.

Social action of one form or another underpins different processes of change. Social action is initiated through a group identifying specific obstacles that prevent non-dominant and disempowered groups from influencing or achieving social change. Removing obstacles is not easy and often the group will have to engage in constructive conflict to overcome and remove the barriers. Such conflict might be in the form of non-violent action (such as that undertaken by groups like the direct action in the disability movement, the Committee of 100 in the movement against nuclear weapons in the 1960s, and Plane Stupid in the struggle against airport expansion). The writings of Saul Alinsky (1971), a US community organiser, are still full of relevant guidance (see also Chapter 13). This form of social change tactic is often associated with radicalism and is often high profile (in terms of attracting the attention of the mass media). In this chapter we consider two further strategies for change that are also forms of social action, namely the forging of alliances, collaborations and counter systems; and accompaniment and advocacy.

Making links, the development of alliances and counter systems

> ## Think!
>
> How do you think alliances might contribute to processes of change? See if you can find some examples in the literature of how organisations have worked together for change. Can you think of examples where alliances might block change? Why might this be?

Forming alliances, and making links across groups, can be thought of in a number of different ways as part of critical community psychological work. Making links between different groups can be a way of securing resources, adding value through the broadening of perspectives, knowledge and interests, or in strengthening an alternative social setting, developing alternatives to the existing social order as in the case of social movements, and thereby forming a critical mass of alternatives that change the power dynamics of any social issue.

Processes of making links and working together

Working with others and facilitating links between groups and organisations involves a number of interrelated steps. Himmelman (2001) describes different kinds of exchanges, each building on the other and increasing the amounts of risk, commitment, and resources that participants must contribute to the exchange (see Table 9.1). Each "*strategy can be assessed and selected in relationship to the challenges, opportunities posed by time, trust and turf*" (Himmelman, 2001, p. 277).

Himmelman argues that meaningful, sustainable and systemic change cannot be achieved without collaboration. However, even collaborations involve different intensities of relationship, as we found when implementing a large portfolio of projects that all involved collaboration between four universities (Kagan & Duggan, 2009). When we tried to make sense of the nature of the collaboration involved, we drew on the work of Corbett and Noyes (2008, p. 6), who offer a continuum of 'relationship intensity' to help understand different types of collaborations. For them, relationship intensity

> ... orders the extent to which participating programs and agencies forfeit some of their identity and defining attributes in an effort to develop a truly blended system. In doing this, the continuum focuses on the character and quality of the relationships among participating programs and agencies; specifically, how closely participating systems are to be blended together.

The continuum is shown in Table 9.2 with reference to types of collaborations within our own programme of projects delivered through collaborations between four universities or higher education institutions (HEI) (Kagan & Duggan, 2009, p. 47). These were either parallel collaborations (each doing their own project addressing the same issue); extended collaborations (two universities working closely together and involving another at a later date to add further expertise); collaboration for evaluation (one or two universities working on a project and involving another specifically to evaluate the work); or integrated evaluation (all universities involved fully collaborative at all stages of planning, delivery and evaluation).

Looking at the HEI collaborations in this way suggests that none of our projects had evolved into unequivocal collaborations. For this to happen, and the inter-university collaborations be sustainable, relationship intensity would need to increase.

In this example, there were limits to the development of the collaborations, due to time (all the projects had to be completed within two years, giving little time to develop relationships and explore

Table 9.1 Characteristics of different types of exchange in collaborative working and associated skills

Form of exchange	Characteristic	Skills needed
Networking: exchanging information for mutual benefit.	Does not require much time, trust or sharing of turf. Useful in initial stages of building working relationships.	Making contact; sharing information; keeping details; maintaining contact (face to face, telephone, email) over time.
Coordination: exchanging information for mutual benefit and altering activities for a common purpose.	Requires more time and trust but does not require sharing turf. Increases efficient use of community resources.	Facilitation of bringing people together, sharing information about practices, identifying gaps and duplication and changing activities so as to avoid duplication.
Cooperation: exchanging information, modifying activities, and sharing resources for mutual benefit and to achieve a common purpose.	Requires significant amounts of time, high levels of trust and a significant sharing of turf. Extends activities available but risks and involvement increase as resources are shared. Pooled resources lead to increased activity.	Implementation of complex organisational processes and agreements in order to expand actions. Conflict management skills needed as exchanges can become more fraught.
Collaboration: exchanging information, altering activities, sharing resources, and willingness to enhance the capacity of another for mutual benefit and common purpose.	Requires highest levels of trust, considerable amounts of time, and extensive sharing of turf. Sharing of risks, resources and rewards but can produce greatest benefit of mutual action.	Openness and willingness to share knowledge, skills and resources. Tenacity in solving problems when the collaboration comes under threat. Organisational analysis and development skills required.

Source: after Himmelman, 2001.

possibilities) and the overall context. Whilst the projects all required collaboration and co-operation between HEIs, the context was one in which the organisations were often in competition with each other for resources. Sometimes being able to demonstrate they have reached a point of collaboration will enable greater access to resources, other times it will not. They were in effect working in 'co-opetition' (Blickstead et al., 2008; Brandenburger & Nalebuff, 1996; also mentioned in Chapter 7) – co-operation in the context of competition, a situation that many community groups also find themselves in.

Table 9.2 Continuum of relationship intensity and type of inter-HEI collaboration

Level of relationship intensity	Characteristics	Inter-HEI collaboration
Communication	Clear, consistent and non-judgemental discussions; giving or exchanging information in order to maintain meaningful relationships. Individual programmes or causes are totally separate.	Parallel collaboration Extended collaboration
Co-operation	Assisting each other with respective activities, giving general support, information, and/or endorsement for each other's programmes, services, or objectives.	Collaboration for evaluation Extended collaboration
Co-ordination	Joint activities and communications are more intensive and far-reaching. Agencies or individuals engage in joint planning and synchronisation of schedules, activities, goals, objectives, and events.	Extended collaboration Integrated collaboration
Collaboration	Agencies, individuals, or groups willingly relinquish some of their autonomy in the interest of mutual gains or outcomes. True collaboration involves actual changes in agency, group, or individual behaviour to support collective goals or ideals.	
Convergence	Relationships evolve from collaboration to actual restructuring of services, programmes, memberships, budgets, missions, objectives, and staff.	
Consolidation	Agency, group, or individual behaviour, operations, policies, budgets, staff, and power are united and harmonised. Individual autonomy or gains have been fully relinquished, common outcomes and identity adopted.	

Source: after Corbett & Noyes, 2008. Reproduced by permission of Manchester Metropolitan University.

Collaborative arrangements can take a number of different forms, ranging from loosely formed communities of interest, to strategic short term alliances, to longer term coalitions, to organisational partnerships (Burton & Kellaway, 1998) and even to the formation or incorporation into wider social movements.

Reflect!

Think of a time where you have collaborated with others in order to achieve something. How did the collaboration help and how did it hinder what you were trying to do? What does this tell you about how *you* collaborate with others?

Communities of interest or communities of practice

Wenger (1998) discusses a form of informal learning which builds on 'legitimate peripheral participation' – the learning emerges through actions and relationships that occur in specific situations.

A community of practice is best understood as a joint enterprise that is understood and negotiated by group members, through, as Duncan, Bowman, Naidoo, Pillay and Roos put it (2007, p. 351), "*a process of mutual engagement that produces a shared repertoire of community resources*" which may be material or knowledge resources.

Wenger, McDermott and Snyder (2002) identify some key features of effective communities of practice. They:

- evolve over time, through design;
- encourage open dialogue between insider and outsider perspectives;
- invite different levels of participation which vary as people come and go;
- develop and value public and private community spaces and grow in both kinds of spaces;
- value the benefits of collaborative practices;
- encourage a combination of familiarity and novelty;
- create a rhythm of ongoing learning which keeps them dynamic and changing.

Thus, communities of practice emerge for collaborative action and the development of relationships. Lawthom (2011) maps the synergies between communities of practice and critical community psychology pedagogy. Positioning learning as fundamentally social it is argued that both approaches emphasise the value of 'de-expertising knowledge'.

Think!

How do the characteristics of communities of practice compare with those of experiential learning (see Chapter 8)? What are the similarities and what are the differences?

Alliances and coalitions

Alliances and coalitions refer to links between groups and organisations that are goal directed and strategic. They work towards and promote a common agenda around particular issues or campaigns. Coalitions can help change processes be more resilient, but they also maximise the efforts and resources of the various parts of the coalition and give greater power to minority voices on an issue. For example, carers' groups might all have their own agendas and concerns but come together in a coalition to fight cuts in public services or resist restrictive legislation. Once the particular campaign is over the coalition may dissolve, or it may have discovered a broader common agenda and contribute to a social movement.

Spangler (2003) points out that coalitions may be built around any issue and at any scale of society from neighbourhood issues to international conflict. The key questions to ask when considering building a coalition are:

● What would the unifying issue(s) be? (Contributors' goals are similar and compatible.)
● What resources could come from other organisations? (Working together will enhance each group's abilities to reach their goals.)
● What obstacles might be encountered? (The benefits of coalescing will be greater than the costs.)

Coalitions can be locally based, and be a potent force for change in neighbourhoods, although Wolff (2001a) reminds us that community coalition building is not a catch-all panacea, and that many fail. By analysing successful coalitions, Wolff (2001b) suggests nine critical dimensions to the success of coalitions and these are summarised in Table 9.3.

Critical community psychologists have a number of different roles to play in building and maintaining effective coalitions. Nelson and Prilleltensky (2005, p. 181) identify a number of roles to be played, including:

1 helping the identification of shared goals and missions;
2 helping bridging differences and creating bonds of collaboration where shared values exist;
3 building relationships and trust amongst members;
4 establishing clear agreements and norms of reciprocity;
5 helping partners share power and resources; and
6 challenging themselves and coalition members to ensure they do not perpetuate oppressive practices.

Further, Foster-Fishman, Berkowitz, Lounsbury, Jacobson and Allen (2001) identify four areas of capacity building for collaboration to which (critical) community psychologists could contribute. These are:

1 building member capacity to collaborate;
2 creating relational capacity;
3 building organisational capacity; and
4 designing and implementing interventions or programmatic capacity.

Partnerships

Partnerships are another, more formal, way of collaborating across organisations. They are often formed as a result of the top down requirements of guidance for the implementation of government policy, but may also form more organically, bottom up.

The Audit Commission (1998) has set out the ingredients for successful partnerships, against which public sector organisations are audited for effectiveness. Table 9.4 outlines key aspects of partnerships.

Over recent years there has been a growth in inter-agency partnership working. Whilst partnerships can be effective and efficient ways of working collaboratively, there is evidence that they can also maintain the status quo rather than promote change. Balloch and Taylor (2001, p. 8) point out:

> ... partnerships have largely left existing power relationships intact. Partnership working has too often been dominated by the more powerful and has not delivered, especially for the communities and service users who are now a required part of most partnerships. By and large they have

Table 9.3 Critical dimensions of successful coalitions

Dimension	Issues for effective practice	Best practice tips
Coalition readiness	There needs to be sufficient energy for forging the coalition, strong leadership, sufficient time for developments and limited history of conflict and competition between partners. New coalitions will be difficult if communities already have lots of coalitions.	Assess communities' assets from the start. Take time to build relationships, mobilise the community. Personally visit key local stakeholders. Build strong personal links with the people to be engaged, mobilised and influenced.
Intentionality	Clear goals, community ownership and belief in what is possible are all in existence.	Use creative ways to identify and reinforce shared vision and mission (visioning). Use symbolic and expressive means of articulating future goals.
Structure and organisational capacity	Sufficient resources, including staffing underpin inclusive decision making and good communications.	Create clear structures and decision making processes. Obtain the core resources needed to run the coalition, including staffing.
Taking action	Concrete outcomes are identified, partners and volunteers are engaged on a regular basis, explicit community change is kept at the forefront of the coalition's work. A mix of advocacy and relationship building is used and power issues addressed.	Create work tasks that set clear goals and objectives and realistic work plans. Identify measurable indicators of success. Publicise and record (in newsletters, annual reports and so on) actions and successes.
Membership	A broad section of the community is involved and recruitment is ongoing, inclusive with necessary supports in place to support the least powerful members.	Attend to open ways of engaging people. Develop an organisational culture that is comfortable and owned by all. Issue specific invitations for membership and welcome them to meetings and events.

continued

Table 9.3 Continued		
Dimension	*Issues for effective practice*	*Best practice tips*
Leadership	Leadership is dispersed around the coalition, is collaborative and constantly bringing new people into leadership roles.	Build personal relationship and maintain contact with interested people. Visit members and issue notes of appreciation. Ensure coalition represents all sections of the community. Introduce reflection to ensure the coalition remains a welcoming organisation.
Resources	Funding is obtained as required and other resources such as time, meeting places and so on are replenished regularly.	Find diverse ways of raising funds and involve as many people as possible in fund raising.
Relationships	Meetings enable trust to grow over time and working relationships to be built, maximising different contributors' strengths. Conflict is recognised but leaders can handle this productively. Informal time together is valued.	Build informal time at the start, during and at the end of meetings. Create occasions for people to come together on a social basis. Join in community events together. Create opportunities for celebrating success.
Technical assistance	The needs of coalitions for training, development and support will change over time and outside expertise be involved as necessary.	Recruit external partners to facilitate development activities and awaydays and to develop skills such as mediating conflict, running meetings and so on.

Source: after Wolff, 2001b.

remained on the margins of processes where the rules of the game are determined by government partners, legitimating rather than making decisions. … If a partnership does not address issues of power it will remain symbolic rather than real.

Indeed, Coleman (2000, p. 60), discussing the mental health user movement, makes a similar distinction between partnerships and alliances, in terms of the locus of power.

… (unlike partnerships) alliances happen between people that have power and people that have no power, and an alliance means that you work together on a particular thing.

Table 9.4 Key dimensions of effective partnerships

Focus	Key aspects of effective partnerships
Reasons to form partnerships	• to deliver co-ordinated packages of services to individuals; • to tackle so-called 'wicked issues'; • to reduce the impact of organisational fragmentation and minimise the impact of any perverse incentives that result from it; • to bid for, or gain access to, new resources; • to meet a statutory requirement.
Functions of partnerships	• to develop a vision for a community – which could be a locality or a group of people with similar needs – and monitor progress towards it; • to formulate medium or long term strategic objectives to turn a shared vision into reality; • to plan the actions necessary to meet agreed strategic objectives; • to carry out joint operations, which could include major capital projects, new services to individuals or new approaches to existing services.
Types of partnership	• separate organisation; • virtual organisation; • co-location of staff for partnering organisations; • steering group without dedicated staff resources.
Key ingredients for successful partnerships	• clear, shared objectives; • a realistic plan and timetable for reaching these objectives; • commitment from the partners to take the partnership's work into account within their mainstream activities; • a clear framework of responsibilities and accountability; • a high level of trust between partners; • realistic ways of measuring the partnership's achievements.
Barriers to effective partnership working	• partners are not committed; • there is little time to learn; • there are conflicting priorities; • managing change is difficult – people do not understand that what they do has to change; • performance frameworks are hindered by unhelpful systems; • difficulty ensuring all partners perform equally.

Source: after Audit Commission, 1998.

> ## Act!
>
> With a colleague design a leaflet that could be used to entice community groups to attend a workshop on forming alliances and partnerships that you are going to run. What would the course contain (that is, what is it that would be useful for community groups to explore and share about the merits of alliances and partnerships)? What knowledge and skills would you hope workshop participants might develop? Was this an easy task? Why or why not?

Working at the ecological edge

One way of thinking about working across organisations or agencies, building coalitions, alliances and partnerships, is to see these processes as creating and maintaining ecological 'edges' (Burton & Kagan, 2000; Kagan, 2007; Kagan & Duggan, 2009; see Chapter 3). The ecological edge is an idea from classical ecology (Odum, 1971) the relevance of which is noted by Levine and Perkins (1997, pp. 111–112)

> 'Ecology' is a fundamental metaphor or analogy in community psychology, embodying both the structure of a scientific paradigm and a specific set of values … We assume that there are enough similarities between the problems that concern community psychologists and those studied by biological ecologists that we may use the concepts to illuminate problems of interest to us.

The transition zone between two or more ecological communities (each characterised by a set of populations living in a particular area or habitat, with elements interacting in an organised way through metabolic flows and transformations) is known as the ecotone. In the ecotone, or transition zone, resources from each contributing community accumulate and the area is more diverse, with more naturally occurring resources than each contributing community alone. This area of rich resources is the ecological 'edge'. Figure 9.1 shows the richness of resources at the 'edge' between the field and the woods (here one of us [CK] is harvesting berries from fruit bushes bordering the woods).

An efficient, productive and sustainable design of ecological development is to increase the contribution the edge makes to the system as a whole (Burton & Kagan, 1996). This metaphor of the ecological edge – or *edge effect* – can be used to think about inter-agency or inter-organisational working, although the mechanisms, transactions and mediations in human systems will differ from those in the natural world.

Community alliances and coalitions will often be forged across various agency or organisational boundaries, disciplinary boundaries, professional boundaries and sector boundaries. Not all cross-boundary work generates 'edges', and practice might be focused on one or more of the different strategies. Table 9.5 summarises three different strategies of working across organisational boundaries with reference to different kinds of projects.

Kagan and Duggan (2009, p. 8) point out:

> At each boundary is the possibility of an 'edge' that maximises resources and enriches ideas and practices. The edge effect is the phenomenon of enrichment through alliances and collaborations. When edge is actually created we notice an increase in energy, excitement and commitment. What characterises all of these boundary settings (whether edge is significantly created or not) is the problem of spanning social entities with greatly differing modes of operation, power structures, cultures, physical environments, practices, values and ideologies.

We have choices about how best to work at the 'edge', and can identify at least three main types of strategies for working across boundaries: working within boundaries, working at the boundary interface, and maximising the 'edge'.

Figure 9.1 The forest edge – abundance at the join of two ecological zones.

Table 9.5 Strategies of working across boundaries of agencies, organisations, disciplines, professions, stakeholders in an issue

Strategy for working across boundaries	Example	Impact
Working within boundaries: development and change targeted at each community separately	Some work we undertook researching the impact of arts projects on the mental health of participants only focused on the projects themselves. A failure to involve the interests of other agencies involved in health and mental health work meant that change would be confined to the arts projects alone and not the wider mental health system.	Unlikely to lead to co-ordinated change in the overall system although may establish the conditions through which the creation of edges is possible in the future.

Table 9.5 Continued		
Strategy for working across boundaries	Example	Impact
Working at the boundary interface: attempts to bridge communities	A project we undertook on the transformation of mental health services in an authority entailed working with and understanding each profession's views separately and separately again from those of service users and family members. The researchers represented the views and interests of different stakeholders to each other.	Energy intensive. Some likelihood of co-ordinated change but effort is likely to be on the margins of each community's area of concern. Sustainability questionable.
Maximising the 'edge': using natural resources – get people from different communities together and maximise the interests and expertise of each	We were involved in a four-university project on aspects of community cohesion: 15 projects were developed, each of which worked across the universities, across disciplines within the universities and each with one or more community partners, on issues driven by the needs of the community partners.	Energy efficient and high likelihood of sustainable and co-ordinated change.
Mixed strategies	Some work with Somali women revealed the need for a project working with older and younger men from two different ethnic communities on intergenerational conflict. Initial work was with each generation in each community separately; then older and young men were brought together and an edge created; following this, work with the generations and communities continued separately, to be brought together at a dissemination event which created a broader edge than before, incorporating older and younger men and women from both communities – work thereafter continued together.	Practical, ideological or value issues may dictate the need to work with communities separately – however, if work continues separately it will be inefficient and make excessive demands on resources and stands in danger of being narrowly focused. Thus the creation of edges, and their maintenance over time is important for more sustainable and widespread change.

Source: after Burton & Kagan, 2000; Kagan & Duggan, 2009.

Example: Higher education and community engagement: urban regeneration and community cohesion

The creation of 'edges' was key to a project in which four universities worked with each other, across disciplines and with community partners – this is the project that was mentioned above. We were responsible for managing and delivering 17 projects concerned with issues facing communities regarding community cohesion and urban regeneration (the UR-MAD project) (Kagan & Duggan, 20098). We had choices to make about how to get started, each recognising the potential 'edges' involved.

Working within boundaries

We could have worked in ways in which development and change was targeted at each partner separately. This strategy, in the UR-MAD project, would have meant we gathered resources within the universities and then explored resources in the community. This is the strategy of "getting our (university) house in order and being clear what universities want from the projects and then seeking community partners". It would have been the universities that defined the agenda and terms of engagement, possibly each one separately, inviting others to join later on.

Working at the interface

We could have worked in ways in which development and change was targeted at each partner separately but with early attempts to bridge from one to another. So each university would have developed its own ideas, using printed material provided about staff interests from the others in order to develop ideas. Community partners might have already been identified or would have had to have been sought at a later stage. Universities would have set the terms of engagement and attempts would have been made to bridge across agencies and groups. Some parts of the community cohesion projects that got off the ground may be described in these terms, especially when other university partners were added at later stages of project development and without discussion.

Maximising the 'edge'

What we did do was to use natural resources – getting people from different communities to work together and to utilise the expertise of each from the start. The projects for which we were responsible started off by maximising the edge, through face to face discussions between partner universities and people working in community organisations. Once the 'edge' had been created and, through a series of interactive meetings, been maximised, the extent to which they continued to work in this way varied: some projects resorted to interfacing at least across some of the boundaries and others prioritised working within boundaries but with some interfacing elements.

Act!

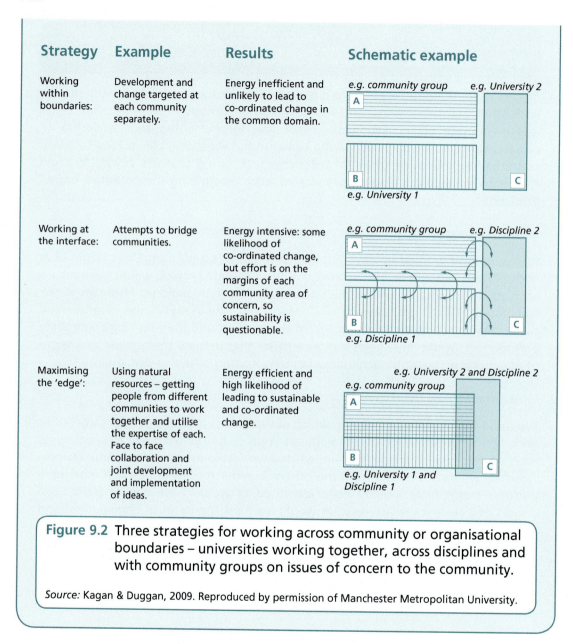

Strategy	Example	Results	Schematic example
Working within boundaries:	Development and change targeted at each community separately.	Energy inefficient and unlikely to lead to co-ordinated change in the common domain.	
Working at the interface:	Attempts to bridge communities.	Energy intensive: some likelihood of co-ordinated change, but effort is on the margins of each community area of concern, so sustainability is questionable.	
Maximising the 'edge':	Using natural resources – getting people from different communities to work together and utilise the expertise of each. Face to face collaboration and joint development and implementation of ideas.	Energy efficient and high likelihood of leading to sustainable and co-ordinated change.	

Figure 9.2 Three strategies for working across community or organisational boundaries – universities working together, across disciplines and with community groups on issues of concern to the community.

Source: Kagan & Duggan, 2009. Reproduced by permission of Manchester Metropolitan University.

Figure 9.2 illustrates the three different ways of working across boundaries with reference to this four-university–community project.

What we recommend, then, are ways of working that create and expand the 'edge', through coalition and alliances, and Table 9.6 summarises different strategies for creating and maximising the 'edge'.

> **Table 9.6** Strategies for creating, maximising and maintaining the 'edge'

Strategy	Methods
Creation and maximisation of edge The maximisation of points of contact between distinct communities and organisations	Location and co-location of projects, teams, events Formation of inter-organisations with membership from more than one sector Creation of new settings (temporary or long standing) that bring elements together Conduct of activity in other locations, that is in territory associated with another sector Creation of multiple points of contact (tessellation)
Maintenance of the edge The preservation of the very best of all adjoining communities	Recognition of 'edge species' and encouragement of them Encouragement of fairness in resource exploitation Pooling of resources between sectors Respect for the uniqueness of each community, or else the edge can become a site of unproductive conflict

Source: after Burton & Kagan, 2000; Kagan, 2007; Kagan & Duggan, 2009.

Example: Intergenerational understanding

A community organisation aimed at developing intergenerational understanding and community spirit in the inner city borough of 'New Borough' was developed. This was a new social setting bringing together older people, teenagers and a number of other community organisations in a new way, around music. An action research process was used and three cycles of this illustrate how alliances were formed, and 'edge effects' maximised.

Stages in project development

1 Gaining the participation of voluntary sector organisations for elderly people and some sponsorship for the project. The researcher made contact, negotiated and persuaded involvement and invested a great deal of time and energy into

gaining participation. The logistics of meeting with organisers and members of dispersed organisations were considerable. Equally, appealing to sponsors who were already over-stretched within the borough required commitment and perseverance as well as good presentation skills.

2 Gaining participation of schools and young people. Further negotiation and persuasion was needed to encourage young people from schools to become involved. The researcher had to be aware of current educational priorities and to be able to convince potential partners of the benefits for the time and efforts expended.

3 A high profile media presence was maintained and the project acquired a high profile venue for the project launch (the local football ground) as part of a sponsorship arrangement.

By the time of the launch, therefore, a number of stakeholders were involved as planned and the organisation was now a complex interweaving of different community partners.

Natural resources used

As far as possible those resources that are already available in the locality were used, including those of schools, youth projects, the media and so on. Where good relationships existed between different agencies and sectors these were supported; where they did not, attempts were made to enable them to develop by strategic use of planning committees and networking events. The project often served to catalyse (speed up) processes that were happening anyway.

Edge effects and energy efficiency

One way of thinking about the work is to see everything that was done as being at the interface of at least two different organisational ecosystems (or parts of them). For example, the project worked at the transition of existing practice and better practice; of statutory organisations and non-statutory organisations; of education and social services; of policing, transport for the elderly, and youth work; of welfare organisations and local communities. The project aimed to maximise the various edges between different parts of the system and to maintain those that were created. A successful intergenerational project was born and teenagers worked with elderly people to produce musical events.

Act!

During the next week look around you and see how many naturally occurring 'edges' you can spot in the world around you. This could include 'edges' in the natural world or at work or amongst your friends and leisure activities. What makes these 'edges'? How long lasting do you think the edges are and what might make them more so?

Alliances, new social settings and connecting with social movements

In Chapter 8 we considered the creation of alternative social settings. New settings can be strengthened through coalitions or alliances with groups or organisations that share common interests or with whom 'edges' can be created. Many social settings will – or could – be connected in some way to some kind of social movement, and one task of the community psychologist might be to identify possibilities for linkages into social movements. Indeed, the very survival of a new social setting might depend on alliances formed and its connection to a social movement and on the nature of that social movement.

Example: Organisation workshop

A residents' group was formed from shared experience planning and organising 'raves'. This often involved the occupation of derelict buildings or open spaces and was considered a public order and trespass offence. Indeed, legislation was passed specifically dealing with the organising of raves (Criminal Justice and Public Order Act, 1994. Part V – Public Order: Collective Trespass or Nuisance on Land: Section 63 – Powers to remove persons attending or preparing for a rave). This residents' group aligned their interests with other landless people's groups in Latin America (particularly the Landless Workers' Movement in Brazil), rather than with other residents' groups in the UK, and became part of the movement for addressing poverty through land rights. This resulted in their finding out about some of the development and change processes originating in Latin America and exploring the use of the organisation workshop enterprise development process originating in Brazil (Carmen, 2000). Their work with the organisational workshop was the first time the process had been used in the UK (see Imagine, 2016 for an evaluation of the organisation workshop – no mention is made in the report of the alliance with the Landless Workers' Movement which spawned the inspiration for the organisation workshop)

Through being part of the social movement, the group has had access to ideas and resources that would otherwise have been inaccessible.

Social movements are, however, varied, and have different concerns, values, ideologies, aims, and so on. Ray (1993), discussing social movements in 'peripheral' states, distinguishes between two tendencies, traditionalising and de-traditionalising. Traditionalising movements are defensive, nationalistic, in support of the status quo and often with anti-liberal tendencies. De-traditionalising movements are more proactive, seek progressive change, often with a human rights dimension and founded on principles of self help.

> ## Example: De-institutionalisation and service transformation: traditionalising and de-traditionalising social movements
>
> In the UK two movements were particularly active in relation to the de-institutionalisation of disabled people. One, traditionalising movement was a coalition of parent led groups who argued for the maintenance of the institutional, protective environments of their adult sons and daughters; the other, a de-traditionalising movement, was a coalition of groups (parents, professionals, social reformers, academics) campaigning for non-institutional, inclusive forms of living. The traditionalising movement was able to harness the interests of community groups, concerned with 'protecting' their locality from settlement by 'undesirable' outsiders. The non-traditionalising movement could harness the interests of community groups concerned with social inclusion and professional interest groups concerned with better quality of life for disabled people. Moreover, the non-traditionalising movement was able to align itself with other forces in social policy that moved (although in a contradictory fashion) in the general direction of increased inclusion (Burton & Kagan, 2006).

Often, new settings make manifest some aspects of the galvanising ideology of the social movement. They therefore feed back into the social movement as persuasive exemplars (images of possibility) and sites to defend (causes celebres). If the social movement has an overarching, transcending philosophy, it is likely to be able to support the setting to grow and develop, but where the social movement has only a limited philosophy, then it is more likely that the setting will become 'stuck' and increasingly take on features of the dominant system. So, when creating settings we can and must pay attention to the social movement dimension.

There is a literature on social movements which holds some useful ideas to help those working with groups and movements to create, develop and sustain alliances. Burton (1999) distinguishes between two complementary traditions. A European tradition (e.g. Melucci, 1989; Touraine, 1981), rooted in social theory and sociology, is concerned with the question: "why do social movements arise?" These theorists emphasise issues of identity in social movements. A North American tradition (e.g. McCarthy & Zald, 1977) emphasises social psychological understanding of how social movements operate, and how they mobilise support.

Reflect!

Social movements often form around big issues (such as gender, disability, land ownership, the environment and so on). What big issues are you concerned about? Can you think of ways you might become part of a social movement linked to this issue? What would the difficulties be?

Accompaniment and advocacy

Critical community psychology is about principled social change and we are committed to this type of community psychology. This also implies learning from other radical movements for social change, and finding space to work in different ways rather than intervening. So, rather than using our expertise to identify, with people themselves, what must change and how; rather than using our research skills to investigate, with people themselves, what is and why; rather than listening as part of a needs assessment prior to designing (participatively or not) an intervention or research project, we could *walk alongside, listen to and witness* the realities of the lives of people living marginalised lives. This is the process of accompaniment, or, with roots in liberation psychology, psychosocial accompaniment. Psychosocial accompaniment does not serve to minimise, re-frame or sympathise with others, deny or normalise their despair and their suffering. Instead, it is an active process of being in the presence of another person and journeying with her or him.

Psychosocial accompaniment

Accompaniment has its roots in a number of different social movements, including peace activism, human rights and social development, as well as social and liberation psychology formulated by Ignacio Martín-Baró. It has been used with communities in marginal situations, with people living during times of war and post conflict, penal servitude, chronic illness, displacement as refugees and asylum seekers, political dissidence, military and paramilitary violence, poverty and homelessness. As Gates (1998) says:

> Accompaniment literally means to <u>walk with</u> or alongside people … [it] is also an act of friendship, and ultimately a mechanism for building solidarity. … Accompaniers also can play an important role in listening to and transmitting the stories of those voices who might not otherwise be heard. … to provide a measure of security to at-risk populations … as observers and witnesses.

Edge, Kagan and Stewart (2004) confirm this approach, suggesting that accompaniment is a process of forming an invited, dialogic relationship that becomes close and continuous, involving presence, listening, witnessing, and the offering of specific, flexible, and strategic support (Edge et al., 2004).

In human rights accompaniment, international observers typically live alongside those most at risk of abuse, violence, torture, even death, in order to learn, support, show solidarity, witness and possibly shield. However, Watkins (2015, p. 327) points out that accompaniers might undertake different kinds of activities, depending on the needs and desires of those accompanied. These can include: providing individual and community witness and support; solidarity in relevant social movements; assistance with networking with communities at a distance suffering similar conditions; research on needed dimensions; and participation in educating civil society about the difficulties suffered and the changes needed to relieve this suffering.

Whatever else they do, accompaniers have to be there, in situations alongside people suffering oppression, witnessing and providing solidarity and helping them find ways of reclaiming their identities and represent their own social worlds.

Sacipa-Rodríguez, Tovar-Guerra, Villareal and Bohórquez (2009, p. 222) outline a process of psychosocial accompaniment as:

> An encounter between the community and the social [i.e. community] psychologists with the goal of constructing liberating knowledge. … The process must be oriented toward helping the community to give new meaning to the feelings associated with the painful experiences it has

lived ... it is necessary to encourage conversations and to promote collective and individual reflections. In this context it is important to have an ethical commitment to be the bridge between the individual subject and their culture in such a manner as to allow both to construct a new order in which interactions and practical dialogs can coexist. ... it is necessary to see the subjects as a reflective and active part of the community because they can transform themselves and the world around them. In this perspective an ethical stance between the social psychologist and the community is fundamental ... we believe that the social psychologist should accompany the community in the construction of feelings and not intervene to make specific changes.

Drawing together literature from the different roots of accompaniment, we can see that the process of accompaniment involves:

- a close and continuous relationship;
- being based on dialogue;
- being by invitation;
- spending time with people in different situations;
- offering specific, flexible and strategic support, long term;
- witnessing;
- listening;
- creating spaces within which people can give their testimonies and assert their rights;
- the recognition that silence can be a form of resistance and agency;
- voicing and transmitting stories of the accompanied;
- monitoring and alerting the wider community to abuses;
- making links so as to reach a position of collective agency; and
- reflexivity, making transparent positions of power and privilege and feelings of fear, stress and fatigue.

Furthermore, accompaniment requires:

- an understanding of history and context;
- the rejection of a hierarchical, outsider, supposedly neutral expert, and instead becoming embedded in the struggle against oppression;
- having to let go of our, the accompaniers', needs, to strategise and intervene on behalf of those accompanied;
- that we accept we are not in a position to propose solutions of problems;
- being open to the impact of the experience;
- being able to experience the pain and struggle of the accompanied; and
- being sensitive to the local political situation and taking seriously the notion of 'doing no harm' and not further endangering people we accompany.

This is not an easy process and Watkins (2015, p. 325) proposes that moving toward accompaniment requires "*both psychic and social decolonization, a shedding of the professionalized role of expertism that is often oriented toward professional aggrandizement*".

In some parts of the world not only those experiencing oppression but also those accompaniers live under conditions of threat and fear for their lives. This is well illustrated by Crosby (2009) as she describes the dangerous context in which a workshop for accompaniers took place in Guatemala.

Even in those parts of the world where threats of violence are less likely, accompaniment can be important. In the UK, for example, people living in poverty are at risk of oppression – and suppression – by the very institutions and professions that are there to support them in moving from poverty. They are also largely invisible to the world around them. The process of accompaniment is one that may enable us to take a step back, to create spaces in which we can begin to understand the multiple experiences of those living poverty, and to scrutinise our own disciplines and practices in the light of this understanding (Edge et al., 2004). Such accompaniment opens the way to solidarity with those living poverty and to joining with them to protest against poverty. As we have said from the outset, such a position is inevitably a political one, a view supported by Gutiérrez (1988, p. 173), who says

> …the solidarity and protest of which we are speaking have an evident and inevitable 'political' character insofar as they imply liberation. To be with the oppressed is to be against the oppressor.

It is difficult to engage in accompaniment within the current organisation of psychological practices, and we have to take seriously the proposition that the discipline and practices of psychology may, themselves, be part of the oppressor. Having said this, though, with personal commitment, moving towards such a practice may be possible – not only possible but it can be a part of the decolonising of psychological knowledge and practice. At the very least, accompaniment of this sort requires

- commitment;
- time;
- a reliable presence;
- openness and willingness to listen, watch and learn;
- negotiation of and joint reflection on relationships as they change over time;
- independence from agency allegiances and responsibilities;
- patience;
- prophetic imagination (a vision explicit or not, about how different – and better – things could be);
- a sense of humour;
- the ability to listen and hear in non-judgemental ways;
- the ability to cherish and not to usurp the cultural resources of those being accompanied;
- the ability to understand the immediate situation in its broader global, cultural and historical context;
- a flexible approach to and understanding of more familiar interpersonal boundaries, including, amongst others, those of 'friend', 'helper', 'client', 'expert', 'facilitator';
- continual reconsideration of ethical judgements.

Becoming an ally (Bishop, 2002) and commitment are the starting points for accompaniment, as well as for solidarity and protest. Bearing witness demands humility and openness to learning ourselves.

Reflect!

How does accompaniment fit with what you have been taught or know about community psychology? Can you see the points of overlap between accompaniment and participative action research? Why do you think some community psychologists argue that accompaniment is not and should not be a legitimate part of community psychology?

Act!

Hold a debate in your class or your workplace, with speakers for and against the motion "Accompaniment is core to community psychology." If possible, ask participants to take the position opposite to the one they actually hold.

Skills needed for accompaniment

Toval Guerra (2014, p. 75) identified the personal resources for those engaged in psychosocial accompaniment in the context of a recovery process involving forcibly displaced people in Colombia. These include: religious beliefs (although in different contexts this may not be so relevant); acknowledgement of moral and practical values; optimism; positive evaluations of adverse situations; good decision making abilities; capacity to initiate effective behaviours; survival skills in aggressive social environments; communication skills; and pursuit of effective personal support. In addition to these personal resources, accompaniers need to be able to take the perspective of the other (that is adopt an 'alterity' stance) through relationships of trust and mutual respect. Nelson, Poland, Murray and Maticka-Tyndale (2004, p. 395) point out

> It would be naïve, however, to think that relationships can always be 'equalized'. It is preferable to acknowledge power imbalances … [and] … in the context of acknowledged unequal power relations, one can work towards embodying active listening, the ceding of decision-making control, and the cultivation of solidarity around shared goals.

Furthermore, Crosby (2009, p. 344) reminds us that accompaniment is a relational activity, requiring not only the building of connections, but also the provision of personal and specialist – often legal – support.

> These struggles for personal and collective liberation are inherently dialogical and relational processes, requiring the building of connections – with other survivors, and with those who can provide accompaniment, including psychosocial and legal support, and the creation of spaces for survivors to give their testimonies and assert their rights. This notion of 'accompaniment' carries within it an assumption of long-term relationships of common cause with survivors, of being present and accountable, and an implication within (albeit from different locations), the struggle for social change.

Example: Precarious housing and vulnerability

We have worked with a group of women living in poverty and alongside other stresses in a low income area of Greater Manchester for some years and have built up strong, horizontal relationships of trust and friendship. One of the women was experiencing considerable duress over a hot summer, with a neighbour who liked to collect and rummage through bags and bags of organic waste, attracting vermin and flies galore, as well as strong smells to the block of apartments. She invited us to spend time with her over the summer as she kept a diary of incidents and tried to request some action from the housing authorities, all to no avail. After a series of incidents she was threatened with eviction and called for an interview with the housing officer. She asked us to go with her – not to intervene, but to provide some support, but most importantly to witness how, as she put it, "people like me are treated by the authorities". This was not a life threatening situation and there was no danger (other than of risk to health and of being exposed) to the accompanier – but provided a unique opportunity to witness what would usually be a private conversation. It was hard to resist trouble shooting and intervening to help resolve the situation, but this is not what the resident wanted. She wanted us to understand, and to bridge her experience to the wider world by using these experiences in our teaching – which we did. Had we not witnessed the smells, the frustrations, the disdain with which the resident was treated, first hand, we would not have been able to convey the emotional layers of living in this kind of precarious housing situation.

Watkins (2015) reminds us that accompaniment often takes place in situations of difficulty and even danger, and whilst those at risk will often have few resources, the solidarity shown through accompaniment enables them, amongst other things, to retain hope that a different future is possible.

Knowledge and accompaniment

Accompaniment as a practice raises fundamental questions about knowledge. It implies an openness to the perspectives of the people accompanied, to their submerged and excluded experience and thought, which can often stand outside the dominant rationality of Western social science. The task here is to develop what Dussel (e.g. 1995, pp. 136–137) terms the *analectical method*, whereby modern rationality is not denied or negated but enhanced through recognition of the knowledge and understanding of the oppressed 'subaltern'. The Other is seen as equal rather than as immature and to be dominated. The Zapatista conception of 'leading by obeying' (*mandar obedeciendo*) is a practical demonstration of this fusion, not just of knowledge but of social practices (Marcos, 2002).

It is not only knowledge of the submerged experiences of those who live through oppression that is exposed through accompaniment. Watkins (2015, p. 329) notes that:

> Many communities suffering from various forms of oppression and scarcity of resources have protested that, to the extent that their difficulties stem from those groups who are relatively advantaged, they would appreciate research and work that focuses on those whose lifestyles are creating suffering for others. While liberation theology and psychology speak of a preferential option for the poor, learning from communities about the sources of their suffering can well return a more economically privileged scholar-activist accompanier back to his or her own community for the work of conscientization and transformation to more just modes of relations with others and the earth.

Think!

Mary Watkins raises the possibility of trans-species and earth-accompaniment (see https://mary-watkins.net/library/Accompaniment-Psychosocial-Environmental-Trans-Species-Earth.pdf). Read what she has to say about this. What do you think – do other species and the earth deserve the protection and solidarity that accompaniment gives? Write a list of the pros and cons of this approach and discuss it with a colleague.

Advocacy

Advocacy is speaking up on behalf of a person or an issue, and/or using evidence, argument and persuasion to achieve change. In relation to a person its aim is to safeguard that person's interests and rights (for example, to protect from abuse or present their vision of a future) if they are unable to do so themselves. In relation to an issue, advocacy stands to benefit all those affected by the issue. Writing in the context of advocacy with and on behalf of disabled people, Brandon, Brandon and Brandon (1995, p. 1) define advocacy as a process that:

> ... involves a person(s), either an individual or group with disabilities or their representative, pressing their case with influential others, about situations which either affect them directly or, and more usually, trying to prevent proposed changes which will leave them worse off. Both the intent and outcome of such advocacy should increase the individual's sense of power; help them to feel more confident, to become more assertive and gain increased choices.

Not only people with disabilities, but all those living in conditions of social marginalisation and their families are often discriminated against in many different ways and have to fight to gain basic rights – to be treated as other members of society in education, employment, housing, relationships, health services, transport and access. Some people are able to speak for themselves in all situations, others need help to express opinions and to have them heard. Sometimes, expert knowledge held by critical community psychologists can strengthen a cause.

Table 9.7 summarises the nature of advocacy arising from some work we undertook on different kinds of advocacy with and for people with learning disabilities in the UK (Kagan, 1997a).

There are several different forms of advocacy, which all overlap in parts. However, each has its own characteristics and issues to be taken into account (Table 9.8).

Reflect!

Are there any types of advocacy you may have received in the past or are receiving at the moment? Critically reflect on the advocacy you may have received. You may want to consider whether it was transformative or ameliorative; how this advocacy could be strengthened and your potential role (including barriers and facilitators) in achieving this.

Critical community psychological practice may involve any or all of these forms of advocacy. All forms require stamina, persistence and commitment. Advocacy can be stressful, take up a lot of time, and be frustrating. It can also be uplifting and rewarding. Advocates need to be resilient and like all forms of community practice, ways of ensuring personal support for the advocate are essential. Support mechanisms can help advocates reflect on their experience, recognise the limits of their advocacy and watch out for emerging conflicts of interest. Advocacy will often test personal values. Grieger and Ponterotto (1998, pp. 30–31) writing about challenging intolerance, consider advocacy to be one of the most aggressive, controversial and public (and personally risky) forms of social action.

> Advocacy and activism in relation to fighting intolerance challenge us to take a moral and ethical stand with regard to the touchiest issues within our organizations, to publicly articulate our stand, and to risk the displeasure, if not the wrath, of those who hold power and authority. It may mean being unpopular, becoming a lightning rod for the anger and resistance of colleagues, and at times, it may mean being willing to put our jobs on the line in order to do the right thing.

Over time, advocacy roles may change and one form of advocacy become another.

Table 9.7 The nature of advocacy

Sources of advocacy	An individual: an interested person, relative, another person living in the same situation or using the same services; service users, professionals or professional advocates (usually lawyers)
	A group: self help group, service users' group, campaigning organisation, or voluntary organisation
Form of advocacy	Arguing a cause
	Representation of an idea or proposal with or on behalf of a person or a group
	Complaints
	Challenge and criticism
	Letters, phone calls, petitions, media coverage
Key issues	Many strong feelings are involved
	Advocacy requires moral and ethical stands to be made
	Advocacy is seldom straightforward
	Advocacy does not always solve the problem
	Advocacy may incur the fury of those who hold power
Content of advocacy	Safeguarding of people's rights
	Representing and enabling expression of a person's interests and views
	Obtaining views, criticism of services, complaints
	Enabling participation in different walks of life
	Enabling consultation, participation in assessment of need, lobbying for change, giving information and advice
	Challenging institutional barriers or policies inhibiting well-being
	Service evaluation
	Development of policies, resolving disputes with families
	Representation within inspection and criminal proceedings

Table 9.8 Types of advocacy, their characteristics and key issues regarding their implementation

Type of advocacy	Key characteristics	Issues
Citizen advocacy	Citizen advocacy is a one to one, long term partnership between a person (usually a service user) and a citizen. She or he gives his/her time without pay and is not connected to the person through a service role. Citizen advocacy is based on the belief that all people have values and rights, irrespective of their disabilities or other support needs. Citizen advocacy's objective is to *empower* those people who have been excluded or kept powerless by linking them to a valued citizen and bring them into full membership of the community.	Citizen advocacy relationships are: • *Unpaid.* • *With minimal conflict of interest.* The advocate's loyalty is to the person he/she represents and is central to the success of the relationship. • *One to one relationships.* The focus is on one individual who is in a relationship with a person who is not socially marginalised. This starts to ensure positive interactions with, and interpretations of people who experience marginalisation. • *Sustained relationships.* The relationship between an advocate and the person represented should have the capacity to develop over a long period.
Self advocacy	Self advocacy can be how a person develops and gains confidence and abilities to express his or her own feelings and wishes. Self advocacy can mean groups of people getting together to collectively speak out about joint concerns.	Self advocacy groups are run by the members, and they determine the direction and purpose of their activities. They can include for example: • Discussion groups in adult education settings • Service user groups • Independent groups supported by volunteers or linked voluntary sector organisations • Residents or tenants associations
Peer advocacy	Peer advocacy involves one to one support by a service user, past or present (or someone who shares similar life experiences), to help another to express and fulfil his/her wishes. Peer advocates do not give advice but introduce people personally to the appropriate agencies in the community who can give the most up-to-date information and support.	• People who have experienced the same or similar problems are uniquely qualified to support an individual through a time of crisis. • User-run peer advocacy is seen as an empowering model for an independent, individual advocacy service. • A peer advocate can bring empathy and strength to a service user. This empowers the service user in ways that are different from an independent advocate.

Type of advocacy	Key characteristics	Issues
Advocacy by friends and families	Friends and family members will have many years' experience of asserting the rights of their friend or relative to services and to a decent standard of living and life opportunities. There will sometimes be conflicts between family advocates and other advocates involved with a person.	• Brandon et al (1995, p.47) point out that family members *"get no training or payment and bring considerable concerns, intimacy and passions to the process of representation as well as despair and exhaustion. Often they are uniquely qualified and involved to make strong cases."* • Despite this, it will not always be in a person's best interests to have their friends or family members advocate on their behalf. Friends and families may be a source of oppression.
Independent advocacy	Independent advocacy is often undertaken by volunteers. It offers a one to one relationship, with advocates assisting a person to express their wishes and feelings. At times it may be necessary for the advocate to speak for the person.	• Individual (volunteer) advocacy often has some elements of professional services i.e. record keeping, accountability to a co-ordinator, supervision of advocates, and payment of expenses, but is undertaken by volunteers. • There is a dilemma about the real independence of agencies providing advocacy services, when much financial support is from statutory services. • Increasingly, services specifically recruit an independent advocate to represent the best interests, or even the perspective, of a person who cannot speak for themselves. This is often done in the midst of conflicting views above what is best for the person, between different professionals or between family members and professionals. This requires high levels of skill.
Professional advocacy	In a human service context, professional advocacy involves a paid person working *independently* of services, representing the interests of a person. (This is different from services staff speaking up on behalf of a service user which should be seen as in-house representation to avoid confusion.) A professional advocate must be working with and for their partner and not as an additional worker for statutory services.	• There is a tendency for professional advocates to adopt an expert model of advocacy which involves them in giving advice, prioritising options, counselling and mediation. • These activities may not encourage empowerment through advocacy. • Where there is funding by statutory services for advocacy workers, there is a danger that the workers have a conflict of interest as paid service workers.

continued

Table 9.8 Continued

Type of advocacy	Key characteristics	Issues
Legal advocacy	Legal advocacy is representation by legally qualified advocates, usually solicitors or barristers.	• Many citizens will require the use of a legal advocate at some time, to move house, to make a will or to represent them in court. • Legal advocacy has an important place in protecting people's rights and interests within the law. • People may need the assistance of other kinds of advocates to access legal advocacy.
Collective advocacy	Collective advocacy is when a group of people come together to pursue an issue which affects more than one individual. This concept overlaps with the work of self advocacy groups. Class advocacy refers to representation affecting a certain group of people, such as homeless people, and may be undertaken by the people themselves or by a campaign group on their behalf.	• Collective advocacy is concerned with *patterns* of problems, difficulties, shortcomings, and possibly with class needs. It focuses on general issues rather than individual difficulties. • Collective advocacy bodies should be independent of direct service provision. • The skills needed in collective advocacy include committee work, managing finances, planning press handouts, the use of the media to influence policies, and campaigning. • There may be overlap between collective and self advocacy processes. • The power of people undertaking collective advocacy can be seen in successful lobbies to change legislation. • Difficulties exist for collective advocacy groups as they have to get close enough to the system to influence its activities but if they get too close, they are in danger of losing their independence and being co-opted into the system they seek to change.
In-house representation (not advocacy)	In-house representation is seen as part of the responsibility of professionals (community psychologists, social workers, nurses and others) to speak up for individual service users.	• There is a conflict of interest as the worker is often paid by the organisation he/she is taking issue with. • Many paid staff working in human services (statutory and voluntary sector) have a significant role to play in representing individuals whom they are working with in a variety of situations. • If advocacy is challenging the employing organisation workers may risk their jobs.

Source: after Kagan, 1997a.

Example: Legal, citizen and independent advocacy

These examples of different forms of advocacy are from projects we have worked on and/or direct work we have undertaken with people with learning difficulties (intellectual disabilities) and other impairments. They illustrate how different forms of advocacy can evolve into others. It is accidental that all of these examples are of work with men.

Robin

Robin lived at home with his elderly mother who had helped him live a full life in the community despite the multiple impairments he had which meant he had been to a special school and it was difficult for him to hold down a job. His brother lived in Australia and had recently convinced his mother to sell up her home and move to Australia (without Robin). No consideration was given to Robin's views or interest in this decision and he stood to lose his home. Ann, his neighbour, got to hear about these plans. She thought, if this were to have happened to her or one of her daughters, who would protest? So she talked to Robin and asked him if he would like his views to be known. He said he would and that what he wanted was to remain in his home. Ann realised preventing the sale of the house was beyond her knowledge and capabilities and, with Robin's permission, she got a solicitor involved. He obtained an injunction on the house sale. A process then followed in which Robin (and Ann his citizen advocate) was fully involved and that resulted in the house being sold but a smaller house, nearby, being bought for Robin with the proceeds and a sum put aside to be held in trust to pay for the personal support that Robin would continue to need. His mother moved to Australia, but with very little spare cash (much to the annoyance of Robin's brother).

Andy

Andy lived in his own flat, supported by social services, who had been in touch with a local independent advocacy service requesting a citizen advocate to spend time with Andy, helping him manage his affairs and continue to live independently. Rose had been his advocate for two years and they spent quite a bit of time together, enjoying a shared interest in music – particularly the music of Cliff Richard. One day Andy went to his bank and withdrew all his money which he then spent on an expensive guitar to add to the two he already possessed. When he told Rose about this, she helped him think about whether or not he did want to spend all his money on the guitar, and what this would mean he would not then be able to do. He decided to take the guitar back to the shop. Rose went with him to assist him in returning the guitar and to put the money back into the bank.

Pete

One of us (CK) was asked to work as an independent advocate for Pete. He was a severely disabled man with no speech but lots of different ways of making his views known. He lived in a staffed house in an ordinary street. The request for advocacy came as there was a conflict between Pete's parents, who considered he lived in a situation that put him at risk and wanted him moved to a segregated institution some 50 miles away, and his sister and the professionals involved with him, who considered he was happy and lived a full life in the community and should not be moved. The advocacy was needed to represent Pete's best interest within this conflict. After spending a lot of time with Pete in different situations, finding out what he did and how he reacted to the different activities and situations in which he was involved, talking to important people in his life, and spending time in the institution to which his parents wanted Pete to move, the advocate concluded, "From Pete's perspective there is no reason to move him from his home and the people and places he knows – although some things could improve" (and these were spelled out). The authorities decided to continue to support Pete in the community. Over time Pete's parents continued to be unhappy with where he lived and abducted him from his home and placed him in the institution. The advocate was still involved and spent time with Pete in the institution. She then became involved in a dispute with the authorities who had failed to protect Pete, leading to this placement that was not in his interests. The advocate's involvement continued in different forms for 14 years and included professional, legal and citizen advocacy. It only ended when Pete died from a non-diagnosed cancer. At this point the role turned into support for his sister who had not been permitted access for three years, so that she could have contact with him during his last months, and advice to her over the advisability of pursuing further complaints about malpractice, leading to his death. (It is worth noting that more recent British legislation (Human Rights Act, 1998; Mental Capacity Act, 2005) would probably have made for a more facilitative context for advocacy in this case, the events of which took place before its implementation.)

Michael

Michael lived independently, with multiple sclerosis, and looked after his mother who had dementia and lived nearby in another authority. As the austerity cuts bit following the 2008 financial crash, services to his mother were severely cut and his own allowance, enabling him to employ an assistant to help him do things that were important to him, was halved. We helped him use the legislation and regulations to challenge both authorities and harnessed the help of legal experts in our writing formal letters in support of maintaining his services to his mother. Services to his mother were maintained but he was unsuccessful in getting his own allowances reinstated.

Advocacy can be a powerful role – it can also fail, as seen above. It can also move from one form to another (for example, individual citizen advocates can refer issues to collective and legal advocates who then develop campaigns). There are some inherent problems in adopting advocacy roles, as all but self and collective advocacy assume that a person is not able to represent their views themselves and that advocates are in a better position to do so. The danger is that advocacy then disempowers, rather than empowers, and places the advocate in the position of power. It can be helpful to supplement advocacy with an analysis of power and to constantly reflect in order to guard against seduction into such a power position and to avoid conflicts of interest. Nevertheless, it can sometimes be vital, especially when working with people or communities with immediate and urgent needs (as in Robin's and Pete's cases above).

Reflect!

Critically reflect on the types of power that you personally have as well as the role that previous and future experiences and choices can play in this. Can you think of examples of marginalised groups who may not have these experiences and choices?

In this chapter we have presented action strategies, demonstrating linkages between development of alliances, accompaniment and advocacy. In the next chapter we look at archival research and analysis and development of policy.

Chapter 10

Action 3: Archive research and policy intervention

Summary

In the last two chapters we have considered different action strategies that are concerned with working directly with people in their current contexts. In this chapter we consider back-stage strategies that go beyond the immediate context and interrogate the data, trends and policies in the background. We provide an overview of largely desk based techniques of investigation into power interests and the ways in which power interests influence policy and the potential for the use of information in the public domain to challenge these interests and underpin action. Techniques include statistical literacy and the processes of policy analysis and development. The possibilities for participatory policy making will also be considered.

Working with archives and big data

A lot of emphasis is given to front-stage, active intervention for change in critical community psychological work. In this section we are going to introduce the idea of back-stage strategies that are sometimes required in the course of wider practices. We will look at archive research: desk research and working with big, and sometimes not so big, data.

Archive research

The word 'archive' is not easy to define as it is used in various ways in different contexts. Here, we are talking about a collection of some sort – a collection of historical documents including photographs, recorded or transcribed interviews, paintings, artefacts – which provides information about a place, institution or group of people. Work with archives can be in preparation for an intervention, particularly at the stages of planning or applying for funds for a project, or can form the intervention itself. Both uses of archives can be participative in their operation and contribute to participants' sense of self-in-context as well as exposing power dynamics that did, and often still do, exist. Certainly, for any heritage project, whether this is for preservation of a building, a landscape, a way of life or cultural traditions, the identification and use of relevant archives will probably be required.

Accessing and using archives

Using archives for background research with local people is not always easy. Sometimes data or documents are held in more than one archive. Table 10.1 offers some general steps to finding and using archives.

Community archives are locally held, usually locally compiled and managed, and help to locate community life in its broad socio-historical context. Both the compilation and the management of archives present opportunities for community engagement. Furthermore, researching within archives can place social justice at the heart, and reveal historical tensions and struggles, often in response to class or colonial oppression relating to (a) particular forms of oppression and redistribution of power or resources, and/or (b) culturally defined groups who are striving for recognition. Archives can interface with social justice in a number of ways. Duff, Flinn, Suurtamm & Wallace (2013, p. 4) discuss the challenges of using archives for social justice purposes:

Table 10.1 Finding and using archives

---

1. Be clear what information you are seeking – or if you do not know what might be available, at least have some broad idea of the aims of your research.
2. Do background research before visiting the archive.
3. Identify relevant archives.
4. Make an appointment to visit an archive and get a registration ticket if required.
5. Ask! Ask archive staff or holders how the archive is organised and how best to search it (although there are some digital archives that behave like other digital repositories, most archives are not searched by keywords). Let the staff know what you are researching.
6. Be prepared to spend a lot of time looking at material that is not directly relevant. Beware of getting side tracked (although this can point to lots of other interesting avenues to pursue).
7. Clarify the rules about note taking and photocopying (many archives only permit note taking in pencil). If there are specific pieces of information you would like to use, check if copyright release is needed – tracing the original owner of the material can be a detective journey in itself. Be particularly careful about the use of images – always check if they are copyright.
8. If you are involving others in accessing the archives, discuss the information you have found and talk about what you now know that you did not before, and how this affects your views of your place in your community. Who has not been involved in using the archive that should have been?
9. Critically reflect on the information you have found. When was it collected, by whom, for what purpose? Who were the informants or original owners of the material? Where do they sit in the social hierarchy? Is the information complete? What might be missing? Often historical records reflect the lives of privileged people – how might you redress this balance?
10. Check if there are other archives you need to access to cross reference your material.

One of the key challenges … is unpacking the dual imperative of archives vis-à-vis social justice. Namely, taking the long historical view afforded by archives while simultaneously engaging present social justice challenges. Through its traditional focus on 'the past,' and a narrowing focus on archival exposure of past injustices, archives safely stay one step behind recognizing and addressing present injustices. The prospect for archives to 'rewrite' the past can manifest both a reality and an illusion. To wit: demonstrating social progress and evolution across time while also fundamentally masking similar current injustices through the control of the record via sensitivity, confidentiality and privacy, security, secrecy and classification, and intellectual property rights justifications, among others. The implicit and explicit danger here is avoiding and voiding linkages between historical and contemporary struggles, thereby helping to sustain the mythology of a disinterested, neutral and honest brokering profession. These dynamics confound social justice objectives, albeit in different forms, locations and intensities across historical and contemporary contexts.

The collection and storing of oral histories is a form of archiving; of recognising and documenting both oppression and resistance; of recovering historical memories and understanding colonial pasts and decolonising possibilities.

Example: Oral history in South Africa

Seedat (2015) describes an oral history project which was part of a broad programme of work and different projects aimed at violence prevention in the final years of the apartheid regime in South Africa. Researchers, teachers and volunteers collected oral histories or accounts from the local community. Some key principles underpinned the work, which are applicable more generally. These included: a focus on gathering informal knowledge on the locality, past and present, and to make it visible inside and outside the area; a determination to be inclusive and authentic and non-accusatory, and to ensure space for conflicting views; a desire for people to identify with what was produced; capturing the language of the people; using a variety of forms of expression including photographs and illustrations; avoiding reproducing apartheid structures, while connecting the local history with the rest of South Africa; collaborating with, and acknowledging, as many people as possible. In the account of the project, Seedat draws attention to the way the work animated the community, to the plans for a range of different forms of recording of the information produced and also to the forces that led to the stalling of the project. He concludes (p. 33):

The elicitation of narratives of past and contemporary events was imbued with (a) transformative meanings of performance involving the 'collection' of stories, artefacts, and other visual materials, (b) interpretation linking past to the present, (c) reflection about the insidious re-inscription of racialized discourse, and (d) social action animating community and solidarity as acts of collective self-definition. Closely linked to the idea of making community, the production of historical narratives was viewed as a public and inclusive endeavour; an endeavour within which community voices both control and drive the process of 'making' narratives. … individual residents were defined as the real knowers … and legitimate bearers of collective and individual narratives and memories, a reclamation of community intellectual and social agency.

Photo-voice, video-voice, participatory film making, sharing artefacts, drawings and so on, are all techniques that can be used to collect accounts of people's lived experiences as part of a local archive. When citizens themselves are the ones collecting the histories, the process can lead to socio-cultural-historical awareness and conscientisation. To make an archive, someone has to catalogue the material. There are different ways of making archived material available, each of which can, in itself be an intervention. For example, participative preparation of booklets, exhibitions, books, films, games and so on, can all be ways of ensuring some permanence to (even a selection of) an archive, whilst at the same time being an engagement, learning and empowerment intervention. Many relevant archives are not held locally. For example, in the UK, every publicly funded qualitative research project is expected to have its raw data archived, so it can be accessed, (re)analysed and used by other researchers. Parry and Mauthner (2004) quite rightly point out a number of ethical problems with this requirement.

Think!

What do you think are some of the ethical issues connected to opening data archives for further and secondary analysis? Read the article by Parry and Mauthner, particularly the sections on ethical issues, as the legal context of different archives will vary. Did you identify all the issues they raise? What did you miss – and why do you think this was?

Reflect!

If you had offered some information or artefacts for a local community archive, would you want any say in who could access these and how? What would your reaction be to a researcher from a different country, say, using your account of living in your community for their own research purposes without you knowing?

Desk (or armchair) research

In many ways desk research is a given. Literature searches, for example, are part of most scientific endeavours and many community practices. Not only are literature reviews important for understanding gaps in knowledge, they are also important as a source of critical appraisal of existing methods and analyses. Curiously, in the field of community psychology few journals actively seek contributions in the form of literature reviews. One exception is the *Journal of Community and Applied Social Psychology*, which explicitly states that it welcomes "*Review articles which survey theoretical developments or topics of major interest*". Other journals will publish empirical reviews, stressing the place of practice in the discipline, and theoretical debates are covered. On the one hand this demonstrates a healthy scepticism for the state of knowledge in the field. On the other hand, being able to carry out a focused and succinct literature review may contribute to influencing policy makers – locally, nationally or internationally.

> ### Example: Mental health and well-being (contributions to policy formulation)
>
> We submitted a review to the UK Government's Department of Trade and Industry's mental well-being policy development through an 'expert' foresight paper. The review was of research on mental health and well-being, drawing on our several years' work in the field (Haworth & Roberts, 2007). The paper was included as part of the overall departmental review.

> ### Example: Gender equity in the workplace
>
> Some of our colleagues were asked by the International Labour Organisation (ILO) to provide an overview of the issues facing small and medium enterprises in their provision of maternity protection. The team provided an overview of the international literature which the ILO was then able to use in their work on gender equity at work. (Lewis, Stumbitz, Miles & Rouse, 2014).

Literature reviews are also necessary, sometimes, to rebut claims made by other people that are inaccurate, partial or have a misleading story to tell, furthering the oppression of marginalised groups.

Literature published in journals is not the only source of material that we need to draw on in understanding the state of existing knowledge. What is known as 'grey literature', that is, reports and other material that is not published academically through peer review (although it may have been reviewed and will usually give information about a review or evaluation process). Many of the different kinds of 'grey' documents will still be copyrighted, but many are not, and increasingly they are openly available through open access or Commons licences. Government documents and reports produced by charities, campaigning groups and think tanks all come under the umbrella of 'grey literature'. In our critical community psychology work, we have often found that 'grey literature' is more informative and illuminating than published work. Many community groups and projects do not have academics associated with them and, even if they do, are not convinced that academic publishing, with its delays and tight controls on access with pay walls etc., is the best way to produce and disseminate information. And for some groups, and in some cultures, the very idea that their knowledge, produced through a collective process, can be authored, is anathema.

As a result, there is a large body of knowledge and recorded experience that is difficult to find and does not feature in the conventional literature. If you know which groups to look for on the internet, for example, it is possible to find all sorts of useful information, such as project descriptions, monitoring or evaluation reports, that can be a source of good ideas as well as being usable to strengthen applications for funding. This might be one reason to build up a Twitter follow list (see Chapter 6).

> ### Example: Supported living groups
>
> We worked with some parents of children with severe learning difficulties about ways in which they might be able to get more involved in planning and even designing services for their adult children. Our role was to record and evaluate the process of service transformation. Whilst the group was pleased to have our reports for their own planning and development, and to share them with other like-minded groups, they "did not see any point" in talking about the process at academic conferences or writing about it in academic journals. So we did not. The lesson we learnt was to negotiate carefully from the start about different concerns and pressures, as well as achieving clarity about who it is that owns both data and their reporting – not always possible and care needs to be taken not to promise things that cannot be delivered.

It may be worth considering some of the issues arising in reading 'grey' or hidden literature:

- Check out the source and authors of the report. If necessary, do some background research to assess any values or positions the group or authors are advocating of which this report is a part.
- Take care not to seek only information that confirms what you think at the start, tempting though it is. However, you do not need to think of being 'even-handed' – it is fine to develop a case from material that is consistent with your argument, but worth thinking about whether or not to include any alternative views (see Psychologists for Social Change's, 2017 paper on universal basic income, which argues for a universal basic income but also includes possible alternative policy solutions).
- Don't rely on Wikipedia without checking the sources, and if necessary finding out who it is that entered the material you are interested in. However, we differ from most academic advice. Wikipedia is an open source repository, which means that ordinary people have contributed material, resulting in a rich resource. So use it, but carefully.
- Always ask if you can use material that you come across. If it is publicly available, acknowledge the sources of your material, even if there is no intellectual property licence attached to it. Never pass the ideas off as your own.
- Be respectful of the material you find if you are using it to make a different argument from that which was intended in the source material.

Act!

See how many different definitions of 'sustainable development' you can find in the non-academic literature. How did you go about finding this information? Did you find material from international bodies as well as local projects? Which were the easiest to find and why might this be?

Working with big and not so big data

Within the community psychological field there are many examples of the use of research designs that incorporate statistical information, whether these be descriptive or inferential. We are (unashamedly) qualitative researchers and will sometimes use research designs that require descriptive statistical analysis but rarely use designs that depend on inferential statistical analysis. So why do we include a section in this book on working with big and not so big data? There are many reasons for this, not least because in our work we need to be able to understand statistical data and their analyses in order to make use of contextual information, but most importantly to be in a position to challenge interpretations of data that are just misleading or even wrong.

In the UK the Government produces heaps of statistics, and with the growth of neoliberalism, 'big data' have taken centre stage, contributing to, for example, a massive array of performance indicators constraining diverse activities including education, employment, climate action, higher education, crime and policing, volunteering, health and well-being. As Milan and van der Velden (2016, p. 63) say, "what is known as big data constitutes a novel, powerful system of knowledge with its own epistemology that is to say a specific way of framing, packaging, presenting and activating information and knowledge".

Of particular interest, in the UK, to community psychologists, are the *Indices of Deprivation*, which rank small neighbourhoods (of on average 1,500 residents) across the country on income; employment; education; health; crime; barriers to housing and services; and living environment. Data are also aggregated up to local authority level. Whilst at first these appear to provide useful information, it is necessary to look behind the headline statistics and interrogate the different measures that make up each of these indices.

Table 10.2 shows how the Indices of Deprivation are compiled.

Think!

To what extent will aggregating data from these different Indices of Deprivation give a meaningful description of deprivation in England. What might make them more meaningful?

We will sometimes judicially use these indices as background information to a project, particularly when requesting funding.

Example: Local heritage project

In an application for funding for a large community regeneration project linked to the acquisition and use of a local heritage site (Kagan & Friends of Hough End Hall, 2015), we used statistical information to make the case:

> Our priority groups were informed by: DCMS* research Taking Part (2014 statistics, 2013/14 quarter 4) which shows those groups are significantly under-represented in heritage activities, arts museums and galleries, digital engagement and volunteering; and the Indices of Multiple Deprivation, 2010, which show parts of our district are in the top 1 per cent and 5 per cent most deprived areas in the country and a third of the population of South Manchester are elderly.

As part of the same project we surveyed the local population about their hopes for the heritage building and used the descriptive statistical results of this as evidence for the uses we were proposing to the funders. During the start-up phase of this project we submitted a petition to the Chancellor of the Exchequer (Government Minister of Finance in the UK), using statistics to argue our case for his support (which we got – it's a long story – see Bulletins at www.houghendhall.org).

*Department of Culture, Media and Sport – this was another digest of statistical information.

Act!

> **Table 10.2** Indices of deprivation in England

The seven domains of deprivation are as follows:

- The **Income Deprivation** Domain measures the proportion of the population experiencing deprivation relating to low income. The definition of low income used includes both those people that are out of work, and those that are in work but who have low earnings (and who satisfy the respective means tests).
- The **Employment Deprivation** Domain measures the proportion of the working-age population in an area involuntarily excluded from the labour market. This includes people who would like to work but are unable to do so due to unemployment, sickness or disability, or caring responsibilities.
- The **Education, Skills and Training Deprivation** Domain measures the lack of attainment and skills in the local population. The indicators fall into two sub-domains, one relating to children and young people and one relating to adult skills.
- The **Health Deprivation and Disability** Domain measures the risk of premature death and the impairment of quality of life through poor physical or mental health. The domain measures morbidity, disability and premature mortality but not aspects of behaviour or environment that may be predictive of future health deprivation.
- The **Crime** Domain measures the risk of personal and material victimisation at local level.
- The **Barriers to Housing and Services** Domain measures the physical and financial accessibility of housing and local services. The indicators fall into two sub-domains: 'geographical barriers', which relate to the physical proximity of local services, and 'wider barriers' which includes issues relating to access to housing such as affordability.
- The **Living Environment Deprivation** Domain measures the quality of the local environment. The indicators fall into two sub-domains. The 'indoors' living environment measures the quality of housing; while the 'outdoors' living environment contains measures of air quality and road traffic accidents.

Weightings of the different indices

The domains are combined using the following weights to produce the overall Index of Multiple Deprivation:

- Income Deprivation (22.5%)
- Employment Deprivation (22.5%)
- Education, Skills and Training Deprivation (13.5%)
- Health Deprivation and Disability (13.5%)
- Crime (9.3%)
- Barriers to Housing and Services (9.3%)
- Living Environment Deprivation (9.3%)

Source: see www.gov.uk/government/statistics/english-indices-of-deprivation-2015.

At other times we will combine data from different sources to get a complete picture of a neighbourhood, whilst at the same time pointing out what aspects of people's lived experiences are not captured by these data, revealing how the statistical information has skewed the representation of the area (for example, Kagan & Duggan, 2010). In our experience of neighbourhood work, existing statistics focus on the deficits of an area and rarely capture the strengths, whether this is in terms of, for example, health, well-being, participation, education. The pictures that are painted of the neighbourhoods in which we work are, then, of problems, inadequacies and deficits, with all the consequences for how this reflects back on the community and how it makes people feel.

Reflect!

If you were to collect some statistical information to draw a picture of the strengths of your area, and to enable comparisons to be made with other areas, what data would you collect? How would you present these data? What might the difficulties of doing this be?

Asserting the inadequacy of statistical information is one form of challenge to the use of statistics. Another form of challenge is to the cases that others make about the world we live in and that reinforce inequities and injustices. These challenges form part of a praxis known as *statactivism*.

Statactivism

Bruno, Didier and Vitale (2014) note that statactivism is a term used as a way of reappropriating statistics' power of denunciation and emancipation, thus ensuring its relevance for critical community psychology. Walker (2017) offers a further explanation:

> statactivism has been defined as collective action using numbers, measurements and indicators as means of denunciation and criticism. What hegemonic logics of quantification have installed, statactivists can dismantle or at least roughen up.

Bruno et al. (2014, p. 213) point out that there is a long history of the link between statistics and social liberation. What statactivism attempts to do is to rally a wide variety of practices, all sharing the goal of placing statistics in the service of liberation. They suggest a number of different techniques adopted by statactivists, including:

- Working to contest, denounce and reject big data representations, on principle.
- Collective action that uses numbers, measurements and indicators as means of denunciating and criticising – exposing the representation of reality and denoting the possibility of a reality other than that of the official one.
- Producing, organising and quantifying original data to make an issue visible or relevant (contemporary examples from the UK might include reporting the financial and social costs of deportation; revealing the numbers living in in-work poverty in particular locations; highlighting the number of precarious workers in the reemployment statistics).
- Using statistical tools to create a shared (sometimes novel) reading of reality. An example here might be the social category of precarious worker, which did not exist in advance of the statistics showing how many people were living in precarity across different professional groups.

Thus, they argue, statistics can be used as a tool for struggle and as a means of emancipation both fiercely individual and expressly collective. Milan and van der Venden (2016, pp. 63, 64, 68, 69) sum up the possibilities:

Postulating a critical/active engagement with data, its forms, dynamics, and infrastructure, data activists function as producers of counter-expertise and alternative epistemologies, making sense of data as a way of knowing the world and turning it into a point of intervention … [thereby it] … supports the emergence of novel epistemic cultures within civil society, contributing alternative narratives of our datified social reality.

In our work on climate change, re-analysis of data, critiques of data interpretation have formed central planks of the climate advocacy work we do. A key question in the field is whether or not climate change can be avoided while growing the economy. We have been engaged in challenging and representing data produced in influential reports as the following example shows.

Example: Statactivism and climate change

An influential report produced by the Global Commission on the Economy and Climate (New Climate Economy, 2014) concluded that

> The decoupling of growth from carbon emissions in some of the best-performing economies, both in Northern Europe and in North America, demonstrates the gains that can be made in incomes, jobs, rates of innovation and profits from a low-carbon, resource-efficient model of growth.

This means absolute decoupling, where the level of carbon emissions decreases yet GDP increases. This seemed to contradict what ecological economists had found. On examining the sources cited in the report (one of which even appeared not to exist), it became clear that while Stern and colleagues draw the conclusion that absolute decoupling is possible, they present no evidence for this, and the (available) sources they do cite, while rather airily talking about 'absolute decoupling', can only show either sectoral reductions (in energy use) or territorial reductions, that leave out all the outsourced emissions that are the sequelae of the rising GDPs (Burton, 2014a).

However, our conclusion was challenged: in 2016 Yeo & Evans (2016) showed that between 2000 and 2014, there were 35 countries where territorial emissions reduced while GDP grew. However, they also reported that

> Only 21 countries decoupled their economic growth from consumption-based CO_2 emissions, between 2000 and 2013. This suggests some countries were only able to decouple by 'offshoring' some of their emissions to other countries. However, major economies including the UK, US, France and Germany still decoupled, even after accounting for the CO_2 contained in imported goods.
>
> *(Yeo & Evans, 2016)*

When we looked in detail at the data, we found the same thing (Burton, 2016a). There did seem to be evidence for absolute decoupling. However, that conclusion relied on country-level data for both GDP and for greenhouse gas emissions. We therefore looked in detail at the quality of that data. We also looked at how it can be interpreted. Our conclusion was complex, challenging not only the detail and quality of the data but also its interpretation. This illustrates the need to look in detail when big data are aggregated, so as to avoid unwarranted claims, but also to reveal the ideological and political drivers of how the data are used.

Whilst big – and not so big – data are important to understand, to challenge and, sometimes, to re-interpret, we should always remember that big data are, by definition, stripped of context and meaning. It is 'thick description' that addresses depth and complexity and makes big data useable (the points made early on by Geertz, 1973). It is stories, intentionally gathered and systematically shared, discussed and analysed for insights that help us understand the nature of social reality, but also, in the context of evaluation, to represent the strengths of an organisation or intervention and its changes over time. Even policy makers, devoted as they are to big data, need such thick description to bring policy needs and possibilities to life.

Policy intervention

In post bureaucratic welfare societies social policy has a major role in determining the well-being of citizens, addressing or creating conditions of social marginalisation and addressing, maintaining or creating inequalities. Furthermore, social policies create, reflect and reproduce subjectivities, embodying the values, beliefs and meanings of a particular society, at a specific point in time (Serrano-García, 2016).

Perkins, García-Ramírez, Menezes, Serrano-García and Stromopolis (2016, p. 6) point out that there is increasing interaction between community psychologists and policy makers, in many different social contexts. Indeed, they suggest that "policy work in community psychology is vital, vibrant and expanding, both geographically and topically". Orford (2008, p. xx) highlights the growing need to look at policy and its impact on poor and disadvantaged groups – in his case in relation to gambling:

> What I have found is that British government policy on gambling is influenced to a greater extent by commercial, now mostly transnational, interests than it is by those of us concerned with personal, family and community health. Perhaps this should not surprise me, but the most alarming aspect is the way that researchers and service providers are encouraged to be complicit with a policy that is increasingly putting people at risk – those on low incomes being most at risk – whilst promoting discourses that exaggerate benefits … I have found myself doing more media work than ever before, giving evidence to government committees and penning editorials. … Much of that activity has been reactive, but it has set me thinking about a more proactive approach.

Think!

Serrano-García (2016) suggests that, "Not only do policies embody values, beliefs and meanings of a particular socio-historical and cultural period but as a result they also influence the development of social relations among participants influenced by these policies." Do you think she is right? How might this work in your own context for policies relating to people who are homeless? Read what Serrano-García has to say about this – how does this differ from what you thought? Why was that? Was there anything particular about your own context that influenced your thinking?

To get embroiled in policy is to work at the intersection of the state (national or local) and citizens and in danger of becoming an ideological agent of the state, supporting policies that endanger the well-being of those we work with. This tension is explored by Burton (2013b, 2013d) who argues that in any policy work we must continually reflect upon the contested nature of both community psychology and social policy, whilst keeping the interests of the disadvantaged central. Opening ourselves and the policies we are engaging with to critical appraisal, he suggests, protects against our slipping into collusion with a disempowering state.

Act!

Write a short review (300 words) of Burton's (2013d) paper, making reference to a policy with which you are familiar. What aspects of his arguments did you agree and disagree with? What does this say about your own world view?

Think!

Academic reviewing holds a privileged position in access to information. What kinds of power does academic reviewing involve? Is this power distributed – and if so, how? Are any groups of people rendered powerless through the process of academic reviewing and/or are some empowered? Have a look at what Jackson, Peters et al. (2018) discuss and compare this with your own thoughts.

Some engagement with policy formulation and analysis enables community psychologists not just to harness social processes for social good, but to reveal where policies and their implementation threaten equalities and well-being. Bishop, Dzidic and Breen (2013) consider that community psychologists have:

> a natural and necessary place within the policy arena. Being able to contend with social complexity and deconstruct social issues in their full provides a sounder foundation and opportunity for second order change.

We can think of policy interventions at three different stages of policy development and practice: policy formulation; policy implementation; and policy analysis. In practice there is often an overlap between the three.

Policy formulation

Dalton et al. (2001) identify the main features of what they refer to as policy research and advocacy:

- speaking out in some form to influence decisions (including judicial decisions), policies or laws;
- seeking to persuade government officials and to influence or inform leaders in the private sector, journalists, or others;
- participating in public decision making and influencing the ways in which an issue of conflict is defined or understood;
- providing empirical research on social issues that may reveal the need for a new policy to address a social problem;
- evaluating existing or innovative programmes, including their intended and unintended consequences; and
- reviewing literature in terms of its implications for policy.

They, along with other commentators highlight the fact that entering the policy arena is to get involved with political decision making. Whilst some psychological contributions to policy making might strive to remain impartial, clarity about the values and principles underpinning critical community psychological practice will, inevitably, mean that work will ally with those on one side of controversial issues. Dalton et al. (2001, pp. 381–382) suggest, however that

> Distortion of research findings is neither ethical nor wise advocacy. To be influential, an advocate must be credible to policy-makers, while also making clear recommendations for action.

In the UK, there has been some debate between scientists and policy makers about the contributions of the former and the understandings of the latter (Sutherland, Spiegelhalter & Bergman, 2013; Tyler, 2013). In a nutshell, the scientists suggest that policy makers do not understand the science that might contribute to policy and policy makers suggest that scientists fail to understand the policy making process. Sutherland, Spiegelhalter and Bergman's case rests on a number of issues relating to understanding empiricist, often highly technical scientific investigations. Whilst some of these apply to critical community psychological practice such as *"bias is rife"*, many do not, such as *"bigger is usually better for sample size"*. There is little awareness of the range of methodological strategies and scientific approaches shown by this group of a zoologist, mathematician and ecologist.

As we know, as critical community psychologists, the decisions we take about how to investigate what social issues will mean that our research will inform particular aspects of controversial social debates. The kinds of research we get involved with will reflect our values and principles and will often make useful contributions to policy debates as they provide information about the most vulnerable. So of more interest, perhaps, is what the policy maker says to the scientists (Tyler, 2013). Tyler's top tips for those trying to influence policy are summarised in Table 10.3.

Decision makers are not being 'irrational' when they fail to act on evidence but rather their rationality is not restricted to a cold consideration of research evidence: they are also responding to their own and others' interests, refracted through the lenses of ideology, amplified by propaganda, yet also subject to particular experiences – which is why it is always important to emphasise the human stories, the emotional, when presenting scientific evidence, or even better to find ways of bringing people in positions of power face to face with those affected, or potentially affected by policies. Policy making is inherently political (French, 2019). Competing interests struggle for influence so the 'policy process' is not a linear one where evidence leads to action. Often the outcome will reflect the balance of interests among the various stakeholders. At different times (depending for example on who is in power and the point in the electoral cycle) the space where policy is debated and made will be relatively open or relatively closed to community interests. Understanding these competing interests is vital for effective intervention in policy making. Serrano-García (2016, p. 2) suggests that community psychologists and policy makers can learn from each other:

> community psychologists have contributed to policy makers' knowledge of community development, empowerment, participation and evaluation research while community psychologists have learned more about political processes, institutionalization, negotiation and conflict resolution.

Whilst recognising the two-way benefits, we do need to be mindful of the point that Tyler makes – "policy makers can be experts too". Engaging with policy makers requires a degree of humility and openness to the possibility that they might have a broad understanding of community psychological processes, even if they do not label them as such.

One of the challenges for us is to ensure that our research reaches decision makers and policy makers in forms that can be easily understood – this is rarely in the form of journal articles. Indeed, writing a policy brief involves thinking carefully about what information to include and what not. A policy brief may be in response to a specific request for a brief or may be unsolicited. In both cases the policy brief sets out a particular issue and makes recommendations for the courses of action to be taken. The steps for writing a policy brief are shown in Table 10.4

Table 10.3 Important things to understand about policy making	
Making policy is really difficult	Public policy is always more complex than it seems, involving a wide range of inputs, complicated interactions with other policies, and varied and unpredictable outcomes. It is rare to have a simple solution to a complex issue.
No policy will ever be perfect	Whatever the decision, the effects of policy are almost always uneven, benefiting some groups and causing problems for others.
Policy makers can be expert too	Many policy makers are experts in their field, with excellent research credentials, and with a good understanding of the research base.
Policy makers are not a homogenous group	Policy makers can include civil servants ranging from senior to junior, generalist to specialist, and to those in connected agencies and regional government; politicians in government and opposition; and all the people who might not directly make the decisions, but as advisers can strongly influence them.
Policy makers are people too	Despite extensive training and the best of intentions, policy makers will sometimes make bad decisions and get things wrong. They may also choose to act in their own interest.
Policy decisions are subject to extensive scrutiny	Policy is regulated by professional guidelines, a variety of checks and balances, and scrutiny that comes from a wide range of institutions and angles.
Starting policies from scratch is rarely an option	Policy makers need solutions that can evolve from within the existing ecosystem.
There is more to policy than scientific evidence	Policies are not made in isolation. First there is a starting point in current policy, and there are usually some complex interactions between policies at different regional scales: local, national and international.
Economics and law are top dogs when it comes to policy advice	When it comes to advice sought by policy makers, economics and law are top dogs. Scientific evidence comes further down the pecking order.
Public opinion matters	Complex policy areas are all heavily influenced by public opinion, which is a critical component of the democratic and policy processes. Public opinion may be sought via elected representatives, public consultations and so on.
Policy makers understand uncertainty	Civil servants are expert at drawing up policy options with incomplete information (which is just as well because complete information is a fantasy). However, policy makers are not fond of information so laden with caveats that it is useless.

Parliament and Government are different	In the UK, the distinction between Parliament and Government is profound. Parliament (many elected members and small staff) – the legislature – debates public issues, makes laws and scrutinises Government. Government (few elected members and large staff) – the executive – is led by select members of Parliament and is responsible for designing and implementing policy.
Policy and politics are not the same thing	Policy is mostly about the design and implementation of a particular intervention. Politics is about how the decision was made.
Policy and science operate on different timescales	If scientists want to engage with policy they need to be able to work to policy makers' schedule which is often in terms of days or weeks. Asking policy makers to work to a slower timetable will result in them going elsewhere for advice. And make your advice concise.
There is no such thing as a policy cycle	In practice, policy making is iterative – the art of the possible. It does not follow an orderly process of starting with an idea, followed by research, design implementation and evaluation.
The art of policy making is a developing science	We live in exciting times for policy making. In the UK, various initiatives for better governance are under way, including ones for opening up the policy making process, and others for building evaluation into policy implementation. Examples in the UK are the *What Works Centres*.
"We need more research" is the wrong answer	Policy decisions usually need to be made pretty quickly, and on incomplete information, so asking for more time and money to conduct research is unlikely to go down well.

Source: derived from Tyler, 2013.

Act!

Take an issue you feel strongly about and that can be informed by community psychological perspectives. Is a policy change needed? Try drafting a policy brief, following the guidelines above. If you cannot think of an example yourself, try writing a policy brief on one of the following: (i) the problem of long working hours; (ii) community involvement in plans for local housing; (iii) the social isolation of older people. How easy was it to do this? What role did your values play in the approach you took to the brief?

Table 10.4 Steps for writing a policy brief

1. Pre-briefing
   a. Decide which agency, department, or organisation you will address the brief to. Make sure the issue is of direct relevance to them and only include multiple agencies if the brief is truly cross-agency.
   b. Contact the agency to find out the name of the person to whom the briefing should be sent. (Note, some departments or agencies do not accept unsolicited briefings – it is as well to find this out before you send them one!). Do some background research into the interests this person has.
   c. Find allies if you can. Policy briefings from coalitions of different groups are likely to be more influential than those from lots of separate groups.
   d. Ask yourself what outcomes you want (for example to change practice, change priorities) and anything you want the person receiving the briefing to do, having considered your brief. If you aren't clear about this, they won't be either. It is not always legislative change that is needed, sometimes it will be enough for Government to authorise changes in how something is done.

2. Writing the briefing
   a. Be brief (3–4 pages maximum), clear and avoid jargon.
   b. Use short paragraphs, headings and subheadings and attach appendices giving further information if necessary.
   c. Structure your briefing to include a summary of issues (without including background information); recommendations for action (possible solutions and concrete next steps – prioritise if there are several); background and rationale (**summarise** background information which will aid understanding, such as a brief (recent) history of the issue, previous policy decisions and their impact, previous research on the issue, or other contextual information).

3. Further information
   a. Include appendices and annexes to the briefing if relevant.
   b. Include a list of your sources.
   c. Include your contact details for people to get back in touch with you and be clear if you are writing on behalf of an organisation. It is better to approach policy makers collectively as they find it difficult to deal with a lot of 'noise' in the system.

4. Presenting the brief
   a. Timing can be important. Be aware of the political agenda. When decision makers are absorbed in a crisis, an election, or other pressing matters will not be the best time. Your message may not chime with some other priority or event, so, where possible, pick your time to present. Jackson (2017, pp. xxv-xxix) describes a striking case of unanticipated bad timing for a major policy report that led to its being sidelined.

    b. Use more than one way of communicating. A press release or a blog post can accompany a more detailed and formal report (but if the report has been commissioned by a government actor, check what is permissible). Could a short video (even you setting out the basic idea for just 2 minutes) help? Consider using social media to increase awareness and coverage of the initiative.

    c. If possible, get the key policy maker to help present the brief. That means they are more likely to both understand it and feel ownership and responsibility for it, making it less likely that it will end up 'orphaned'.

5. Follow up

    a. Request a report on what happened to your policy brief and look out for opportunities to attend consultation or briefing sessions about the issue of concern. Be persistent.

    b. Keep allies abreast of developments as and when they occur.

    c. Celebrate success. But if there is no success, don't be downhearted, look for examples of successful policy impact.

Example: Psychological impact of austerity

In the UK critical community psychologists have been centrally involved with a network seeking to influence policy in a number of ways. Psychologists for Social Change is

> a network of applied psychologists, academics, therapists, psychology graduates and others who are interested in applying psychology to policy and political action. We believe that people's social, political and material contexts are central to their experiences as individuals. We aim to encourage more psychologists to draw on our shared experience and knowledge to engage in public and policy debates.
>
> *(www.psychchange.org/)*

The group has: responded to policy initiatives (for example offering a critique of an influential policy initiative on the origins of happiness and the Government's green paper on transforming children and young people's mental health provision); argued for psychological impact assessment of policies (for example the impact a universal basic income might have); and evaluated how austerity policies and practices have had an unequal impact in society, disadvantaging poorer people and contributing to social inequality and weakening social justice (see https://psychagainstausterity.files.wordpress.com/2015/03/paa-briefing-paper.pdf).

Think!

Look at any recent piece of social policy (you will find lots of examples on websites for government departments). Is there *any* evidence that community psychologists were involved in the policy making process? You might look at works used in the policy development process, or groups or organisations consulted. Why do you think community psychology is as (in)visible as it is? What policy areas might critical community psychology be relevant to? What tensions might there be in becoming more involved in social policy processes?

Policy formulation may not always be the most effective way of influencing key policy makers, and collective advocacy and lobbying – talking to elected representatives, using social media to raise wider awareness of issues – can be just as important. It partly depends what the aims of the intervention are – for example, do you want to change behaviour, cultural awareness or the culture itself (which sometimes is needed before behaviour change can happen), or democratic processes? If it is all three, then multi-pronged interventions will be needed. Although, as in many areas of practice, compromise might be needed in policy formulation, one thing that should not be compromised is the fundamental values underpinning your work – you will regret helping to shape policies that contradict your values!

Example: Professional body divestment from fossil fuels

Two of us (MB, CK) have been working on cultural change and policy developments in relation to our global climate emergency. One area of activity is to get organisations to divest from investment in fossil fuels. Our own professional body (the British Psychological Society – BPS) has substantial investments, but there was no clarity about how many of these were in fossil fuels, or even what the investment policy was. Our aim was to ensure that the BPS had an investment policy that excluded fossil fuel investment and that any funds invested in such companies were reduced to zero. We initially tried just asking the BPS for information, and sent through a policy briefing asking for divestment and for an ethical policy that precluded further investment in fossil fuels – only to be fobbed off by the claim this was a matter only for trustees. We complained to the President about this stance and to the newly appointed CEO. We wrote letters to the BPS' magazine; wrote to each of the trustees with briefings about the issue and what they could do about it; allied with MedAct which campaigns for fossil fuel divestment and climate change mitigation on health grounds, built a list of BPS members who supported the campaign and presented the Society with a petition calling our aims. After two years of persistent prodding and asking for updates, and apropos no explanation, the BPS issued an Ethical Investment Policy which included not investing in companies engaged in extraction of fossil fuels.

This is an example of what eventually was a successful campaign to change the professional body's policy relating to climate mitigation. It is an important example, because if we take *stewardship* seriously as a core critical community psychology value (which we do), there is an onus on all of us to do what we can, in whatever capacity we can, to influence policy and practice on climate mitigation. Whilst we were active in this intervention, there were different roles for other participants in the intervention, ranging from co-signing letters to signing our petition. Not everyone has to be active in an intervention (see Chapter 5 on the nature of participation), but in this case, the weight of opinion from members was probably an important factor in the change.

Whilst there was some involvement of Society members in this policy change, it could not really be called participatory policy making. If policy ideas either emerge from the grass roots through a wide campaign of involvement, or involve a broad range of stakeholders at an early stage, the process could be called participatory policy making. Participatory policy making involves a reversal of the usual power relations, with ordinary people living in communities holding the greatest decision making power, and government (or local government) representatives serving these interests. Michels and De Graaf (2010) suggest that participatory policy making is closely linked to better democracy, insofar as it enables:

- greater inclusion (allowing different voices to be heard), thereby strengthening social capital and deliberative democracy;
- development of civic skills (such as the running of meetings, dissemination of views) and civic virtues (feeling of being a public citizen and participating in public life), thereby strengthening participatory democracy and social capital;
- deliberation where rational decision is based on public reasoning (via exchange of arguments and shifts of preferences), thereby strengthening deliberative democracy;
- legitimacy, giving support for both process and outcomes, thereby strengthening participatory democracy.

Participatory policy making is not easy: it is time consuming and requires a lot of resources. In Greater Manchester, a participatory policy making process was enacted at regional level via the People's Plan, involving a great number of volunteers and civil society groups. The resultant plan differed from the formal, non-participative strategic policy framework, highlighting not only the merits of a participatory process, but also the gulf between the power brokers and citizens.

Example: The People's Plan of Greater Manchester (People's Plan, 2017)

The People's Plan: Greater Manchester was an independent public engagement by and for the citizens and civil society of Greater Manchester (ten local government administrative areas), at the time of some limited devolution from central government. The Combined Authority (the coalition of ten administrative areas) issued a Greater Manchester Strategic Plan. The People's Plan was an attempt to do the same, but from the grass roots.

> The approach taken has been unusual and experimental in GM. It is not the work of one organisation or committee, but of a broad alliance of willing volunteers – citizens, groups and networks from civil society and communities, experts from think-tanks and academia, business people and trade union members, activists and artists, technology and media professionals and more. With very limited financial resources, the potential and capacity of this approach to deliver was unknown and the risks have required a certain amount of courage; but the many challenges have also strengthened belief in the need for, and value of, this collaborative approach. From October to December 2016 volunteers organised a programme of varied public meetings;

alongside this the People's Plan website provided an online survey, with prepared questions and open inputs covering six major themes – homes, health and care, transport, democracy, environment, jobs and economy.

(Peoples Plan, 2017, p. 3)

The conclusion of the detailed analysis highlighted the differences between policy makers and citizens.

Policy makers have had a concept of how to try and build a city-region economy on growth and jobs for market income; but they have not been able to close gaps in economic output and income, or create jobs for citizens in the northern boroughs. Our citizens have a different vision of a more sociable city-region for individual and community well-being, where decent homes and tenants' rights, sustainably funded public health and care, better connected and cheaper transport, healthy environment and renewable energy, better skills and fairer jobs take precedence and are delivered with a strengthened local democracy. In a democracy, our citizens' priorities need to be taken seriously.

(People's Plan, 2017, p. 30)

For participatory policy making to have an impact, there must be a level of openness to citizen engagement, and a willingness to shift priorities by the formal policy makers and politicians. In Greater Manchester, the process continues, perhaps with some recognition from the authorities that citizens will no longer accept what is on offer. In more recent policy consultations (not the same as participation we know), policy makers have received responses in the thousands – rather than the tens which was more usual.

Act!

In small groups, take an area of policy that is important to your community (such as policy to lower levels of crime and increase community safety; decrease homelessness; increase the levels of social housing available). Design a participatory policy process. What resources would you need? Who would you involve? What questions would you ask? How will you analyse the responses? How will you try to ensure your recommendations are adopted?

Think!

Find two sets of advice on formulating policies (you can find lots on the internet). How do they differ? Why might this be? Have a look at who is giving this advice and consider what their agendas might be. If you read these sets of advice through a community psychology lens, would you add anything? Why/why not? Consider what you know about formal policies developed in your context and consider whether the advice you have found fits your understanding.

It is one thing to be involved in policy formulation and development, but perhaps more often critical community psychologists will find themselves involved in policy implementation.

Policy implementation

Some community psychological practice will involve developments in relation to specific policy implementation. This is most likely when community psychologists are employed in particular service development areas. Conflicts can emerge between the interests of the employer and the values of the community psychologist, especially if the implementation of particular policies might increase inequalities. This might be one reason why community psychologists can be ambivalent about engaging with policy arenas. However, sometimes policy implementation will lead to substantial increases in wellbeing and social inclusion with a decrease in marginalisation. Community psychologists can then be in a position to use their expertise and skills to ensure most effective implementation.

One of the current trends in policy implementation, particularly in the context of public services, is what is known as co-production (Beebeejaun, Durose, Rees, Richardson & Richardson, 2014). Boyle and Harris (2009, p. 3), strong advocates for co-production, suggest

> the key to reforming public services is to encourage users to design and deliver services in equal partnership with professionals. The time seems to have arrived for the idea that the users of public services are an immense hidden resource which can be used to transform services – and to strengthen their neighbourhoods at the same time.

The idea is that power between professionals and those using public services is equalised as they design (and sometimes deliver) a particular service together. Another way to think about this is that those using services are invited to participate, as equals, in the design and delivery of the services they use. We are most familiar with the situation in the UK, but co-production ideas are implemented in many other places (see, Howlett, Kekez & Poocharoen, 2017, for example, for case studies of co-production in Croatia and Thailand). Mayer and McKenzie (2017) reported that young men who co-produced local mental health services had increased self-efficacy and self-esteem and the professionals involved experienced a shift in their professional identities. Co-production can apply equally to research, wherein those who would usually be the focus of the research, or the beneficiaries of research, themselves co-produce the research design and practice with researchers.

Implicit in the idea of co-production is an equalising of power relations between those experts by experience and those experts by training. From the outset there are power asymmetries and it can be very difficult to resolve these. One approach to examining the power balance in either normal forms of policy implementation or co-produced ones, is the process of boundary critique which we have explored in Chapter 7. In the following example we can see the boundaries of place, people and practice being expanded.

Example: INTEGRATE: young people and mental health

MAC-UK INTEGRATE (Duncan, Zlotowitz & Stubbs, 2017) adopts a community psychological and co-produced approach to working with excluded and vulnerable young people, including those in contact with the criminal justice system. These young people often experience multiple risk factors for poor mental health, exacerbated by services that are experienced as 'hard-to-reach', leading to wide health inequalities. The MAC-UK INTEGRATE approach harnesses the power of young people themselves to be part of the solution. INTEGRATE seeks to wrap holistic and responsive support, including mental health and emotional well-being provision, around excluded young people. Work starts with meeting young people where they are (and not where the services are) and gaining trust – a process which cannot be short-cut and is essential to later work – if and when the young people want it. Young people choose, design and run a range of activities from music or sport to drama based on their passions and interests. Their help is actively requested in all aspects of the activities and young people can take up explicit leadership roles such as 'Head of Music' or 'Gym Project Lead', promoting a sense of ownership and responsibility. Young people can be employed on an ad hoc and part-time basis to carry out some of the project work. In addition, young people co-produce training workshops, campaigns and lobbying activities. See www.centreformentalhealth.org.uk/sites/default/files/mac_uk_anniversary_evidence_summary_0.pdf for further information.

Think!

Read the evaluation of MAC-UK at www.centreformentalhealth.org.uk/sites/default/files/mac_uk_anniversary_evidence_summary_0.pdf. Is co-production the same as participation? What are the similarities and differences? Is the promise of equal power delivered through co-production? If so, how?

Co-production is challenging, and it is essential to consider, amongst other things (Kagan, 2013):

- how co-production is understood by all parties;
- how power asymmetries will be reduced;
- who is and is not to be involved;
- who decides who is to be involved (as users either by experience or expertise);
- the relative balance of needs and wants;
- how the different world views of experts by experience and by expertise will be resolved;
- where activities and meetings will take place;
- the role of gatekeepers with respect to inclusion or information;
- the ease with which people can cease to be involved with co-production;
- the role of cost-cutting in co-production;
- the different capacity building needs of all parties (and where this will come from);
- who it is that decides what success looks like.

Reflect!

Think of a service you have received or delivered – this could be something to do with health, childcare, education, housing – anything at all. What would this have looked like if you had co-produced this service as either a service beneficiary or provider? What would it take to include more co-produced elements in the service?

Policy implementation invariably involves alliances and coalitions between internal agents (community members), external agents (outsiders) and representatives of the local or national state. Montero (2013) describes such an alliance, or social consortium, highlighting the complex role that community psychologists can play in bringing those with different interests together whilst maintaining the participation of community members at the core. In Montero's example, the social consortium itself becomes a constituted community association. This is important in a locality with few organised groups, but need not always be the case. The final responsibility for delivering change (in Montero's case, housing) might lie with a pre-existing community group which enjoys the trust of the different stakeholders.

Act!

In pairs, identify a policy that needs to change. On a large sheet of paper, write down the different community level stakeholders in different places on the sheet and draw lines indicating connections between them. Now add external stakeholders, again drawing interconnecting lines. Finally add local or national (even international if relevant) interests and complete your diagram by drawing lines connecting them to others concerned. What do you think of this web of policy interest? If you wanted to influence policy, where would you start? Why?

Sometimes, to make a difference, the only feasible option is to take on a management role in a service delivery organisation. This can bring its own problems and dilemmas, for example diversion into serving the system as system, with its often perverse incentives in the form of performance indicators and so on. So it is essential to be clear about what the ends are, to constantly remain open to alternative perspectives, especially from those affected by the system. Nevertheless, a role as an internal change agent, in management, is a feasible role for critical community psychologists.

Policy formulation and implementation are both important roles for critical community psychologists. The other policy arena that is relevant is policy analysis (which will often overlap with both formulation and implementation).

Policy analysis

Policy analysis is an important critical community psychological role to be played in the exposure of disempowering and contradictory aspects of policy and their implementation. This critique can come from experience in implementation, or in a textual analysis of legislation and associated regulations, which can reveal the ideological base of particular policies and the disempowering consequences for particular groups affected by policy implementation. The UK based policy and advocacy group Psychologists for Social Change give a rationale for policy analysis:

> There is growing awareness that politicians need to consider the well-being of their citizens, and that policy decisions should go beyond 'bottom line' economic arguments. As psychologists, we are in a position to analyse the evidence in policy recommendations, governmental speeches and investment in local and national schemes ... [and] ... draw attention to the impact that policy might have on marginalised groups and individuals. Recently, there has been political recognition that the organisation of our society is not working for many people. We hope that this strategy will celebrate psychologically informed and evidence based policies that will have a positive impact on people's well-being. However, we will also hold to account and critical appraise those policies that do not consider the mental health [and well-being] implications. We also have a firm commitment to articulating clear routes to the prevention of mental health problems ... in

developing our own policy recommendations, we will demonstrate how they might improve people's agency, security, connection, sense of meaning and trust.

(www.psychchange.org/formulating-policy.html)

Policy analysis can take place at an early, proposal or consultation stage; at the time of legislation, via its implementation; or after it has been in force for some time. Initial analyses are best understood as impact assessments. In the UK equality impact assessments and environmental impact assessments are widely understood – psychological impact assessments, less so. For this it is necessary to have some community psychological criteria against which to assess the likely impact. Table 10.5 offers a framework for interrogating policy.

Example: Universal basic income

Universal basic income (UBI) is a policy idea that is being promoted in many different places. Psychologists for Social Change produced a community psychological impact assessment of the policy. Part of this was to draw on psychological knowledge about social recognition and redistribution of social resources, including wealth. However, we were also able to examine the impact of some alternative policy proposals (Psychologists for Social Change, 2017).

Table 10.5 Criteria for critical community psychological policy impact analysis

1. Boundaries
   a. Are there some people who are excluded who should be included?
   b. Are there some people who are included who should not be?
   c. What are the consequences of the above boundary decisions?
2. Well-being
   a. To what extent will this policy enhance people's agency?
   b. To what extent will this policy enhance people's sense of security?
   c. To what extent will this policy enable people to have a sense of purpose?
   d. To what extent will this policy enable people to have a sense of trust?
3. Results
   a. Will this policy lead to increased participation?
   b. Will this policy lead to increased skills in the community?
   c. Will this policy lead to increased empowerment?
   d. Will this policy lead to increased community connections?
4. Wider impact
   a. Will this policy lead to greater social equity?
   b. Will this policy lead to increased social capital (bonding, bridging, linking)?
   c. Will this policy lead to increased social trust?
   d. Will this policy lead to long lasting protection of the environment and community resilience?

Example: Valuing People (VP)

Burton and Kagan (2006) reviewed the contradictory policy mix in the UK Government's policy framework for learning disability. They were concerned to decode Valuing People (VP) (Department of Health, 2001) in terms of the dominant ideologies and interests that had influenced policy formation in order to try to diagnose its strengths and weaknesses. This required contextualising Valuing People in terms of the policy mix of the Blair government, wider ideologies in human services, and the situation of modern welfare states in a context of neoliberal globalisation. While this was an ambitious project it did help to establish some of the challenges in inclusion of people with learning disabilities (an avowed policy aim). A key finding was that there was an alliance of convenience between the market oriented ideology that had dominated since the late 1970s and the agendas of individualisation (personalisation in later jargon) and self determination. This, supported by a romantic image of learning disability, potentially made it harder to work collectively for a radically improved situation. Allied to this was a selective understanding of human rights which again minimised economic and social rights. Burton and Kagan's analysis drew upon ideological analysis (see Jameson, 2009, for an overview) as well as direct knowledge from being embedded (Burton) and closely engaged (Kagan) in the field. The analysis was not entirely negative, however; the overall direction of Valuing People was endorsed while adopting a sanguine viewpoint on its limitations and chance of overall success.

Thomas and Robertson (1992) point to the ways in which such analyses of social policies can highlight hidden agendas, in contrast to explicitly stated objectives. They offer a framework for analysing social policies that addresses each stage of policy development: problem identification; policy formulation and adoption; policy implementation; policy outcomes; and policy evaluation (but bear in mind, as discussed above, policy making rarely follows such a cycle).

Table 10.6 summarises the steps of policy analysis proposed by Thomas and Robertson (1992).

As we can see, analysis of policy and involvement in all stages of policy development are complex and have a number of different components. Policy analysis is one of the more distal, macro-level community psychological interventions, but can contribute to further innovations in policy formulation and social change. The work ranges from involvement in decision making within local services and social institutions to involvement in legislation and associated regulations. Our discussion of it here has been confined to national and sub-national policy. However, international and global policy increasingly has direct and indirect impact on the lives of people who are socially marginalised, and Perkins et al. (2016, p. 6) point out that community psychologists also have a role in analysing and influencing these policy arenas. They report that community psychologists, in alliance with others from other disciplines are working on:

> …inherently international policies, such as those affecting climate change and that provoke wars and widespread violence while causing extreme poverty that forces millions of people to be displaced and shortens the life spans of entire communities. The neoliberal, pro-global capital-market policies that are restricting services and rights of citizens are also an example of this.

Table 10.6 Social policy analysis

Policy analysis stage	Questions to ask in policy analysis
Problem identification	How are issues identified as problems requiring governmental or institutional action?
	What are the assumptions made about the causes and locations of the problems?
	What organisational pressure points or public issue have influenced the identification of the problem?
	Who has been involved in the identification of the problem?
	How has the socio-political context influenced the identification of problems?
Policy formulation and adoption	Who is participating in the policy development and are some important stakeholders excluded from this process?
	What values appear to form the basis for the policies and what are the desirable outcomes emanating from these values?
	What discrepancies are there between existing conditions and the desirable outcomes?
	How do socio-political and historical contexts limit the options considered and boundaries on, for and within policy formulation?
Policy implementation	What goals are set for each policy? What procedures and timescales are proposed for achieving each goal and how are these to be implemented?
	How will different people be affected by these procedures?
	Which institutions or organisations are assigned responsibility for implementing the policy and what does this reveal about hidden agendas?
	How will the policy be shaped by these particular institutions and organisations and what might the impact on different groups of people be?
	What organisational energy, enablers, constraints or inertia might influence implementation?
	Who will be excluded from participation in the light of the above?
	How have these decisions been influenced by the historical and socio-political contexts?

Policy analysis stage	Questions to ask in policy analysis
Policy outcomes	What are the effects of the policy on relevant social, political and/or economic processes?
	What are both the intended and the unintended outcomes?
	How does this policy complement or contradict other policies?
	How has the policy been affected by changes in the socio-political context?
Policy evaluation	How is the policy being monitored?
	How effective are the implementation mechanisms?
	Have the policy objectives been achieved?
	What is the impact of the policy on different groups affected by it?
	What have been the organisational issues in policy implementation?
	How cost-effective is the policy?
	What unintended effects have been created by the policy?
	How have changes in the socio-political context affected the impact of the policy?
Dissemination of policy information	How have the results of policy analysis been communicated to different interested parties beyond those concerned with formulating and implementing the policy?
	How have the most disadvantaged been assisted by this policy analysis?
	What recommendations for change have emerged from the policy analysis?
	What mechanisms are in place for influencing future decisions in relation to the policy?
	How will the socio-political context influence adoption of recommendations for change?

Source: after Thomas & Robertson, 1992, p. 40.

This work is carried out without negating our value base and principles and while continuing to side with those most unequally and disadvantageously affected. In many places, local and sometimes national governments consult about proposals for new policies, and these afford opportunities to give feedback, submit research evidence or advocate on behalf of community groups (better still – to help groups to advocate on their own behalf).

Act!

See if there are any live consultations about local or national policies where you live. Complete the consultation. What opportunities were there to introduce community psychological ways of thinking into this consultation? How else might you bring community psychological understanding to the attention of the policy makers?

271

The agenda of policy analysis, and policy critique, raises the question of when, how and if community psychologists should get involved in the local or state apparatus (see Burton, 2013d). It also raises again the question of the boundaries between critical community psychology and political activism. We are clear that there is a distinction, but as in other cases, having made the distinction it can be appropriate to blur it. This goes in two directions. Political campaigning can be the pursuit of goals that emerge in community psychological work by other means. Colleagues of ours for example, working on educational inclusion, have taken part in direct action against segregation and been prosecuted. Alternatively, political action can benefit from critical community psychology when community psychological methods and concepts contribute to political campaigning.

Example: Climate change

We have been involved in local action on climate change, bringing a critical community psychological perspective. We have used group facilitation techniques to improve the running of planning meetings and to develop alternative policy frameworks. Understanding of how local government works has contributed to the design of both tactics and strategy. Skills of policy analysis have been applied to policy consultations – for example a regional economic strategy that included a sustainability rhetoric but manifestly was still locked into the dominant paradigm with its discredited assumptions of global competitiveness and endless economic growth.

It is not always easy – or even desirable to see the different action strategies as separate from each other. For example, policy analysis can lead to advocacy, which in turn contributes to the furtherance of critical consciousness (and indeed may be preceded by conscientisation).

Example: Seroxat and SSRI Users' Group

The Seroxat Users' Group (described in Burton, Kagan & Duckett, 2012; Duckett, 2012) is one example of an integrated strategy for change. Through a process of policy research and advocacy the work of this group has involved the lobbying of the judiciary, social policy makers, the mass media, corporations and so on to redress the social harm done by a multinational pharmaceutical company. Specifically, the group is seeking to stop doctors prescribing dangerous anti-depressant medication (SSRIs) which cause physiological and psychological harm (such as increasing the risk of patients attempting suicide). The group has engaged in efforts to persuade those who occupy positions of power to effect change on their behalf (by amending social policy, publishing the group's cause, changing corporate and professional practice, instigating criminal proceedings and so on). One of us (PD) has been involved in working for the group as an expert witness in a way that is helpful to the group's cause.

This chapter has completed the chapters in the section 'Act!' and has covered a number of different strategies for change. In the next part of our book, we turn to 'Reflection', which we begin by considering how to evaluate action.

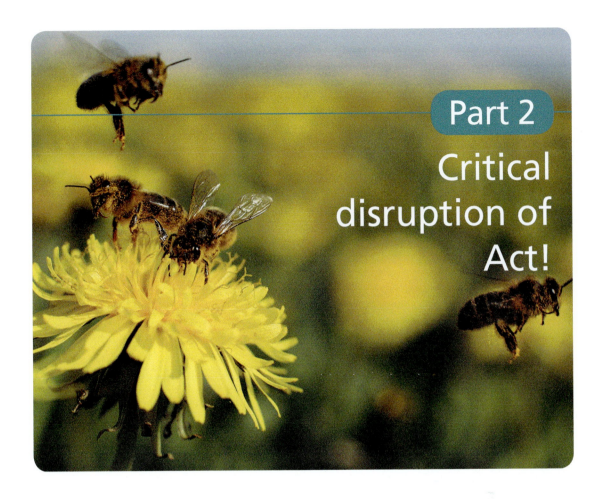

Part 2
Critical disruption of Act!

In Part 2 we have discussed the importance of social action of various kinds. We have engaged critically with these concepts, but here we consider whether we have engaged so critically with the belief system that underpins Part 2. Doing so might provide a useful disruption to some of the assumptions that may underlie those chapters, the main one being that action is good.

Action has been the *sine qua non* of community psychological work which might explain why action research has become a central, defining feature of the discipline. It is interesting to note that our discussion of resistance throughout has been largely in terms of it being a type of change process. We see resistance in two ways, as a sign that something is going wrong in terms of people's commitment to a project, or that the direction the project is taking might be misguided. This might be because for community psychologists, to engage in a project that results in inaction could be viewed as a negative outcome (although perhaps our discussion of the concept 'accompaniment' (see Chapter 9) hints at an alternative orientation). So perhaps we conceptualise resistance either as action in disguise or as a sign that action is endangered. Making a link with cultural theories of social action, we could consider the cultural and political preconditions that permit or encourage such a stance to be adopted towards action in critical community psychology. In doing so we might find that action, change and progress have become particularly culturally valued under a capitalist consumer economic system.

Under consumer capitalism (Stiegler, 2006; Burton, 2009c), the system needs the consumer to purchase new products and discard old products on a regular basis. This produces mountains of waste and consumer capitalism promotes an extravagance of both consumption and waste. For consumer capitalism to thrive, social conditions need to be created for us not only to consume more and more (and more often), but also to discard more and more (and more often). If we do not become rapidly dissatisfied with our old goods, we will not have the desire (or the room) to rapidly acquire new goods. A delayed purchase for the consumer is a delayed profit for the capitalist system. Consumerism creates (or at least exploits the opportunities created by) social conditions to encourage people to behave as consumers in this way by a number of means. First, it ensures that material goods have an in-built obsolescence. Second, it creates the perception of an insecure, unpredictable future. Third, it exploits prior norms or activism, grounded in the norms established by the 'work ethic'.

In-built obsolescence is most easily achieved for foodstuffs as they truly are turned into waste in use. However, even here, the imposition of 'use by' and 'best before' dates ensures that these consumables will be turned into waste expeditiously. The effect in the UK is that a third of all food that is bought is thrown away and never actually eaten either because it had spoiled, too much was cooked or the 'best before' date had been exceeded (Smithers, 2017). For non-foodstuffs, the goods must be socially regulated to ensure they are disposed of in a timely fashion. This can be achieved both by the fashion industry and by technological innovation – both achieving the same thing – to ensure goods are labelled 'out of date' and consumers are implanted with the desire to buy replacements.

Academics are subject to a similar process – to produce new knowledge to supplant old knowledge. This can be seen in the publications of old text with some minor revisions which are then marketed and consumed as 'new editions' but also more broadly in the sheer volume of publishing activity. Duckett (2009) summarised the problem identified by others:

> It is estimated that five million journal papers are published each year (Canagarajah, 1996). On their website, Blackwell Publishers proudly announce that they are "the home of over one million articles from over 850 journals" (Blackwell, 2008). More 'information' has been produced in the past thirty years than was produced in the past 5,000 years such that now a Sunday newspaper can contain more information for consumption in one day than a 'cultivated' person in the eighteenth century would have been expected to 'consume' in a lifetime (Ramonet, 1999). Of course, the point at which the production of knowledge outstrips the point at which all of that knowledge can be consumed has long been passed. Most knowledge produced now is being produced (by effect rather than intent) as waste. It has been observed that more than half of all published academic journal articles will never be cited nor, presumably, read (other than by copyeditors) and much of the work that is cited is seldom fully engaged with and may, in fact, not have been read by the author who cites it. It is likely that only a small percentage of academic texts are actually read and a smaller percentage (probably a tiny f[r]action) actually influences the academic field in any noticeable way (Bauman, 2007).

Of course, our textbook is now in its second edition. We did see the need to update the content of the book, largely in response to: (a) major social and political events (e.g. the growth of nationalism exemplified by Brexit in the UK) and to shifting political priorities (e.g. the crisis of climate change); (b) previous omissions (expanded sections on social policy and working on big data sets); and (c) a need to address theoretical positions (e.g. colonialism) that became more salient to us as a writing team when two of us (Asiya and Paul) moved from the UK to China and Australia. However, this opens us to the criticism that we too have become subject to the project of rabid capitalist consumptive practices as we have added another publication to the stockpile. The question is begged as to whether we might have worked harder to have updated our text in a way that might have immunised ourselves to the criticism that we are feeding the very system we are aiming to critique.

To encourage consumerism, being content with what you have got has to be unsettled. Being content with the first edition of the book was not in our gift: our original publisher did not keep the book in print, driven by the never ending machine of the academic publishing industry. Positioning social change as a dominant and positive social norm achieves this such that people are encouraged to change their appearance, their job, their house, their mobile phone and so on and that not changing is equated with stagnating and as a warning sign that you are faltering or failing in some way. So, change is embraced as a cultural norm by an economic system that seeks to regulate behaviour to accommodate the production of excess.

Chronic uncertainty

Carpe diem (seize the day) has become a prominent leitmotif of modern living in the industrialised West. The future is constructed as uncertain, unpredictable and unstable such that one should live for today rather than for tomorrow. These features of modern life are expressed potently in the labour market of many Western nations where jobs are becoming short term and insecure. For example, in the UK 90 per cent of the net rise in jobs during 1992 to 1994 were in non-permanent, insecure employment (Trades Union Congress, 1995). In March 2019 official employment figures stand at their highest since 1975. But at the same time in-work poverty and child poverty has increased (Joseph Rowntree Foundation, 2018), due to a combination of factors, including low paid work, welfare changes and austerity. Between 1981 and 2001 the UK labour market lost 2.3 million full-time jobs and gained 2.7 million part-time jobs, creating a new 'class' – the precariat (Ford, 1995; Standing, 2018). The increased insecurity of the labour market has been driven by economic demands, ushered in largely by the corporate world, for high profit growth achieved through reduced wage bills (Harvey, 2005a; Glyn, 2006). Thus, a corporation requires a flexible labour force that can be hired and fired quickly to ensure the profit margins of the corporation are protected. "Profitability is maximised while the risk of fluctuating demand has been displaced to the labour force." (Hutton, 1995, p. 171).

Work ethic

The work ethic, traceable as far back as the sixteenth century and embedded in Protestant Christian ideology (Weber, 1904/1930; Tawney, 1938), has been a value that helped discipline agricultural workers into the new requirements of factory work. The work ethic remains embedded in social policy today. Politicians in the UK have talked about an unacceptable culture of 'worklessness' (cf. Martín-Baró's 1987 critique of the myth of the lazy Latino), where work is socially lauded and worklessness is condemned. It becomes every citizen's duty not only to work, but to want to work. The citizen is required to be an active contributor to the economy, even to the extent of calls to raise the retirement age (despite widespread youth unemployment).

These conditions (in-built obsolescence, insecurity and the work ethic) provide fertile ground for capitalist consumerism which requires consumers to constantly renew (to cast out the old and bring in the new), make their choices for today not tomorrow (to replace the comfort of long term security with the pleasure derived from instant gratification) and remain active in the economy (both as workers and as shoppers). Combined, these conditions create a hegemonic discourse that promotes activity and change as important features of social life that must be encouraged and limits the discourses permissible around the notion of resistance other than that we have entered into (that resistance is problematic, a sign that something is wrong). In this regard, it is interesting to see how the concept of procrastination has become transformed.

> Contrary to an impression made common in the modern era, procrastination is not a matter of sloth, indolence, quiescence or lassitude; it is an active stance, an attempt to assume control over

the sequence of events and make that sequence different from what it would be were one to stay docile and unresisting, To procrastinate is to manipulate the possibilities of the presence of a thing by putting off, delaying and postponing its becoming present, keeping it at a distance and deferring its immediacy.

(Bauman, 2000, p. 156)

The art of procrastination was the act of delaying action through engaging in contemplation – to stop and to sit and to think so as to gain a better understanding of where we are and where we are going.

This is an unfamiliar practice for community psychologists who have embraced the notion, extolled by Kurt Lewin and others, that we learn through doing. This leaves little room, or an awkward room, for us to procrastinate. Moreover, a contemporary rendering of procrastination positions it not as a virtue but as a vice, perhaps because it disrupts the social conditions required for the smooth functioning of a consumer capitalist economic system. This might restrict our ability to explore the art of procrastination as a form of political resistance (the employment of delaying tactics) and the notion of silence and invisibility as political activity (going underground, the politics of silence and so on) in their own right rather than as a precursor to action (or as a form of action). It might also prevent us from considering non-participatory, non-action research as having merit. Indeed, the philosophical ruminations and esoteric language associated with critical psychology can be (and in our experience often are) caricatured by community psychologists as an exemplar of the problem of thought without action. The readiness of community psychologists to act is sometimes caricatured by critical psychologists as an exemplar of the problem of action without thought. Einstein's aphorism on the criminality of thought without action and the insanity of action without thought captures an element of the antagonism between community psychology and critical psychology (community psychologists are seen as acting too quickly and critical psychologists as acting too slowly), but also points to how the orientation towards action has become sufficiently moralised so as to operate as an axiom (a critically unexamined, self-evident truth) in community psychology.

Here is a collection of some resources with a short description to assist in your reading of Part 2 (Chapters 6, 7, 8, 9 and 10).

Films

- *Made in Dagenham* (2010). Directed by Nigel Cole. This is the story of Rita O'Grady who worked for the Ford Motor Co. plant in Dagenham, England. Despite performing the specialised task of sewing upholstery for car seats, women at that time were classified as unskilled labour and paid much less than men. Rita agrees to bring the women's grievances to Ford. The meeting goes badly and, outraged by the company's lack of respect for them, Rita leads her colleagues to strike.
- *Blue Gold: World Water Wars* (2008). Directed by Sam Bozzo, this is a documentary examining the environmental and political implications of the planet's declining water supply. The film also highlights some success stories of water activists around the world, and makes a strong case for community action. https://vimeo.com/208683543
- *The Shape of Water* (2006). Directed by Kum Bhavnani, this is a documentary exploring the narratives of powerful, imaginative and visionary women confronting the destructive development of the Third World and has themes of new traditions, social justice, peace and the environment. www.theshapeofwatermovie.com/aboutfilm.html

- *Bread and Roses* (2000). Directed by Ken Loach, this is a film about the struggle of two Mexican labourers in Los Angeles for the right to form a union. It depicts an episode in the ongoing Justice for Janitors campaign, which is run by the Service Employees International Union. The film presents a contemporary account of the ways in which union activity is related to legal status.
- *I, Daniel Blake* (2016). Directed by Ken Loach. This is a film about the indignities of relying on state welfare in austerity Britain. Whether young or older, austerity policies have had a devastating effect on people's psychological health, social connections or well-being. A must to see how the 'system' can degrade people.
- *Community psychology in practice.* Watch PD giving an account of an unsuccessful attempt at changing policy regarding the UK Government and legislation around the intersection between the Department of Health, health regulators and Big Pharma. https://youtu.be/3NKx0T6CN6k

Toolkits

- *Community Toolbox.* This is a useful source of ideas for tools and techniques for social change. Have a look at this regularly and learn new things. https://ctb.ku.edu/en
- *Collaboration.* There is also a large compendium on building community consensus at www.nationalassembly.org/wp-content/uploads/2018/06/TheNewCommunityCollaborationManual.pdf
- *Participatory action research.* Some useful resources for participatory action research can be found at www.participatoryactionresearch.net/publications
- *Action Learning and Action Research.* ALARA (the Action Learning and Action Research Association) is an excellent source of innovative and value based, participatory work across the world. See www.alarassociation.org/
- *World Café events.* For lots of good ideas about how to run a World Café event see www.theworldcafe.com/
- *Families and Schools Together.* This programme takes a socioecological view of the child and implements a programme that links families within communities in order to strengthen both families and communities (it focuses on areas of social difficulty where many families are under stress). It builds on the experiences of families themselves rather than experts. www.familiesandschools.org/
- *New Economy Organisers Network.* Ideas for campaigners, activists and organisers. https://neweconomyorganisers.org/resources/
- *Participation in policy making.* The Northern Bridge Doctoral Training Programme, which is a consortium of UK universities training scheme for doctoral students across the disciplines, has an excellent Public Policy Engagement Toolkit, with links to examples of good practice. Whilst this has a UK focus which reveals itself in some of the areas of policy influence (such as Parliamentary Select Committees) that might not exist elsewhere, the resources are widely applicable. http://toolkit.northernbridge.ac.uk/engagingwithpolicymakers/

Other resources

- *The Life and Work of Paulo Freire.* For lots of interesting material about the life and work of Paulo Freire see www.freire.org/, and see also the blogspot: http://pfiucla.blogspot.com/
- *Rural Women Making Change (Canada) Project.* www.worklifecanada.ca/rural_women/rural_women_making_change
- *The Lawrence Textile Strike.* You may want to look into detail at this strike which concerned immigrant women workers in Lawrence, Massachusetts in 1912. The strike was led by the Industrial

Workers of the World (an international union) and was prompted by one mill owner's decision to lower wages when a new law shortening the workweek went into effect. The strike gained momentum in the town, growing to more than 20,000 workers at nearly every mill within a week and lasted more than two months. The strike defied the assumptions of conservative unions within the American Federation of Labour, by proving that immigrant, largely female and ethnically divided workers could be organised. The Lawrence strike is often known as the 'Bread and Roses Strike'. There is an interesting account of this in the following book: Watson, B. (2005) *Bread and Roses: Mills, Migrants, and the Struggle for the American Dream.* New York: Viking.

- *Vandana Shiva* is a prominent activist and anti-globalist. She writes, protests and documents issues such as farming practices and water. She suggests that a more sustainable and productive approach to agriculture can be achieved through reinstating a system of farming in India that is more centred around engaging women. She advocates against the prevalent "patriarchal logic of exclusion", claiming that a woman-focused system would change the current system in an extremely positive manner. See her talking at www.bbc.co.uk/programmes/p010d95m or www.bbc.co.uk/programmes/p03jrn5r

Anti-consumerist resources for you to critically consider:

- 'No Money Man', Mark Boyle, has spent a year spending no money. See the following link for short-videos of some of his experiences: www.theguardian.com/environment/2009/nov/09/mark-boyle-money
- An antidote to Black Friday's consumerism mayhem – www.buynothingday.co.uk/
- The Billboard Liberation Front: www.billboardliberation.com/
- The Earth Day: www.earthday.org/earthday/

Practical ideas

The Centre for Well-Being adopts a multi-dimensional approach to well-being – aiming to provide a good evidence base. Have a look at the community well-being work and see how you think this chimes with critical community psychology. Is there anything missing? https://whatworkswellbeing.org/

Re-drawing boundaries of critical community psychology

- *New Economics Foundation.* Works on the ways to make the economy work for everyone and for their well-being: https://neweconomics.org/
- *198 Methods of Nonviolent Action* from the work of Gene Sharp. www.peacemagazine.org/index.php?id=2083
- *Campaigning effectiveness* in the non-governmental sector (NCVO), www.ncvo.org.uk/practical-support/information/campaigning, and see also:
  - www.ncvo.org.uk/images/documents/practical_support/campaigning/campaigning_for_change_learning_from_the_US.pdf
  - www.ncvo.org.uk/images/documents/practical_support/campaigning/Trustee_guide_to_campaigning_and_influencing.pdf
- *Extinction Rebellion.* Urgent action on climate change. See the blog https://xrblog.org/
- *Accompaniment.* Mary Watkins speaks about her recent work on "Accompaniment: Psychosocial, Trans-species, and Earth Based." www.youtube.com/watch?v=Onyngjgw4lA
- *Using archives.* Some useful information about the general use of archives can be found at https://archiveshub.jisc.ac.uk/guides/usingarchives/

- *Qualitative data archives*. There seems to be an appetite for opening qualitative data to further and secondary analysis – Ask yourself *"what are the ethical issues in doing this?"* See for example:
  - UK: www.ukdataservice.ac.uk/get-data/other-providers/qualitative
  - Canada: http://leddy.uwindsor.ca/qualitative-data
  - USA: https://qdr.syr.edu/
  - Australia: https://legacy.ada.edu.au/

Policy ideas

- *Psychologists for Social Change*. There are a number of resources on the site of Psychologists for Social Change. For their briefing on the adverse effects of austerity policies on poorer people in the UK see https://psychagainstausterity.files.wordpress.com/2015/03/paa-briefing-paper.pdf
- *Steady State Manchester*. Seeks to influence policy at a city-region level. See www.steadystate manchester.net for lots of examples of policy interventions and an extensive blog and twitter feed, amongst other activities, that seek to influence culture around climate change and a slow down of economic growth. Two of the authors (MB and CK) are members of the Steady State Manchester collective.
- *Co-production*. For a discussion of the difference between co-production and participation see www.youtube.com/watch?v=iJjmFYSB_qo
- *Policy brief*. The UK Government has issued some advice about writing a policy brief. Consider how this differs from the guidance given in this chapter and why this might be. www.parliament. uk/mps-lords-and-offices/offices/bicameral/post/about-post/writing-a-policy-brief/
- *The Global Journal of Community Psychology Practice* has published two special issues about social policy and community psychology. See Volume 4(2) 2013; and Volume 7(1S) 2016 for a range of discussions from different parts of the world. www.gjcpp.org

Part 3

Reflect!

Contents

This section of the book is about looking back and examining what happened as a result of action, what roles and skills are used in community psychology practice and the role of reflecting on practice.

Chapter 11

Evaluation

Summary

In this chapter we look at different processes of evaluation, each with their own rationale and method. We overview different systemic models of evaluation, and specifically discuss 'theory of change' and realistic evaluation approaches as well as evaluation through systematisation of experiences. Throughout, we take a decolonising stance and promote the role of participation in evaluation as well as capacity building for evaluation and the centrality of reflection.

Evaluation is a key component of an action research cycle and is also a form of reflection. Furthermore, it can be an intervention in itself and lead to change (Cook, 2015; Miller, 2017). Evaluation technically refers to assessing the value (or worth) of something, but we use the term to mean how we know what difference a project or activity has made or is making. Increasingly, policy and practice claims to have been evaluated or piloted although the mechanism by which this happens is not always transparent. In critical community psychology, we not only evaluate our own practice as an integral part of action oriented work, but are also frequently invited to undertake evaluation research with and for other projects. In this chapter we will look at helpful evaluation frameworks including some from our own work and will examine our own roles as evaluators in relation to both our own and others' practice.

Act!

Using the web, locate an evaluation of a community based intervention. Key words you may want to use within a search include 'evaluation', 'community' and 'intervention'. What model of evaluation was used? Who conducted the evaluation (those internal or external to the project)? What was the evaluation for? How were the results of the evaluation used? Can you detect the values underpinning the evaluation? What do you think the risks to making values explicit might be?

Apart from the evaluation of our own practice, community psychological roles include those of evaluators, researchers and capacity builders (in this context, capacity building for evaluation). The National Council for Voluntary Organisations (NCVO), a national umbrella organisation for third sector organisations in the UK, issues guidance for evaluation, and hosts over 100 resources for evaluation in the form of guidelines, models, reports and discussion papers for community and voluntary sector organisations (see www.scribd.com/lists/17786361/NCVO-Charities-Evaluation-Services). There are other compendia of evaluation research too (see, for example, Shaw, Greene & Mark, 2006), and many published guides to different kinds of evaluation. We will discuss the approaches to evaluation we have found to be most useful, combining evaluation approaches that reflect our critical community psychological orientation; take a decolonising and systemic approach; attempt to understand experience in context; are participative and inclusive; and focus on collective action and continual learning. As usual, context is always central to the work.

Purpose of evaluation

Evaluation can be formative (at early stages, informing the direction of the project); summative (at the end, informing the extent to which the project did what it set out to do); or ongoing (as part of the everyday project activity, assessing how the project is working, its progress, the obstacles facing it and its impact).

Formative evaluation often involves those internal to a project whilst summative evaluation frequently brings in external 'experts', or 'objective evaluators' to assess the project. Formative evaluation can take the form of a needs assessment, or of a 'test run' wherein, for example, ways of working are assessed through a pilot project, prior to being extended to the whole project. The purpose of formative evaluation is to improve procedures, to identify potential barriers to implementation and to find better ways of doing something. Summative evaluation takes place at the end of a project and provides information on a project's efficacy – the extent to which it produces the results it aims for – and the extent to which goals were met. It assesses whether project objectives were achieved, the cost effectiveness of the project – often compared with other projects with similar aims – and outcomes for those benefiting or affected in some way from the project activities. The purpose of a summative evaluation is to provide evidence about what difference was made and how important it was, once an activity is completed.

> ## Think!
>
> Can formative and summative evaluations be separated? What would an evaluation that was entirely formative look like? What would one that was solely summative look like?

Whilst formative and summative stages are pretty well understood by most community projects, the idea of evaluation being a continuous (rather than one-off) process is less well understood; yet it is this type of evaluation that best reflects a critical community psychological approach and will give the most useful information. Ongoing evaluations, built into planning from the start, need to be flexible and adaptable as circumstances change, and to speak to the different interests involved – they need to be responsive (Stake, 1980) and guard against replicating existing power relationships. They require a commitment to ongoing critical reflection, thoughtful gathering of information and openness to learning. It would be a mistake to think that the processes of implementation of a project are confined to formative evaluation. At any point, evaluation can focus on processes, outcomes or impact of an action project, all aimed, not just at recording results, but at continual learning, project improvement and further action.

A decolonising stance for evaluation

Whilst every aspect of critical community psychological praxis tries to incorporate a decolonising stance, it is perhaps when discussing evaluation that this comes most clearly to light. Evaluation is an integral part of both action research and action learning cycles, and all the challenges of involvement and engagement of others, discussed in previous chapters also apply to evaluation. However, often critical community psychologists will be invited to evaluate projects of which they have not been a part, and it is here that the dangers of replicating power imbalances, and dominant epistemologies, are most stark. Almost by definition, when conducting an evaluation as an external commentator, we are expected to retain a degree of objectivity, to position the project and those working in and affected by it, as 'other', which affects what we seek, what we see and hear and the sense we make of our findings. There is the danger of what Fricker (2007) describes as epistemic injustice. She focuses on two kinds of epistemic injustice:

- Testimonial injustice – which considers who could/should have, or has, a voice; who is excluded; and how this is justified (see also the discussion of boundary critique in Chapter 7).
- Hermeneutic injustice – which considers the extent to which significant areas of social experience are obscured due to prejudicial flaws in interpretation. In practice, there may be an absence of knowing that this injustice has occurred, allied to a lack of opportunities and skills necessary to participate in understanding and interpreting findings.

These injustices can occur, even when we think we are participatory in our approach, as participation can also reproduce relations of power (Jovchelovitch, 2007). To try to ensure we introduce epistemic justice requires us to, first, address the boundary issues of whose voices are heard, and how; second, to understand those cultural forces at play, and to recognise that culture is intertwined with power, oppression and exploitation, which in turn need to be located within historical, social and political contexts (Reyes Cruz & Sonn, 2011); and third, to explore, wherever we can, the intersections of gender, age, race and disability (Kessi, 2017). The implications of this include ensuring our methods chime with the traditions, beliefs and worldviews of the community we are working with (Chilisa, 2012). Critical reflexivity is central to every point of evaluation, including the cultural assumptions we bring, how we are positioned in terms of the cultural practices we surface, and how we are positioned in different power hierarchies. The very nature of evaluation as a social process particularly of external evaluation, is often one of power, with the potential to ruin a project and those working in or affected by it. When we are invited to work with a project to undertake an evaluation, we need to understand how those internal to the project make sense of both the purpose and the practice of the evaluation; and to ensure that our methods are such that marginalised knowledges can be brought to the fore – which often means going beyond questionnaires, interviews and focus groups, the mainstays of many evaluations. The use of indigenous methodologies (Chilisa, 2012; Gaotlhobogwe, Major, Koloi-Keaikitse and Chilisa, 2018) to enable people to express themselves, such as proverbs, folklore, songs, and dance, and the creative invention of methods is as important in evaluation as it is in other parts of critical community psychological praxis.

Think!

Kessi (2017, pp. 509–512) describes some case studies where photo-voice was used. She argues that these illustrate in a very potent way how community members understand forms of violence and oppression that exist in their communities. How does her use of photo-voice address (a) testimonial and (b) hermeneutic injustices?

> ## *Reflect!*
>
> If you were in a position to conduct an evaluation, how might you ensure you adopt a decolonising stance? In each of the following sections, ask yourself this question.

Principles of evaluation

Our approach to evaluation is holistic, rather than reductionist (splitting things down into disconnected elements), focusing on multiple stakeholder and organisational perspectives, organisational change processes, outcomes and both intended and unintended impact. Throughout, attention is paid to the role of power and to ourselves within the evaluation process. From a similar standpoint, Taylor, Purdue, Wilson and Wilde (2005, p. 2) identify the following key characteristics of evaluation:

- it is a continuous process informing planning and delivery as the project develops;
- it involves all those with an interest in the project in defining the questions they want answered;
- it uses imaginative and creative approaches, which engage those involved;
- it helps projects to be more accountable to the wider community;
- it is used to challenge discriminatory and oppressive policies and practice, and to overcome inequality and disadvantage;
- it highlights and celebrates successes and achievements;
- it encourages an honest appraisal of progress, learning from what has not worked as well as what has.

We would add two characteristics to this list:

- it is culturally safe and appropriate, learning about the historical, social and cultural dynamics as well as the intersections of, for example, race, gender, age, (dis)ability and class;
- it incorporates environmental considerations as a matter of course.

The American Evaluation Association has published some interdependent, and interconnected, guiding principles for evaluators, which chime with community psychological approaches (American Evaluation Association [AEA], 2018; Sheldon & Wolfe, 2015) and are useful to consider. These principles are for those who are undertaking commissioned evaluations, more than those building evaluation into a process of action, but probably still stand. Each principle has a number of sub-statements attached to it that clarify its meaning and give direction for action, and it is in the sub-statements that we can see, amongst other things:

- a grounding in explicitly stated and communicated values as well as details of the evaluation approach and ethical considerations;
- consideration of the boundaries of competencies and the importance of ongoing capacity building;
- open communication;
- a requirement to understand and take account of power, stakeholder interests and potential risks that might arise from the evaluation.

The key principles, which would be difficult to disagree with, are as follows:

A Systematic inquiry: evaluators conduct systematic, data-based inquiries about whatever is being evaluated.

B Competence: evaluators provide competent performance to stakeholders.

C Integrity/honesty: evaluators ensure the honesty and integrity of the entire evaluation process.
D Respect for people: evaluators respect the security, dignity and self-worth of the respondents, pro-gramme participants, clients and other stakeholders with whom they interact.
E Responsibilities for general and public welfare: evaluators articulate and take into account the diversity of interests and values that may be related to the general and public welfare.

Of paramount importance, underpinning these principles, are a concern with the public good, includ-ing cultural, social, economic and political resources as well as natural resources involving shared materials such as air, water and a habitable earth (reflecting the value of stewardship a well as a concern for the planetary boundaries of practice); and the importance of a culturally competent evalu-ator (drawing on further guidelines about cultural competence (AEA, 2011)). This is an acknowledge-ment that evaluation reflects culture and cannot be culturally free, just as evaluators often embody cultural privilege, and there is danger of perpetuating power inequities. To be culturally safe, evalua-tion, and, indeed critical community psychological praxis, needs to recognise historical and contempo-rary injustice, the role that practices such as evaluation often play, not in liberation, but in furthering oppression.

Reflect!

How do you feel about these guidelines? To what extent do you think they are suf-ficient to underpin a critical community psychological approach to evaluation? Why or why not?

There is little in this guidance, other than in exhortations to respect diversity and difference, about working **with** stakeholders in evaluation, as partners or co-evaluators.

Smits and Champagne (2008) identify the key components of a practical participatory evaluation model, including stages of initiation; interactive data production; knowledge co-construction; local context of action and instrumental use. Table 11.1 explains these stages with reference to examples of evaluation in practice.

Act!

Look carefully at Table 11.1. Write a summary of the evaluation in terms of power. Where does power lie – who has it and who does not? What notice has been taken of historical and cultural factors? Who are the main beneficiaries of the evalua-tion? Could there be different beneficiaries? What advantages were there in 'out-siders' to the team conducting this evaluation?

Needless to say, the stages do not always proceed smoothly. For example, in an ongoing project around homelessness in Manchester, we negotiated to evaluate a co-produced approach to homeless-ness. City-wide stakeholders had agreed to work as part of a wider charter on homelessness (https://charter.streetsupport.net/). Our community psychological approach was to adopt a transparent and value based evaluation by working with both the driving group and the action groups (who included experts by experience). We are having to continually account for the participatory approach which is ongoing and inclusive. In an evaluation of arts and mental health, referred to in Chapters 7 and 13 (Sixsmith & Kagan, 2005), a failure to gain full commitment and understanding of the possible posi-tive benefits of evaluation from internal project members at the start meant that much work had to be done to overcome reluctance to take part in the evaluation. On another occasion, a failure on our part

Table 11.1 Stages of practical participatory evaluation

Stage	Example (Kagan & Siddiquee, 2004)
Initiation Respond to a trigger (need to find a solution for a problem that has not been resolved – need for project improvement or demonstration of efficacy). Recruit external evaluators and gain internal commitment. Identify external capabilities and internal knowledge about evaluation.	*A community development project wanted to find out how its website was being used – and could be better used – to enhance community development practice. The whole team was committed to improvement. A tender was issued and our team was commissioned after a selection and interview process that in part explored technical expertise of evaluation and knowledge of community development practice.*
Interactive data production Evaluators, practitioners, and other stakeholders collaborate in an interactive and reflexive dialogue about methods of collecting data and throughout data collection process. While data are collected questions emerge and are answered by evaluators, practitioners and other stakeholders when necessary.	*Methods of data collection, content of questionnaires, telephone and face to face interviews were explored and agreed collaboratively between web manager and evaluators.* *A series of meetings and discussions took place during data collection processes to resolve any difficulties that were arising.*
Knowledge co-construction Data are analysed and interpreted in the light of the practitioners' knowledge of the field and the evaluators' knowledge of scientific design limitations. During discussion of results the co-constructed knowledge can be translated into decisions relevant to the specific context.	*Further meetings took place as data were analysed and sense made of data collaboratively. Findings were shared with other team members and discussion held about how to interpret findings and what further information would be needed to collect. Workshops were held with wider groups of community development workers and those interested in evaluation to contribute to interpretation of findings.*
Local context of action External constraints are identified that influence the relevance and potential of co-constructed knowledge to lead to proposals for actionable knowledge or change. These might include resources (money, time, expertise), policies, project terms of reference, other stakeholder agendas (such as the acceptability of proposals for funders).	*The feasibility of different solutions to issues that were emerging was discussed in meetings between evaluators and the whole team as well as between evaluators and the web manager. Policy context, the realities of community development in the field (for example in terms of access to web resources) and resources as well as the project's priorities were all taken into account in the formation of recommendations.*
Instrumental use Decisions are made about which actionable knowledge should be carried through into an actual action targeting the initial problem.	*A plan of action was prepared by the web manager and discussed with an incoming new chief executive who was able to 'fast track' an understanding of potential for change within the organisation from the full evaluation report, although the work had taken place prior to her arrival.*

Source: derived from Smits & Champagne, 2008.

to gain full understanding of the local context and failure to involve key stakeholders in presenting recommendations from an evaluation, meant that in the short term change did not take place (see the witness support examples in Chapter 7 and see Kagan, Caton & Amin, 2001), although in the longer term the work did lead to new beneficial developments. In another evaluation, although there was commitment from those who commissioned the project, this was not shared by key gatekeepers with different agendas and thus access for data collection for change was not easy and recommendations were only partially implemented (Kagan & Siddiquee, 2005). In each of these cases (and many others) critical reflection enabled us to better understand the historical, cultural and political contexts, epistemic (in)justice, and both proximal and distal obstacles to change, usually through the exercise of power by those with vested interests (see Chapter 12). This is the key to the prefigurative action research process outlined in Kagan and Burton (2000).

The concept of prefigurative *action* was explored in Chapter 3: prefigurative *action research* helps us relate the experience of a project to its wider social (historical, cultural, political) and societal context, and to an implicit or explicit programme of action towards a more just society – the 'utopian horizon'. What this means is that if a piece of critical community research or evaluation does not contribute to the anticipated change, all is not lost. Through careful and critical reflection, we can learn about what obstructs, suppresses or limits the possibilities for change. We can also consider whether or not the 'time was right' for the intervention or whether there are other blocks to progress that need to be dismantled. We have an ethical responsibility to try to ensure that evaluations are carried out diligently and provide useful information. From a social justice perspective, Morris (2015) distinguishes four types of social justice, and suggests that if these were taken into account, this would contribute to ethical practice. These are:

1 relational justice – includes people's perceptions of fairness in the ways they were treated, especially in terms of dignity and respect;
2 informational justice – includes the perceptions of fairness of the information used as a basis for making decisions or framing interpretations;
3 procedural justice – includes how people view the fairness of the procedures used in the evaluation, used to determine the outcomes they receive;
4 distributive justice – includes people's beliefs about the fairness of their work-related outcomes, such as pay or recognition.

Act!

There are lots of reasons why evaluations falter: they may not lead to change, may be disrupted or may be incomplete. Make a list of the different reasons evaluations may falter – in each case, how might you try to ensure this does not happen?

Evaluation frameworks

From the many frameworks for evaluation, we are going to discuss those we have found most useful in our praxis, evaluating a wide range of different projects and action processes.

Systemic approaches to evaluation

Any change activity is embedded in a web of relationships both internal and external to a particular project or organisation. Evaluation, if it is to be systemic or holistic, needs to try to take account of these complexities. Three 'ideal types' of evaluation can be identified, that when

Reflect!

combined create a holistic framework for evaluation. By ideal types, we mean conceptual models that highlight distinct approaches: however, in the real world of application these are rarely implemented in a pure form and elements from each are often combined. The three ideal types of systemic evaluation are 'stakeholder evaluation', 'goal based evaluation' and 'organisational evaluation' (Boyd et al., 2007).

Stakeholder evaluation

Stakeholder evaluation involves the identification of relevant stakeholders and the elicitation of stories and accounts of their experiences, reflecting their different perspectives. Within these stories, both common and separate experiences can be detected and examples of good and bad practice articulated. In addition to views about what *is* happening, views about what *ought* to be happening can be sought, and the differences between the two can help identify plans for future action (see the discussion on boundary decisions in Chapter 7). Figure 11.1 summarises the stakeholder evaluation.

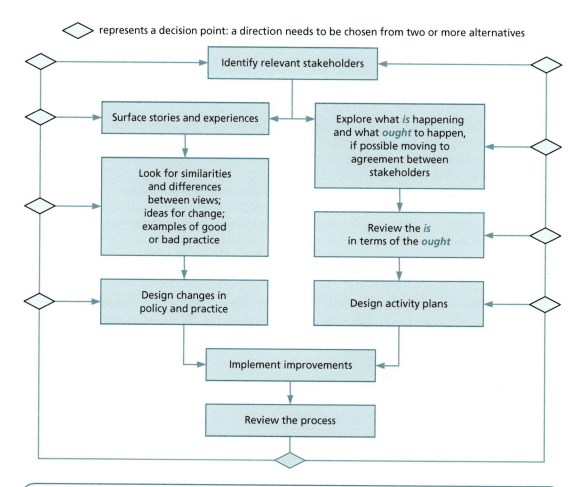

Figure 11.1 Stakeholder evaluation.

Source: after Boyd et al., 2007. Reproduced with permission from the Operational Research Society.

Goal based evaluation

Goal based evaluation begins with asking people to identify a general goal, which is then translated into objectives. Indicators reflecting each objective are agreed and information collected against these objectives enabling an assessment of performance towards objectives to be made, and proposals for change identified. Figure 11.2 summarises the goal based ideal type evaluation.

Organisational evaluation

Organisational evaluation enables the performance of a project to be compared with other similar projects. External evaluators can be helpful in doing organisational evaluations since specialist knowledge

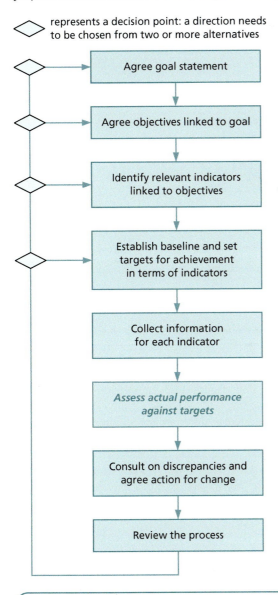

⬦ represents a decision point: a direction needs to be chosen from two or more alternatives

Agree goal statement

Agree objectives linked to goal

Identify relevant indicators linked to objectives

Establish baseline and set targets for achievement in terms of indicators

Collect information for each indicator

Assess actual performance against targets

Consult on discrepancies and agree action for change

Review the process

Figure 11.2 Goal based evaluation.

Source: after Boyd et al., 2007. Reproduced with permission from the Operational Research Society.

Reflect!

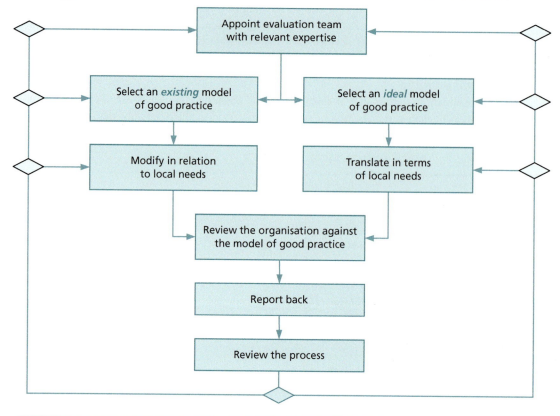

◇ represents a decision point: a direction needs to be chosen from two or more alternatives

Figure 11.3 Organisational evaluation.

Source: after Boyd et al., 2007. Reproduced with permission from the Operational Research Society.

about best practice elsewhere may be needed. An existing model of best or good practice is then selected and the current project assessed in comparison with this. Figure 11.3 summarises organisational evaluation.

These ideal type evaluation frameworks can be integrated in different ways. Stakeholder evaluations can be a part of goal based or organisational evaluations; organisational evaluations can include stakeholder and goal based evaluation processes. Each can stand alone, or goal based evaluation can follow stakeholder evaluation and both lead to organisational evaluation. Sometimes it is worth conducting a stakeholder evaluation in the early stages of the project and goal based evaluation towards the end.

Think!

Why are these frameworks called systemic frameworks? What is their link to systems thinking? If you have not encountered it, see what you can find out about community operational research, which is a field related to community psychology but which takes a particular approach to understanding (and changing) human experience.

Reflect!

If you were to design an evaluation of your own work, what kind of evaluation would it be? If you have shown a preference for goal based, stakeholder or organisational evaluation, why might this be? To what extent is your choice of evaluation due to your preferences, the nature of the work being evaluated or the purpose for which you might evaluate?

All of these evaluation frameworks go beyond the assessment of worth or utility of an activity. Instead, evaluation is seen as the deliberate, organised collection and assessment of information about an activity in order to provide feedback, create understanding and enable judgements to be made about the activity. There are different – often divergent – interests at play in all evaluations and this makes evaluation a political activity. The very act of evaluation can be, in and of itself a change activity (Miller, 2017). These evaluation frameworks could be implemented in a critical community psychological way, or they could not. Similarly, each could be implemented in a participatory way or not.

Act!

Take each of these systemic evaluation framework diagrams and add those steps or elements that would be necessary in order to implement the framework in a critical community psychological way, taking a decolonial and participatory stance, and maximising epistemic justice. Was this easier to do for some frameworks than others? Why was this?

Evaluation is often confused with monitoring and audit. Both monitoring and audit tend to collect static, numerical data, collected at a particular point in time. These data are often in the form of indicators – events that can be measured and applied over various different situations or occasions, ostensibly to enable comparisons within or between people, projects or organisations. Most monitoring or audit indicators are devoid of meaning and complexity, often addressing the only activities that can be measured without considering context, power or stakeholder differences. In higher education, for example, not just in the UK but elsewhere too, indicators or performance metrics become the drivers of activity, suppressing innovation and community engagement (Brown, 2015; Kagan & Diamond, 2019). In the community sector, in the UK, there is usually the need to demonstrate the social value of any activity, particularly if funding is sought, through evaluation. This sounds interesting – a need to look at how any activity contributes to social, environmental or economic benefits. In practice, this has meant that some innovative work does get funded, but, increasingly, social value is linked to monetary value. As Social Value UK (n.d.) says:

> Social value is the quantification of the relative importance that people place on the changes they experience in their lives. Some, but not all of this value is captured in market prices. It is important to consider and measure this social value from the perspective of those affected by an organisation's work.

The widespread use of indicators, metrics, and the commodification and financialisation of experience is **not** a part of critical community psychological praxis.

> ## *Reflect!*
>
> What monetary value would you put on: your increased confidence as you study critical community psychology; enjoying the company of older people; working with people who are homeless on an access to health project; or going for a bike ride? What did you decide what each activity was worth? Why is this approach not a critical community psychological one?

Politics of evaluation

Power is played out in various ways in evaluations. In our evaluation activity we seek to enable those most marginalised to have a voice and to enable community groups to develop the ability to undertake their own evaluations – to collect good, relevant information, using a range of different methods, and make good sense of it, and attempt to take a decolonial and epistemic justice stance. As we will see, this ideal position is often not realised in practice.

Although, as outlined above, evaluation research has moved beyond 'scientific, objectivist' approaches, in practice there are increasing pressures for community projects to provide valid and reliable data, proving their project's worth to funders, in order to help them make decisions about whether to continue to invest in an activity or not. Ellis (2009, p. 1) draws attention to the increasing dominance since 1990 of business models in the voluntary and community sector, with a growing emphasis on organisational performance and value for money, so that by 2006 monitoring and evaluation was becoming an accepted part of organisational life, even if the rhetoric was not matched by development of practice. (See, too, the discussion of audit and social value, above.) However, whilst the sector's demand for new skills and information was largely driven by upward compliance and reporting mechanisms, there was considerable interest in evaluation for internal benefit. In practice, however, time constraints and limited resources meant that many projects under-used evaluation findings, particularly for learning.

In contrast to this functional and utilitarian pressure to evaluate, Taylor et al. (2005, p. 2) emphasise the developmental, learning aspects of evaluation of neighbourhood based community projects.

> Evaluation by members of a project or organisation will help people learn from their day-to-day work. It can be used by a group of people or by individuals working alone. It assesses the effectiveness of a piece of work, a project or a programme. It can also highlight whether your project is moving steadily and successfully towards achieving what it set out to do, or whether it is moving in a different direction. You can then celebrate and build on successes as well as learn from what has not worked so well.

In our critical community psychological work we can encourage this perspective if we are involved from the outset in a project, and can adopt a developmental approach to our own work. Sometimes, though, we are invited in to a project specifically to undertake evaluation – often once the project has been in operation for some time. We are invited as external evaluators with specific research expertise and thus 'objectivity' to appeal to funders. These invitations often come when a project is nearing the end of a funding cycle or is fighting for its survival. At times, evaluations are requested by commissioners, rather than projects themselves, in order to inform future funding or project specifications. On all of these occasions, different interests are vested in the process and outcome of the evaluation, and, because evaluation is seen as an add-on, rather than an integrated part of the activity, information to feed into an evaluation is frequently inadequate and the opportunities to contribute to project improvement are limited.

Example: Men in sheds

We (RL) responded to a tender to evaluate the effectiveness and impact of an innovative intervention for older men to combat loneliness and isolation (Fisher et al., 2018). In this particular initiative, a national organisation had invested monies into schemes across the UK. In the locality we were exploring, the sheds were diverse and had different working practices and cultures. The men, and shed facilitators, who were key participants, were not included in the rationale nor the preparation for an evaluation. Consequently, the need for an evaluation and access to the important stakeholders was re-negotiated at each step. Whilst the small numbers of men and prior knowledge pointed toward qualitative evaluation, at the funders' behest, the work contained quantitative measures. These proved difficult to administer and justify to the older men. We used mixed methods and managed to gain access through perseverance.

Example: English as a second language through volunteers

We were asked to evaluate a project through which volunteers had helped refugees learn English (Lawthom, Porretta & Kagan, 2009). Again, the project workers thought their work was innovative and wanted to demonstrate this in order to attract more funding. Very little information had been collected during the project which inevitably impoverished and limited the evaluation.

On both these occasions we were invited in to evaluate by those who had been responsible for delivering the projects and with a strong interest in 'proving' the value of the work. We had to be clear from the outset, that we could not guarantee positive appraisals, and that the evaluations might well draw attention to ways in which the projects might be more effective. There were missed opportunities in both projects: if we had been involved at the start it might have been possible to work together to understand the potential of evaluations for continual improvement and help the projects build in data collection from the outset – and sense making or reflection – into their everyday activity. They may then have been in the position of being able to demonstrate both how they achieved their targets and the value of their work beyond their immediate goals.

A further problem can arise if those who are running a project are also doing the evaluation – self evaluation. Whilst this can be a valuable source of learning, it can be difficult to stand back from the emotional investment in how the project works and be open to the possibility of bad news about its effectiveness. For this reason it is important to create ways of working where a culture of trust and non-threatening inquiry is the norm, and to be careful to distinguish between commitment and dogmatism. Partnering between internal and external evaluators can be helpful here.

Sometimes an evaluative intervention can be used to unblock a situation, as illustrated by some work on a city-wide response to climate change.

> ### Example: Climate change
>
> A local authority commissioned consultants from another area of the country to write a plan about responding to the challenge of climate change (a central government requirement). Local activists thought the plan was weak and lacked local stakeholder input. We (MB) worked with other activists producing our own evaluation of the plan together with an alternative set of proposals (Call for Real Action Collective, 2009). We presented it as a constructive contribution and did so publicly. Following discussions the insiders and outsiders worked together to produce the next phase of the plan. This time a lot of different people contributed.

The uninvited evaluation had been a helpful change tool, supported by both campaigning and the capacity of each side to work flexibly and to understand the other's standpoint. This makes the point that evaluation is invariably political in nature, having to contend with questions of power and interest, as well as the formal, technological, content of the evaluation.

Act!

See if you can explain (i) what evaluation can and cannot achieve and (ii) why ideally evaluators should be involved with a project from the start. Imagine you are producing a brochure about your approach to evaluation of community projects. Draft two paragraphs outlining (i) what it is reasonable to expect of evaluation and (ii) the importance of early involvement for evaluation.

What is to be evaluated?

Evaluation can focus on various points in the sequence of change. The outcomes for people affected might be examined and so might the processes of change. As Burton and Kagan (1995, p. 312) say:

> Both process and outcome are important. While we want to emphasise the outcomes [of an intervention], especially those that affect the person's quality of life, we also want to know something of the processes by which these outcomes were attained. Without some analysis of process, we will find it difficult to understand what to do next time to secure a better set of outcomes.

In our experience most commissioners of evaluations are more concerned with outcomes than with process issues. However, it is by understanding process issues that we learn most about how to improve and enhance the effectiveness of an intervention. Different perspectives on evaluation guide decisions about what is to be evaluated.

'Theory of change' perspectives on evaluation

It is, in many situations, rather simplistic to assume there is a straightforward and direct relationship between what is done within a project and its impact. Most social projects are more complex than this. A critical community psychological approach would be concerned to examine how the historical, social and cultural context affects both what has been done and what is possible to do, and their effects. Most social change programmes and critical community psychological practice involve complex situations that are best thought about as soft and open systems (see Chapters 3, 6). Within multi-layered contexts, multiple activities take place involving people in different ways, and with different consequences arising for different stakeholders. When it comes to evaluation we have to try to disentangle some of these relationships, and to begin with asking the questions:

- What is this programme trying to do?
- What effects are intended and what theory do we have about how they might come about from the project activities?

In other words, what is the theory of change underpinning the activity or project that is to be evaluated (Murray & Stewart, 2006)?

Reflect!

Think of a time you were the beneficiary of a project. For example, you might have been to a fitness class, a local park may have been regenerated, or you went into a school to hear children read. Can you see how a theory of change perspective might apply? Was this easy? Why or why not?

In the UK, funders, commissioners and policy makers increasingly expect a theory of change perspective to be brought to bear on funding bids as well as reports or accounts of projects. It is not always clear, though, that they expect anything other than a simple logical account of how the inputs to a project will lead or have led to any project results. Whilst it is certainly possible to build complexity, a thorough understanding of context and of power, into theory of change approaches, these often go beyond formal requirements. For relevant and effective praxis, though, the complexity should remain.

Example: Higher education and community engagement: evaluating a portfolio of projects

We had responsibility for delivering a portfolio of 17 projects concerned with urban regeneration (or renewal) and community cohesion. Each project was driven by the needs of partnering community groups and involved people from four different universities working in interdisciplinary groups. One of our tasks was to conduct an evaluation of these projects (Kagan & Duggan, 2009). They were all different – variously involving children, unemployed people, people with mental health difficulties or who lived in poverty, and migrant communities. The projects included research, development activities, training, action research and arts activities. All in all, an evaluator's nightmare! One of the first things we did was to ask each individual project to articulate its 'theory of change' – what should change, how and why. We then compiled an overall theory of change. Initially this was expressed as:

Through the development of an 'ecological edge' via collaboration, staff from the four universities will gain from working effectively together with community groups on issues of need identified by those groups, and will enable exchange of knowledge and expertise to strengthen the work of both the community groups and the universities, as well as building understanding of the role of community cohesion, health and well-being, crime and enterprise in urban regeneration and thus lead to further collaborative developments.

(p. 13)

This theory of change statement outlines the mechanisms (working together, collaboration, developing an 'ecological edge') by which the outcomes (addressing needs of community groups, gains for the university staff, better understanding of community cohesion etc.) and outputs (exchange of knowledge and expertise, strengthening work of community groups, further collaborative developments) of the portfolio of projects were to be achieved. The evaluation essentially tested this theory of change and enabled us to say something about the overall efficacy of the portfolio of projects, and to contribute to learning within the university about how this kind of work might work more effectively in the future. It is worth noting that the 'theory of change' statement says nothing about context, and little about just how knowledge will strengthen communities. The evaluation tried to examine enabling and obstructive aspects of the context. The full evaluation was, in effect, an elaboration on the initial theory of change, describing what happened and explaining it in theoretical terms.

Think!

Look at the theory of change statement in the above example. Identify those parts of the statement that might underpin explorations of power; cultural dynamics; positionality; marginalisation; voice. Were some of the themes impossible to detect? Why was this?

It is not easy to compile theory of change statements but the process of trying to do them, and of revising them as a project proceeds, really does help clarify what can be expected of an intervention and why. This then helps to avoid unrealistic expectations and hopes about what a change intervention might achieve: it helps retain a realistic stance towards the work with which we are involved.

Realistic or realist perspectives on evaluation

In complex situations a number of different theories of change might apply, reflecting different strands of activity and guiding evaluation questions to be asked. Pawson and Tilley (1997, 2004) describe an approach to evaluation called *realist evaluation*, which also stresses the role of theory for understanding a proposed change and informing evaluation. They suggest that social programmes can themselves be seen as theories, embedded in social systems. These systems are open, permeable and plastic, constantly changing, and change is triggered by the reasoning and resources of those touched by the programme.

However, realist evaluation resonates with community psychological approaches as it recognises the crucial and complex role that an understanding of context plays in project delivery and in evaluation.

> Realist evaluation is a species of theory-driven evaluation. [along with other approaches such as theory of change evaluation] ... In all of these perspectives social programmes are regarded as products of the human imagination: they are hypothesis about social betterment. Programmes chart out a perceived course whereby wrongs might be put to rights, deficiencies of behaviour corrected, inequalities of condition alleviated. Programmes are thus shaped by a vision of change and they succeed or fail according to the veracity of that vision. Evaluation ... has the task of testing out the underlying programme theories. When one evaluates realistically one always returns to the core theories about how a programme is supposed to work and then interrogates it – is that basic plan sound, plausible, durable, practical and, above all, valid?
>
> (Pawson & Tilley, 2004, p. 2)

Pawson and Tilley draw attention to the different aspects of a programme that need to be understood for evaluation, namely mechanisms, context, outcome patterns and context–mechanism–outcome pattern configurations.

1   **Mechanisms** are those aspects of programmes that bring any effects (known elsewhere as processes).
2   **Context** refers to the circumstances under which any mechanisms can become active. Pawson and Tilley (2004, p. 8) note that "... what is contextually significant may not only relate to place but also to systems of interpersonal and social relationships, and even to biology, technology, economic conditions and so on".
3   **Outcome patterns** are project achievements. They are likely to be mixed (hence pattern), because of the variations in mechanisms and contexts that lead to different outcomes.
4   **Context–mechanism–outcome pattern configurations** (CMOC) bring together mechanisms, contexts and outcome patterns in meaningful ways to underpin the evaluation. CMOC are described in the following way (Pawson & Tilley, 2004, p. 9):

> [CMOCs] comprise models indicating how programmes activate mechanisms amongst whom and in what conditions, to bring about alterations in behavioural or event or state regularities. These propositions bring together mechanism-variation and relevant context-variation to predict and to explain outcome pattern variation. Realist evaluation thus develops and tests CMOC conjectures empirically.

For Pawson and Tilley, context is inextricably linked to mechanisms and outcome patterns and any complex programme is likely to have a number of context–mechanism–outcome pattern configurations which will underpin an evaluation. When we have worked with projects on evaluation, we often have to spend quite a bit of time discussing with those involved in the projects their theories of what should happen, how and why. Sometimes evaluations get stalled and the work comes more to resemble project or organisational development.

Reflect!

> ## Example: Arts for health and well-being
>
> We evaluated a group of projects in the field of arts for health (Kilroy, Garner, Parkinson, Kagan & Senior, 2007). Six projects had been selected from a much greater number of projects, all of which had responded to invitations to be part of the overall evaluation. Thus, internal commitment was high. When the researchers visited the projects, none could clearly articulate why their projects might have certain kinds of health benefits (a 'theory of change'). We implemented an appreciative inquiry process (Cooperrider & Whitney, 2005) with each project, in order to be sure that people internal to the projects and the researchers shared understanding of the underlying values and objectives of the project, and could get an agreement of how the projects might be evaluated. In two of the projects this work led initially not to evaluation activities, but instead to some team development, whilst latent conflicts within the projects could be resolved. In one case, through detailed examination of the context in which it was embedded, a new set of objectives and overall aim or purpose was articulated, and the process became one of project or organisational development.

Working out the theory of change or CMOC towards the start of a project helps us to get an overview of the evaluation task, the scale of complexity, and how reflection and learning emerge from and contribute to the evaluation activities. We like to sketch the skeleton of these relationships in a diagram, similar to programme logic models (McLaughlin & Jordan, 1999). Figure 11.4 presents a model we used as part of an evaluation plan for researching the impact of participatory arts on well-being and social inclusion (Sixsmith & Kagan, 2005).

This diagram links the context with the resources and activities undertaken in the arts workshops with the outcomes for participants in terms of both health and well-being and social inclusion as well as community and service development. The workshop and its outcomes, in turn, lead to intermediate and final outcomes. It is the intermediate outcomes that suggest themes for exploration of impact – and the activities that suggest a focus for exploring processes of project implementation. The reflective feedback loops – of reflections by artists and researchers through their action research process, involving regular feedback – contribute to double loop learning for the projects (Argyris & Schön, 1996; Suárez-Herrara, Springett & Kagan, 2009) which encourages participants to question in depth the role of the framing of the project's goals, strategies and assumptions. It is a deep form of learning, beyond individual learning.

Act!

Using the framework (or programme logic model) illustrated in Figure 11.4 devise the components of an evaluation of a 'good cup of tea'. What are the inputs (ingredients, equipment, skills)? What are the processes (how is the cup of tea produced – you may want to include the growing, picking, processing and transport of tea, or just begin at the point of buying the tea from a shop)? What are the intermediate outcomes (what is produced as a result of the process)? What are the outcomes (what impact does the tea have on whom)? You might want to consider the following:

Costs: for example, ingredients and time; skills of tea maker;

Gains and losses: Who gains and loses from this cup of tea? What do the tea drinkers think? What do the tea producers think?

Stakeholders: What is a cup of tea (to different people)? What is the process of serving tea – what are the steps?

Measures: What hard measures of inputs and outcomes might you use (for example quantities, temperature, time, costs)?

Resources: What is the quality of hardware (e.g. cups, kettle)?

Context: What else might have led to people's satisfaction with the tea? What else might affect the making of the tea?

The logical framework model is one way of outlining the different components of a project that can contribute to an evaluation and enable theory of change statements to be produced. Another way is to use a diagram embodying metaphorical thinking. In Figure 11.5 we have used the image of a stack of parts, maybe a building? There is a foundation block, supporting another block by pillars, with different features of the environment also outlined. This picture comes from the higher education and community engagement project outlined previously. It is used to suggest the aspects that can be included in any evaluation of this kind of work. Implicit in the diagram is the idea that organisational functioning enables community impacts to be supported, and this all takes place within a complex, multi-faceted university context.

At its best, evaluation can and should always be, in part at least, about project improvement and development (as in double loop learning), at its most powerful when there is participation in the evaluation. Suárez-Herrara et al. (2009, p. 322) illustrate this process:

> [in participatory evaluation] stakeholders develop a dynamic process through which the social production of knowledge occurs, contributing to a collective conception of learning about themselves, the organization in which they are involved and ultimately the essential features underlying the phenomena being evaluated. Therefore, participatory evaluation becomes praxis in fostering the creation of an organizational learning process … whereby different types of knowledge, created by a sustainable network of stakeholders working together through communicative actions and supportive partnerships, are used towards a political articulation of action.

Participatory evaluation can be seen, from this perspective, as a learning process in which reflection, negotiation, dialogue, decision making, knowledge creation and power dynamics are all explored and subject to change. Indeed, in the organisation workshop example above, it was clear that the evaluations acted as catalysts for change and development within the projects: the evaluation created learning environments for intentional change, and the evaluator shifted *"from being a principal investigator and participant observer to becoming responsible for accomplishing tasks related to learning, mediation, teaching, local development, social change, education and promotion of interactive learning environments"* (Suárez-Herrera et al., 2009, p. 330).

Systematisation of experiences

Whilst not strictly evaluation, as Jara (2012) notes, systematisation of experiences goes alongside both participatory research and evaluation as a tool for continual learning and improvement of practice. Like evaluation, it is a tool for understanding reality in order to change it. Systematisation focuses entirely on the experiences of those involved in an intervention. It is a process of reconstruction of specific, concrete experiences, critical-analytical reflection and shared learning.

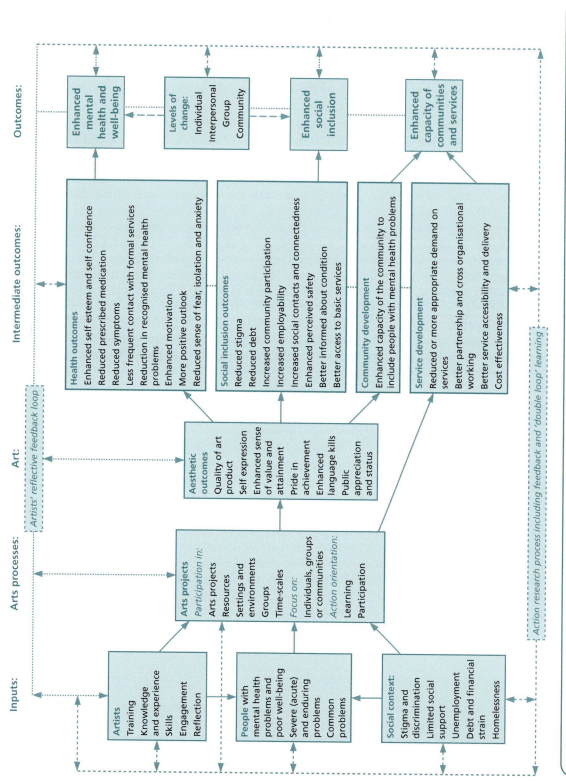

Figure 11.4 Evaluation of community arts projects: links between project activities and outcomes in terms of enhanced mental health, social inclusion and capacity of communities.

Source: Sixsmith & Kagan, 2005. Reproduced by permission of Manchester Metropolitan University.

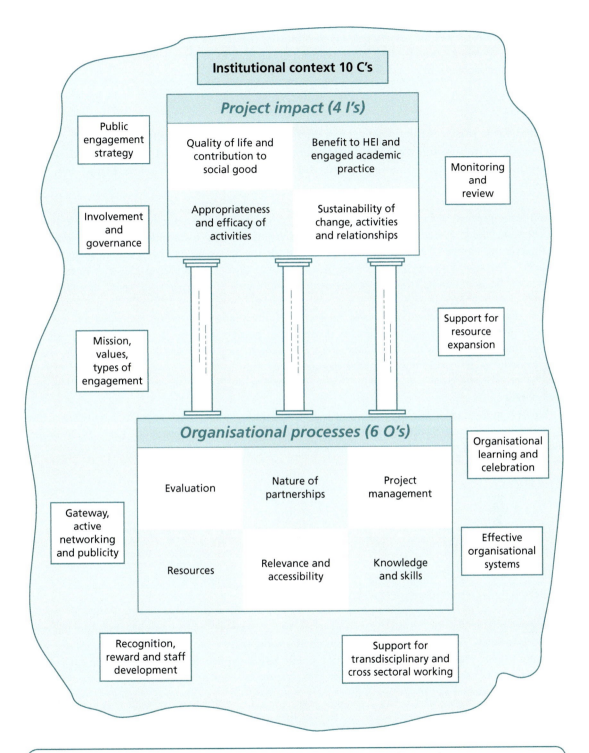

Institutional context 10 C's

Project impact (4 I's)

Quality of life and contribution to social good

Benefit to HEI and engaged academic practice

Appropriateness and efficacy of activities

Sustainability of change, activities and relationships

Public engagement strategy

Involvement and governance

Mission, values, types of engagement

Monitoring and review

Support for resource expansion

Organisational processes (6 O's)

Evaluation

Nature of partnerships

Project management

Resources

Relevance and accessibility

Knowledge and skills

Gateway, active networking and publicity

Recognition, reward and staff development

Organisational learning and celebration

Effective organisational systems

Support for transdisciplinary and cross sectoral working

Figure 11.5 Dimensions of HEI–community engagement for evaluation.

Source: Kagan & Duggan, 2009. Reproduced by permission of Manchester Metropolitan University.

Note: "C's", "I's" and "O's" represent, respectively, contexts, impacts and organisational processes.

Systematisation takes as a starting point that those involved in any activities will almost certainly have quite different perceptions and interpretations of the same experiences, but when these are shared and reconstructed, new understandings emerge.

Act!

Next time you are doing something with someone else – it could be a friend, colleague or family member, talk afterwards about what you did, thought and felt about the activity. To what extent did you both agree with each other. Why/why not?

Without the process of sharing, participants might never know there were other ways of experiencing the same thing. Systematisation goes beyond sharing, though, to a critical analysis, comparing what actually happened with the initial intentions of the intervention (bringing in an evaluative element). Through a process of ordering and reconstruction, new understandings emerge, which must then be communicated back to the wider community and beyond, in order to extend the learning.

Systematisation is particularly useful, as a means of bringing to the fore, historical and cultural contexts of people's shared experiences: through the process of critical questioning, it seeks to extract and demonstrate the knowledge that is found in practice (Streck & Jara, 2015). Thus, new knowledge is to be found in reflecting upon concrete experiences, and this in turn leads to further conscientisation and action. Thus, systematisation is the integration of participatory action–reflection.

We saw in Chapter 8 the importance of recording and registering experience as part of an action strategy, and that these recordings would form the foundation of later discussion. Table 11.2 outlines the process of a full systematisation of experiences.

Think!

What is the role of intersubjectivity in producing a systematisation of experiences? What theoretical resources can help inform how new knowledge emerges when people share and recollect their experiences?

Participation and evaluation

Participation in evaluation, in itself, can lead to the development of understanding, skills and changed attitudes towards evaluation. This is evident in the process of evaluation known as empowerment evaluation (Fetterman & Wandersman, 2005) which makes explicit the link between the capacity to undertake evaluation within a project and the effectiveness of the project.

As Wandersman et al. (2005, p. 27) put it:

Empowerment evaluation is an evaluation approach that aims to increase the likelihood that programs will achieve results by increasing the capacity of program stakeholders to plan, implement and evaluate their own programs.

The principles of empowerment evaluation are similar to those outlined near the start of this chapter, but incorporate community psychological values. Smith (2007) recognises the role that values play in

Table 11.2 Outline of systematisation of experiences

Step	Considerations
The starting point: living the experience	• All those involved in the systemisation should take part in the activity • The focus is on people's own practice – Consider your own practice and focus on what you do; what you think; how you feel • All those participating should have been involved in the practice, although some external facilitation may be required • Keep records of experiences via diaries, photos, project materials etc.
Initial questions: defining the framework and planning the systematisation	• Understanding systematisation – exploring the meaning of systematisation, its benefits, and what is involved • Objectives of this systematisation – taking into account the purpose of the project or intervention • What experiences will be included? – it is not necessary to try to cover the entire experience of a project or an intervention • What is the context – international, national, local, organisational • What information will be drawn on and shared? • Who will participate (sometimes it is necessary to have a representative of a group if the number of people involved is high)
Recuperation of the lived experiences – telling the history	• Reconstruct the history – share memories of what happened and when • Identify the most significant events or moments – use pictorial methods and diagrams as needed • Ask key questions (make them open not closed), participants interview each other • Organise the information – this could be in chronological stages, stories etc and present these visually if possible
Critical analysis through deep reflection	• Interpret the experience; analyse significant elements; conclude • Discuss the experiences described, look for relationships between different components and ask critical questions (these will vary depending on the focus of the systematisation) • Consider what made particular things happen – when things changed, why did they? What impact did these changes have on the project? • What tensions or contradictions emerged? • Ask what worked and what did not work and why • Consider what might be done differently in the future – what would be done the same • What recommendations could be made to others doing something similar?
Sharing the lessons learned – where have we got to?	• Formulate conclusions • Communicate learning • Produce a full systematisation that includes all stages of the systematisation in a detailed way; write a summary of conclusions and recommendations • Plan and disseminate learning via different media, including for example, radio, workshops, a book

Source: derived from Jara, n.d. and Luger & Massing, 2015.

Note: whilst each systematisation will be sensitive to its own context, the table shows the general pattern.

empowerment evaluation and argues that it is necessary to assess the underlying values when considering the efficacy of the approach. The principles of empowerment (Wandersman et al., 2005, p. 30) are:

- improvement;
- community ownership;
- inclusion;
- democratic participation;
- social justice;
- community knowledge;
- evidence based strategies;
- capacity building;
- organisational learning;
- accountability.

In contrast to a number of other approaches to evaluation that emphasise external expertise and independent judgement, and that encourage dependency on these external experts, empowerment evaluation utilises internal resources, engenders self determination and capacity building, and is achieved through collaboration and reflection. Most importantly, empowerment evaluation is a participative process.

Reflect!

Can you think of any situations where evaluation might lead to disempowerment? What might you, as an evaluator, do to minimise this possibility?

Participation and empowerment in evaluation

All evaluation involves some participation and Rebien (1996) argues that consistency in approach cannot be achieved across different kinds of evaluations. Smits and Champagne (2008, p. 428) distinguish between participation in evaluation as an *end* – as in empowerment evaluation (Fetterman & Wandersman, 2005) – or participation as a *means* of getting better information or implementing evaluation findings.

> When a major goal is to generate more social justice for disenfranchised minority groups, it is called empowerment evaluation. ... When the participative process aims to increase the use of evaluation results through the involvement of intended users, it is known as PPE (Practical Participatory Evaluation).

Example: Gardening as a tool for participation

We worked participatively with some local activists who were attempting to improve their local environment through gardening. The evaluation was planned collaboratively, there was some shared responsibility for collecting information, and the report and a conference presentation were given together (Kagan & Stewart, 2007).

Rebien (1996) outlines three criteria for distinguishing those evaluations that are participatory from those that are not, or involve very low levels of participation:

- Stakeholders must have an active role as subjects in the evaluation process, rather than having just passive roles as sources of data.
- At least representatives from the following stakeholder groups should participate: beneficiaries, project field staff, project management and funders.
- Stakeholders should participate in at least three stages of the evaluation process – designing terms of reference, interpreting data and using evaluation information.

Gregory (2000) points out, however, a number of barriers to participation that make Rebien's (1996) conditions difficult to implement. First, the evaluator generally has status due to their position, with an assumed superiority of wisdom and expertise, rendering other participants in the process relatively acquiescent and engendering a relationship of dependence that can be difficult to overcome. Second, if only certain representatives of stakeholders are to be involved, issues of representation and reporting come into play. It can be difficult to know who is included and who is not – who is represented and who is not. It might emerge that some important stakeholder groups are not included. This brings into play the role of boundary critique again (see Chapter 7), as decisions are made about who may and who may not participate (also see discussion on epistemic justice above).

Reflect!

Reflect on your own status and position. What are the potential strengths and limitations of your status in terms of facilitating participatory evaluation and how could you minimise your limitations? Furthermore, what methods could you use to ensure you included all stakeholders in an ongoing evaluation?

Third, the focus on encouraging participation on functional tasks and the acquisition of practical skills may prevent participants actively and critically engaging with the full evaluation process, restricting their abilities to engage with evaluation in the future. Limiting participation to only some parts of the process prevents people from gaining insight into the whole evaluation process and range of methodological strategies. It is unclear why they should not also be encouraged to collect information as part of the evaluation, a method we have advanced in several different studies (Kilroy et al., 2007; Sixsmith & Kagan, 2005; Woolrych & Sixsmith, 2008; Sixsmith, Callender, Hobbs, Corr & Huber, 2014; Stewart & Kagan, 2007).

Fetterman, Rodríguez-Campos, Wandersman and O'Sullivan (2014, pp. 144–145) draw attention to the value of differentiating stakeholder approaches, so that evaluators can select the most appropriate. The three different approaches to stakeholder involvement are as follows:

1   Collaborative approach: Collaborative evaluators are **in charge** of the evaluation, but they create an ongoing engagement between evaluators and stakeholders, contributing to stronger evaluation designs, enhanced data collection and analysis, and results stakeholders understand and use. Collaboration can range from consultation to full-scale involvement at every stage of the evaluation.
2   Participatory approach: Participatory evaluators **jointly share** control of the evaluation. Participatory evaluations range from stakeholders participating in the evaluator's agenda to participation in an evaluation that is jointly designed and implemented by the evaluator and stakeholders in the programme. Control passes from the evaluator to stakeholders over time.
3   Empowerment approach: Empowerment evaluators view **programme staff members, programme participants and community members as in control** of the evaluation. However, empowerment evaluators serve as critical friends or coaches to help keep the process on track, rigorous, responsive and relevant. Empowerment evaluations are conducted within the conventional constraints

and requirements of any organisation. However, stakeholders determine how best to meet those external requirements and goals.

Even if full participation of all stakeholders in all aspects of the evaluation is desired, there are a number of barriers that may prevent this ideal being reached (Gregory, 2000).

Structural barriers reflect the exercise of power. One power issue – of who is in and who is out – has been considered above. Power differentials between different stakeholders in an evaluation make participation by some groups more likely, and more likely to be taken seriously, than that of others, reflecting the ways in which social relations are organised outside the evaluation. Sometimes, projects themselves, or those commissioning evaluations, explicitly want the 'power' of an external evaluator involved. There is a wider social context at play here, in which beliefs about the role that objectivity or independence play in getting at the 'truth' prevail. We recognise this reality and if accepting this kind of research brief we always endeavour to work in ways by which projects or local people gain benefit along the way. Challenges for evaluators are to recognise the political nature of evaluation, continually reflect on boundary questions and find diverse ways to involve all those affected by an evaluation who wish to be involved.

Administrative barriers reflect the practical realities of undertaking participative evaluation. Formal and informal gatekeepers can enable access to participants, but can also hinder involvement. The gatekeepers' perceptions of legitimate involvement can mean that some people are invited to participate whilst others are not. Apart from gatekeeper attitudes which may prevent them facilitating participation, there might be practical difficulties. It might be too difficult – or too time consuming – to involve all those who could be involved, in meaningful ways. However, if different means of securing participation are not tried, the claim of disinterest and an unwillingness to participate might be wrongly raised. Participation from the outset can often lead to productive outcomes.

Example: Disability and resilience across the life course

In our work exploring how disabled people are resilient with a disability charity, we used participation from the outset. The disability charity brief was framed in terms of wanting to explore resilience as an individual characteristic. Through the competitive tendering process, which we won, we explained our interdependent approach to resilience. The model proposed engaged a disability group of experts by experience, who acted as a community of practice across all stages. Being transparent about the concept of resilience and engaging commissioners and disability experts from the outset enabled a clear map of the process. The work yielded a toolkit, involved disabled people across the life course in learning about research, and shifted the charity's initial view of resilience. Whilst we have many tales of less successful processes and outcomes, this project was a success (Runswick-Cole, Goodley & Lawthom, 2013).

Social barriers can operate if there is insufficient understanding of the social context – of social, political and cultural factors that might affect involvement, or of the biases and prejudices. Guba and Lincoln (1989) recommend intense involvement and participant observation by the evaluators in a setting prior to the evaluation taking place, or the involvement of local community members to sensitise evaluators to the intricacies of the context. Such local informants, however, would thereby be in a privileged position and this might have an impact on the evaluation process. Our own approach to evaluation generally involves considerable time 'penetrating the situation' and listening to different perspectives on the issue under evaluation, as well as observations made in various relevant settings. We should not forget, though, that this very experience puts us in a powerful position as we gain a broad understanding of context in which to embed other evaluation information.

Example: Resilience and disability

In this work we spent considerable time getting to think about how resilience works at different stages of life. This involved talking to diverse people, reading background material, using a wider global internet based mail list, or listserve, to elicit understanding and so on, and talking to key informants from different stake-holder groups. This meant that our questions were informed: we were aware of different perceptions and we were able to ask different questions across the informants to reveal the various facets of resilience. We had to make decisions about what to do with this information, which did not strictly inform the work and often became entangled with advocacy. We were fully aware of our status as objective researchers from the university, yet we also recognised ourselves as allies and advocates for the disabled experts by experience. Recognising this power does not diminish it, but engages with transparency.

Resistance to involvement as a barrier to participation in evaluation

Some people will not want to participate and might be suspicious of the whole evaluation endeavour. They may even try to sabotage the evaluation. Such resistance may be a positive way to reclaim power in a particular situation. On the other hand it might constitute a cynical manipulation of power and a silencing of others, particularly if one group of people is preventing others from participating. A fine understanding of the context might help disentangle the two possibilities. Sometimes both processes occur at the same time, as in the following example.

Example: Contested change in a psychiatric service

An evaluation of a change in service delivery for people with mental health difficulties living in the community, commissioned by the service manager and involving the major stakeholder groups, was undertaken (Knowles, 2001). Considerable hostility was expressed by the highest status group – the psychiatrists. The competence of the researcher was called into question on more than one occasion; there was some refusal to meet and give necessary information; the view that their position on the matter should prevail whatever the views of anyone else was forcibly expressed; other professionals were intimidated. It was only through the involvement of one of the most highly respected psychiatrists in the country on the project steering group that the psychiatrists agreed to co-operate with the evaluation and abide by the changes that arose from it. It was our understanding of the status concerns of psychiatrists that led us to appoint the relevant person to the steering group and thus weaken resistance.

Some people in some communities may experience 'participation fatigue', particularly when invited to participate in evaluation of public services from which they have seen no benefit in the past (Kagan, Caton & Barnett, 2005), and in these circumstances pressure to participate may become coercive (Gregory, 1997).

As evaluators we can try to maintain a perspective that encourages participation as an end in itself, and not just the means by which we might obtain better evaluation data (see Chapter 5). The questions to ask ourselves are *"why should people participate – what will they gain from so doing?"* and *"are we sure we are not wasting people's time in asking them to participate?"* In this way we might be able to avoid what is becoming known as the tyranny of participation (Cooke & Kothari, 2001) – which we referred to in Chapter 7 when we discussed decision making processes behind action planning.

Not everyone we work with accepts that participation enhances evaluation. We have been asked on more than one occasion questions of the ilk: *"If anyone can do research or evaluation, what is the role of the evaluator with a PhD?"* Tilakaratna (1990) considers this dilemma and identifies the tasks of the evaluator – or outside knowledge professional – as:

- assisting people to collect data and then to process and analyse the information using simple methods which enables them to systematise their knowledge;
- linking the local situation (which the people know best) to the larger external situation (about which the outsider may know more);
- improving people's access to new information and formal knowledge (for example, technology);
- introducing local people to experiences from outside their environment;
- throwing up relevant issues or problems for local people to reflect on and analyse and then assisting them in coming to their own conclusions;
- disseminating to wider audiences (including policy makers and intellectuals as well as participation workers seeking to facilitate local participation).

As we have seen, whilst we might aspire to working in a participatory way, in practice there are often compromises to be made. It can be useful to think of participative evaluation as a continuum with different degrees of involvement.

1 Voice.
2 1 plus: Partnership in decision making.
3 2 plus: Collaboration in the process of collecting information.
4 3 plus: Involvement in analysis of information and sense making.
5 4 plus: Collaboration in dissemination of the information through written reports, oral presentations or other media.
6 5 plus: Evaluation research that is directed and controlled.
7 6 plus: Evaluation research that is fully owned.

A different continuum might reflect participation as a means and participation as an end, as illustrated in Figure 11.6. Some evaluation activity will sit at one end or the other: many will be somewhere in between with partial participation.

Think!

Participation is a slippery concept. With reference to evaluation, does participation refer to the role project managers play in commissioning the evaluation; the involvement of the evaluator(s) in the project; the involvement of project workers in the evaluation; the involvement of project beneficiaries in the evaluation; or any combination of these? How do these different types of participation reflect (or not) principles and values of community psychology?

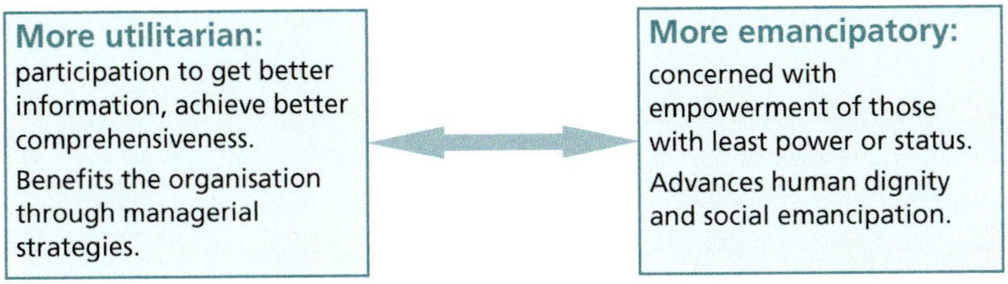

More utilitarian:	More emancipatory:
participation to get better information, achieve better comprehensiveness. Benefits the organisation through managerial strategies.	concerned with empowerment of those with least power or status. Advances human dignity and social emancipation.

Figure 11.6 A participatory continuum: participation as a means and participation as an end.

Capacity building for evaluation

Participative evaluation more than any other system of evaluation, reflects, community psychological values and principles. However, it is not so easy to catalyse people's learning about evaluation. It might be necessary as part of an evaluation activity, or even more generally, to engage in capacity building for evaluation (Boyd et al., 2001, 2003; Dabelstein, 2003; Johnson, 2000; Preskill & Boyle, 2008). This includes addressing knowledge about evaluation, skills in carrying out evaluations and feelings and beliefs about evaluation. Table 11.3 outlines arenas of understanding and knowledge (cognitive aspects), skills and abilities (behavioural aspects) and feelings (affective aspects) that might be addressed through capacity building.

Example: Capacity building for evaluation

We undertook a capacity building programme for evaluation in the voluntary, community and public sectors (Boyd et al., 2001, 2003, 2007). Initially we consulted with 50 projects about their views on evaluation and what they would find useful from a series of learning events. These consultations took the form of three hour workshops with as many people as possible from the projects, and we summarised the issues arising from each workshop. Our seven-person interdisciplinary team (plus some members of our steering group drawn from local projects) then examined these summaries in detail, clustering issues in different ways until we were happy that they could be addressed by discrete learning events. The clusters were: relationships with others (including participation, inclusion, stakeholder issues, multi-agency issues, funders); toolbox (different methods of collecting information and making sense of it as well as communicating findings); ways evaluation should happen (processes of evaluation, limits and expectations of evaluation, reflection, learning, links with planning); and things to be evaluated (including activities, experiences, organisational structures and processes, internal and external dynamics).

We then considered issues to be taken into account for designing the learning events and agreed they should: aim for fairly large events to maximise shared learning (up to 50 people) with scope for subgroups; be fun, enlivening, engaging, energetic, participative and challenging, yet instil confidence – help people to learn; be mixed rather than explicitly targeted at a particular audience, such as funders, in order to help people come across new ideas; stress partnership and collaboration; be flexible in order to respond to different demands; and take a broad view of evaluation that includes, for example, planning.

Nine learning events included introductions to evaluation; participation in decision making; planning and choosing evaluation approaches; use of statistics and other methods of collecting information; mixing qualitative and quantitative methods; embedding evaluation in learning; planning and project improvement; sustainability; and networking for future support for evaluation.

This capacity building project was conceived as an action research project with cycles of planning, delivery of training workshops, thinking about sustainability and a follow-up with different projects a year later.

Preskill and Boyle (2008, p. 447) outline additional strategies for capacity building. These include:

1 Internship: participating in a formal programme that provides practical evaluation experience for novices.
2 Written materials: reading and using written documents about evaluation processes and findings.
3 Technology: using online resources such as web sites and/or e-learning programmes to learn from and about evaluation.
4 Meetings: allocating time and space to discuss evaluation activities specifically for the purpose of learning from and about evaluation.
5 Appreciative inquiry (AI): using an asset based, collaborative, narrative approach to learning about evaluation that focuses on strengths within the organisation.
6 Communities of practice: sharing evaluation experiences, practices, information, and readings among members who have common interests and needs (sometimes called learning circles).
7 Training: attending courses, workshops and seminars on evaluation.
8 Involvement in an evaluation process: participating in the design and/or implementation of an evaluation.
9 Technical assistance: receiving help from an internal or external evaluator.
10 Coaching or mentoring: building a relationship with an evaluation expert who provides individualised technical and professional support.

Skills for evaluation

Evaluation skills are always needed in the evaluation of critical community psychological work. The theory of change and systemic approaches to evaluation include the identification of indicators – not confined to numerical indicators – of change – in terms of processes, outputs, outcomes and impacts on beneficiaries. Once the focus of change and relevant markers have been identified, the task is to find a way of collecting information that will inform the indicator and to progress towards anticipated change as well as any unintended effects of the intervention. These can include a wide range of different data collection and analysis methods and we will often use mixed methods of collecting different kinds of information. If a systematisation of experiences approach is used, then those participating in the intervention will need skills of recording (indeed, careful records are needed for all evaluations),

> **Table 11.3** Cognitive, affective and behavioural aspects of capacity building for evaluation

Cognitive aspects Understanding about…	Affective aspects Feelings or beliefs that…	Behaviour aspects Ability to…
Purpose and potential of evaluation	Evaluation can be enjoyable and lead to learning	Negotiate and clarify different expectations about evaluation
Differences between formative and summative evaluation	Evaluation can be useful	Identify a 'theory of change' statement
Nature of objectives, goals, processes, experiences and other outputs and outcomes	Evaluation can be integrated with other project activities and is an important part of project work	Articulate and communicate underlying values
Strengths and weaknesses of different evaluation approaches	Evaluation need not be stressful	Articulate project processes and outcomes and their links, as well as key aspects of the context
Different methods of engagement and participation	Evaluation works best when owned by those being evaluated	Involve different stakeholders including those most marginalised
Strengths and weaknesses of different methods of collecting information	Evaluation contributes to the project's effectiveness	Decide on key evaluation questions
Sources of power and powerlessness	Evaluation is most worthwhile if built in from the start and adequately resourced	Decide if external expertise is needed
How to use information and data in a meaningful way	There are a diversity of people involved in and affected by the work being evaluated	Decide if there will be formative and summative aspects to the evaluation
Political and ethical issues in evaluation	Power inequalities will affect what is seen and heard	Decide on specific indicators and methods of collecting data
Relevant historical, cultural and social dynamics	Evaluation is enriched by the inclusion of different types and sources of knowledge	Identify stakeholder interests
Creative invention of methods	Epistemic justice will be best served if voice and interpretation of findings involves all stakeholders	Write an evaluation plan and budget if required
The role of participation, reflection and learning from evaluation		Collect and record information
The importance of securing resources for evaluation		Make sense of information, analysing both quantitative and qualitative information
Relevant legislation and regulations that needs to be taken into account (e.g. in the UK the Data Protection Act; safeguarding children and vulnerable adult regulations)		Interpret results and draw up options for change or recommendations
		Communicate evaluation results appropriately to a range of different audiences
		Critically reflect on own positions of power throughout the evaluation process, as well as own historical and cultural roots, and how these impact on the evaluation

Source: derived from Preskill & Boyle, 2008, p. 450.

Reflect!

interpersonal communication and a willingness to listen and to share, visualising, and synthesising information. When deciding on methods, it is as well to have in mind the different audiences to which an evaluation might speak as well as the different agendas of those involved in the planning of the evaluation.

We have argued elsewhere that *pragmatic concerns, linked to the problem in hand, determine the most appropriate method* (Kagan, Burton & Siddiquee, 2017, p. 41). And, it can be useful to categorise different methods as one of the three 'E's' Creswell (2002) identified: experiencing, enquiring and examining. Experiencing includes those methods in which the evaluators are also participants and can draw on their own involvement. Enquiring includes the collection of new information in a variety of different forms. Examining includes those methods that rely on the use of existing records and information. We summarise below some of the data collection methods that we have used in different evaluation projects, organised according to Creswell's three 'E's'.

Example: Methods for evaluation

We have used the following methods across various evaluations:

Experiencing:	Enquiring:	Examining:
Participant observation	Interviews: unstructured and informal; semi-structured; structured and formal; email or internet	Archives
Performance and other creative arts including photography, film making, writing		Minutes of meetings
		Statistical databases
	Narratives (new) and story-telling	Texts and maps
Story-telling		Monitoring information
Self-reflection	Focus groups and group discussions	Attendance registers
Intentional conversations		Audio and videotapes or films (CDs and DVDs)
Team reflections	Large scale, whole system events	
Field notes	Questionnaires – standardised and custom made	Artefacts – project photographs, project products, diaries etc.
Collaborative and appreciative inquiry		Existing narratives
	Diaries	Worker and beneficiary reflections
	Guided conversations	Diaries
		Field notes of observations, feelings, reflections

As with all social research methods, there are advantages and limitations to using different kinds of information and part of the critical reflection in relation to evaluation is to consider, on an ongoing basis, whether or not the methods chosen will give the intended insights. One difference between evaluation and other research projects is that many different audiences are likely to see and consider the results of evaluations. It is, therefore, important that the possibilities and limitations of method are understood and that evaluation findings are illustrated, so that it is clear how recommendations are built on what kinds of evidence. Interpretation of different kinds of information is another capacity building task that needs to be directed at recipients of, not just participants in, evaluation – another capacity building task.

The different facets of evaluation can be summed up by the injunction to ask the simple questions *why? who? what? how?* and *where/when?* in relation to any evaluation task. Figure 11.7 illustrates what we have called the evaluation wheel (Boyd et al., 2001).

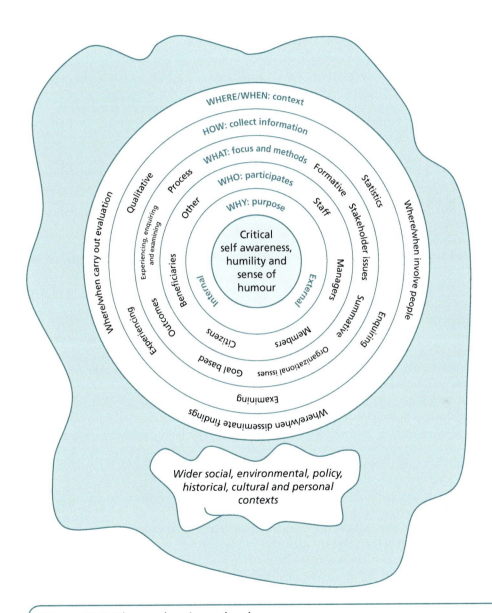

Figure 11.7 The evaluation wheel.

Act!

How might you undertake an evaluation of this book – who would be involved? Would you evaluate the content or the process?

Reflect!

Whatever kind of evaluation is undertaken, a key requirement is for a critical reflection and a critical reflexive stance throughout, which does not happen automatically. Critical reflection is a skill to be learned, practised and continually improved upon, and includes:

- ability to understand and question how beliefs, assumptions, social and historical location and previous experiences brought to a social situation influence understanding;
- ability to articulate and interrogate positionality (including the ways one's own and others' age, class, race, (dis)ability and gender, for example, intersect) in any social situation;
- ability to understand how our own historical and cultural roots affect how we frame and interpret things;
- ability to listen to alternative framings of reality and come to grips with multiple standpoints;
- ability to question what we think of as real, essential, true and necessary;
- ability to ground interpretations in relevant theory.

Chilisa, Major and Khudu-Petersen (2017, pp. 329–330) offer the following set of questions through which indigenous and non-indigenous researchers can reflect on their work and place themselves along a continuum of least to most indigenised methodologies.

1 Does the research have social relevance and is it transformative?
2 Is the decolonisation and indigenisation intent explicit?
3 Does the research take a stance against political, academic and methodological imperialism of its time?
4 Does the research highlight potential areas of Western research incompatibility with local and indigenous epistemologies as well as areas of convergence?
5 Is there any concept or variable that is unique to the local phenomenon of study?
6 Does the unique concept or variable contribute to building a new theory or modifying existing ones?
7 Is there a local perspective or indigenous conceptual or theoretical framework that is used to inform a reflection on the specific context?
8 Are there unique ontological, epistemological, cultural and value assumptions that inform the study that are different from the global generic or other cultural approaches?
9 What are the local or indigenous methods that are in contrast to globally applicable methods that are generic?
10 What are the locally relevant constructs that are in contrast to globally applicable approaches that are generic?
11 Does the research contribute towards a new research approach that develops from an indigenous conceptual or theoretical perspective?
12 Does the research contribute towards the documentation and restoration of historical marginalised indigenous knowledge, cultures and values?

These skills require a good sense of self awareness, and Evans, Malhotra and Headley (2013) suggest that whilst the descriptive and personal reaction aspects of reflection are relatively easy to acquire, the interpretive, reflexive and decisional aspects are harder.

Think!

Read the article by Gaotlhobogwe, Major, Koloi-Keaikitse and Chilisa (2018). Is the approach being offered a decolonial or postcolonial approach? What is the difference between decolonial and postcolonial goals and methods? Which is it that critical community psychology aspires to and why?

As we have seen, evaluation cannot easily be reduced to a series of steps in community psychological work. In this chapter we have covered the purposes and principles of evaluation, and outlined some possible frameworks and perspectives with which to position evaluation. In emphasising the process of evaluation, issues such as what to evaluate, who participates, the politics of evaluation and capacity building for evaluation arise. We go on now to reflect on other roles and skills for critical community psychology.

Chapter 12

Change, influence and power

Summary

In this chapter we will be looking at different ways of thinking about the nature of social change, strategic approaches to change and resistance to change. We will revisit the idea of action research as a change process and consider the role of social movements with reference to power and ideology. The manifestation of power threads throughout critical community psychological praxis and we will discuss social influence and different approaches to understanding power, powerlessness and empowerment.

Throughout the book we have touched on two interrelated themes, social change and social power. These are of such fundamental importance that in this chapter we seek to deepen and broaden some of the many ways of understanding them. That this comes after the practical sections may seem strange, but we took the view that (in the event of the book being read in linear fashion, cover to cover) this treatment will make most sense after a consideration of many practical examples of critical community psychology in action.

The nature of social change

There are several different theories of social change (Boudon, 1986) that seek to understand the content of social transformation, the function of social transformation and the causes of social change. Much of this work is embedded in the philosophy of history. For our purpose, we will adopt a rather broad definition of social change – a transformation in the social relations between people as a result of changes in social structures, social norms and social institutions. Social change might occur as a result of material circumstances. For example, an economic depression can lead to changes in how social institutions function (such as changed priorities in educational institutions and welfare delivery).

Reflect!

Technological developments can also result in powerful processes of social change (such as the invention of steam power and then electricity that supported the first and second industrial revolutions and, most recently, the development of new communication technologies that have supported the third and fourth industrial revolutions – digital technologies and new digital communication and networking). Environmental degradation can result in social change (such as global climate change leading to new legislation on energy use). Social groups – people who come together with a common purpose of influencing others – can also initiate and implement social change. Typically, it is the influence of such social groups that effects material, technological, political and environmental changes that in turn result in further processes of social change.

Think!

Take one of the following and try to identify the major forces that contributed to the particular change:

Increased presence in the workplace of women in the West
Increased population mobility from the early 1990s
The process of the departure of the United Kingdom from the European Union ('Brexit')
Falling birth rate in southern European countries
Decrease in organised religion in the UK
Rapid increase in literacy in Cuba in 1961

We can think about change in lots of different ways and at different levels. It is rare that a process of change can be delineated clearly as having a start and an end point. Indeed, from a critical community psychology perspective it may be most helpful to think about change as a direction of movement, towards liberation and against oppression, not as an end point to be achieved or not. Any work we do is part of a process in time – something has gone before and something will follow it. It therefore becomes difficult to assert our effectiveness in 'achieving' change. Whilst we might be required to record our social impact by those that commission our work, or by our employers, we should either resist doing so or at least do so with scepticism for five reasons:

1 Change is effective if it is owned by those affected by it. In the process of empowerment we have to be prepared to give up power (whether real or imagined) and let those we work with move forward through discovery not instruction.

2 Those who are affected by change are not always in a position to give feedback or recognition of the part we have played, either because they do not see it or because they are not able to articulate what it is that has made a difference. It is also easy to be seduced by the thanks that people may give us, attributing far more to our efforts than is warrantable. Receiving a thank you for creating a positive change can be as much a part of existing systems of privilege (where it is assumed the most important work has been done by the most important people) as it is a true reflection of the work done.

3 Any work we do is only part of what is going on at any one time. Social life is multivariate and we cannot lay claim to everything that happens.

4 We are rarely true insiders to the communities and groups with which we work and we will seldom have to live directly with the consequences of change. Having said this we must recognise that we are part of the processes, and it is through careful and continual reflection that we can get a realistic sense of our efficacy.

5 Change does not always occur immediately or in the area where we intervened. We therefore talk of 'slow fuse' change and 'ripple effects' to capture, respectively, the less immediate effects of change in time and in space (Burton & Kagan, 1995, Chapter 11).

Thomas and Veno (1992, p. 4) draw our attention to some important aspects of change that we are asked to take into account in our work.

> Attempts by psychologists to influence the process of social change to promote well-being of community members must take into account [the fact that] that change:
>
> 1. Is normal
> 2. Carries no implicit trauma
> 3. Comes in a diverse range of patterns and a range of alternatives open to any society
> 4. Whether one assumes change or persistence as the basis of society, has important practical as well as theoretical consequences

Here, the assumptions of persistence reflect conservative values and change represents a more radical set of values. However, the concept of change has shifted in recent years, particularly since the first edition of this textbook. It has somewhat shifted into the mainstream and might now occupy a more conservative role than it once did. The corporate sector, in particular, has increasingly valorised social change with the notion of 'disruptive innovation' taking hold in technology companies (famously encapsulated at Facebook by their corporate motto 'Move Fast and Break Things') and taking hold in the corporate sector during the early years of the millennium. Here change is adopted by the corporate sector to protect and promote corporate power in competitive consumer markets. This does not turn us away from the concept of social change, but it has reminded us that change is complex and situated. Adopting a critical community psychological approach, we acknowledge and are mindful of the shifting political and economic context in which the central tenets of our work are located. Moreover, when we work for change as critical community psychologists, change has a purpose, that of improving the situation of people and communities. This contrasts with much of the dominant discourse about change which can articulate it in essentially value neutral terms. As we have said elsewhere: always ask "so what?" about change you are planning or implementing.

Reflect!

Can you think of a time when change has been good for you? Would everyone involved in or affected by that change think it was good? Why or why not?

Many of the principles of (critical) community psychology are implicitly about change, such as, for example, empowerment and prevention. Change can take place at individual, interpersonal, group, collective or systems levels. Community psychology would tend to focus on group, collective and/or systems levels, whilst recognising that change at the other levels will also inevitably occur. Change at a systems level will frequently be multi-pronged. A good example of this is in the work of Tommy MacKay, an educational psychologist working in Dumbarton, Scotland.

MacKay (2008) argues that psychologists should agree to a values framework. This would then allow them to impact positively on well-being and human welfare. Noting a great deal of functional illiteracy in a disadvantaged area in Scotland, MacKay proposed to eradicate illiteracy. A large and long term literacy initiative was undertaken over ten years involving 63,563 young people and children. Specific aims were to raise the reading attainment of all children and reduce reading failure. The work involved five studies which explored methods of teaching, attitudes and individual support for illiteracy. In one study children had to make declarations of future reading ability (individually or as whole group chants). This powerful experience changed attitudes and beliefs, impacting upon early literacy skills. This kind of work demonstrates that long term change involves not only individual change but organisational change. Changing one aspect of a system impacts upon the wider system.

Another example is the work we undertook with working parents of disabled children to discover what needed to change in employment practices and policy to enable parents to continue to work whilst caring for disabled children.

Example: Caring to work

In an action research study we undertook that aimed to prevent a decline into poverty for working parents of disabled children, a multi-pronged change programme working with individuals, families, services, employing organisations and policy makers was needed (Kagan, Lewis & Heaton, 1998; Kagan, Lewis, Heaton & McLean, 1999). We worked with groups of parents to find out about what made it possible for parents of disabled children to continue to work, and brought groups together so that they could share their experiences. We then worked with a small number of parents to design a framework for employers and for professional service agencies to audit their practices in terms of support for working parents of disabled children. We piloted and refined the audit process with three large national employers and then made the process widely available, offering support where needed. In addition, we involved policy makers in discussion of the implications of the research and this resulted in a change to the national Childcare Strategy in favour of recognising the needs of disabled children beyond the start of school age.

Whilst this systems level and complex change is the focus of community psychology, we recognise that other kinds of psychologists, also concerned with change, might focus more on individual, family or organisational change. However, the distinctions between levels of change are not always clear, and Kagan, Tindall and Robinson (2009) have shown how counselling psychologists, for example, might adopt a more community psychological stance. MacKay's work, above, illustrates a community level concern of educational psychologists. Goodley and Lawthom (2005) note the similarities between community psychology and disability studies in understanding social change. Using a paradigmatic model based on Burrell and Morgan (1979), change in critical community psychology work may shift between functional and radical change processes and between individuals, groups and communities. It is worth reminding ourselves that people are still at the heart of critical community psychological change: the changes brought about at systems level above were all mediated by people doing things differently.

The Freirean concept of conscientisation (see Chapter 8) is about experiences through learning. Individual contradictions in experience through dialogue lead to political awareness and to people becoming part of the process of changing the world around them. So this is an approach (again participatory) which may begin at the individual level but through which group action leads to social change. Much of Freire's work in Latin America and Africa demonstrates how individual growth can be inextricably linked to collective change.

Act!

Write a manifesto for change outlining the key positive features of change from a community psychological perspective. Imagine you are doing this in order to contribute to the growth of community psychology as a practice by convincing others (employers, government, other projects or organisations) about the impact community psychology could make on society.

Incremental or radical change

Change can be bit by bit, chipping away at how things are done within an existing system, in which case it is incremental change, sometimes referred to as 'first order change' (Levy & Merry, 1986). In contrast, radical, or second order change, creates a paradigm shift in how things are done – radically altering the system. Incremental change is often ameliorative, making some adjustments but having little effect on the overall system. Ameliorative change is sometimes thought of as putting a sticking plaster over the wound instead of dealing with the cause of the injury. Radical change, on the other hand is thought to be transformative and the proper, urgent business of critical community psychology.

> Time is short and the suffering vast. ... If we continue to use our limited community psychology resources only to ameliorate conditions and to tend to the wounded, who will work to transform the very conditions that create exploitation and distress in the first place?
>
> (Prilleltensky, 2008, p. 132)

Radical change, however, is not without its risks. Disruption to systems can lead to disruptions that shift the ground you and your colleagues work on to a point that can lead to your role becoming either redefined or redundant so that you are no longer in a position to promote social change. Given that the status quo is what it is (usually because some groups' interests are served by things being as they are, and those groups are usually powerful – at least sufficiently powerful to maintain the status quo), becoming involved in radical social change can result in a robust response from such groups and this can place you and those you work with in a vulnerable position (and may dilute the possibilities for change). One of us (author X) has had the experience of challenging racial and disability discrimination in their university workplace, a challenge that resulted in institutional reports, external investigations and a number of academic staff being found to have discriminated against disabled and black students. Those staff were required to undertake training in disability and racial awareness, much to their annoyance. The effect of this was that those staff and their colleagues worked to isolate and marginalise author X to the point at which author X was forced to leave the university. Thereafter, author X had no further opportunity to tackle discriminatory practices in that university.

In our experience, though, the distinction between ameliorative and transformational change is not always easy to maintain. In a complex system, chipping away at different parts of the system, bit by bit, whilst each individual change is incremental and ameliorative, over time the culmination of the incremental changes creates a radical transformation. There is nothing wrong in itself with ameliorative intervention and change. It is right to offer help to those in need and this is the moral basis that also underpins the more systemic interventions and aspirations of critical community psychology. In some cases community psychologists have made transformative claims for interventions that in reality are only ameliorative. This is at worst disingenuous and at best mistaken: either way it 'devalues the coin' of truly transformative change. Making grandiose claims without a thorough political analysis of the systemic reality will make critical community psychology and its practitioners lose credibility with those who they wish to help liberate and those who exercise power. If we cannot live up to the transformative pretension, better that we limit our aspirations to the ameliorative. However, ameliorative changes can under some circumstances combine transformatively.

> ## Example: Deinstitutionalisation and service transformation
>
> We (MB and CK) worked as a small part of the large scale transformation of services for and with people with learning difficulties and their families in the 1980s and 1990s. At the start of the 1980s in the North West of England some 1,700 people lived in large institutions away from other people and a further thousand or so lived in hostels catering for 12–30 people. By 2002 130 people remained in institutions and no new hostel accommodation had been provided. The majority of people were either living in family homes or in what was known as domestic scale accommodation (no more than five people living together in one housing unit). There was no doubt about it, there had been radical change, but made up of lots of small change activities, including policy development; staff training and recruitment; changes in the use of welfare benefits; involvement of people with learning difficulties on decision making bodies; organisational development and consultancy with local services; visits to and from progressive practitioners from other countries; and experimentation with new service delivery models (Kagan, 1997b; Kagan, McLean, Gathercole & Austin, 1988, 1990). Any one of these changes alone would have made little differences to people's lives. Each on its own could have been called ameliorative. Taken together they not only transformed people's lives and the service system in the North West, but they acted as demonstration projects for a radical overhaul of new national policy, which had far reaching transformative impact (although not without its faults – Burton & Kagan, 2006).

Linear and non-linear change

Some approaches to change assume that once a goal is set, progress towards it can be made in a steady way. This is known as goal directed, means–end or rational change. In human systems change rarely occurs like this. Instead, a general direction for a complex system is set, and progress is messy with different parts proceeding at different paces: progress is made, it falters, diversion sets in and so on. This is known as holistic, organic (sometimes irrational) change.

If we are serious about thinking of critical community psychology in a systemic way then it is those processes of organic change that we must get to grips with. Communities (of whatever kind) can be thought of as akin to organisations. This then opens up the literature on organisational change for the critical community psychologist. As if to make the point about the overlap between these two types of system (community and organisation), organisational theorists have found it illuminating to consider work organisations as communities, insofar as they can both be understood in terms of capability, commitment, contribution, continuity, collaboration, and conscience (Brown & Isaacs, 1994).

Reflect!

When you think about the course of your life, would you describe it as linear or non-linear change? What do you think has influenced this pattern?

Stage approaches to change

The metaphor of stages or steps can also be used to understand change. In its pure form a stage approach would indicate some kind of hierarchy – first stages must be attained before later ones are possible. However, other stage perspectives on change adopt a more flexible approach. Discrete stages may be useful to delineate but progress through them does not necessarily take place in an orderly way and earlier stages can be revisited at any time, rather like painting a wall in contrast to building a wall with bricks.

One influential stage theory of change is that of Kubler-Ross (1969), drawing initially on stages that people pass through as they cope with grief and loss. Change theorists argue that the same emotional stages occur during organisational (and hence community) change. The original stages are: denial, anger, bargaining, depression, acceptance. Rashford and Coghlan (1989) in the context of organisational change, suggest a reduction of these stages to: denying, dodging, doing and sustaining. The advantage of outlining these stages is that it encourages us not only to anticipate, but also to make sense of particular stakeholder reactions to change.

Example: Contested change in a psychiatric service

We were invited to undertake an action research project on organisational change in a psychiatric service in a town in the North West of England. Changes already made by the service organisation had changed the power relations between different professional groups (Knowles & Kagan, 1995a,b). We examined the changes made, made recommendations for further change, examined their impact and so on. One of the most powerful of the internal stakeholder groups was the psychiatrists. At one point our researcher found herself in a room with a psychiatrist who was banging on the table and raging that he would expose her incompetence and undermine everything she was doing. Following this meeting, he did, indeed, do what he could to belittle the rigour of the study and the personal qualities of the researcher. This was upsetting and we wondered if we should put up with this kind of abuse. Understanding, though, that anger and resistance is a normal reaction to change, enabled us to see these dynamics as part of a process and not as personal attacks. This insight has stood us in good stead on many occasions – if we can ride the anger and channel it into constructive dialogue, then we are able to move to more positive stages of change. It also highlights the need for a thick skin and for support in work around change. In this case we had established a steering group for the project that included a leading academic psychiatrist in the country with a strong reputation for promoting new models in the community. It was difficult for the psychiatrists on the ground to undermine what we were doing when we had the support of the steering group.

Once the 'dodging it' or resistance stage is overcome, this does not mean it will not re-emerge as change proceeds. Resistance is not always a force to be overcome and indeed is often the site of progressive change (see later on in the chapter) – the tricky part is working out where the power interests lie and whose interests resistance serves.

Another stage model of change, moving from individual to collective action in a community setting is offered by Holland's work in inner city London (Holland 1991, 1992). Holland used a model called Social Action Psychotherapy (which is an approach of conscientisation with women collectively). Over a ten year period, this long term project identified the stages of working on individual issues, and found commonality with others with similar experiences, collectively identifying and mobilising for change. Women's distress was resolved and channelled into social action. Women collectively began to set up their own services providing support to each other. A similar approach was followed by Mel-luish and Bulmer (1999) with a group of unemployed men in Nottingham. We do not wish to suggest that following this sequence of stages is inevitable, although in both cases the community psychologists took the view that until a start had been made on addressing individual level issues, it was not feasible to work on the more collective plane. In other contexts individual and socio-political issues have been addressed at the same time (Agger & Buus Jensen, 1996; Burton, 2004b) rather as ecological cultivators might overlap crop rotations using techniques such as undersowing (Fukuoka, 1985a, 1985b), or in the case of the community therapy approach developed in the Pirambu favela, Fortaleza, Brazil (Barreto, 2011; Camarotti et al., 2004) as fully interlocked elements of the same reality that cannot be dissolved into either individual or collective moments.

Reflect!

Think about what you know about people and change. Do you think that personal issues must be resolved BEFORE group or collective issues can be addressed? Can you think of any examples where personal change has led to collective change or where collective change has taken place even though personal issues are unresolved?

Strategic change

Pettigrew, Ferlie and McKee (1992) summarised some of the dimensions of change to take into account in strategic change management. Known as Pettigrew's triangle, these facets can be summarised as context, process and content of change.

Context of change refers to the 'why and when' of change, and includes both inner and outer contexts. Outer contexts are those external to the organisation (or community) and may include wider economic forces and social policy shifts. They may also include whatever else is going on in other linked organisations (including competition for resources) and open up the possibility of thinking about the political environment in which the organisation is embedded. Inner contexts are those influences internal to the organisation, such as interpersonal dynamics, internal resources, capabilities and skills, and organisational politics and culture.

Content refers to the 'what' of change, and invites consideration of the areas of transformation and the tools and techniques needed to make change happen.

Process refers to the 'how' and who' of change and refers to the ways in which those different stakeholders involved in the change interact and behave as they negotiate proposals for change and implement agreed tactics.

Different levels of change can be seen: individual, interpersonal, group, organisation, system, policy, societal; or individual, interpersonal, collective. They are often linked to each other and can be difficult to untangle. We have argued in Chapter 11, in relation to evaluation, that sometimes it is necessary to try to articulate the kind of change we anticipate: only by doing this can we properly evaluate our work.

Act!

Talk to an older adult – maybe a relative – about some of the social changes they have seen over their lifetime. How would you describe these changes? Can you think of key events or actions that speeded up the process of change or slowed it down?

Resistance to change

Resistance is, in itself, a change process – particularly when it is resistance by oppressed persons against some imposition by the state or other powerful group (such as landowners, employers and so on). Foucault's (1976, p. 95) assertion that *"where there is power there is resistance"* is a useful reminder that resistance, just like power, is ever-present. Resistance can, therefore, be the space wherein those who are oppressed act for their own liberation.

In our critical community practice, resistance to change is a dynamic to be anticipated, worked with and taken seriously, as it can sometimes indicate incomplete commitment or even a completely misguided direction for change at any particular point in time. Our point is that we do not have a perfect understanding of what needs to change and the 'victims' of a change programme must be listened to as a valid and essential source of knowledge about what is at stake. However, we need to be very careful here to distinguish between those that have illegitimate power or other resources in a situation and fear it being taken away, and those that are already disadvantaged and rightly fear that the change planned will worsen their situation. Not all voices are equally valid and it is a heavy responsibility weighing up which are and which are not. This is not something to be done on your own and we would argue not to be done by community psychologists as a unidisciplinary group. This whole question is complicated by the bigger picture in which a variety of groups may be facing threats to their interests.

> ## Example: Deinstitutionalisation and service transformation
>
> In the 1980s programmes of closure of institutions that had oppressed disabled people for generations, groups of organised workers faced job losses or changes of role and location. This was in the context of the beginnings of the neoliberal assault on organised labour and the welfare state. A future for disabled people that did not include a positive future for those that delivered care was not something to aspire towards. Accordingly, the better programmes of institutional closure and replacement (including the one we were a part of described above) included programmes that offered 'positive futures for staff', engaging them in the change and offering them retraining, new, more satisfying roles, and so on (Kagan, 1997b).

Veno and Thomas (1992, p. 23) outline some of the challenges presented by resistance to change.

> Psychologists acting as change agents face a wide array of resistance when trying to facilitate change. The sources of this resistance include value systems, social stratification and opposition to the goals of change…

Veno and Thomas draw on an early analysis of resistance to social change to suggest that resistance takes place when change is perceived to threaten people's basic security; or is not understood; or is imposed from above.

We have already seen above that stakeholders may have emotional reactions to change that stimulate their active opposition, played out in a range of different interpersonal ways, particularly if their power base is under threat in some way. Even when we manage to work in collaborative ways, bringing together different stakeholders in dialogue, it will still often be necessary to deal with resistance within groups. As Burns (2007, p. 144) says:

> Those with a vested interest in the status quo often mount an attack on the 'methodology' because they do not like the 'challenging' work that the group is doing. It is often easier to attack the method than to attack the sense making that the [co-operative] inquiry is doing.

Resistance can also operate through strong gate keeping. Those with the power to do so can prevent actions happening or people being involved in a piece of work.

Example: Indian dancing in a day centre

One of our students was working as a volunteer in a day facility for people with enduring mental health difficulties, taken on by the manager in order to stimulate change. There were few activities and few people other than those with mental health difficulties and paid staff involved in the work of the centre. After speaking to a number of the people using the centre, she proposed running some Indian dance sessions for those using the centre as well as for people who had had nothing hitherto to do with the centre. The centre members thought this a good idea and the front line staff did too. The centre manager would not permit it to go ahead. No reasons were given, just something vague like "it would be difficult to do and people may not be interested." On reflection, it seemed that his resistance was, in large part, because the very essence of the centre he was in charge of was being questioned: its purpose, its operation, member satisfaction and locus of ideas for change.

Example: Irish folk singing with older Irish migrants

One of our students wanted to explore cultural well-being with older Irish migrants, using singing and cultural memory. She was herself Irish and a trained folk singer. She spent much time accessing and volunteering in day centres and community centres and running workshops. Eventually she gained access to a group of older Irish migrants who were keen to have someone Irish work with them. The planned project which involved singing was not something the other participants felt confident in – and although managers there agreed it would be a good idea, the singing never got off the ground. Indeed, the day centre participants persuaded the student to enter an Irish beauty contest as this better suited their memories of Ireland! Despite promises that they would sing it never happened. The resistance was powerful and reflected confidence and interest in singing. Change cannot always happen in a planned way – the student was forced to rethink the project. (She established a community choir with open access and no auditions that has gained a strong reputation for its wide repertoire.)

Reflect!

Consider when a personal course of action has not gone the intended way. Can you pinpoint whether particular stakeholders impeded the process in any way? What was the resistance to change and how (if at all) did you resolve it?

If we work collaboratively, undertaking stakeholder analyses, it is sometimes possible to anticipate resistance from those with vested interests, or that stand to lose from an intervention. Then our plans for action can take these into account. We have found it useful to co-opt those who might resist, so that their blocking does not interfere with the actual processes of change.

> ### Example: Leisure advocacy
>
> We (MB and CK) initiated a project that sought to use principles and processes of citizen advocacy to increase the leisure participation of people with learning difficulties in one part of a Northern town. One of the local social service managers was hostile to the project, arguing that the slow, person centred ways of working would lead to little change and be a waste of public money. We invited him to join the management group of the project. Although his criticisms were still voiced, he could not stop his staff co-operating with a project of which he was a part. He was also exposed to some of the exciting changes that were achieved. Within three years he had 'mainstreamed' many of the ideas and they became part of the service (Kagan, 1990). Far from continuing to resist, he ended up embracing the practices and had also brought a different set of skills and knowledge to the project.

This co-option was strategic and, in the end, helpful. In many forms of participatory community work there is suspicion that the very invitation to participate is nothing other than co-option and an attempt to silence people rather than give them voice – a realistic concern that we have to be aware of. We must interrogate our practices so that we do not inadvertently end up doing this. It is our value systems that will be our best guard against co-option.

One way of identifying the motivations behind co-option is to ask, (1) *"what change is being planned and who will it affect?"* and (2) *"what is the position of those to be co-opted vis a vis this direction of change? Are they on the receiving end of the change, and if so is this co-option a way to defuse resistance to a change that is not in their interests?"* The ideal of everyone agreeing and working co-operatively together rarely, if ever, happens and working with the complexity of people's views, positions and actions, recognising the reality of irreconcilable interests, is at the core of critical community psychological work.

Action research as change

The different types of change outlined above, focusing on systems change but incorporating ideas from knowledge about organisational change (learning organisations, strategic change, stages of change, resistance to change) can all be accommodated in action research, which itself embraces a strong action learning (Revans, 1980) component. Indeed, action research and action learning are closely aligned in much of the work on systemic organisation change, brought together through the work of the Action Learning and Action Research Association (ALARA – www.alarassociation.org; Burns, 2007; Shankar, Dick, Passfield & Swepson, 2002).

Kagan, Burton and Siddiquee (2017) have outlined different forms of action research of relevance to community psychologists, distinguishing between practical and emancipatory and participatory action research. Whilst they can be distinguished as ideal types, they have a number of features in common:

Reflect!

- value based, future oriented practice;
- cross disciplinary;
- cyclical process;
- combined methods of data collection;
- learning through dialogue and sharing;
- combining theory and action;
- context bound;
- concerned with change;
- sustainable over time.

Stringer (1999, p. 17) summarises very well the application of action research to change in community contexts:

> Community-based action research is a collaborative approach to inquiry or investigation that provides people with the means to take systematic action to resolve specific problems. This approach to research favours consensual and participatory procedures that enable people (a) to investigate systematically their problems and issues, (b) to formulate powerful and sophisticated accounts of their situations, and (c) to devise plans to deal with the problems at hand.

Social movements, power and ideology

In the above discussion we have sometimes considered change within project or problem situations with reasonably identifiable boundaries. In other cases, however, we are concerned with multiple dimensions of change involving multiple actors and interest groups. When considering large scale change of this sort, as well as when looking at the community dimension of change projects, we consider an understanding of social movements is critical.

Social movements typically arise in a situation where people have a grievance (for example the mothers of the disappeared in Argentina, the families of those killed on the Pan-American aeroplane over Lockerbie, school children concerned about climate change), an unfulfilled need (the crofters' movement in the Scottish highlands and islands at the beginning of the twentieth century, the unemployed movement, the suffragettes), or an alternative social project (the Campaign for Nuclear Disarmament (CND), the Co-operative Movement). For them it is essential that they maintain cohesion while gaining influence in a situation where they have relatively limited power. A key to this is their use, implicit or explicit, of ideology.

While not usually considered within the field of social movements, the insights of Gramsci (1971; see Burton & Kagan, 1996) are invaluable to understand the relationships between ideology and the lived world in which social movements operate. Gramsci uses the concept of ideological hegemony to explain how order is maintained in modern capitalist societies by the organisation of consent. His understanding of hegemony is not just about beliefs and ideas, but concerns the whole of society, permeating it, and even defining the nature and limit of common sense. Ideology, which is more than ideas, acts as a kind of 'social cement', unifying a bloc of varied social groups and interests. In this, a hegemonic social group exercises leadership and power, not through crude ideological domination, but rather through the combination of key elements from the ideologies of those social groups that form an alliance or social bloc with it. Elsewhere we have identified the following postulates about the exercise of ideological hegemony in relation to social settings (Burton, 1994; Burton & Kagan, 1995):

1 Ideological hegemony, with its ideological coalitions, has boundaries other than those of the setting. Therefore, change efforts at the ideological level must focus both on the internal coalitions

of the setting and on other external interest groups who can be empowered in the process of cohering in a hegemonic coalition.

2   Ideological coalitions are likely to have varying degrees of hegemony. The effective range of their hegemony over diverse interest groups will vary as will the intensity with which such groups identify with the hegemonic ideology.

3   In order to continue uniting diverse interests under changing conditions, the dominant group will need what we call *necessary hegemony*, i.e. a sufficient degree of hegemony (in range and intensity) to handle threats to the hegemonic view. Where there is a deficit in the necessary hegemony of the dominant group in the coalition then there can be signs of hegemonic strain with the breakdown of ideology and the splitting off of components of the coalition.

4   We therefore have a basis for the succession of hegemonic groups and their wider coalitions. The more successful hegemonists will be able to alter both the ideology and the assemblage of allied groupings to adapt to changing conditions, protecting a core ideology and the core membership of the alliance. It is this active engagement that Gramsci refers to with the metaphors of the 'Modern Prince' and the 'War of Position'.

Devine et al. (2009) and Dussel (2008) present recent applications of these ideas to the field of politics and social change.

Social influence

In psychology, the understanding of how social change occurs has tended to emphasise social influence. The classic studies of conformity of Asch and Sherif in the USA are included in most programmes of study in psychology. There the emphasis was on how people become pressurised by majorities within groups to conform to their norms. Subsequent European work took a different approach, contextualising the closed world of the social psychology experiment within the wider society and also seeking to understand the ways minority groups influence majority groups. Majority and minority do not just refer to how many people are in each group but also to the political, cultural and economic resources available to that group. Thus, it often makes more sense to refer to dominant and non-dominant groups. For example, the British in a colonial town in the period of the British Empire were in the minority, but were nevertheless the dominant group, whereas in some neighbourhoods in the UK Muslims are now in the majority, but are not necessarily the dominant group.

> ### *Think!*
>
> Think of instances in which a minority group has been or might be more influential than the majority. Describe a personal situation in which you were influenced by a minority view. How did this come about?

Moscovici contrasted the different social change processes involved in minority (non-dominant) group influence and majority (dominant) group influence (Moscovici, Lage & Naffrechoux, 1969). In doing so, he proposed a two-process model to understand how social influence creates social change. This model asserts that majority influence happens through a process of normative social influence that occurs at a public level whereas minority influence happens through a process of informational social influence that occurs at a private level. When we are influenced by a majority group we might change our behaviour but we might not necessarily change our beliefs. For example, someone might be convinced not to act or speak in a racist manner but might still privately hold racist beliefs. The way people's public behaviour changes without a concurrent change in their beliefs causes problems when social scientists seek to survey people's attitudes. The results of such surveys might say more about how respondents' verbal behaviour conforms to public norms than it does about their actual private beliefs. In contrast, minority influence occurs because a minority group has not only influenced how a person might behave but also changed that person's beliefs. So social change through majority group influence can be weaker and more unstable than that arising from minority group influence.

It is not always easy to discern when a group is a minority or a majority. A minority group might find that it engages in a process of social change as though it were perceived as a majority group because the change proposed fits within the ethos of the dominant culture. Thus, the influence of social movements such as the Pride movement, disability movement, the women's movement and so on might have created a change in public behaviour but not private attitudes because its agenda of celebrating diversity is a dominant cultural norm (certainly in the West since the 1970s).

Under *normative* social influence, people's behaviour changes as a result of their moving closer towards a social norm. The motivation for doing so is to be more socially accepted (by the dominant group) and to avoid appearing to be too different from others (other dominant group members or those who subscribe to dominant group norms). This is the process seen to be at the heart of the classic studies in social psychology on conformity and social influence. In the contemporary UK, the thinking underpinning normative social influence is at the heart of 'nudge' politics (Hallsworth & Sanders, 2016).

Example: The behavioural insights team

In the UK the Behavioural Insights Team began life at the seat of Government, in the Cabinet Office. It is now called a social purpose company, part funded by the Cabinet Office, employees and the innovation quango, Nesta. Its brief is to "generate and apply behavioural insights to inform policy, improve public services, and deliver positive results for people and communities". The team has been nicknamed the 'nudge unit' as one of the strands of their work is to encourage behaviour change in the direction of Government priorities, nudging people to change their behaviour and thereby changing social norms (and vice versa).

Normative social influence contrasts with *informational* social influence where behaviour change is achieved by people being persuaded of the need to change their behaviour based on the information they are presented with – they are convinced by the argument that underpins the requested change in behaviour (rather than the more simplistic – "do it because everyone else does") under normative social influence. Here we see a change in behaviour that is much stronger and more stable than that often induced by normative social influence.

Moscovici argued that a minority can influence a majority when the minority is seen as strong, self confident and consistent in the call for change but flexible and appearing to be willing to compromise and negotiate at the same time.

Act!

Read the article by Halpern (2019). Does 'nudge' politics reflect normative or informational social influence? Taking a critical community psychological perspective, list five ethical issues that arise from the article. On balance, do you think 'nudge' politics is a good thing? Why?

Reflect!

There has been quite a rapid, recent growth in public concern over the pollution caused by plastics, particularly single use plastics, despite the damage they cause having been known for a long time. How do you explain this?

Act!

Using some of the above ideas draw up a plan of action to try to mobilise interest in a social issue (such as climate change; the challenge of peak oil production; people trafficking; violence towards women; biodiversity loss). What steps might you take to galvanise interest in the issue? What difficulties would there be in implementing your plan? Try your ideas out on some friends and see what they think of them.

Social change tactics

A group can engage in a process of social change by using a variety of tactics. In Chapters 8, 9 and 10 we discussed six action strategies for change: furthering critical consciousness; creation of alternative social settings; development of alliances and coalitions; accompaniment and advocacy; working with archives and big data; and analysis of policy. Within these strategies lie the tactics of change outlined by Dalton et al. (2001): social action, community development, consciousness raising and policy research and development. These different change tactics use power in different ways. Social action (campaigns against a practice, situation, policy or plan) tends to be confrontational, using coercive power based on the strength of the mobilisation. Community development engages in the control of participation but, unlike social action, creates change through promoting people's participation in the proposed change process. With its emphasis on strengthening the bonds between community members, it often relies on personal power. Consciousness raising, along with policy research and advocacy, places more of an emphasis on the role of the power of persuasion, but also employs authoritative forms of power based on perceived competence and legitimacy. Thus, the emphasis is on influencing those in power to reconsider their policies and practices through persuading them to change. Advocacy is not primarily about engaging in bargaining or engaging in coercion, but is based on seeking to persuade with information (such as with the use of empirical research, individual testimony and theoretical models) and reasoned arguments.

Social power is relational (it exists between people, not within people) and sits within a complex mix of cultural, economic, historical, political and social forces. Community can serve to place boundaries around groups in such a way as to benefit those with power. Power and community combine to manufacture social exclusion (which we discuss in Part 1, Chapters 4 and 5). However, power can also find its expression in promoting social change to remove those barriers and to promote a fair and balanced distribution of power and resources.

Social power, powerlessness and empowerment

Social power can be defined as the capacity to produce change in people's social relations (what they do, how they are seen by others and how their social networks function) and in the social and material conditions in which they live (such as their income, housing, access to resources, services and so on). In the West (post-industrialised countries where democratic political systems and capitalist economic systems dominate) it is more typically defined as the ability to impose one's will on others, even in the face of resistance. So, you have social power if you are able to get another person or group of people to act, think or reflect in a way that they might not ordinarily do. Weber (1946, p. 152) stated this in terms that point more to its coercive nature:

> By power is meant every opportunity/possibility existing within a social relationship, which permits one to carry out one's own will, even against resistance, and regardless of the basis on which this opportunity rests.

There are three important dimensions to social power. The first is that it is relational. By saying that one person or one group has power implies there are other people or groups who are involved in a power relationship with them (i.e. over whom power is exerted) and that power cannot exist unless those relationships exist. The second is that power operates reciprocally. Having power over others nearly always comes with those others having some form of power over you. For example, an employer controls wages, working conditions, conditions for promotion and so on. However, the worker has control over some aspects of the labour process – they can withdraw their labour, go slow, even sabotage production, although this depends on collective strength, through for example joining a trade union or other social movement organisation. The reciprocity will not be equally balanced and 'the balance of power' constitutes the third important dimension that needs to be considered. So an employer's ability to hire or fire might be more powerful than the employee's ability to withdraw their labour (such as during times of high unemployment when employees can become trapped in their job because of a lack of availability of alternative jobs). The dimension of balance is a consequence of power being both relational and reciprocal.

Reflect!

Think of a situation wherein you think you have exerted power or influence. Identify (i) the relational aspects; (ii) reciprocity; (iii) balance of power. What can you learn about powerlessness from this analysis?

Taxonomy of power

In addition to identifying different dimensions of power, there have been a number of attempts to produce a taxonomy of social power to capture all of the different ways a person or a group gets others to do something they might not ordinarily do.

Power can come in many different forms. Person A might get person B to do something by force, by persuasion, by exercising authority or by manipulation. So, to get someone to go through a doorway, you could physically push them (force), you could encourage them (persuasion), you could command them (authority) or you could trick them by telling them that there is a reward on the other side (manipulation).

Each of these forms of power might contain further distinct strands. Wrong (1979) draws out five different ways in which authority might operate: how person or group A is able to command person or group B to do something (see Figure 12.1).

Personal power is the way B does what A wants because of B's admiration, friendship and liking of A. This might be due to A having charismatic qualities or because A acts as a role model for B. Coercive power is where B does what A wants because they are threatened with a punishment. This is where power resembles the use of force, but is mediated by B being requested to do something (A doesn't force B to do something; A asks B to do something and makes clear the negative consequences

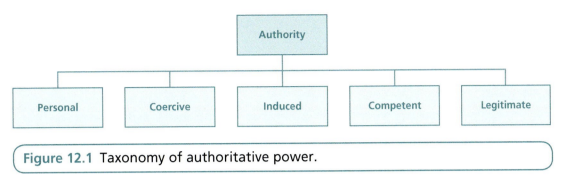

Figure 12.1 Taxonomy of authoritative power.

of not doing so). Induced power is where a reward rather than punishment is promised. Legitimate power is where neither a punishment nor a reward is necessarily offered. Instead, the differing social roles that A and B occupy require that B complies with A's requests (such as the roles of teacher–pupil, parent–child, employer–employee). Finally, A might be able to direct B because A is perceived as having the competence to do so (such as with a driving instructor). Here B follows A's command because of the perception that A is in a better position than B to know what B should do. The intensity and extensiveness of authoritative power is at its greatest when all these forms are used together but the combination of legitimate and personal power is often enough to ensure authoritative power works; indeed, this combination is often when authoritative power works most effectively (in terms of ensuring compliance without damaging social relationships). Thus, a charismatic teacher may be able to exercise authority over her pupils particularly effectively.

Act!

Undertake a quick literature search of 'power' and 'community psychology'. Can you find three different ways that power is featured in community psychology? Write these down and see how they are similar and how they are different from each other. Do you think there are different ways of thinking about power in community psychology? Which fits the perspective of critical community psychology best and why?

A widely used taxonomy of social power was developed initially by French and Raven (1959). It is shown in Table 12.1.

Through reflection, we can become aware of the type of influence we are exerting and what consequences this has. However, French and Raven's analysis of power, while influential has not been without its criticisms. Martín-Baró (1989, pp. 107–109) identifies two of them. First, emphasising power as influence over change means that those exercises of power that do not involve change are not explored.

> Every act of influence implies a power, but not every power is channelled into influence, understood as the production of a change in the person affected. Power can act without it meaning a change in the person affected. This happens, for example, when a state of things imposed by those with power is simply accepted, when the exercise of power impedes the possibility that someone takes a decision … or through the exercise of power the alternatives are eliminated. The worker who has to choose between accepting a low salary without protest or ending up unemployed and who has no other way of securing food and maintaining their family, really lacks choice and whoever places him before this false dilemma is in reality imposing a behaviour (acceptance of low salary) and denying other possibilities for action.
> (Martín-Baró, 1989, pp. 107–108, our translation)

Table 12.1 Sources of social power and their consequences

Type of power	Characteristic	Likely consequence
Expert power	Perception that someone is competent due to their specialist or expert knowledge	May induce passivity if knowledge is not shared. Expert power can be useful when challenging other expert positions.
Legitimate power	Perception that a person has a right to exercise influence by virtue of her position or role	May be disempowering to the most marginalised. However, it may also be utilised to good effect in challenging institutional power.
Reward power	Perception that a person has the ability and resources to obtain rewards	Can lead to manipulation.
Referent power	Influence is linked to perceptions of shared experience or commonality	If genuine, can be supportive and empowering.
Coercive power	Influence is based on fear and the perception that the person is able to implement some kinds of sanction such as withholding of resources	Can lead to further oppression. Likely to generate resistance.

Second, their analysis is psychological, appearing to assume that the path of power passes necessarily through the consciousness of people. So all the unconscious ways in which power operates remain beyond the French and Raven analysis. Other well known analyses (e.g. Lukes, 1974; Wrong, 1979) emphasise the way that power and domination become internalised, so in effect the person's own decisions are nevertheless influenced by the external operation of explicit and implicit power. Foucault (1976) and Habermas (1984) in their different ways emphasise the role of language in the maintenance and reproduction of social power. In keeping with the reproduction–transformation account of society put forward in Chapter 3, then, power should be seen as both systemic in nature and exercised by people.

However, we can use the taxonomies of French and Raven, Wrong and others, not as representations of reality so much as heuristic devices, models that help us understand and explore how power operates. In reality the different forms of authoritative power as well as power through force, persuasion and manipulation described by Wong are not discreet – they can overlap considerably and one form of power can readily transform itself into another. If repeated often enough, persuasion might transform into legitimate or competent authority. Further, an inducement might become coercive if its threat of withdrawal becomes perceived as a punishment. Competent authority might transform into legitimate power if those who have perceived competence become a professional body (such as has happened with the discipline of psychology). Competent power might also transform into coercive power if that professional organisation attains legislative powers. In the UK clinical psychologists, social workers, police officers and doctors variously have, for example, powers to detain people under mental health or immigration legislation, or to remove children from their family homes under child protection legislation. Their professional competence enables them to exercise coercive power due to the legislation. At the same time there are other legislative requirements within which professionals must work, to guard against the deprivation of liberty, aiming to prevent people being unlawfully detained or removed. The power of knowledge and information, then, underpins professional action (how can legislative requirements be met so that detention or removal can take place?).

Reflect!

Choose a social role that you occupy (e.g. employee, student, mother). List the types of authoritative power (i.e. coercive, induced, legitimate, competent, personal) you are subjected to and that you subject others to whilst occupying that role. To what extent does the exercise of authoritative power depend upon your compliance?

The social structure of social power

The relational nature of power, the forms of its reciprocation, and the means by which it is balanced, are structured within the context and interplay of cultural, economic, historical, political and social forces. The power exerted by one group over another might be determined by the particular nature of the social relationship between those two groups, the way these relationships have been socially structured. Relationships of authority might be clear to map and be clearly understood. Others might be less easy to discern and might be the result of quite complex histories of power relations and struggles. For example, the complex history of colonialism (such as the British occupation of India and Africa), feudalism (which led to the social stratification of society by social class) and patriarchy (where men occupy positions of power over women) all may define how contemporary power relations are configured and resisted through the fight against racism, classism, sexism and social inequalities. Economic power lies at the heart of many structural aspects of power.

Think!

Why might it be that societies differ in the influence exerted by older people? How is the power held (or not held) by elders linked to historical factors, cultural factors, economic factors and social relationships? What implications does this analysis have for work you might undertake as a critical community psychologist working with older people?

At this point, we return to the approach we first used when looking at the concept of community in Part 1, the need to look at the good and the bad side. It is useful to remind ourselves that there are two ways of viewing social power. There is the consensus view which sees social power as benign and the conflict view which sees social power as reflecting irreconcilable interests – for example those of different classes. The consensus view tends to see social power as used for good, helping organisations, communities and society as a whole to operate smoothly. In contrast, the conflict view holds that social structures reflect and promote the uneven distribution of resources and serve the vested interests of politically and economically dominant groups: there is therefore conflict between the social power of different groups in the social structure. The difference between these two theoretical approaches can been seen in the classic works of Talcott Parsons (1957) and C. Wright Mills (1956). Mills saw power relations as resulting in a zero sum game where the ultimate effect is the production of winners and losers. For example, the exercise of power of shareholders in a corporation who support a buyout of a corporation which leads to job losses for employees of that corporation produces clear winners (shareholders increase their profits) and losers (employees lose their jobs). Parson's approach to power relations is founded on the belief that they produce winners and winners, such that the exercise of power by group A will ultimately benefit both group A and group B: a win–win situation. For example, the wielding of power of teachers over students is believed to lead to benefits for the teacher (ability to control the class) and for the students (clear tuition and guidance to help their learning).

Just as with the concept of community, by which those who live in safe communities tend to view the concept of community as benign and those who live in unsafe communities tend to view the concept of community as malign, those who have social power (that is, through their economic wealth or cultural dominance) tend to hold a consensus view of power while those who have less social power (that is, through their economic poverty or cultural exclusion) tend to hold a conflict view of social power. Critical community psychology tends to side with those who have less social power and thus a conflict theory approach to power is more pronounced (although the insights from consensus theory are not ignored). Foucault's writing on power is particularly influential in this regard. Foucault theorised that power and knowledge are inextricably linked. He argued that belief systems (such as those transmitted by social institutions) gain momentum, and thus power, as more and more people come to accept the views associated with that belief system as common sense and the social roles that develop from that belief system as natural (such as the hegemony of the medical institutions and the legitimate and competent authority role of medical doctors). Within those belief systems (or discourses) moral positions are adopted (ideas form as to what is right, what is wrong, what is normal and what is abnormal) and other discourses become obscured and ultimately rendered unthinkable.

Think!

Look at a critical psychology text and then consider the profession of psychology. Can you identify the power that is held by the profession in the society from which you come? How does the power of psychology compare with other professions or occupations? What implications does this have for a critical community psychology?

Foucault (1980) further argued that the existing power relations are sustained by the use and abuse of symbolic constructions that naturalise those power relations so they are not questioned because they are seen as 'normal', or that obfuscate them so they pass unnoticed. Foucault's analysis of power raises (as we have done in Chapters 4 and 5) the question as to how concepts such as community might function to disguise coercion and oppression towards some social groups and to disguise social structures that result in social and political exclusion. Foucault's work also makes the notions of resistance and defiance central to a conceptualisation of power and argues that such notions both define power and are inseparable from it. However, Foucault's argument is sometimes used in a reductionistic way to suggest that power is 'nothing but' the exercise of the power of words to shape perceptions of reality. This approach loses sight of the Marxist roots of Foucault's work and also of the similarities between his perspective and that of Gramsci and critical theorists such as Habermas. It may help to consider that power is *produced* on the basis of the structural relations in society but *reproduced* through a variety of mechanisms, including language.

Power analysis

What we can call power analysis helps to explore the flow of power in any particular situation, to identify barriers to and enablers for change and to interrogate one's own position in any particular work process. Smail (1999) has drawn attention to what he calls the 'impress of power'. He distinguishes

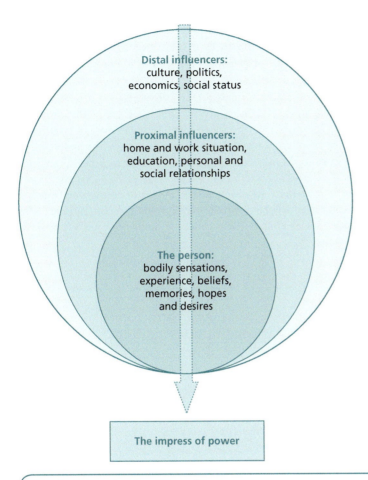

Figure 12.2 The impress of power.
Source: after Smail, 1999.

between distal and proximal influences on people's lives and notes that distal influences (over which an individual can have little influence) exert the most influence over most people's lives. Figure 12.2 outlines the impress of power.

Act!

Power mapping is closely linked to the impress of power. Consider the following scenarios and complete a power map (see Figure 7.5) for each:

1 Some youths harass a Chinese migrant worker who runs a takeaway food business. After five months of this they attack him, breaking his cheek bone and arm. The police respond to the community meeting held to express concern about the situation by asking "what do you expect if you live around here?"
2 In an area where there are few places for children to play, a proposal has been made to build offices on the spare land. The local small action group opposing this development cannot get others to join in – people ask "what's the point?"

> 3 An asylum seeker and her family of three children under 12 years old are threatened with deportation. There is a local campaign to enable her to stay and the core of the campaign rests on arguing what a good citizen she is because of all the work she does in the community.

When reflecting upon our own power in our roles as community psychologists, especially to try to minimise this, it can be useful to think of the different forms of power that can be exercised over others. As we have seen, there are a number of sources of social power that we can deliberately use for change or inadvertently slip into through custom. Many of these are framed as 'power over' (someone or something) – a dominant approach in Westernised societies (as we describe earlier). An alternative way of thinking about power is in terms of 'power to' (do something). This is of course very much a theme of this book – we seek to achieve principled change together with groups and communities who need to achieve principled and progressive social change. In the next chapter we review the skills required within community psychology work.

Chapter 13

Capability: roles, skills and reflections on learning for community psychologists

Summary

In this chapter we unpack some of the skills involved in critical community psychology, which cross over and are integrated with the action strategies and processes covered in Part 2. Our honest engagement with the project work undertaken has often demonstrated issues and problems which have required us to reflect, develop and change. These reflections upon learning are essential for value based community psychology work. The chapter is organised around, first, a discussion of what we mean by capability (rather than competencies), followed by an explicit consideration of the roles and skills often utilised in community psychology. Finally, we review what reflection on learning and practice can offer.

Throughout this book the *Think!*, *Act!* and *Reflect!* boxes have been an explicit strategy to include you in this text. Our hope is that, in addition to any knowledge you might have gleaned, your skill base will have strengthened through this engagement.

A capability perspective

A capability perspective on critical community psychology praxis presents critical community psychology as a situated, relational practice, rather than one in which practice resides in the efforts of individual practitioners. Practice is not understood in terms of the characteristics of the person, but rather in terms of the interactions and transactions with other people and also with the particular context (situational, cultural, historical) and the opportunities afforded by that context (Burton & Kagan, 1995). Capability embraces competence and the skills that contribute to competence. However, capability also embraces the competence of others with whom, or for whom, we work, which in turn throws up opportunity, rendering us capable (or not). For example, we may have the skills to undertake small group work: however, if the communities we are working with do not wish to take part in small groups, or do not themselves have the skills of participating in small groups, our capability is limited, and we will need to change tack. Our actions are not free standing and acontextual: our own competence is a result of our relationships with others. Remove the competence of those around us and we become incompetent. Capability underpins our ability to respond effectively to others in different situations: it includes roles and skills and incorporates the following qualities – qualities of being rather than actions:

- adaptability;
- flexibility;
- responsibility;
- sensitivity;
- potentiality;
- positionality;
- criticality;
- fluidity;
- reflexivity.

Competence not competencies

Having competence – a part of capability – is not the same as acquiring competencies. There has been a lot of discussion at community psychology conferences and in the literature about the nature of competencies in community psychology (for example, Dzidic, Breen & Bishop, 2013; Francescato & Zani, 2013; Akhurst, Kagan, Lawthom & Richards, 2016), following the publication of draft competencies by the Society for Community Research and Action (SCRA, 2012) (Dalton & Wolfe, 2012). These competencies are organised in terms of foundational principles; community programme development and management; community and social change; and community research. Each section is subdivided into a number of different *abilities*. The focus is very much on the abilities of the practitioner and whilst the authors claim they are not intended to lead to accreditation and assessment, it is easy to see this is where they might lead.

We have argued elsewhere (Akhurst et al., 2016) that there are a number of characteristics of a competencies approach to learning and career development that do not fit easily with the very community psychological principles and ethics enshrined in the approach taken in this book. To take a competencies stance is to:

- adopt behavioural notions of skills acquisition;
- see curricula designed to achieve the goals of policy makers or employers and which place emphasis on achieving economic competitiveness;
- open the possibility that they be used for evaluation of accreditation standards;
- see community psychological practice as static at any point in time and adopt 'expert' notions of progression by suggesting different levels of competence.
- accept that competency curricula have a "focus on training rather than education; an approach that stresses and enables measurement, comparison and assessment of behaviours that lie above or below an invisible line of expert-defined acceptability" (Akhurst et al., 2016, p. 6).

From our experience of introducing community psychology degree programmes in the UK, we see the discourse and practice of competencies as part of the neoliberal agenda applied to higher education. Competencies require the deconstruction and commodification of practice into units of behaviour that can be measured, assessed, and, if necessary, found wanting. Learning is thereby reduced to blocks of proficiency and feeds into an alienated engagement with learning. Learning itself can be erroneously understood as a set of categories or blocks to be passed, and ticked off, rather than as an ongoing process. We can see the seep of neoliberal rather than liberatory values into the capability and capacity building debates, when we see that SCRA has also produced a 'value proposition' for community psychology (Society for Community Research and Action [SCRA], n.d.). Value propositions come from the business world of business strategy, marketing and competitiveness (Osterwalder, Pigneur & Clark, 2010).

Think!

Search for any definition of 'value proposition' on the internet, and discuss in small groups the extent to which this is or could be aligned to critical community psychological capability. Does it matter what we call it, if it summarises the practice niche for critical community psychology? Why or why not?

SCRA's value proposition includes an overall statement of what it is that community psychologists do and the value they bring, as well as the skill sets they have. This is shown in Table 13.1.

Table 13.1 Value proposition for community psychology: skills

Community Psychology Skill Sets

In addition to a solid grounding in the science of psychology, most Community Psychologists are trained to:

- Plan and conduct community-based applied research including needs assessment and planning studies.
- Evaluate programs/services: Develop evaluation designs. Collect, analyze, report, and interpret evaluation data.
- Incorporate psychological, ecological, and systems level understanding into holistic, sustainable community development processes.
- Contribute to organizational assessment, program planning and development.
- Locate, evaluate, and apply information from diverse information sources to new situations.

Many community psychologists also are trained to:

- Facilitate small and large group processes.
- Communicate effectively; disseminate information in both technical and lay language with diverse stakeholder groups.
- Build community and organizational capacities.

As they gain experience, community psychologists also:

- Build and maintain collaborations with a network of clients, communities, organizations, and other involved professions. Negotiate and mediate between different stakeholder groups around a particular issue.
- Apply leadership, supervisory and mentoring skills.
- Develop organizational and community resources.
- Develop additional skill sets, consistent with individual interests and organization need.

Source: SCRA, n.d.

Reflect!

Of course we understand that community psychologists have to be able to summarise what it is that they know and can do and to differentiate this from other community practitioners, and that employers need to be clear about the expectations for community psychologists they employ.

In keeping with the emphasis on a decolonising, liberatory and participative praxis advocated in this book, we suggest that, rather than competencies that stand in danger of revealing (community) psychology's positivist heritage, community psychology would "benefit from iterative-generative reflective practice and being attuned to underlying world views and values, which then enables (them) to be receptive and responsive to the contextual requirements of the social settings in which we engage" (Dzidic et al., 2013, p. 7).

Example: Designing community psychology programmes

When we designed our community psychology courses at undergraduate and post-graduate levels (Kagan, Lawthom, Siddiquee, Duckett & Knowles, 2007; Kagan & Lawthom, 2014), we adopted a liberation-psychology lens, through which we saw that far from training in competencies, students learnt to be reflective practitioners in action through the very processes of conscientisation, deideologisation and problematisation they advocate for others. The approach we took included:

- a pedagogical approach that stresses experience, action and self reflection;
- a pedagogical approach that challenges and facilitates an understanding of the world and our place in it;
- an androgogical approach that recognises students as adult learners with as much to offer each other as to learn from each other;
- a teaching practice that explores the role of power and encourages a different relationship with tutors, not placed as experts but as co-learners.

It is worth noting there is no professional route to qualified community psychology status in the UK, and it was difficult to sustain the postgraduate courses as the department chose to provide only those courses that led directly to professional psychology status. Nevertheless, past students attest to the value of their learning experiences, for work as community practitioners with other job labels. It was the combination of the articulation of values, coupled with fields of interdisciplinary knowledge, understood within particular social contexts and anchored by reflexivity, that underpinned students' claim for the unique skills sets of critical community psychology practitioners.

Both the competencies and the value proposition were developed by SCRA at a specific time, within a particular cultural and social context (USA), where community psychology is a recognised career track that students can choose. A similar concern to articulate competencies has arisen in Italy, where too there is the promise of a recognised career route (Francescato & Zani, 2013). Our, and many other places' context is different and it is beholden on readers to consider the distinction between competence and competencies in their own situations.

Act!

Write either a rap or a short sketch to capture the difference between competence and competencies. Make it as funny as you can and include the idea of capability if you can. Perform your act to your colleagues. How would you communicate the difference between competence and competencies to community partners if they were to ask you what critical community psychologists can do?

> ## *Reflect!*
>
> Think of your own context. How have neoliberal values and assumptions influenced your educational contexts? What would 'competence', 'competencies', 'skills', 'aptitudes' and 'functions' of community psychology mean in this context? Who needs to know what it is that community psychologists can do and why?

In our capability approach, function (roles) and competence (skill) sit alongside reflection and reflexivity – all components of critical community psychological capability.

Roles for facilitating change

The discussion of the action strategies (in Chapters 8, 9 and 10) embraces a number of different areas of skill and a range of different roles that might be played by critical community psychologists. Critical community psychology roles are similar to those of other community practitioners but differ from other psychology roles. Following Ife (1995) we suggest that the roles community psychologists can play concern facilitation, education, representation and technical roles. Figure 13.1 summarises the different roles that can be adopted (Kagan, Duckett, Lawthom & Burton, 2005; Kagan, Lawthom et al., 2007). It is important to recognise that different roles may well be played simultaneously – they are not mutually exclusive.

Many critical community psychologists are based either in community practice or in universities. We have found it useful to consider, in universities, the role of scholar activists (for example, Clennon, 2018) or pracademics (Corbett, 2011); and in practice, the roles of activist scholars.

Facilitation roles

Facilitation roles are those concerned with getting to know people, enabling participation and building consensus – those activities linked to the development of new social relations and new social settings and the development and maintenance of alliances. These roles include negotiating with solidarity actions, groups and organisations, forming alliances and coalitions, working effectively with groups, and inspiring and motivating others to action. This includes a range of participative techniques – often referred to as 'community animation'. They require commitment, energy and enthusiasm and the ability to develop rapport and listen sensitively to other people. These skills are learned and often need reflecting upon – for example, *"Did I listen and how? Did I build on peoples' existing knowledge and experience and how? What did I bring to the relationship(s)? What were my prior assumptions?"*

Learning or educational roles

Educational roles underpin the furtherance of critical consciousness. They might include giving information, facilitating dialogue and awareness, working with conflict, mounting training workshops and assessing the need for further training and/or experience. They also include continuing development and self-learning. Key to educational roles is the ability to problematise and to enable others to develop greater understanding of the wider historical, cultural and social contexts of their lives and of action. These roles require the ability to communicate clearly – language that works in an academic context does not transfer easily to other contexts. Similarly, other language skills are useful in certain settings. These skills are learned and often need reflecting on – for example: *"Did I provide the conditions for learning and understanding? Did I build on people's knowledge and experience? What have I contributed to the learning situation and what have I learnt from it?"*

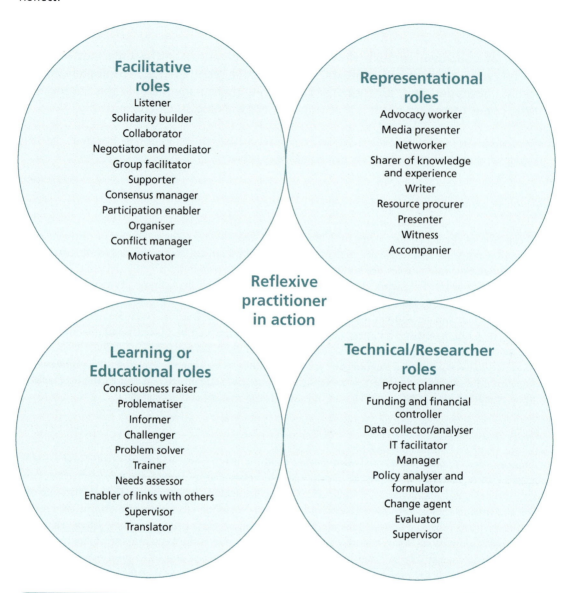

Figure 13.1 Roles of critical community psychologists.

Source: after Kagan, Lawthom et al., 2007. Reproduced by permission of Manchester Metropolitan University.

Representational roles

Representational roles are those that enable effective communication of the ways in which social issues affect people's lives. They include support for people in being able to express their views, but also presentation (through, for example, writing, public talks) of issues. Using different media, and the support of others using the media are an important part of representational roles and these activities underpin action strategies of accompaniment, advocacy and analysis of policy. Representation requires being able to communicate to different audiences using appropriate language. When working with others and acting on behalf of others, it is crucial to use the right pitch. These skills are learned and often need reflecting on – for example: "*What assumptions did I bring? Did I enable people's own positions to be understood? Did I communicate effectively? Do I have the skills to communicate differently in different situations?*"

Technical roles

Technical roles include project management and implementation, and research and evaluation. They may involve specialist knowledge (legislation, computers, funding availability, for example) and, although sometimes seen as routine, are usually essential for effective action. Technical roles include good organisation, resource procurement (e.g. funding), financial management, supervision of workers. Technical roles (as others) may be roles that access to education and privilege has enabled, and they may often be used in capacity building with others. Policy analysis and formulation are technical roles. These skills are learned and often need reflecting on – for example: "*Was I proficient in my actions? What resources did I bring to the situation? What power did I wield in the situation? How might I involve other people more in these tasks?*"

Whilst roles can be described in terms of tasks, the social psychological way of understanding roles is to see them as relational, in juxtaposition to other roles, and embedded in social situations. There are social rules affecting both these situations and how different roles are played in particular contexts (Harré, 1993). It is the role-rule contexts that influence the expectations placed on those occupying particular roles, as well as how roles are played and the conflicts experienced within and between roles. It can be useful to think who the role partners are for any given role at a particular point in time, and where the potential for conflict might be, either between different and multiple roles occupied by the community psychologist or between different role partners. Closely allied to the concept of role is the concept of social practices – a constant flow of 'doings and sayings', culturally based patterns of behaviour which may or may not be ritualistic. Büchs and Koch (2017) point out that social practices integrate the micro (such as subjective accounts of identities and values) with the macro (such as objective structures or systems). See also the discussion of ideology–action–structure complexes in Chapter 3.

Act!

Take any of the community psychological roles outlined in Figure 13.1 (these could be roles you actually occupy or hypothetical ones). Answer the following questions in relation to the role.

- Who are your role partners?
- In what settings do you meet?
- What do the different role partners expect of you in your chosen role? What would be inappropriate to do in this role?
- What are the social rules that influence appropriate and inappropriate ways of playing your chosen role?
- How important are role partners in determining appropriate and inappropriate ways of playing your chosen role?
- How many of these roles are social practices, linked to custom and practice, social conventions, social attitudes (such as what is expected according to age, gender and so on)?

As critical community psychologists working from universities or from within public services, we often encounter considerable role conflict as scholar activists, pracademics, or activist scholars, and have to find ways of resolving this.

Role conflict and role strain can be due to a number of things. There may be different priorities between the critical community psychologist and community partners (for example community psychologists might want to address large scale transformational change whereas community partners might be concerned with a specific local issue).

Time and other resources might not be adequate. Many projects need a longer time than is available. It can be difficult to justify time spent building trust with community partners, and the challenge for us is to continue to push for legitimation of this kind of activity within the academe and other professional contexts. Role strain and conflict can be linked to identity, and sometimes role conflict challenges our core identity. At these times it is clarity about values that enables us to gauge the best way to resolve such conflict.

Resolution of role strain and conflict can involve prioritising, compromise, skills development, negotiation, clarification of expectations and resource procurement. The ways in which we play our roles and deal with conflict and strain are closely linked to our positionality (see Chapter 6). Once again, perhaps the most important skill in relation to our roles is that of continual reflection so we are not caught out and find ourselves in a conflict situation we were not expecting.

Reflect!

Think about some situations where you have experienced role conflict. Are there some forms of role conflict you would rather avoid than confront? Why might this be? What ways of resolving role conflict do you tend to prefer? Why might this be?

Skills for facilitating change

As we have suggested above, skills are a part of capability – they are not characteristics of a person but rather of the person in constant interaction with situations. When we talk about skills, we do not mean to imply that community psychology can only be 'done' by experts who have been trained and assessed as having reached a specified level of competence. Nor do we want to imply that some people will be naturally good at community psychology – effectiveness is not just a personal quality, but a *relational and situational* quality. Instead, we are using the term skills to imply that whatever it is we are doing, we could learn, grow and do it better. As teachers of critical community psychology we do not employ an 'expert' perspective where we expect students to learn to do things as we do. Instead we adopt a mutuality and reciprocity perspective. We work with students (and each other) to share our existing knowledge and enable them (and us) to combine these knowledges and develop critical reflections on the activities undertaken. We do not shy away from discussing with them some of the difficulties and dilemmas we face. At times, in some situations, with some people, working on some issues, we are clumsy and inept. However, over time we have learnt to reflect on what we have done and the impact it has and, if necessary, to grow our competence or redress a problematic situation. To do this we need a range of skills and the ability not only to reflect but also to be flexible and change tack as required.

In Chapter 9, we discussed using a 'communities of practice' approach to learning. This sees participation within the setting (not mastery) as key to learning and identity change (Lawthom, 2011). Whilst there are a number of skills which may be of use, we have organised critical community psychology skills into four overlapping groups: interpersonal skills, social problem solving skills, organisation skills and research skills. In all these clusters, a broad repertoire of ways of relating to and working with and alongside others is central. In the previous chapters we have discussed a range of different strategies and skills, with illustrations from practice. Whilst some roles demand some technical skills – such as time management, administration, writing bids for funding – and some research skills, nearly all the other activities involve relating to others – and in some forms of critical community praxis, these technical skills do too. All of the skills can be deployed in different combinations in relation to the different roles and activities undertaken.

Interpersonal skills

This group of skills ranges from interpersonal communication – one-to-one and group listening (and talking) skills – to group and individual conflict resolution skills. It includes motivating and activating others, supporting, enabling participation, basic counselling skills and the ability to develop rapport and relationships with a wide range of people. It also includes challenging, persuading, explaining, informing and both representing and advocating for others. Problematisation and other techniques need careful use of different kinds of questions, as well as active listening. An understanding of group dynamics underpins working with groups, from formation to long term work. Group work is often at the heart of critical community psychological work and includes, for example, setting up groups, organising agendas and notes, securing venues, chairing, facilitating, making sure people feel able to be involved, using experiential processes, summarising discussions, managing conflict, building consensus and achieving goals. There are many guides to developing good group work skills – it is strange there seem to be no guides specifically devoted to group work and community psychology, although most texts have a section on working with groups. A sound knowledge of good governance in informal and formal community organisations is required. Interpersonal skills also include consciousness raising, working with co-operation and collaboration and network development and support. In a great deal of community psychology, as we have seen, there is reliance on discussion and dialogue. As we saw in Chapter 8, skilful use of other creative and experiential techniques adds to our repertoires. In our own work we have used, or supported research students in using, participatory theatre, table top games, sewing, creative writing, singing, dancing, storytelling, photography and film work, poetry or sport as methods both of engagement and of action and dissemination. The recent turn to performativity in social science (Gergen & Gergen, 2011; Douglas & Carless, 2013; Clennon, Kagan, Lawthom & Swindells, 2016; Kagan & Duggan, 2011) embraces skills that can enable people to express themselves through everyday practices or beyond words. Whilst most of these debates are in relation to research, they also apply to action research and community practice. We might not always need, ourselves, to be skilled in all these ways of enabling participation – but we may need to know others who can. It is also important to be aware of our limitations and either develop skills that are lacking, or involve those who have them, so that our work remains as broadly relevant as possible. Working across languages, or with interpreters, is particularly challenging and a reliance on words and their meanings can lead to misunderstanding and mis-representation, further supporting the use of methods that are not dependent on words.

Social problem solving skills

Social problem solving includes skills of resource procurement, planning, observing and understanding influences on people's behaviour, strategic decision making and creative thinking about methods of working and for enabling participation. It also includes the cognitive skills of multi-level systems analyses, identifying relevant stakeholders in a community as well as ways of maximising resources (human, social and material) locally. Different training techniques are also included in social problem solving skills, although they clearly also involve interpersonal communication.

> ### Example: Games for conscientisation
>
> We and our students have developed a number of different board and card games that can be used for training or for conscientisation. We have piloted these games in a number of different fora, including running sessions at international conferences with people from many different countries. The games have included those designed to explore and understand: the nature of community psychology perspectives; experiences of living in urban areas of dereliction; experience of living with long term impairments over the life course; variations in life opportunities due to social class; challenges of urban regeneration or renewal; experiences of parents with the label of learning difficulties; abuse of older people; power, control and decision making in organisational alliances. We have used table top games in a number of different national contexts, and this has exposed the importance of grounding them in local practices. For example, we worked in Uganda with speech and language professionals from all over East Africa, to introduce them to the idea of 'social model' and non-stigmatising approaches to impairment and disability. We made a table top game using local materials (fabric, chalk, shells and stones), and modelled the game on a local, well known game. Our game involved turn taking with a throw of a simple dice made of local wood. One participant, from Rwanda had never experienced this kind of game. So whilst it was familiar to people from Uganda and Kenya (former UK colonies) it was not a familiar form to those from Rwanda (former German/Belgian colony).

Gaming, of course, need not be limited to table top games. Role play games, digital games, social gaming are all being used, increasingly, not just for education and training, but to facilitate engagement and participation in cultural and social change and the design of civic space (Bagni et al., 2017). There will be times when we have to give formal presentations and, again, we will need to be able to design and communicate different kinds of information for different audiences. Sometimes this might include working with electronic communication systems; other times we may need to use different kinds of aids. When working with cash poor community organisations technology cannot be a priority, so being able to talk without overheads, and being able to use flipcharts and boards, is a real skill (and increasingly rare in academic circles).

Act!

Take a critical community psychological issue and invent a table top board game that is designed to (a) raise awareness about the issue; and (b) help people identify some courses of action to address the issue. Examples might include: the impact of income inequality; gender and climate change; indigenous communities fighting fracking or oil pipelines; the rise of extremism. Are there any issues that could not be cast into a game format? What are the advantages and disadvantages of using games like these to work with people in communities?

Organisation skills

This group of skills includes all those necessary for managing projects (including the supervision of workers as appropriate). It includes office administration, financial management, use of computers and new technology, managing pressure and multi-task workloads. The procurement of resources – physical, financial and human resources – would also be a part of organisational skill. This means that finding office space, applying for grant funds and so on may be needed. It also includes inter-agency working, building of relationships and links with other professionals or interest groups, locally, nationally and internationally, and the forming of inter-agency alliances. At a personal level, organisational skills include time management and stress management skills.

> ### Example: Arts in the city
>
> One of our students was working with a community arts project that served as a vital resource for local people in a part of the city where there were few community resources. The group needed to find funds for materials and for the hire of a room. She worked on identifying different sources of funding and making applications for funding. Had she not been there to do this, no further funds would have been found as there was no-one else to do the work.

Act!

Do you know how to establish a formal community organisation in your own context? Try to find some guidelines that tell you about different organisational forms – in the UK this might be a charity, a community interest company, a community benefit company, a charitable incorporated organisation or a co-operative, but is likely to differ in different places. Draw up a table comparing the different organisational forms and their merits.

Research skills

Research skills enable choices to be made regarding elements of action research, the purpose and execution of monitoring and evaluation of project work, collecting background information and understanding the limitations of different styles of work. Skills of designing relevant projects, collecting different kinds of information and analysing, interpreting and presenting the information collected are all included in research skills. Furthermore, skills of spreading information, writing different kinds of reports, giving oral, visual and written presentations are included. The understanding and use of statistical information and methods will form a part of this group of skills. Research skills include those of facilitating participation by people from marginalised groups in any or all of the stages of research, and of sharing information with others. They also include making applications for funding and developing collaborative bids for funding to underpin research. Research skills for critical community psychology are broad, and need not be confined to ones already available. The creative invention of methods is to be encouraged as well as the use of creative methods themselves.

> ## Example: Creative methods to enable voice and participation
>
> Richards, Lawthom and Runswick-Cole (2018) describe the use of creative methods to enable people with learning difficulties to engage in participatory research and to find a voice. The consequences of direct and indirect stigmatisation affect people's social relationships and strengthen barriers to full inclusion. The men in this project used a series of visual and creative methods to challenge some of these misconceptions by telling stories through art, demonstrating skill through photography, using poetry to talk about sexual identity and improvising drama and filmmaking to challenge stigma, and through sculpture expressed their voices. The project was developed in alliance with a local museum in which the men exhibited their work, thereby reaching a public audience.

Skills do not exist in a vacuum and we take the view that even if a person is able to use their skills in a particular context, they may not transfer to other, new contexts. Community psychological skills are firmly located in, and a result of particular contexts.

Reflect!

Are there any situations in which, even though you know you have the skills, you are unable to use them? What gets in the way (for example, other people and how they behave, lack of confidence, anxiety, the role you occupy and so on).

Act!

Make a list of all the skills you think are relevant to critical community psychology. Draw on other community psychology texts to help you do this. Assess the extent to which you already have these skills and what you might need in terms of development to gain more skills. Draw up an action plan for how you will develop these skills over a period of time. Include who or what is needed to make this plan work.

The context of community psychological action

As we have seen the meaning of context for community psychology is multi-layered. The immediate physical and social context may affect action. For example, if a geographical community is very hilly, or it rains a lot, it may be difficult for infirm elderly members of the community to take part in a house to house survey as part of some action. The social situation, including the meaning of different social situations, as well as the penetrability of the situation may also inhibit participation. Sometimes, situations will prevent people from using the skills that they have; in addition, if we think of critical community psychology skills as relational skills, they are always developed and used in particular social contexts.

The policy context may mean that the community psychologist might have to explain policy changes – assuming they know about them! It might also mean that only some things are possible or that particular alliances need to be forged.

Cultural contexts need to be understood for culturally safe and appropriate practices to take place. Culture varies in obvious ways with ethnicity and minority groups. However, the cultural context of the majority population, in all its complexity, also needs to be understood. Culture varies with the many stratifications in a society and a neighbourhood (see Ferreira Moura et al., in press for diverse cultural perspectives on poverty in Brazil). There are different cultural practices and traditions across class, age, gender and other forms of social identity. At times we need to adopt an anthropological stance, and slowly get to understand some of the cultural complexities of the neighbourhoods and groups with which we work. We need to be open and honest and collaborate with those who can 'translate' (actually or figuratively) for us. To understand cultural contexts is to understand the norms, values, rituals and symbolic transactions of the groups with whom we work and the social practices of the people within them.

Example: Organisational culture and blocks to service development

One of our doctoral students was working on introducing a new way of thinking about and delivering services to two people with profound and multiple impairments who relied on 24-hour support. Initially the project was designed as an action research project to introduce a process known as essential lifestyle planning with and for these two in a complex, multi-agency service. Before the research had got very far a number of barriers in the current practices within the service and the way the overall service operated were identified and it became clear that there needed to be a cultural change in the organisation. Staff and managers needed to move from being satisfied with the view that "this is how things have always been done" to practices that allowed staff autonomy and permission and space to innovate. The student's work became a study in cultural change in the organisation.

To a certain extent the above example is also one of understanding the historical context – what had gone on in the past – in order to create change in the present. In critical community psychological work we need to have a grasp, not only of the immediate and recent past affecting people's lives, but also of the longer term historical context and future possibilities. Some of this understanding can be gleaned from books and reports but a great deal comes from the people themselves, their accounts and their family and community stories. It is with historical understanding that sense can be made of the present. To illustrate this, we return to an example we first cited in Chapter 4.

Example: Inner city disturbances

In 1981 in several major cities in the UK there were some inner city disturbances. Disaffected, mostly young, men took to the streets in protest about how the police were using stop and search powers disproportionately to stop young black men. As the disturbances grew, simmering dissatisfaction with the lack of connections between the police and communities fuelled further conflict on the streets. Manchester was one of the cities where the disturbances took place. We (CK) were a part of the enquiry panel into the causes of the disturbances and the experiences of those affected, many of whom took part in the disturbances. It was only through a thorough understanding of a century of population, labour and social changes that sense could be made of what had led up to the disturbances and what might need to be in place for the future. The historical factors included the processes of post World War II migration to Manchester; slum clearance programmes; changes in patterns of work; changes in patterns and control of housing; and changes in policing. A large part of the report that was produced set out this historical background, against which contemporary experience could be understood.

> ## Think!
>
> Choose a social issue of relevance to the area in which you live. What is the historical context of this issue? Has there been a particularly pertinent struggle and, if so, who was involved? What are the historical antecedents of what is there today? What new light does this shed? (Some examples might be a proposal to change the use of some land; the imminent closure of a school; concerns about levels of crime or about homelessness.)

In order to understand the impact of the context on our use of skills, we need to adopt a reflective and reflexive stance, and understand both our potential and our limitations. Indeed, critical self awareness, alongside the personal qualities of humility and a sense of humour are at the heart of community psychological action, itself bound by the values of justice, stewardship and community. Figure 13.2 summarises action in community psychology. Community psychological skills, roles, actions, and values are presented as a series of concentric circles that should be conceived as spinning not static circles, with critical self awareness, humility and sense of humour at the core, and all within the immediate and wider context.

> ## Reflect!
>
> Examine the diagram in Figure 13.2. Are there any parts you do not understand? Seek out someone with whom to discuss this so that you are a little clearer. Are there any parts that make you think "Yes, I can see this is important, but I couldn't do it"? Why might this be, and what impact do you think it will have on your work?

We have argued, above, that the roles and skills involved in critical community psychology shift over time but are also distributed across people, which allows collaboration and participation to happen more easily. Recognising the importance of combining popular knowledge and experience with 'expert' knowledge and experience and allowing people to acknowledge the learning they are bringing to the table encourages this process of working in partnership. Central to developing skills is the ability to reflect – without reflection on and with others, it is difficult to learn.

Reflexivity as part of practice

The idea of reflecting on practice is a consistent thread throughout our book. Reflection upon the process of working with others and reflecting on self (in terms of skills and development) are fundamental to working as a critical community psychologist – indeed to good practice generally. Indeed, "a continuous commitment to reflective practice means not only that we get the benefits of reflection on an ongoing basis, but also that we can develop our knowledge, skills and confidence in reflective practice over time" (Thompson & Thompson, 2008, p. 12).

The ideas of reflective practice emerge from the work of John Dewey (1916/1966) and Donald Schön (1983). Schön's interest was around how knowledge was utilised in practice, the translation of a body of knowledge into action. Schön and others were highly critical of technical rationality – the idea that theory and knowledge can be applied directly to practice. Shifting away from established 'right answers' and theoretical 'high ground', Schön (1983) likened reality to working in the 'swampy lowlands' of practice. Schön's model was that professional knowledge bases utilised professional

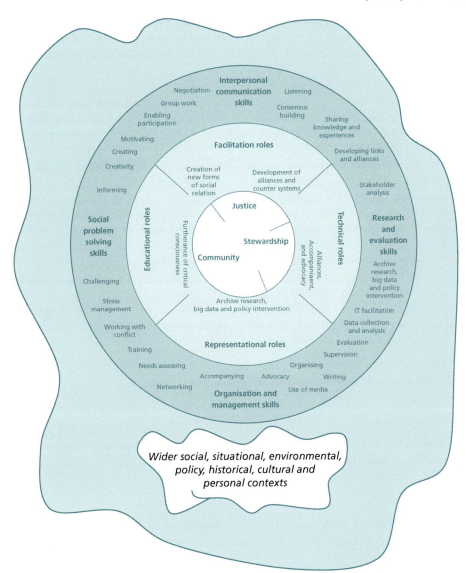

Figure 13.2 Community psychological action: skills, roles and action with values and critical self awareness at the core and within a multi-layered context.

'artistry', drawing upon natural and social science where appropriate. In applying this to critical community psychological practice, we would be interested in the 'swampy lowlands' of the context, and keen to collaborate with others using knowledge bases. A key idea useful to our practice is his distinction between reflection-in-action (thinking *in situ*) and reflection-on-action (reflection after the event which involves sense making, review and learning).

Some of the skills we covered earlier may well require reflection-in-action – changing a course of action (such as communication) in order to better meet the requirements. Reflection-on-action may well occur after the event as we consider the skills we have or need to develop and the roles we occupy. Indeed, this reminds us of the action research cycle which draws on reflection throughout.

The ideal scenario would be a reflection-in-action interconnecting with reflection-on-action – facilitating the integration of theory and practice. The notion of praxis is one we have utilised to outline the reciprocal nature of theory and practice. Griseri (1988, p. 213) defines this fusion of theory and practice in the following way,

> By praxis I mean a personal theory-in-action that someone uses to get on with their life. Long before anyone learns anything about the formal theory of dynamics, they may learn how best to throw a stone so that it will skim along the top of a still pond.

A distinction is made between the terms 'reflective' and 'reflexive'. Reflectivity conjures up self awareness or a sense of thinking, whilst reflexivity is a term more allied with qualitative methodologies which privileges its employment as a useful research tool. Reflexivity here is seen as a way of factoring oneself into the situation (Fook & Askeland, 2006). Both senses are useful for reflective and reflexive practice. In critical community psychology work, being reflective about what we can and cannot do enables practice, whereas reflexivity is about considering how we impact and are impacted upon by practice. Case (2017) suggests reflexivity is one way of 'navigating ethically important moments' through exploration of one's own biases, values and skills, but also, crucially, in order to anticipate adverse impacts we might have on those affected by our research or action. Through reflexive work, we are then able to determine a course of action that will uphold the dignity and interests of our participants. Thompson and Thompson (2008) advocate using open knowledge as the basis for mindful (and good) practice. This entails openness in three senses:

- open knowledge – which is open to challenge and scrutiny;
- open mindedness – in the sense of not having fixed or preconceived ideas;
- openness to learning: being willing to learn from mistakes and reflect on what went well.

Whilst Schön's ideas are helpful in encouraging reflection, a criticism levelled at the work is around individualism – that it pays little attention to wider contexts. This atomism (a notion of seeing society as no more than a collection of individuals) fails to acknowledge the impact of wider social processes.

Think!

Take a few minutes to think about any of the chapters you have read. What models, theories, approaches explicitly engage with this contextual awareness?

We are arguing that reflective practice is not atomistic, and engages with social and political awareness. Harré (2011), writing in the context of being a sustainability advocate, suggests three levels of reflection-on-action directed at social change. These are

- personal (changes in lifestyle commitments linked to the change issue);
- group (change with and in groups of like-minded people but also of non-like-minded people); and
- civic (changes in public attitudes, government, corporations and large institutions).

Regular reflection on all three levels contributes to decision making, sense of purpose and, not least, enjoyment. Action for change should be an enjoyable and fulfilling activity – if it is not, why do it?

Of course, as covered in the skills section above, and threaded throughout the book, raising consciousness and conscientisation enables us as critical community psychologists, and not only those with whom we work, to develop and grow. The following example illustrates this.

> ### Example: Arts and mental health
>
> A commission was obtained to evaluate the impact of participatory arts projects on the health and well-being of its participants (planning and action stages had been completed). Prior to undertaking the evaluation, it was evident that there was a need to provide an evidence base for funders. As researchers working on this evaluation, we set out to work in a collaborative way with participants of the various arts projects. It was hoped that this would result in greater participant involvement in the evaluation and would foster esteem and the gaining of skills. However, as gatekeepers providing access to the arts projects, the artists involved were concerned about the impact of this on their (the artists and participants) relationships and participant well-being. Consequently, participants of the arts projects were unable to contribute to the design and planning stages of the evaluation, and as the evaluation progressed certain restrictions in terms of data collection and analysis also emerged. However, over time a collaborative relationship with the artists was generated. Reflecting on the situation, we recognised that there were considerable tensions between the group of researchers and the group of artists. These differences were underpinned by differences in discourses, knowledge and value systems. Furthermore, there were also schisms within the research team itself, due to pre-existing relations and depth of experience. To resolve this issue, we employed both discussion and other team building workshops and, as a result, trust and a common understanding emerged from which the evaluation could progress.

The case study above illustrates something which Mezirow (1983) terms perspective transformation. This entails ways in which processes of reflection can result in radically different understandings. In working with artists our assumptions about their world view needed to change. Transformation can enable rather different understandings to emerge. In thinking about the process we likened the approach to double loop learning (Argyris & Schön, 1978). Whilst single loop learners adjust behaviour to suit fixed goals, norms and assumptions, double loop learners review and re-negotiate goals, norms and assumptions. In the arts project, evaluation involved double loop learning (Lawthom, Sixsmith & Kagan, 2007) and, in this case, appreciative inquiry. This is illustrated in Figure 13.3.

Seeing reflexivity here as embedded in practice (our practice, art practice, research practice, for example) allows ongoing insight into processes, outcomes and selves. We reflected on ourselves, the different groups we traversed, and at later points in the project, the civil level, as we sought to influence policy makers and health commissioners.

Reflexivity does not have to be done alone: peer discussion and peer review all enable collective reflexivity (Case, 2017).

Constraints on working as a community psychologist and spaces for resistance

Process tools such as SWOT analysis or force field analysis should enable some useful reflection on how change occurs in critical community psychology and what the constraints are. However, the role itself may entail role conflict (as we detailed earlier). The importance of context in understanding is a

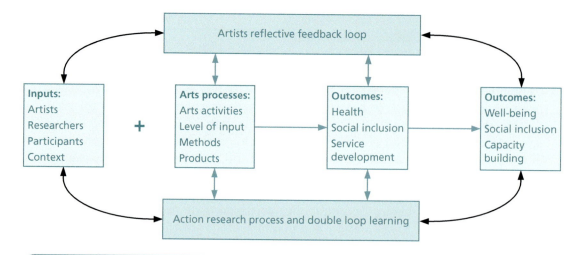

Figure 13.3 Participative evaluation model for arts and health.

Source: Lawthom, Sixsmith & Kagan, 2007. Reproduced by permission of Manchester Metropolitan University.

key principle within critical community psychology. This also extends to working as a critical community psychologist. Working as a critical community psychologist in the UK feels different from other parts of the world. The policy context and development of the discipline differ across countries. Burton and Kagan (2003, p. 12) speculate about the slower start in the UK:

> The conservatism of the British universities and of the British Psychological Society (BPS) probably acted as a brake on the development of community psychology.

It was not until 2010 that a community psychology section was formed within the BPS, open to all members. It is a small section and whilst the majority of members are clinical psychologists (as in professional psychology in the UK), there are members from other practitioner groups, including counselling, organisational, educational, social and sports psychology. There are also members with no professional affiliation. The issue of validating community psychology through formal professional channels indicates a fundamental paradox for critical community psychology and its ways of working. Formalising the role and possibly recognising a structured career path could well stifle the very ways of working we have outlined throughout this book. In the UK currently the regulation of practising psychologists occurs under an organisation called the Health and Care Professionals Council (HCPC) – an acronym which asserts a focus on health and professions, not on community psychology with a focus on well-being and de-expertising (giving and sharing knowledge). It also denotes a set of competencies which practitioners need to attain (rather than ongoing skill development – although there are requirements for continuing professional development). Working with values entails a rather different approach. There has been a sustained focus on developing a values based UK community psychology which can encompass critical community psychologists working in academia and in clinical settings. The Birmingham Manifesto (Collective of Authors, 2007) posits a set of roles/identities and areas in which community psychologists can and should work. The roles encompass being citizens, 'experts' and workers (within any setting).

> *Citizens*: We are all citizens and it is fundamentally in this role that we should be organising and participating in counter-systemic struggles, whether on burning excessive hydrocarbons, opposing more wars, solidarity with progressive social movements and so on.

Experts: As psychologists we have some legitimacy and expertise. We know and can say with authority that commercialisation is poisoning childhood. We know and can say with authority that restrictions on abortion harm women. We know and can say with authority that Britain's asylum laws destroy family life. We don't have to be pompous about it, just claim the expertise we can for the good of the cause.

Workers: We are workers who sell our labour power; some are only one or more pay cheques away from destitution. We should defend the interests of ourselves and of other workers world wide using the vehicle developed for this, the trade unions.

In addition to a recognition of multiple roles, the manifesto argues that community psychology activity should focus in on particular arenas.

The priority areas include war and imperialism, sites of counter-system resistance, action on global warming and the environment and public services. *"If we are to survive and thrive, people and societies need to make change happen: as psychologists, we must play our part"* (Collective of Authors, 2007, p. 12).

How to play the part in an increasingly regulated and professionalised setting seems difficult, but in setting out a clear agenda progress seems possible. The relatively recent organisation within community psychology currently can be seen as a potential opportunity. Such an opportunity was taken by Burton and Kagan (2007) when they created a space within *The Psychologist* (the BPS publication sent to all 25,000 members) to make visible the controversies around psychological torture. They advocated that socially responsible psychologists should build a coherent stance with a clear ethical code which prohibits both interrogation and funding from state security organisations and which encourages involvement in humane policies of detention. This is clearly a value based position. They used the same space in 2018 to try to find out how the BPS invested its money and to get them to adopt a policy of divestment in fossil fuels. After some persistence and a refusal to be relegated to *The Psychologist*'s online version, this campaign was successful.

Another initiative was the York statement on poverty. This was produced at the 2017 annual UK community psychology conference in a large workshop session (about 30 people) and focused on the role of psychology in relation to poverty (see www.compsy.org.uk).

As community and critical psychologists we believe that psychologists have a fundamental responsibility to join with others to end poverty and societal inequality independent of absolute wealth, which we believe are personally, collectively and socially destructive.

We believe mainstream psychology to be complicit with the prevailing psychologically toxic neoliberal economic order and believe psychology has allowed itself to be used to hide systemic effects of poverty and inequality and instead position poverty as a consequence of individual psychological dysfunction.

We call for the radical transformation of psychology so that it has the resources necessary to expose the personally, collectively and socially destructive effects of poverty and inequality and the proactive deployment, with allies, of this transformed psychology to end poverty and societal inequality and the exploitation, exclusion, oppression, distress and illness which result from them (UK Community Psychology Network, 2007).

Burton, Kagan and Duckett (2012, p. 5), referring to this statement, note the failure over time to do anything more with the statement in an organised, collective way. They suggest this is due, in part, to those constraints on the current effectiveness of community psychologists seeking to engage politically, discussed throughout the book and particularly in Chapter 2.

An initiative that is more active began in relation to austerity policies which have taken hold since 2010. A group of psychologists and their allies, including groups and individuals affected by the policies, formed *Psychologists Against Austerity* (PAA), producing an important and politically visible report on the adverse psychological impact of austerity policies. The group has become *Psychologists for Social Change* and has branches round the country, including both members of the professional body and those not. Our point is, sometimes it is possible to use spaces to organise within the professional body and sometimes it is better outside.

Reflect!

Reflect on the various restrictions which may prevent you from becoming politically engaged (not necessarily in politics in the formal sense of the word, but in terms of challenging an established practice or way of thinking). When reflecting on this, you may want to consider an issue of social justice which you are passionate about, and to then consider ways in which you can transform this passion into some form of action (e.g. writing an opinion piece or developing a group around the issue for example).

Think!

Think about the other forms of psychology that you have learnt about. How do you see community psychology versus the other kinds of psychology you have learnt about? What are the similarities and differences in terms of the skills you would need to develop if you were working within these various branches?

Ethical issues

Psychological research and practice always attend to ethical issues (see British Psychological Society, 2018). The rather linear way in which this is proposed assumes that a research question is mooted and from this grows the subsequent research design which can then be subject to ethical scrutiny. Action research entails a rather different, less linear conceptualisation of ethics which is ongoing. Ethics in community psychology is always tied to values and principles and these provide the strongest guide to ethical practice. At the broadest level this may mean we should 'do no harm' but it also entails considering one's own practices, being reflexive and attuned to ethics throughout the process, not just at the start of a piece of work. The participation and involvement in decision making of those affected by any issue or practice also provides an ethical safeguard. However, it is important to remember that in complex situations, there are different stakeholders with different perspectives and ways need to be found to embrace as many as possible whilst challenging those perspectives that compromise our values. Wide involvement in decision making throws up ethical dilemmas for which there are no simple solutions (as discussed in Chapter 7). Sometimes our work has to fit formal ethical frameworks and this in turn can lead to rather strange developments in practice.

> ### Example: Arts for health and well-being
>
> We were researching, through processes of participatory evaluation, six different kinds of arts projects that focused on enhancing health and well-being (Swindells et al., 2013). Two projects involved people with mental health problems and staff supporting them; two involved elderly people and project workers supporting them; and two were focused on cultural change in health settings, including staff

attitudes. There were some similarities and some differences in the means of collecting different kinds of data with each of the pairs of projects. We obtained approval from the National Health Service ethics panel on condition that we identified and collected data from a control group. This made no sense to us. Our research paradigms were not experimental. Whilst we were using some standardised questionnaires as part of some of the data collection, these had norms associated with them against which our data could be compared if necessary. We were faced with the decision about whether or not to withdraw our projects or meet the requirement. After a lot of discussion in the team, we compromised and identified a control group of health professions students, some of whom would have mental health difficulties, and from whom we could collect some identical data over time. Whilst this could appear to be a waste of these students' time (breaching the value of stewardship) we thought we might be able to say something about how their courses affected their well-being and make some useful recommendations. We did recognise, however, that the groups were not really comparable. This compromise seemed the best thing to do to ensure we could continue to work with the original six projects which we would not have been able to do had we withdrawn. This 'control group' was accepted and several years later we were still trying to work out if we could say anything sensible about our comparison data! (We have already said lots of useful things about the original project data and helped those projects move forward more effectively as well as developing some models for best practice for the arts and health field more generally.)

Example: Health, refugees and asylum seekers

In a recently funded project (see Fang, Sixsmith, Lawthom, Mountian & Shahrin, 2015) we were exploring the pathways through which Iraqi and Somali asylum seekers and refugees negotiated health care. The work involved interviewing health and voluntary providers and accessing asylum seekers and refugees through community and third sector style organisations (not the health service). The research demanded a lengthy ethical process and panel style interview (common in gaining health service ethics approval) and demanded that we simplify the information (for potential participants) and translate it (which we had planned to do). The simplification of the information we felt was insulting for individuals who often came to the UK with a high level of qualification but it was necessary to do. The translation was an integral part of the planned work anyway but we were thinking that it would be good to get the translations checked through the process. The ethics panel informed us that they were not concerned with checking the translation, only that we had done it. It would have been possible to translate almost anything to show the panel. Having jumped through the requisite hoops we were allowed to proceed.

Risk

Allied to ethics is the understanding of risk. Learning and doing community psychology is not a pre-packaged body of knowledge which can be 'banked'. The unpredictability of working with others, in a variety of settings, and the nature of collaboration, entails risk. Risks to participants in our work are usually addressed through a consideration of ethics, and ongoing reflexivity, but risks to us, the community psychologists, must also be laid bare. Risks of confrontation, exclusion and conflict are risks which can be key to the collaborative process. Risk within the process is an everyday possibility which comes with the nature of the territory although there are some ways in which risk can be theorised and considered within a project. Critical community psychological work is often 'detached' work, without a clear organisational base. This raises questions about how the health and safety of those working can be assured. There are no easy answers to how personal risks, beyond those of everyday life, can be managed in these kinds of situations, but it is possible to think through some of the issues in advance and as the work progresses. We ask students, researchers and community based co-researchers, who are not working with a formally constituted project, to go through a risk assessment process and to make sure that they use monitoring and reporting processes if risks are deemed to be larger than normal, and we do this ourselves.

Act!

Either take an area of your own work or take any of the examples of practice given in this book. Complete a risk assessment as if you were to undertake the work. How easy is it to assess risks to you as a community psychologist? What kinds of risks do you face in this example?

It is not always easy to assess the risks of a situation and the most important safeguard, for all involved, is discussion with colleagues or supervisors.

However, risks can change over time. In Table 13.2 we give some examples of some of the kinds of risks we have encountered in our work.

Power (again)

> Life is a corrupting process from the time a child learns to play his mother off against his father in the politics of when to go to bed; he who fears corruption fears life.
>
> (Alinsky, 1971, p. 24)

Power has been a central theme throughout our book. We have explored it in relation to community psychology generally (Chapter 5), decision making (Chapter 7) and participation (Chapter 8). We have also considered how we as community psychologists have roles which are subject to power. At times, the privileged position from which we speak allows us a rare platform from which to talk.

The power ascribed to academics is often liberal – the power to speak, profess and intellectualise. A more radical approach to community organising is Alinsky (1971). Alinsky opens his book with a statement of purpose:

> What follows is for those who want to change the world from what it is to what they believe it should be. The Prince was written by Machiavelli for the Haves on how to hold power. Rules for Radicals is written for the Have-Nots on how to take it away.
>
> (Alinsky, 1971, p. 3)

Table 13.2 Examples of risks faced and their mitigation in community practice

Situation/issue	Risk and resolution of risk
Researchers conducting street interviews about crime, perceived safety, and its resolution in area of high crime	Risk of intimidation or victimisation. Researchers carried research materials in shopping bags, dressed informally and worked in pairs.
Researcher facing intimidation and assaults on her expertise by high status stakeholder in community change project	Risk of embarrassment, humiliation and discrediting – resolved through regular, daily discussion with other researchers. Risk of project being obstructed by denigration by group of professionals – resolved by appointing member of the stakeholder's profession, with high credibility and respect, to steering group.
Community co-researchers filming daily life around their neighbourhoods	Risk of upsetting other people – permissions gained from all caught on film. Risk of becoming distressed through awareness of the bleakness of local lives – resolved through regular discussion and sense making with other members of the team.
Researcher transcribing an interview material about being a victim of violent crime late at night at home, alone	Risk of strong emotion linked to the realisation of the vulnerability of people living alone – resolved through transcribing only during the day and in the workplace.
Researcher interviewing working mother in the evening at her own home and accepting lift home from man she had only just met (assumed to be husband) who was in the house at the time	Risk to personal safety. No precautions taken but thereafter, researcher ensured details of her whereabouts were held by housemate and that she had made arrangement for getting home if she was interviewing in the evenings.
Researcher working with elderly women from an ethnic minority community with male community leaders	Risk of incurring anger from male community leaders and of participants not being allowed to participate. Resolved through contact and permissions obtained from community leaders before the work began.
White undergraduate female student wanting to carry out participant observations of aggression meted out to mixed race couples in a nightclub run by local black people	Risk of personal violence. Permission not granted to proceed.
Researcher working with co-researchers collecting narrative accounts from people working in forced labour conditions	Risk of exposing and thwarting strong business interests and of violence and intimidation of both researchers and participants; and risk of exposure of unauthorised immigration status. Precautions taken: participants briefed as to risks prior to taking part; details of interviews held in project office but no personal details kept of participants; narrative accounts collected were hosted by a pre-existing project that is valued by business community; detailed discussion with project team before and after all data collection sessions – ongoing reflexive process. Support for participants from host project.

His 'rules' derive from many successful campaigns where he helped poor people fighting power and privilege. When we were undertaking an action project on community organising, we were concerned that Alinsky stressed conflict over collaboration in his rules. Zacharzewski (2011) discusses a revision to the rules by Tessy Britton. Space precludes a consideration of all of the 'rules' but here are two:

- *Rule 1: Alinsky (Old/Conflict):* "Power is not only what you have, but what the enemy thinks you have." Power is derived from two main sources – money and people. 'Have-Nots' must build power from flesh and blood. If your organization is small, hide your numbers in the dark and raise a din that will make everyone think you have many more people than you do.
  Rule 1: Britton (New/Collaborate): "Power involves creating spaces where ideas, energy and people are connected together from within all sections of the community and local government to create positive communities." This involves careful facilitation and creating safe spaces where everyone can share their opinions and contribute positively. There is no enemy in a community.
- *Rule 2: Alinsky (Old/Conflict):* "Never go outside the expertise of your people." It results in confusion, fear and retreat. Feeling secure adds to the backbone of anyone.
  Rule 2: Britton (New/Collaborative): "Always reject ignorance in favour of building skills and knowledge." There are many new ideas and methods that result in creative solutions that make people and communities stronger.

In advocating these rules, both Alinsky and Britton are arguing for grassroots organising, but have quite different ways of understanding the power dynamics at stake.

Reflect!

Consider a time in which you have participated in a local change project – maybe you have taken part in a protest or have worked with local people to ensure that new migrants are welcomed. Whatever it is, how did power and privilege affect the work? What difference would conflict tactics have made, and what difference would collaborative tactics have made? Can you think of situations where conflict might be more useful than collaboration?

The scholar activist or pracademic roles discussed earlier in the chapter may be the stance to adopt for those of us working from universities.

Example: Living with multiple sclerosis

A doctoral student working with people diagnosed with multiple sclerosis adopted a scholar activist approach. The work incorporated quality of life measures which contrasted with participants' self assessments. Service provision quality was a big issue and the scholar activist incorporated an action research approach in bringing together providers and participants. The student also agitated with professionals, politicians, policy makers and regulators for better services and continues to do so.

We are arguing here for doing and acting, not simply just writing and thinking.

Think!

Look up Alinsky's rules and consider their relevance for contemporary organising. Are the rules gender-neutral? How might these tactics link to critical community psychology and what limitations might they have?

In considering power in our book, we have explored the context and policy of project work. We argue that power analysis always needs foregrounding.

Prefigurative learning

Thompson and Thompson (2008) note that the Schön model outlined earlier does not fully explore the potential to anticipate. Reflection-for-action refers to planning, thinking ahead about what may happen and possibly anticipating future scenarios. Writers in other domains have termed this 'clinical forethought' (Benner, Hooper-Kyriakidis & Stannard, 1999) or prefigurative action research (Kagan & Burton, 2000). Many of the actual case examples utilised in our book draw upon this framework as a way of engaging critically with community psychology, linking local projects with wider agendas. (See Chapter 2 for discussions of prefigurative action and learning.) Mead (1978) described prefigurative learning as a process of deconstruction whereby the events of the past are understood. She advocated that society needed to discover prefigurative ways of teaching and learning that will keep the future open, so that children will learn how to learn and discover the value of commitment, rather than be told what to learn or be committed to. Mead was writing in the seventies about the possibility of cultural shift. The idea of prefigurative learning is one which allies well with processes of both reflection and action and is commensurate with Freire's (1972a, 1972b) notion of learning and development, although this is not without its critics.

For example, Smith (2002) questions the formality of Freire's approach,

> ... his approach is still curriculum-based and entail transforming settings into a particular type of pedagogical space. This can rather work against the notion of dialogue (in that curriculum implies a predefined set of concerns and activities). Educators need to look for 'teachable moments' – but when we concentrate on this we can easily overlook simple power of being in conversation with others.
>
> (Smith, 2002, p. 197)

We would argue that the approach we have taken in the text and the worked practical examples utilised reflect this approach to learning. However, reading is no substitute for doing. As Harré (2011, p. 163) says: *Only being able to do a little is never a reason not to do the little you feel that you can.*

In this chapter, we have proposed a number of interrelated skills that community psychologists need to develop. We have also stressed the centrality of reflection (both personal and in conjunction with others). There are no simple criteria in use and we would not want to enter the world of competency based professional training. What is provided here is a resource of possible skills and roles which may be developed. In the second half of the chapter, we outlined the importance of reflexivity and mapped some of the overarching concepts which frame praxis – for example, power, values, ethics. Before we finish our book, and mindful of the power of critique, in the next chapter we present the case for and against community psychology. After we provide a critical disruption chapter for this third part of our book, we offer one last critical reflection where we consider the use of critical community psychology, in one final flourish of critical disrupting. In doing so we do not want you to disengage from critical community psychology, we wish to further engage your interest. We want also to encourage action and doing as we ask you to consider your next steps on the road to critical community psychology.

Part 3

Critical disruption of Reflect!

In this section we consider some of the dangers inherent in the roles adopted by community psychologists that ask them to engage in evaluation research, to reflect on the actions of others and of themselves, and to promote 'community focused skills'. The dangers become pronounced when we consider each as a form of hidden political activity that may unconsciously serve particular ideological interests. We then briefly consider how a discipline that purports to be driven by ethics and values might become problematic if as a result the discipline's politics become obscure and contradictory. Finally, we critically reflect on the dangers of the type of critical reflection we have been seeking to encourage in this book.

Evaluation and the audit culture

Community psychology provides a useful disciplinary framework for evaluative work as it promotes rich, sophisticated means and methods of understanding issues in organisational change through adopting holistic rather than reductionist methods of inquiry. As such, we might be valuable resources for organisations and communities that are undergoing or anticipating change. We might also be effective in creating value for ourselves given the emphasis we place on promoting social change. But the role of evaluator of change is also being created for us through the dominant social norm of social change (see our critical disruption of Part 2).

Reflect!

The promotion of social change and of evaluation may be said to have contributed to an audit culture. An audit culture is one in which the majority of social institutions in a society are having their aims and activities made transparent so that they can be measured and made accountable to the institution's stakeholders. An audit culture employs values of transparency and democracy, uses the rhetoric of 'improving quality' and of 'empowerment' and appears to have much synergy with a critical community psychological framework.

During the 1980s and 1990s, the term 'audit' expanded from its original application in financial accountancy to a broader signifier for social and political accountancy, particularly of professional organisations. So, financial audits have expanded out from the material and into the social world (e.g. 'health and safety audits', 'environmental audits' and so on). Described in less politically neutral terms, the audit as a social practice first shifted from management where it was used primarily to assessing the financial 'health' of the private corporation to becoming used to assess 'value for money' delivered by public institutions to then becoming a political tool of neoliberal governmentality which signified an ideological shift from government directly managing the activities of social institutions to social institutions self-monitoring and self-regulating within broader parameters set by both state and market. In the UK, this widened role for audit particularly caught hold during the early 1980s under political reforms undertaken by the Thatcher government which planned to reduce public expenditure through promoting efficiencies in the state by subjecting public institutions (such as education, health care, housing and social services) to the disciplines of the 'free market' in the belief that this would engender a new culture of fiscal responsibility and efficiency gains. The audit culture has directly contributed to the growth in evaluation research.

Auditing and evaluation can embed new forms of power relationships (based on increased competitive individualism) and new forms of subjectivities (based on the self regulating consumer) into existing social relations in the public sphere. In terms of the latter, reflectivity, reflexivity (see Chapter 13) and self criticism become valorised as the professional becomes self monitoring, self auditing within the discreet parameters set by neoliberal government (the promotion of consumerism and competitive individualism). For example, teachers and researchers in higher education are increasingly encouraged to adopt the social role of an entrepreneur (who tests their ideas out in the marketplace and seeks to become a strong competitor for research funding and future teaching positions). Students are also extolled to engage in personal development planning as a way of mapping the self and reflecting on professional improvement.

The audit culture has noticeably affected the spheres of psychological practice in many ways. In higher education in the UK, Australia and elsewhere, academics are now audited on their teaching performance (through student evaluation and external examination), their research performance (through research assessment exercises) and their overall job performance. Parallel developments have affected the fields of health and social welfare. Among the consequences of the new audit culture in higher education has been a transformation of the academic peer review process from a collegial activity (a means by which academics could support the academic rigour and quality of the work of their peers) to a competitive activity (a means by which academics could subject the work of their peers to competitive funding). As a consequence, some academics found their roles transformed from scholars into professional managers and entrepreneurs as they became employed by their institution to ensure the institution performed well in such audits and competed successfully for funding sources. It has also subjected the work of academics and other professionals to crude, quantified forms of measurement. Some commentators have cited the encroachment of these auditing practices in higher education as resulting not only in the increased surveillance of academic activity but also in the introduction of new forms of coercive and authoritarian governmentality (Shore & Wright, 1999).

Under this audit culture, evaluation work has become a dominant social practice through it becoming (covertly) both a political activity and a cultural artefact. So, rather than evaluation being a politically neutral form of empirical inquiry, it is increasingly becoming a political practice that employs systems of power to regulate behaviour and a means to impose neoliberal systems of power (based on the idea of the self-regulation of the market) more broadly into society. As such, critical community psychologists can become incorporated into auditing processes that are little more than highly formalised and theatrical, strictly choreographed and ideologically loaded political rituals (Abélès, cited in Shore & Wright, 1999). This might explain some of the problems we have described in Chapter 12 where critical community psychologists sometimes clash with organisations when their methods of evaluation and the results they produce fall out of kilter with those desired by an institution. The kernel of our concern was contained in Part 2 where we described community audits, and mentioned, in passing, how audit tools appear to jar a little with critical community psychology values. Those concerns have become harder for us to avoid following our focus on 'skills' in Part 3.

Auditing skills

One particular audit that higher education has undergone, that may make other elements of the material we have included in Part 3 of our book particularly problematic, is the skills audit. Four of us work in an academic context where skills, perhaps obviously, are central to our work as we seek to enhance the skills of psychology students to enable them to acquire effective roles when they work in community settings with disenfranchised and disempowered groups. So, interpersonal communication skills, problem solving skills, organisational skills and research skills all become important when we occupy facilitating, educational, representational and technical roles. However, all this happens in a culture where the concept of 'skills' is becoming increasingly ideological and is seated within reinforced hierarchies of competence whereby trainees are subject to stricter and more precisely defined areas of competence that both weaponise auditing regimes and restrict the opportunities for challenges to professional power. For example, the professional accreditation requirements of psychology training in Australia have undergone a renewed focus on key competency areas for both generalist and specialist psychologists and these competencies must be demonstrated by students before they can apply for membership to, and thus to become agents of influence in, those professional bodies. Moreover, the concept of competence has been appropriated by conservative political thinkers (e.g. Jordan Peterson) so that social inequalities have become rearticulated as the just outcomes of naturally distributed levels of competence in the population, the so-called hierarchies of competence. Though we have sought, in Chapter 13, to obviate this perversion of our argument around competency and capability, our ideas may still be subverted by the overarching political context in which we are now working.

The Dearing Report (Dearing, 1997), still influential in UK higher education, set out a number of 'key skills' to be acquired by university students: numeracy, information technology, communication and learning to learn. The last of these is part of an underlying ecology of the 'learning society' and a political project known as Lifelong Learning. It is the process rather than the content of learning that becomes prioritised in an era in which specific knowledge is believed to become obsolete through fast moving technologies and where work skills can become transitory due to the short term, insecure nature of employment contracts dominating the labour market. Learning to learn is viewed as valuable in the context of 'market-driven skills' in an insecure labour market. The Dearing Report also placed work-based learning centre stage, stating it should be embedded into the university curriculum so as to bring vocational and academic qualifications into closer alignment. These initiatives are largely 'employer driven' and are focused on making students 'employable'. In relation to the broader labour market, they are supply-led (aimed at increasing the numbers of people ready for employment) rather than demand-led (aimed at increasing the employment opportunities ready for people) in their focus. As such, this focus on skills stresses the responsibilities and duties of citizens to play an active part in the labour market (to acquire the skills employers require them to have). Through such social policy, employment has become a duty of 'citizenship' (Kagan & Diamond, 2019).

Reflect!

This is the political backdrop to the 'skills' culture in the UK, in which community based, competencies and skills focused learning initiatives in community psychology perhaps sits comfortably. However, this background should alert us to the problem of learning and skill development becoming decontextualised and re-conceptualised as the responsibility and immutable psychometric property of the individual. This leads to a propensity for individuals rather than employer organisations and government being made culpable for skills deficits in the labour market and, ultimately, unemployed people becoming viewed as culpable for their own unemployment. It begs the question as to whether critical community psychologists might embrace learning initiatives blinkered to the political ideologies upon which they are based. One particularly political ideology is the rhetoric of 'Third-Way politics'. This 'new' politic is described as resolving the tensions between the heightened individualism of the political right and the welfarist policies of the political left. It fully emerged onto the political landscape with the start of the Clinton administration in the USA in 1992 and the Blair government in the UK in 1997 and continues to this day. This new political vision is said to lead to a consensual, conflict-free form of governance as 'the Third Way' challenges the idea that politics is about conflict and change (the world around us is changing so fast and so dramatically that all we can do, perhaps, is keep up with it in the best way we can).

Third-way politics has come under considerable critique for flattening the political landscape and the paralysis it seeks to impose on political dissent, while objectively reinforcing the neoliberal hegemony. There is a danger that community psychology might be inheriting such political ideologies through unreflexively adopting particular practices. Thus, the problem we may be facing is that community psychology might appear to become depoliticised (publicly, at least). This may have happened by the readiness of the field to define itself as driven by ethics and values more than it is ready to define itself as driven by politics and ideology.

Both ethics and values can be employed as political smoke screens. Where research is viewed as having produced or as likely to produce politically sensitive findings, ethics can be employed to censor such research (by either forbidding it to happen or by directing attention away from what is found). Such may have happened with the social psychological work of Milgram and Zimbardo which showed how good people can do evil things when subject to bureaucratic systems of authority. The result of their work was at the time, and still is, politically unpalatable. Society was still seeking to comprehend the horrors of the Holocaust during the Second World War and work that suggested those actions were perpetrated by ordinary people (people like you and like us) rather than by evil people was socially unpopular and politically unconscionable (Bauman, 1989). Social scientists rescued the public and the politicians from such an analysis through miring Milgram and Zimbardo's work with the charge of unethical conduct (both experiments entailed participants undergoing psychological distress and offered them limited rights to withdraw). Ethics concealed the political ramifications of the research (that social institutions can turn 'good' people 'evil'). In this way, social ethics can operate to conceal politics (Pels, 1999). The deployment of values can work in a similar way.

In the UK, the then Prime Minister Tony Blair famously stated that he wanted to replace politics with values. Since that time, politics in the West is increasingly galvanised around loose value propositions that are neatly spun into political slogans (e.g. a 'Fair Go for all' in Australia). Community psychology might appear to be showing the same ambition. The tendency for community psychologists to talk of values rather than politics might obfuscate critical thinking in the field as it replaces (at least in a public sense) political sensibility and activism with personal belief and consensual norms. This can lead to the politics of the field becoming obscured or even contradictory. For example, at a session at a European community psychology conference some delegates from the USA began using the discourse of valuing diversity to argue for the inclusion of mainstream psychological research being conducted in the USA into European community psychology. In this discourse, the value of diversity was stripped of its political meaning – the power relations that define how difference leads to disadvantage – so as to prize open space (in this instance, in European community psychology) to further extend the reach of dominant systems (USA mainstream psychological research). The value of diversity disguised a politics of domination.

Critical disruption of critical reflection

To end this chapter of critical disruption, we provide a critical disruption to our critical reflections. We have placed an emphasis on critical thinking throughout all three parts of our book. As such, we are positioning our work in the new branch of community psychology that is increasingly being referred to as critical community psychology. We are not claiming to define critical community psychology as at the time of writing it is not an established field in itself (indeed, the decision to entitle our text 'critical community psychology' was something of a leap of faith) but more of an approach adopted by some community psychologists. We have briefly mentioned the tension between these two forms of psychology in our critical disruption of Part 2. However, we need to consider whether the critical perspective we are advocating for community psychology might actually operate more as a comfort than a challenge to the social systems that create the inequalities we are so keen to redress.

It could be argued that the presence of critical voices is required by a system that purports to be open, free and democratic (which are dominant cultural values – rhetorically at least – promoted by Western democracies and neoliberalism), something termed 'repressive tolerance' by Marcuse (1965). The inclusion of a critical perspective into the mainstream gives the mainstream the appearance of being imbued with liberal values (a tolerance of diverse views and support for freedom of thought and freedom of speech). The incorporation of critical perspectives into a system can give that system the veneer of respectability but also a degree of control over the location of the critiques that might challenge that system. Thus, a critical perspective, rather than threaten a dominant system of thought (such as individualism), can also promote that system of thought by giving the impression that it is a democratic system.

However, certain forms of criticality will be denied access through the restriction of freedom of speech created by libel, slander and anti-terrorism laws. This might happen overtly (through the imposition of legal controls over publication – patrolled by publishing corporation lawyers) or through self censorship (academics self monitoring their activities through engaging in 'reflexivity' guided by concerns over career development). A critical perspective that attempts, as ours does, to provide some critical disruption to dominant social systems, might paradoxically be more of a hindrance than a help to those who struggle against such social systems. Having our critical reflections published might be the first indication that the balance of interests that our work promotes might have already tilted away from those with the least power and towards those with the most.

Here is a collection of some resources with a short description to assist in your reading of Part 3 (Chapters 11, 12 and 13).

Many of these resources are UK based – have a look for something similar in your own country.

General resources

- The UK Government has a National Audit Office which is charged with scrutinising public spending for Parliament. They assert that the independent public audit perspective helps Parliament hold government to account and improve public services. www.nao.org.uk/
- The Office for National Statistics provides up-to-date statistical information about UK economics and society. Key terms you might want to search include 'Quality of Life' and 'Well-being'. www.ons.gov.uk
- The Office for Disability Issues (ODI) is a Government office working towards equality for disabled people. www.gov.uk/government/organisations/office-for-disability-issues
- The UK Evaluation Society has a capability framework for the conduct of quality evaluations. www.evaluation.org.uk/index.php/news-resources/ukes-publications/77-ukes-capabilities-framework

Reflect!

- The National Council for Voluntary Organisations has a number of resources for evaluation in the charity and non-governmental sector. www.ncvo.org.uk/practical-support/consultancy/ncvo-charities-evaluation-services
- On ethics beyond psychology, the Social Research Association's guidelines on ethics and safety in conducting social research raise broader considerations of use to critical community psychologists. Have a look and compare them with psychology guidelines. http://the-sra.org.uk/research-ethics/ethics-guidelines

Films

- *Lagaan* (2001). Directed by Ashutosh Gowariker, the film is set in the Victorian period of the British Raj in India and focuses on an Indian village's fight against British oppression.

Books

- Alinsky, S. (1971) *Rules for Radicals: A Pragmatic Primer for Realistic Radicals*. New York: Vintage.
- Hsiao-Hung Pai writes and is an activist on migrant labour issues. She is best known for her book *Chinese Whispers: The True Story Behind Britain's Hidden Army of Labour*.
- Have a look at the open source e-book by Nikki Harré (2011) http://elibrary.bsu.az/books_400/N_350.pdf. Complete the worksheets on becoming a sustainability advocate and draw up an action plan for personal action, bearing in mind that she suggests that *"Only being able to do a little is never a reason not to do the little you feel that you can"* (p. 163).
- Listen to Carolyn Kagan and Mark Burton talking about working as scholar activists and about liberation psychology. www.open.edu/openlearn/health-sports-psychology/social-psychology-and-politics/content-section-5.3; www.open.edu/openlearn/health-sports-psychology/social-psychology-and-politics/content-section-5.1

Chapter 14

Critical disruption: does critical community psychology have an adequate praxis?

Summary

In this final critical disruption we seek to stand back from the whole book, and also from the whole enterprise we have termed critical community psychology to ask some more fundamental questions about it like: *Do we believe that critical community psychology really is something that can live up to the rather bold claims it makes for itself – implicitly or explicitly?*

The case for and against community psychology

Throughout this text we have encouraged you to *Think!, Act! & Reflect!* and the critical disruption sections aimed to present a critical voice as integral to community psychology. The role of the critical community psychologist (in the model we have presented) is ostensibly non-professional, whilst using a range of skills, and the practices employed need critical reflection. Critical community psychologists as individuals can of course reflect on practice (as covered above) and many of the tools covered encourage group and collaborative reflection and reflexivity. An underpinning assumption in this text is about the indivisibility of what is individual and what is social. So in moving beyond individual critical community psychologists, what are the critiques of the discipline? Critics come from within community psychology and outside. Prilleltensky and Nelson (1997), community psychology insiders, note the gap between desired aspirations and actions of community psychology. They argue that ameliorative ways of working need to give way to transformative change. Duckett (2005), too, questions the extent to which interventions in community psychology have resulted in any meaningful resistance against, in this case, political violence.

Other critics position themselves outside of community psychology. Parker (2007) reviews a number of psychological interventions claiming to be empowering, among them critical psychology, discursive psychology and positive psychology. Parker's critique of community psychology rests on three problems. The first issue is around 'action research' where community psychologists often need to work within the constraints of a funding agenda. Here, funders can prescribe, monitor and potentially control communities. Parker acknowledges that non-funded work allows individuals the role of community activists and hence more freedom. Working as a community psychologist, however, can produce dissent as different communities are identified to work with, masking class politics. In this account the community psychologist may ultimately end up being seen as a traitor, or dilemmas of representation may rear their ugly head. The second issue is around the identification of 'good citizens' who will engage in community projects and build 'social capital'. Clifford and Marcus (1986) discuss the historical relationships between anthropology, ethnographic research and colonialism, noting that 'action research' was a colonial favourite when understanding local 'native' perceptions of colonial power required observation, interference and control as efficient methods. Parker relates colonial relations to oppression then and now. The modern day equivalent sees the notion of 'community' as some kind of assessment of citizenship – those who participate being viewed as good and deserving of support. The wider neoliberal agenda of service privatisation forces people to rely on self resources and can fit neatly into the ethos of 'action research' (Parker, 2007). The building up of networks and 'social capital' is here framed as informal welfare support and entrepreneurial opportunities are all that individuals without 'capital' can access (Cooke & Kothari, 2001).

The third issue pivots around inclusion. Community psychologists are so keen to be 'constructive' that they privilege what 'works' rather than problems people have. Notions of community can be suffocating for some and social capital (the 'glue') can also exclude dissimilar community members. We discuss some of these issues in Part 1 of our book. Community psychologists often have to occupy a difficult space between community members' concerns and others. Parker cites the UK disabled people's movement as demonstrating disability 'action research' (see Goodley & Lawthom, 2005). Here, the drivers for the movement developed outside of psychology thereby avoiding psychologisation.

Community psychology then often glues together the two terms 'community' and 'psychology' in such a way as to psychologise what a community is – to treat the community as something that can be conceptualised and studied by psychologists on their own terms – and then to use that psychologised image of the community to understand the individuals that comprise it (Parker, 2007, p. 145).

This bleak critique is not levelled at all community psychologists (and indeed we would argue that the approach developed here falls outside that critique of 'liberal' community psychology) but presents some serious challenges. (Here we use liberal in the economic and social sense – liberalism emphasised individual freedom and arose with modern capitalism which required freedom of labourers to enter into employment contracts, freedom of trade and emancipation from landed power interests. This is different from the rather sloppy use of 'liberal' in North America and the UK to mean progressive reformer, although the origins are the same – see Wallerstein, 2004.)

Are there any alternatives? Parker advocates that psychologists themselves read and are politicised, thereby allowing them to prioritise social change, in contrast to psychological knowledge being utilised as a conservative response to political problems. In this text, we have aimed to contextualise knowledge with political history and real-life examples, many of them illustrating a collaborative approach where the issue has been defined by those outside academia or the professions. We have done this with some caution as we recognise that on its own each example, severed not only from a full explanation of the work involved but also from its connection with other social change currents, may fall foul of Parker's critique. It is a risk we thought worth taking.

Community psychology as oppression or liberation

So is critical community psychology a resource for liberation, or does it actually serve instead to help disguise the overall oppression in the system – or, worse, is it part of the panoply of tools by which the dominant interests obtain consent for policies and practices of exploitation and oppression? Theorists and practitioners from differing contexts have rather different approaches to this.

Moane (2003) notes the potential of community psychology to engage with liberatory psychology. Certain kinds of community psychology models such as action research and empowerment models have the potential to improve social conditions and bring about social justice. The project of liberation would be enhanced here if liberatory psychology was utilised. Whilst Lykes and Moane (2009) suggest a hybrid feminist liberatory psychology, Whelan and Lawthom (2009) draw attention to the pedagogical alignments between the goals of feminism and community psychology. This is conceptualised as a fundamental commitment to political activism (in terms of dealing with oppression). Whilst there are areas of difference between the approaches (Bond & Mulvey, 2000), theorists have noted the ways in which particular pedagogies have promoted social change. Moane (2006) maps out social change oriented pedagogies and Duckett (2002) argues that the pedagogy of critical community psychology promotes collaborative, participatory projects. Can community psychology be oppressive and/or liberatory? Evans, Duckett, Lawthom and Kivell (2017, p. 110) suggest that critical community psychology for transformation is possible under some circumstances, and with the critical community psychologist working as a problematising agent.

> Political analysis and critique of the status quo are fundamental to transformative community research and action. However, analysis and critique are not enough: We also must engage as co-researchers and activist scholars in solidarity with community efforts to transform oppressive systems and structures.

The issues of both power and contextual awareness are key. Painter, Terre Blanche and Henderson (2006, p. 216) mount a critique of ways in which community psychology has been employed in the South African context. They position community psychology as an American (USA) product located in clinical training and conventional academic programmes. From this position, it:

> ...reproduced many problematic assumptions about knowledge production and application, social action, and psychology as a profession – not to mention assumptions about 'community', 'culture' and 'race'.

Other critics such as Seedat, Duncan and Lazarus (2001), Pretorius-Heuchert and Ahmed (2001) and Hamber, Masilela and Terre Blanche (2001) identify limitations of community psychology. First, categories of community, culture and race have at times reinforced the divisions around race and culture defined in apartheid. Second, as with other forms of psychology in South Africa, the practitioners tend to be white and middle class. Third, there has been little translation of macro-level critical theory into actual political practice. In the words of Hamber et al. (2001), then, "South African community psychologists, despite some noble efforts to engage with 'relevant' social issues, have historically fallen prey to ... individualizing, idealist, and relativizing tendencies" (quoted by Painter & Blanche, 2004).

An issue which is central both to community psychology and to the question of oppression or liberation is that of context or location. Just as in critical community psychology we have extolled the value of assessing and paying attention to the context in which the work takes place, the context is also very relevant to the wider project of critical community psychology. Hence, the location of community psychology within a clinical discipline in the above South Africa example may well promote more of an oppressive regime than a liberatory one. (See Reich et al. (2007) for further examples of differences and tensions between different (national) contexts).

Reflect!

What do you know about community psychology in your context? Is it visible in academic and/or practice settings? What factors do you think have resulted in this?

Seedat, Duncan and Lazarus (2001) distinguish between distributive equality (issues of political representation and social justice) and distributive sufficiency (does community psychology theorise how liberation can be achieved and has it integrated radical perspectives?). The authors argue that in the South African context community psychology has not even approached distributive sufficiency. For our context, the issues are rather differently framed. Burton, Kagan and Duckett (2012, p. 13) argue

> Community psychology is a construction – historically and societally bounded. This determines its politics. To the extent that the battle of ideas steps up, so will the contradictions that affect community psychology and its practitioners. One response would be quietist distraction (for example the study of the community as object) while at the other extreme would be naïve attempts at activism. The latter have to be encouraged since this is how learning takes place, overcoming naïveté through praxis, but this is only likely to yield much if community psychologists are able to step outside the isolation of being psychologists.

The dichotomy of liberation–oppression is perhaps a static and somewhat false one. There are nuances to this debate as we have shown throughout the text. In attending to our positionality as agents of change and maximising awareness of skills and learning, we can hope to be attentive to the practices we engage in, the values we embrace and the context in which we work. It is not only social justice that we need to be working towards – it is increasingly clear that environmental justice is fundamental to human flourishing within planetary boundaries (Harré, Madden, Brooks & Goodman, 2017; Watkins, 2015), which opens up new and wide vistas for critical community psychological practice. Evans et al. (2017, p. 121) place practitioners at the heart of practice.

It is not easy to learn how to utilise our technical or professional skills to work hand in hand with community groups for social justice rather than social maintenance. But if we do not embark upon a type of critical community praxis that transforms ourselves as well as reality, it will be hard to develop a community psychology that will contribute to transformative social change.

Is there an adequate praxis for community psychology?

The claims we have made in the book and are now interrogating can be summarised as follows:

- Critical community psychology is an alternative to psychology's individualism and positivism.
- Critical community psychology can link what people feel, think, experience with an understanding of the complex dynamics of social systems.
- Critical community psychology can support people effectively as they struggle together for social justice: it contributes to principled social transformation.
- Critical community psychology really exists.

The project perhaps looks pretty preposterous. If it weren't so implausible that a small group of professionals could really make a difference in a world characterised by immense and absolutely ruthless power interests (Klein, 2007; Napoleoni, 2008) the proposition would look rather arrogant. As it is it just looks a bit naïve. But these claims in turn rest on one fundamental question, does critical community psychology have an adequate praxis? Praxis means the unity of theory and practice and using this term is meant to ensure that neither does theory end up as abstract, divorced from reality, inaccessible, nor does practice end up as mindless activism with nothing to guide it in its choice of strategy because it has no understanding of the sources of oppression or of the factors that keep it in place. An adequate practice means more than just good theoretically grounded practice. It also means adequate connection with those who are affected and an adequate access to sources of power without which change cannot take place.

But the verdict also depends on the scope of the above claims. On one level they can all be supported – this book amasses evidence for each of the claims, so long as they are kept within modest bounds. So critical community psychology is an alternative way of doing psychology – alternative for example to individualistic pathologising approaches in clinical psychology and mainstream psychology more generally, and to collusion with policy initiatives that disempower communities. It also recognises the limits of ameliorative community psychology and at its best shows another way, as many of the examples in the book suggest. It does wear its qualifier, 'critical', to indicate that it is not complacent and is not presenting a finished product that is the answer to all social problems.

And we remain dissatisfied. Orford (1998) asked if we have a theory of community psychology. He tentatively suggested "yes" by presenting Holland's use of Burrell and Morgan's (1979) framework for categorising organisational theory as a guide to the change process and by presenting Hagan and Smail's (1997) work on power mapping. However, this is hardly a basis for a theory, or for what is really needed, a 'metatheory' that loosely integrates understanding of the different levels and processes of the construction, destruction and reconstruction of lived community in a socio-economic context, to guide oppressed and disadvantaged groups and communities, with their intellectual allies (i.e. in this instance critical community psychologists) in their resistance and struggle for a better life – that is, the metatheory becoming praxis.

A content analysis of the 'best praxis' in this book would discover a preponderance of

- Latin American innovations from the 1960s onwards;
- management and organisational studies;
- concepts imported from politics, ecology and the social sciences.

What does this tell us? First, it suggests that there is little of any real use in the mainstream of psychology: mainstream psychology, as a discipline centred on individualism, adaptation, pathology, can hardly be expected to provide much in the way of helpful concepts and tools for social transformation. So, like practitioners in the mainstream of psychology, we borrow from outside psychology. We attempt to do this critically, mindful of the original context of the concepts and tools, of their potential mismatch (incommensurability) with our context of application, in terms of logical fit, purpose and embedded assumptions (Burton & Kagan, 1998). We are, however, fairly relaxed about this, recognising that the context of discovery does not have to infect the context of application (Mackenzie, 1981) as long as that original context of its discovery is fully understood and disrupted when necessary. So although action research has roots in colonial administration and industrial management (social science in the service of power interests – for which see: Cooke & Kothari, 2001; Kagan, Burton & Siddiquee, 2017), it has its uses in focusing and organising liberatory action (Fals Borda, 1988; Fals Borda & Rahman, 1991) and has potential for linking local action with more ambitious social and political change (Kagan & Burton, 2000; Burns, 2007).

Second, however, it indicates that there is a real gap in the repertoire of tools for creating real social change. Is this a consequence of the history of ossification of social change into three main paradigms, each of which is plainly exhausted? They were the two socialisms – Leninist and social democratic, and the post 1968 identity-politic. It is perhaps for this reason that the Latin American tradition of praxis (Dussel, 2008; Flores, 2009) has such an appeal for us. It appears to integrate the best of these traditions in a democratic and participatory way, with careful attention to the situation of the excluded Other. Yet this in itself suggests a further critically disruptive insight.

The Latin American tradition has its roots in work with excluded and marginalised communities: poor and illiterate peasants in Brazil's North East (Paulo Freire), peasant and worker movements in Colombia (Orlando Fals Borda), victims of war and state terror in the Southern Cone and Central America (Elizabeth Lira, Maria Langer, Ignacio Martín-Baró). In large part this work (picked up and developed by writers such as community social psychologist Maritza Montero and philosopher

Enrique Dussel) predates 1990, a watershed year after which neoliberalisation, rather than rolling back the collective gains of the post World War Two period, became embedded, rolled out, as the Washington Consensus (Harvey, 2005a, 2007), the only way to think (*el pensamiento único*), as the hegemonic ideology (Devine et al., 2009). Arguably this has taken us to a much more thoroughly globalised context of oppression that has implications for the aims and the very viability of critical community psychology (Freitas, 2009).

A new context: extreme and globalised oppression

Here are some examples of how the challenges facing communities, especially oppressed and disadvantaged ones are now more extreme and driven by globalised forces. This was always to some extent the case (think of the Black Death, or 1492) but we seem to be witnessing a step change that perhaps renders the Latin American praxis tradition with its key characteristics of problematisation, conscientisation, reflection–action–reflection, less potent as a vehicle for resistance and collective social progress.

One major challenge is *organised gang violence and the drug trade*. The *maras*, violent street gangs in Central American countries, arrived after the failed insurgencies and civil wars of the 1980s. They have their origins in the violent gang culture of the United States cities where Central American refugees settled and in the subsequent policy of deportation of these young people. Their presence has changed and complicated radically the local politics of community development in those countries. A related but in some ways distinct development has been the growth of the drugs trade which in countries such as Colombia and Mexico has corrupted the state while the drug gangs terrorise the poor communities. The impact of institutionalised violence has been explored by community psychologists, but the projects described tend to be more ameliorative than transformational (Estrada et al., 2007; Schrader McMillan & Burton, 2009).

The enormous growth of *people trafficking* can be traced to the collapse of the soviet bloc and the subsequent opening of new territories to unleashed, unmitigated capitalism with the collapse of local economies, the (relative) opening of borders, and the growth of international communications. Everything is a commodity in this new system and people do not just sell their labour power but in many cases become products that are sold on the market (Craig et al., 2007; Napoleoni, 2008).

Climate change, a direct result of the system of global capitalism (Bellamy Foster, 2009) threatens us all but most immediately those living precariously in the global South. Even in the North, we have seen what are almost certainly the first results of a worsening weather pattern. Combined with state negligence and support for the free market, there have been losses of homes and ways of life in places as widespread as Melbourne, New Orleans and Cumbria. Islanders living on small land masses are particularly vulnerable, losing homes and livelihoods through floods and typhoons. Since the publication of the first edition of our book, the existential threats have accelerated, exacerbated by the entrenchment of anti-climate change sceptics, particularly in the USA under the Trump administration.

Rethinking the amelioration–transformation distinction

These three examples do not make critical community psychology irrelevant but they do illustrate the extent of the challenge, a challenge that perhaps forces a rethink of the distinction between amelioration and transformation. Would it make more sense to think in a more nuanced way? Figures 14.1 and 14.2 attempt this by distinguishing between two dimensions of change – its extent and its scope. This framework could be extended to indicate the strength of the countervailing forces – development of force field analysis for today's troubled times.

Extent of change / Scope of change	No change – status quo preserved	Changes of a 'quantitative' nature – no change in social relations but an improvement in experience	Changes of a 'quantitative' nature – involving a change in social relations
Parochial/short term focus	**Collusion**		
Medium range focus (city- or region-wide/ medium term)		**Amelioration**	
Long range focus (national or international/long term)			**Transformation**

Figure 14.1 Rethinking the amelioration–transformation distinction.

Note: The arrow indicates a dimension from collusion with the status quo through amelioration towards transformation. Oppressive and destructive forces are more likely to oppose change projects the further towards the right and bottom of the matrix.

But, none of this is specific to critical community psychology: instead it describes the context for any project that aspires to resistance or radical change. If community psychologists want to play a role in such struggles that's great, but maybe we should not be over-confident that we have anything very special to contribute – maybe this book is just a toolkit of local to meso range tricks and techniques. We just hope, they might be of use.

Reflect!

Scope of change \ Extent of change	No change – status quo preserved	Changes of a 'quantitative' nature – no change in social relations but an improvement in experience	Changes of a 'quantitative' nature – involving a change in social relations
Parochial/short term focus	e.g.	e.g. Providing Indian dance classes in a local centre	e.g. Working with artists on arts for health evaluation
Medium range focus (city- or region-wide/ medium term)	e.g. Litter reduction campaigns	e.g. Teaching refugee women internet skills for empowerment (Siddiquee & Kagan, 2006)	e.g. The re-provision of learning difficulties provision in NW
Long range focus (national or international/long term)	e.g. Roll-out of Computerised Cognitive Behaviour Therapy nationally	e.g.	e.g. Work with victims of torture leads to collective empowerment and national rejection of impunity (Lira)

Figure 14.2 Rethinking the amelioration–transformation distinction – with examples.
Note: The same matrix as that in Figure 14.1 with examples from the book and elsewhere.

Final word

In our first edition of this book we likened our rubber ducks on the cover to our vision for critical community psychology:

> rather like the unsinkable and tenacious ducks we hope that streams of critical community psychology reach other shores. Unlike the duck armada, we hope we do not end as battered and bruised as we swim with and against the tides…

In 2018 it has become clear that circumstances have changed and our little bobbing rubber ducks have now taken on a rather unpleasant portent. Our ducks have been joined by a mass of plastic flotsam that is now in our oceans – 8 million metric tonnes per year (Jambeck et al., 2015). So, as a metaphor, our armada has taken on a new meaning and much more of a sinister quality as it now toughs out the ocean currents accompanied by its entourage of plastic waste dumped into our oceans as effluent of a capitalist economies that show no sign of retraction. In this second edition of our text, climate change and the destruction of the natural environment has become a much more central concern for us and is fast becoming an overriding context and challenge for community psychology.

Reflect!

What do you make of the book cover? Bees on the cover seem visually like a rather odd choice for a text on critical community psychology. However, bees both provide inspiration and present a warning. Bees live in colonies, working in different roles for the common good. They are exemplars of community, of solidarity and of complex social organisation. However, throughout the world, bees and other insects are under threat. They are under threat from the activities of people: through their use of pesticides to extract maximum productivity (and often profits) from crops; and along with many other animal and plant species from the warming of the climate. They are fighting for their very survival, and their survival underpins our survival.

In this second edition of our book, we offer bees in their natural habitats as a metaphor for critical community psychology: of both hope for a future of solidarity and working for the common good, and of despair for the human destruction of the world on which we live.

To us the bee suggests,

- sociability (community): conviviality and co-operative, collective action;
- activity (social justice) the satisfaction of necessary and common needs;
- ecology (stewardship): the natural world of interdependence, and its fragility.

The bee is also the symbol of our city, Manchester, that we want to see continuing to lead through example, as a society characterised by fairness, equality and guardianship of the natural world. There have been two bombings in recent years in Manchester – 1996, with no loss of life, and 2017 in which 22 people died. Since then, the Manchester Bee symbol has become popular as a symbol of resilience and solidarity among cultures.

For us, community psychology has been a force for change in psychology and critical community psychology has largely emerged from a response to a frustration with the pace and nature of that change (it has not been quick enough and sufficiently substantive). But, we wonder how much of our work has remained locked into an insular intradisciplinary struggle to change the way psychology conceptualises and intervenes in the problems of living, and whether our work will get sucked down the sink hole along with psychology as a whole as we all get overtaken by the existential crisis our species faces as the speed of climate change continues unabated. Things have changed at such a rapid pace in so many ways since the first edition of our text. Whilst the foundational ideas and our learning from our praxis remain, as we finish this second edition we remain hopeful but have a growing fear that all our efforts will be for nought if we all get trumped.

References

All links checked and working on 22 March 2019.

Agger, I., & Buus Jensen, S. (1996). *Trauma and healing under state terrorism*. London, England: Zed.

Ahmed Iqbal Ullah Race Relations Resource Centre. (2013). *Wangari Maathai & the green belt movement*. Available at https://prezi.com/ilx0yojudfjb/wangari-maathai-the-green-belt-movement/.

Akhurst, J., Kagan, C., Lawthom, R., & Richards, M. (2016). Community psychology practice competencies: Some perspectives from the UK. *Global Journal of Community Psychology Practice*, 7(4), 1–15, online.

Aldrich, C. (2005). *Learning by doing: A comprehensive guide to simulations, computer games, and pedagogy in e-learning and other educational experiences*. Chichester, England: Wiley.

Alinsky, S. (1971). *Rules for radicals: A pragmatic primer for realistic radicals*. New York, NY: Vintage.

American Evaluation Association (AEA). (2018). *Guiding principles for evaluators (updated)*. Fairhaven, MA: American Evaluation Association. Available at www.eval.org/p/cm/ld/fid=51.

American Evaluation Association (AEA). (2011). *Statement on cultural competence in evaluation*. Fairhaven, MA: American Evaluation Association. Available at www.eval.org/ccstatement.

Angelique, H., & Culley, M. (2007). History and theory of community psychology: An international perspective of community psychology in the United States. In S. Reich, M. Riemer, I. Prilleltensky & M. Montero (Eds.), *International community psychology: History and theories*. New York, NY: Springer.

Archibald, T. (2019). What's the problem represented to be? Problem definition critique as a tool for evaluative thinking. *American Journal of Evaluation*. doi:109821401882404.

Arcidiacono, C., Tuozzi, T., & Procentese, F. (2016). Community profiling in participatory action research. In L.A. Jason & D.S. Glenwick (Eds.), *Handbook of methodological approaches to community-based research: Qualitative, quantitative and mixed methods*. New York, NY: Oxford University Press.

Argyle, M., Furnham, A., & Graham, J.A. (1981). *Social situations*. Cambridge, England: Cambridge University Press.

Argyris, C., & Schön, D. (1996). *Organizational learning II: Theory, method and practice*. Reading, MA: Addison Wesley.

Argyris, C., & Schön, D. (1978). *Organizational learning: A theory of action perspective*. Reading, MA: Addison-Wesley.

Armistead, N. (ed.) (1974). *Reconstructing social psychology*. Harmondsworth, England: Penguin.

Arnstein, S.R. (1969). A ladder of participation. *Journal of the American Planning Association*, 35(4), 216–224.

Audit Commission (1998). *A fruitful partnership. Effective partnership working*. Management Paper. London, England: Audit Commission.

References

Austin, A. (2018). *Social exclusion: Black people have everything to lose under Trump*. Available at www.demos.org/publication/social-exclusion-black-people-have-everything-lose-under-trump.

Australian Bureau of Statistics (2018). Press release issued on 29th November 2018 cat. no. 3302.0.55.003: Life tables for Aboriginal and Torres Strait Islander Australians, 2015–2017. Canberra, Australia: Australian Bureau of Statistics. Available at www.abs.gov.au/ausstats/abs@.nsf/Lookup/by%20Subject/3302.0.55.003~2015-2017~Media%20Release~Life%20expectancy%20lowest%20in%20remote%20and%20very%20remote%20areas%20(Media%20Release)~15.

Baachi, C. (2012). Introducing the 'what's the problem represented to be?' approach. In A. Bletsas & C. Beasley (Eds.), *Engaging with Carol Bacchi: Strategic interventions & exchanges* (pp. 21–24). Adelaide, Australia: University of Adelaide Press.

Bagni, F., Bojic, I., Duarte, T., Preis Dutra, J., Gaule, S., van Heerden, A., … Psaltoglou, A. (2017). Design principles for co-creating inclusive and digitally mediated public spaces. In C. Smaniotto Costa & K. Ionnidis (Eds.), *The making of the public space: Essays on emerging urban phenomena. Culture & territory.* (pp. 25–40). Lisbon, Portugal: Edições Universitárias Lusófona.

Balloch, S., & Taylor, M. (2001). *Partnership working: Policy and practice*. Bristol, England: Policy Press.

Banister, P., Burman, E., Parker, I., Taylor, M., & Tindall, C. (1997). *Qualitative methods in psychology: A research guide*. Buckingham, England: Open University Press.

Barker, R.G. (1968). *Ecological psychology: Concepts and methods for studying the environment of human behavior*. Stanford, CA: Stanford University Press.

Barreto, A.P. (2011). *Terapia comunitária passo a passo*. Fortaleza, Brazil: Grática LCR.

Bauman, Z. (2007a). *Liquid times: Living in an age of uncertainty*. Cambridge, England: Polity Press.

Bauman, Z. (2007b). *Consuming life*. Cambridge, England: Polity Press.

Bauman, Z. (2005). *Liquid life*. London, England: Wiley.

Bauman, Z. (2001). *Community. Seeking safety in an insecure world*. Cambridge, England: Polity Press.

Bauman, Z. (2000). *Liquid modernity*. Cambridge, England: Polity Press.

Bauman, Z. (1996). *Alone again – Ethics after certainty*. London, England: Demos.

Bauman, Z. (1989). *Modernity and the Holocaust*. New York, NY: Cornell University Press.

Beebeejaun, Y., Durose, C., Rees, J., Richardson, J., & Richardson, L. (2014). 'Beyond text': Exploring ethos and method in co-producing research with communities. *Community Development Journal, 49*(1), 37–53.

Beetham, D., Blick, A., Margetts, H., & Weir, S. (2008). *Power and participation in modern Britain: A literature review for Democratic Audit*. Wembley, England: Creative Print Group.

Bell, B. (2014). *The global disability rights movement: Winning power, participation and access*. Available at www.huffingtonpost.com/beverly-bell/the-global-disability-rig_b_5651235.html?guccounter=1.

Bell, D.M. (2016). A raison d'être for making a reggae opera as a pedagogical tool for psychic emancipation in (post)colonial Jamaica. *International Journal of Inclusive Education, 20*(3), 278–291.

Bellamy Foster, J. (2009). *The ecological revolution: Making peace with the planet*. New York, NY: Monthly Review Press.

Bender, M.P. (1976). *Community psychology*. London, England: Methuen.

Benner, P., Hooper-Kyriakidis, P., & Stannard, D. (1999). *Clinical wisdom and interventions in critical care*. Philadelphia, PA: W.B. Saunders.

Bennett, K., Beynon, H., & Hudson, R. (2000). *Coalfields regeneration: Dealing with the consequences of industrial decline*. Bristol, England: Policy Press and the Joseph Rowntree Foundation.

Benneworth, P. (2013). University engagement with socially excluded communities: Toward the idea of the 'engaged university.' In P. Benneworth (Ed.), *University engagement with socially excluded communities* (pp. 3–32). New York, NY: Springer.

Bhambra, G.K., & Holmwood, J. (2018). Colonialism, postcolonialism and the liberal welfare state. *New Political Economy*, 23(5), 574–587.

Bhana, A., Petersen, I., & Rochat, T. (2008). Community psychology in South Africa. In S. Reich, M. Riemer, I. Prilleltensky & M. Montero (Eds.), *International community psychology: History and theories*. New York, NY: Springer.

Bhaskar, R. (1998). *The possibility of naturalism: A philosophical critique of the contemporary human sciences* (3rd ed.). London, England: Routledge.

Bhaskar, R. (1979). On the possibility of social scientific knowledge and the limits of naturalism. In J. Mepham & D.H. Ruben (Eds.), *Issues in Marxist philosophy: Epistemology, science, ideology* (Vol. 3) (pp. 107–139). Brighton, England: Harvester.

Bhatia, S., & Sethi, N. (2007). History and theory of community psychology in India: An international perspective. In S.M. Reich, M. Riemer, I. Prilleltensky & M. Montero (Eds.), *International community psychology* (pp. 180–199). Boston, MA: Springer. https://doi.org/10.1007/978-0-387-49500-2_9.

Billig, M. (2008). *The hidden roots of critical psychology*. London, England: Sage.

Bishop, A. (2002). *Becoming an ally: Breaking the cycle of oppression in people* (2nd ed.). Nova Scotia, Canada: Fernwood Publishing.

Bishop, B.J., Dzidic, P.L., & Breen, L.J. (2013). Multiple-level analysis as a tool for policy: An example of the use of contextualism and causal layered analysis. *Global Journal of Community Psychology Practice*, 4(2), 1–13.

Blake, R., & Mouton, J. (1961). *The managerial grid*. Houston, TX: Houston Gulf.

Blanchard, A. (2006). Virtual behavior settings: An application of behavior setting theories to virtual communities. *Journal of Computer-Mediated Communication*, 9(2), online.

Blanden, J., Gregg, P., & Machin, S. (2005). *Intergenerational mobility in Europe and North America*. London, England: Centre for Economic Performance, London School of Economics and Political Science.

Blickstead, J.R., Lester, E., & Shapcott, M. (2008). *Collaboration in the third sector: From co-opetition to impact driven cooperation*. Toronto, Canada: Wellesley Institute. Available at www.wellesleyinstitute.com/wp-content/uploads/2011/11/collaborationinthethirdsector.pdf.

Boal, A. (1995). *The rainbow of desire: The Boal method of theatre and therapy* (Adrian Jackson, Trans.). London, England: Routledge.

Boggs, C. (2001). Social capital and political fantasy: Robert Putnam's 'Bowling alone'. *Theory and Society*, 30(2), 281–297.

Bond, M.A., & Mulvey, A. (2000). A history of women and feminist perspectives in community psychology. *American Journal of Community Psychology*, 28(5), 599–630. doi:10.1023/A:1005141619462.

Boudon, R. (1986). *Theories of social change: A critical analysis*. London, England: Policy Press.

Bourdieu, P. (1986). The forms of social capital. In J. Richardson (Ed.) *Handbook of theory and research for the sociology of education* (pp. 241–258). New York, NY: Greenwood.

Boyd, A., Geerling, T., Gregory, W.J., Kagan, C., Midgley, G., Murray, P., & Walsh, M.P. (2007). Systemic evaluation: A participatory, multi method approach. *Journal of the Operational Research Society*, 58(10), 1306–1320.

Boyd, A., Geerling, T., Gregory, W.J., Kagan, C., Midgley, G., Murray, P., & Walsh, M.P. (2003). Participative learning for evaluation: A systems approach to the development of evaluation capability in community health projects. In A. Erasmus & P. du Toit (Eds.), *Proceedings of Action Learning, Action Research and Process Management/Participatory Action Research (ALARPM/PAR) Conference, Pretoria*. Available at https://e-space.mmu.ac.uk/25916/.

Boyd, A., Geerling, T., Gregory, W., Midgley, G. Murray, P., Walsh, M., & Kagan, C. (2001). *Capacity building for evaluation: Report to the Manchester, Salford and Trafford Health Action Zone*. Hull, England: University of Hull.

Boyd, N.M., & Bright, D.S. (2007). Appreciative inquiry as a mode of action research for community psychology. *Journal of Community Psychology*, 35(8), 1019–1036. doi:10.1002/jcop.20208.

Boyle, D., & Harris, M. (2009). *The challenge of co-production. How equal partnerships between professionals and the public are crucial to improving public services*. London, England: NESTA. Available at https://media.nesta.org.uk/documents/the_challenge_of_co-production.pdf.

Bradshaw, J.R. (2015/1972). The taxonomy of social need. In R. Cookson, R. Sainsbury & C. Glendinning (Eds.), *Jonathan Bradshaw on social policy: Selected writings 1972–2011* (pp. 1–12). York, England: University of York/White Rose Research Online. Available at http://eprints.whiterose.ac.uk/112541/.

Brandenburger, A., Nalebuff, B. (1996). *Co-opetition: A revolution mindset that combines competition and cooperation*. New York, NY: Currency Doubleday.

Brandes, D., & Norris, J. (1998). *The gamesters' handbook 3*. London, England: Nelson Thornes.

Brandon, D., Brandon, A., & Brandon, T. (1995). *Advocacy: Power to people with disabilities*. Birmingham, England: Venture Press.

Branic, N. & Kubrin, C. (2018). Gated communities and crime in the United States. In G. Bruinsma & S. Johnson (Eds.), *The Oxford handbook of environmental criminology* (pp. 405–427). Oxford, England: Oxford University Press.

Bridger, A.J., Emmanouil, S., & Lawthom, R. (2017). Trace.space: a psychogeographical community project with members of an arts and health organisation. *Qualitative Research in Psychology*, 14(1), 42–61.

British Psychological Society. (2018). *Code of Ethics and Conduct*. Leicester, England: British Psychological Society. Available at www.bps.org.uk/news-and-policy/bps-code-ethics-and-conduct.

Brodie, E., Cowling, E., & Nissen, N. (2009). *Understanding participation: A literature review*. London, England: NCVO. Available at www.bl.uk/collection-items/understanding-participation-a-literature-review.

Bronfenbrenner, U. (1994). Ecological models of human development. In *International encyclopedia of education* (Vol. 3, 2nd ed.). Oxford, England: Elsevier. Reprinted in M. Gauvain & M. Cole (Eds.), *Readings on the development of children* (2nd ed., 1996, pp. 37–43). New York, NY: Freeman. Available at http://edfa2402resources.yolasite.com/resources/Ecological%20Models%20of%20Human%20Development.pdf.

Bronfenbrenner, U. (1979). *The ecology of human development*. Cambridge, MA: Harvard University Press.

Brown, J., & Isaacs, D. (1994). The core processes of organizations as communities. In P.M. Senge, A. Kleiner, C. Roberts, R.B. Ross & B.J. Smith (Eds.), *The fifth discipline fieldbook: Strategies and tools for building a learning organization*. London, England: Nicholas Brealey Publishing.

Brown, R. (2015). The marketisation of higher education: Issues and ironies. *New Vistas*, 1(1), online.

Brown, R., & Carasso, H. (2013). *Everything for sale? The marketisation of UK higher education*. Abingdon, England: Routledge.

Bruno, I., Didier, E., & Vitale, T. (2014). Statactivism: Forms of action between disclosure and affirmation. *PArtecipazione e COnflitto – PArticipation and COnflict*, 7(2), 198–220.

Büchs, M., & Koch, M. (2017). *Postgrowth and wellbeing*. Cham, Switzerland: Springer International Publishing.

Burchardt, T., Le Grand, J., & Piachaud, D. (1999). Social exclusion in Britain 1991–1995. *Social Policy and Administration*, 33(3), 227–244.

Burns, D. (2007). *Systemic action research: A strategy for whole system change*. Bristol, England: Policy Press.

Burrell, G., & Morgan, G. (1979). *Sociological paradigms and organisational analysis*. London, England: Heinemann.

Burton, M. (2016a). *New evidence on decoupling carbon emissions from GDP growth: What does it mean?* Available at https://steadystatemanchester.net/2016/04/15/new-evidence-on-decoupling-carbon-emissions-from-gdp-growth-what-does-it-mean.

Burton, M. (2016b). *Intervening at the regional level: Building momentum for another possible regional economy: opportunities and traps*. Paper presented at the 5th International Degrowth Conference, Budapest. Available at www.academia.edu/28426063/Intervening_at_the_regional_level_Building_momentum_for_another_possible_regional_economy_opportunities_and_traps.

Burton, M. (2015). Building consensus for another possible economy at municipal level. In J. Condie & A.M. Cooper (Eds.) *Dialogues of sustainable urbanisation: Social science research and transitions to urban contexts* (Chapter 63, pp. 282–285). Penrith, Australia: University of Western Sydney. Available at www.academia.edu/attachments/38876891/download_file?st=MTQ0Nzc2Mz Q4Nyw3OC4xNDkuMjEwLjE1LDEwMzk5OTM%3D&s=swp-toolbar.

Burton, M. (2014a). *Less levity Professor Stern! Economic growth, climate change and the decoupling question*. Available at https://steadystatemanchester.net/2014/09/21/less-levity-professor-stern-economic-growth-climate-change-and-the-decoupling-question/.

Burton, M. (2014b). Social reproduction. In T. Teo (Ed.), *Encyclopedia of critical psychology* (pp. 1802–1804). New York, NY: Springer. Available at https://link.springer.com/referenceworkentry/10.1007/978-1-4614-5583-7_266.

Burton, M. (2013a). A renewal of ethics. *The Psychologist*, 26(11), 802–807. Available at https://thepsychologist.bps.org.uk/volume-26/edition-11/renewal-ethics.

Burton, M. (2013b). The analectic turn: Critical psychology and the new political context. *Les Cahiers de Psychologie Politique*, 23, online. Available at http://lodel.irevues.inist.fr/cahierspsychologie politique/index.php?id=2465.

Burton, M. (2013c). Liberation psychology: A constructive critical praxis. *Estudos de Psicologia (Campinas)*, 30(2), 249–259.

Burton, M. (2013d). In and against social policy. *Global Journal of Community Psychology Practice*, 4(2). Available at www.gjcpp.org/pdfs/burton-v4i2-20130522.pdf.

Burton, M. (2009a). *A green deal for the Manchester-Mersey bioregion: An alternative regional strategy*. Manchester, England. Available at http://greendealmanchester.wordpress.com/about/.

Burton, M. (2009b). *Concepts for bioregional development*. Available at http://greendealmanchester.wordpress.com/concepts-for-bioregional-development/.

Burton, M. (2009c). *Sustainability: Utopian and scientific*. Available at https://greendealmanchester.wordpress.com/sustainability-utopian-and-scientific/.

Burton, M. (2004a). Viva nacho! Liberating psychology in Latin America. *The Psychologist*, 17(10), 584–587.

Burton, M. (2004b). Liberation social psychology: Learning from the Latin American experience. *Clinical Psychology (Clinical Psychology Forum)*, 38(June 2004), 32–37.

Burton, M. (2000). Service development and social change: The role of social movements. In C. Kagan (Ed.), *Collective action and social change*. Manchester, England: IOD Research Group. Available at www.compsy.org.uk/conf11.doc.

Burton, M. (1999). *Service development and social change: The role of social movements*. Paper presented to UK National Community Psychology Conference, Manchester, January. Available at www.compsy.org.uk/Community%20Psychology%20Conference,%20Manchester,%201999.pdf.

Burton, M. (1994). Towards an alternative basis for policy and practice in community care – with special reference to people with learning disabilities. *Care in Place: International Journal of Networks and Community*, 1(2), 158–174.

Burton, M., & Kagan, C. (2009). Towards a really social psychology: Liberation psychology beyond Latin America. In M. Montero & C. Sonn (Eds.), *The psychology of liberation. Theory and application* (pp. 51–73). New York, NY: Springer.

Burton, M., & Kagan, C. (2008). *Societal case formulation*. Available at www.compsy.org.uk/Societal%20case%20formulation%20expanded%20version%202008.pdf.

Burton, M., & Kagan, C.M. (2007). Psychologists and torture: More than a question of interrogation. *The Psychologist*, 20(8), 484–487.

Burton, M., and Kagan, C. (2006). Decoding Valuing People. *Disability and Society*, 21(4), 219–313.

Burton, M., & Kagan, C. (2005). Liberation social psychology: Learning from Latin America. *Journal of Community and Applied Social Psychology*, 15(1), 63–78.

Burton, M., & Kagan, C. (2003). Community psychology: Why this gap in Britain? *History and Philosophy of Psychology*, 4(2), 10–23.

Burton, M., & Kagan, C. (2000). *Edge effects, resource utilisation and community psychology*. Paper presented to European Community Psychology Conference, Bergen, Norway. Available at www.compsy.org.uk/edge.htm.

Burton, M., & Kagan, C. (1998). Complementarism versus incommensurability in psychological research methodology. In M. Cheung-Chung (Ed.), *Current trends in history and philosophy of psychology*. Leicester, England: British Psychological Society.

Burton, M., & Kagan, C. (1996). Rethinking empowerment: Shared action against powerlessness. In I. Parker and R. Spears (Eds.), *Psychology and society: Radical theory and practice*. London, England: Pluto Press.

Burton, M., & Kagan, C. (1995). *Social skills and people with learning disabilities: A social capability approach*. London, England: Chapman and Hall.

Burton, M., & Kagan, C. (1982). Looking at environments (i). The physical and social environments of the mental health services. *Nursing Mirror*, August.

Burton, M., & Kellaway, M. (Eds.). (1998). *Developing and managing high quality services for people with learning disabilities*. Aldershot, England: Ashgate.

Burton, M., Irvine, B., & Emanuel, J. (2014). *The viable economy* (1st ed.). Manchester, England: Steady State Manchester. Available at https://steadystatemanchester.files.wordpress.com/2014/11/the-viable-economy-master-document-v4-final.pdf.

Burton, M., Kagan, C.M., & Duckett, P. (2012). *Making the psychological political: Challenges for community psychology*. Presented at the 2nd International Conference of Community Psychology 2008, Lisbon. *Global Journal of Community Psychology Practice*. 3(4), online.

Burton, M., Boyle, S., Harris, C., & Kagan, C. (2007). Community psychology in Britain. In S. Reich, M. Riemer, I. Prilleltensky & M. Montero (Eds.), *International community psychology: History and theories*. New York, NY: Springer.

Call for Real Action Collective (2009). *Call for real action: First report*. Available at http://calltorealaction.wordpress.com/first-report/.

Camarotti, M.H., Siva, M.H., Medeiros, R.A., Lins, R.A., Barros, P.M., Camorotti, J., & Rodgruigues, A. (2004). Terapia comunitaria: Relato de la experiencia en Brasilio-Distrito Federal [Community therapy: Report of an experience in Brasilia-Distrito Federal]. In A. Sanchez Vidal, A. Zambrano Constanzo & M. Palacín Lois (Eds.), *Psicología comunitaria Europa: Communidad, poder, ética y volores* [European community psychology: Community, power, ethics and values] (pp. 362–376). Barcelona, Spain: Publicacions de la Universitat de Barcelona.

Campbell, C.D. (2000). Social structure, space, and sentiment: Searching for common ground in sociological conceptions of community. In Chekki, D.A. (Ed.), *Community structure and dynamics at the dawn of the new millennium*. Connecticut: JAI Press Inc.

Campbell, C., & Jovchelovitch, S. (2000). Health, community and development. *Journal of Community and Applied Social Psychology*, 10, 255–270.

Campbell, C., & Murray, M. (2004). Community health psychology: Promoting analysis and action for social change. *Journal of Health Psychology*, 9(2), 187–195.

Canagarajah, A.S. (1996). 'Nondiscursive' requirements in academic publishing, material resources of periphery scholars, and the politics of knowledge production. *Written Communication*, 13, 435–472.

Carlquist, E., Nafstad, H.E., & Blakar, R.M. (2007). Community psychology in a Scandinavian welfare society: The case of Norway. In S.M. Reich, M. Riemer, I. Prilleltensky & M. Montero (Eds.), *International community psychology* (pp. 282–298). Boston, MA: Springer. https://doi.org/10.1007/978-0-387-49500-2_14.

Carmen, R. (2000). A future for the excluded? Learning from Brazil. *Development, 43*, 47–50.

Carmen, R., & Sobrado, M. (2000). *A future for the excluded: Job creation and income generation by the poor. Clodomir Santos de Morais and the organization workshop*. London, England: Zed Books.

Carson, R. (1962). *Silent Spring*. New York, NY: Houghton Mifflin.

Case, A.D. (2017). Reflexivity in counterspaces fieldwork. *American Journal of Community Psychology, 60*(3–4), 398–405.

Chatterjee, H.J., & Camic, P.M. (2015). The health and well-being potential of museums and art galleries. *Arts & Health, 7*(3), 183–186. doi:10.1080/17533015.2015.1065594.

Checkland, P., & Scholes, J. (1990). *Soft systems methodology in action*. Chichester, England: John Wiley.

Cheong, P.H. (2006). Communication context, social cohesion and social capital building among Hispanic immigrant families. *Community, Work and Family, 9*(3), 367–387.

Chilisa, B. (2012). *Indigenous research methodologies*. Thousand Oaks, CA: SAGE Publications.

Chilisa, B., Major, T.E., & Khudu-Petersen, K. (2017). Community engagement with a postcolonial, African-based relational paradigm. *Qualitative Research, 17*(3), 326–339.

Chomsky, N. (1992). *Chronicles of dissent: Interviews with Noam Chomsky by David Barsamlan*. Boston, MA: South End Press.

Chouchani, N., & Abed, M. (2018). Online social network analysis: Detection of communities of interest. *Journal of Intelligent Information Systems* (Aug 2018a), online. Available at https://link.springer.com/article/10.1007/s10844-018-0522-7.

Clennon, O. (2018). *Black scholarly activism between the academy and grassroots*. New York, NY: Palgrave Macmillan.

Clennon, O.D., Kagan, C., Lawthom, R., & Swindells, R. (2016). Participation in community arts: Lessons from the inner-city. *International Journal of Inclusive Education, 20*(3), 331–346.

Clifford, J., & Marcus, G. (1986). *Writing culture: The poetics and politics of ethnography*. Berkeley: University of California Press.

Cohen, A. (1986). *Symbolising community boundaries. Identity and diversity in British cultures*. Manchester, England: Manchester University Press.

Cohen, A.P. (1985). *The symbolic construction of community*. London, England: Routledge and Kegan Paul.

Coleman, R. (2000). Self-help and social change. In C. Kagan (Ed.), *Collective action and social change*. Retrieved from www.compsy.org.uk.

Collective of Authors. (2007). *The Birmingham Manifesto*. Available at www.compsy.org.uk/The%20Birmingham%20Manifesto.pdf.

Collins, K., & Ison, R. (2009). Jumping off Arnstein's ladder: Social learning as a new policy paradigm for climate change adaptation. *Environmental Policy and Governance, 19*(6), 358–373.

Committee on the Rights of Persons with Disabilities. (2017). Observations by the United Kingdom of Great Britain and Northern Ireland on the report of the Committee on its inquiry carried out under article 6 of the Optional Protocol. United Nations, Convention on the Rights of Persons with Disability. Available at https://tbinternet.ohchr.org/_layouts/treatybodyexternal/TBSearch.aspx?Lang=en&TreatyID=4&DocTypeCategoryID=7.

Cook, J.R. (2015). Using evaluation to effect social change: Looking through a community psychology lens. *American Journal of Evaluation, 36*(1), 107–117.

Cooke, B. (2001). The social psychological limits of participation? In B. Cooke & U. Kothari (Eds.), *Participation: The new tyranny?* London, England: Zed Books.

References

Cooke, B., & Kothari, U. (2001). *Participation: The new tyranny?* London, England: Zed Books.

Cooperrider, D.L., & Whitney, D.K. (2005). *Appreciative inquiry: A positive revolution in change.* San Francisco, CA: Berrett Koehler.

Corbett, C.J. (2011). Review of pracademics and community change: A true story of nonprofit development and social entrepreneurship during welfare reform by O. Cleveland and R. Wineburg [Lyceum Books; www.lyceumbooks.com]. *Global Journal of Community Psychology Practice, 1*(3), online.

Corbett, T., & Noyes, J.L. (2008). *Human services systems integration: Conceptual framework.* Institute for Research on Poverty Discussion Paper 133-98. Available at www.irp.wisc.edu/publications/dps/pdfs/dp133308.pdf.

Cornwall, A. (2008). Unpacking participation: Models, meanings and practices. *Community Development Journal, 43*(3), 269–283.

Cosgrove, L., & McHugh, M.C. (2000). Speaking for ourselves: Feminist methods and community psychology. *American Journal of Community Psychology, 28*, 816–838.

Craig, G., Gaus, A., Wilkinson, M., Skøivánková, K., & McQuade, A. (2007). *Contemporary slavery in the UK.* York, England: Joseph Rowntree Foundation.

Crespo, I., Pallí, C., Lalueza, J. (2002). Moving communities: A process of negotiation with a Gypsy minority for empowerment. *Community, Work and Family, 5*(1), 49–66.

Creswell, J.W. (2002). *Educational research: Planning, conducting, and evaluating quantitative and qualitative research.* Upper Saddle River, NJ: Merrill-Pearson Education.

Crosby, A. (2009). Anatomy of a workshop: Women's struggles for transformative participation in Latin America. *Feminism and Psychology, 19*(3), 343–353.

Crow, G., Allan, G., & Summers, M. (2001). Changing perspectives on the insider/outsider distinction in community sociology. *Community, Work and Family, 4*(1), 29–48.

Crowther, J., Martin, I., & Shaw, M. (1999). *Popular education and social movements in Scotland today.* Leicester, England: NIACE.

Dabelstein, N. (2003). Evaluation capacity development: Lessons learned. *Evaluation, 9*(3), 365–369.

Daher, M., & Haz, A.M. (2011). Changing meanings through art: A systematization of a psychosocial intervention with Chilean women in urban poverty situation. *American Journal of Community Psychology, 47*(3–4), 322–334.

D'Alisa, G., Demaria, F., & Kallis, G. (Eds.). (2014). *Degrowth: A vocabulary for a new era.* Abingdon, England: Routledge.

Dalton, J., & Wolfe, S. (2012). Education connection and the community practitioner: Competencies for community psychology practice – draft, August 15th 2012. *The Community Psychologist, 45*(4), 7–14.

Dalton, J., Elias, M., & Wandersman, A. (2001). *Community psychology: Linking individuals and communities.* Belmont, CA: Wadsworth.

Daly, H.E., & Farley, J. (2011). *Ecological economics: Principles and applications.* Washington, DC: Island Press.

Danziger, K. (1994). Does the history of psychology have a future? *Theory and Psychology, 4*, 467–484.

Danziger, K. (1990). *Constructing the subject: Historical origins of psychological research.* Cambridge, England: Cambridge University Press.

Darling, F.F. (1970). *Wilderness and plenty.* London, England: Oxford UP.

Davey, B. (2015). *An introduction to ecological economics. University of Nottingham/FEASTA.* Available at www.feasta.org/2015/09/14/an-introduction-to-ecological-economics/.

Davies, N. (1998). *Dark heart: The shocking truth about hidden Britain.* London, England: Vintage Press.

Deal, M. (2003). Disabled people's attitudes toward other impairment groups: A hierarchy of impairments. *Disability and Society, 18*(7), 897–910.

Dearing, R. (1997). *National Committee of Inquiry into Higher Education.* Norwich, England: HMSO.

Debord, G. (1983). *Society of the spectacle* (K. Knabb, Trans.). London, England: Rebel Press.

Değirmencioğlu, S.M. (2007). Moving but not yet talking: Community psychology in Turkey. In S.M. Reich, M. Riemer, I. Prilleltensky & M. Montero (Eds.), *International community psychology* (pp. 356–362). Boston, MA: Springer. https://doi.org/10.1007/978-0-387-49500-2_19.

Department of Health (2001). *Valuing People: A strategy for learning disability services in the 21st century* (Cm 5086). London, England: Department of Health.

Desai, P., & Riddlestone, S. (2002). *Bioregional solutions: For living on one planet.* Schumacher Briefings 8. Dartington, England: Green Books.

Devine, P., Pearmain, A., & Purdy, D. (Eds.). (2009). *Feelbad Britain: How to make it better.* London, England: Lawrence and Wishart.

Dewey, J. (1946). *The problems of men.* New York, NY: Philosophical Library.

Dewey, J. (1916/1966). *Democracy and education. An introduction to the philosophy of education.* New York, NY: Free Press. (First published in 1916 in New York by Macmillan).

Douglas, K., & Carless, D. (2013). An invitation to performative research. *Methodological Innovations Online, 8*(1), 53–64.

Doyal, L., & Gough, I. (1991). *A theory of human need.* Basingstoke, England: Macmillan.

Duckett, Paul (2012). Seroxat: A story about UK pharmacological corporations, UK politicians, academics and other corrupt bastards. In C. Walker, K. Johnson & L. Cunningham (Eds.), *Community psychology and the socio-economics of mental distress: International perspectives* (pp. 16–31). Basingstoke, England: Palgrave Macmillan.

Duckett, P.S. (2009). Critical reflections on key community psychology concepts: Off-setting our capitalist emissions? *Forum Gemeindepsychologie, 14*(2). Available online from: www.gemeinde psychologie.de/fg-2-2009_06.html.

Duckett, P.S. (2005). Globalised violence, community psychology and the bombing and occupation of Afghanistan and Iraq. *Journal of Community and Applied Social Psychology, 15*(5), 414–423.

Duckett, P. (2002). Community psychology, millennium volunteers and UK higher education: A disruptive triptych? *Journal of Community and Applied Social Psychology, 12*(2), 94–107.

Duckett, P.S. (1998). What are you doing here? 'Non disabled' people and the disability movement, a response to Fran Bransfield. *Disability and Society, 13*(4), 625–628.

Duckett, P.S., & Schinkel, M. (2008). Community psychology and injustice in the criminal justice system. *Journal of Community and Applied Social Psychology, 18*, 518–526.

Duckett, P., Sixsmith, C., & Kagan, C. (2008). Researching pupil well-being in UK secondary schools: Community psychology and the politics of research. *Childhood, 15*(1), 91–108.

Duff, W.M., Flinn, A., Suurtamm, K.E., & Wallace, D.A. (2013). Social justice impact of archives: A preliminary investigation. *Archival Science, 13*(4), 317–348.

Duncan, G., Zlotowitz, S., & Stubbs, J. (2017). *Meeting us where we're at. Learning from INTEGRATE's work with excluded young people.* London, England: Centre for Mental Health. Available at www.centreformentalhealth.org.uk/sites/default/files/centreformentalhealth_meeting_us_where_were_at_briefing_.pdf.

Duncan, N., Bowman, B., Naidoo, A., Pillay, J., & Roos, V. (2007). *Community psychology: Analysis, context and action.* Capetown, South Africa: UCT Press.

Durkheim, É. (1894/1982). *The rules of sociological method and selected texts on sociology and its method.* London, England: Macmillan (Original publication 1894).

Durose, C., & Richardson, L. (2015). *Designing public policy for co-production: Theory, practice and change.* Bristol, England: Policy Press.

Dussel, E. (2013). *Ethics of liberation in the age of globalization and exclusion* (A.A. Vallega, Ed.). Durham, NC: Duke University Press.

References

Dussel, E. (2008). *Twenty theses on politics*. Durham, NC: Duke University Press.

Dussel, E. (2000). Europe, modernity and eurocentrism. *Nepantla: View from the South*, *1*(3), 465–478.

Dussel, E. (1995). *The invention of the Americas: Eclipse of 'the other' and the myth of modernity*. New York, NY: Continuum.

Dzidic, P., Breen, L.J., & Bishop, B.J. (2013). Are our competencies revealing our weaknesses? A critique of community psychology practice competencies. *Global Journal of Community Psychology Practice*, *4*(4), 1–10, online.

Edge, I., Kagan, C., & Stewart, A. (2004). Living poverty: Surviving on the edge. *Clinical Psychology*, *38*(June), 28–31.

Ellis, J. (2009). *Monitoring and evaluation in the third sector: Meeting accountability and learning needs*. Paper presented to NCVO/VSSN Conference: Researching the Voluntary Sector, 2009. www.ces-vol.org.uk retrieved 29 September 2009.

Engeström, Y. (1999). Activity theory and individual and social transformation. In Y. Engeström, R. Miettinen & R-L. Punamäki (Eds.), *Perspectives on activity theory* (pp. 19–38). Cambridge University Press.

Engeström, Y., & Miettinen, R. (1999). Introduction. In Y. Engeström, R. Miettinen & R-L. Punamäki (Eds.), *Perspectives on Activity Theory* (pp. 1–16). Cambridge University Press.

Escobar, A. (2007). Worlds and knowledges otherwise: The Latin American modernity/coloniality research program. *Cultural Studies*, *21*(2), 179–210.

Estrada, A.M., Ibarra, C., & Sarmiento, E. (2007). Regulation and control of subjectivity and private life in the context of armed conflict in Colombia. *Community, Work and Family*, *10*(3), 257–281.

European Environment Agency. (2013). *Late lessons from early warnings: Science, precaution, innovation* (Publication 1/2013). Copenhagen, Denmark: European Environment Agency. Available at www.eea.europa.eu/publications/late-lessons-2.

Evans, K. (1997). "It's alright round here if you're local": Community in the inner city. In P. Hoggett (Ed.), *Contested communities: Experiences, struggles, policies* (pp. 33–50). Bristol, England: Policy Press.

Evans, S.D., Malhotra, K., & Headley, A.M. (2013). Promoting learning and critical reflexivity through an organizational case study project. *Journal of Prevention & Intervention in the Community*, *41*(2), 105–112.

Evans, S.D., Duckett, P., Lawthom, R., & Kivell, N. (2017). Positioning the critical in community psychology. In M.A. Bond, I. Serrano-García, C.B. Keys & M. Shinn (Eds.), *APA handbook of community psychology: Theoretical foundations, core concepts, and emerging challenges* (pp. 107–127). Washington, DC: American Psychological Association.

Falkembach, E.M.F., & Torres, A.C. (2015). Systematization of experiences: A practice of participatory research from Latin America. In H. Bradbury (Ed.), *The SAGE handbook of action research* (3rd ed., pp. 76–82). London, England: SAGE Publications Ltd.

Fals Borda, O. (1988). *Knowledge and people's power: Lessons with peasants in Nicaragua, Mexico and Colombia*. New York, NY: New Horizons Press.

Fals Borda, O., & Rahman, M.A. (1991). *Action and knowledge: Breaking the monopoly of power with participatory action-research*. London, England: Intermediate Technology Publications.

Fang, M.L., Sixsmith, J., Lawthom, R., Mountian, I., & Shahrin, A. (2015). Experiencing 'pathologized presence and normalized absence'; understanding health related experiences and access to health care among Iraqi and Somali asylum seekers, refugees and persons without legal status. *BMC Public Health*, *15*(1), online. Available at http://bmcpublichealth.biomedcentral.com/articles/10.1186/s12889-015-2279-z.

Fanon, F. (1967). *Black skins, white masks*. New York, NY: Grove.

Farias, L., & Perdomo, G. (2004). Moral dilemmas of community leaders and sense of community. *Journal of Prevention and Intervention in the Community*, *27*(1), 25–37.

Feeney, M. (2019). Tea in the Pot, 'third place' or social prescription? Exploring the positive impact on mental health of a voluntary women's group in Glasgow. In L. McGrath & P. Reavey (Eds.), *The handbook of mental health and space: Community and clinical applications*. Oxford, England: Routledge.

Felton, B.J., & Shinn, M. (1992). Social integration and social support: Moving 'social support' beyond the individual level. *Journal of Community Psychology, 20*(2), 103–115. doi:10.1002/1520-6629(199204)20:2<103::AID-JCOP2290200202>3.0.CO;2-4.

Ferreira Moura, J., Morais Ximenes, V., Camurça Cidade, E., & Barbosa Mepomuceno, B. (in press, 2019). *Psychosocial implication of poverty: Diversities and resistances*. New York, NY: Springer.

Fetterman, D., Rodríguez-Campos, L., Wandersman, A., & O'Sullivan, R.G. (2014). Collaborative, participatory, and empowerment evaluation: Building a strong conceptual foundation for stakeholder involvement approaches to evaluation (A response to Cousins, Whitmore, and Shulha, 2013). *American Journal of Evaluation, 35*(1), 144–148.

Fetterman, D.M., & Wandersman, A. (Eds.). (2005). *Empowerment evaluation principles in practice*. New York, NY: Guildford Press.

Filipe, A., Renedo, A., & Marston, C. (2017). The co-production of what? Knowledge, values, and social relations in health care. *PLOS Biology, 15*(5), e2001403. doi:10.1371/journal.pbio.2001403.

Fisher, A.T., Sonn, C., & Bishop, B.J. (Eds.). (2002). *Psychological sense of community. Research, applications, and implications*. New York, NY: Springer.

Fisher, J., Lawthom, R., & Kagan, C. (2016). Delivering on the Big Society? Tensions in hosting community organisers. *Local Economy: The Journal of the Local Economy Policy Unit, 31*(4), 502–517.

Fisher, J., Lawthom, R., & Kagan, C. (2014). Revolting tales of migrant workers and community organisers: A UK community psychological perspective. *Australian Community Psychologist, 26*(1), 37–50.

Fisher, J., Lawthom, R., Hartley, S., Koivunen, E., & Yeowell, G. (2018). *Evaluation of Men in Sheds for Age UK Cheshire final report*. Manchester, England: Manchester Metropolitan University.

Flores, J.M. (2009). Praxis and liberation in the context of Latin American theory. In M. Montero & C. Sonn (Eds.), *Psychology of liberation: Theory and applications*. New York, NY: Springer.

Fook, J., & Askeland, G.A. (2006). The 'critical' in critical reflection. In S. White, J. Fook & F. Gardner (Eds.), *Critical reflection in health and social care*. Maidenhead, England: Open University Press/McGraw Hill Education.

Foot, J., & Hopkins, T. (2010). *A glass half-full: How an asset approach can improve community health and well-being* (p. 32). London, England: IDeA (Improvement and Development Agency). Available at www.assetbasedconsulting.net/uploads/publications/A%20glass%20half%20full.pdf.

Ford, J. (1995). Middle England: In debt and insecure? *Poverty, 92*, 11–14.

Foster-Fishman, P.G., & Behrens, T.R. (2007). Systems change reborn: Rethinking our theories, methods, and efforts in human services reform and community-based change. *American Journal of Community Psychology, 39*(3/4), 191–196.

Foster-Fishman, P.G., Nowell, B., & Yang, H. (2007). Putting the system back into systems change: A framework for understanding and changing organizational and community systems. *American Journal of Community Psychology, 39*(3/4), 197–216.

Foster-Fishman, P., Berkowitz, B., Lounsbury, D.W., Jacobson, S., & Allen, N.A. (2001). Building collaborative capacity in community coalitions: A review and integrative framework. *American Journal Community Psychology, 29*(2). 241–261.

Foucault, M. (1980). Two lectures. In C. Gordon (Ed.), *Power/knowledge: Selected interviews*. New York, NY: Pantheon.

Foucault, M. (1976). *The history of sexuality, Volume 1: An introduction* (R. Hurley, Trans.). London, England: Penguin.

References

Foweraker, J. (1995). *Theorizing social movements*. London, England: Pluto.

Francescato, D. (2000). Community psychology intervention strategies as tools to enhance participation in projects promoting sustainable development and quality of life. *Gemeindepsychologie*, 6(2), 49–58.

Francescato, D., & Aber, M.S. (2015). Learning from organizational theory to build organizational empowerment. *Journal of Community Psychology*, 43(6), 717–738. doi:10.1002/jcop.21753.

Francescato, D., & Zani, B. (2013). Community psychology practice competencies in undergraduate and graduate programs in Italy. *Global Journal of Community Psychology Practice*, 4(4), 1–12, online.

Francescato, D., Arcidiacono, C., Albanesi, C., & Mannarini, T. (2007). Community psychology in Italy: Past developments and future perspectives. In S.M. Reich, M. Riemer, I. Prilleltensky & M. Montero (Eds.), *International community psychology* (pp. 263–281). Boston, MA: Springer. https://doi.org/10.1007/978-0-387-49500-2_13.

Francescato, D., Gelli, B., Mannarini, T., & Taurino, A. (2004). Community development: Action research through profiles analysis in a small town in Southern Italy. In A. Sanchez Vidal, A. Zambrano Constanzo & M. Palacin Lois (Eds.), *Psicologia comunitaria Europa: Communidad, poder, ética y valores* (pp. 247–261). Barcelona, Spain: Publicacions Universitat de Barcelona.

Freire, P. (1994). *Pedagogy of hope*. New York, NY: Routledge.

Freire, P. (1972a). *Pedagogy of the oppressed*. Harmondsworth, England: Penguin.

Freire, P. (1972b). *Cultural action for freedom*. Harmondsworth, England: Penguin.

Freire, P., & Faundez, A. (1989). *Learning to question: A pedagogy of liberation*. Geneva, Switzerland: World Council of Churches.

Freitas, M.F. de Q. (1994). Prácticas en comunidad y psicología comunitaria [Practices in community and community psychology]. In M. Montero (Ed.), *Psicología Social Comunitaria: Teoría, método y experiencia*. Guadalajara, Mexico: Universidad de Guadalajara.

Freitas, M.F.Q. (2009). (In) Coerências entre prácticas psicossocias em comunidade e projetos de transormação social: Aproximaçãos entre as psicologias socais da libertação e comunitaria. *Psico*, 36(1), 47–54.

Freitas, M.F.Q. (2000). Voices from the South: The construction of Brazilian community social psychology. *Journal of Community and Applied Social Psychology*, 10(4), 315–326.

French, J.R.P., & Raven, B.H. (1959). The bases of social power. In D. Cartwright (Ed.), *Studies in social power*. Ann Arbour, MI: University Michigan Press.

French, R.S. (2019). *Policy and politics: Evidence-based policy – Older than advertised and weaker than we could wish*. Available at https://discoversociety.org/2019/01/02/policy-and-politics-evidence-based-policy-older-than-advertised-and-weaker-than-we-could-wish/.

Fricker, M. (2007). *Epistemic injustice: Power and the ethics of knowing*. Oxford, England: Oxford University Press.

Fryer, D. (2008). Some questions about 'the history of community psychology'. *Journal of Community Psychology*, 36(5), 572–586.

Fukuoka, M. (1985a). *The one-straw revolution: An introduction to natural farming*. New York, NY: Bantam Books.

Fukuoka, M. (1985b). *The natural way of farming: The theory and practice of green philosophy*. Tokyo, Japan: Japan Publications, 1985. Available at www.rivendellvillage.org/Natural-Way-Of-Farming-Masanobu-Fukuoka-Green-Philosophy.pdf.

Fynn, A. (2013). Using appreciative inquiry (AI) to evaluate an education support ngo in Soweto. *Psychology in Society*, 44, online.

Gaotlhobogwe, M., Major, T.E., Koloi-Keaikitse, S., & Chilisa, B. (2018). Conceptualizing evaluation in African contexts: Conceptualizing evaluation in African contexts. *New Directions for Evaluation*, 2018(159), 47–62.

Gates, A. (1998). *Letter from Alice Gates*. Available at www2.oberlin.edu/external/EOG/SEPA/Gates-letter.html.

Geertz, C. (1973). *Thick description: Towards an interpretative theory of culture*. New York, NY: Basic Books.

Gergen, M., & Gergen, K.J. (2011). Performative social science and psychology. *Forum Qualitative Sozialforschung/Forum: Qualitative Social Research*, 12(1), online. Available at www.qualitative-research.net/index.php/fqs/article/view/1595.

Gilchrist, A. (2004). *The well connected community: A networking approach to community development*. Bristol, England: Policy Press.

Global Footprint Network. (n.d.). *Ecological footprint: Global Footprint Network*. Available at www.footprintnetwork.org/our-work/ecological-footprint/.

Glyn, A. (2006). *Capitalism unleashed*. Oxford, England: Oxford University Press.

González Rey, F. (2017). The topic of subjectivity in psychology: Contradictions, paths and new alternatives. *Journal for the Theory of Social Behaviour*, 47(4), 502–521.

González Rey, F. (2015). Human motivation in question: Discussing emotions, motives, and subjectivity from a cultural-historical standpoint: Human motivation in question. *Journal for the Theory of Social Behaviour*, 45(4), 419–439.

Goodings, L., & Tucker, I. (2019). Social media and mental health: A topological approach. In L. McGrath & P. Reavey (Eds.), *The handbook of mental health and space: Community and clinical applications*. Oxford, England: Routledge.

Goodley, D., & Lawthom, R. (2011). Disability, community and empire: Indigenous psychologies and social psychoanalytic possibilities *International Journal of Inclusive Education*, 15(1), 101–115.

Goodley, D.A., & Lawthom, R. (2005). Epistemological journeys in participatory action research: Alliances between community psychology and disability studies. *Disability and Society*, 20(2), 135–151.

Gough, I. (2017). *Heat, greed and human need: Climate change, capitalism and sustainable wellbeing*. Cheltenham, England: Edward Elgar Publishing.

Gramsci, A. (1971). *Selections from the prison notebooks* (Q.H. a. G.N. Smith, Trans.). London, England: Lawrence and Wishart.

Gramsci, A. (1968). Soviets in Italy (Writing from 1919 and 1920). *New Left Review* (1st series), 51, 28–58.

Gray-Rosendale, L.A., & Harootunian, G. (2003). *Framing feminisms: Investigating histories, theories, and moments of fracture*. New York: State University of New York Press.

Gregory, A. (2000). Problematizing participation. A critical review of approaches to participation in evaluation theory. *Evaluation*, 6(2), 179–199.

Gregory, A. (1997). Evaluation practice and the tricky issue of coercive contexts. *Systems Practice*, 10(5), 589–609.

Gridley, H., & Breen, L. (2008). So far and yet so near? Community psychology in Australia. In S. Reich, M. Riemer, I. Prilleltensky & M. Montero (Eds.), *International community psychology: History and theories*. New York, NY: Springer.

Grieger, I., & Ponterotto, J.G. (1998). Challenging intolerance. In C.C. Lee & G.R. Walz (Eds.), *Social action: A mandate for counsellors* (pp. 17–50). Alexandra, VA: American Counselling Association and ERIC Counselling and Student Services Clearinghouse.

Griseri, P. (1988). *Managing values: Ethical change in organisations*. Basingstoke, England: Macmillan.

Grosfoguel, R. (2008). Transmodernity, border thinking, and global coloniality: Decolonizing political economy and postcolonial studies. *Revista Crítica de Ciências Sociais*, 80. Available from *Eurozine* at www.eurozine.com/transmodernity-border-thinking-and-global-coloniality/?pdf.

Grover, R. (1995). *Communities that care: Intentional communities of attachment as a third path in community care*. Brighton, England: Pavilion Publishing.

Guba, E.G., & Lincoln, Y.S. (2001). *Guidelines and checklist for constructivist (A.K.A. fourth generation) evaluation*. Evaluation Checklists Project. www.wmich.edu/evalctr/checklists/constructivisteval. pdf retrieved 2 January 2009.

Guba, E.G., & Lincoln, Y.S. (1989). *Fourth generation evaluation*, Newbury Park, CA, Sage Publications.

Gutiérrez, G. (1988). *A theology of liberation*. Maryknoll, NY: Orbis Books (Revised from first English translation in 1973 published by Orbis from the original Teologia de la liberación, Perspectivas: CEP, Lima).

Gutiérrez, G. (1973). *A theology of liberation* (M. O'Connell, Trans.). New York, NY: Orbis.

Habermas, J. (1984). *The theory of communicative action: Reason and rationalisation in society*. Boston, MA: Beacon Press.

Hagan, T., & Smail, D. (1997). Power-mapping: Background and basic methodology. *Journal of Community and Applied Social Psychology*, 7, 257–267.

Hallsworth, M., & Sanders, M. (2016). Nudge: Recent developments in behavioural science and public policy. In F. Spotswood (Ed.), *Beyond behaviour change: Key issues, interdisciplinary approaches and future directions*. Bristol, England: Policy Press.

Halpern, D. (2019, January 24). Chances are you've been nudged by the government without realising. *The Times*. Available at www.thetimes.co.uk/article/chances-are-you-ve-been-nudged-by-the-government-without-realising-vznvb2gq0?utm_source=newsletter&utm_campaign=newsletter_119&utm_medium=email&utm_content=119_5010928&CMP=TNLEmail_118918_5010928_119.

Hamber, B., Masilela, T.C., & Terre Blanche, M. (2001). Towards a Marxist community psychology: Radical tools for community psychological analysis and practice. In M. Seedat (Ed.), N. Duncan & S. Lazarus (Cons. Eds.), *Community psychology: Theory, method and practice* (pp. 51–66). Cape Town, South Africa: Oxford University Press.

Hanks, K., & Belliston, L. (2006). *Rapid Viz: A new method for the rapid visualization of ideas*. Menlo Park, CA: Crisp Publications.

Hanley, L. (2017). *Estates: An intimate history*. London, England: Granta Books.

Harré, N. (2011). *Psychology for a better world. Strategies to inspire sustainability*. Auckland, New Zealand: Auckland University Press. Available at http://elibrary.bsu.az/books_400/N_350.pdf.

Harré, N., Madden, H., Brooks, R., & Goodman, J. (2017). Sharing values as a foundation for collective hope. *Journal of Social and Political Psychology*, 5(2), 342–366.

Harré, R. (1993). *Social being* (2nd ed.). Oxford, England: Blackwell.

Harrison, A.K. (2008). Racial authenticity in rap music and hip hop. *Sociology Compass*, 2(6), 1783–1800.

Harvey, D. (2007). *A brief history of neoliberalism*. Oxford, England: Oxford University Press.

Harvey, D. (2005a). *Spaces of neoliberalization*. Heidelberg, Germany: University of Heidelberg Press.

Harvey, D. (2005b). The sociological and geographical imaginations. *International Journal of Politics, Culture and Society*, 18(3/4), 211–255.

Hassan, A., Fatimilehin, I., & Kagan, C. (2019). 'Geedka shirka' (under the tree): Cultural, migratory and community spaces for preventive interventions with Somali men and their families. In L. McGrath & P. Reavey (Eds.), *The handbook of mental health and space: Community and clinical applications*. Oxford, England: Routledge.

Hawe, P., Shiell, A., & Riley, T. (2009). Theorising interventions as events in systems. *American Journal of Community Psychology*, 43(3–4), 267–276.

Haworth, J.T., & Roberts, K. (2007). Leisure: The next 25 years. For *Science review for the DTI Foresight project on Mental Capital and Mental Wellbeing*. London, England: DTI.

Hawtin, M., Hughes, G., & Percy-Smith, J. (1994). *Community profiling: Auditing social needs*. Buckingham, England: Open University Press.

Hernández, E. (2004). Metadecision: Training community leaders for effective decision making. *Journal of Prevention and Intervention in the Community*, 27(1), 53–70.

Hillery, G.A. (1955). Definitions of community: Areas of agreement. *Rural Sociology 20*, 111.

Himmelman, A. (2001). On coalitions and the transformation of power relations: Collaborative betterment and collaborative empowerment. *American Journal of Community Psychology, 29*(2), 277–284.

Hodgson, F.C., & Turner, J. (2003). Participation not consumption: The need for new participatory practices to address transport and social exclusion. *Transport Policy, 10*(4), 265–272.

Holland, S. (1992). From social abuse to social action. In J. Ussher & P. Nicholson (Eds.), *Gender issues in clinical psychology* (pp. 68–77). London, England: Routledge.

Holland, S. (1991). From private symptom to public action. *Feminism and Psychology, 1*(1), 58–62.

Hollander, N.C. (1997). *Love in a time of hate: Liberation psychology in Latin America.* New Brunswick, NJ: Rutgers University Press.

Holmgren, D. (2008). *Future scenarios: Mapping the cultural implications of peak oil and climate change.* www.futurescenarios.org/, retrieved 3 October 2009.

Holmgren, D. (2007). *Essence of permaculture.* Hepburn, Australia: Holmgren Design Services. Available at https://holmgren.com.au/essence-of-permaculture-free/.

Hook, D., Kiguwa, P., & Mkhize, N. (2004). *Introduction to critical psychology.* Lansdowne, South Africa: UCT Press.

Howlett, M., Kekez, A., & Poocharoen, O.-O. (2017). Understanding co-production as a policy tool: Integrating new public governance and comparative policy theory. *Journal of Comparative Policy Analysis: Research and Practice, 19*(5), 487–501.

Hu, C., Zhao, L., & Huang, J. (2015). Achieving self-congruency? Examining why individuals reconstruct their virtual identity in communities of interest established within social network platforms. *Computers in Human Behavior, 50*, 465–475.

Humphrey, J.C. (2000). Cracks in the feminist mirror: research and reflections on lesbians and gay men working together. *Feminist Review, 66*, 95–130.

Hutton, W. (2007, February 18). 'Open the gates and free people from Britain's ghettos', *The Observer*; also available online at http://observer.guardian.co.uk/comment/story/0,2015638,00.html (Accessed 5 June 2009).

Hutton, W. (2002). *The world we are in.* London, England: Little Brown.

Hutton, W. (1995). *The state we're in.* London, England: Little Brown.

Hytner, B., D'Cocodia, L., Kagan, C., Spencer, L., & Yates, W. (1981). *Report of the Moss Side Enquiry to the Leader of the Greater Manchester Council.* Manchester, England: Greater Manchester Council.

Ife, J. (1995). *Community development. Creating community alternatives: Vision, analysis and practice.* Melbourne, Australia: Longman.

Illich, I., Zola, I., McKnight, J., Caplan, J., & Shaiken, S. (1977). *Disabling professions.* London, England: Marion Boyars.

Imagine. (2016). *Marsh Farm organisation workshop: Evaluation report.* Bristol, England: Imagine/Office for Civil Society. Available at www.corganisers.org.uk/what-is-community-organising/stories/marsh-farm-organisation-workshop/.

Intergovernmental Panel on Climate Change (IPCC). (2018). *Global warming of 1.5°C: Summary for policymakers.* Geneva, Switzerland: United Nations Intergovernmental Panel on Climate Change. Available at www.ipcc.ch/report/sr15/.

Jackson, K.T., Burgess, S., Toms, F., & Cuthbertson, E.L. (2018). Community engagement: Using feedback loops to empower residents and influence systemic change in culturally diverse communities. *Global Journal of Community Psychology Practice, 9*(2), 1–21.

Jackson, L., Peters, M.A., Benade, L., Devine, N., Arndt, S., Forster, D., ... Ozoliņš, J. (John). (2018). Is peer review in academic publishing still working? *Open Review of Educational Research, 5*(1), 95–112.

Jackson, M. (2003). *Systems thinking: Creative holism for managers*. Chichester, England: John Wiley.

Jackson, T. (2017). *Prosperity without growth: Foundations for the economy of tomorrow* (2nd ed.). London, England: Routledge. Preface available online at www.book2look.com/embed/eFJiPjyMKG&euid=68185891&ruid=68174127&referurl=www.routledge.com&clickedby=H5W&biblettype=html5.

Jahoda, M., Lazarsfeld, P., & Zeisel, H. (2002). *The sociology of an unemployed community*. Chicago, IL: Aldine.

Jambeck, J.R., Geyer, R., Wilcox, C., Siegler, T.R., Perryman, M., Andrady, A., ... Law, K.L. (2015). Plastic waste inputs from land into the ocean. *Science, 347*(6223), 768–771.

Jameson, F. (2009). Ideological analysis: A handbook. In F. Jameson (Ed.). *Valences of the dialectic* (pp. 215–363). London, England: Verso.

Janis, I. (1982). *Groupthink* (2nd ed.). Boston, MA: Houghton-Mifflin.

Jara, O. (2012). Systematization of experiences, research and evaluation: Three different approaches. *International Journal for Global Development Education Research (Revista Internacional sobre Investigación En Educación Global y para el Desarrollo)*, 1(February), 71–84.

Jara, O. (n.d.). *Orientaciones teórico-practicas para la sistematización de experiencias* [A theory-practice guide to the systematisation of experiences]. San José, Costa Rica: Centro de Estudios y Publicaciones Alforja. Available at http://centroderecursos.alboan.org/ebooks/0000/0788/6_JAR_ORI.pdf.

Johnson, B. (1992). *Polarity management: Identifying and managing unsolvable problems*. Amherst, MA: HRD Press. www.polaritymanagement.com.

Johnson, D. (2000). Laying the foundation: Capacity building for participatory monitoring and evaluation. In M. Estrella, J. Blauert, D. Campilan, J. Gaventa, J. Gonsalves, I. Gujit, D. Johnson & R. Ricafort (Eds.), *Learning from change: Issues and experiences in participatory monitoring and evaluation* (pp. 217–228). London, England: Intermediate Technology Publications.

Johnson, D.W., & Johnson, F.P. (1996). *Joining together: Group theory and group skills* (6th ed.). Boston, MA: Allyn and Bacon.

Johnston, C., & Mooney, G. (2007). 'Problem' people, 'problem' places? New Labour and council estates. In R. Atkinson & G. Helms (Eds.), *Securing an urban renaissance*. Bristol, England: Policy Press.

Joseph Rowntree Foundation (JRF). (2018). *Budget 2018: Tackling the rising tide of in-work poverty*. York, England: Joseph Rowntree Foundation. Available at www.jrf.org.uk/report/budget-2018-tackling-rising-tide-work-poverty.

Jovchelovitch, S. (2007). *Knowledge in context: Representations, community and culture*. London, England: Routledge.

Junqué, M., & Baird, K.S. (Eds.). (2018). *Ciudades sin miedo: guía del movimiento municipalista global* (Primera edición). Barcelona, Spain: Icaria Editorial (English edition is *Fearless cities: Guide to the global municipalist movement*. (2019). London, England: New Internationalist).

Jurgenson, N. (2009). Facebook, the transumer and liquid capitalism. *Sociology Lens*. www.sociologylens.net/article-types/opinion/facebook-the-transumer-and-liquid-capitalism/3108.

Kagan, C. (2013). *Co-production of research: For good or ill?* Presented at the Postgraduate Policy Research Conference, Edge Hill University. Available at https://e-space.mmu.ac.uk/609524/1/Co%20production%20reserach%20ormskirk%20b%2013.pdf.

Kagan, C. (2008). Broadening the boundaries of psychology through community psychology. *Psychology Teaching Review, 14*, 28–31.

Kagan, C. (2007). Working at the 'edge': Making use of psychological resources through collaboration. *The Psychologist, 20*(4), 224–227.

Kagan, C. (2006a). *Making a difference: Participation, well-being and levers for change* (intelligence report). Liverpool, England: RENEW.

Kagan, C. (2006b, January 11). Health hazards. *New Start*. Available at www.compsy.org.uk/stress.html.

Kagan, C. (2002). *Have we been here before? A community psychological perspective on regeneration and empowerment*. Paper presented to Harvester Housing Seminar, Manchester, England.

Kagan, C. (1997a). *Agencies and advocacies: Experience in the North West*. Whalley, England: North West Training and Development Team.

Kagan, C. (1997b). *Regional development for inclusion: Community development and learning disabled people in the North West of England*. Manchester, England: IOD Research Group.

Kagan, C. (1990). *Network development: An experiment in case management?* Whalley, England: North Western Regional Health Authority (N.W.D.T.).

Kagan, C. (1986). *Towards leisure integration and advocacy (BLISS)*. Manchester, England: Manchester Polytechnic.

Kagan, C., & Burton, M.H. (2018). Putting the 'social' into sustainability science. In W. Leal Filho (Ed.), *Handbook of sustainability science and research* (pp. 285–298). Cham, Switzerland: Springer International Publishing.

Kagan, C., & Burton, M. (2014). Culture, identity and alternatives to the consumer culture. *Educar Em Revista (Brazil)*, 53(Dossier: Educação, Cotidiano e Participação: desafios e contribuições para a formação). Available at http://ojs.c3sl.ufpr.br/ojs/index.php/educar/article/view/36583.

Kagan, C., & Burton, M. (2010). Marginalisation. In Nelson & Prilleltensky (Eds.), *Community psychology: In pursuit of liberation and well-being* (2nd ed.). Basingstoke, England: Palgrave Macmillan.

Kagan, C., & Burton, M. (2000). Prefigurative action research: An alternative basis for critical psychology. *Annual Review of Critical Psychology*, 2, 73–87.

Kagan, C., & Diamond, J. (2019). *Rethinking university-community engagement: Reflections on higher education policy and practice in England*. London, England: Palgrave Macmillan.

Kagan, C., & Duggan, K. (2011). Creating community cohesion: The power of using innovative methods to facilitate engagement and genuine partnership. *Social Policy and Society*, 10(03), 393–404.

Kagan, C., & Duggan, K. (2010). *Birley Fields development: Impact on the local community. Working paper 1: Context setting*. Manchester, England: Research Institute for Health and Social Change. Available at https://e-space.mmu.ac.uk/117657/1/978-1-900139-43-4.pdf.

Kagan, C., & Duggan, K. (2009). *Breaking down barriers: Universities and communities working together. Urban regeneration: Making a Difference – Community Cohesion Thematic Evaluation Report*. Manchester, England: RIHSC. Available at https://e-space.mmu.ac.uk/83457/1/978-1-900139-29-8.pdf.

Kagan, C., & Friends of Hough End Hall. (2015). *Community alliances against big business*. Presented at the 2nd UK Community Psychology Festival, Manchester, England.

Kagan, C., & Kilroy, A. (2007). Community psychology and well-being. In J. Haworth & G. Hart (Eds.), *Wellbeing: Individual, community and social perspectives*. London, England: Palgrave Macmillan.

Kagan, C., & Lawthom, R. (2014). *From competencies to liberation*. Presented at the Symposium on Liberation Psychology, International Congress Community Psychology, Fortaleza, Brazil. Available at www.researchgate.net/publication/308967854_From_Competencies_to_Liberation_community_psychology_learning.

Kagan, C., & Lewis, S. (1995). Families, empowerment and social change: Empowerment and counter-hegemonic action. In S. Lewis, C. Kagan & M. Burton (Eds.), *Families, work and empowerment: Coalitions for social change*. Manchester, England: IOD Research Group. https://e-space.mmu.ac.uk/41686/.

Kagan, C., & Lewis, S. (1990). 'Where's your sense of humour?' Swimming against the tide in higher education. In E. Burman (Ed.), *Feminists and psychological practice*. London, England: Sage. Out of print but online at https://ericaburmancom.files.wordpress.com/2013/01/fppmerged.pdf.

Kagan, C., & Scott-Roberts, S. (2002). *Family based intervention for children with cerebral palsy and their inclusion in the community: Occupational and community psychological perspectives.* Manchester, England: COP Research Group. Available at https://e-space.mmu.ac.uk/41781/.

Kagan, C., & Siddiquee, A. (2005). *Review of the East Manchester Neighbourhood Nuisance Team.* RIHSC occasional papers 03/05. Manchester, England: RIHSC. Available at https://e-space.mmu.ac.uk/24693/.

Kagan, C., & Siddiquee, A. (2004). *Final report of evaluation of the Standing Conference for Community Development web-site.* RIHSC occasional papers. Manchester, England: RIHSC/SCCD. https://e-space.mmu.ac.uk/24636/.

Kagan, C., & Stewart, A. (2007). *The In Bloom competition: Gardening work as a community involvement strategy.* Presented at the 2nd International Community, Work and Family conference, Lisbon.

Kagan, C., Burton, M., & Siddiquee, A. (2017). Action research. In C. Willig & W. Stainton-Rogers (Eds.), *The Sage handbook of qualitative research in psychology* (2nd ed., pp. 55–73). Thousand Oaks, CA: SAGE Inc.

Kagan, C., Caton, S., & Barnett, M. (Eds.). (2005). *Regenerating professionals? Report of Sustainable Communities Summit 2005 fringe event.* RIHSC occasional papers on community engagement. Manchester, England: RIHSC. https://e-space.mmu.ac.uk/41863/.

Kagan, C., Caton, S., & Amin, A. (2001). *The need for witness support.* Manchester, England: IOD Research Group. https://e-space.mmu.ac.uk/41755/.

Kagan, C., Lewis, S., & Heaton, P. (1998). *Caring to work: Accounts of working parents of disabled children.* London, England: Family Policy Studies Centre/Joseph Rowntree Foundation.

Kagan, C., Tindall, C., & Robinson, J. (2009). Community psychology: Linking the individual with the community. In R. Woolfe, S. Strawbridge & B. Douglas (Eds.), *Handbook of counselling psychology* (3rd ed.). London, England: Sage.

Kagan, C., Caton, S., Amin, A., & Choudry, A. (2004). *'Boundary critique', community psychology and citizen participation.* RIHSC occasional papers 5/04. Manchester, England: RIHSC. https://e-space.mmu.ac.uk/41847/.

Kagan, C., Duckett, P., Lawthom, R., & Burton, M. (2005). Community psychology and disabled people. In D. Goodley and R. Lawthom (Eds.), *Disability and psychology: Critical introductions and reflections.* London, England: Palgrave.

Kagan, C., Duggan, K., Richards, M., & Siddiquee, A. (2011). Community psychology. in P. Martin, F. Cheung, M. Kyrios, L. Littlefield, M. Knowles, B. Overmier & J.M. Prieto (Eds.), *The IAAP handbook of applied psychology* (Chapter 19). Oxford, England: Blackwell.

Kagan, C., Lawthom, R., Knowles, K., & Burton, M. (2000). *Community activism, participation and social capital on a peripheral housing estate.* Paper given at the European Community Psychology Conference, Bergen, Norway, September 2000.

Kagan, C., Lewis, S., Heaton, P., & McLean, I. (1999). *Community, work and family audit 1: Employing organisations.* IOD occasional papers 4/99. Manchester, England: IOD Research Group. https://e-space.mmu.ac.uk/41735/.

Kagan, C., McLean, T., Gathercole, C., & Austin, M. (1990). *Report on the work of the North Western Development Team for 1988–1990.* Whalley, England: North West Regional Health Authority.

Kagan, C., McLean, T., Gathercole, C., & Austin, M. (1988). *North Western Development Team annual report.* Whalley, England: North West Regional Health Authority. pp. 23.

Kagan, C., Lawthom, R., Siddiquee, A., Duckett, P., & Knowles, K. (2007). Community psychology through community action learning. In A. Bokszczanin (Ed.), *Community psychology: Social change in solidarity.* Opole, Poland: University Opole.

Kane, L. (2001). *Popular education and social change in Latin America.* London, England: Latin America Bureau.

Kawachi, I., & Berkman, L.F. (2001). Social ties and mental health. *Journal of Urban Health*, 78(3), 458–467.

Keenan, H.B. (2017). Unscripting curriculum: Toward a critical trans pedagogy. *Harvard Educational Review*, 87(4), 538–556. doi:10.17763/1943-5045-87.4.538.

Kelly, J.G. (2006). *Becoming ecological: An expedition into community psychology*. Oxford, England: Oxford University Press.

Kelvin, P. (1971). *The bases of social behaviour: An approach in term of order and value*. London, England: Holt, Rinehart and Winston.

Kessi, S. (2017). Community social psychologies for decoloniality: An African perspective on epistemic justice in higher education. *South African Journal of Psychology*, 47(4), 506–516.

Kilroy, A., Garner, C., Parkinson, C., Kagan, C., & Senior, P. (2007). *Towards transformation: Exploring the impact of culture, creativity and the arts on health and well-being. A consultation report for the Critical Friends event*. Manchester, England: RIHSC/Arts for Health. Available at https://e-space.mmu.ac.uk/24673/1/Critical_friends_report_final_amendments.pdf.

Klein, K., & D'Aunno, T. (1986). Psychological sense of community in the workplace. *Journal of Community Psychology*, 14, 365–377.

Klein, N. (2015). *This changes everything: Capitalism vs. the climate*. London, England: Penguin Books.

Klein, N. (2007). *The shock doctrine: The rise of disaster capitalism*. London, England: Penguin Books.

Knowles, K. (2001). *Evaluation of reorganisation of community psychiatric nursing services*. Unpublished PhD thesis, Manchester Metropolitan University, Manchester.

Knowles, K., & Kagan, C. (1995a). *Psychosocial rehabilitation in and with communities*. Paper presented to 1st International Conference of A.R.A.P.D.I.S.: Psychosocial Rehabilitation in and with Communities, Barcelona, Spain.

Knowles, K., & Kagan, C. (1995b). *Making your voice heard: Involving service users in the planning and development of services*. Paper presented to 1st International Conference of A.R.A.P.D.I.S.: Psychosocial Rehabilitation in and with Communities, Barcelona, Spain.

Knowles, M. (1980). *The modern practice of adult education: From pedagogy to andragogy* (2nd ed.). New York, NY: Cambridge Books.

Kolakowski, L. (1972). *Positivist philosophy: From Hume to the Vienna Circle*. Harmondsworth, England: Penguin.

Kolb, D.A. (1984). *Experiential learning: Experience as the source of learning and development*. New Jersey: Prentice-Hall.

Kothari, A., Demaria, F., & Acosta, A. (2014). Buen vivir, degrowth and ecological swaraj: Alternatives to sustainable development and the green economy. *Development*, 57(3–4), 362–375.

Kowalsky, L.O., Verhoef, M.J., Thurston, W.E., & Rutherford, G.E. (1996). Guidelines for entry into an Aboriginal community. *The Canadian Journal of Native Studies* 16(2), 267–282.

Kropotkin, P.A. (1912). *Fields, factories, and workshops; Or, industry combined with agriculture and brain work with manual work* (new revised and enlarged ed.). New York, NY: Thomas Nelson and Sons.

Kubler-Ross, E. (1969). *On death and dying*. New York, NY: Macmillan (Republished 1997, Touchstone).

Kundera, M. (1978). *The book of laughter and forgetting*. New York, NY: Columbia University Press.

Labra, I. (2001). *The development of power in grassroots groups. Skills and knowledge within a self-managed production environment*. Paper presented to the conference on Work, Skills and Knowledge, Swiss Development Corporation, Interlaken Switzerland, September 2001.

Lambert, S., & Hopkins, K. (1995). Occupational conditions and workers' sense of community: Variations by gender and race. *American Journal of Community Psychology*, 23, 151–179.

References

Langer, E.J., & Rodin, J. (1976). The effects of choice and enhanced personal responsibility for the aged: A field experiment in an institutional setting. *Journal of Personality and Social Psychology, 34*, 191–198.

Lave, J., & Wenger, E. (1990). *Situated learning: Legitimate peripheral participation*. Cambridge, England: Cambridge University Press.

Lawthom, R. (2011). Developing learning communities: Using communities of practice within community psychology. (Special edition: Inclusive communities). *International Journal of Inclusive Education 15*(1, February), 153–164.

Lawthom, R., Porretta, B., & Kagan, C. (2009). *Inclusion and integration through ESOL*. Manchester, England: RIHSC.

Lawthom, R., Sixsmith, J., & Kagan, J. (2007). Interrogating power: The case of arts and mental health in community projects. *Journal of Community and Applied Social Psychology 17*(4), 268–279.

Lawthom, R., Kagan, C., Baines, S., Lo, S., Sham, S., Mok, L., Greenwood, M., Gaule, S. (2015). Experiences of forced labour amongst UK based Chinese migrant workers: Exploring vulnerability and protection in times of empire. In L. Waite, G. Craig, H. Lewis, & K. Skrivankova (Eds.), *Vulnerability, exploitation and migrants* (pp. 174–186). London, England: Palgrave Macmillan UK.

Lawthom, R., Kagan, C., Baines, S., Sham, S., Mok, L., Lo, S., Greenwood, M., & Gaule, S. (2013). Experiences of forced labour amongst Chinese migrant workers: Emotional containment in a context of vulnerability and protection. *International Journal Work, Organisation and Emotion, 5*(3), 261–280.

Lawthom, R., Woolrych, R., Fisher, J., Murray, M., Smith, H., Garcia-Ferrari, S., … Pereira, G. (2018). Making methods age friendly: Methods, movement, and mapping. *Innovation in Aging, 2*(suppl_1), 242. doi:10.1093/geroni/igy023.906.

Lazarus, S., Bulbulia, S., Taliep, N., & Naidoo, A.V. (2015). Community-based participatory research as a critical enactment of community psychology. *Journal of Community Psychology, 43*(1), 87–98.

Leonard, P. (1984). *Personality and ideology: Towards a materialist understanding of the individual*. London, England: Macmillan.

Leonard, P. (1975). Towards a paradigm for radical practice. In M. Bailey & M. Brake (Eds.), *Radical social work*. London, England: Edward Arnold.

Levin, M., & Greenwood, D. (2018). *Creating a new public university and reviving democracy. Action research in higher education*. New York, NY: Berghahn Books.

Levine, M., & Perkins, D.V. (1997). *Principles of community psychology*. New York, NY: Oxford University Press.

Levy, A., & Merry, U. (1986). *Organizational transformation: Approaches, strategies, theories*. New York, NY: Praeger.

Lewin, K. (1997). *Resolving social conflicts and field theory in social science*. Washington, DC: American Psychological Association. (Reprints of books originally published in 1948 and 1951).

Lewin, K. (1951). *Field theory in social science: Selected theoretical papers* (D. Cartwright, Ed.). New York, NY: Harper and Row. (Reprinted 1975 Greenwood Press and as Lewin, 1997).

Lewin, K. (1943). Defining the field at a given time. *Psychological Review, 50*, 292–310. (Republished in Lewin, 1997).

Lewis, S., Stumbitz, B., Miles, L., & Rouse, J. (2014). *Maternity protection in SMEs: An international review*. Geneva, Switzerland: International Labour Office.

Lira, E. (2000). Psicología del miedo y conducta colectiva en Chile [The psychology of fear and collective behaviour in Chile]. In I. Martín-Baró (Ed.), *Psicología social de la guerra*. San Salvador, El Salvador: UCA Editores.

Lira, E., & Castillo, M.I. (1991). *Psicología de la amenaza política y el miedo*. Santiago, Chile: ILAS.

Lira, E., & Weinstein, E. (2000). La tortura. Conceptualización psicológica y proceso terapéutico. In I. Martín-Baró (Ed.), *Psicología social de la guerra* (3rd ed.). San Salvador, El Salvador: UCA Editores.

Lloyd, M. (2001). The politics of disability and feminism: Discord or synthesis? *Sociology, 35*(3), 715–728.

Locke, A., Lawthom, R., & Lyons, A. (2018). Social media platforms as complex and contradictory spaces for feminisms: Visibility, opportunity, power, resistance and activism. *Feminism & Psychology, 28*(1), 3–10. doi:10.1177/0959353517753973.

Lowndes, V. (2000). Women and social capital: A comment on Hall's 'social capital in Britain'. *British Journal of Political Science, 30*, 533–540.

Luft, J. (1969). *Of human interaction*. Palo Alto, CA: National Press Books.

Luger, A., & Massing, L. (2015). *Learning from our experience: A guide to participative systematisation. Horizon 3000*. Available at www.knowhow3000.org/wp/wp-content/files/KM/KM%20public/Manuals%20%26%20Handbooks/ENG_MAN_Learning-From-Our-Experience-A-guide-to-participative-sistematisation_2015.pdf.

Lukes, S. (1974). *Power: A radical view*. London, England: Macmillan.

Luque-Ribelles, V., García-Ramírez, M., & Portillo, N. (2009). Gendering peace and liberation: A participatory-action approach to critical consciousness acquisition among women in a marginalized neighborhood. In M. Montero & C.C. Sonn (Eds.), *Psychology of liberation: Theory and applications*. New York, NY: Springer.

Lykes, M.B., & Moane, G. (2009). Editors' introduction: Whither feminist liberation psychology? Critical explorations of feminist and liberation psychologies for a globalizing world. *Feminism and Psychology, 19*(3), 283–297.

Lynd, R.S., & Lynd, H. (1929). *Middletown: A study of contemporary American culture*. New York, NY: Harcourt Brace.

MacGillivary, A., Weston, C., & Unsworth, C. (1998). *Communities count: A step by step guide to community sustainability indicators*. London, England: New Economics Foundation.

MacKay, T. (2008). Can psychology change the world? *The Psychologist, 21*(11), 928–931.

Mackenzie, D. (1981). Notes on the science and social relations debate. *Capital and Class, 14*, 46–60.

Malm, A. (2016). *Fossil capital: The rise of steam-power and the roots of global warming*. London, England: Verso.

Mantilla, G.E.V. (2010). Community systematization and learning: Project management for change. *Community Development Journal, 45*(3), 367–379.

Marcos, Subcomandante Insurgente. (2002). *Our word is our weapon: Selected writings of Subcomandante Insurgente Marcos*. New York, NY: Seven Stories.

Marcuse, H. (1965). Repressive tolerance. In R.P. Wolff, B. Moore & H. Marcuse (1969). *A critique of pure tolerance* (pp. 95–137). Boston, MA: Beacon Press. Available at www.marcuse.org/herbert/pubs/60spubs/65repressivetolerance.htm.

Martin, B. (1994). Plagiarism: A misplaced emphasis. *Journal of Information Ethics, 3*(2), 36–47. Available at: www.uow.edu.au/arts/sts/bmartin/pubs/94jie.html.

Martín-Baró, I. (1996). Toward a liberation psychology. In A. Aron & S. Corne (Eds.), *Writings for a liberation psychology*. New York, NY: Harvard University Press (Originally published as Hacia una psicología de la liberación. *Boletin de Psicología (UCA), 22*, 219–231). Available at www.uca.edu.sv/deptos/psicolog/hacia.htm.

Martín-Baró, I. (1989). *Sistema, grupo y poder: Psicología social desde Centroamérica II*. San Salvador, El Salvador: UCA Editores.

Martín-Baró, I. (1987). El latino indolente. Carácter ideológico del fatalismo latinoAmericano. In M. Montero (Ed.), *Psicología política LatinoAmericana* (pp. 135–162). Caracas, Venezuela: Panapo. (Translated as The lazy Latino: The ideological nature of Latin American fatalism. Chapter 12 of Martín-Baró (1996)).

References

Martín-Baró, I. (1983). *Acción e ideología: Psicología social desde Centroamérica I*. San Salvador, El Salvador: UCA Editores.

Maton, K.I. (1989). Community settings as buffers of life stress? Highly supportive churches, mutual help groups and senior centers. *American Journal of Community Psychology, 17*, 203–232.

Mayer, C., & McKenzie, K. (2017). '...It shows that there's no limits': The psychological impact of co-production for experts by experience working in youth mental health. *Health & Social Care in the Community, 25*(3), 1181–1189.

Mayo, M. (1994). Community work. In Hanvey, C., & Philpot, T. (Eds.), *Practising social work*. London, England: Routledge.

Mayo, P. (1999). *Gramsci, Freire and adult education: Possibilities for transformative action*. London, England: Zed Books.

McCarthy, J.D., & Zald, M.N. (1977). Resource mobilization and social movements: A partial theory *American Journal of Sociology, 82*(6), 1212.

McGill, I., & Brockbank, A. (2004). *The action learning handbook: Powerful techniques for education, professional development and training*. London, England: Routledge Falmer.

Mckenzie, L. (2015). *Getting by: Estates, class and culture in austerity Britain*. Bristol, England: Policy Press.

McLaren, P. (2000). *Che Guevara, Paulo Freire and the pedagogy of revolution*. Lanham, MD: Rowman and Littlefield.

McLaren, P., & Leonard, P. (Eds.). (1993). *Paulo Freire: A critical encounter*. London, England: Routledge.

McLaughlin, J.A., & Jordan, G.B. (1999). Logic models: A tool for telling your programs performance story. *Evaluation and Program Planning, 22*(1), 65–72.

McMillan, D.W., & Chavis, D.M. (1986). *Sense of community: Definition and theory*. London, England: Routledge.

McNulty, D. (2005). *Dreams, dialogues and desires. Building a learning community in Blackburn with Darwen*. Leicester, England: NIACE.

Mead, M. (1978). *Culture and commitment*. New York, NY: Anchor Press.

Meadows, D.H. (2009). *Thinking in systems: A primer* (D. Wright, Ed.). London, England: Earthscan. Available at https://wtf.tw/ref/meadows.pdf.

Meari, L. (2015). Reconsidering trauma: Towards a Palestinian community psychology. *Journal of Community Psychology, 43*(1), 76–86.

Melluish, S., & Bulmer, D. (1999). Rebuilding solidarity: An account of a men's health action project. *Journal Community and Applied Social Psychology, 9*(2), 93–100.

Melucci, A. (1989). *Nomads of the present: Social movements and individual needs in contemporary society*. Philadelphia, PA: Temple University Press.

Merriam, S.B., Johnson-Bailey, J.; Lee, M-Y; Kee, Y., Ntseane, G., & Muhamad, M. (2001). Power and positionality: Negotiating insider/outsider status within and across cultures. *International Journal of Lifelong Education, 20*(5), 405–416.

Mewett, P.G. (1986). Boundaries and discourse in a Lewis crofting community. In A.P. Cohen (Ed.), *Symbolising community boundaries: Identity and diversity in British cultures*. Manchester, England: Manchester University Press.

Meyrowitz, J. (1986). *No sense of place: The impact of electronic media on social behaviour*. New York, NY: Oxford University Press.

Mezirow, J. (1983). A critical theory of adult learning and education. In M. Tight (Ed.), *Education for adults: Volume 1: Adult learning and education*. London, England: Croom Helm.

Michels, A., & De Graaf, L. (2010). Examining citizen participation: Local participatory policy making and democracy. *Local Government Studies, 36*(4), 477–491.

Mickelson, K.D., & Kubzansky, L.D. (2003). Social distribution of social support: The mediating role of life events. *American Journal of Community Psychology, 32,* 265–281.

Midgley, G. (2000). *Systemic intervention: Philosophy, methodology and practice.* New York, NY: Kluwer.

Midgley, G. (1992). Pluralism and the legitimation of systems science. *Systemic Practice and Action Research, 5*(2), 147–172.

Midgley, G., & Ochoa-Arias, A.E. (Eds.). (2004). *Community operational research: OR and systems thinking for community development.* New York, NY: Kluwer Academic/Plenum.

Midgley, G., Munlo, I., & Brown, M. (1998). The theory and practice of boundary critique: Developing housing services for older people. *Journal of the Operational Research Society, 49,* 467–478.

Milan, S., & van der Velden, L. (2016). The alternative epistemologies of data activism. *Digital Culture and Society, 2*(2), 57–74.

Miller, R.L. (2017). The practice of programme evaluation in community psychology. Intersections and opportunities for stimulating change. In M.A. Bond, I. García de Serrano, & C. Keys (Eds.), *APA handbook of community psychology* (1st ed., pp. 107–121). Washington, DC: American Psychological Association.

Mills, C.W. (1956). *The power elite.* New York, NY: Oxford University Press.

Moane, G. (2011). *Gender and colonialism: A psychological analysis of oppression and liberation.* Basingstoke, England: Palgrave Macmillan.

Moane, G. (2009). Reflections on liberation psychology in action in an Irish context. In M. Montero & C.C. Sonn (Eds.), *Psychology of liberation: Theory and applications.* New York, NY: Springer.

Moane, G. (2006). Exploring activism and change: Feminist psychology, liberation psychology, political psychology. *Feminism and Psychology, 16*(1), 73–78.

Moane, G. (2003). Bridging the personal and the political: Practices for a liberation psychology. *American Journal Community Psychology, 31*(1/2), 91–101.

Mollinson, B. (1988). *Permaculture: A designer's manual.* Tyalgum, Australia: Tagari.

Montero, M. (2013). Social consortium: A partnership of community agents. *Global Journal of Community Psychology Practice, 4*(2). Available at www.gjcpp.org/pdfs/Montero-v4i2-20130531.pdf.

Montero, M. (2009). Methods for liberation: Critical consciousness in action. In M. Montero & C. Sonn (Eds.), *Psychology of liberation: Theory and applications.* New York, NY: Springer.

Montero, M. (2006). *Hacer para transformar: El método en la psicología comunitaria.* [Action for transformation: Method in community psychology]. Buenos Aires, Argentina: Ed. Paidós.

Montero, M. (2004a). *Introducción a la psicología comunitaria: Desarrollo, conceptos y procesos* [Introduction to community psychology: development, concepts and processes]. Buenos Aires, Argentina: Paidós.

Montero, M. (2004b). Relaciones entre psicología social comunitaria, psicología crítica y psicología de la liberación: una respuesta latinoAmericana. *Psykhe (Chile), 13*(2), 17–28.

Montero, M. (2000a). Participation in action research. *Annual Review Critical Psychology, 2,* 131–143.

Montero, M. (2000b). Perspectivas y retos de la psicología de la liberación. In J.J. Vazquez (Ed.), *Psicología social y liberación en América Latina* (pp. 9–26). Mexico City, Mexico: Universidad Autonoma de Mexico, Unidad de Iztapalapa.

Montero, M. (1998). Psychosocial community work as an alternative mode of political action (the construction and critical transformation of society). *Community, Work and Family, 1*(1), 65–78.

Montero, M. (1996). Parallel lives: Community psychology in Latin America and the United States. *American Journal of Community Psychology, 24,* 589–606.

Montero, M. (1994). Consciousness raising, conversion, and de-ideologization in community psychosocial work. *Journal of Community Psychology, 22*(1), 3–11.

Montero, M. (1982). La psicología comunitaria: orígines, principios y fundamentos teóricos [Community psychology: origins, principles and theoretical foundations]. *Boletín de AVEPSO, 5*(1), 15–22.

References

Montero, M., & Montenegro, M. (2006). Critical Psychology in Venezuela. *Annual Review of Critical Psychology*, 5, 257–268. Available at https://discourseunit.com/annual-review/5-2006/.

Montero, M., & Varas-Díaz, N. (2007). Latin-American community psychology: Development, implications and challenges within a social change agenda. In S. Reich, M. Riemer, I. Prilleltensky & M. Montero (Eds.), *International community psychology: History and theories*. New York, NY: Springer.

Montero, M., Sonn, C., & Burton, M. (2016). Community psychology and liberation psychology: Creative synergy for ethical and transformative praxis. In M.A. Bond, I. García de Serrano, & C. Keys (Eds.), *APA handbook of community psychology* (1st ed., Vol. 1). Washington, DC: American Psychological Association.

Moon, J.A. (2004). *A handbook of reflective and experiential learning: Theory and practice*. Abingdon, England: Routledge and Falmer.

Morris, M. (2015). More than the Beatles: The legacy of a decade for community psychology's contributions to evaluation ethics. *American Journal of Evaluation*, 36(1), 99–107. doi:10.1177/10982 14014557808.

Moscovici, S., & Zavalloni, M. (1969). The group as a polarizer of attitudes. *Journal of Personality and Social Psychology*, 12, 125–135.

Moscovici, S., Lage, E., & Naffrechoux, M. (1969). Influence of a consistent minority on the responses of a majority in a color perception task. *Sociometry*, 32, 365–380.

Murray, H., & Stewart, M. (2006). Who owns the theory of change? *Evaluation*, 12(2), 179–199.

Murtagh, B. (1999). Listening to communities: Locality research and planning. *Urban Studies*, 36(7), 1181–1193.

Napoleoni, L. (2008). *Rogue economics: Capitalism's new reality*. New York, NY: Seven Stories.

Natale, A., Di Martino, S., Procentese, F., & Arcidiacono, C. (2016). De-growth and critical community psychology: Contributions towards individual and social well-being. *Futures*, 78–79, 47–56. doi:10.1016/j.futures.2016.03.020.

New Economics Foundation (NEF). (2008a). *A green new deal. Joined-up policies to solve the triple crunch of the credit crisis, climate change and high oil prices: The first report of the Green New Deal Group*. London, England: New Economics Foundation.

New Economics Foundation (NEF). (2008b). *Co-production: A manifesto for growing the core economy*. London, England: New Economics Foundation.

New Economics Foundation (NEF). (1998). *Participation works! 21 techniques of community participation for the 21st century*. London, England: New Economics Foundation.

Nel, H. (2018). A comparison between the asset-oriented and needs-based community development approaches in terms of systems changes. *Practice*, 30(1), 33–52.

Nelson, G., & Prilleltensky, I. (Eds.). (2005). *Community psychology: In pursuit of liberation and well-being*. New York, NY: Palgrave/MacMillan.

Nelson, G., Poland, B., Murray, M., & Maticka-Tyndale, E. (2004). Building capacity in community health action research: Towards a praxis framework for graduate education. *Action Research*, 2, 389–408.

Neuwirth, R. (2006). *Shadow cities*, London, England: Routledge.

New Climate Economy. (2014). *Better growth, better climate*. New Climate Economy. Available at http://newclimateeconomy.report/2014/.

Nisbet, R.A. (1967). *The sociological tradition*. London, England: Heinemann.

North, P. (2010). Eco-localisation as a progressive response to peak oil and climate change: A sympathetic critique. *Geoforum* 41(4), 585–594. Published online at http://dx.doi.org/10.1016/j.geoforum.2009.04.013.

Odum, E.P. (1971). *Fundamentals of ecology* (3rd. ed.). Philadelphia, PA: Saunders Press.

Odum, H.T.O., & Odum, E.C. (2001). *A prosperous way down: Principles and policies*. Boulder: University Press of Colorado.

Office for National Statistics. (2018). *Labour market profile: Manchester* [Nomis: official labour market statistics]. Available at www.nomisweb.co.uk/reports/lmp/la/1946157083/report.aspx?town=Manchester#tabempunemp.

Oldenburg, R. (1989). *The great good place: Cafes, coffee shops, bookstores, bars, hair salons, and other hangouts at the heart of a community.* New York, NY: Marlowe and Company.

Oldenburg, R. (1997). Our vanishing third places. *Planning Commissioners Journal, 25,* 6–10.

Oldenburg, Ray (Ed.). (2001). *Celebrating the third place: Inspiring stories about the 'great good places' at the heart of our communities.* New York, NY: Marlowe & Co.

O'Leary, T., Burkett, I., Braithwaite, K., Carnegie United Kingdom Trust & IACD. (2011). *Appreciating assets.* Retrieved from https://d1ssu070pg2v9i.cloudfront.net/pex/carnegie_uk_trust/2011/06/14151707/pub1455011684.pdf.

O'Neil, J., & Marsick, V.J. (2007). *Understanding action learning.* New York, NY: Amacom.

Orford, J. (2008). *Community psychology: Challenges, controversies and emerging consensus* (2nd ed.). Chichester, England: Wiley.

Orford, J. (1998). Have we a theory of community psychology? *Clinical Psychology Forum 122,* 6–10.

Orford, J. (1992). *Community psychology: Theory and practice.* Chichester, England: Wiley.

Osterwalder, A., Pigneur, Y., & Clark, T. (2010). *Business model generation: A handbook for visionaries, game changers, and challengers.* Hoboken, NJ: Wiley.

Packham, C. (1998). Community auditing as community development. *Community Development Journal 33*(3), 249–259.

Pahl, K. (2004). Narratives, artefacts and cultural identities: An ethnographic study of communicative practices in homes. *Linguistics and Education. 15*(4), 339–358.

Pahl, R. (1970). *Patterns of urban life.* London, England: Longmans.

Painter, D., & Blanche, M.T. (2004). Critical psychology in South Africa: Looking back and looking forwards. *South African Journal of Psychology, 34*(4), 520–543. doi:10.1177/008124630403400402.

Painter, D., Terre Blanche, M., & Henderson, J. (2006). Critical psychology in South Africa: Histories, themes and prospects. *Annual Review of Critical Psychology, 5,* 215–235.

Parker, I. (2007). *Revolution in psychology: Alienation to emancipation.* London, England: Pluto.

Parker, I.A. (2005). *Qualitative psychology: Introducing radical research.* Maidenhead, England: Open University Press.

Parker, I.A. (1999). *Deconstructing psychology.* London, England: Sage.

Parker, I., & Spears, R. (Eds.). (1996). *Psychology and society: Radical theory and practice.* London, England: Pluto Press.

Parry, O., & Mauthner, N.S. (2004). Whose data are they anyway? Practical, legal and ethical issues in archiving qualitative research data. *Sociology, 38*(1), 139–152.

Parsons, T. (1957). The distribution of power in American Society. *World Politics, 10*(1), 123–143.

Pawson, R., & Tilley, N. (2004). *Realist evaluation.* Available at www.communitymatters.com.au/RE_chapter.pdf.

Pawson, R., & Tilley, N. (1997). *Realistic evaluation.* London, England: Sage.

Pearce, J. (2010). Co-producing knowledge: Critical reflections on researching participation. In J. Pearce (Ed.), *Participation and democracy in the twenty first century* (pp. 34–50). Basingstoke, England: Palgrave Macmillan.

Pearce, J., Raynard, P., & Zadek, S. (1996). *Social auditing for small organisations: The workbook for trainers and practitioners.* London, England: New Economic Foundation.

Pearpoint, J., O'Brien, J., & Forest, M. (1993). *Path: A workbook for planning possible positive futures: Planning alternative tomorrows with hope for schools, organizations, businesses, families.* Toronto, Canada: Inclusion Press.

Pels, P. (1999). Professions of duplexity: A prehistory of ethical codes in anthropology. *Current Anthropology*, 40, 101–136.

People's Plan. (2017). *People's Plan: Greater Manchester*. Manchester, England: PeoplesPlanGM. Available at www.peoplesplangm.org.uk/wp-content/uploads/2017/04/PEOPLES-PLAN-April-2017.pdf.

Perkins, D.D., García-Ramírez, M., Menezes, I., Serrano-García, I., & Stromopolis, M. (2016). Community psychology and public policy: Research, advocacy and training in international contexts. *Global Journal of Community Psychology Practice*, 7(1), *online*. Available at www.gjcpp.org/en/article.php?issue=21&article=124.

Petras, J., & Veltmeyer, H. (2005). *Social movements and state power*. London, England: Pluto Press.

Petras, J., & Veltmeyer, H. (2001). *Globalization unmasked: Imperialism in the 21st century*. London, England: Zed Books.

Pettigrew, A., Ferlie, E., & McKee, L. (1992). *Shaping strategic change*. London, England: Sage.

Phythian, G. (2018). *Peterloo: Voices, sabres and silence*. Stroud, Gloucestershire, England: The History Press.

Portes, A., & Landolt, P. (1996). The downside of social capital. *American Prospect*, 26, 18–22.

Potter, J. (2001). Wittgenstein and Austin. In M. Wetherell, S. Taylor & S. Yates (Eds.), *Discourse theory and practice*. London, England: Sage.

Preskill, H., & Boyle, S. (2008). A multidisciplinary model of evaluation capacity building. *American Journal of Evaluation*, 29(4), 443–459.

Pretorius-Heuchert, J., & Ahmed, R. (2001). Community psychology: Past, present, and future. In M. Seedat, N. Duncan & S. Lazarus (Eds.), *Community psychology, theory, method, and practice. South African and other perspectives*. Cape Town, South Africa: Oxford.

Priestley, M. (2006). Disability and old age: Or why it isn't all in the mind. In D. Goodley & R. Lawthom (Eds.), *Disability and psychology: Critical introductions and reflections*. Basingstoke, England: Palgrave Macmillan.

Prilleltensky, I. (2008). The role of power in wellness, oppression, and liberation: The promise of psychopolitical validity. *Journal Community Psychology*, 36(2), 116–136.

Prilleltensky, I., & Nelson, G. (1997). Community psychology: Reclaiming social justice. In I.D. Fox & I. Prilleltensky (Eds.), *Critical psychology: An introduction*. London, England: Sage.

Psychologists Against Austerity (PAA). (2015). *The psychological impact of austerity* (p. 16). London, England: Psychologists for Social Change. Available at https://psychagainstausterity.files.wordpress.com/2015/03/paa-briefing-paper.pdf.

Psychologists for Social Change. (2017). *Universal basic income: A psychological impact assessment*. London, England: PSC. Available at www.psychchange.org/uploads/9/7/9/7/97971280/ubi_for_web_updated.pdf.

Public Health England. (2018). Local authority health profiles. Available at https://fingertips.phe.org.uk/profile/health-profiles.

Putnam, R.D. (1995). Bowling alone: America's declining social capital. *Journal of Democracy*, 6, 65–78.

Quijano, A. (2000). Coloniality of power, Eurocentrism, and Latin America. *Neplanta*, 1(3). Available at www.decolonialtranslation.com/english/quijano-coloniality-of-power.pdf.

Radford, J. (2008). Psychology in its place. *Psychology Teaching Review*, 14, 38–50.

Rappaport, J., & Seidman, E. (Eds.). (2000). *Handbook of community psychology*. New York, NY: Kluwer/Plenum Publishers.

Rashford, N.S., & Coghlan, D. (1989). Phases and levels of organisational change. *Journal of Managerial Psychology*, 4(3), 17–22.

Ravetz, J. (2000). *City region 2020: Integrated planning for a sustainable environment*. London, England: Earthscan.

Ray, L.J. (1993). *Rethinking critical theory: Emancipation in the age of global social movements.* London, England: Sage.

Raynes, N., Kagan, C., Varela-Raynes, A., & Bolt, B. (2013). *From generation to generation via Intergen: An intergenerational approach to active ageing.* Paper presented to International Initiative on Ageing, Istanbul. Available from http://fromgeneration2generation.org.uk/intergen-evidence-base/.

Reason, P., & Bradbury, H. (2001). Introduction: Inquiry and participation in search of a world worthy of human aspiration. In P. Reason & H. Bradbury (Eds.), *Handbook of action research: Participative inquiry and practice.* London, England: Sage.

Rebien, C.C. (1996). Participatory evaluation of development assistance: Dealing with power and facilitative learning. *Evaluation, 2*(2), 151–172.

Reich, S., Riemer, M., Prilleltensky, I., & Montero, M. (Eds.). (2007). *International community psychology: History and theories.* New York, NY: Springer.

Revans, R. (1980). *Action learning: New techniques for management.* London, England: Blond and Briggs, Ltd.

Revenson, T., D'Augelli, A., French, S., Hughes, D., Livert, D., Seidman, E., et al. (Eds.). (2002). *Ecological research to promote social change: Methodological advances from community psychology.* New York, NY: Kluwer Academic/Plenum Publishers.

Reyes Cruz, M., & Sonn, C.C. (2011). (De)colonizing culture in community psychology: Reflections from critical social science. *American Journal of Community Psychology, 47*(1–2), 203–214.

Richards, M., Lawthom, R., & Runswick-Cole, K. (2018). Community-based arts research for people with learning disabilities: Challenging misconceptions about learning disabilities. *Disability & Society,* 1–24, online.

Riley, V. (1998). Listening to caregivers: The community, work and family interface. *Community, Work and Family, 1*(1), 95–98.

Robertson, N., & Masters-Awatere, B. (2007). Community psychology in Aotearoa/New Zealand. In S. Reich, M. Riemer, I. Prilleltensky & M. Montero (Eds.), *International community psychology: History and theories.* New York, NY: Springer.

Rockström, J., Steffen, W., Noone, K., Persson, Å., Chapin, F.S.I., Lambin, E., ... Foley, J. (2009a). Planetary boundaries: Exploring the safe operating space for humanity. *Ecology and Society, 14*(2), art. 32, online. doi:10.5751/ES-03180-140232.

Rockström, J., Steffen, W., Noone, K., Persson, Å., Chapin, F.S., Lambin, E.F., ... Foley, J.A. (2009b). A safe operating space for humanity. *Nature, 461*(7263), 472–475.

Rogers, C. (1969). *Freedom to learn.* Ohio, OH: Merrill (Reprinted as Rogers & Frieberg, 1994).

Rogers, C., & Frieberg, H.J. (1994). *Freedom to learn* (3rd ed.). Ohio, OH: Merrill/Macmillan.

Runswick-Cole, K., Goodley, D., & Lawthom, R. (2018). Resilience in the lives of disabled children: A many splendoured thing. In K. Runswick-Cole, T. Curran, & K. Liddiard (Eds.), *The Palgrave handbook of disabled children's childhood studies* (pp. 425–442). doi:10.1057/978-1-137-54446-9_27.

Sacipa-Rodríguez, S., Tovar-Guerra, C., Villareal, L.F.G., & Bohórquez, V. (2009). Psychological accompaniment: Construction of cultures of peace among a community affected by war. In M. Montero & C. Sonn (Eds.), *Psychology of liberation: Theory and applications.* New York, NY: Springer.

Sale, K. (1985). *Dwellers in the land.* San Francisco, CA: Sierra Club.

Sampson, E.E. (2000). Reinterpreting individualism and collectivism: Their religious roots and monologic versus dialogic person-other relationship. *American Psychologist, 55*(12), 1425–1432.

Sánchez, E., Cronick, K., & Wiesenfeld, E. (1988). Psychosocial variables and participation: A case study. In D. Canter, M. Kramping & D. Stea (Eds.), *New Directions in Environmental Participation* (Vol. 3). Aldershot, England: Avebury.

Sarason, S.B. (1988). *The psychological sense of community: Prospects for a community psychology* (2nd ed.). San Francisco, CA: Jossey-Bass.

Sarason, S.B. (1974). *The psychological sense of community: Prospects for a community psychology.* San Francisco, CA: Jossey-Bass.

Sarason, S.B. (1972). *The creation of settings and the future societies.* San Francisco, CA: Jossey Bass.

Schön, D.A. (1983). *The reflective practitioner: How professionals think in action.* New York, NY: Basic Books.

Schrader McMillan, A., & Burton, M. (2009). From parent education to collective action: 'Childrearing with love' in post-war Guatemala. *Journal of Community and Applied Psychology, 19*(3), 198–211.

Seedat, M. (2015). Oral history as an enactment of critical community psychology: Oral history as critical enactment. *Journal of Community Psychology, 43*(1), 22–35.

Seedat, M., Duncan, N., & Lazarus, S. (Eds.). (2001). *Community psychology: Theory, method and practice.* Cape Town, South Africa: Oxford University Press.

Seidman, E. (1988). Back to the future, community psychology: Unfolding a theory of intervention. *American Journal Community Psychology, 16*(1), 3–24.

Seidman, E. (1986). Justice, values and social science: Unexamined premises. In E. Seidman & J. Rapaport (Eds.), *Redefining social problems.* New York, NY: Plenum Press.

Sen, R., & Goldbart, J. (2005). Partnership in action: Introducing family-based intervention for children with disability in urban slums of Kolkata, India. *International Journal of Disability, Development and Education, 52*(4), 275–311.

Serrano-García, I. (2016). Social policy: The tightwire we walk (A commentary). *Global Journal of Community Psychology Practice, 4*(2), online. Available at www.gjcpp.org/pdfs/Serrano-Garcia-v4i2-20130613.pdf.

Sève, L. (1975). *Marxism and the theory of human personality.* London, England: Lawrence and Wishart.

Shankar, S., Dick, B., Passfield, R., & Swepson, P. (Eds.). (2002). *Effective change management using action learning and action research.* Lismore, Australia: Southern Cross Press.

Shaw, I., Greene, J., & Mark, M. (2006). *Sage handbook of evaluation.* London, England: Sage.

Sheldon, J.A., & Wolfe, S.M. (2015). The community psychology evaluation nexus. *American Journal of Evaluation, 36*(1), 86–89. doi:10.1177/1098214014558503.

Shiell, A., & Riley, T. (2017). Methods and methodology of systems analysis. In M.A. Bond, I. Serrano-García, C.B. Keys, & M. Shinn (Eds.), *APA handbook of community psychology: Methods for community research and action for diverse groups and issues* (pp. 155–169). Washington, DC: American Psychological Association.

Shore, C., & Wright, S. (1999). Audit culture and anthropology: Neo-liberalism in British higher education. *Journal of the Royal Anthropological Institute, 5*, 557–575.

Siddiquee, A., & Kagan, C. (2006). The internet, empowerment, and identity: An exploration of participation by refugee women in a Community Internet Project (CIP) in the United Kingdom (UK). *Journal Community and Applied Social Psychology, 16*(2), 189–206.

Silverman, T. (2001). Expanding community: The internet and relational theory. *Community, Work and Family, 4*(2), 231–238.

Sixsmith, J., & Kagan, C. (2005). *Pathways Project evaluation: Final report.* Manchester, England: RIHSC.

Sixsmith, J., Callender, M., Hobbs, G., Corr, S., & Huber, J.W. (2014). Implementing the National Service Framework for long-term (neurological) conditions: Service user and service provider experiences. *Disability and Rehabilitation, 36*(7), 563–572. doi:10.3109/09638288.2013.804594.

Sloan, T. (2005). Globalization, poverty and social justice. In G. Nelson & I. Prilleltensky (Eds.), *Community psychology: In pursuit of liberation and well-being.* Basingstoke, England: Palgrave Macmillan.

Smail, D. (1999). *The origins of unhappiness.* London, England: Constable (Reproduced in *Power, responsibility and freedom.* Available at https://the-eye.eu/public/WorldTracker.org/Sociology/

David%20Smail%20-%20Power%2C%20Responsibility%20and%20Freedom%20-%20 Internet%20Publication%20%282005%29.pdf.

Smail, D. (1993). Putting our mouths where our money is. *Clinical Psychology Forum, 61,* 11–14.

Smith, M.K. (2002). 'Paulo Freire and informal education', *Encyclopaedia of informal education.* http://infed.org/mobi/paulo-freire-dialogue-praxis-and-education.

Smith, N.L. (2007). Empowerment evaluation as evaluation ideology. *American Journal of Evaluation, 28*(2), 169–178.

Smithers, R. (2017, January 10). UK throwing away £13bn of food each year. *Guardian.* Available at www.theguardian.com/environment/2017/jan/10/uk-throwing-away-13bn-of-food-each-year-latest-figures-show.

Smits, P.A., & Champagne, F. (2008). An assessment of the theoretical underpinnings of practical participatory evaluation. *American Journal of Evaluation, 29*(4), 427–442.

Social Value UK. (n.d.). *What is social value?* Available at www.socialvalueuk.org/what-is-social-value/.

Society for Community Research and Action (SCRA). (2012). Competencies for community psychology practice: Draft August 15, 2012. *The Community Psychologist, 45*(4), 7–14.

Society for Community Research and Action (SCRA). (n.d.). *An evidence informed community psychology value proposition.* Available at www.scra27.org/files/4513/9007/7333/Evidence_based_CP_Value_Proposition__Final_20110829.pdf.

Spangler, B. (2003). Coalition building. In G. Burgess & H. Burgess (Eds.), *Beyond intractability.* Boulder: Conflict Research Consortium, University of Colorado. Available at www.beyondintract ability.org/essay/coalition_building.

Sprigings, N., & Allen, C. (2005). The communities we are regaining but need to lose. A critical commentary on community building in beyond-place societies. *Community, Work and Family, 8*(4), 389–411. doi:10.1080/13668800500263032.

Stake, R.E. (1980). Program evaluation, particularly responsive evaluation. In W.B. Dockerell & D. Hamilton (Eds.), *Rethinking educational research.* London, England: Hodder and Stoughton.

Standing, G. (2018). *The precariat: Today's transformative class.* Available at www.greattransition. org/publication/precariat-transformative-class.

Steffen, W., Richardson, K., Rockström, J., Cornell, S.E., Fetzer, I., Bennett, E.M., … Sorlin, S. (2015). Planetary boundaries: Guiding human development on a changing planet. *Science, 347*(6223), 1259855–1259855. doi:10.1126/science.1259855.

Stewart, A., & Kagan, C. (2008). *The 'In Bloom' competition: Gardening work as a community involvement strategy.* Manchester, England: RIHSC. Available at https://e-space.mmu.ac. uk/41941/1/978-1-900139-24-3.pdf.

Stiegler, B. (2006). The disaffected individual in the process of psychic and collective disindividuation. Extract from the 3rd chapter of *Mécréance et Discrédit: Tome 2. Les sociétés incontrôlables d'individus désaffectés* (Paris, France: Editions Galilée, 2006), published as a working paper for the Ars Industrialis seminar, 'Suffering and consumption', February 25, 2006, translated by Patrick Crogan & Daniel Ross. Available at http://tinyurl.com/yjregfv.

Streck, D.R., & Jara, O. (2015). Research, participation and social transformation: Grounding systematization of experiences in Latin American perspectives. In Hilary Bradbury (Ed.), *The SAGE handbook of action research* (3rd ed., pp. 472–480). London, England: SAGE Publications Ltd.

Stringer, E. (1999). *Action research* (2nd ed.). Palo Alto, CA: Sage.

Suárez-Herrara, J.C., Springett, J., & Kagan, C. (2009). Critical connections between participatory evaluation, organizational learning and intentional change in pluralistic organization. *Evaluation, 15*(30), 321–342.

Suffla, S., Seedat, M., & Bawa, U. (2015). Reflexivity as enactment of critical community psychologies: Dilemmas of voice and positionality in a multi-country photovoice study. *Journal of Community Psychology, 43*(1), 9–21.

References

Sultana, F. (2007). Reflexivity, positionality and participatory ethics: Negotiating fieldwork dilemmas in international research. *ACME: An International E-Journal for Critical Geographies, 6*(3), 374–385.

Sutherland, W.J., Spiegelhalter, D., & Bergman, M.A. (2013). Twenty tips for interpreting scientific claims. *Nature, 503,* 335.

Swindells, R., Lawthom, R., Rowley, K., Siddiquee, A., Kilroy, A., & Kagan, C. (2013). Eudaimonic well-being and community arts participation. *Perspectives in Public Health, 133*(1), 60–65.

Synnot, B., & Fitzgerald, R. (2007). *The toolbox for change: A practical approach.* Brisbane, Australia: Danjugah.

Szreter, S. (2002). The state of social capital: Bringing back in power, politics, and history. *Theory and Society, 31,* 573–621.

Taket, A., & White, L. (2000). *Partnership and participation. Decision making in the multiagency setting.* Chichester, England: John Wiley.

Tanguay, J. (2012). *Well-being in Vanuatu.* Vanuatu: VKS Studios. Available at www.youtube.com/watch?v=jtnLl1Jp0K0.

Tawney, R.H. (1938). *Religion and the rise of capitalism: A historical study.* Harmondsworth, England: Pelican.

Taylor, M., & Burns, D. (2000). *Auditing community participation: An assessment handbook.* Bristol, England: Policy Press.

Taylor, M., Purdue, D., Wilson, M., & Wilde, P. (2005). *Evaluating community projects: A practical guide.* Available at www.jrf.org.uk/sites/files/jrf/1859354157.pdf.

Taylor-Gooby, P., & Dale, J. (1981). *Social theory and social welfare.* London, Edward Arnold.

Therborn, G. (2009). The killing fields of inequality. *Soundings, 42,* 20–32.

Therborn, G. (1980). *What does the ruling class do when it rules? State apparatuses and state power under feudalism, capitalism and socialism.* London, England: Verso.

Thomas, D., & Veno, A. (1992). *Psychology and social change: Creating an international agenda.* Palmerston North, New Zealand: Dunmore Press.

Thomas, D.R., & Robertson, N. (1992). A conceptual framework for the analysis of social policies. In D. Thomas & A. Veno. (1992). *Psychology and social change: Creating an international agenda.* Palmerston North, New Zealand: Dunmore Press.

Thompson, J.B. (1990). *Ideology and modern culture: Critical social theory in the era of mass communication.* Cambridge, England: Polity Press.

Thompson, S., & Thompson, N. (2008). *The critically reflective practitioner.* Basingstoke, England: Palgrave Macmillan.

Tiffany, G. (2009). *Community philosophy: A project report.* York, England: Joseph Rowntree Foundation.

Tilakaratna, S. (1990). *A short note on participatory research.* Paper presented to a seminar of Sri Lankan social scientists and community specialists in January 1990. www.caledonia.org.uk/research.htm.

Tönnies, F. (1887/2002). *Community and society.* Newton Abbott, England: David and Charles (First published in 1887 as *Gemeinschaft und Gesellschaft,* Leipzig, Germany: Fues's Verlag).

Topping, A. (2008, March 12). Communalist revolution. *Society Guardian.* Available at www.guardian.co.uk/society/2008/mar/12/regeneration.communities.

Touraine, A. (1988). *The return of the actor: Social theory in post-industrial society.* Minneapolis: University of Minnesota Press.

Touraine, A. (1981). *The voice and the eye: An analysis of social movements.* Cambridge, England: Cambridge University Press.

Toval Guerra, C. (2014). Personal resources and empowerment in a psychosocial accompaniment process. In S. Sacipa-Rodríguez & M. Montero (Eds.), *Psychosocial approaches to peace-building in Colombia* (pp. 75–87). Cham, Switzerland: Springer.

Trades Union Congress (1995). *Britain divided: Insecurity at work*. London, England: TUC.

Trickett, E.J., Barone, C., & Watts, R.J. (2000). Contextual influences in mental health consultation: Toward an ecological perspective on radiating change. In J. Rapaport & E. Seidman (Eds.), *Handbook of community psychology*. New York, NY: Kluwer Academic/Plenum Publishers.

Tyler, C. (2013, December 2). Top 20 things scientists need to know about policy making. *Guardian*. Available at www.theguardian.com/science/2013/dec/02/scientists-policy-governments-science.

UK Community Psychology Network. (2007). *York Statement on Poverty – September 2007*. Available from www.compsy.org.uk.

UK Government. (2015). *The English Indices of Deprivation: Statistical release*. London, England: Ministry of Housing Communities and Local Government. Available at https://assets.publishing.service.gov.uk/government/uploads/system/uploads/attachment_data/file/465791/English_Indices_of_Deprivation_2015_-_Statistical_Release.pdf.

Ulrich, W. (2005). *A brief introduction to critical systems heuristics (CSH)*. ECOSENSUS project website, The Open University, Milton Keynes, England, October 14, 2005. Available at http://projects.kmi.open.ac.uk/ecosensus/publications/ulrich_csh_intro.pdf.

Ulrich, W., & Reynolds, M. (2010). Critical systems heuristics. In M. Reynolds & S. Holwell (Eds.), *Systems approaches to managing change: A practical guide*. (pp. 243–292). London, England: Springer.

Veno, A., & Thomas, D.R. (1992). Psychology and the process of social change. In D.R. Thomas & A. Veno. (1992). *Psychology and social change: Creating an international agenda*. Palmerston North, New Zealand: Dunmore Press.

Vergara-Camus, L. (2014). *Land and freedom: The MST, the Zapatistas and peasant alternatives to neoliberalism*. London, England: Zed Books.

Vidales, R. (2014). Memory, narrative and the social transformation of reality. In S. Sacipa-Rodríguez & M. Montero (Eds.), *Psychosocial approaches to peace-building in Colombia* (pp. 89–110). Cham, Switzerland: Springer.

Wainwright, H. (2009). *Reclaim the state: Experiments in popular democracy*. London, England: Seagull Books.

Walker, C. (2017). *Attacking the neoliberal university from 'within' – Statactivism, critical praxis and the National Senior Managers Survey*. Presented at the 3rd UK community Psychology Festival, Bristol, England: UWE//BPS Community Psychology Section. Available at http://eprints.uwe.ac.uk/33503/6/CPF%20Book%20of%20Abstracts.pdf.

Walker, C., Hart, A., & Hanna, P. (2017). *Building a new community psychology of mental health: Spaces, places, people and activities*. London, England: Palgrave Macmillan.

Walker, I., & Smith, H.J. (eds). (2002). *Relative deprivation: Specification, development, and integration*. Cambridge, England: Cambridge University Press.

Wallerstein, I. (2004). *World systems analysis*. Durham, NC: Duke University Press.

Wallerstein, I. (1996a). *Historical capitalism, with capitalist civilization*. London, England: Verso.

Wallerstein, I. (1996b). *World-systems analysis: An introduction*. Durham, NC: Duke University Press.

Wandersman, A., Snell-Johns, J., Lentz, B.E., Fetterman, D.M., Keener, D.C., Livet, M., Imm, P.S., Flaspohler, P. (2005). The principles of empowerment evaluation. In Fetterman, D., & Wandersman, A. (Eds.), *Empowerment evaluation principles in practice*. New York, NY: Guildford Press.

Watkins, M. (2015). Psychosocial accompaniment. *Journal of Social and Political Psychology*, 3(1), 324–341.

Watson, B. (2005). *Bread and roses: Mills, migrants, and the struggle for the American dream*. New York, NY: Viking.

Watson, E.R., & Foster-Fishman, P.G. (2013). The exchange boundary framework: Understanding the evolution of power within collaborative decision-making settings. *American Journal of Community Psychology*, 51(1–2), 151–163.

References

Weber, M. (1946). *From Max Weber: Essay in sociology* (Hans H. Gerth & C. Wright Mills, Trans. & Ed.). New York, NY: Oxford University Press.

Weber, M. (1904/1930). *The Protestant ethic and the spirit of capitalism.* London, England: George Allen and Unwin University Books. (Ethik und der Geist des Kapitalismus, Archiv für Sozialwissenschaft und Sozialpolitik, 20.).

Weil, S.W., & McGill, I. (Eds.). (1989). *Making sense of experiential learning. Diversity in theory and practice.* Milton Keynes, England: Open University Press.

Wenger, E. (1998). *Communities of practice: Learning meaning and identity.* New York, NY: Cambridge University Press.

Wenger, E.C., McDermott, R., & Snyder, W.C. (2002). *Cultivating communities of practice: A guide to managing knowledge.* Cambridge, MA: Harvard Business School Press.

Wertsch, J. (1990). The voice of rationality in a sociocultural approach to mind. In Moll, L.C. (Ed.), *Vygotsky and education.* New York, NY: Cambridge University Press.

Whelan, P. & Lawthom, R. (2009). Transdisciplinary learning. Exploring pedagogical links between feminism and community psychology. Special Issue of *Feminism and Psychology, 19*(3), 414–418.

Whyte, W.F. (1943). *Street corner society* (4th ed., 1993). Chicago, IL: University of Chicago Press.

Wilcox, D. (1994). *Guide to effective participation.* York, England: Joseph Rowntree Foundation. Available at http://partnerships.org.uk/guide/.

Wilkinson, R. (2005). *The impact of inequality: How to make sick societies healthier.* London, England: Routledge.

Wilkinson, R.G. (1996). *Unhealthy societies: The afflictions of inequality.* London, England: Routledge.

Wilkinson, R., & Pickett, K. (2009). *The spirit level: Why more equal societies almost always do better.* Harmondsworth, England: Penguin.

Wilkinson, R.G., Kawachi, I., & Kennedy, B.P. (1998). Mortality, the social environment, crime and violence. *Sociology of Health and Illness, 20*(5), 578–597.

Williams, C.C., Aldridge, T., Lee, R., Leyshon, A., Thrift, N., & Tooke, J. (2001). Local exchange and trading schemes (LETS): A tool for community renewal? *Community, Work and Family, 4*(3), 355–361.

Williams, R. (1980). *Problems in materialism and culture: Selected essays.* London, England: Verso. (Reissued as *Culture and materialism,* Verso radical thinkers series, 2005).

Williams, R. (1976). *Keywords: A vocabulary of culture and society.* Glasgow, Scotland: Collins Fontana.

Willmott, P. (1989). *Community initiatives. Patterns and prospects.* London, England: Policy Studies Institute.

Wittgenstein, L. (1953). *Philosophical investigations.* Oxford, England: Blackwell.

Wolff, T. (2001a). Community coalition building: Contemporary practice and research: Introduction. *American Journal Community Psychology, 29*(2), 165–172.

Wolff, T. (2001b). A practitioner's guide to successful coalitions. *American Journal Community Psychology, 29*(2), 173–191.

Woolrych, R.D., & Sixsmith, J.A. (2008). *Final report: Understanding health and well-being in the context of urban regeneration.* Manchester case study for HEFCE: Urban Regeneration – Making a Difference Project. Manchester, England: RIHSC.

Woolrych, R., Sixsmith, J., & Kagan, C. (2007). *The impact of regeneration on the well-being of local residents: The case of East Manchester.* Manchester, England: RIHSC. Available at https://e-space. mmu.ac.uk/41939/.

Worley, C. (2005). It's not about race. It's about the community: New Labour and community cohesion. *Critical Social Policy, 25*(4), 483–496.

Wrong, D.H. (1979). *Power: Its forms, bases and uses.* Oxford, England: Blackwell.

Yeo, S., & Evans, S. (2016). *The 35 countries cutting the link between economic growth and emissions*. Carbon Brief Website. Available at www.carbonbrief.org/the-35-countries-cutting-the-link-between-economic-growth-and-emissions.

Zacharzewski, A. (2011). *Democracy for new radicals*. Available at www.demsoc.org/blog/2011/05/03/democracy-for-new-radicals.

Zald, M.N., & McCarthy, J.D. (1988). *The dynamics of social movements: Resource mobilization, social control, and tactics*. Lanham, MD: University Press of America.

Zambrano, A.C. (2007). Participación y empoderamiento comunitario: Role de las methodology's implicativas. In A.C. Zambrano, G.O. Rozas, I.F. Magaña, D.S. Asún & R.A. Pérez-Luco (Eds.), *Psicología comunitaria en Chile: Evolución, perspectivas y proyecciones*. [Community psychology in Chile: Development, perspectives and projections]. Santiago de Chile: RIL editores.

Zúñiga, R. (1975). The experimenting society and radical social reform: The role of the social scientist in Chile's Unidad Popular experience. *American Psychologist, 30*(2), 99–115.

Index

Page numbers in **bold** denote tables, those in *italics* denote figures.

people diagnosed with MS 364; obligation of local authorities to improve 131; for people living with dementia 124; struggle to improve *59*

racism 14, 37, 84, 97, 114; anti-racism 35, 37; fight against 337; racism-imperialism 31
racist 110; anti-racist 37; attitudes and behaviour 37; beliefs 331; effects of cultural norms 77; graffiti 204; ideas 84
radical (transformative) change 60, 115, 169, 185, 231, 322–3, 348, 375, 378, 381; community 34; deciding and acting together lead to 102; meso-level interventions contribute to 146; social movements concerned with 35
really social psychology 21, 62, **64–8**; *see also* critical community psychology
referent power **336**
reflecting 16, 107, 166, 304, 360; change 11; community psychologists' roles 281, 354, 357; community psychologists' skills 281, 345–6; context of CP 183; critique of CP 27, **64–8**, 375–6; evaluation 298; power 13, 163, 308, 337–40; professional improvement 368; reflexivity **157**, 201, 232, 285, 342, 344–5, 354, 356–7, 362, 365, 368, 371, 375; resources **24**, 38, *39*, 45, 82, 101, 123, 185, 215, **221**, 228–9, 333, **336**, 337; social influence 145, 331–2; working constraints 357–8
reflection, critical 10, 41, 62, 163, **188**, 189, 284, 289, 314, 316, 348, 365, 367, 371, 375; and indigenous people 4, 26–7, 38, 88, 90, 96, 114, 316, 350
reflexivity **157**, 201, 232, 342, 344, 362, 368; collective 357; and colonialism 21, 199, 274, 337, 376; component of critical community psychological capability 345; critical 285; engaging in 371; group 375; importance of 365; as part of practice 354, 357; way of factoring oneself into the situation 356
refugees 14, 78, 80, 154, 231, 295, 361, 380; women 2, *382*
relationship intensity 214, **216**
representational roles *346*, *355*, 369
research ethics 155, 167, 201, 232–3, 236, **237**, 248, 262, 274–275, 280, 286, 289, **313**, 332, 359–61

research skills 16, *181*, 191, **215**, 231, 234, 240, 291–2, 312, **313**, 349, 351, 360, 365, 369
resource cycling 43, 47, 154
respect 15, 39, 45, 47, **92**, 139–40, 142, 201, **227**, 250, 289, **363**; diversity and difference 61, **68**, 190, 287; lack of 277; mutual 94, 190, 234
reward power **336**
rich pictures 142–3, 145, *149*
rich settings 206
rights *see* human rights
risk 62, 70, 91, 103, 109, 136–7, *153*, 263, 362, 376; of attempted suicide 272; displaced to labour force 275; examples of 242, **363**; factors 56, 265; for group members 194, 214; health 234; high 47; to jobs **240**; of losing valuable information 201; making values explicit 283; personal 236; populations at 231–2, 235, 255; potential, for stakeholders 286; of premature death **252**; project 166, **363**; in radical change 323; sharing **215**; of victimisation **252**
role-conflict 348
role-rule contexts 51–3, 206, 209, 347
role strain 348
roles, critical community psychologists' 39, 45, 317, 345, 354
rubber ducks 382–3
rural life 38, 72–3, 91, 191, 278

safety 73, 87, *302*; audits 368; cognitive in conducting social research 374; community profiling 130–1, 135; crime and **134**, **363**; emotional, social barriers providing 99; issues **135**; maps of crime 96, **133–4**, 136, 166–7, *173*, *174*, 189, 251, **252**, **363**; for people with dementia and their carers 137; researchers' risks 194, 201, 214, 236, 283; social (community as) 98–100, 264; witness support 160, 166, **173**, *174*, 175, 288; at work 126, 362
scholar activists 3, 345, 348, 374
school-based projects **121**, **133**, 137, 141, 146, 209, 228, 330
scientific knowledge 57, 105, 123, *125*
self, sense of 70, 87, 316
self-advocacy **238**, 240
self-awareness 193, 316, 356; critical *315*, 354, *355*

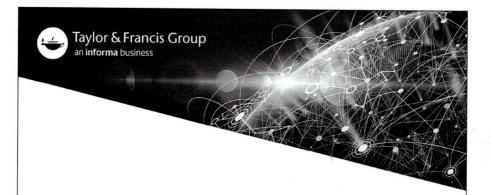